Infancy: Development from Birth to Age 3

Dana Gross
St. Olaf College

Boston   New York   San Francisco
Mexico City   Montreal   Toronto   London   Madrid   Munich   Paris
Hong Kong   Singapore   Tokyo   Cape Town   Sydney

Senior Acquisitions Editor: *Stephen Frail*
Series Editorial Assistant: *Allison Rowland*
Executive Marketing Manager: *Pamela Laskey*
Production Supervisor: *Liz Napolitano*
Editorial Production Service: *Nesbitt Graphics, Inc.*
Composition Buyer: *Linda Cox*
Manufacturing Buyer: *JoAnne Sweeney*
Electronic Composition: *Nesbitt Graphics, Inc.*
Interior Design: *Nesbitt Graphics, Inc.*
Photo Researcher: *Sarah Evertson*
Cover Designer: *Linda Knowles*

For related titles and support materials, visit our online catalog at www.ablongman.com.

Between the time website information is gathered and then published, it is not unusual for some sites to have closed. Also, the transcription of URLs can result in typographical errors. The publisher would appreciate notification where these errors occur so that they may be corrected in subsequent editions.

Library of Congress Cataloging-in-Publication Data was not available at press time.

ISBN 10: 0-205-41798-1
ISBN 13: 978-0-205-41798-8

Printed in the United States of America

10   9   8   7   6   5   4   3   2   1   RRD-VA   11   10   09   08   07

Dedication

To John, Rolf, and Simon

CONTENTS

PREFACE

The focus of this book is on current research, practice, policy, and theory about development from birth to 3 years of age. It developed in response to my experience using other infancy books in my own courses with undergraduates. In trying to find a book that was appropriate in content and presentation for my students, I discovered that many of the available texts were either too advanced or too basic. The overly advanced books tended to be encyclopedic in their coverage, often gave only minimal coverage to important practical topics, and seemed not to have been written with teaching and learning in mind. The overly basic books tended to leave out information about how research is conducted, focused almost exclusively on practical topics, and lacked advanced critical thinking approaches. Some books adopted a chronological approach that missed opportunities to highlight the coherence, continuity, and change in specific aspects of development from birth to age 3. This book aims to find a useful middle ground that will provide students with enough information about research in order to understand methodological issues, explore both practically and theoretically important topics, and engage students in thinking critically about development from birth to age 3.

Engaging, Thought-Provoking Chapter Openers

I usually begin each of my classes the way that each chapter in this book begins—with a thought-provoking, real-life scenario that highlights and introduces key issues and concepts. In nearly 20 years of teaching, I have found that this approach draws students into the topic from the beginning and that they are able to relate subsequent material to specific questions that were raised at the outset. Examples of these scenarios include infants being sent to wet nurses in eighteenth-century Paris (Chapter 1), linguist Werner Leopold's classic longitudinal study of his infant daughter Hildegard's development as a bilingual child (Chapter 2), and health and physical growth—including brain development—in an infant adopted from an East European orphanage (Chapter 5). Chapter 9 begins with questions about baby shower gifts and the things that all infants need, Chapter 10 asks us to consider what it is that makes the thousands of infants who are named Jacob or Emily each year unique, and Chapter 12 invites us to ponder likely entries in a musical Toddler Top 20.

The Broader Historical Context

In many of the chapters, I have included relevant historical information that provides a broader perspective and highlights how far we have come in our understanding of the first 3 years of life. This is seen most prominently in Chapter 1, which contains a comprehensive chronology and many examples of historical perspectives on childhood and the study of child development, but other chapters also contain the historical context for current practices. Chapter 2, for example, considers the remarkable discoveries about genetics that have resulted from the Human Genome Project. Chapter 3 reminds us that we did not always understand the vulnerability of the prenatal period, while Chapter 4 discusses trends in childbirth procedures and options. Chapter 11 describes current research on early child care and early intervention as well as trends in women's employment, maternity leave policies, and child care for infants and toddlers. Chapter 12, which focuses on the presence and role of music, media, and computers in the lives of the very youngest children, recounts the recent history of technology and programming aimed specifically at the under-3 audience.

Policy Considerations

Policy considerations are also included in a number of chapters, in part because these are questions that are gaining prominence in the field of child development and in part to answer "so what?" questions. My students, like students everywhere, want to know more than just what the research shows—they want to know what we can *do* with our knowledge. In Chapter 5, for example, we learn that awareness of the harm caused by lead exposure led to changes in legislation regarding formulas for paint and gasoline, that public health campaigns to keep babies safer by placing them on their backs to sleep led to reductions in the rate of Sudden Infant Death Syndrome, and that awareness of the benefits of human milk led to Healthy People 2010 goals to increase breastfeeding rates in the United States. In Chapter 11, we compare the implications of parental leave policies in the United States and in a wide range of other countries. In Chapter 12, we explore issues surrounding television for infants and toddlers, including a policy statement on this topic from the American Academy of Pediatrics, and we consider evidence that helps us evaluate campaigns designed to provide infants with greater exposure to the music of Mozart.

Practical and Theoretical Issues

There is also a balance in this book between practical and theoretical issues. In Chapter 6, for example, we consider the implications of motor and locomotor development for parents and caregivers who want to make the environment safe for babies and toddlers on the go. Chapter 9 describes some of the factors that can smooth young children's transition to being a sibling, incorporating the new sibling system into existing family relationships. In Chapter 8, we learn about prelinguistic communication and the value of using gestures to help toddlers and caregivers communicate before real words or signs appear.

Diversity and Multicultural Experience

My students, like students everywhere, want to understand interconnections between cultural, institutional, familial, and personal experiences. To address these concerns, issues of diversity and multicultural experience are incorporated into virtually every chapter, illustrating how nature and nurture work together. In Chapter 5, we examine nutritional needs and dietary patterns in the United States as well as the effects of malnutrition, which is a significant problem for infants and toddlers in many other parts of the world. Chapter 7 introduces the notion of diversity by comparing examples of guided participation in different cultures. As we see in Chapter 8, English is only one of the languages in the world, and many infants and toddlers grow up in a bilingual or multilingual community. Chapter 9 reminds us that there is also diversity in infant-caregiver relationships and that, across cultures, there are different expectations and beliefs about infants and the roles that mothers and fathers play in their care and development. Chapter 9 also considers aspects of diversity that are clearly not beneficial, including maternal depression, maltreatment, and early institutionalization. In Chapter 11, our review of child care discusses the inclusion of children with disabilities, and our examination of early intervention addresses the impact of poverty on development from birth to age 3.

Pedagogical Elements

Last, but certainly not least, I have included a number of pedagogical elements that I was not able to find in most of the other infancy books that I had used or examined. Each chapter contains a chapter outline, summary and conclusion section, questions for reading and discussion, and clear definitions of key words. With critical thinking skills in mind, many of the questions at the end of each chapter invite students to apply their knowledge or consider it in light of other evidence.

In conclusion, I hope that you enjoy and learn from this book. We know so much about the first 3 years of life, but in many ways the study of infants and their development is still in its own infancy. As new discoveries are made, it is my wish that the chapters in this book will enable you to appreciate and make sense of that information, evaluating it and applying it to the babies and toddlers that you know. I would love to hear from you, if you have comments or suggestions. Feel free to get in touch at grossd@stolaf.edu.

Dana L. Gross

ACKNOWLEDGEMENTS

I would never have been inspired to write this book if it were not for all of the students who have explored the fascinating journey from birth to the age of 3 years with me. I am grateful for the many ways in which they have made me a better teacher and for their comments on earlier drafts of chapters in this book. I also received invaluable feedback and encouragement from the members of the Kokoro writing group—Mark Allister, Maggie Broner, Phyllis Larson, and Dolores Peters. My colleague Rebecca Starr offered helpful insights about Chapter 12. I also feel fortunate to have received so many specific and useful comments from a small army of anonymous reviewers. Darla Frandrup provided constant support in numerous ways, and several others, notably, Ashley Allen, Beth Hendrickson, and Bethany Jacobson, also helped with preparation of the final manuscript. Marcie Mealia was instrumental in encouraging me to act on my desire to find the "perfect" infancy book by developing my very own. Along the way, many people at Allyn & Bacon provided guidance, information, and support for this book. I want to thank several in particular: Karon Bowers, Stephen Frail, Deborah Hanlon, Carolyn Merrill, Tom Pauken, Allison Rowland, and Lara Torsky.

CHAPTER 1

Beliefs About Babies: Historical Perspectives on Children and Childhood

S uppose you heard about parents, living in a large city, who sent their newborn infant to live with an unrelated woman in the countryside until the age of 2 to 3 years, never paying a visit to their child during that time. The woman—the family's wet nurse—would have responsibility for all aspects of caring for the baby, especially nursing the infant with her own breast milk. Paid to care for several infants in this way, she might supplement their diet with a concoction called pap, consisting of a small amount of milk, simmered with flour, honey, and perhaps a bit of watered-down wine or beer. She might chew bread or meat, allowing the food to mix with her saliva, before placing it in the infant's mouth. If the infant became ill, the wet nurse might pray to a saint to provide a cure.

Would you approve of this diet and the care being provided? Would you have any concerns about the baby's well-being? How would you feel about the parents, knowing that they had made these arrangements partially in order to make it easier for the mother to return to an active social life and partially in order not to violate a taboo against sexual relations while nursing? Would your opinion of the parents change if you were told that 95 percent of children born in their city that year were nursed by wet nurses for similar reasons and under similar circumstances?

As someone living in the twenty-first century, you almost certainly find this scenario objectionable, but if you were living in Paris, France, in the eighteenth century, you probably would see very little to criticize (Fontanel & d'Harcourt, 1997). You might even feel envious or embarrassed if your family could not afford to hire a wet nurse. Moreover, in the absence of specialized pediatric medicine, which was not developed until the late nineteenth century, you probably would not find fault with the wet nurse's efforts to remedy the infant's illness. These divergent views about the proper care and feeding of infants reflect prevalent popular and scientific beliefs then and now. Our focus in this opening chapter is on the events that have transformed, and continue to transform, our thinking about infancy and childhood. We will consider historical changes in views about the nature of children and childhood itself, as well as transformations in family structure, health, and education. These evolving perspectives and practices are fascinating, but they are not the only reason to study infants and their development from birth to age 3. Let's look at a few other reasons first.

Why Do We Study Infants?

Why are you interested in studying infant development? Do you want to understand a particular infant or toddler better? Are you planning to work with infants and toddlers in your future career? Do you want to learn how to be an effective parent for children you plan to have someday? There are many, many reasons to study infants.

Development as Transformation

One of the most basic reasons to study development during the first 3 years of life is the significant transformation that occurs in every developmental domain. Even a casual observer of the same child from birth to the age of 3 years would be able to identify dramatic physical changes that occur. Infants not only gain weight and grow in length, but they also learn new skills and demonstrate increasing coordination and intentionality in using those skills. Infants who initially can only swipe at toys that are attached to the front of their car seat or high chair are soon able to be selective in the way that they touch and manipulate those toys. By 3 to 4 months of age, initially immobile newborns learn to roll over, then crawl, and are on their way to independent walking by the time they celebrate their first birthday. The ability to communicate through language also emerges during the first three years of life, opening new opportunities to understand as well as influence young minds. Even before they can communicate through language, however, babies express their feelings and show preferences for parents and other caregivers, reflecting a capacity for memory and for forming special relationships. Which transformations during infancy do you find the most interesting?

Impact of Early Experience

A second reason to study infant development is to understand the impact of early experience on development. From birth to age 3, there is tremendous variability in infants' early experiences and the settings in which they spend time. Some infants are cared for at home by parents, grandparents, or other adults, whereas other infants enter full-time group childcare at an early age. How do parents' choices affect their children's early development? Are there long-lasting effects of early experiences? Does early enrichment, such as watching "brain boosting" videos and DVDs, make a difference later in childhood? Is it possible to overcome the negative effects of early deprivation and adversity, as experienced by infants living in orphanages and other institutional settings? Infants who are born preterm are more likely than ever before to survive; how does their early arrival affect their subsequent development? These and other examples that you may wonder about raise important questions about the degree to which humans are resilient early in life and the extent to which we remain open to the effects of experience during childhood and beyond.

Many infants and toddlers are cared for by their grandparents.

Research Methods and Tools

A third reason to study infants is that we currently have more tools and information available to guide our inquiry than at any previous time. Imaging techniques provide glimpses of the developing fetus, and other prenatal tests give expectant parents and doctors more information than ever before. Advances in technology enable researchers to examine the infant brain and to understand how it is shaped by experience. New understanding of genetics offers intriguing possibilities to predict and even influence infants' health from the earliest point in development. As we will see in Chapter 2 and throughout the rest of this book, researchers' selection of particular methods and tools enable them to ask infants profound questions long before the subjects of their studies are able to utter their first word.

Interdisciplinary Collaboration

Finally, this is an ideal time to study infants because, as you may have noticed in other courses that you've taken, there is heightened interest in interdisciplinary collaboration. Pediatricians, early childhood educators, social service providers, researchers in child development, and public policy makers have never been more open to sharing knowledge and working together to improve the conditions in which infants live and, hopefully, thrive. As we will see, even economists have recently become involved in evaluating intervention programs for infants and toddlers in an effort to identify programs that are worthwhile and cost-effective. Historians, too, have taken an interest in understanding changes in children's experiences over time, as well as reconceptualizations of the nature of childhood and children (Elder, Modell, & Parke, 1993).

Recurring Themes in the Study of Child Development

As long as there have been infants, there have been beliefs about the factors that affect their development. These beliefs have been incorporated into formal theories in disciplines such as psychology and sociology as well as folk theories held by parents and members of society in general. Theories about child development are usually specific to particular developmental domains, which means that they tend to focus on topics such as language, memory, or emotion, rather than explain or unify multiple areas of development. For that reason, we will introduce specific theories in the chapters about the domains to which the theories pertain. In this section we briefly touch on some of the factors that all developmental theories address—themes that we will return to throughout our study of infant development.

The Path of Development: Stages versus Continuous Change

The field of child development has many theories that describe development as occurring in a **stagewise** fashion, with qualitatively different abilities or characteristics emerging out

Development from birth to age 3 may seem either abrupt or continuous, depending on how frequently children are observed.

of the transition from one stage to the next. Stage theories capture the sort of impression that infrequent observations of the same child over the first 3 years of life might create. At an early visit, the infant would appear to be focused inward, oriented toward his or her own fingers or toes; he or she might show a strong desire to remain close to the parents. A visit several months later, by contrast, would reveal an infant who seems intent upon crawling or cruising away from the caregiver in order to explore the environment. In this sense, the child would appear to possess a qualitatively different set of motivations and abilities at the second visit than at the first. By the time of a third visit, when the child is 3 years old, the intermittent visitor would notice the emergence of language abilities and new forms of play, suggesting that the child had entered a new stage of development.

To parents, or to an observer who sees the child more frequently, daily exposure to the infant would show that there were many subtle changes from birth to the time when independent crawling or walking began. In addition, they would know that the acquisition of new abilities did not occur all at once but was the result of days, weeks, or even months of practice and, initially, failure. Seen in this way, it would appear that development is relatively **continuous**, without clearly marked stages.

As we will see in the remainder of this book, theories differ in terms of whether they describe development as stagewise or continuous. Researchers' beliefs about whether development is stagewise or continuous may influence the measures and designs they use in their studies and the inferences they draw from their data. We will examine some of these issues when we consider research methods in the next chapter.

Heredity and the Environment

In every domain of development, there has been debate about whether the amazing transformations during the first three years of life are the result of childrearing practices and experiences in the environment (**nurture**) or whether they occur relatively independently of experience (**nature**) and are the result of some predetermined "program," whether the source of that program is viewed as divine or biological. Researchers have moved away from the strong version of this debate, and no one would plausibly argue today that development is affected only by the experiences parents provide. Nor would anyone seriously assert that parents' contributions are unimportant in children's development. Instead, the debate has become more nuanced, with both sides recognizing that there is an interaction of heredity and the environment.

This does not mean, however, that the nurture camp has ceased exploring the effects of experience; indeed, it has become even clearer that there are many coexisting, interacting environmental influences in children's lives (Bronfenbrenner & Morris, 1998). As many scientists studying development have noted, children are influenced by environments in both direct and indirect ways, including settings in which they never spend time, such as their parents' workplace. Parents who have stressful jobs, for example, may be more impatient and less sensitive interacting with their infants at home than parents whose work is less emotionally draining. The quality of the care that infants receive is also affected by the wider neighborhood or community in which they live, as well as the cultural context and even the historical period.

The nature proponents, for their part, have also continued to provide new levels of analysis. Early research in embryology provided a foundation that has been built upon by modern-day studies of prenatal development, aided by high-tech tools that enable researchers to view the developing fetus with increasing clarity and precision. Early twentieth-century notions about the brain's development during infancy have been expanded and modified as well by recent advances in neuroscience.

Thanks to the Human Genome Project, we know more than ever before about the genetic material that provides a "blueprint" for development. The evidence is clear that even some aspects of development that appear to be "pre-wired" are influenced by experience. Dietary regulation, for example, can alter the effects of a genetic predisposition

From birth, babies are prepared to respond to and elicit responses from parents and other caregivers.

for the disease phenylketonuria (PKU), preventing mental retardation that would occur otherwise. Exposure to alcohol during the prenatal period, as another example, can "anesthetize" the fetus, interfering with the movement of arms and legs and changing the course of the brain's development and later functioning. Children's biological characteristics, such as whether they are "easy" or "difficult" babies, have an impact on the responses they elicit from parents and other caregivers. Thus, as we will see in the remainder of this book, it is now clear that development occurs as a result of nature *and* nurture.

Active or Passive Development?

Throughout history, parents, philosophers, social reformers, and scientists have tended to view infants as relatively incompetent, passive creatures, playing only a minimal role in their own development. The childrearing advice given to parents tended to reflect this perspective, and parents were seen as the most important agents in the processes of education, socialization, physical development, and personality formation.

There is clear evidence, however, that from birth babies are prepared to respond to and elicit responses from parents and other caregivers. Even very young infants are capable of communicating many of their needs nonverbally by cooing, crying, and reaching. They also learn about the physical world as they act upon and explore it using different methods at different ages, first mouthing objects and later fingering, grasping, banging, and dropping them. Theories of infant development today, therefore, incorporate infants' surprisingly sophisticated capabilities, and empirical studies are designed to measure changes that result from infants' own actions as well as the actions of their caregivers.

Normal and Atypical Development

Just as we now know that infants are much more capable than previously thought, it is also clear that infants develop at different rates. Parents of two or more children can usually report which one rolled over, sat up, or began walking first, and when two or more parents are together, they inevitably make comparisons between their infants. Parents who conclude that their child is precocious may feel a sense of pride or validation of their parenting, even when the milestone is something over which they have no direct influence, such as the eruption of the child's first tooth. It can be worrisome, though, if the baby seems significantly slower to develop than other babies, and parents may wonder if their infant is within the normal range of development. Infants with atypical development, whether in the physical, cognitive, or socioemotional domain, present a challenge to parents and caregivers, but they also can and should be included in activities and programs with more typically developing children. In the chapters that follow, we will consider recent research on atypical development in infancy, focusing on practical issues as well as the implications for theories about normal development.

Culture and Context

Across contemporary cultures, there are many differences in the way that parents care for and interact with their infants (DeLoache & Gottlieb, 2000; McAdoo, 1999; Shore, 2004).

The diversity and validity of Native American family life has not always been recognized or supported in the United States.

In some cultures, in contrast to typical arrangements in the United States, infants and parents share the same bed, even when there would be room in the house for children to sleep elsewhere by themselves (Morelli et al., 1992). In addition, although many U.S. parents play games and engage in pretend play with their infants and toddlers, these practices are not universal (Roopnarine, Johnson, & Hooper, 1994). In the rest of this book, we will examine some of these differences and consider what they reveal about the nature—and nurture—of infant development.

We will also endeavor to understand the richness and diversity of parenting practices within the United States. As we discuss family life, for example, we need to remember that, before European immigrants arrived in the New World, there were numerous and diverse Native American cultures. Daily family life and customs involving marriage, birth, and childrearing reflected the worldviews that prevailed in each culture and geographical region. In some groups, each nuclear family functioned as a separate unit and lived in its own dwelling, but in others households consisted of several nuclear families sharing a common long house. In many Native American cultures, elaborate ceremonies involving members of the community were performed at the birth of a child, and other adults in the community were often responsible for guiding and supporting the child at significant milestones in his or her life, practices that remain important today (Gill, 2002).

The diversity and validity of Native American family life has not always been recognized or supported. For much of U.S. history, American Indians were encouraged or coerced to follow European patterns of childrearing, and differences among tribes were either dismissed or not recognized. It was not until 1978, when the Indian Child Welfare Act was passed, that the intrinsic value of American Indian cultures and extended families was recognized at the federal level. Although there are still concerns about interpretation and implementation, the law has resulted in fewer children being removed from their families, a practice that had occurred in the past for as many as 25 to 35 percent of all American Indian children (Goodluck, 1999).

A history of family disruption is also part of the experience of the majority of African Americans, a phenomenon that can be traced back to the practice of slavery. As historians have noted, however, there were also African Americans who were free while others were enslaved, and it is important to recognize differences in past experience as well as the great diversity in family structure and parenting style that exists among contemporary African American families (Hatchett & Jackson, 1999; McAdoo, 1999).

Similarly, whereas some Mexican American families and families of Spanish descent have been in the United States since the eighteenth and nineteenth centuries, there are also many who immigrated during the second half of the twentieth century from Mexico as well as Puerto Rico, the Caribbean, and Central and South America (McAdoo, 1999). As we will see, researchers now recognize that there are many different parenting styles among these groups (Chahin, Villarruel, & Viramontez, 1999; Martinez, 1999; Suárez, 1999).

Great diversity of experience, beliefs, and behaviors are also found among families who are often grouped together as Asian American. Chinese immigrants, for example, began arriving in the United States in 1820 but were actively prevented from coming to and being integrated into the United States after 1882, when the Chinese Exclusion Act was passed (Lin & Liu, 1999; Ou & McAdoo, 1999). Vietnamese families, by contrast, largely immigrated to the United States in three distinct waves during the 1970s and 1980s (Gold, 1999). Differences in family structure, social class, and educational background prior to immigration, as well as differences in community sponsorship and support, have had a significant impact on each of these groups' experience in their new home.

In summary, the United States is becoming a more diverse nation in an increasingly interconnected world. Awareness of cultural and ethnic diversity is essential if we are to understand the many different settings in which infants develop. This awareness also reminds us that ideas about proper childrearing practices are often a function of time and place. As we will see next, historical comparisons, such as the image of an eighteenth-century infant being sent off to a wet nurse, may also help us perceive both change and continuity in perspectives on infants and their development.

Historical Perspectives on Infancy and Early Childhood

Views about children and their development have changed throughout history. In the past, like today, there was not always agreement concerning the proper care of infants and the role of children in society. It is possible to summarize major trends and turning points in perspectives on infants and their development. As we do so, it is important to remove the sentimental lens through which we may view children and families, especially when we consider times that some now regard as "simpler" days. From the vantage point of the mid-twentieth century, for example, some historians (Ariès, 1962) painted a picture of medieval times as a freer, more equitable era for children, suggesting that they were better off before adults removed them from the working world and sequestered them in school for years of compulsory education. This nostalgic interpretation has been challenged, however, by subsequent historical research which shows that children in the past were more likely to be killed, abandoned, exploited, and abused (Boswell, 1988; De Mause, 1974; Hawes & Hiner, 1985).

Historical Studies of Children and Childhood

Given that parents and children who lived in earlier times cannot be observed or interviewed, how do historians know what their lives were like and what adults of the time thought about them? Three major sources of information have been used: (1) **literary evidence**, including parents' diaries and letters, childrearing advice written by midwives, ministers, and doctors, and children's books; (2) **quantitative archival evidence**, such as census data, tax records, and legislative and court records; and (3) **material culture**, such as toys, clothing, furniture, and works of art. When interpreting these sources, historians are aware—and we should be too—that many of the details about daily life probably were not recorded, because they were viewed as ordinary and unimportant. It is also possible that diaries included entries about problems that parents encountered with their infants, rather than successes, leading modern readers to assume that there was a greater prevalence of problems than successes (Pollack, 1983). Where records do exist, they generally represent families who were educated, wealthy, or prominent. It is also important to recognize that beliefs and behavior do not always match; as is true today, even when parents had childrearing manuals and were able to read them, it cannot be assumed that they followed the advice they contained (Colón & Colón, 2001; Hulbert, 2003; Pollack, 1983; Schulz, 1985).

Historians thus continue to debate the interpretation of evidence. Some have argued that, despite social and technological changes, examining available materials in their entirety reveals significant continuity and surprisingly little change in parent-child relationships, even when the time span considered covers the years 1500 to 1900. According to some historians, for example, far from tolerating or ignoring child abuse and abandonment, in the past most parents, and society as a whole, looked at these practices with horror and outrage, much as parents and other adults do today. As another example, there is evidence that parents who sent their infants to wet nurses were nevertheless emotionally attached to them and took steps to remove their children from these arrangements if they discovered conditions of neglect or abuse (Pollack, 1983).

As we shall see, there is compelling evidence that parents have always wondered about their children's development, even before birth, and have taken steps to promote their well-being. As we shall also see, views about proper childrearing methods and even definitions of childhood itself have often changed because they are cultural inventions, constructions that reflect a society's basic shared beliefs and values at a particular point in time (Borstelmann, 1983; Cahan et al., 1993; Colón & Colón, 2001; Hulbert, 2003; Kessen, 1979). Indeed, the impermanence of childrearing beliefs and practices is reflected in an interesting reversal that occurred by the nineteenth century in Paris; wealthy women began nursing their own infants, and poorer mothers who worked outside of the home were the ones hiring wet nurses (Colón & Colón, 2001).

Many scholars have documented the history of children and childhood, but a complete consideration of these historical studies is beyond the scope of this chapter. Instead, we will focus on three key issues: changing views of children, family life, and education. In addition, although we will consider some aspects of childhood in ancient Greece and Rome, as well as medieval and Renaissance Europe, our main focus will be on the United States and the time from the nineteenth century to the present. Table 1.1 shows a chronology of events that affected children in the United States from the seventeenth century to the present time.

TABLE 1.1   A Chronology of Childhood and Child Development in the United States

1619	Poor English children are shipped to Virginia for their families' financial gain; indentured service and apprenticeships await them.
	Twenty Africans—the first slaves brought to the colonies—arrive in Virginia.
1624	In Jamestown, Virginia, the first African American child is born to slave parents.
1642	Massachusetts statute requires parents and masters to teach children to learn to read and to learn a trade.
1660	Fertility rate is approximately 9.0 (average number of children born to white women).
1662	Virginia law specifies that a mother's status as slave or free person determines her children's status.
1688	The first formal antislavery resolution is passed by the Quakers of Pennsylvania.
1721	Inoculation for smallpox is introduced in Boston.
1776–1830s	Public schools are established in North Carolina, Vermont, Virginia, New York, Massachusetts, and Pennsylvania.
1777	Vermont is the first state to abolish slavery.
1800	Fertility rate is 7.0 (average number of children born to white women).
1819	Civilization Fund forces Indian people to cast aside their religious views, practices, and languages; Indian children are separated from their families and sent to off-reservation boarding schools in which their native language is forbidden.
1820s–1840s	Infant school movement is imported from Europe.
1824	Bureau of Indian Affairs is established.
1830	Indian Removal Act forces most of the Indian population in the southeastern United States to move to Oklahoma.
1833	American Anti-Slavery Society is created; leaders from 10 states meet in Philadelphia.
1836	Massachusetts is the first state to adopt a compulsory school attendance law.
1842	In Massachusetts and Connecticut, the working day for children under 12 years of age is limited to 10 hours.
1850s–1870s	Organizations for the protection of poor, abused, abandoned, and orphaned children are founded, including the New York Children's Aid Society, the New York Catholic Protectory, and the New York Society for the Prevention of Cruelty to Children.
1856	In Wisconsin, the first kindergarten opens, based on the philosophy of Frederich Froebel.
1863	Abraham Lincoln signs the Emancipation Proclamation, freeing slaves in all U.S. states.
1865	Slavery in the United States is outlawed when the 13th Amendment is ratified. The Bureau of Refugees, Freedmen, and Abandoned Lands is established to assist former slaves.
1882	The Chinese Exclusion Act limits immigration and integration into the United States.
1880s	Pediatrics becomes organized, with journals and professional societies established.
1890	Fertility rate is 3.9 (average number of children born to white women).
1890s	Milk stations (milk depots) are established in major American cities to dispense bacteria-free milk and advice about infant feeding and hygiene.
1897	National Congress of Mothers is founded (later renamed National Congress of Parents and Teachers).
1906–1912	Organizations promoting the moral and physical well-being of children and youth are established, including the Playground and Recreation Association of America, Boy Scouts of America, Campfire Girls, and Girl Scouts of America.

(continued)

TABLE 1.1   Continued

1914	U.S. Children's Bureau, created in 1912, publishes *Infant Care*, a child care manual urging parents to adopt a child-centered approach in which they place the child's welfare at the center of family life.
1918	Mississippi adopts compulsory school attendance law, the last state to do so.
1920	Fertility rate is 3.2 (average number of children born to white women).
1928	The National Foundation for Infantile Paralysis (later renamed the March of Dimes) is established to raise funds for research into the causes and prevention of poliomyelitis.
1934	Indian Reorganization Act is enacted to enable conservation and development of American Indian lands and resources by and for American Indian communities; required "pedigree papers" to be issued by each tribe.
1935	Social Security Act provides aid to dependent children, maternal and child health programs, disabled children's programs, and child welfare services.
1940	Inequalities among children, especially rural, low-income, migrant, and minority children, are noted in White House Conference on Children in a Democracy.
1946–1964	"Baby Boom" changes U.S. demographics in post–World War II period.
1950	Midcentury White House Conference on Children and Youth is held.
1953	Department of Health, Education, and Welfare is established. Dr. Jonas Salk reports success of polio vaccine.
1954	*Brown v. Board of Education* court case leads to end of racial segregation in schools.
1964	Head Start is established as part of the War on Poverty to serve low-income children between the ages of 3 and 5 years.
1972	Smallpox vaccination is discontinued in the United States due to eradication of the virus. American Indian Education Act incorporates Indian language and culture into education.
1973	Children's Defense Fund begins advocacy of children's issues, especially those concerning low-income and disabled children.
1977	Zero To Three is founded by child development experts to disseminate information about the significance of the first three years of life. World Health Organization (WHO) efforts result in the eradication of all smallpox viruses, except for samples stored for government research purposes.
1978	Louise Brown, first "test-tube" baby (from *in vitro* fertilization) is born in England. Pregnancy Discrimination Act prohibits employment discrimination on the basis of pregnancy or childbirth. Indian Child Welfare Act strengthens families by ending the practice of removing Indian children from their homes and placing them with non-Indian families off the reservation.
1979	Department of Health and Human Services (DHHS) is created when a separate Department of Education is established. Within the DHHS, the Administration for Children and Families is organized to oversee a number of programs and services, including Head Start.
1980	The WHO recommends that all countries stop vaccinating for smallpox.
1990	Americans with Disabilities Act (ADA) is passed to protect the civil rights of all individuals with disabilities. Children with disabilities are covered by the Individuals with Disabilities Education Act (IDEA). Native American Language Act is passed to preserve native languages.

TABLE 1.1   Continued

1991	Poliomyelitis is eliminated from the Americas, leading the March of Dimes to refocus its efforts, becoming the March of Dimes Birth Defects Foundation.
1992	European Union mandates a paid 14-week maternity leave.
	American Academy of Pediatrics recommends that all infants be placed on their back or side to sleep to prevent Sudden Infant Death Syndrome.
	U.S. Family and Medical Leave Act is passed to enable up to 12 weeks of unpaid, job-protected leave to care for a newborn infant, a newly adopted child or a foster child, or a spouse or parent with a serious health condition.
1994	Early Head Start is established to serve low-income pregnant women and families with infants and toddlers from birth to age 3.
1996	American Academy of Pediatrics recommends that all infants be placed on their back to sleep to prevent Sudden Infant Death Syndrome.
1997	State Children's Health Insurance Program (SCHIP) is established to provide health insurance to children in families without other means of obtaining health insurance.
	White House Conference on Early Childhood Development and Learning is held.
1998	European Union institutes a three-month parental leave.
2000	Human Genome Project completes "working draft" of the human genome.
	Fertility rate (average number of children born to all women over a lifetime) is 2.1.
2001	Canadian Employment Insurance Act expands paid leave benefits from six months to one year for mothers as well as fathers.
2002	SCHIP coverage provides prenatal and delivery care for low-income women.
2004	California is the first U.S. state to enact a paid family leave policy.
2005	American Academy of Pediatrics endorses the use of pacifiers and back-sleeping for all infants and recommends that infants not sleep with parents in order to prevent Sudden Infant Death Syndrome.

Source: Based on Bremner et al., 1970; Harjo, 1999; Hawes & Hiner, 1985; Helfand, Lazarus, & Theerman, 2001; Hulbert, 1999; Low & Clift, 1984; Mathews, MacDorman, & Menacker, 2002; Noymer, 2002; Population Reference Bureau/Child Trends, 2002; and Silvey, 1999.

Views of Children

At many points in history, parents and other adults have debated the true nature of children, and at any given time, differing attitudes and opinions have coexisted. Some have regarded children as innocent, naïve, and unformed, whereas others have viewed them as possessing innate, sometimes undesirable characteristics and predispositions that need to be modified through parents' actions. As we will see, views of children at any given time determine the degree to which systems and policies are in place to protect them and promote their development.

Ancient Greece and Rome.   Stages of growth and development were noted in ancient times, and distinctions were made between infants, young children, and adolescents. Children in ancient Greece and Rome were valued as the future of society, but they were generally regarded as property and had few rights (Borstelmann, 1983). In ancient Sparta, the concept of citizenship included the production of healthy offspring who would, in turn, serve the state as adults. Boys in particular were valued as future warriors, and parents were required to have infant males inspected to be sure that they were healthy and sufficiently well formed to benefit from rigorous training and education; infants who did not pass this inspection were abandoned and left to die of exposure (Colón & Colón, 2001).

Early Roman law also required that citizens produce heirs (three offspring were considered the necessary contribution to the state). Parents were legally required to raise all healthy male infants and at least one of the female infants born to them. Infants were abandoned for a number of reasons, including gender, poverty, illegitimacy, and birth defects (Boswell, 1988). Over time prohibitions against abandonment were themselves largely abandoned, but infanticide and maltreatment of infants and young children were practiced for many years before Roman emperors, beginning around the year AD 100, acted to protect children through legal reforms (Colón & Colón, 2001).

Medieval Europe.   In medieval Europe (approximately 500 to 1300), plagues killed many people, and fewer written records remain than from ancient Greece and Rome (Boswell, 1988). According to the documents that did survive this era, **infant mortality rates** (the number of deaths per 1,000 live births, before the age of 1 year) were high, and perhaps as many as one or two of every three children died in the first year of life (comparison statistics for infant mortality at other times in history are shown in Table 1.2). Parents used the only means available to them, usually charms and amulets of various kinds, to protect their infants from harm and sickness (Fontanel & d'Harcourt, 1997). One of the "ailments" that parents feared during the Middle Ages (and well into the mid-nineteenth century) was teething. Infants who were teething often suffered from fevers, convulsions, and diarrhea brought on by parasites, cholera, or respiratory diseases, so many parents erroneously believed that teething per se could prove fatal. Remedies for teething and its accompanying illnesses included placing leeches on the baby's gums, hanging amulets around the baby's neck, or following other superstitious practices that were thought to transfer the baby's ailment to some other person or object (Fontanel & d'Harcourt, 1997; Howe, 1998).

Given the high rate of infant mortality, there was great concern about the souls of deceased infants. Parents whose infants became ill often went on a religious pilgrimage or prayed to the "first pediatricians of Christianity"—saints specializing in children and their illnesses, including Saint Quintin (whooping cough), Saint Blaise (sore throats), Saint Apollonia (toothaches), Saint Nicholas (colic and diarrhea), and Saint Medard (parasitic worms). One healing pediatric saint was Saint Guinefort, a greyhound who had been killed while defending his young. In praying to Saint Guinefort, parents hoped that he would remove the sick creature (a changeling) that had been left in their child's place by forest sprites and return their real child. If the child recovered, it was taken as proof that Guinefort had defeated the devilish forest sprites and their real child had been returned. If the child died, on the other hand, parents could tell themselves that the child had not been theirs. In the thirteenth century, the Church,

TABLE 1.2   Infant Mortality Rates in Historical and International Perspective[a,b]

Historical Era	Infant Mortality Rate

Number of deaths per 1,000 live births by the age of 1 year:

United States

1920	100.0
1940	47.0
1945	38.3
1984	12.6
1990	8.9
2002	7.0

2000 International Comparisons[b]

Number of deaths per 1,000 live births by the age of 5 years:

Industrialized Countries[c]	6
Latin America/Caribbean	37
East Asia/Pacific	44
South Asia	100
Middle East/North Africa	64
Former USSR/Central Eastern Europe	38
Sub-Saharan Africa	175

Notes: (a) Based on information in Hawes & Hiner, 1985; and Mathews, MacDorman, & Menacker, 2002. (b) Population Reference Bureau/Child Trends, 2002. (c) Western Europe, the United States, Australia, and Israel.

bothered by the idea of a dog-saint, tried to bring an end to these practices (Boswell, 1988; Fontanel & d'Harcourt, 1997).

In early medieval Europe, just as in ancient times, infants were still abandoned and left to die of exposure, and laws even supported parents' rights to sell their children into servitude (Boswell, 1988). By the beginning of the seventh century, another form of abandonment— **oblation**—had been established. Oblation was the permanent "donation" of an infant or very young child to a monastery. The practice removed the requirement of servitude per se, but by law, oblates were required to remain in the monastery for the remainder of their lives. In comparison with other forms of abandonment, oblation offered parents assurance that their child would survive, be well fed, and even receive some education as part of a "family" in which all of the children were adopted (Boswell, 1988).

As early as the eighth century, the Church showed concern for abandoned infants by establishing asylums and orphanages. In response to alarm about the numbers of infants who were drowned or left to die of exposure, and to offer parents an alternative to infanticide, between 787 and 1421, infant asylums were founded, first in Italy and later in other major European cities (Boswell, 1988; Colón & Colón, 2001; Fontanel & d'Harcourt, 1997).

In some wealthy families, infant abandonment functioned as a way of reducing the number of possible heirs among whom the father's property and wealth would need to be divided. Changes in inheritance laws in some parts of Europe, such as England, allowed a single heir to be designated, resulting in a reduction in infant abandonment (Borstelmann, 1983). Among poor families, the practice of infant abandonment declined when opportunities developed for impoverished children to earn a living by becoming servants in the households of wealthy families. In other parts of Europe that did not experience an increase in prosperity, or where overpopulation was a problem, however, abandonment and infanticide, especially of illegitimate children, appear to have continued. Legislation in the thirteenth century focused on whether abandoned infants should be baptized, and the main consequence for parents who knowingly abandoned their infants was loss of the right to control or reclaim the child in the future. Poverty-stricken parents (usually fathers) had the legal right to sell their children (Boswell, 1988).

The Renaissance. During the Renaissance (approximately 1300–1500), as in previous times, children continued to be abandoned and left at the doors of churches or in publicly run foundling homes. These institutions, which were the precursor to orphanages and children's hospitals, developed systems through which mothers could anonymously leave their newborns. In some cases, there was a depository with a revolving tray on which the infant could be placed and transferred indoors, out of the harsh elements (Boswell, 1988; Colón & Colón, 2001; Fontanel & d'Harcourt, 1997). Sadly, infants taken into these foundling homes may have been more likely to die than infants who previously had been abandoned surreptitiously and then rescued by adoptive parents. Records from the fourteenth century show that, as a result of poor hygiene and an absence of effective medical care, 20 to 40 percent of infants died within a year, many within a month, of arriving in the foundling home. By comparison, the mortality rate among infants sent to wet nurses during the same time was about 17 percent (Boswell, 1988).

Many Renaissance thinkers contemplated ways to create a perfect society, as exemplified by Sir Thomas More's *Utopia* (1516). More's book, like much literature from the late Renaissance, pondered human values, the difference between good and evil, and the path to virtue. Religious reformers in Europe asserted that parents had a duty "to produce good Christian souls, along with good, healthy human beings of limitless potential" (Colón & Colón, 2001, p. 284). The ideal child was described as pious, disciplined, obedient, and teachable. The debate about whether infants were inherently innocent or corrupt continued in Europe and was exported to Puritan colonies that were established in the New World by the middle of the seventeenth century.

Colonial America. For Puritans in the New World, infancy began in the womb and prayers were needed because infants were believed to be conceived in sin. Prenatal care, therefore, was both physical and spiritual (Beales, 1985). At birth, children were regarded as "innocent vipers," likely to commit evil but not yet able to understand the nature of their acts, ignorant of Scriptures and inherently sinful but capable of becoming enlightened and restrained. Pious parents had two tasks, instruction and discipline (Moran & Vinovskis, 1985). Puritan attitudes about these tasks are reflected in advice from John Robinson, minister of the Plymouth Colony (1625), who wrote, "And surely there is in all children, though not alike a stubbornness, and stoutness of mind arising from natural pride, which must, in the first place be broken and beaten down" (cited in Moran & Vinovskis, 1985, p. 26).

Despite the harshness of these words to our twenty-first-century ears, there is evidence that Puritan parents were devoted to and loved their children. Given the likelihood that at least some of their children would not live beyond their first year, parents showed love and concern for their infants' souls by baptizing them early, usually within 1 to 2 weeks of their birth (Beales, 1985). Other signs of Puritans' love for their children included expressions of grief in letters and diaries after a child had died and the common practice of naming subsequent children after deceased siblings (Beales, 1985). The care and training of children were the nuclear family's responsibility, but concerns about spoiling them with too much affection led some Puritan families to send their offspring to live with other Puritan families for a time (Beales, 1985; Hareven, 2000; Pollack, 1983).

Throughout the colonial period, epidemics of smallpox, diphtheria, scarlet fever, yellow fever, intestinal diseases, and influenza occurred in waves. Smallpox was particularly deadly, especially for young children; some parents inoculated their children against the disease after the practice was introduced in Boston in 1721, but the practice was controversial (Colón & Colón, 2001; Schulz, 1985). Children also died of ordinary childhood diseases, including measles, whooping cough, and mumps (Schulz, 1985). Slave children often suffered from malnutrition, with the result that the mortality rate for young black children was twice that of white children (Schulz, 1985). In addition, because colonial children's homes were not "baby-proofed," many young children died or were seriously injured in accidents in and around the home (Colón & Colón, 2001; Schulz, 1985).

Unlike the Parisian parents described at the beginning of this chapter, most Puritan parents did not employ wet nurses (Finkelstein, 1985). Instead, mothers nursed their infants themselves, a practice that was thought to impart the mother's positive qualities and pious attitudes to the child early on. Coincidentally and fortuitously, antibodies in the mother's milk also afforded infants at least some degree of temporary immunity from the diseases surrounding them (Beales, 1985).

During the seventeenth and eighteenth centuries, Puritan parents' diaries became increasingly focused on childhood and childrearing as abstract concepts. Whereas earlier diaries noted children's specific misbehaviors and parents' responses to those actions, for example, later records described general approaches to childrearing and philosophies about discipline. Parents increasingly wrote about their efforts to train their children to think and behave in morally correct ways (Pollack, 1983).

During the nineteenth century, an increasingly romantic view of childhood emerged, and young children came to be seen as the redeemers of a more complex, possibly corrupt, industrialized society (Borstelmann, 1983). In a sense, childhood was discovered anew. The home was envisioned as a refuge from the outside world (Hareven, 1985, 2000), and the mother's role as moral guardian was sentimentalized and emphasized in numerous publications. In *The Mother at Home* (1834), for example, the Rev. John Abbott wrote, "O mothers! . . . There is no earthly influence to be compared with yours. There is no combination of causes so powerful, in promoting the happiness or the misery of our race, as the instructions of home" (p. 167).

Beginning in the 1890s, advice about infant care, feeding, and hygiene was dispensed to immigrant parents in locations that included New York City's Ellis Island.

Before the age of 5 or 6 years, children were regarded as creatures that were under the control of animal impulses. For this reason, infants and very young children were thought to need "guidance, not repression, activity rather than confinement, sensitive tutoring from a totally available, benevolent mentor" (Finkelstein, 1985, p. 124). Because mothers were viewed as inherently gentle and morally superior, they were seen by many as the ideal agents to protect children through a concentrated, socially isolated relationship in an environment that they controlled (Finkelstein, 1985).

As we will see later in this chapter, the sentimentality directed toward motherhood began to change toward the end of the nineteenth century, as scientific professionals emerged to assist mothers in making the right choices for their children. Mothers themselves played a central role in bringing about this collaboration. As early as 1888, for example, a group of affluent, educated New York City mothers established the Society for the Study of Child Nature. Soon after that, mothers' clubs and child study groups were formed across the country. The National Congress of Mothers (later renamed the National Congress of Parents and Teachers) was founded in 1897, as "the widespread mood of a closing century coalesced into a self-conscious institutionalized movement for a new era" (Hulbert, 1999, p. 21). At the 1899 National Congress of Mothers, Dr. Luther Emmett Holt, one of America's first pediatricians and author of *The Care and Feeding of Children* (1894), reflected this mood when he endorsed systematic, scientific study as the best way to promote children's health and development (Hulbert, 1999).

Holt's advice found a receptive audience because scientific study had shown that bacteria in urban milk supplies were the likely source of fatal infections and diseases in infants. To address this problem, child-health activists established milk stations, first in New York City during the 1890s, and later in other U.S. cities. As milk stations became more widespread, advice about infant care, feeding, and hygiene was dispensed along with the milk (Colón & Colón, 2001; Halpern, 1988).

As waves of new immigrants arrived in the United States and settled in urban areas with large populations, members of the clergy, educators, and social observers became concerned about the children. Disease and illness, including cholera, tuberculosis, and infant diarrhea, were rampant; hunger and malnutrition were common (Berrol, 1985). In response to these conditions, from 1800 until 1835, clergy members established protective settings, such as Sunday schools for infants in the factories where their parents worked (Finkelstein, 1985).

Another sign of concern for child welfare at the end of the nineteenth century was the emergence of the Progressive Movement, which was active from the 1890s until the 1920s. The available evidence suggests that Progressives were motivated by a mixture of feelings, including humanitarian altruism, concern, fear, confusion, and a desire to exert control over the changing urban environment (Cohen, 1985). Regardless of their motives, members of the Progressive movement were involved in the establishment of a growing number of private and public institutions, all of which existed to counteract the negative influence of the adult world on children (Finkelstein, 1985).

Public policy and interventions addressing the problems of children and families became established during the twentieth century, and many are now a familiar part of twenty-first-century life. Continuing their activities from the beginning of the twentieth century, women's organizations throughout the country called for and organized child study initiatives to document and solve child welfare problems (Cravens, 1985). They also lobbied for federal support of studies of children's health and development. In 1912, they were rewarded by the establishment of the United States Children's Bureau, which was designed to serve as a clearinghouse for information about the best childrearing practices. In 1914, the Children's Bureau published the first edition of *Infant Care*, a manual distributed at no cost to millions of new parents (Cohen, 1985; Cravens, 1985). The federal government lacked the funds to produce significant change, however, and in the end philanthropic foundations formed partnerships with universities in support of the scientific study of children and their development (Cravens, 1985). We shall return to the scientific study of child development later in this chapter. For now, we will look at some of the ways in which family life has varied.

Family Life

Immigrants to the New World in the early seventeenth century brought their old customs, beliefs, and childrearing practices with them. It is difficult to generalize about their experience in the American colonies because, like today, childhood and family life were affected by the characteristics of the local community (Beales, 1985; Schulz, 1985). The best records of colonial families come from Puritans who settled in New England.

In the seventeenth century, most New England women married in their late teens or early twenties and began having children within the first year of marriage. Women typically continued having children, at two-year intervals, until they were in their late 30s or early 40s (Beales, 1985). Families thus had a relatively large number of children, by today's standards, but the high rate of infant mortality (between 10 and 30 percent of infants did not survive beyond the age of 1 year) meant that the household itself was not necessarily that large at all times (Schulz, 1985). The basic family unit was the nuclear family, with kinship networks nearby providing an important source of support (Hareven, 1985, 2000).

The Industrial Revolution changed family life dramatically in the United States. At the beginning of this period, most children lived in rural areas and grew up farming with their parents and a relatively large number of siblings (in 1865, 82 percent of families had five or more children). By the mid-twentieth century, by contrast, most children had fewer siblings (in 1930, 57 percent lived in families with three or fewer children) and lived in urban areas with populations of 10,000 or more (Hernandez, 1997). In the 1930s, the effects of the Great Depression on family life are well documented but beyond the scope of this chapter. In general, it appears that children born during the years of greatest economic hardship were more negatively affected than children whose first years of life occurred when their families—and the country as a whole—were more affluent (Elder, 1974; Elder & Hareven, 1993). This finding, which will be echoed again whenever we discuss the effects of poverty and parenting stress due to financial hardship, reflects the unique vulnerability of the youngest children in families—infants and toddlers (Shonkoff & Phillips, 2000).

A defining demographic trend—the Baby Boom—occurred in the years following World War II (1946–1964), with the peak occurring in 1957. Babies born at this time, unlike those born during the Depression, entered a world in which the United States was experiencing a new child-centered period of prosperity. During the Baby Boomers' formative years, families, schools, and community life were transformed in important ways. There was an increase in the proportion of Americans marrying and a decline in the number of childless couples. The average age at which women married decreased from 21.5 in 1940 to 20.1 in 1956 (Strickland & Ambrose, 1985). For comparison, the corresponding age was 23 in 1970 and 25 in 2003 (Fox, Connolly, & Snyder, 2005). In addition, more couples were having their first child within 13 months of their marriage, and more than half of women marrying for the first time gave birth to their first child before they were 20 (Strickland & Ambrose, 1985).

Studies of childrearing patterns in the 1950s suggest that middle-class parents, especially young, first-time mothers, regarded their role in ways that were different from prewar parents. Many parents at this time were influenced by Dr. Benjamin Spock's (1946) *The Common Sense Book of Baby and Child Care*, which sold more than 28 million copies and, by 1976, had become the best selling book in the twentieth century, after the Bible. In addition to medical advice, Spock urged parents to adopt a child-centered, "commonsense" approach for socializing children, intended to minimize confrontation and conflict in the family. He encouraged mothers to monitor their children's growth and development and to gently and tactfully guide them toward becoming a cooperative member of a happy family (Strickland & Ambrose, 1985). Spock's goals also included alleviating mothers' anxiety about childrearing, since he believed that anxiety itself could be harmful to children's development. Ultimately, the book was intended to help parents create a more democratic society (Hulbert, 2003; Strickland & Ambrose, 1985). As shown in Table 1.3, Spock's advice about toilet training also reflected attitude changes in the 1940s (Brazelton et al., 1999).

There is some evidence to suggest that Spock's advice made an impression on parents in the late 1940s and 1950s. One review of the parenting literature of the time, for example, indicates that middle-class and working-class parents appear to have exchanged positions with respect to permissiveness with their children. Whereas middle-class mothers before 1945 had been less permissive than mothers of the working class, after 1945, the trend was in the other direction (Bronfenbrenner, 1958, cited in Strickland & Ambrose, 1985).

TABLE 1.3   Changes in Attitudes and Advice about Toilet Training

Years	Attitudes and Advice
1920s/1930s	A rigid, parent-centered approach to toilet training was recommended. This view was in keeping with the theoretical positions of well-known child development experts, such as John B. Watson.
1940s/1950s	Experts, including Benjamin Spock, rejected absolute and rigid rules for toilet training. It was believed that rushing children or being too harsh with them might fail and lead to behavioral problems. Parents were advised to look for "signs of readiness" in their child and to communicate with them in order to enlist their cooperation before beginning training.
1950s/1960s	Pediatricians, such as T. Berry Brazelton, proposed a child-oriented gradual method. Based on notions of child readiness, this approach integrated physical, emotional, and cognitive elements. Child readiness was believed to be present in most children by the age of about 18 months. Surveys from 1951 to 1961 showed that approximately one-half of children were continent during the day by the age of 27 months, and nearly all children (98 percent) were fully toilet trained by the age of 36 months.
1960s/1970s	Experts, such as Nathan Azrin and Richard Foxx, used applied behavior analysis as the basis for structured-behavioral toilet training. In published reports, their method was said to achieve toilet training with normal, healthy toddlers in an average of 3.9 hours. The Azrin-Foxx method incorporated notions of child readiness with principles of applied behavior analysis.

Source: Based on Brazelton et al., 1999.

Spock's advice was not the only factor shaping middle-class parents' attitudes and childrearing behaviors (Strickland & Ambrose, 1985). Postwar economic prosperity also affected patterns of childrearing (Elder et al., 1993; Potter, 1954, cited in Strickland & Ambrose, 1985). Greater affluence made it possible, for example, for families to buy washing machines and other conveniences. These trends suggest that parents who read Spock's advice may have followed it because it coincided with changing middle-class attitudes about children and families as well as economic and social conditions that made it possible for them to do so (Strickland & Ambrose, 1985).

By contrast and if they were aware of it, for families living in poverty, the new, child-centered approach probably did not seem very commonsensical. One study from the 1960s compared white and black mothers in Chicago in terms of their exposure to Spock's book. Whereas 77 percent of white, middle-class mothers had read *Baby and Child Care*, only 32 percent of black, middle-class mothers had. Similar patterns were found among working-class mothers, with 48 percent of white, working-class mothers reporting that they had read Spock's book, as compared to 12 percent of black, working-class mothers (Blau, 1971, cited in Strickland & Ambrose, 1985).

It is reasonable to assume that other groups who were not benefiting from postwar prosperity, such as migrant worker families, were also likely to be indifferent to or unaware of the new approach to childrearing. As shown in a landmark television documentary in 1960, "Harvest of Shame," migrant children often began working in the

In 1960, the landmark television documentary "Harvest of Shame" publicized the transience, poverty, and poor living conditions of many children in migrant worker families.

fields by age 7 or 8 and experienced transience, poverty, and poor living conditions from birth. Middle-class Americans who saw this program were shocked to discover that only 1 out of every 500 migrant children finished grade school (Strickland & Ambrose, 1985).

There was growing awareness, then, that not all American children were being nurtured by parents who had the knowledge, skills, and time to implement the new, common-sense approach to childrearing. At the level of the federal government, there was increasing evidence of the harm being done to Baby Boom children growing up in environments filled with poverty, discrimination, and a lack of opportunity or hope. This awareness led to political support for a "war on poverty," an effort to create a "Great Society" in an America that would be rid of poverty and racial injustice. As part of the "war" effort, Project Head Start was created in 1964 to serve preschool-age children of low-income families (we will discuss the more recently established Early Head Start program for infants and toddlers in Chapter 11).

The compensatory model of Head Start sought to provide the best childrearing advice and comprehensive services for economically disadvantaged families. What was the nature of this advice, and what were the experts telling parents about infant development and care during this time? One review of the U.S. Children's Bureau *Infant Care* manual and *Parents* magazine from 1955 through 1984 shows that there was not a simple, direct relationship between what experts knew and the information that was communicated to parents (Young, 1990). Information about biological aspects of infant development (perception, cognition, and temperament) was most accurately and consistently communicated to parents, but coverage of the mother-infant relationship, child care, feeding, and fathers grew, shrank, or remained the same as a function of the "broader cultural context and demographic changes" (Young, 1990, p. 17).

As shown in Table 1.4, advice concerning the mother-infant relationship from the mid-1950s until the early 1970s emphasized the mother's role over all other influences; by

TABLE 1.4   What Child Development Experts Told Parents (Usually Mothers) in *Infant Care*

Topic	1955	1980
Newborns . . .	. . . are more passive than active.	. . . learn through their own actions, but parents need to provide stimulation.
Temperament . . .	. . . each baby is different.	. . . refers to your baby's distinctive style. Which type is your baby?
Feeding . . .	. . . your baby with breast milk is the natural way. The breast is the center of his emotional world.	. . . with sensitivity is more important than whether you give your baby breast milk or formula. Unless you feel strongly about not breast feeding, however, you should plan to nurse your baby.
The Mother-Infant Relationship . . .	. . . is the reason your baby is happy and secure. Your baby needs you as much as he needs food or air.	. . . is only one of several important influences on your baby's emotional health.
The Father-Infant Relationship . . .	. . . can be a great help to you, but do not expect your baby's father to share equally in caring for him.	. . . provides a unique and necessary complementary relationship to the relationship that you have with your baby. Your baby's father can share the role of primary caregiver with you.
Nonparental Child Care . . .	. . . is like boarding your baby away from home.	. . . will not harm your baby as long as you choose the right setting. Use our checklist to judge your baby's child care setting.
Infants . . .	. . . are able to see light and color. They have an awakening memory around the age of 6 months.	. . . are able to track objects, make associations between events, and discriminate patterns. They learn best when you interact with them and respond to their actions. Watch to see what your baby is interested in and take your cue from him or her.

Source: Based on Young, 1990.

the 1970s, experts recognized that the mother-infant relationship is only one of many important relationships influencing the child's development. Advice about the father's role revealed another shift, from the 1950s and 1960s when "mothers were encouraged to include fathers in the care of the baby but not to expect fathers to share equally in the care of the infant," to the mid-1980s when "new parents were told that fathers could share in the role of primary caretaker" (Young, 1990, p. 23).

The postwar trends that produced the Baby Boom generation were not duplicated by young adults in the later 1960s and 1970s. As we noted previously, the average age for first marriage increased steadily, and many young adults postponed having children or even decided to remain childless. Between 1957 and 1976, marriage and parenthood came to be viewed as a personal choice and less as a "natural" accompaniment of adulthood. Social regard for families remained high, but there was more tolerance of a range of choices about whether and when to start a family (Arnett, 2000; Douvan, 1985).

Education

Popular press reports in recent years about brain development from birth to age 3 have heightened many parents' desire to expose their infants to stimulating experiences that will increase their intelligence. Despite the fact that brain development does not end at age 3, many new parents now feel pressure to make the most of their infant's first brain-building months and years. Let's look now at historical evidence concerning parents' beliefs about the importance and the possibility of educating very young children.

One of the most influential philosophers and educators in the late seventeenth and early eighteenth century, John Locke, believed that children could (and should) be educated as soon as possible. In Locke's *Essay Concerning Human Understanding* (1690), he described children as tabula rosa—"blank slates"—and argued that children's behavior and knowledge are derived from experience, rather than being innately predetermined. In *Some Thoughts Concerning Education*, Locke (1693) advised against forcing or coercing children or acting in any way that would discourage their natural curiosity (Hulbert, 1999; Moran & Vinovskis, 1985).

Another widely read publication, many years later, was Jean Jacques Rousseau's (1762) *Émile, or On Education*. In *Émile*, Rousseau asserted that parents need to be aware of and shape children's natural tendencies in order to create morally desirable individuals embodying traits of humility, chastity, and honesty. Instead of confining infants in swaddling clothes, for example, Rousseau advised parents to adopt natural childrearing practices that would allow the infant to be active and free to move. These views gained favor in Europe as well as in the American colonies and influenced beliefs about child development and the role of parents by the end of the nineteenth century (Hulbert, 1999).

Puritan parents in the New England colonies taught their children to read very early in life, at least by 4 or 5 years of age. The preferred reading material was the Holy Scriptures, and their primary motivation was to improve their children's souls and moral character (Moran & Visnovskis, 1985). Males were usually better educated than females, so fathers at first played the dominant role in educating children in colonial New England. This appears to have changed in the mid-seventeenth century, as men became less involved in the church and were increasingly viewed as less suitable moral educators, while women continued church membership at high levels and became increasingly literate. By the late seventeenth century, Puritan ministers had become accepting of women as educators, inside the home and in local schools that were established as the population increased. At the end of the eighteenth century, public schools and churches in New England had primary responsibility for educating children, but the family was still expected to teach very young children the alphabet and provide them with the foundations of literacy (Moran & Visnovskis, 1985). As we will see next, public and private institutions came to play an increasingly significant role in family life and in children's development.

Early in the nineteenth century, many educators believed that children as young as 18 months could be educated and taught to read at an early age; these educators strongly supported the **infant school movement** and imported it from Europe in the 1820s (Hareven, 2000). In America, infant schools offered poor children aged 2 to 4 years an early education as a way of compensating for their disadvantaged family life (Moran & Vinovskis, 1985). By the 1830s and 1840s, middle-class children were enrolled as well. In Massachusetts, as many as 40 to 50 percent of 3-year-olds attended infant schools, and most American parents believed that very young children could and should be taught to read (Moran & Vinovskis, 1985).

Not everyone supported the infant school movement. In the 1830s, physicians, educators, and authors of popular childrearing books began to express concerns about systematic efforts to encourage young children's intellectual development (Hareven, 2000). Some even warned that early childhood education would lead to insanity (Finkelstein, 1985). As a result, attendance began to drop at infant schools throughout the country, and by 1860, almost no 3- or 4-year-olds attended schools in Massachusetts or anywhere else in America (Moran & Vinovskis, 1985).

Between about 1840 and 1860, there was growing support for the expansion of schools and education for children, as long as it did not begin before the age of 6 or 7 years, and as long as it built children's character by providing a refuge from the adult world (Finkelstein, 1985). School attendance was not yet the norm, however, and only 50 percent of children ages 5 to 19 were enrolled in school in 1870 (Hernandez, 1997).

Laws concerning compulsory education, child labor, and the treatment of juvenile delinquents were enacted, although these changes were gradual and there was sometimes wide variation across the United States. Massachusetts, for instance, was the first state to pass compulsory school attendance laws in 1836, whereas Mississippi, acting in 1918, was the last state to do so (Bremner et al., 1970, 1971; Hawes & Hiner, 1985). One clear, if not surprising, result of this legislation was a sharp increase in school attendance. Enrollment rates for children ages 7 to 13, which had hovered around 50 percent in the mid-1800s, rose to 95 percent by 1940 and to 99 percent by 1949 (Hernandez, 1997).

By the beginning of the twentieth century, early childhood education had also taken root, as seen in the expanding kindergarten movement. The concept of the kindergarten, imported from Germany, was based on Friedrich Froebel's theories about the necessity and centrality of play in early childhood (Cohen, 1985). The first kindergartens in the United States were opened in the mid-1850s, with a curriculum that explicitly rejected the earlier infant school emphasis on precocious learning (Finkelstein, 1985). Instead, kindergartens were intended to protect impoverished children from the city streets and to facilitate immigrant children's assimilation into American culture. Immigrant neighborhoods in many cities had private charity kindergartens as well as kindergartens in public schools. By the late 1870s, the organized play and socialization available in kindergartens came to be seen as a necessity for all young children, regardless of their family's economic resources (Cohen, 1985; Finkelstein, 1985).

Progressives directed some of their efforts at the youngest members of society, creating day nurseries for the young children of working, often destitute mothers and, in 1898, founding the National Federation of Day Nurseries (Cohen, 1985). The original purpose of these day care settings was to contribute to the moral elevation of impoverished families and children, but, by the 1920s, public and private attitudes had changed again. Day care came to be regarded as "a custodial place of last resort for needy, pathological families" (Ashby, 1985, p. 497).

As we have seen, views of childhood have evolved throughout history. Significantly, there is little debate today about whether children are inherently innocent or sinful. In fact, "the transition from a moral and religious to a more secular and scientific view of childhood is one of the great revolutions" of the twentieth century (Smuts & Hagen, 1985, p. 6). Let's look now at the fascinating transition to the scientific study of infants and children, from the perspective of those who studied them.

The Development of Child Development

During the twentieth century, parents increasingly turned to professionals with expertise in the field of child development to provide guidance and answer questions about childrearing. Increasingly, professionals in child development moved away from an examination of and intervention in children's external worlds and toward the consideration of children's internal, psychological experiences. To understand the history of the scientific study of infants and children requires some understanding of the emergence of child development and its introduction into the United States at the beginning of the twentieth century, as well as an awareness of the emergence of pediatric medicine, since many researchers in child development focused their attention on early physical growth and motor development.

It has become commonplace for parents to bring their infants and children to visit a pediatrician, not only in times of sickness but also for preventative well-child care. This is an experience that most children growing up in previous eras would not have had. Although parents sought advice from local experts, such as midwives, clergy, and older relatives, it would not have occurred to them to consult a pediatrician, because physicians who focused exclusively on children did not exist. In 1880, child specialists called themselves *pediatrists* rather than pediatricians, and there were fewer than 50 such specialists in the United States, none of whom saw children on a full-time basis. It was not until the 1930s and 1940s, in fact, that pediatrics emerged as a secure, established part of medicine (Cravens, 1985; Halpern, 1988).

As many historians have noted, pediatrics developed in response to health-related social problems, such as those we have already discussed concerning the children of immigrants (Halpern, 1988; Sears, 1975). The same influence of real-world problems was evident in the origins of helping professions such as education and social work and, to a great extent, in the discipline of child development. As one historian observed, "[d]uring the first two decades of the twentieth century, these professions began relevant research to improve their abilities, but their main influence on the future science was their rapidly expanding services for children in the schools, hospitals, clinics, and social agencies. . . . [I]t was in the next decade, the 1920s, that scientists from several nonprofessionally oriented ("pure science") disciplines began to join the researchers from the child-oriented professions to create what we now view as the scientific field of child development. . . . But . . . child development is a product of social needs that had little to do with science qua science. . . .

The field grew out of *relevance*" (Sears, 1975, p. 4, original author's emphasis). Let's look more closely now at several of the key figures in the history of child development in order to find out who they were and how they contributed to the scientific study of children in the United States.

G. Stanley Hall

In order to understand how scientific approaches to the study of child development were introduced into the United States, we need to consider the central role played by G. Stanley Hall, the first professor of psychology in the United States, the first president of the American Psychological Association, and an organizer of the Child Study Section of the National Education Association. According to one source, "Hall did more than any other founder of U.S. psychology to develop the new . . . child psychology" (Cravens, 1985, p. 423).

Hall became aware of child psychology during post-doctoral studies in Germany with Wilhelm Wundt (generally credited with establishing the first psychology laboratory in 1879). Returning to the United States in 1880, Hall was convinced that the new science of psychology had the potential to create better individuals and thus a better society. He also believed that scientific research and the study of children could transform educational practices. In his own research, Hall used a questionnaire method—an early aptitude test— that he brought back from Europe to study children's thinking and to help teachers understand the concepts children had learned by the time they entered school (Cairns, 1998).

Together with Dr. Luther Emmett Holt, pediatrician and author of *The Care and Feeding of Children* (1894), Hall appeared at numerous meetings of child study groups and at conferences held by organizations such as the National Congress of Mothers. During 1893 to 1894 alone, Hall gave 34 major public speeches to such groups (Hulbert, 1999). Whereas Holt was influenced by John Locke's views about parents' ability to shape their children, especially during the period of infancy, "Hall took a more Rousseau-like tack, championing the child's own natural impulses and rich imagination as the best guide to his growth" (Hulbert, 1999, p. 25). In his most important book, *Adolescence: Its Psychology and Its Relation to Physiology, Anthropology, Sociology, Sex, Crime, Religion, and Education* (1904), Hall echoed the views of European embryologists and other scientists when he argued that the life cycle consists of stages of predictable and naturally unfolding maturation.

Hall trained many of the first child psychologists in America, including John Dewey, who later became one of the most influential psychologists in the field of education in the early twentieth century. In 1916, in keeping with the spirit of the times and consistent with principles that Hall espoused, Dewey asserted that children's experiences in school could contribute to a better society. The key was for teachers to discern the subject matter of education "from the child's immediate environment and from the child's current interests" (Cairns, 1998, p. 56), avoiding the temptation to impose their own agendas on their pupils.

Hall is also remembered as the American psychologist who arranged a meeting at Clark University, in 1909, between Sigmund Freud and the leading psychologists in North America (Cairns, 1998). This too is evidence of Hall's contributions to the field of child development, since the basic premise of Freud's theory is that experiences early in life, especially infancy and toddlerhood, are of great consequence for subsequent development and functioning (Cairns, 1998). Even psychologists who did not endorse Freud's psychosexual perspective—and there were many who did not—agreed with this basic premise, as do child development experts today.

James Mark Baldwin

Like Hall, James Mark Baldwin was a pioneer in organizing psychological science in North America. Known primarily for his later theoretical work, in his early years Baldwin founded an experimental laboratory at the University of Toronto in which he began a research program on infant psychology (Cairns, 1998, p. 44). Among the topics that Baldwin explored in the early 1890s were the ontogeny of movement patterns and handedness. In one study of handedness, Baldwin observed the development of his own infant daughter's reaching behavior under systematic, controlled laboratory conditions. In order to eliminate any hand preference that might result from the way that parents carry their infants, Baldwin even specified that his wife should give their daughter equal time in her left and right arms (Harris, 1985). Influenced by theories of evolution, Baldwin considered research on "handedness" in animals to be relevant to his study of human infants.

Baldwin also brought evolutionary concepts into his theoretical work on cognitive development in books such as *Mental Development in the Child and the Race* (1895), in which he asserted that intellectual development in the individual could not be considered without also contemplating the evolution of the mind in the human species (or "race"). Baldwin described how development progresses from infancy to adulthood in a series of stages, the first of which he called the sensorimotor stage, a term that was later used by Jean Piaget in his theory of infant intelligence, which we will discuss in greater detail in Chapter 7 (Cairns, 1998).

Baldwin's other major theoretical work, *Social and Ethical Interpretations of Mental Development* (1897), broke new ground by articulating the relation between social institutions and individuals. Baldwin held that, beginning in infancy, social development occurs through a dialectical process in which the child moves from an initial, self-focused stage and eventually reaches a more empathic stage that incorporates the views of other people (Cairns, 1998; Wertsch & Tulviste, 1992). Ripples from this sociocultural approach emerged again years later in the work of Russian psychologist Lev Vygotsky, whose theory we discuss in Chapter 7.

John B. Watson

As the United States became a major center, along with Europe, for the scientific study of children, the American public became more aware of the implications and applications of this new science as it entered their homes, schools, and communities. Not everyone in the United States shared Hall's enthusiasm for European traditions in psychology. One influential dissenter was John B. Watson, who carried out research at Johns Hopkins from 1916 until 1920 and then wrote books about the "purely American" psychological perspective of behaviorism. He also gained wide recognition in the 1920s and 1930s for popular-press publications in which he advised parents to apply behaviorist theory to the important job of childrearing.

As a behaviorist, Watson rejected the European traditions and methods that other American psychologists had imported, including questionnaire research and the use of introspection (self-reflection) as a way of tapping the contents of the mind. The only way to produce scientific data, in his view, was to employ behavioral, noncognitive methods—namely, observation. From 1916 until 1920, Watson focused his observations on infants, studying their behavioral and emotional responses to stimuli that he presented. Watson chose to study infants because he believed that the conditioning of basic emotions (love, fear, and rage) early in life provided the foundation for later behavior and personality.

The empirical study for which Watson is probably best known is a case study of conditioned fear in an infant he referred to as "little Albert" (Watson & Rayner, 1920). In his work with Albert, Watson paired the presentation of an aversive stimulus (a loud noise that made Albert fearful and upset) with a previously neutral stimulus (a white rat). Following a series of pairings, the rat alone began to elicit a fear response from the child, supporting Watson's behaviorist prediction. Although the details of Watson's experiment have been embellished and even distorted over the years (Harris, 1979), it led to many subsequent studies by other psychologists, especially in the 1920s and 1930s, and remains a part of the standard coverage of behaviorism in many psychology courses.

Watson did share at least one belief with Hall and others who promoted the new science of psychology—the conviction that psychological science could and should be applied across a wide range of everyday settings, including the home. The advice that he offered, however, differed dramatically from the views that his peers endorsed. In a best-selling book, *Psychological Care of Infant and Child* (1928), Watson argued that parents, especially mothers, should avoid smothering their children with too much affection. The danger, he wrote, was that the child would become conditioned by this love, the result being an unhealthy dependence on and need for attention and affection from others. Watson urged parents to be emotionally cool with their children and to adhere to strict schedules. Despite an absence of empirical evidence, Watson's views were widely disseminated to the public, at least some of whom must have been impressed by their apparent scientific legitimacy.

Arnold Gesell

The field of child development did have real scientists working in it, including Arnold Gesell, a former student of Hall. Gesell founded a child study laboratory at Yale in 1911, in which he carried out methodologically rigorous and innovative studies of early physical growth and motor development (he was one of the first to compare the development of twins and to use motion pictures in his research). Gesell published the results of his research in 1928, in *Infancy and Human Growth*, a book in which he charted and compared normal and "exceptional" infants in terms of their physical, motor, and perceptual development. Gesell came to the opposite conclusion that Watson did regarding the role of experience in early development, asserting that infants have an innate ability to develop in optimal ways, despite variability in experience. At the same time that Gesell posited a key role for maturation in development, however, he also suggested that experience may modify the functioning of

Arnold Gesell founded a child study laboratory at Yale University in 1911 and carried out innovative studies of early physical growth and motor development.

some inborn maturational mechanisms. (We will consider current studies of early motor development in Chapter 6.)

Child Research Institutes: Investigation and Dissemination

As the discipline of psychology emerged and gained strength in America, child development experts became more interested in solving children's problems from within than through social engineering and public policy (Bornstein, 2006; Cravens, 1985). Child research institutes, including those at Columbia University, Yale University, and universities in Iowa and Minnesota, were established in the 1920s and 1930s with funds provided by the Laura Spelman Rockefeller Memorial (Schlossman, 1985). The dual mission of these institutes was research and dissemination of useful findings to the general public, but more attention and resources were directed to basic research documenting the growth and development of "normal" children. Each institute developed its own character, and researchers at each institute became known for carrying out particular kinds of studies. Researchers at Iowa, for example, studied growth and physical maturation, as well as the care and feeding of infants and children. Behavioral and emotional development were explored at Columbia, Johns Hopkins, University of Minnesota, University of California, and Washington University (St. Louis). Mental testing and studies of intelligence and IQ were associated with researchers at Iowa, Berkeley, Minnesota, and Stanford. Two institutes—Berkeley and Fels—began systematic longitudinal studies (Cairns, 1998).

A significant amount of research and theoretical work in child development during this time was influenced by Freud's (1910) psychoanalytic theory or variations of it (Emde, 1992). Social learning theory emerged as a hybrid of behaviorist and psychoanalytic thinking, and researchers sought to apply concepts from this new perspective (e.g., reinforcement, imitation, and observational learning) to problems like childhood aggression, usually focusing on school-age children.

Parents Magazine began publishing in the late 1920s and was initially affiliated with the Laura Spelman Rockefeller Memorial and, by association, the child development research institutes it had funded. The success of the magazine surprised even those who had published it, signifying the strong interest in scientifically derived information about parenting and child development (Schlossman, 1985).

The scientific journal *Child Development* was launched in 1930, and in 1933, the Laura Spelman Rockefeller Memorial, in conjunction with the National Research Council, played a crucial role in helping to establish the interdisciplinary professional organization that became associated with *Child Development*, the Society for Research in Child Development (Cravens, 1985). The Memorial also funded programs to recruit future professionals and to develop parent education programs.

In the years following the Depression (1930–1945), numerous federal agencies were established and legislation was enacted to address child welfare problems, especially those resulting from economic devastation caused by the Depression. In addition to child labor laws, federal day care programs were established in the 1930s through the Works Progress Administration; the 1935 Social Security Act offered coverage for dependent, rural, and disabled children; free lunches were offered daily to poor children in New York City; and the Emergency Maternal and Infant Care (EMIC) Program was established in 1943 to provide free health care for the wives and infants of lower-ranking men serving in the military during wartime. Records show that the EMIC program was effective at reducing infant and maternal mortality rates; infant mortality, for example, fell from 47 per 1,000 live births in 1940 to 38.3 in 1945 (Ashby, 1985).

Child Development after World War II

Social learning theorists continued to study topics such as aggression but also explored the development of gender-role typing and conscience, as well as the relation between parental attitudes, beliefs, and childrearing practices and children's social development. These studies were unusual at the time for their multimethod approach, in which the researchers interviewed parents, observed children's play behavior, and observed parent-child interactions. Social learning research also highlighted the importance of studying the mutual, bidirectional influence of parent and child. This was a departure from previous approaches, which had assumed that the direction of influence flowed from parents to children (Bornstein, 2006; Cairns, 1998).

In the 1950s and 1960s, work began on a topic that was even more central to the study of infant development, the infant-caregiver attachment relationship. Harry Harlow studied the formation and consequences of attachment in rhesus monkeys at about the same time that John Bowlby used his clinical observations of the mother-infant relationship to construct a theory of attachment in humans. Bowlby detailed his theory in several important books, including the multivolume *Attachment and Loss,* most notably, *Attachment* (vol.1, 1969) and

Separation: Anxiety and Anger (vol. 2, 1973). We will discuss the extensive attachment literature in Chapter 9. For now, it is sufficient to note that Bowlby's theory incorporated ideas from his own psychoanalytic background, from studies of imprinting and bonding in animals, and from theories of cognitive development in infancy (Bretherton, 1992).

The rest of the story of the field of child development will be told in the remaining chapters of this book, as we consider the period of infancy from a topical perspective. In Chapter 2, we'll discuss the methods that researchers use to study infant development. In Chapters 3, 4, and 5, we'll learn about the biological beginnings of infancy, including prenatal development and health, nutrition, and physical growth from birth to the age of 3 years. Chapters 6, 7, and 8 will bring us into the cognitive domain, where we'll explore sensation, perception, and motor development, as well as learning, intelligence, and language. The social world of emotions and relationships is the focus of Chapters 9 and 10, while Chapters 11 and 12 examine institutions that are now commonplace in the lives of children younger than 3—childcare, early childhood education, and electronic media.

WRAPPING IT UP: Summary and Conclusion

How has infancy and childhood changed over time? Children who lived in the past cannot be observed or interviewed, of course, so our answers to this question are based on indirect sources, such as parents' diaries, childrearing books, toys, paintings, and records of births and deaths. As imperfect as these sources are, they reveal both differences and similarities between the present and the past. We know, for example, that parents in the past gave birth to more children than today, but that many of those children died in infancy. Despite high rates of infant mortality, parents in the past appear to have grieved over each loss, just as parents do today. We have learned that infant abandonment was once a common practice in many parts of the world, but that concern about the vulnerability of infants and children gradually led to institutional and legal forms of protection. We have also seen that increasing belief in the importance of infancy and early childhood gave rise to organized efforts to train and educate children early in life so that they would grow up to be moral, responsible, and capable adults.

We have seen that childrearing advice—now more typically referred to as parenting advice—has sometimes been inconsistent or faddish. As a result, it has often produced confusion among parents who merely want to know what the experts think (Hulbert, 1999, 2003). Holt, the highly regarded pediatrician and author of *The Care and Feeding of Children* (1894), for example, warned parents about the health risks of kissing children and the dangers of making infants nervous and irritable by playing with them (Cairns, 1998). In popular magazines in the 1920s, the behavioral psychologist John B. Watson instructed parents to put their young children on strict schedules, to avoid being overly affectionate toward them, and to ignore their own emotional responses to their young children (Watson, 1928).

In the 1930s and 1940s, by contrast, experts recommended that parents respect their children as unique individuals, watch for signs of their natural unfolding, and ensure that their children's needs were met while avoiding intervention and conflict. These views were disseminated in childrearing books with titles such as *Babies Are Human Beings* (1938), *Keep Them*

Human (1942), *Infant and Child in the Culture of Today* (1943), and *Our American Babies* (1944). Similar views were also presented in another parenting book that we considered earlier in this chapter—Dr. Spock's *The Common Sense Book of Baby and Child Care* (1946).

Given the extreme positions that have sometimes been presented, it is reasonable to wonder how many parents actually followed the experts' advice—a question that is just as relevant today as it was when Watson urged parents to avoid expressing too much emotion in their interactions with their children. For a more recent example, consider the medium of television. When it became established, public television programs, like *Sesame Street* (which first aired in 1969), were developed with the assistance of child development experts. Knowing that knowledgeable professionals had been involved in the production of these educational programs, many parents felt confident that they would have positive effects on their children. In recent years, electronic media, including public television programs, have been created with toddler and even infant audiences in mind. Although some of these programs have been designed by experts in child development, at least one other set of experts—the American Academy of Pediatrics—issued a policy statement advising parents not to use these forms of media with children under the age of 2 years. As in the past, therefore, parents may wonder which position is correct and how to apply the experts' recommendations in their own lives. There is, it seems, no end in sight to the search for information and advice about infants and young children.

This book is not intended to be a parenting manual, but we will periodically consider how the findings might be interpreted and used by parents or adults who work with infants and toddlers. For some topics, we will see that there may be more than one right answer, that the right answer varies according to the characteristics of the children in question, or that we may not know enough yet to be able to provide definitive answers for anyone. Like parents of infants, then, we will sometimes need to accept this uncertainty while continuing to ask questions and evaluate the answers that we obtain. As we do, we will presume that objective evidence is more valid than appeals to emotion, tradition, or unsupported beliefs. Above all, our focus will be on current findings from systematic studies by researchers whose work uses recognized, accepted research methods, the topic of our next chapter.

THINK ABOUT IT: Questions for Reading and Discussion

1. Imagine that you are a historian in the twenty-*second* century and your topic is the history of infancy and early childhood. What sorts of literary evidence, quantitative evidence, and material culture—evidence and artifacts being created today—might you use to study parenting in the twenty-first century? What sorts of conclusions might be drawn from these sources about our current society's attitudes about infants and their development? What would be the advantages and disadvantages of using these kinds of materials instead of observing infants directly?

2. Children in the United States and many other industrialized countries are becoming toilet trained at increasingly older ages (Bakker & Wyndaele, 2000; Brody, 1999). Whereas 92 percent of 18-month-olds were toilet trained in 1957, in 1999, only 2 percent of 2-year-olds,

and 60 percent of 3-year-olds were reliably toilet trained. (It is not until the age of 4 years that most U.S. children—98 percent—are finally out of diapers.) Use the information in this chapter to identify some of the factors that might be responsible for this trend.

3. What is the most surprising thing about the history of infancy and childhood that you have learned from this chapter? How does this information affect your views about infants and development from birth to age 3?

4. What do you think was the most important factor influencing the establishment and growth of the field of child development in the United States? Is this factor still important today? Are current conditions right to continue supporting the field of child development? Explain.

5. Do you think that today's parents would support an infant school movement? Why or why not?

6. Which of the recurring themes in the study of child development do you think is the most important? Explain.

7. When you think about the recurring themes in the study of child development, how do you tend to view the key debates in the field? That is, do you tend to believe more strongly in nature or in nurture as an influence on development? Do you tend to view babies as active or passive participants in their own development? How important do you think culture and the historical era are? Compare your views with the views of others taking this course. In addition, after you have finished this book, take another look at your notes to see if your ideas have changed.

KEY WORDS

Continuous (5)	Characterization of development as a gradual, smooth process of change
Infant mortality rate (14)	Number of deaths per 1,000 live births, usually reported with reference to the age of 1 year
Infant school movement (25)	An early nineteenth-century movement, imported to the United States from Europe, in which educators believed that children as young as 18 months could be educated and taught to read
Literary evidence (10)	Written information, including parents' diaries and letters, childrearing advice written by ministers and doctors, and children's books
Material culture (10)	Physical evidence, such as toys, clothing, furniture, and works of art
Nature (5)	Biological factors influencing development
Nurture (5)	Environmental and experiential factors influencing development
Oblation (15)	Medieval European practice involving the permanent "donation" of an infant or young child to a monastery
Quantitative archival evidence (10)	Official sources of written information and data, including census data, tax records, and legislative and court records
Stagewise (4)	Characterization of development as occurring in distinct phases, with qualitative differences between stages

2

Research Methods

Research methods have evolved since the time when child development experts first began to study infants and toddlers. These changes may be highlighted by considering a classic investigation of early language development that involved two languages, two countries, and one little girl.

When Hildegard Rose Leopold was born in 1930, her father, a German linguist, took an immediate and intense interest in her language development. In family conversations, Werner Leopold spoke only German, while his American wife Marguerite spoke only English. By keeping detailed records, beginning when Hildegard was 8 weeks old, Werner Leopold sought to document the development of a child growing up in a bilingual home. According to one source, Leopold took copious notes about Hildegard's vocalizations on slips of paper that he carried with him and spent weekends meticulously recording the notes (Hakuta, 1986). Unlike most language researchers today, who tend to specialize in the study of just one aspect of language, such as the acquisition of word meaning or grammar, Leopold made observations about all aspects of his daughter's language development. The result, *Speech Development of a Bilingual Child: A Linguist's Record* (1939, 1947, 1949), was a four-volume publication covering nearly 900 pages!

Leopold's pioneering study provided an important foundation for research on childhood bilingualism, but his approach was extremely labor-intensive and, in the end, provided information about only one child. What alternative research methods might he have used to answer the same set of questions? In this chapter we will consider the range of options that researchers have available when they embark on a journey of scientific inquiry, whether their focus is on the development of language, cognition, perception, motor skills, or relationships. As we do, we will encounter several classic studies that changed our understanding of the development of infants and young children. We will see that in the past, as is true today, choosing among the options requires researchers to make three major decisions about their study: the type of setting, the research design, and the measures that will be used.

Research Settings

Werner Leopold observed and made notes about his daughter's language development in ordinary settings, including their home in the United States and their living quarters during extended visits to Germany (Hakuta, 1986). Even without such ready access to infants, some researchers choose to carry out studies in their participants' homes and in other everyday settings rather than in a laboratory. In light of the extra effort that would appear to be involved, why do they elect those settings, and how do they compare to laboratories?

Naturalistic Studies

In some studies researchers observe infants in **naturalistic settings**—their usual surroundings, such as their own home or their regular childcare center. In some naturalistic research, like a classic study of language acquisition that we will discuss in Chapter 8 (Brown, 1973), children's spontaneous behavior is recorded as they interact with their parent or caregiver. This was also the case when Fernald and Morikawa (1993), in a cross-cultural study of Japanese and European American families, observed 6-, 12-, and 19-month-old infants and their mothers as they played with toys at home and compared the dyads' conversations and play themes. In many studies using **naturalistic observation**, researchers remain relatively passive observers in the sense that, apart from being physically present, they do not intervene in or try to influence the situation. One example of this is a study that took place in a health clinic and involved the observation of the type and duration of emotion expressions of 2- to 7-month-old infants in response to the acute pain of a diphtheria-pertussis-tetanus (DPT) inoculation (Izard, Hembree, & Huebner, 1987). Although the researchers in this study undoubtedly had their own emotional reaction to observing babies cry in pain, they were careful not to show these feelings or to intervene in any way as the infants' parents comforted them.

If researchers are becoming familiar with the setting or gathering ideas for future studies, they may write a **narrative record**—a detailed description of the range of behaviors they observe. By contrast, to answer questions about specific, well-defined behaviors, they use techniques that allow them to focus on just those target behaviors. In **event sampling**, for example, a small number of behaviors are identified and the researcher notes each time they occur by making a mark on a prepared checklist. It is essential to have a clear verbal description of the target behaviors so that they can be measured accurately. This description is known as an **operational definition**. Operational definitions can help researchers differentiate between behaviors that may appear to be similar in a number of ways, such as aggression and rough-and-tumble play ("play-fighting"). In an observational study of children's physical interactions on the playground, for example, researchers, as well as the children's teachers, might want to compare the frequency of each type of behavior. To do this, aggression might be defined as "physical contact between two or more children, accompanied by angry facial expressions and resulting in physical injury, negative emotions, and the cessation of interaction between the children, perhaps with the intervention of teachers or other adults." Rough-and-tumble play, by contrast, might be defined as "physical contact between two or more children, accompanied by smiles and laughter, not resulting in physical injury or negative emotions, and leading to continued interaction between the children" (Pellegrini, 1998; Pellegrini & Smith, 1998).

In an observational study of the development of pride, researchers might use an operational definition that includes a set of predetermined behaviors, such as erect posture, smiling, and verbal expressions such as "I did it!"

Operational definitions are necessary in all studies, whether they take place in a naturalistic setting or in a laboratory. Clear operational definitions help guard against **observer bias**—the phenomenon in which researchers' expectations or beliefs influence the way they record or interpret behavior. Because different observers may focus on different aspects of a behavior, good operational definitions ensure that the same criteria are used by all members of the research team. Researchers involved in one classic study of children in six cultures—the United States, India, Japan, Kenya, Mexico, and the Philippines—were able to compare interactions in settings in which children spent a typical day by specifying operational definitions for more than 30 possible behaviors, including "observing," "ignoring," "insulting," and "assaulting," as well as "helping," "nurturing," "suggesting," "commanding," "greeting," and "imitating" (Whiting et al., 1966).

Research need not be as ambitious as the six-culture study in order to benefit from clear operational definitions. In one recent laboratory study of toddlers' responses to their mother's verbal and nonverbal behavior during a challenging puzzle task, the researchers coded children's display of feelings of pride and shame during the session (Kelley, Brownell, & Campbell, 2000).

> *Pride* was coded when at least three of the following five behaviors occurred within 30 s[econds] following a child-produced success outcome: erect posture (i.e., shoulders back and head up), smile (either open or closed mouth), eyes directed at the experimenter or mother, points to outcome or applauds, or positive self-evaluation (e.g., "Yeah!" or "I did it!"). *Shame* was coded when at least three of the following five behaviors occurred within 30 s following a child-produced task failure: body collapsed, corners of the mouth down

In one observational study of infants' reactions to pictures in books, researchers both videotaped and took notes about children's manual exploration and vocalizations.

turned/lower lip tucked between teeth, eyes lowered with gaze downward or askance, withdrawal from the task situation, or negative self-statements (e.g., "I'm no good at this"). (p. 1065)

Because pride and shame are familiar emotions, differences between them may seem intuitive or obvious, but the use of clear operational definitions made it possible for the different members of the original research team to use the same criteria to categorize children's emotional displays. (Table 2.1 shows an example of a checklist that might have been used to record data about these behaviors.) Clear operational definitions also make it possible for subsequent researchers to make direct comparisons between their findings and those of the original researchers, whether they are studying pride and shame in a laboratory or in a naturalistic setting.

In some naturalistic studies, researchers take an active role and try to elicit particular child behaviors by creating specific experiences. Jean Piaget (1954), for example, whose well-known research on cognitive development we will discuss in Chapter 7, studied his own children in naturalistic settings but tested their reactions to the appearance and disappearance of objects that he selected and manipulated as well as objects that they encountered on their own.

When Piaget conducted his research, audio- and video-recording equipment was not as readily available as it is today. Like Werner Leopold, Piaget had to record his observations in writing. Contemporary researchers in naturalistic studies still take notes but primarily for the purpose of providing contextual information later, during the coding of audiotape or videotape records. In one study of infants' reactions to pictures in books, researchers both videotaped and took notes about children's manual exploration and vocalizations (DeLoache et al., 1998). Because this study compared infants in the United States and on the Ivory Coast of Africa, notes taken in these settings, especially notes about the presence and function of pictures and picture books in each culture, provided useful information later.

TABLE 2.1   Example of a Prepared Checklist for Use in Event Sampling

To code displays of **pride**, in the 30 seconds following a child-produced success outcome, make a mark for every instance of the behaviors listed.[a]

Success Outcome #	Erect Posture Smile	Eye Contact	Positive Self-Evaluation
1			
2			
3			
4			
5			

Note: (a) Adapted from information in Kelley, Brownell, and Campbell, 2000.

Co-sleeping is a less common practice in the United States than it is in many other parts of the world.

Some naturalistic studies, like DeLoache and collegues' picture book study, explore phenomena through **ethnographic research**, in which researchers make detailed observations or conduct interviews in everyday settings in order to understand patterns of behavior. Ethnographic research can be carried out in the researcher's own culture, as was done in one study of Girl Scout cookie sales in the United States (Rogoff et al., 2002). In most ethnographic research, however, researchers from one (usually Western) culture study behavior in a different (usually non-Western) culture. Ethnographic methods are a staple of anthropological research—Margaret Mead's famous (1928, 1930) studies of child and adolescent development in Samoa and New Guinea are an example of this tradition—but many psychologists, child development researchers, and pediatricians have also used this method to provide comparative data on topics such as sleeping, feeding, discipline, parent-infant interaction, and other fundamental aspects of caring for infants (DeLoache & Gottlieb, 2000; Morelli et al., 1992; Rogoff et al., 1993; Small, 1998; Winikoff, Castle, & Laukaran, 1988).

Results of ethnographic studies can be surprising to anyone who believes that caring for infants is just commonsense or to anyone who assumes that the way infants in their own culture are cared for is the "natural" or the "best" way. One revealing ethnographic study compared infants' sleeping arrangements in rural Guatemala and in middle-class homes in the United States (Morelli et al., 1992). The researchers reported that U.S. parents tended to promote their infants' independent sleeping at an early age, whereas Mayan parents in Guatemala slept with their children in the same bed, typically until the next child in the family was born. In addition, whereas U.S. parents tended to express concerns about co-sleeping, Mayan parents regarded the typical U.S. practice as cold and neglectful. These findings are consistent with anthropological research suggesting that, around the world, more families would prefer the Mayan practice of co-sleeping than the U.S. sleeping arrangements.

Ethnographic studies can also reveal aspects of development that are universal, occurring at about the same age or in the same way, regardless of cultural practices. As we will see in Chapter 8, for example, there are cross-cultural variations in how much parents speak to their infants and in the degree to which they believe infants are capable of understanding language. Despite these variations, the process of language acquisition is remarkably similar across numerous cultures that have been studied (Slobin, 1985).

Naturalistic studies are appealing for a number of reasons (see Table 2.2). First, once infants become accustomed to the presence of researchers and their recording equipment, their behavior is likely to be representative of their usual behavior. This may happen more quickly than in the past, since tape recorders and camcorders have become quite small and many families use them to make their own home movies. Second, parents may be more at ease when observed in their own home rather than in an unfamiliar laboratory. Because infants and toddlers respond to their parents' emotional cues (as we will see in Chapters 9 and 10), it is clearly preferable to observe parents and their young children in settings in which parents feel comfortable. A third reason some researchers use naturalistic settings is to generate ideas about spontaneously occurring phenomena that could be studied further in a more controlled laboratory setting. One researcher who used both naturalistic and laboratory settings was Mary Ainsworth, whose groundbreaking work we will discuss in Chapter 9. Some of her earliest observations of infant-caregiver interactions were carried out in children's homes (Ainsworth, 1967), but her later research resulted in the development of the Strange Situation—a standard laboratory procedure for investigating the infant-caregiver relationship (Ainsworth et al., 1978).

Laboratory Studies

One potential problem with naturalistic settings is the degree to which they vary across dimensions that may make a difference in children's behavior. Parent-infant interactions in a home where a boisterous older sibling is playing nearby or a telephone is ringing frequently, for example, are likely to be different from interactions in a home in which there are few distractions and little background noise. By using a standard **laboratory setting**— a specially designed research space—researchers are able to eliminate extraneous nuisance factors, such as ringing telephones and barking dogs. This allows them to focus on the influence of selected **independent variables**—the conditions that they are interested in studying—in order to see how they affect behaviors of interest—the **dependent variable**.

TABLE 2.2   Comparison of Naturalistic and Laboratory Studies

Naturalistic	Laboratory
Infants' behavior is likely to be typical	Strange environment may elicit strange behavior
Parents may feel comfortable in own home	Parents may feel anxious, self-conscious
Variations may exist across settings	Testing environment can be controlled, standardized for all participants
Good source of ideas for further study	Ideal for studying behavior that occurs only infrequently in naturalistic settings
Requires adjustment to equipment and researchers	Equipment and researchers can be hidden
High external validity, low internal validity	Low external validity, high internal validity
An integral part of ethnographic research	Ideal for normative studies and studies requiring specialized equipment and stimuli

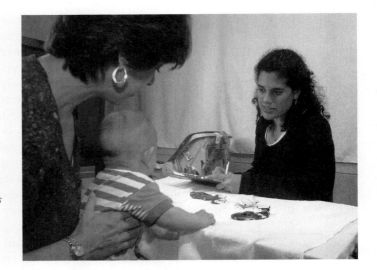

In laboratory settings, researchers have a high degree of control over the environment. This enables them to provide certain types of toys and observe how infants respond, as this researcher is doing.

Researchers who want to study the effect of older siblings on infants' interactions with their mothers, for example, might use the independent variable of "group composition" to compare infant-mother pairs with infant-mother-sibling trios in terms of the amount of physical contact that occurs between the infant and mother (the dependent variable). In other studies using laboratory settings, researchers may intentionally vary other conditions, such as the presence and type of toys, or the amount of potentially distracting background noise. When these factors are systematically varied, their influence on the infant's behavior (the dependent variable) can be more clearly understood.

The focus of the investigation may also influence researchers' choice of a laboratory setting instead of a naturalistic setting. Researchers studying the development of perceptual abilities, for example, often show babies specially designed video displays (e.g., Arterberry & Yonas, 1995) or examine their crawling and reaching behavior in specially designed environments (e.g., Arterberry, Yonas, & Bensen, 1989; Eppler, Adolph, & Weiner, 1996). As we will consider later in this chapter and in Chapters 4 and 6, researchers who study newborns' perceptual abilities typically record behavioral measures, such as heart rate or sucking rate in response to carefully presented stimuli (e.g., Moon, Cooper, & Fifer, 1993). Similarly, as we will see in Chapter 3, researchers who explore prenatal development or fetal responses to external stimuli depend on ultrasound scanners and fetal heart rate monitors. Studies like these clearly require the presence of specific equipment that is not found in infants' homes or in child care centers.

Some researchers are interested in charting normative development, such as determining the average age for the development of walking or the acquisition of aspects of language. For greatest accuracy, these researchers need to observe or test large samples of infants, bringing in dozens or even hundreds of infants and exposing them to the very same laboratory situation.

Another advantage of laboratory settings is that recording equipment and observers can be disguised or hidden from view. As a result, infants in laboratory settings do not need to become accustomed to the visible presence of a stranger and may interact with their parent in ways that are similar to their behavior at home.

A final advantage of laboratory settings is that they make it easier for researchers to study behaviors that may occur infrequently in the natural environment. One researcher who wanted to understand the development of toddlers' locomotor responses to obstacles, for example, set up barriers of different heights and materials (e.g., opaque versus transparent) in a narrow laboratory hallway and asked parents to call to their children from the other side of the barrier, encouraging them to cross over it (Schmuckler, 1996). Because parents of infants and toddlers usually "baby-proof" their homes, removing furniture that affords climbing and installing safety gates at the top and bottom of staircases, it is unlikely that the researcher would have been able to observe infants climbing and stepping over barriers in a naturalistic setting—especially since parents would normally actively discourage those behaviors.

As we noted earlier, many researchers choose laboratory settings because they allow a significant degree of control over the conditions in which participants' behavior will be observed, such as ensuring that the temperature and background noise level in the room are the same for everyone. In laboratory settings, it is also easier for researchers to manipulate selected independent variables, such as the effect of a mother's presence versus absence on her young child's free play behavior. The greater the degree of control researchers have over independent variables, the more confident they can be that any differences they find between groups, such as differences in free play behavior between a mother-present and a mother-absent group of toddlers, may be attributed to the independent variable under study, in this case, the presence or absence of the mother. When researchers have this sort of control, their studies are said to have a high degree of **internal validity**—the degree to which differences in the dependent variable (free play behavior) are actually due to differences in the independent variable (mother's presence versus absence). A study is said to have low internal validity when alternative explanations can cast doubt on the true effects of the independent variable. In our example, this might happen if there were an unintended difference between the mother-present and mother-absent groups of toddlers, such as the presence of familiar versus unfamiliar toys, that could have influenced the toddlers' motivation to play.

If internal validity is so desirable, why does research also take place outside of controlled laboratory settings? One reason is that the internal validity of a study is related to that study's **external validity**—the degree to which the findings can be extended, or generalized, to other samples and settings. If mother's presence versus absence has an influence on free play behavior for only one sample of toddlers, for example, but not other samples in subsequent studies, the original study would be said to have low external validity because the results apply so narrowly. Studies need to have both internal validity and external validity, so researchers must consider both when designing and carrying out their investigations.

As we have seen, the choice of a research setting has a significant impact on researchers' ability to conduct their studies and to draw conclusions from their data. When selecting a setting, researchers need to consider their specific needs and goals. The choice need not be an either/or one, however. Behaviors that are documented in both naturalistic and laboratory settings may ultimately be more convincing and informative about that aspect of development than behaviors that are seen in only one setting.

Research Designs

There are a number of alternative research designs that Werner Leopold might have used to study the language development of his bilingual daughter. Each design has its strengths and weaknesses, of course, and researchers need to keep these in mind as they consider their options.

Case Studies and Single-Subject Research

The approach Werner Leopold took is an example of a **case study**—an in-depth examination of a single individual. Well-known case studies were carried out in psychology by Sigmund Freud and Jean Piaget. Susan Curtiss (1977) studied the language development of Genie—an abused, socially isolated, apparently nonverbal girl who came to the attention of authorities at the age of 13 years (also see Rymer, 1993). One often cited case study of an infant was published by Charles Darwin about his son, Doddy. Although Darwin was not the first to carry out detailed observations of his own child, when his article appeared in 1877 (based on notes he had taken while observing his son 37 years earlier!), it gave legitimacy to the systematic study of children. As a celebrity of his time, Darwin's publication also inspired many parents to write their own **baby biographies** (observational records of their infants' early development). These parents didn't realize, of course, that Darwin had followed in the footsteps of others, such as Dietrich Tiedemann (1787), who is generally acknowledged as having published the first psychological diary of longitudinal development in children (Cairns, 1998).

Parents who wrote baby biographies in the nineteenth century were unaware of the methodological rigor that such studies need in order to be considered scientifically useful, but a number of researchers at that time began to use methods from other sciences to study individual infants' behavior and development. In the 1880s, William T. Preyer broke new ground by applying methods and concepts from embryology to the study of postnatal behavior and development (Cairns, 1998). Preyer's work suffered from technological limitations and theoretical biases that led him to the erroneous conclusion that the normal human infant hears nothing at birth. Nevertheless, many of his observations about infant development were surprisingly accurate, and he is generally reported to have been a meticulous, careful observer (Cairns, 1998). Preyer outlined rules for his observations that are consistent with observational methodology used by researchers today, including comparing different people's observations in order to achieve accurate information.

Another well-known study of an individual infant's development was begun in 1893 by Milicent Washburn Shinn (the first woman to earn a Ph.D. in psychology from the University of California). Shinn's (1900/1985) book, *The Biography of a Baby*, was based on a day-by-day account of her niece Ruth's first year of life. Shinn was aware of Tiedeman's work and at first consciously modeled her biography on Preyer's records. Shinn also recognized that her niece did not represent all babies and might even differ greatly from others. Still, like her predecessors, she believed that the case study approach offered unique advantages, explaining, "If I should find out that a thousand babies learned to stand at an average of 46 weeks and two days, I should not know as much that is important about standing, as a stage in human progress, as I should after watching a single baby carefully through the whole process of achieving balance on his little soles" (p. 11).

In the case studies that we have considered so far, researchers documented the naturally occurring behavior and development of a single child, without intervening or otherwise manipulating the child's experience. In other case studies, researchers do intervene or study the effects of an experimental manipulation on a single participant; these studies are referred to as **single-subject research** (Miller, 1998). A good example of single-subject research is the therapeutic work of Ivar Lovaas (Lovaas & Smith, 1989; McEachin, Smith, & Lovaas, 1993), who used principles of operant conditioning (rewards and punishment) with children with autism to reduce undesirable behaviors (e.g., temper tantrums, rocking, repetitive finger movements) and increase desirable behaviors (e.g., language, eye contact).

To understand how this approach worked, we will consider the hypothetical therapeutic goal of increasing eye contact. Working with one child at a time, researchers record the initial, baseline level of eye contact and then begin systematically rewarding the child each time he or she engages in that behavior. At first, rewards are given for even slight approximations of the target behavior, such as looking at the therapist for a second and then looking away. Eventually, rewards are given only for the complete behavior that is being targeted, such as looking at the therapist for several seconds without looking away. Throughout the sessions, the duration of the child's eye contact is recorded and, if the treatment has been successful, it will be evident to anyone examining the record.

Single-subject research gives the researcher more control and internal validity than a case study that is primarily descriptive. As shown in Table 2.3, however, both types of studies have limitations, beginning with concerns about external validity—the degree to which the particular individual under study is representative of other people. Indeed, the more unique the subject of the study, the less likely the results can be tested and replicated in future research. Another concern with these studies is the possibility that the researcher may be theoretically biased when interpreting the data. Although the evidence with respect to Werner Leopold suggests that he was an objective observer (Hakuta, 1986), it is easy to imagine that case studies, especially those carried out by parents, might not always provide an accurate record. Case studies and single-subject research are valuable, however, for the detail that they provide about individual children. They may also point researchers to aspects of development that can be fruitfully studied with larger samples.

Quasi-Experimental Studies

Many researchers use a **quasi-experimental design** (sometimes referred to as a nonexperimental design) to collect information about groups of participants that are already formed before the study begins. For practical reasons, this design is used in the investigation of preexisting group variables such as culture, race/ethnicity, and gender, where participants cannot be randomly assigned to a group. For ethical reasons, this design is the only option available for topics such as the effect of preterm birth, prenatal exposure to alcohol, or the impact of child abuse, since researchers cannot ethically induce these experiences (see Table 2.3). In quasi-experimental studies, researchers compare the groups that they select in terms of dependent variables of interest, such as physical growth, motor development, or language acquisition.

If Werner Leopold had used a quasi-experimental design, he might have studied children whose parents had already decided to bring them up in bilingual homes and compared their language development with the language development of children growing up in monolingual homes. (For both practical and ethical reasons, it would not be possible to randomly

TABLE 2.3   Comparison of Three Research Methods

Case Study/Single-Subject	Quasi-Experimental	Experimental
Permits in-depth study of a single individual	Compares pre-existing groups	Creates groups for comparison, using random assignment
External validity may be low, especially if individual is very unique	External validity is high	External validity may be low
Internal validity is high in single-subject experiments, but not in descriptive case studies	Internal validity may be low; inferences about cause and effect can not be drawn	Internal validity is high; conclusions about cause and effect can be made
May suggest topics for research with larger samples	The only design available for many topics, where ethical or practical considerations make random assignment to groups impossible	The best design for topics that allow experimental manipulation and random assignment to groups

assign children and their families to monolingual or bilingual groups.) The results of this hypothetical study would indicate whether there is a relationship between the number of languages to which a child is exposed from birth and the child's language development.

If Leopold had found that children in monolingual homes were more advanced in their language development than children from bilingual homes, he might have concluded that learning more than one language during childhood is detrimental to language development. This finding would not permit him to infer, however, that early exposure to more than one language *causes* slower language development than early exposure to just one language. Alternative explanations would still need to be considered, such as the impact of other differences between the two groups of families. These differences might include the children's intellectual abilities, parents' attitudes about the language(s) they speak, families' economic resources, or even the amount of verbal interaction each child experiences.

Unless Leopold could rule out the effect of these other differences, a study like this one would suffer from low internal validity. There are some steps that could be taken to strengthen any causal inferences that might be drawn. One approach would be to equate the families in each group on other factors that could be related to child language outcomes. This would leave only the number of languages in the child's home—one or two—to vary between the families. Another approach would involve use of statistical procedures to "partial out" the effect of nonlanguage differences between groups. Even with these adjustments, Leopold would never be able to remove the influence of all of the potentially important factors, and any causal conclusions would still need to be viewed as tentative.

Experimental Studies

In contrast to quasi-experimental studies, inferences about cause and effect can be drawn from studies using an **experimental design**—a design that examines the effect of an independent variable on a dependent variable (see Table 2.3). Experiments differ from quasi-experiments in employing **random assignment** (using a random number table or another nonsystematic procedure) to place each participant into one of two or more groups that represent different aspects of the independent variable. When random assignment is used, each participant has an equal chance of ending up in each of the groups being compared in the experiment. In our earlier discussion of laboratory studies, there were two conditions of the independent variable being compared—presence versus absence of the mother—and the dependent variable was the child's free play behavior. If children were randomly assigned to either the mother-present or the mother-absent condition, and if a greater quantity or higher quality of play behavior were found for children whose mothers were present, the researchers could conclude that the presence of a child's mother increases or improves the child's play behavior. In fact, the researchers in this example could be relatively confident that something about maternal presence *caused* the difference in play behavior between the two groups of children. The researchers would still need to determine *how* maternal presence exerts its effects—through the mother's direct involvement in the child's play, as a result of suggestions that she makes to the child from the sidelines, or just by providing a secure, comforting presence in the room.

How might Werner Leopold's study have been adapted to an experimental design? One way would be to bring young children growing up in bilingual homes into a laboratory setting and explore their ability to learn a set of new words, made up by the researcher (words like *bleg*, *thrip*, and *lart*). All of the children would be shown an object to accompany the new word, but half of the children would be taught the new word by their mother, whereas the other half would be taught by an unfamiliar person (the researcher). If Werner Leopold used random assignment, potentially important differences between the two groups of children might still exist, but their influence could be controlled through random assignment, ensuring that each child would have an equal chance of being taught by either a familiar person or an unfamiliar person. Random assignment would also ensure that potentially important differences across children would be distributed across the two teaching conditions. The results of this hypothetical experiment would indicate whether bilingual children learn new words better when they are taught by a familiar or an unfamiliar person.

As a result of random assignment, an experiment like this one would have a relatively high level of internal validity. It could be criticized for having relatively low external validity, however, because even if the findings were replicated in other samples of bilingual children studied by other researchers, the use of nonsense words would limit its generalizability to children's acquisition of real languages in naturalistic settings. The best plan, since no research design is without weaknesses, may be to use more than one approach and determine whether the results of different kinds of studies using different measures tend to agree or disagree (Brewer & Hunter, 1989).

Research Designs for Studying Development

Implicit in all developmental research is the goal of understanding how behaviors and abilities change with age and experience. When Werner Leopold studied his daughter's language development, he chose an intensive approach when she was a newborn and continued recording his observations into her adolescence. As Hildegard's father, Leopold's choice of a years-long design may seem like an obvious one. Numerous other researchers have also studied their subjects over a span of months or even years, although not all have gathered the staggering quantity of data that Leopold amassed. We will look at several classic examples of longitudinal studies next and consider the advantages and disadvantages of this research design (see Table 2.4).

Longitudinal Research

In **longitudinal research**, investigators study the same sample of children (or adults) over time, measuring their behavior or ability at specified intervals. Roger Brown (1973) used a longitudinal design to study language development in three children he referred to as Adam, Eve, and Sarah. Brown and his research team visited the children's homes approximately every 2 weeks, beginning when they were around 2 years of age, and audiotaped their interactions for approximately 2 hours on each visit. As a result of this design, Brown was able to show that, although each child developed language at a different rate, they acquired aspects of language in a similar order. One advantage of longitudinal research, then, is the ability to chart individual change or stability over time.

Data from longitudinal studies can reveal relations between early functioning and later development. This has been demonstrated in ongoing longitudinal studies of the infant-caregiver relationship in which the infants are now in their twenties. We will discuss the evidence for long-term continuity in and consequences of these early relationships in Chapter 9. Longitudinal studies of intelligence, by contrast, in which measures in infancy are compared with measures in childhood and adolescence have generally produced only modest evidence of continuity over time. One of the problems in this research is a lack of **measurement equivalence**—correspondence between the measures, or dependent variables, used at two different points in time (Miller, 1998). Whereas IQ tests in childhood and

TABLE 2.4   Comparison of Three Developmental Research Designs

Longitudinal	Cross-sectional	Microgenetic
Charts individual change or stability over time	Does not provide information about individual change or stability	Ideal for studying infants' rapidly developing skills, showing individual change or stability
Can reveal relations between early functioning and later development; is ideal for showing long-term effects of interventions	Does not provide information about participants at later ages	Focuses on a short period of time, not usually linked to performance at later ages
Time consuming, expensive, susceptible to attrition of participants over time	Economical and efficient, with lower chance of attrition	Time consuming and labor intensive study of a relatively small sample; likelihood of attrition is low
Results may apply only to the cohort of participants studied	Does not differentiate between differences due to age and differences due to cohort	Results may apply only to individuals involved in study

beyond typically rely on verbal ability, intelligence tests for babies tend to focus on nonverbal, motor abilities. We will consider whether and how infant intelligence predicts later intelligence in Chapter 7.

Longitudinal designs are also well suited to studies of the effects of interventions on development. Ramey and his colleagues, for example, used a longitudinal design to study children from the time they were 6 weeks of age until they entered adolescence (e.g., Ramey & Campbell, 1991; Ramey et al., 2000; Ramey & Ramey, 1998a). By comparing children randomly chosen to participate in an early childhood education program and children randomly chosen to receive pediatric and social work services, nutritional assistance, and home visits, the researchers were able to assess the influence of the education program in a number of developmental domains. (We will discuss this research program in greater detail in Chapter 11.)

Longitudinal studies are not ideal for all researchers or all research questions. One disadvantage is that they are time consuming. In order to gather data about how a given behavior or ability changes across childhood and into adolescence, researchers need to commit themselves to studying the same group of individuals for nearly two decades. Researchers who have been involved in some of the most ambitious longitudinal studies, such as the Stanford Studies of Gifted Children, the Oakland (Adolescent) Growth Study, the Berkeley Growth and Guidance Studies, the Fels Research Institute Study, and the Seattle Longitudinal Study, have grown old with their subjects and in some cases have been outlived by them. This problem is obviously less relevant when the research question concerns development from birth to the age of 2 or 3 years, since intervals of even a few months can reveal dramatic developmental change (Miller, 1998).

Keeping track of all of the participants in a longitudinal study over many years can be expensive, and some of the participants may decline to continue in the study or become unavailable for a variety of reasons. In addition, in some longitudinal studies, such as those investigating intelligence or cognitive abilities, it may be unclear whether participants' performance improves as a result of the development of more advanced abilities or as a result of repeated exposure to the measures of those abilities, a phenomenon known as a **practice effect**. Again, these problems tend to be of less concern for researchers studying developmental change over the period of infancy (Miller, 1998).

Finally, it is not always clear in longitudinal research whether the results obtained for a particular group or generation, known as a **cohort** of participants (such as infants born in the same year), are generalizable to other groups. Although it applies to all longitudinal research, the reason for concern about generalizability to other cohorts may be especially evident when considering studies that were begun in the 1920s or 1930s, like the Stanford Studies, the Oakland Growth Study, the Berkeley Growth and Guidance Studies, and the Fels Research Institute Study. The individuals in these studies experienced a particular set of historic events, including the Great Depression, World War II, the Korean War, and the Vietnam War, and they lived in a society that has changed dramatically, especially in terms of technology and educational and work opportunities for girls and women. It is reasonable, therefore, to ask whether and how the course of their development compares to the development of children born in the 1960s, the 1990s, or the twenty-first century. In Chapter 12, we will consider some of the ways in which infants born in the twenty-first century constitute a unique cohort.

Cross-Sectional Research

Given the practical limitations of longitudinal studies, it is not surprising that most developmental researchers choose to conduct **cross-sectional research** instead. In cross-sectional designs, two or more age groups of participants are compared in terms of their behavior or ability at the same point in time. If Werner Leopold had used a cross-sectional design, he could have gathered data covering the same range of ages by comparing different groups of English-German bilingual children between 8 weeks and 14 years. Instead of spending 14 years, he could have finished his study in just a single year.

Cross-sectional studies can provide important converging evidence for longitudinal findings. This was true of cross-sectional studies that later replicated Brown's (1973) findings regarding early language acquisition. In comparison to longitudinal studies, cross-sectional research is clearly less time consuming, and typically less expensive and more flexible because new variables can be explored in subsequent cross-sectional studies. In addition, the problems of participant loss and practice effects are of less concern in cross-sectional studies than in longitudinal research.

It is important to remember that even when cross-sectional studies reveal differences between age groups, it cannot be assumed that the differences are due to developmental change. If researchers are not careful when selecting their sample, they will have difficulty disentangling the influence of age from the influence of other "nuisance" variables. In Werner Leopold's research, these nuisance variables might include differences in the families' economic resources or in the amount of English and German to which children in various families are exposed. Another potential problem with cross-sectional designs, especially in studies comparing a wide range of ages and older samples, such as 10-, 20-, 30-, and 40-year-olds, is that age differences may actually stem from generational differences—**cohort effects**. Infancy researchers, fortunately, are probably safe in assuming that 12-, 18-, and 24-month-olds represent the same cohort (Miller, 1998).

Microgenetic Research

Cross-sectional studies reveal age differences and suggest developmental differences, but they do not provide information about *how* development occurs. Researchers who want to understand developmental processes as they occur within the same individual have turned recently to what might be thought of as a very short-term longitudinal design—**microgenetic research**. In microgenetic studies, participants are observed in a relatively large number of sessions over a short period of time, with the researchers gathering a rich set of data on which fine-grained analyses can be performed. Microgenetic analyses are applicable across many different developmental domains and can be used in a wide variety of settings, including those outside of a laboratory (Siegler, 2006).

The microgenetic method has been used to shed light on older children's cognitive development and problem solving (Fletcher et al., 1998; Siegler, 1996, 2006; Siegler & Crowley, 1991). In one study comparing normally achieving children and children with mental retardation, the microgenetic approach was applied over a period of 12 weeks to document changes in the strategies that children used to solve math and reading problems. The results revealed a number of similarities between the two groups of children that had not been detected in other studies using less dense sampling (Fletcher et al., 1998).

In studies of infants, the microgenetic approach has proved especially fruitful in documenting learning and development—significant changes in behavior that often occur in a relatively brief period. The microgenetic approach has been used to investigate the onset of walking (Adolph, 1995) and reaching (Thelen & Smith, 1994) as well as the development of infants' manual and oral exploratory responses to objects presented over several sessions (Jones, 1996). In other studies, patterns of vocalization and emotional communication have been analyzed by scrutinizing videotapes of mother-infant play that were made over a period of 4 to 7 months (Pantoja, Nelson-Goens, & Fogel, 2001).

If Werner Leopold had been able to use modern video technology to record samples of his daughter's language, and if his study had covered a vastly briefer period of time (e.g., 24 to 30 months of age), it would have been similar to some contemporary microgenetic studies. Microgenetic studies generally have a much smaller number of participants than cross-sectional studies. This is due to the dense sampling of behavior and detailed analysis of videotapes, which often makes them both expensive and labor intensive. Still, the new insights that they may provide make them an attractive option for many researchers today.

In addition to selecting a setting and design, researchers also need to choose a response measure. The age and abilities of the research participants play an important role in this choice, and as we will see next, infants present special challenges to researchers. There are advantages to studying infants, however, because unlike older children and adults, they are often unaware that they are participating in research. This means that researchers are more likely to see infants exhibiting their natural behaviors, even in unfamiliar laboratory settings.

Research Measures

The specific question the researcher is asking has an influence on the measures chosen in a study. In studies of infant-parent relationships, for example, it makes sense to measure behaviors that occur in the course of infant-parent interactions, such as play, emotional communication, and physical contact. In investigations of language development, by contrast, researchers quite reasonably focus on aspects of communication, both verbal and nonverbal. In this section we will examine examples of the range of response measures that are used in studies with infants. We will see that some researchers choose to measure behaviors that infants display spontaneously, while other researchers focus on behaviors that they teach infants to perform. Finally, some researchers forego direct observation of infant behaviors altogether and gather parental reports about their infants or examine data and records that other researchers have gathered.

Behavioral Responses

Newborn and very young infants are capable of making a number of behavioral responses, such as looking and sucking, that researchers can use to investigate their perceptual and cognitive abilities. Thus, if responses do not depend on more advanced behaviors, such as the ability to reach or crawl, it is possible to ask even very young infants specific questions and end up with useful, interpretable answers.

New technology allows researchers to measure electrical activity in the infant's brain, using electrodes that rest on the scalp in a special cap.

Spontaneously Occurring Behaviors.   Almost any behavior that infants display sponta-neously can be used as a dependent variable. Some researchers use psychophysiological measures to gauge infants' responses to stimuli. Heart rate is the most popular of these measures, primarily because it can be recorded in response to any sort of stimulus, whether it involves infants' vision, hearing, or sense of taste, touch, or smell (Miller, 1998). When infants are orienting and attending to stimuli, their heart rate tends to slow down. Heart rate is also attractive to researchers because it can be used with infants of any age and does not depend on motor skills. Changes in heart rate can be measured even when overt behavioral changes are not apparent (Bornstein & Lamb, 1992). Some researchers have combined measures of heart rate and other behavioral responses in the same study. These studies have shown, for example, that infants who do not show behavioral signs of stress when their par-ent leaves the room sometimes have changes in heart rate that are consistent with a psycho-logical stress reaction.

Other studies using psychophysiological responses have measured levels of the stress hormone cortisol in the saliva of infants and young children (Andersson, Bohlin, & Hagekull, 1999; Larson et al., 1998). Cortisol levels can be measured between 15 and 45 minutes after a stressful event, whether the stress is the result of a medical procedure like circumcision, a painful inoculation, a distressing separation from the parent, or interactions in a play group of unfamiliar children in an unfamiliar setting. Cortisol can be gathered from saliva that collects in flavored dental pads the child has chewed or sucked on. Cortisol levels fluctuate naturally during the course of the day, however, so researchers need to be aware of these normal rhythms when examining their data.

Some researchers measure electrical activity in the infant's brain, using sensitive electrodes that rest on the scalp. Recording of the spontaneous natural rhythms of the brain are made using **electroencephalography, or EEG** (Johnson, 1998). The EEG procedure is attractive because it is both noninvasive and relatively inexpensive. It is not well suited to the study of cognition, because it does not reveal brain activity in response to particular stimuli, but it is sensitive to state changes and can be used in studies of social and emotional development (Nelson & Bloom, 1997). Electrical activity resulting from the presentation of discrete stimuli can be measured with the cortical **event-related potential, or ERP**. The ERP has been useful in studies of infants' cognitive abilities, including attention, memory, and language comprehension (Nelson, 1994, 1995; Nelson & Bloom, 1997). The primary difficulty in applying ERP methodology to infants is that muscle or eye movements can produce responses that are not related to the stimulus under study, and the results may lead researchers to disregard a participant's entire data set (Johnson, 1998; Nelson & Bloom, 1997; Shonkoff & Phillips, 2000). We will examine brain development as well as more recently developed measures such as MRI scans in Chapter 5.

Another commonly used measure is infants' spontaneous looking behavior—or **visual fixation**. This measure is typically used in laboratory studies of perception and cognition, where researchers present carefully constructed stimuli and note the direction and duration of infants' looking behavior. We will discuss the development of perceptual abilities in detail in Chapter 6. For now, it is sufficient to note that even newborn infants are able to shift their attention from one object or one display to another, and this ability improves with age. By noticing where and for how long infants gaze, researchers have been able to answer many fundamental questions about perceptual abilities in infancy.

Much of contemporary research in infant perception is built on the pioneering work of Robert Fantz (1961), who developed the **visual preference method**—a technique in which infants' looking behavior is used to determine their ability to perceive and notice differences between stimuli presented in a laboratory setting. Fantz designed a special looking chamber in which infants lie on their back and look at two visual stimuli that are presented simultaneously, such as a bull's-eye and a solid circle. (The position of the bull's-eye and the circle are alternated so that the researcher can detect responding that is based on a preference for displays on the baby's right side, rather than a preference for pattern complexity.) The stimuli cannot be *examined* simultaneously, however, so infants are required to move their head slightly in order to look at the entire display. In Fantz's studies the dependent variable was the duration of the infants' look at each stimulus. (Looking down into the chamber, it is possible to see where the infant is looking during each moment of the session). If infants looked longer at one stimulus, such as the bull's-eye, Fantz inferred that they preferred that stimulus. Using this method, Fantz—and many researchers after him—tested infants' ability to discriminate between pairs of stimuli varying in numerous ways, including complexity, familiarity, and symmetry.

The usefulness of the visual preference method is limited, however, if an infant does not show a clear preference for one of the two stimuli. The absence of a preference could reflect something as uninteresting as an infant's preference for stimuli that are shown on the right side; since the two stimuli appear equally often in the left and the right positions, a strong right-side preference would result in similar looking times for the two stimuli. Absence of a preference could also indicate that the infant could not tell the difference between the two stimuli or that the infant noticed the difference but did not prefer one more than the other (Miller, 1998).

Infants' spontaneous looking behavior is also a frequent measure in studies in which infants are shown just *one* stimulus at a time in a procedure known as the habituation and dishabituation method—the most commonly used method in the study of infant perception and cognition (Kellman & Arterberry, 1998). **Habituation** refers to the phenomenon in which infants gradually lose interest in a stimulus after repeated presentations. The first time the stimulus is shown, infants show an **orienting response** and may momentarily cease any ongoing activity in order to give close visual attention to the new stimulus (Haith & Benson, 1998; Miller, 1998). After numerous presentations, the orienting response weakens, but it can be reactivated by replacing the first stimulus with a different one. The recovery of attention when a new stimulus is introduced is known as **dishabituation**. Researchers infer that infants who become habituated to one stimulus, such as a photograph of a woman's face, and show dishabituation when that photograph is replaced by, for example, a photograph of a different woman's face are able to detect differences between the two stimuli.

If infants fail to show dishabituation, it may mean that they cannot detect a difference between the old and new stimuli. It may also indicate, however, that changes in looking behavior were not a sufficiently sensitive measure of infants' orienting response. Because the orienting response is also characterized by subtler physiological changes, researchers often use heart rate as an index of infants' habituation-dishabituation response (Miller, 1998). Other behaviors, such as sucking rate, can also be used to detect decreasing and increasing amounts of responsiveness to stimuli during habituation and dishabituation.

Habituation measures are valuable because they can be used with infants only a few months or even a few days old (Aslin, Jusczyk, & Pisoni, 1998). In addition, given that orienting responses, habituation, and dishabituation are naturally occurring behaviors, researchers do not have to teach infants to respond in these ways. Habituation-dishabituation measures do have some drawbacks, however, including attrition rates of 50 percent or higher. These rates reflect the requirement that infants remain in a stable state for as long as 10 to 15 minutes in order to complete all parts of the sequential task (Aslin et al., 1998; Kellman & Arterberry, 1998). Another potential limitation is the existence of individual differences among infants in how quickly they habituate and dishabituate. This variability may reflect individual differences in infants' ability to process information about the world, and as we will see in Chapter 7, some researchers have reported finding correlations between infants' efficiency of habituation and cognitive abilities later in childhood (Colombo, 1993; Colombo & Janowsky, 1998; McCall & Carriger, 1993). The creative, evolving nature of research is exemplified by this application—a method that was developed primarily to study infant perception is now being used to explore the foundations of intelligence.

Conditioned Behaviors.   In some studies, researchers *do* teach infants how to respond. A procedure known as **conditioned headturning** has been used to assess infants' ability to hear differences between auditory stimuli. When infants turn their head to look in the direction of a new sound or speech sample, they are rewarded with an entertaining sight, such as an animated toy moving inside a lighted display case. Infants who are rewarded with this sight every time they hear that sound or speech sample—and only when they hear that sound or speech sample—soon learn to turn their head after they hear it, in anticipation of the "show." Once this headturning response has been conditioned and can be elicited reliably, a different sound (or speech sample) can be presented or alternated with the original one. Infants who do not turn their head in response to the new stimulus are assumed to be able to discriminate between the one used in conditioning and the new stimulus, whereas infants who turn their head, looking for the entertaining display, are thought not to be able to make this discrimination (Miller, 1998).

The conditioned headturning procedure and its variations work because infants are able to notice and remember associations between their responses to specific events, such as the presence of a particular sound, and the consequences of their response. Some variations on the basic conditioned headturning procedure have made the task so complex that it cannot be used with infants younger than 4 or 5 months of age, but the simple version of the procedure has been used with infants as young as 2 to 3 months old. Once the conditioning phase is completed, the technique has the advantage of a low attrition rate and great flexibility in the stimuli that can be used (Aslin et al., 1998; Miller, 1998).

Parental Reports

Researchers working with infants and very young children typically see them for only brief periods of time. During that time, infants may not reveal their true range of abilities due to the interference of factors such as behavioral state changes or wariness in the presence of an unfamiliar researcher or strange laboratory setting. One way to gather more representative data is to use **parental reports**—to enlist infants' parents or caregivers, who have almost unlimited access and opportunity to observe their behavior and development. As we have seen, Werner Leopold may be the best example of a parent who used every opportunity to notice and record his child's development!

Some researchers have trained parents to keep diaries in which they systematically record observations about one aspect of the infant's development, such as memory, in everyday settings (Ashmead & Perlmutter, 1980). In other studies, parents provide researchers with reports, often in checklist form, about whether or not their child has achieved particular milestones in the development of motor skills, social interaction, or language and communication. As they use these measures, researchers need to keep in mind that parental reports do have some limitations. The principal disadvantage is that, for a variety of reasons, parents may misunderstand instructions or fail to give accurate reports about their children's behavior and development. As we'll see in Chapter 10, when we compare parental ratings with other approaches to studying infant temperament, some researchers have discovered that it can be useful to employ multiple methods, such as direct observation in a laboratory setting as well as parents' ratings of their child's behavior in everyday contexts.

Archival Research

Finally, some researchers are interested in understanding the period of infancy at different points throughout history. Infants from the past obviously cannot be compared directly with infants living today, but as we saw in Chapter 1, archival records can be used.

Archival research may use official sources of information, such as census records or birth certificates from different points in time, to answer questions about changes in birth-weight, family size, maternal age, and rates of infant mortality or infant growth. Archival research can also be based on information found in popular child care manuals from the past, parents' diaries, or even cultural artifacts such as children's literature, works of art, advertisements, and furniture (Calvert, 1992; Fontanel & d'Harcourt, 1997; Smuts & Hagen, 1985).

Archival studies often make fascinating reading and may reveal changes in beliefs about the essential nature of babies and their development. The history of devices used to restrain and prop up infants, for example, shows that parents in the Middle Ages, and even in the seventeenth and eighteenth centuries, "had no faith that children would come to walking of their own accord" (Calvert, 1992, p. 34). Parents believed that, without active intervention, babies might never abandon their animalistic form of crawling on all fours. As a result, they used contraptions of all kinds, like those shown in Figure 2.1, to hold their infants upright before they began to walk on their own and to guide their first steps. Histories of feeding practices, rich in details about the practice of wet-nursing and the development of bottles, nipples, and alternatives to breast milk, are equally revealing (Fontanel & d'Harcourt, 1997). More recently, an examination of *Parents* magazine revealed significant differences in the advice being given to parents of infants from 1955 to 1984 (Young, 1990).

Issues in Research with Infants

As we have just seen, infants' nonverbal responses can be illuminating, but infants are not always cooperative research participants. Moreover, researchers working with infants can never actually know what they are perceiving, feeling, or remembering—all response measures require inference and interpretation. As we have noted, parents can sometimes help researchers interpret infants' behavior, but studies of infants entail special ethical concerns, and researchers need to take precautions to help parents understand their role as the child's advocate in the research setting. In addition, because babies just 1 month apart may be at quite different developmental stages, researchers working with newborns and very young infants must work hard just to find new participants.

Behavioral State

Unless researchers are studying sleep, they need participants to be awake and alert in order to provide data. Newborn infants, however, sleep an average of 16 to 17 hours each day and move in and out of as many as 10 different states of arousal (Freudigman & Thoman, 1998; Louis et al., 1997; Thoman, 1990). These **behavioral states** include four awake states, three transition states between sleep and waking, two sleep states, and one transition sleep state. Of these 10 states, the awake/alert state, in which the infant's eyes are open and bright and the infant is engaged in attentively scanning the environment, is the most optimal one for nearly all research questions. Unfortunately for researchers, less than 10 percent of the average newborn infant's day is spent in this state (Louis et al., 1997; Thoman, 1990).

FIGURE 2.1   Nineteenth-century prints illustrating a turnstile and slide walker—devices used to hold infants in an upright position before they learned to walk independently.
Source: Reprinted by permission of Roger-Viollet Agence Photographique.

A regular, predictable pattern of sleep/wake states depends upon neurological development. This is one of the reasons it can take several months before an infant gets "on a schedule." Some infants show greater regularity at an earlier age than others (Freudigman & Thoman, 1998; Ingersoll & Thoman, 1999; Larson et al., 1998; Thoman, 1990; White et al., 2000; Whitney & Thoman, 1994). One neonatal assessment that takes this variability across infants into account—the Brazelton Neonatal Behavioral Assessment Scale (NBAS)—uses it to help new parents become sensitive to their infant's behavioral patterns and capabilities (Brazelton & Nugent, 1995). (We will discuss sleep/wake states and the Brazelton NBAS in more detail in Chapter 4.)

Newborn infants who have been fed recently are likely to drift into a sleep state, but infants who are hungry are also unlikely to be attentive research participants. To compensate for these tendencies, parents sometimes offer pacifiers to help their baby remain alert and nonfussy (Franco et al., 2000), but pacifiers cannot be used in all studies. It may help to shift the infant's position (Myers et al., 1998), but this cannot be done in all studies. It is also a good idea to make the experimental session as short as possible. Even with these steps, researchers who work with newborns must accept the reality that attrition of participants will be commonplace. Indeed, in some studies with newborns (e.g., Moon, Cooper, & Fifer, 1993), as many as 50 percent of infants (22 out of 44 tested) do not complete the procedure due to factors such as drowsiness, crying, needing a diaper change, or spitting up.

FIGURE 2.2   In some laboratory studies, infants are shown side-by-side video displays and the amount of attention they give to them is compared to determine whether they prefer one display more than the other.

Inference and Interpretation

Another challenge facing researchers working with infants and preverbal children is the problem of inference and interpretation. The measures that researchers use to study infants are necessarily indirect, since participants cannot respond verbally to questions about what they perceive, think, or feel. Instead, as we noted, researchers rely on nonverbal responses, such as changes in heart rate and cortisol levels, as well as behaviors such as sucking, looking, and in some studies, reaching, crawling, or walking.

In many studies of infant perception and cognition, researchers measure the duration of infants' visual gaze toward stimuli. In these studies, which we will discuss further in Chapters 6 and 7, differences in the amount of time infants spend looking at different stimuli are inferred to reflect their awareness of or preference for aspects of the stimuli that the researcher has manipulated, such as size, complexity, and familiarity. In some studies, infants who look longer at "impossible" events—such as a solid object that appears to pass through another solid object—are described as expressing surprise (e.g., Baillargeon, 1994a, 1994b, 1999). In other studies, the duration of infants' looking behavior when stimuli like dolls or small toys are introduced or taken away is said to reveal an early understanding of addition and subtraction (e.g., Simon, Hespos, & Rochat, 1995; Wynn, 1992). Inferences like these are not universally accepted, and researchers continue to debate the meaning of infants' behavioral responses (Haith & Benson, 1998; Wakeley, Rivera, & Langer, 2000a, 2000b; Wynn, 2000).

Ethical Concerns

An important issue that is relevant in all studies, including those with infants, concerns **research ethics**—a set of principles and guidelines for conducting acceptable research activities. Before researchers conduct their studies, they are required to obtain approval from an independent Institutional Review Board (IRB). Members of the IRB are independent in that they must not be part of any research team whose proposal they review. In considering whether or not to approve proposals, members of the IRB determine whether and how the researchers' plans meet a set of guidelines for ethical conduct in research, guidelines that have been specified, for example, by the American Psychological Association or the Society for Research in Child Development (SRCD, 2000). Guidelines from SRCD specify that researchers studying child behavior and development must use the least harmful and least stressful procedures whenever possible. The rationale for any proposed exposure to physical or psychological stress must be extremely clear and compelling; even then, the IRB may not give approval to these kinds of studies if the risk imposed on participants is not outweighed by the potential value of the study's findings.

All ethical guidelines for research with humans specify that **informed consent** be obtained from participants (an exception is usually made, however, for studies in which behavior is observed in naturalistic settings and in which participants' identities are not known to the researchers). The ethical requirement of informed consent depends on research participants being able to understand the procedures involved in a study and any risks those procedures might entail and knowing that they are free to withdraw or decline to participate without any negative consequences. It is generally assumed that children cannot give informed consent, but children who can answer questions verbally are able to give their **assent**—or agreement—to participate in research (Thompson, 1990). In addition, they can indicate (e.g., by saying "I don't want to play this game anymore") that they wish to discontinue participating.

In studies with infants, not even assent is possible, so researchers need to obtain the informed consent of their participants' parents. In doing so, researchers must explain all procedures clearly, indicate any potential risks that may result from participation, and make clear the parents' right to stop participation on their infant's behalf. It is also essential that parents giving their informed consent are told exactly how their rights to privacy will be maintained. If the infant's behavior is videotaped, for example, parents need to be told who will have access to the videotape, how their family's identity will be protected, how long the videotape will be kept by the researcher, and what will happen to the videotape after the study is completed.

It is also essential that the researcher make clear any benefits—or lack of benefits—associated with the study. Parents who bring their infants to participate in a study in a university setting or health clinic, for example, may also bring unfounded expectations that their infant's intelligence or health will be enhanced as a result of their participation. In studies involving infants who are at risk, due to conditions such as preterm birth or prenatal exposure to drugs or alcohol, researchers need to be extraordinarily clear when obtaining informed consent if infants will be randomly placed into either a potentially helpful treatment group or a comparison group that will not receive treatment. If, in the course of such a study, researchers become convinced that there is no doubt about a treatment's effectiveness, ethical guidelines direct them to offer the treatment to all participants.

Finally, researchers need to be cautious when communicating with parents about any developmental problems that they suspect an infant may have, if those problems become evident during the course of a study. Because young infants' state of arousal has a significant impact on their ability to attend to stimuli, they may not always display their "best" performance. If parents express concerns about their child's development, researchers may provide information or referrals to qualified specialists. As a rule, however, unless researchers have the necessary expertise and are using recognized assessment tools, it is best if they give parents only general feedback about their infant's performance in the study. By contrast, researchers who strongly suspect that an infant has been abused or neglected should take steps to notify the local child protection agency.

Where Do Babies Come From?

Unlike researchers studying college students, who often participate in studies as a requirement for an academic course or to receive extra credit, researchers studying infants have the additional challenge of finding their participants. Some researchers keep track of birth announcements, while others recruit participants from child care centers, parenting groups, health clinics, and hospitals. Still others place advertisements in newspapers or parenting magazines. In some studies, researchers may have funds with which to pay families for their participation. When researchers report the findings of their studies in published articles or at professional conferences, they need to provide information about the source and characteristics of their sample. This information is useful to the wider community of researchers, since it is informative about the external validity of the study and the ethnic, racial, and socioeconomic diversity of the participants.

WRAPPING IT UP: Summary and Conclusion

Naturalistic studies offer some advantages over studies that are carried out in controlled laboratory settings. Researchers often prefer laboratory settings, however, for the consistency and uniformity of experience that they provide across research participants. There are also trade-offs involved in decisions about conducting case studies as opposed to studies with larger samples, such as quasi-experiments and experiments.

Longitudinal studies reveal continuity and change within the same individuals, but they are more time consuming and expensive than most researchers desire, making cross-sectional approaches the more frequent choice. Some researchers are turning to microgenetic research to illuminate the process through which development occurs over a relatively short period of time.

The specific question the researcher is asking has an influence on the measures chosen in a study. Some measures rely on infants' natural, untrained responses to stimuli presented in a laboratory setting. Infants can also be trained to perform behaviors, such as sucking or turning their head, as a way of signaling that they detect differences between stimuli. Parental reports about their infants' behavior and development can provide useful information, especially when researchers train parents to observe specific aspects of their child's development and record these observations in structured diaries.

Researchers working with infants face special challenges, including the tendency for newborns to shift frequently between behavioral states. Researchers who work with very young infants can take steps to increase the chance that participants will be able to complete their studies, but they must also accept the reality that loss of participants will be commonplace. To the extent that researchers studying infants rely on indirect measures, they are basing their conclusions on inference and interpretation, and different researchers may have different interpretations of the same evidence. Ethical guidelines for research with children specify ways in which researchers need to be thoughtful about ethical issues as they design and carry out their research. Because infants are unable to give either informed consent or assent to participate in studies, researchers need to obtain informed consent from their parents.

The choices that researchers make as they plan and carry out their studies depend on a number of factors, including the availability of infants. Even with ready access to infants, as in the case of Werner Leopold's study of Hildegard, researchers breaking new ground may face limitations in terms of knowledge and instrumentation. It seems unlikely, for example, that a modern-day Werner Leopold would choose to record his observations on individual slips of paper. Because the choices available to researchers are one indicator of how much is already known about the topic under study, accepted measures and standard laboratory procedures tend to exist only for topics that have been under investigation for many years. Even for well-established topics, there is still room for innovation as new technologies and more sensitive measures become available.

Research is a creative endeavor, and existing methods can be applied to new topics, especially when there is communication between researchers studying different aspects of development, such as perception and emotion, or language and social interaction. Throughout the remainder of this book, we will see examples of methodological cross-fertilization at the same time that standard methods for studying early development in particular domains are highlighted.

It has been noted that "all methods must cope with the fact that human infants are nonverbal, relatively immobile, and only intermittently cooperative experimental subjects" (Kellman & Arterberry, 1998, p. 317). It is a testament to researchers' creativity and doggedness, then, that so many choices exist today.

THINK ABOUT IT: Questions for Reading and Discussion

1. Which do you think are more valuable—naturalistic studies or laboratory studies? If you were the parent of an infant, would you allow a research team to observe you and your child in your home, or would you prefer to participate in a study in a laboratory setting? Explain your answers.

2. What are some of the ethical issues that researchers should consider when carrying out case studies, especially when the individual being studied is at risk or may have been deprived of normal care early in life? From an ethical standpoint, how would you evaluate Werner Leopold's study of his bilingual daughter?

3. Some researchers use deception in their studies. Under what circumstances do you think that this is appropriate? Would you agree to participate—or have your child participate—in a study that you knew involved some sort of deception? Why or why not?

4. Some studies examine basic issues, such as infants' ability to discriminate between two speech sounds. Other studies explore applied issues, such as the impact of child care on infants' development. How can the relative value of basic and applied studies be determined? If you were in charge of allocating funds for research, would you divide the money equally between these types of studies or not? Explain your answers.

5. What sorts of issues should ethnographic researchers be sensitive to when observing behavior and development in a culture other than their own?

6. Can you think of a way that Werner Leopold could have carried out his study using ethnographic research methods? Could archival research have been used in a study like his? Would psychophysiological measures have been useful? Explain your answers.

7. How could psychophysiological measures be combined with either behavioral responses or parental reports to increase our understanding of infant behavior and development?

KEY WORDS

Archival research (56)   Research that replaces the direct observation or assessment of research participants with examination of records or artifacts

Assent (59)   Verbal agreement to participate in research, obtained when participants are unable to give informed consent

Baby biography (44)   Observational records made by parents or other caregivers of an infants' early development

Behavioral state (56)   Any of 10 distinct levels of arousal observed in newborn infants, including four awake states, three transition states between sleep and waking, two sleep states, and one transition sleep state

Case study (44)   Also referred to as the clinical method, this is an in-depth examination of a single individual

Cohort (49)   A particular group or generation of participants, such as infants born in the same year

Cohort effects (50)   A problem in cross-sectional research, in which age differences may actually stem from generational, or cohort, differences

Conditioned headturning (54)   A technique in which infants are taught to turn their head every time they hear a particular signal—and only when they hear that signal. Once this headturning response has been conditioned and can be elicited reliably, a different stimulus is presented or alternated with the original signal. Infants who do not turn their head in response to the new stimulus are assumed to be able to discriminate between the signal used in conditioning and the new stimulus, whereas infants who turn their head are thought not to be able to make this discrimination

Cross-sectional research (50)   A developmental design in which two or more age groups of participants are compared in terms of their behavior or ability at the same point in time

Dependent variable (41)   The main behavior or response of interest in a study, this is the researchers' measure of the impact of the independent variable(s)

Dishabituation (54)	Infants' recovery of attention when a new stimulus is introduced
Electroencephalography (EEG) (52)	A measurement of electrical activity and spontaneous natural rhythms in the brain
Ethnographic research (40)	A technique for exploring the interaction of culture and biology, in which researchers from a Western culture make observations or conduct interviews in everyday settings in non-Western cultures
Event-related potential (ERP) (53)	A measurement of electrical activity resulting in the brain from the presentation of discrete stimuli
Event sampling (37)	A technique in observational research in which a small number of behaviors are identified and the researcher makes a note each time they occur by making a mark on a prepared checklist
Experimental design (46)	A design that examines the influence of an independent variable on a dependent variable
External validity (43)	The degree to which the findings of one study can be extended, or generalized, to other samples and settings
Habituation (54)	The phenomenon in which infants gradually lose interest in a stimulus after repeated presentations
Independent variable (41)	Aspects of a research setting that researchers identify or vary, such as presence or absence of an infant's mother, in order to determine their effect on behaviors of interest
Informed consent (59)	A key requirement in ethical research, based on research participants being able to understand the procedures involved in a study and any risks those procedures might entail and knowing that they are free to withdraw or decline to participate without any negative consequences
Internal validity (43)	The degree to which differences in the dependent variable are actually due to differences in the independent variable
Laboratory setting (41)	A specially designed research space that enables researchers to control or eliminate the influence of irrelevant or distracting factors
Longitudinal research (48)	A developmental design in which investigators study the same sample of children (or adults) over time, taking measures of their behavior or ability at specified intervals
Measurement equivalence (48)	Correspondence between the measures, or dependent variables, used at two different points in time
Microgenetic research (50)	A developmental design in which participants are observed over a period of time, perhaps 10 or more sessions, with the researchers gathering a rich set of data on which fine-grained analyses can be performed
Narrative record (37)	A detailed description of the range of behaviors researchers observe
Naturalistic observation (37)	Studies in which researchers remain relatively passive observers in the sense that, apart from being physically present, they do not intervene in or try to influence the situation
Naturalistic setting (36)	Studies in which researchers observe infants in their usual surroundings, such as their own home or their regular child care center
Observer bias (38)	The phenomenon in which researchers' expectations or beliefs influence the way they record or interpret behavior

Operational definition (37)   A clear, concrete verbal description that enables target behaviors and outcomes to be measured accurately

Orienting response (54)   Infants' behavior the first time a stimulus is presented, characterized by momentary cessation of any ongoing activity in order to give close attention to the new stimulus

Parental reports (55)   Data provided about infants' behavior and development by their parents or caregivers

Practice effect (49)   Improvement in participants' performance as a result of the repeated exposure to the measures of those abilities

Quasi-experimental design (45)   A design in which researchers collect information about groups of participants that are already formed before the study begins

Random assignment (47)   The equivalent of flipping a coin, this technique is used to ensure that each child has an equal chance of being placed into the different groups being compared on a specific dependent variable. As a result of this precaution, potentially important differences across children are distributed across the different groups

Research ethics (59)   A set of principles and guidelines for conducting acceptable research activities

Single-subject research (45)   A variation of the case study, in which researchers intervene or study the effects of an experimental manipulation within a single participant

Visual fixation (53)   Infants' looking behavior at stimuli presented in laboratory settings

Visual preference method (53)   A technique in which infants' looking behavior is used to determine their ability to perceive and notice differences between stimuli presented in a laboratory setting

CHAPTER

3

Genetics, Conception, and Prenatal Development

All parents hope that their infant will be healthy at birth. Expectant parents can do much more than simply hope, however, if they want to increase the chance that their baby will have a healthy start in life. As we will discuss in this chapter, there are many ways to safeguard prenatal development, and the vast majority of pregnancies in the United States and other developed countries end with the birth of a healthy, full-term baby.

Recent medical advances and greater understanding of genetics have prompted some parents to go even further, beyond basic prenatal care, in their efforts to maximize their child's health and potential. Some couples, for example, have placed ads in college and university newspapers: "Egg donor wanted. Agents working on behalf of a couple who wish to become parents are looking for a woman younger than 30, five feet nine or taller, with college-level athletic ability, SAT scores of at least 1400, and a good family medical history. In exchange for providing eggs, the donor will receive payment of $50,000." Ads like this are thought provoking on a number of levels (Kolata, 1999). First, there are ethical issues surrounding egg donation. Some ethicists have raised questions about the practice, especially when compensation to the donor reaches five figures. There are also legal issues, such as the donor's liability if a child cannot be produced from her egg, or if the child turns out not to be what the parents wanted, in terms of health, abilities, or even physical appearance (ESHRE Task Force on Ethics and Law, 2002). Finally, the ad raises questions about genetics, conception, and human development. Is it really possible to achieve the kind of control that these prospective parents desire? As we will see in this chapter, parents have a better chance of using genetic information to influence their future child's health than his or her athletic ability, intelligence, or height. Even so, advances in the study of genetics, conception, and prenatal development are bringing us closer to understanding that a person's genetic endowment is only one of multiple influences on development and behavior.

Genetics and the Human Genome

All forms of life—plants, animals, and people—possess genetic information that specifies their potential characteristics. Across the twentieth century, a number of significant milestones were achieved in the study of genetics. One important step occurred when the cellular basis of heredity was shown to be **chromosomes**, physical structures consisting of **deoxyribonucleic acid (DNA)**. The genetic code of a cell is carried by DNA, strands of four basic molecules—adenine (A), thymine (T), cytosine (C), and guanine (G). In 1953, Watson and Crick described the molecular basis of DNA—a double-helix structure that resembles a twisted ladder. The molecules out of which DNA is comprised are always paired together in the same way—A with T, and C with G—to form the rungs of the DNA ladder. The sequence of the rungs varies, however, and provides a unique set of instructions for inherited characteristics. With this knowledge, it became possible to define a **gene** as a segment of DNA in a specific location on a chromosome.

Further studies showed that DNA duplicates itself during the lifelong process of growth through cell division known as **mitosis.** In mitosis, the chromosomes in a cell are duplicated and a copy of each chromosome moves to either end of the cell. When the chromosomes are organized in this way, the cell then divides in two, producing two identical cells. The original cell and its copy each contain a complete set of the original cell's 46 chromosomes (Dennis & Gallagher, 2001).

Another phase of the science of genetics began when researchers determined the mechanism by which cells "read" the information in genes and created technologies of cloning and sequencing. The first animal to be cloned, in 1997, was a sheep named Dolly (Schnieke et al., 1997). Since then, other animals, including mice, cows, cats, and rabbits, have been cloned (Evans et al., 1999; McCreath et al., 2000; Shin et al., 2002). Even before this milestone was achieved, there was great debate about the ethical and practical issues associated with human cloning, especially in light of research with cloned mice suggesting that there may be long-term negative effects of cloning, even when prenatal development and birth are normal (Ogonuki et al., 2002).

All living things have their own way of packaging DNA in chromosomes; mosquitoes have six chromosomes, pea plants have 14, cats have 38, and dogs have 48 (Dennis & Gallagher, 2001). Human cells contain 46 chromosomes, arranged in 23 pairs—one pair of **sex chromosomes** (XX in females and XY in males) and 22 pairs of **autosomes** (any of the chromosomes other than the sex-determining chromosomes). The arrangement of chromosome pairs, with one member of each pair coming from each parent, is shown in the karyotype (pictorial display of chromosomes) in Figure 3.1 on p. 68.

On June 26, 2000, two independent groups of scientists announced that they had completed the Human Genome Project (HGP)—a "working draft" of the DNA sequence of the 30,000 to 40,000 genes in the human genome (Dennis & Gallagher, 2001; International Genome Sequencing Consortium, 2001; Venter et al. 2001; Wolfsberg, McEntyre, & Schuler, 2001). This discovery, in turn, ushered in an era of "postgenomic science" (Baltimore, 2001, p. 814), in which research efforts are focusing on ways to use genomic information to diagnose, treat, and even prevent inherited diseases (Dennis & Gallagher, 2001). An important step in this phase of genomics began in 2001, when a

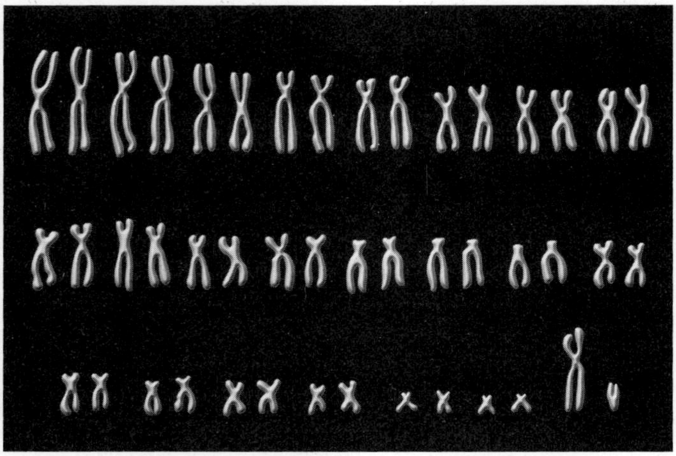

FIGURE 3.1 A karyotype shows the 23 pairs of chromosomes that humans usually have; this karyotype is from a male, as shown by the presence of one X chromosome and one Y chromosome in the 23rd pair.

group of researchers from Canada, China, Japan, Nigeria, the United Kingdom, and the United States completed work on a human haplotype map, or HapMap, that describes more than 1 million markers of genetic variation (International Genome Sequencing Consortium, 2001).

Genetics and Disease

Genes influence many human characteristics, including eye color, the ability to perceive color, and even more importantly, physical development and health. There are many well-known hereditary diseases, but even rare conditions may significantly affect the lives of infants and their families. This was the case for one set of new parents who were not able to identify their daughter Gabby's condition—hereditary sensory autonomic neuropathy (HSAN) Type 5—until she reached the age of 1 year. Initially, they and Gabby's pediatrician thought that she simply had a high tolerance for pain because as a newborn she continued sleeping peacefully even when her heel was pricked to draw blood for a routine health screening. As they would later discover, Gabby was unable to feel pain at all, despite having other senses that functioned normally.

As scientists learn more about human genetics, it may be possible to treat hereditary conditions such as HSAN Type 5 and even predict which prospective parents are most likely to pass on genes for inherited disorders of all types. For now, however, because there is no cure, all that Gabby's parents can do is monitor her carefully and give her swimming goggles to wear so that she will not accidentally poke, scratch, or otherwise damage her eyes (Freed, 2004).

How close are we to understanding the genetic basis of human characteristics—and to helping children like Gabby or even to providing the couple advertising for an egg donor with the child they desire? The answer depends on which characteristics are examined. Table 3.1 shows examples of congenital human diseases (diseases present from birth) with

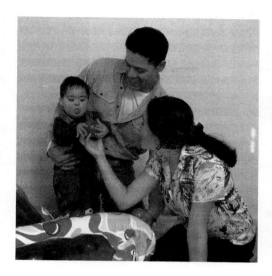

Infants born with Down syndrome have distinctive facial features and mild to severe mental retardation; like other babies, they benefit from interactions with involved parents in a loving, stimulating environment.

a known genetic basis. A very small number of diseases, such as Huntington's disease and achondroplasia (both caused by genes located on chromosome 4), are inherited when a child receives a single dominant gene. All individuals inheriting this gene develop the disease and, if they have offspring of their own, have a high probability of passing it on to the next generation. (Huntington's disease is a degenerative neurological disease with symptoms not appearing until middle adulthood, whereas achondroplasia is a form of dwarfism that is apparent from birth.) Other diseases, such as Tay Sachs disease (chromosome 15), Noonan syndrome (chromosome 12), sickle-cell anemia (chromosome 11), and a form of hearing loss in newborns (chromosome 13), occur only when a child receives two recessive genes for the disease, one from each parent. Still other diseases, such as hemophilia and Duchenne muscular dystrophy, are the result of **sex-linked inheritance** of recessive genes. These diseases (and harmless traits such as red-green color blindness) are transmitted when boys receive a single defective X chromosome from their mother. Girls receive a second, nondefective X chromosome from their father and thus do not usually inherit the characteristic.

Research is under way to discover whether and how the X chromosome might be involved in Autism Spectrum Disorders and Fragile X syndrome, both of which are more prevalent in boys. Autism and Fragile X are neurodevelopmental disorders that cause severe and pervasive deficits in cognition, emotion, language, and social functioning, but impairment can range from mild learning disabilities to more severe problems. This variability suggests that, even if a link to the X chromosome is discovered, there may be other genetic and environmental factors involved. Candidates being explored include chromosomes 7, 10, and 19 (NIH/NIMH Human Genetics Initiative, 2005).

Very few diseases and complex human traits are determined simply. Instead, most complex characteristics with a heritable component, such as intelligence, personality, and psychopathology, appear to be influenced by multiple genes, interacting in ways that are poorly

TABLE 3.1   Examples of Congenital Human Diseases with a Genetic Basis

Disease	Characteristics	Genetic Factors	Prevalence
Achondrioplasia (dwarfism)	Disorder of bone growth, short stature and shortened arms and legs	Chromosome 4, dominant trait	1 in 25,000 births
Asthma	Chronic respiratory disease	Chromosomes 5, 6, 11, and 14, recessive trait	1.4 percent of U.S children
Cystic fibrosis	Overproduction of mucus, which interferes with lung function	Chromosome 7, recessive trait	1 in 2,000 births
Duchenne muscular distrophy	Muscle weakness and respiratory failure leading to death by early adulthood	X chromosome, recessive trait	1 in 3,500 males
Hemophilia	Excessive bleeding	X chromosome, recessive trait	1 in 10,000 births
Huntington's disease	Progressive neurological disease, usually appearing in middle adulthood	Chromosome 4, dominant trait	1 in 10,000 births
Noonan syndrome	Multiple malformations of the body and face, short stature, developmental delays, and learning disabilities	Chromosome 12, dominant trait	1 in 2,500 births
Phenylketonuria (PKU)	Metabolic disorder resulting in mental retardation without a diet free of phenylalanine	Chromosome 12, recessive trait	1 in 10,00 to 1 in 25,000 births
Sickle-cell anemia	Deformation of red blood cells, resulting in oxygen deprivation and possible death	Chromosome 11, recessive trait	1 in 500 African Americans
Tay Sachs disease	Progressive neurological disease, death by age 5	Chromosome 15, recessive trait	1 in 3,000 Eastern European Jews

Source: Adapted from National Center for Biotechnology Information, 2002.

understood at the present time. Part of the continuing work of the Human Genome Project, therefore, is the complete specification of the genes on all 24 human chromosomes. The first chromosomes to be mapped in this way were chromosome 22 (Dunham et al., 1999), chromosome 21 (Hattori, Fujiyama, Taylor, Watanabe, Yada, Park, et al., 2000), and chromosome 20 (Deloukas, P., Matthews, L.H., Ashurst, J., Burton, J., Gilbert, J.G., Jones, M., et al., 2001).

It has been known for many years that an extra chromosome 21 causes **Down syndrome**. Individuals born with Down syndrome have mild to severe mental retardation and distinctive facial features. Many people with Down syndrome also have physical malformations, including heart defects and intestinal obstructions. The risk of Down syndrome increases with maternal age, but other, still unidentified factors are thought to play a contributing role as well. As chromosome-mapping continues, it is possible that this research will shed increasing light on Down syndrome and other chromosomal abnormalities.

Studies of twins and of families in which specific diseases are more common than in the population at large have also contributed to our understanding of the genetic basis for many heritable conditions. It is now known, for example, that juvenile onset (Type I) diabetes (also known as diabetes mellitus) is a complex trait, a disease that is thought to be caused by mutations in several genes on chromosomes 6, 7, and 11. Genes on chromosome 20 are implicated in adult onset (Type 2) diabetes, obesity, cataracts, and eczema.

Even as the human genome becomes more fully understood, it is important to remember that most traits and abilities are produced through the process of **multifactorial transmission**—the interaction of genes and the environment. As a result, even identical twins, who inherit an identical genotype (genetic potential), may possess different phenotypes (the expression of characteristics that are possible for a given genotype), especially if their environments and experiences differ markedly. Consider, for example, the case of identical twins with the same genetic predisposition to develop Type 2 diabetes, a disease that is made worse by obesity. If one twin maintained a healthy weight, followed a nutritious diet, and exercised, but the other twin did none of these things, the second twin would be more likely than the first to develop Type 2 diabetes.

Multifactorial transmission is also operating in schizophrenia, a form of psychopathology for which studies of families, twins, and adoptees have produced a compelling case for strong—but not deterministic—genetic factors. The rate of schizophrenia in the general population is relatively low (1 percent), as compared with the rate among children born to a schizophrenic parent (13 percent) and the rate among individuals with an identical twin who develops schizophrenia (48 percent). Even in the case of identical twins, however, their identical genetic inheritance does not correspond to identical outcomes. As one researcher noted, in schizophrenia "the implicated predisposing genetic factors combine in additive and interactive ways with known, as well as still unknown, environmental factors, acting prenatally, perinatally, and postnatally" (Gottesman, 2001, p. 870).

The more knowledge people have about their genetic predispositions, the more steps they may be able to take to prevent diseases that they may be at risk of developing. They may also be more likely to get regular screening tests for diseases that develop over time. If the disease is detected, they have a better chance of receiving early treatment.

Genetics and Prenatal Development

The genetic basis of conception and prenatal development is also becoming more clearly understood. Using animal models, researchers have made important discoveries about genes that determine the structure of specialized body structures, such as arms, legs, eyes, and parts of the brain (Cunningham et al., 2002). One group of scientists working with mice, for example, discovered a gene that controls the development of the hippocampus, a brain structure that is crucial for higher cognitive functions such as learning and memory (Zhao et al., 1999). The function of the gene was determined by inactivating it; when this was done, the researchers observed that embryos lacking the gene developed a malformed hippocampus.

Another group of researchers "knocked out" two genes in zebrafish and discovered that the resulting embryos failed to develop any sort of head or trunk—they were simply overgrown tails (Gonzalez et al., 2000). Researchers who wish to study humans cannot perform these kinds of experiments, of course, but further investigation may yield evidence about the genetic basis of prenatal development and naturally occurring birth defects in a range of mammals, including humans. We will discuss birth defects later in this chapter, but first let's consider the usual course of conception and prenatal development.

Conception

The role of sexual intercourse in conception has been apparent to humans throughout recorded history, but ideas about the process through which conception occurs have reflected different notions about the roles of males and females in society. In antiquity, Aristotle believed that the woman's role was simply to be a receptacle in which the child could develop. The process of conception was viewed (incorrectly) as beginning with the production of the man's sperm—in the brain—and concluding with its journey "along the ears and then . . . down to the testicles via the spinal cord" (Fontanel & d'Harcourt, 1997, p. 10). Hippocrates gave more importance to the woman's role, supporting the idea that the fetus was the result of the union of male *and* female "seeds." This debate continued over the years, even into the seventeenth century, when the woman's passive role was asserted by "animalculists," who argued that the man's spermatozoa (referred to as "animalcules") required only an empty chamber in which to grow into a child. "Ovists" of the time argued for the opposite view; they held that a tiny but fully formed fetus existed in the ovum produced by the woman (Fontanel & d'Harcourt 1997).

The basic process of fertilization is well understood, yet it remains a source of fascination, and researchers continue to learn about the **ovum** (female sex cell) and **sperm** (male sex cell). It has been known for many years, for example, that a woman's eggs are nearly as old as she is. This is because the ovarian structures that contain the genetic components of the ova are formed during the fetal period. As a result, a woman's follicles—ovarian structures containing immature eggs—exist even before birth. Sperm, by contrast, are made over a period of just 60 to 90 days, and new sperm are always being produced. New research suggests, however, that the cells that nurture growing sperm—Sertoli cells—are formed primarily during the first 6 to 9 months of life. One implication of this recent finding is that some male fertility problems may actually begin in the prenatal period, when the testes are still developing, rather than in puberty, or later, when mature sperm are produced (Timmons, Rigby, & Poirer, 2001).

Fertilization becomes possible when an egg matures in one of the ovaries, a process that occurs over a continuous 28-day cycle. During the first week in the cycle, the hypothalamus and pituitary release luteinizing hormone (LH) and follicle-stimulating hormone (FSH) into the woman's bloodstream. These hormones in turn bring about the production and secretion of ovarian hormones, including estradiol and progesterone. By the end of the first week of the cycle, these hormones result in the selection and subsequent growth of the follicle containing the egg that will be released during that cycle (Colón, 1997).

Initially, each unreleased egg has a full set of 46 chromosomes. By the end of two weeks, in response to a midcycle release of LH, the sex cells of the egg (also known as gametes) divide through the process of **meiosis**. Meiosis begins with duplication of the set of 46 chromosomes in the egg, as occurs in mitosis. But the cells then divide twice, yielding four sex cells, each of which has one set of 23 chromosomes. Meiosis differs from mitosis in another way as well; the chromosomes in each sex cell are more than just a copy of the original chromosomes. This is because the pairs of chromosomes exchange pieces of their genetic material during the first meiotic division. The outcome of this process is the production of chromosomes with new combinations of genes and, in offspring, new traits that may not have been present in either parent (Dennis & Gallagher, 2001).

A few hours after meiosis has completed, ovulation occurs: the egg is released from the ovary, and cilia (tiny hair cells) facilitate its travel through the fallopian tube, where it remains for one to two days. As the egg follows this path, the follicle in which it matured becomes a corpeus luteum and secretes hormones that prepare the uterine environment for possible implantation and pregnancy. The corpus luteum secretes these hormones for a period of only 14 days, however, and without fertilization it deteriorates (Colón, 1997; Gilbert, 2000). If the egg is not fertilized by sperm during this time, it too begins to disintegrate, and the woman experiences her typical monthly menstrual flow. The 28-day cycle then begins again.

If sperm are present, there is a chance that the egg will be fertilized. Although approximately 100 to 300 million sperm are released during a single ejaculation, only a few hundred travel as far as the fallopian tube, and only one sperm ultimately penetrates the membrane surrounding the egg. Their journey is possible because sperm have "tails" and can move through the cervix and the uterus, toward the fallopian tubes. Sperm locomotion is also assisted by hormones that affect the characteristics of the uterine environment. These hormones include estrogen, which is produced by the female's ovaries, and oxytocin, which is produced by the pituitary. The influence of the uterine environment is so strong that even sperm with deformed tails or other abnormalities may succeed in reaching and fertilizing the egg. As we will discuss later in the chapter, the notion that only the fittest sperm succeed in fertilizing an egg has been rejected. We now know that, like women, men who are trying to conceive a child need to be aware of and limit their exposure to potentially dangerous environmental influences.

Sperm undergo the process of meiosis in the sperm-producing cells in the testes, before they are released through ejaculation. The mechanisms that determine which single sperm will join its 23 chromosomes with the 23 chormosomes of the egg are not completely understood (Colón, 1997). When a sperm penetrates the membrane of the ovum, the membrane itself changes, and no other sperm may enter the ovum thereafter. The cell that results when the ovum is fertilized is known as a **zygote**. Because an ovum always contributes an X sex chromosome, the sex of each zygote is determined by the sex chromosome carried by the father's sperm. If the sperm carries a Y chormosome, the resulting zygote will be XY, or a male. If the sperm carries an X chromosome, however, the zygote will be XX, or a female.

Twins and Other Multiples

Sometimes more than one ovum is released at ovulation (this is especially likely to occur if the woman is taking fertility-enhancing drugs). When this happens, if each ovum is fertilized by different sperm, the resulting offspring are as closely related to one another as if they were siblings born years apart. Siblings resulting from two different eggs are referred to as **dizygotic twins** (two zygotes), or fraternal twins. Less frequently, a single fertilized ovum divides into two separate fertilized cells. Because these cells are fertilized by a single sperm, they are genetically identical, and the twins that result are referred to as **monozygotic twins** (one zygote), or identical twins. In approximately 40 percent of all twin pregnancies, only a single child is born. The "vanishing twin" phenomenon occurs in dizygotic twins when they carry different variants of a gene on chromosome 3 (PPAR-gamma), causing one twin to develop at the expense of the other. When twins have the same variant of this gene, they usually develop at the same pace (Busjahn et al., 2000; Landy & Keith, 1998). Monozygotic twins are always the same sex (two boys or two girls), but dizygotic twins, as well as triplets, quadruplets, and other multiples resulting from different sperm fertilizing each ovum, may be the same sex or different sexes.

Sex Chromosome Abnormalities

In some cases, when a problem occurs during meiosis, the embryo that develops has an abnormal number of chromosomes—either too many or too few—a condition known as aneuploidy. Instead of dividing evenly, the egg may have an extra X chromosome or the sperm may have both an X and a Y chromosome. An egg with a normal X chromosome that is fertilized by a sperm with both an X and a Y chromosome will produce a male with the XXY pattern, a condition known as Klinefelter syndrome. Klinefelter syndrome is thought to be the most common chromosomal abnormality, occurring as frequently as 1 in every 500 male births. A sperm cell with a normal X chromosome that fertilizes an egg with more than one X chromosome will produce a female with an XXX pattern. This condition, known as Turner syndrome, occurs in approximately 1 out of every 2,500 female births. The characteristics of these and other common sex chromosome abnormalities are shown in Table 3.2. The risk of misalignment of chromosomes during meiosis increases with age and is more common among women over age 35 (Hodges et al., 2002).

Infertility and Assisted Reproduction

There are many reasons for infertility, but one common cause is a previous sexually transmitted disease. Approximately 2 percent of U.S. women of reproductive age have an infertility-related medical appointment each year, and 13 to 15 percent receive infertility services at some point in their lives. In addition, approximately 7 percent of married couples in the United States in which the woman is of childbearing age report that they have not become pregnant, despite not using contraception for the previous 12 months (Centers for Disease Control & Prevention, 1995). In the past, these couples would have remained childless or created a family through adoption. Today, however, **assisted reproductive technology (ART)** makes it possible for many of these men and women to conceive their own biological children.

TABLE 3.2   Sex Chromosome Abnormalities

Abnormality	Characteristics
Syndromes affecting females:	
Turner syndrome (XO syndrome)	Short stature, delayed growth of the skeleton, shortened fourth and fifth fingers, broad chest, possible heart defects; infertility common due to ovarian failure; pubertal development depends on treatment with estrogen
XXX syndrome (triple X syndrome)	Mild to moderate mental retardation, tall stature, webbed neck, speech and cognitive delays, sterility
XXXX syndrome (poly-X syndrome)	Mild to severe mental retardation, some physical abnormalities, facial features similar to those seen in Down syndrome, sterility
XXXXX syndrome (poly-X syndrome)	Same as XXXX syndrome but with five X chromosomes present
Syndromes affecting males:	
Klinefelter syndrome (XXY syndrome)	Signs and symptoms vary and are not present in all cases; possible breast enlargement, lack of facial and body hair, rounded body type, possible language impairment, infertility
XYY syndrome (polysomy Y syndrome)	Increased height, speech delays, learning disabilities, mild to moderate mental retardation, behavioral disturbance

Source: Based on Hodges et al., 2002.

As defined by the 1992 Fertility Clinic Success Rate and Certification Act, ART includes all fertility treatments in which both egg and sperm are handled. Intrauterine insemination (IUI, also referred to as artificial insemination), in which sperm is placed into a woman's uterus to facilitate fertilization, is thus not considered an ART procedure. As

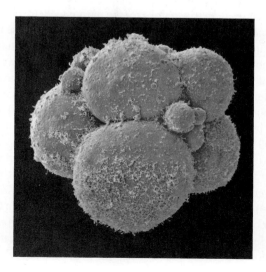

By approximately 1 week after conception, the process of mitosis has produced a hollow spherical cluster of cells called a blastocyst.

TABLE 3.3   A Number of Assisted Reproductive Technology (ART) Procedures Are Available to Achieve Conception Despite Fertility Problems

ART Procedure	How It Works
In vitro fertilization (IVF)	An ART procedure in which eggs are removed from a woman's ovaries and fertilized outside of her body, with the resulting embryo transferred into the woman's uterus through the cervix
Gamete intrafallopian transfer (GIFT)	An ART procedure in which eggs are removed from a woman's ovary, combined with sperm, and transferred (still unfertilized) into the woman's fallopian tube through an incision in her abdomen
Zygote intrafallopian transfer (ZIFT)	An ART procedure in which eggs are collected from a woman's ovary and fertilized outside her body, with the zygote transferred into the woman's fallopian tube through an incision in her abdomen
Intracytoplasmic sperm injection (ICSI)	An ART procedure in which a single sperm is injected directly into a woman's egg in order to achieve fertilization

Source: Adapted from Centers for Disease Control & Prevention, 2001; and Colón, 1997.

described in Table 3.3, a number of ART procedures are available to couples today. The procedure that received the most initial publicity was in vitro fertilization (IVF), which resulted in the birth of the world's first "test-tube" baby in 1978 (Steptoe & Edwards, 1978). Other ART procedures that have been developed since that time include gamete intrafallopian transfer (GIFT), zygote intrafallopian transfer (ZIFT), and intracytoplasmic sperm injection (ICSI).

A woman's chances of becoming pregnant and having a live birth after using ART are influenced by a number of factors, including the woman's age, the cause of infertility, the quality of the embryos, and the number of embryos that are transferred. Success rates (defined as the percentage of egg retrievals that result in a live birth) for the most widely used ART procedures (IVF, GIFT, and ZIFT) range between 25 and 30 percent (Centers for Disease Control & Prevention, 2001, 2003). To maximize birth rates, physicians performing embryo transfer procedures often transfer several embryos. Although this increases the chance that a live birth will occur, it also increases the risk of multiple births. In fact, pregnancies achieved through ART, which uses drugs to induce ovulation, are more likely to result in multiple births than pregnancies occurring without intervention. These procedures are responsible for a marked increase in triplet and higher-order multiple births since the 1980s (Centers for Disease Control & Prevention, 2000b; Schieve et al., 1999). ART procedures are generally thought to be safe for the babies conceived through them (Tournaye & Van Steirteghem, 1997); complications during pregnancy and delivery and after birth may occur, however, when multiple fetuses are carried and when the babies are born preterm (Colón, 1997; Goldenberg & Jobe, 2001; Koivurova et al., 2002; Schenker & Ezra, 1994). We will discuss preterm infants in more detail in Chapter 4.

Regardless of the number of ova, the sex of the zygote, and the process through which conception has been achieved, fertilization initiates a series of changes, culminating in the implantation of the egg in the mother's uterine wall and a period of prenatal development.

Prenatal Development

As late as the nineteenth century, the fetus was shown as a tiny, fully formed human being, frolicking in the mother's uterus. The period of gestation was viewed as a time when the miniature person simply grew larger and waited to be born. Many people believed that miscarriages and birth defects could be prevented by satisfying the cravings of pregnant women and protecting them from unnecessary emotional upsets. These beliefs influenced thinking about pregnancy as recently as the late nineteenth- and early twentieth-century. Doctors from this time placed prohibitions on expectant women that, today, seem quite absurd, including warnings about dancing, singing, swimming, riding on streetcars, and leaving the house after sunset. Most doctors of the time placed sexual intercourse off limits as well (Fontanel & d'Harcourt, 1997).

The stages of prenatal development are clearly understood today, and most pregnant women are advised to continue their normal activities—including work, travel, aerobic exercise, and sexual intimacy—until the first signs of labor begin (American College of Obstetricians and Gynecologists, 1994, 2003). There is now compelling evidence that pregnant women who exercise regularly tend to have fewer problems during pregnancy and labor (Brankston et al., 2004; Leiferman & Evenson, 2003). There may even be sustained benefits after birth for children whose mothers exercised regularly during pregnancy (Clapp, 1996). Women with preexisting health problems and those experiencing complications during pregnancy need to follow their obstetrician's advice and limit their activities accordingly. As we will discuss later in the chapter, all pregnant women need to avoid **teratogens**—substances, such as alcohol, drugs, nicotine, and radiation, that are known to harm the developing fetus (Shepard et al., 2002). Table 3.4 shows some agents that are known or suspected to be teratogenic. Most teratogens produce their effects during specific critical periods of development, with the greatest damage typically occurring during the earliest part of pregnancy.

From the perspective of the expectant mother, pregnancy is usually experienced as three equally long trimesters, with the total period of gestation lasting 280 days, counting from the last menstrual period. From the perspective of the developing child, by contrast, the actual period of gestation is about 266 days (time since conception), and the three stages are unequal in length and characterized by unique events.

The Germinal Stage, Fertilization to 2 Weeks

The **germinal stage** begins with fertilization of an ovum by a sperm cell and ends at approximately 2 weeks. At approximately 30 hours postconception, the zygote divides in two through mitosis, forming two identical sets of chromosomes. The originals and the copy are then divided into two separate cells. At approximately 60 hours postconception, each of these cells undergoes the same mitotic process, resulting in a cluster of four identical cells. The process of mitosis repeats itself over and over again until, by about one week postconception, there are almost one hundred identical cells organized into a hollow spherical structure called a **blastocyst**. The cells in the blastocyst then begin to differentiate into an inner cell mass, which subsequently develops into the embryo, and an outer group of cells, the trophoblast (Gilbert, 2000).

During the process of early cell division and differentiation, the zygote travels through the fallopian tube to the uterus, where it begins the process of implantation in the uterine wall between the seventh and ninth day after conception. The mother's ovaries secrete hormones

**TABLE 3.4   Agents That Are Known or Suspected
to Be Teratogenic**

Teratogenic Agent

Drugs and Chemicals
Alcohol
Cigarette smoke
Cocaine
Cortisone
Diethylstilbesterol (DES)
Heroin
Lead
Methylmercury
Penicillamine (antibiotic)
Retinoic acid (Accutane, an acne medication)
Streptomycin
Tetracycline (antibiotic)
Thalidomide (sedative)
Trimethadione
Valproic acid (antiseizure medication)

Infectious Diseases
AIDS/HIV
Cytomegalovirus (CMV)
Herpes simplex
Parvovirus
Rubella (German measles)
Toxoplasmosis
Syphilis

Source: Adapted from Gilbert, 2000; not all known or suspected teratogens are listed.

that maintain the uterine lining and prevent it from being shed. Hormones produced by the corpus luteum also help to maintain the uterine lining, especially during the first trimester of the pregnancy. The germinal stage concludes at approximately 2 weeks postconception, after the blastocyst has become attached to the uterine lining, which provides it with nutrients and oxygen. As many as 55 percent of zygotes never reach this stage of development (Colón, 1997).

Sometimes implantation of the fertilized egg occurs outside of the uterus, a condition known as an ectopic pregnancy (also referred to as a tubal pregnancy). This potentially life-threatening condition is the leading cause of pregnancy-related deaths in the first trimester. There has been a fivefold increase over the past 20 years, with the result that approximately 10,000 ectopic pregnancies occur each year in the United States. The cause is often unknown, but tubal damage from sexually transmitted infections is thought to be responsible for many cases. The condition has also been attributed to fertility drugs, previous operations on

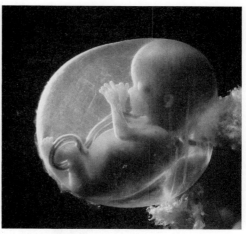

During the embryonic stage of prenatal development, major organ systems and structures develop, and the embryo is especially vulnerable to the effects of teratogens. At 8 weeks postconception, the embryo is 1 inch long and weighs about 1/30 of an ounce.

In the fetal stage of prenatal development, the major body parts and systems that were established during the embryonic stage grow and mature. At birth, the typical newborn is 20 inches long and weighs $7\frac{1}{2}$ pounds.

the fallopian tubes, endometriosis (when uterine tissue implants outside the uterus), and cigarette smoking (Centers for Disease Control & Prevention, 1995).

The Embryonic Stage, 2 to 8 Weeks

A zygote that has become implanted is referred to as an embryo. The **embryonic stage** begins approximately 2 weeks after conception and ends in the eighth prenatal week, when the first bone cells replace cartilage in the embryo's skeleton. Major organ systems and structures develop during this stage, and the embryo is especially vulnerable to the effects of teratogens. The type of defect (the heart versus the eyes or palate) depends on which structures and organs are developing at the time of exposure to the teratogen.

Growth in the embryonic stage is rapid and follows two principles that are also evident in development after birth. According to the **cephalocaudal principle**, development occurs first in the embryo's anterior region (head) and later in the direction of the embryo's posterior region (feet). In the early weeks of the embryonic stage, development of the embryo's lower regions lags behind development of the head, which is disproportionately large. Following the **proximodistal principle**, development begins in the center of the body and continues outward to the extremities. Thus fingers and toes develop later than and depend upon the earlier development of arms and legs.

As shown in Figure 3.2, a number of supporting structures begin to develop early in the embryonic stage. The **placenta** develops from cells in the trophoblast and from cells in the uterine lining; it contains a vast network of blood vessels and is connected to the

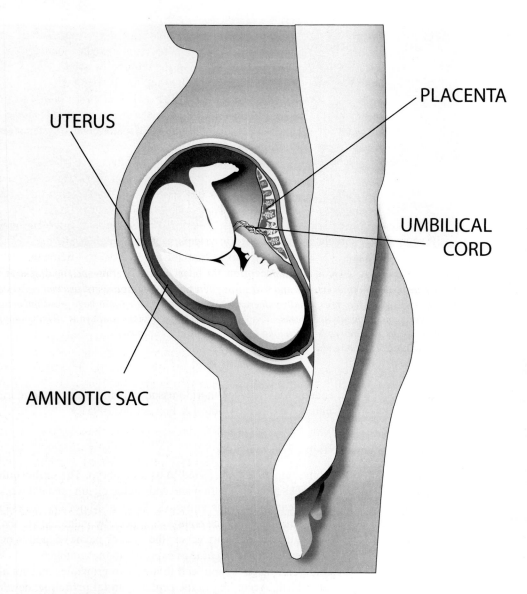

UTERUS

PLACENTA

UMBILICAL CORD

AMNIOTIC SAC

FIGURE 3.2   Each part of this system plays an important role in maintaining the pregnancy and promoting the development of the embryo and fetus.

embryo by the **umbilical cord**. Together, these structures bring oxygen and nutrients from the mother to the embryo and carry waste products from the embryo to the mother. The amniotic sac and its outer membrane, the chorion, envelop the embryo in amniotic fluid, which is replenished constantly during the pregnancy. The fluid acts as a barrier and a cushion and thus offers some degree of protection for the embryo at the same time that it helps to maintain a relatively constant temperature in the womb. The yolk sac is the source of red blood cells.

There is an invariant timetable for the development of major organs, systems, and body parts during the embryonic stage. In the third week after conception, the embryo's cells begin to differentiate. The upper layer of cells gives rise to the **ectoderm**—the source of the brain and spinal cord, sensory organs, and skin, nails, hair, and teeth. The brain and spinal cord develop from an ectodermal neural plate that thickens and then folds upon itself to become a neural tube. Later in the chapter we will discuss neural tube defects, a common and serious malformation that originates at this point in gestation. The middle layer—the **mesoderm**—is the source of the circulatory and excretory systems, as well as muscles and the skeleton. The respiratory and digestive systems are formed from the lower layer, or **endoderm**.

In the fourth week after conception, the heart begins beating and the digestive system begins to develop. These changes are followed by the beginnings of arms, legs, eyes, ears, and tissue that develops into the lower jaw and larynx (week 5). During weeks 6 to 8, development occurs in the circulation system as well as in the nose, upper lip, tongue, palate, trachea, teeth, fingers, and toes. Eyelids begin to form, facial features continue to develop, and the gastrointestinal tract separates from the genitoruinary tract. Long bones begin to form, muscles are able to contract, and the umbilical cord is well developed (Gilbert, 2000).

One of the most significant developments during the embryonic stage—one that has a profound, lifelong impact from the moment of birth (or even earlier, if the parents learn the sex of their unborn child)—occurs when the embryo's reproductive system becomes differentiated as male or female. During the first 6 weeks of prenatal development, the primitive sex glands (known as gonads) of genetically male (XY) and genetically female (XX) embryos are undifferentiated. Then, at approximately 6 to 8 weeks, in response to the Y chromosome, the gonads in genetically male (XY) embryos begin developing into testes. The testes subsequently produce testosterone, the hormone that leads to the development of the male reproductive tract (the Wolffian duct system) and penis. At the same time, the testes also produce Müllerian Inhibiting Substance (MIS), a hormone that prevents the Müllerian duct system (the female reproductive tract) from developing (Ahmed & Hughes, 2002).

In genetically female (XX) embryos, in the absence of testosterone and MIS, the gonads begin developing into the Müllerian duct system, the Wolffian ducts degenerate, and the ovaries begin producing female hormones. For many years, it was believed that females are created by "default"—that female characteristics develop in the absence of a Y chromosome or if the embryo is not exposed to male hormones. Evidence in support of this view came from cases in the 1950s in which genetically female human embryos, whose mothers were treated with male hormones to prevent miscarriage before the third prenatal month, were born with masculinized external genitalia. By contrast, female embryos exposed to male hormones later, after the reproductive system had completed the process of differentiation, were not affected by those hormones and developed normally.

Recent discoveries about factors controlling embryonic growth and differentiation, however, have made it clear that normal female reproductive system development depends on the *presence* and functioning of specific genes and molecules. There is evidence that HOX genes are involved in the development of the Müllerian system and are necessary for both appropriate embryological reproductive tract development and adult function (Taylor, 2000). It is also becoming clear that molecules known as the Wnts are responsible for embryological growth and differentiation of the midbrain, central nervous system, kidney, and limbs and that some of these molecules are needed for normal development of the reproductive system. Without the influence of Wnt-4, Wnt-5a, and Wnt-7a, female (XX) embryos do not develop normally (Heikkila, Peltoketo, & Vainio, 2001; Vainio et al., 1999).

Taken together, these studies highlight the importance of timing in understanding the effects of experience on embryological development. They also show that sexual differentiation, like other aspects of prenatal development, is affected by genetic and physiological factors within the embryo as well as by the biochemical and hormonal environment in which the embryo is developing.

The Fetal Stage, 8 Weeks to Birth (38 Weeks)

During the **fetal stage** of prenatal development, the major body parts and systems that were established during the embryonic stage grow and mature. The magnitude of growth that occurs during this last stage is readily apparent when comparing the 8-week-old fetus, which is approximately 1 inch long and weighs approximately 1/30 of an ounce, with the full-term newborn, which is typically 20 inches long and 7 1/2 pounds.

As in the embryonic stage, the timetable for development during the fetal stage is orderly and predictable, but the changes are more subtle. At about 9 to 12 weeks after conception, the fingers and toes are more clearly defined, tooth buds appear, and reflexes such as sucking and swallowing are developing. The eyelids close and will remain sealed shut until about the 28th week. The liver is now capable of producing red blood cells. Around 13 to 16 weeks, the fetus's head is covered with soft down known as lanugo, which will later cover the entire body; the skin on its body is almost transparent. Hair appears on the fetus's head, and eyebrows and eyelashes appear. The fetus swallows amniotic fluid, and meconium (a fetal waste product) is made in the intestinal tract. A 20-week-old fetus becomes increasingly active and has identifiable patterns of low and high activity, which may correspond to later sleep and wake states. Individual patterns of activity and responsiveness seem to correspond to differences in activity level and responsiveness after birth (DiPietro et al., 1996).

By about 24 weeks, fingerprints and toe prints are visible, as are fingernails, toenails, and nipples. The fetus's skin is protected by a waxy coating called vernix. With intensive care, survival is possible if the child is born at this stage. As we will discuss in Chapter 4, infants born this early are extremely fragile and, if they survive, often have complications that affect their health and development for years. The fetus is able to hear and responds to sounds that are transmitted through the uterine wall. Fetuses often show an increase in activity and greater responsiveness to sounds between weeks 28 and 32, and the eyelids open and close. The fetus has a rudimentary ability to regulate body temperature. Bones at this stage are fully developed but are still soft.

A baby born at 36 weeks has an excellent chance of survival but is likely to be small. The average fetus at this stage weighs about 5 lb. 12 oz. to 6 lb. 12 oz. and is about 16 to 19 inches long. By 38 to 40 weeks, the fetus is considered full term. The lanugo covering will have disappeared from most of the baby's body. (The newborn's physical appearance and abilities, as well as the process of labor and birth, are covered in Chapter 4.)

Although brain development begins during the embryonic stage, with the formation of the neural tube and brain stem and the production of brain cells called **neurons** (approximately 250,000 to 500,000 per prenatal minute), the most rapid prenatal period of brain development occurs during the last 2 months. It is during this time that the number of brain cells increases most rapidly, and the interconnection of those cells begins. By about 5 months after conception, the majority of brain cells that make higher-level thinking possible are in place. The functional connections among those cells depend primarily on experience that occurs after birth, however, with the most significant connections being formed during the first 2 years of life (Black, 1998; Johnson, 1997; Shonkoff & Phillips, 2000). In this way, the brain differs from other major organs because it is not completely developed by the time the child is born, a point that we will discuss at greater length in Chapter 5.

Most pregnancies today are healthy, and, as we saw in Chapter 1, infant mortality rates have dropped significantly, especially in the United States and in other developed countries. But complications still occur, sometimes for unknown reasons. In some cases, these complications are so serious that they lead to fetal death and endanger the mother. In other cases, the problems are evident in birth defects that may adversely affect the child's chances of survival and quality of life.

Miscarriage. Miscarriage is defined as pregnancy that ends before 20 weeks, but most miscarriages occur during the first 12 weeks. Most miscarriages occur when the pregnancy is not progressing normally. As many as 70 percent of all first-trimester miscarriages are believed to be caused by chromosomal abnormalities in the fetus. A faulty egg or sperm cell, formed during meiosis, may be the cause. When chromosomal abnormalities exist, embryonic and fetal development does not progress normally; in some cases an empty amniotic sac may be formed around an embryo that never developed or that stopped developing in the earliest stages.

During the second trimester, problems with the woman's uterus are a more common cause of miscarriages, although chromosomal abnormalities still account for up to 20 percent of cases. Uterine abnormalities that have been linked with miscarriage include a small or abnormally shaped uterus, or a uterus that has tumors or scar tissue from past surgeries. In some second-trimester miscarriages, the level of the hormone progesterone is insufficient to support the pregnancy. Immune system problems, which may interfere with the flow of blood in the placenta, are another cause of early miscarriage. In approximately 70 to 80 percent of such cases, subsequent miscarriages can be avoided if the woman takes low doses of aspirin and a blood-thinning drug called heparin (Hill, 1998). Low levels of folic acid may be responsible for some early miscarriages; by adding 400 micrograms of folic acid to her daily diet even before becoming pregnant, a woman can reduce her chances of a miscarriage at the same time that she reduces the risk of a defect in the formation of the neural tube, a problem that we will discuss shortly.

Stillbirth. When a fetus dies after 20 weeks, it is referred to as a stillbirth. Stillbirth is less common than miscarriage and is estimated to occur in approximately one in 200 pregnancies. As many as half of all stillbirths occur in pregnancies that appeared to be normal. The reasons for stillbirth are not always known, and in more than 30 percent of cases, the cause cannot be determined. One common cause of stillbirth is a placental problem, such as placental abruption, in which the placenta peels away from the uterine wall before delivery. This problem, which most frequently occurs around the 35th week of pregnancy, causes heavy bleeding and is life-threatening for both mother and baby. Fetuses who are small for gestational age or not growing properly may die from lack of oxygen; this problem is often seen in women who have high blood pressure. Fetal deaths that occur between 24 and 27 weeks are frequently caused by bacterial infections, which may go undetected if they cause no symptoms in the mother. Birth defects caused by chromosomal abnormalities may also lead to stillbirth, but they are more likely to result in miscarriage before 20 weeks.

Birth Defects

Approximately 4 million babies are born each year in the United States (Hamilton et al., 2005; Martin et al., 2005). Most expectant parents today can assume that their baby will develop normally and be born healthy, but approximately 120,000 U.S. babies every year are affected by birth defects (Centers for Disease Control & Prevention, 2006). This number represents a significant decline in the rate of birth defects since 1979, but they continue to be the leading cause of infant death in the United States (Centers for Disease Control & Prevention, 2006; Yang, Khoury, & Mannino, 1997). Researchers collect data about the prevalence of two major categories of birth defects: structural defects and birth defects resulting from chromosomal abnormalities. As shown in Table 3.5, the most common defects include those affecting the heart, the mouth and face, and the musculoskeletal system. The most common type of defect resulting from a chromosomal abnormality is Down syndrome (Centers for Disease Control & Prevention, 2006). We will take a closer look at two of these defects—those affecting the neural tube and the heart.

TABLE 3.5   Prevalence of Selected Major Birth Defects

Category	Estimated Prevalence
Heart and circulation system	17 per 10,000 live births
Cleft lip/palate	17 per 10,000 live births
Down syndrome	14 per 10,000 births
Muscles and skeleton	14 per 10,000 live births
Gastrointestinal tract	8 per 10,000 live births
Eye	2 per 10,000 live births
Club foot	58 per 100,000 births
Anencephaly	10 per 100,000 births
Spina bifida	19 per 100,000 births

Source: Adapted from Centers for Disease Control & Prevention, 2006; and National Center for Health Statistics, 2001.

Neural Tube Defects

Neural tube defects (NTDs) are birth defects that involve abnormal development of the neural tube. As we discussed earlier, the neural tube forms during the first few weeks of the prenatal period and is the structure that eventually becomes the brain and spinal cord. In the United States, approximately 4,000 pregnancies per year are affected by NTD, of which approximately 1,500 end in miscarriage or stillbirth. Several types of NTDs exist. Two types, spina bifida and anencephaly, make up 90 percent of all NTDs. A third type of NTD, encephalocele, accounts for the remaining 10 percent (Mathews, 2003).

Spina bifida is sometimes referred to as "open spine" because it is a defect caused by failure of the fetus's spine to close properly during the first month of pregnancy. Infants born with spina bifida sometimes have an opening on their spine, a condition that leads to nerve damage and varying degrees of permanent paralysis. Newborns with spina bifida usually undergo surgery to close the spinal opening within 24 hours of their birth in order to prevent further damage. Prognosis for infants with spina bifida depends on the number and severity of abnormalities (National Institute of Neurological Disorders and Stroke, 2001).

Anencephaly is a much more serious form of NTD, one which usually leads to still-birth or death within a few hours or days after birth. In anencephaly, the anterior end of the neural tube fails to close; as a result, there is an absence of a major portion of the brain, skull, and scalp. Infants with this condition lack a forebrain and a cerebrum (the areas of the brain that are responsible for thinking). There may be a semifunctional brain stem, which makes it possible for the baby to breathe and respond to sound or touch reflexively. The brain tissue that exists may be exposed, without any bone or skin present (National Institute of Neurological Disorders and Stroke, 2001).

In encephalocele, the infant's brain tissue protrudes through abnormal openings in the skull. The symptoms vary in severity, with the prognosis depending on the specific brain tissue involved, the location of the skull openings, and whether there are other malformations of the brain. Babies born with encephalocele usually survive but may suffer mental retardation (National Institute of Neurological Disorders and Stroke, 2001).

In another, rarer defect called hydranencephaly, the infant's brain is filled with sacs of cerebrospinal fluid rather than the cerebral hemispheres that normally develop during the fetal stage. Unlike the NTDs we have just considered, which have their origin in events occurring in the third to fourth week after conception, hydranencephaly is thought to be caused by infections or traumatic events occurring after the 12th week of pregnancy. Hydranencephaly is present at birth, but symptoms may not appear until the infant is a few weeks or even a few months old. At this time the infant may develop seizures and hydrocephalus (an extremely enlarged head) due to the accumulation of cerebrospinal fluid in the brain. Hydrocephalic infants often have other serious symptoms, including visual impairment, deafness, blindness, paralysis, and lack of growth. Shunts may be surgically implanted to relieve the build-up of fluid, but the prognosis for children with hydranencephaly is often poor. Death may occur before the age of 1 year (National Institute of Neurological Disorders and Stroke, 2001).

In 1992, after estimates that 50 percent or more of NTDs could be prevented if women consumed an adequate amount of folate, the B vitamin folic acid (beginning before they became pregnant), the United States Public Health Service recommended that women of childbearing age increase their daily consumption of folic acid to 400 micrograms (4,000 daily micrograms were recommended for women who have previously had an NTD-affected pregnancy). In 1998, the U.S. Food and Drug Administration required that all enriched cereal grain products have folic acid added (National Center for Health Statistics, 2002). How effective has this requirement been? Initial results suggest that it has had a positive impact (Centers for Disease Control & Prevention, 2004). Comparisons of data from 1995 and 1998 show that there was an increase (from 64 to 75 percent) in folic-acid awareness among women who had recently delivered a live-born infant, as well as an increase in folate intake of U.S. women of childbearing age (Ahluwalia, & Daniel, 2001; Centers for Disease Control & Prevention, 2004). The rate of all NTDs decreased by 26 percent between 1990 and 2000 (Centers for Disease Control & Prevention, 2004; Honein et al., 2001; National Center for Health Statistics, 2001).

Unfortunately, folic acid awareness differs among groups of women. Women who have less than a high school education, those who are African American or Hispanic, those who receive no prenatal care during the first trimester, and those whose pregnancies were not intended are generally less aware of the benefits of folic acid (Ahluwalia & Daniel, 2001; American Academy of Pediatrics, 1999b; Farley, Hambidge, & Daley, 2002). Hope for changing these statistics comes from a study in 14 Texas-Mexico border counties in which the rate of NTDs was high. The study, which focused on women who had already had an NTD-affected pregnancy, found promising results. After the intervention, a large percentage (89 percent) of the women who had had a subsequent pregnancy had taken folic acid before conception, and only 1 case of NTD occurred out of 124 pregnancies that resulted in live births (Centers for Disease Control & Prevention, 2000c). These findings suggest that even high-risk women can reduce their risk of NTDs if they are given information and guidance.

Congenital Heart Defects

Approximately 7,000 babies are born each year with congenital heart defects (Centers for Disease Control & Prevention, 2000a, 2006). The extent of the defect can range from mild and undetected to severe and life threatening. The defects can include holes in the chamber walls, inadequate blood flow, or abnormalities of the valves.

Congenital heart defects are often caused by environmental influences. Women who contract rubella (German measles) during the first trimester of pregnancy are at risk of having a baby with a heart defect. Women with diabetes also have an increased risk (Wren, Birrell, & Hawthorne, 2003). Certain prescription medications have also been implicated, as well as alcohol and drugs such as cocaine. Advances in genetic research and studies of affected families also point to a role for genetics, a role that is likely to become clearer in coming years (Schott et al., 1998).

Some heart defects may be diagnosed during the fetal stage of development, using tests we will discuss later in this chapter. New diagnostic tests and surgical treatment over the past 40 years have led to improved survival rates for children with even the most serious heart defects. Half of the surgeries for congenital heart defects are now performed on children under the age of 2 years (Centers for Disease Control & Prevention, 2006).

In Chapter 4, we will discuss another factor that has led to a reduction in deaths due to birth defects—new technology that has made it possible to save preterm infants and others born at risk. Overall, infant deaths due to birth defects have been reduced by half since 1960, largely as a result of new prenatal diagnostic and treatment options that we will discuss next.

Prenatal Diagnosis and Treatment

Expectant parents have a number of options available for assessing fetal development and detecting potential problems. In some cases, there are treatments, including hormones, medication, and even fetal surgery, that can correct defects before the child is born.

Advances in research on the genetics of human disease have led to the development of tests that offer expectant parents the chance to assess the health of a fetus and determine whether the child carries the code for a genetic disease, a disease for which the parents may not even realize they are carriers. However, prenatal genetic testing, especially for conditions that do not develop until adulthood, is controversial. The American Academy of Pediatrics (2000c) recommends that these tests be performed only in specific circumstances, primarily when there are immediate medical benefits that can prevent the disease, delay its onset, limit its severity, or prevent secondary disabilities. Genetic tests are not without limitations, and not all genetic mutations that cause disease are understood or detectable at the present time. As a result, expectant parents should receive counseling as part of any prenatal genetic testing they might undertake (Cunniff & Committee on Genetics, 2004).

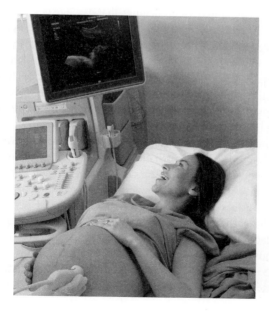

Many infants' first "baby pictures" are produced through ultrasound—a low-risk procedure in which sound waves are bounced off of the developing fetus and converted into an image on a video monitor.

Preimplantation Genetic Diagnosis (PGD)

When a couple has a known high risk of having a child with a serious genetic disorder, such as when both potential parents are carriers of a recessive gene mutation or when one parent has a dominant gene mutation, what can be done to avoid passing on the same genetic potential to their offspring? One relatively new procedure they might consider is **preimplantation genetic diagnosis (PGD)**. In PGD, a biopsy is performed on blastocysts resulting from in vitro fertilization (American Academy of Pediatrics, 1994). Blastocysts that are not carriers of the genetic mutation for the disease are selected for transfer to the woman's uterus, while blastocysts that are carriers of the mutation, and those for which the genetic status cannot be determined, are not implanted. Since PGD was developed in the late 1980s, it has resulted in the birth of approximately 700 healthy babies worldwide (Star Tribune, 2002; ESHRE PGD Consortium Steering Committee, 2002).

In 1999, researchers used PGD for the first time to enable a couple, both carriers of the recessive genetic mutation for sickle-cell anemia to conceive a healthy (mutation-free) child. In that trial, three healthy embryos were transferred to the uterus, resulting in healthy twins delivered at 39 weeks gestation (Xu et al., 1999). Other successful applications of PGD have focused on beta thalassemia, a severe form of anemia that is usually fatal in adolescence or early adulthood (Chamayou et al., 2002).

PGD has also been used, in one family, to select embryos that were free of a genetic mutation that causes early-onset Alzheimer's disease around age 40 to 50. Four mutation-free embryos were selected for transfer, resulting in the birth of a healthy child (Verlinsky et al., 2002). Given this success, the same family used PGD again to produce a set of mutation-free twins (Star Tribune, 2002).

PGD was employed in another family to produce a second child, but in this case the procedure selected embryos that could serve as potential stem cell donors for an older sibling requiring treatment for Fanconi anemia, a recessive genetic defect that prevents cells from repairing damaged DNA or removing toxic molecules that damage cells (Damewood, 2001; Verlinsky et al., 2001). Both parents were carriers of the mutation that causes the disease, and the only chance to save the first child was a compatible stem cell transplantation from the umbilical cord blood of a healthy sibling. (Without such a transplant, children with Fanconi anemia usually die before they reach early adulthood). Out of 30 embryos obtained in four IVF attempts, five compatible embryos were produced and, eventually, a healthy child was born, achieving the dual objective of saving the first child and producing a child that would be free of the life-threatening disease.

In response to the Alzheimer's PGD case, some bioethicists have asked whether it is ethical for parents to conceive children, knowing that early-onset dementia will prevent one of the parents from caring for them within several years (Towner & Loewy, 2002). Others have noted that the PGD procedure simply adds a new dimension to the debate about the rights of parents with disabling diseases to have children. Some have drawn parallels to the debate about using ART procedures for posthumous reproduction, such as when a surviving spouse elects to retrieve a deceased or dying spouse's stored sperm, ova, or embryos in order to produce a child (Benshushan & Schenker, 1998).

With a combined cost of $10,000 or more for each IVF and PGD, and no guarantee of success on the first attempt, these procedures are likely to appeal to only a small segment of the population, at least at the present time. As genetic research unveils more about the genetic basis for an increasing number of human characteristics, however, some bioethicists envision the potential misuse of PGD by couples like those described at the beginning of this chapter who placed the ad for an egg donor. What would prevent parents who want "perfect" children from using PGD to select other traits? Using preimplantation diagnosis for sex selection for nonmedical reasons has been discouraged by the Ethics Committee of the American Society of Reproductive Medicine, but there is no consensus at yet about this application of PGD (ESHRE PGD Consortium Steering Committee, 2002; Savulescu & Dahl, 2000). Preimplantation sex selection of embryos conceived through IVF does, in fact, occur in cultures in which families have a strong preference for sons rather than daughters (Malpani, Malpani, & Modi, 2002). Most clinics performing PGD, however, reserve the procedure for serious diseases such as cystic fibrosis, Tay-Sachs disease, Huntington's disease, and sickle-cell anemia (Cunniff & Committee on Genetics, 2004).

Ultrasound

In **ultrasound** (also called ultrasonography), sound waves are bounced off the developing fetus and converted into an image called a sonogram that can be viewed on a special video monitor. The examiner holds an instrument called a transducer and moves it across the woman's abdomen. The most advanced ultrasound technology produces a three-dimensional image that is almost photographic in the amount of detail that it shows. Ultrasound has been used for more than 30 years, across the prenatal period, without any identified risks for baby or mother.

Some experts recommend that ultrasound be used only for specific medical reasons, such as cases in which there may be an ectopic pregnancy or multiple pregnancy, or when the due date and fetal age are in question (American College of Obstetricians and Gynecologists, 1997). Despite this recommendation, nearly 70 percent of pregnant women in the United States have an ultrasound exam (Centers for Disease Control & Prevention, 2006; Martin et al., 2005). An ultrasonogram can also be used to identify a miscarriage, diagnose birth defects, check fetal well-being, and assist with other prenatal diagnostic tests, such as amniocentesis and chorionic villus sampling, which we will discuss shortly (Cunniff & Committee on Genetics, 2004). Recent studies have shown that ultrasound is an effective early screening tool between 11 and 13 weeks for Down syndrome (Cicero et al., 2001; Malone et al., 2005; Reddy & Mennuti, 2006).

Depending on the reason for the ultrasound, the procedure may take as little as 15 minutes or as much as several hours. One drawback to ultrasound is that it may miss some birth defects, perhaps as many as 25 to 50 percent (Grandjean, Larroque, & Levi, 1999). It may also lead to the opposite problem—a mistaken diagnosis of a birth defect that does not actually exist. The accuracy of an ultrasound diagnosis is affected by the training and experience of the examiner (Reddy & Mennuti, 2006).

Maternal Blood Screening

The **maternal serum alpha fetoprotein (MSAFP)** test, also referred to as the triple screen, is used routinely on most pregnant women. The MSAFP can detect neural tube defects, such as spina bifida or anencephaly. The test, which requires only a small blood sample from the mother, can also aid in the detection of Down syndrome. The blood sample is used to determine the level of alpha fetoprotein (AFP), a small amount of which normally crosses the placenta and enters the mother's bloodstream. High levels of AFP may indicate that the fetus has a neural tube defect, whereas low levels may signal Down syndrome. As part of the triple screen, the maternal blood sample is also analyzed for human chorionic gonadotropin (HCG), a hormone produced in the placenta, and estriol, an estrogen produced by both the fetus and the placenta. Abnormal levels of HCG and estriol may indicate fetal spinal defects and chromosomal abnormalities. The test is most accurate when performed between 16 and 18 weeks of gestation, but results can be affected if fetal age is miscalculated. If problems are suspected, a follow-up test or ultrasound may be used to gather more information (American Academy of Pediatrics, 1994; American College of Obstetricians and Gynecologists, 1996; Cunniff & Committee on Genetics, 2004; Pilu & Hobbins, 2002).

Chorionic Villus Sampling (CVS)

In **chorionic villus sampling (CVS)**, a small amount of the chorion tissue surrounding the amniotic sac is extracted, using a needle guided by ultrasound. The test is usually performed between 10 and 12 weeks after the mother's last menstrual period. CVS can diagnose or rule out birth defects due to chromosomal abnormalities and it is offered to women who will be 35 or older at the time of delivery, as well as to women with a previous child or pregnancy with a birth defect or chromosomal abnormality (American Academy of Pediatrics, 1994; Cunniff & Committee on Genetics, 2004). Some early (1991) studies suggested that when CVS is performed before the 10th week after the last menstrual period, there is a risk (1 out of every 1,700 procedures) that the baby will be born with missing or shortened fingers or toes or perhaps abnormalities of the tongue and lower jaw. More recent studies of the safety of CVS have found no increased risk of these defects (World Health Organization/PAHO Consultation on CVS, 1999). The accuracy rate for CVS is greater than 99 percent.

Amniocentesis

Amniocentesis is a test that is usually conducted in the second trimester (15 to 18 weeks postconception) of pregnancy. It involves inserting a thin, hollow needle, guided by ultrasound, into the uterus and removing a sample of the amniotic fluid surrounding the fetus. The sample of fluid is analyzed for chromosomal disorders, including Down syndrome. Amniocentesis also poses a small risk of miscarriage, however, and is not used for low-risk pregnancies. Because the risk of Down syndrome increases as a function of maternal age (from 1 in 1,250 children born to mothers in their 20s to 1 in 100 children born to mothers age 40), it is routinely offered to women who will be 35 or older at delivery. Amniocentesis may also be recommended if a woman has had a previous child or pregnancy with a birth defect or chromosomal abnormality, or if other prenatal screening tests have suggested that a chromosomal abnormality or birth defect may exist. Amniocentesis has an accuracy rate of nearly 100 percent in diagnosing chromosomal abnormalities (American Academy of Pediatrics, 1994; Cunniff & Committee on Genetics, 2004).

Fetal Echocardiography

When a cardiac defect is suspected, fetal echocardiography—a special kind of ultrasonography that provides information about structural defects or rhythmic disturbances—can be used. This procedure is usually performed after 20 weeks' gestation for cases in which a standard ultrasound has indicated potentional malformations. It may also be performed when there has been prenatal exposure to a known teratogen, when there is a family history of congenital heart defects, or when a fetal chromosomal abnormality or disease has been diagnosed. The procedures may also be used to evaluate fetuses whose mothers have diseases associated with fetal structural heart defects, such as diabetes (Cunniff & Committee on Genetics, 2004).

Fetal Therapy

When defects are detected during the fetal stage, can anything be done to correct them before the child is born? The answer depends on the nature of the problem, but the options for fetal therapy—interventions carried out during the prenatal period in order to correct known defects or prevent health problems after birth—are expanding.

If the problem is a disease caused by faulty genes, it may some day be possible to perform gene therapy—inserting healthy genes into the cells of a person's body. Results of studies with laboratory animals have been promising. Researchers working with diseased human lung cells grafted into a living mouse have had success "fooling" the body into repairing genetic codes that cause cystic fibrosis (Liu et al., 2002). Gene therapy has also been used to correct sickle-cell disease in mice that were bioengineered to contain a human gene for sickle-cell disease (Pawliuk et al., 2001). This form of gene therapy is known as somatic gene therapy because the targeted genes are in cells other than the sperm or eggs. Somatic gene therapy is still experimental, but if it becomes widely available in the future, it will help only the individual who has been treated. In order to prevent the genetic code from being inherited by the patient's offspring and all future descendants, germline gene therapy—changing the genes in sex cells—would be needed. This form of gene therapy entails numerous practical and ethical concerns, however, and is not being actively researched (Dennis & Gallagher, 2001).

Some health problems, such as HIV and heart rhythm disturbances, can be treated or prevented by giving drugs or other substances to the mother. Other potential problems, such as structural malformations, can be treated surgically before birth through fetal surgery—surgery performed on a fetus that remains connected to the placenta and is returned to the uterus following the procedure. Experimental trials were initiated in the 1960s but began in earnest in the 1980s. Since that time, with the development and refinement of ultrasound technology, operations on fetuses have succeeded more often, but there is still much about the physiology of the maternal-fetal-placental system that is not understood, and the field of fetal medicine is both technically challenging and ethically complex. While some applications of fetal surgery, including repairing blocked urinary tracts, have produced such reliable results that they are now regarded as nearly routine procedures, others have not lived up to expectations and continue to generate controversy among doctors and medical ethicists (Bruner et al., 1999; Evans et al., 2002; Simpson, 1999; Sutton et al., 1999; Wilson, 2002).

One controversial application of fetal surgery is treatment of congenital diaphragmatic hernia (CDH), a condition diagnosable by ultrasound, in which the fetus's abdominal organs migrate into the chest through a hole in the diaphragm, frequently resulting in respiratory failure in utero. Despite the development of new surgical procedures, research has shown that CDH continues to be associated with very high (75 percent) fetal mortality rates, whether it is treated prenatally or after birth. Critics thus question the value of the fetal treatment, since babies born with CDH need surgery after birth, even if they were operated upon prenatally (American Academy of Pediatrics, 1999a; Casper, 1998; Harrison et al., 2003; Peek & Elliott, 2004). Critics also point out that some open-uterus surgical procedures may lead mothers to risk their own lives in vain hope of saving their fetuses. Most fetal treatment facilities emphasize closed-uterus forms of treatment, with only a few medical centers actively engaged in research on open surgical techniques (Casper, 1998).

More consistently positive outcomes may be achieved through prevention efforts that promote healthy behaviors in pregnant women. As we have seen, a woman's nutrition, even before she becomes pregnant, may have a profound impact on the health and development of her unborn child. Besides having an adequate daily intake of folic acid, what can be done to achieve a healthy pregnancy and baby?

Prenatal Influences

Pregnancy is not always apparent to women during the first trimester, especially if the pregnancy is unintended, as may be true in as many as one-third to one-half of pregnancies in the United States (Alan Guttmacher Institute, 1999). Statistics indicate that unintended pregnancy is more prevalent among women younger than 20 years, African American women, women with lower levels of education, and lower income women (Beck et al., 2002). In general, these are the same groups of women who are likely to receive prenatal care late or not at all (Beck et al., 2002; Lewis, Mathews, & Heuser, 1996; National Center for Health Statistics, 2000). Women who receive less than adequate prenatal care are also less likely to follow a schedule of well-child visits with a pediatrician later (Kogan et al., 1998).

Since 1990, the number of pregnant women seeking prenatal care during the first trimester has increased steadily. In fact, in 2004, the vast majority (83.9 percent) of pregnant women began prenatal care during the first trimester, but some women (3.6 percent) did not seek care until the third trimester or did not receive prenatal care at all (Hamilton et al., 2005). Prenatal care that begins early in the pregnancy educates women about pregnancy and prenatal development; without this information, they may be less likely to consume a healthy, nutritious diet and more likely to ingest alcohol or drugs and expose themselves (and their fetuses) to potentially harmful environmental influences.

Nutrition

Only a few generations ago, women were routinely advised by their doctors to gain no more than 15 pounds during their pregnancy (Eisenberg, Murkoff, & Hathaway, 1991). We now know that babies whose mothers gain fewer than 20 pounds are at greater risk of being preterm and are more likely to grow slowly during the prenatal period than babies whose mothers gain between 25 and 35 pounds (Ehrenberg et al., 2003). Women who were underweight or overweight before becoming pregnant, as well as adolescents and women carrying twins or other multiples, may be advised to gain more or less weight (Martin et al., 2005; Schieve et al., 2000). For all women, weight gain should be slow and steady; the amount gained during the entire first trimester should be approximately 3 to 4 pounds. In the second trimester, women should gain a total of 12 to 14 additional pounds. About 1 pound per week should be added during the seventh and eighth months and only about 1 or 2 pounds for the entire ninth month (Eisenberg, Murkoff, & Hathaway, 1991). Women who gain more weight or gain a significant amount of weight early should consult their doctor to rule out any medical problems. Although they should be careful about the amount and type of food they eat thereafter, they should not try to lose weight during the remainder of their pregnancy. Losing weight before becoming pregnant is a good idea because children born to women who are overweight or obese before becoming pregnant are more likely to have birth defects and to develop health problems that include a greater risk of becoming overweight by 2 to 3 years of age (Salsberry & Reagan, 2005; Watkins et al., 2003).

It is often said that pregnant women are "eating for two," but the second diner requires only about 300 extra calories each day. Just as it is important to gain the right amount of weight and to put it on at the right rate, it is also critical that the foods women consume are of high nutritional value. Because many foods in the United States have been fortified since the 1930s, pregnant women consuming recommended servings also receive the benefits of vitamins A and D in cow's milk, and thiamin, niacin, riboflavin, and iron in flour and bread products (Centers for Disease Control & Prevention, 2002a; United States Food and Drug Administration, 1996).

Salty foods should be eaten in moderation, but it is crucial that the salt pregnant women do consume is iodized, because a deficiency of the micronutrient iodine interferes with the normal functioning of the thyroid and the production of thyroid hormone. Low levels of thyroid hormone (a condition referred to as hypothyroidism) cause a range of serious problems, including miscarriage, stillbirth, abnormalities in fetal brain development, and a form of mental retardation known as endemic cretinism (Cao et al., 1994; Haddow et al., 1999; Hetzel, 1999).

Women in the United States generally get enough iodine, which has been added to salt since 1924. Iodine deficiency still poses a significant risk of preventable brain damage in many parts of the world, however, and it is estimated that nearly 50 million people worldwide suffer from some degree of brain damage caused by iodine deficiency disorder. Fortunately, the number of countries with salt iodization programs has risen since 1991, and global rates of mental retardation and cretinism have begun to fall (World Health Organization, 2001, 2002). Where iodized salt is not yet available, doses of iodized oil may be injected or administered orally to pregnant women, with the same preventative effects (World Health Organization, 1996).

To help develop the blood supply for the fetus and mother, iron-rich foods should be consumed every day, and they should be eaten at the same time as foods rich in vitamin C to increase the body's absorption of iron. The need for iron is greater during pregnancy than at any other time in life, and many women in the United States and other developed countries take a daily prenatal vitamin supplement to ensure that their iron intake is sufficient. Iron deficiency is the most common nutritional disorder in the world. According to the World Health Organization (2002), 50 percent of pregnant woman worldwide suffer from iron deficiency, a condition that is thought to contribute to preterm birth, low birthweight, and 20 percent of all maternal deaths, primarily in developing countries.

Pregnant women need to be careful not to consume too much of certain nutrients. Women who consume more than twice the recommended daily amount of vitamin A in the first 2 months of pregnancy, for example, have a heightened risk of giving birth to babies with birth defects such as cleft lip or palate, hydrocephalus, or heart defects. The only food that provides very high amounts of vitamin A is liver, and although it has not been proved that eating liver causes birth defects, pregnant women are advised to limit their consumption (Rothman et al., 1995).

Alcohol and Drugs

The fetus and mother have separate circulatory systems, but small molecules, such as oxygen and nutrients, are able to cross through the cell membranes. Unfortunately, alcohol and drugs are also able to pass through the cell membranes of the placenta and may damage the developing child. The extent and type of damage that occurs depends on the timing, duration, and degree of exposure, with greater damage generally resulting from sustained exposure to larger doses earlier in the prenatal period.

It is difficult to obtain accurate reports, but some experts believe that between 13 and 20 percent of pregnant U.S. women consume alcohol and more than 5 percent use illicit drugs, putting their fetuses at risk for a wide range of serious medical problems (Ebrahim & Gfroerer, 2003; Martin et al., 2005; National Institute on Drug Abuse, 1996). There is an ongoing debate about how to ensure that fewer babies are exposed to these risks. On one side are those who advocate criminal punishment (for child abuse or child endangerment) for pregnant women who drink alcohol or take drugs. On the other side are those who argue that the best way to prevent or minimize damage to babies is to treat pregnant women for their addictions; according to this view, pregnant women will not seek this kind of help—or prenatal care—if they are in danger of being prosecuted as criminals. One recent survey shows that there is substantial support among doctors for mandatory alcohol and illicit drug screening of pregnant women as a way of reducing the devastating effects on their children (Abel & Kruger, 2002). Although there is not agreement about the best way to address the problem of prenatal exposure to alcohol and drugs, everyone agrees that too much preventable damage is being done.

Alcohol.   Prenatal exposure to alcohol is the leading preventable cause of birth defects, mental retardation, and neurodevelopmental disorders (American Academy of Pediatrics, 2000b). Alcohol is used by more pregnant women than are drugs such as cocaine and marijuana, and it produces the most serious neurobehavioral effects in the fetus (National Organization on Fetal Alcohol Syndrome, 2002). **Fetal alcohol syndrome (FAS)**, first clinically described in 1973, is a constellation of physical, behavioral, and cognitive abnormalities caused by prenatal exposure to alcohol (Jones & Smith, 1973). Children with FAS typically

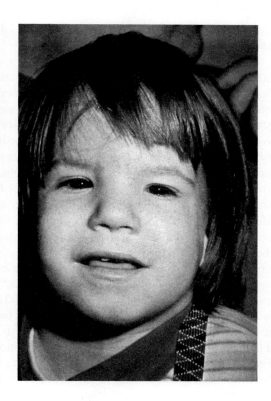

Prenatal exposure to alcohol produces fetal alcohol syndrome—a constellation of physical, behavioral, and cognitive abnormalities that are typically accompanied by the distinctive facial features seen in this child.

have small brains and growth deficiencies before and after birth, as well as poor coordination, attention-deficit hyperactivity disorder, and distinctive facial abnormalities. FAS is the leading known cause of mental retardation in the United States (Gilbert, 2000; Jacobson & Jacobson, 2000). As many as 12,000 infants are born with FAS each year, and another 50,000 show signs of other fetal alcohol effects, including conditions referred to as alcohol-related neurodevelopmental disorder (ARND) and alcohol-related birth defects (ARBD) (American Academy of Pediatrics, 2000a; Jacobson & Jacobson, 2000; National Organization on Fetal Alcohol Syndrome, 2002; Shonkoff & Phillips, 2000).

Attempts to increase public awareness of the risks to unborn children have reached many but not all women. Data from the 1990s suggest that the number of women drinking during pregnancy may have declined, but that the number of pregnant women binge drinking has not declined (Ebrahim, Decoufle, & Palakathodi, 2000; Ebrahim, Diekman, Floyd, & Decoufle, 1999; Ebrahim & Gfroerer, 2003; Martin et al., 2005). These trends suggest that many women still are not aware of the irreversible harm that can be done by consuming alcohol during pregnancy. Effects of prenatal alcohol exposure vary according to the timing, amount, and duration of exposure (Shonkoff & Phillips, 2000). Studies using animal models are shedding light on the mechanisms of fetal damage at different stages of development. It is clear, however, that there are differences between women in the effects of alcohol on their fetuses, even when the timing, amount, and duration of exposure are similar. No amount of alcohol, therefore, is regarded as safe. Given that even some over-the-counter medications may contain alcohol, it is a good idea for pregnant women to read labels care-fully and seek medical advice about safe alternatives.

Illicit Drugs.   Determining the effects of individual illicit drugs, such as cocaine, mari-juana, and heroin, on prenatal development can be difficult because pregnant women taking these substances often expose their fetuses to more than one drug, as well as alcohol and nicotine (Lester et al., 2002, 2004; Messinger et al., 2004). In addition, they are less likely to receive early prenatal care or to consume a healthy diet, and the fathers of their babies are also more likely to have a history of drug and/or alcohol use as well as physical abuse (Frank et al., 2002). Experiments with animals can reveal the effects of drugs in isolation, but even correlational (nonexperimental) evidence from research with humans indicates that illicit drugs are potent teratogens, causing miscarriage, stillbirth, and birth defects, as well as developmental problems in infancy and beyond. One valuable longitudinal study—the Maternal Lifestyle Study—is charting the development of approximately 800 babies who were exposed to cocaine and other drugs during the prenatal period (Lester et al., 2002).

According to recent estimates, approximately 1 million children have been born after prenatal exposure to cocaine since the 1980s, when a "crack epidemic" resulted from the availability of a cheap, smokeable form of cocaine (Singer et al., 2002). Women who use cocaine during their pregnancy are at increased risk of giving birth to babies who are preterm or low-birthweight, and the effects increase with greater exposure (Chiriboga et al., 1999). Cocaine-exposed babies tend to have a smaller head circumference and are at greater risk of dying from Sudden Infant Death Syndrome (SIDS) than are unexposed babies. Prenatal exposure to cocaine is associated with lower arousal, poorer quality of movement and self-regulation, greater excitability, and abnormal reflexes at the age of 1 month (Lester et al., 2002). There is also evidence from longitudinal research that chil-dren exposed to cocaine in utero are twice as likely to have significant delays in mental skills by the age of 2 years and may have continued learning difficulties and a need for special educational services when they reach school age (Delaney-Black et al., 1998; Singer et al., 2002).

Experiments with animals indicate that cocaine produces these effects by interfering with the development of neural systems in the fetal brain, with the most serious alterations seen during the period corresponding to the first trimester of pregnancy (Levitt, Reinoso, & Jones, 1998). Damage may also occur when cocaine constricts the vascular system, decreasing blood flow through the placenta, and producing low levels of oxygen in the fetus (Eyler et al., 1998; Singer et al., 2002). One longitudinal study that followed children to age 3 found developmental delays due to prenatal exposure to cocaine only for infants who were also low birthweight and who experienced nonoptimal caregiving after birth (Messinger et al., 2004). These findings offer hope that at-risk newborns—those who are known to have been prenatally exposed to cocaine or other substances—may be helped through early interventions (Frank et al., 2002).

Like cocaine, methamphetamine ("speed," or "ice") is a nervous system stimulant that has negative effects on the developing fetus. Heroin abuse can also cause serious com-plications during pregnancy, as well as problems with learning and attention underlying cognitive development after birth (Moe & Smith, 2003). Pregnant women trying to detox-ify from heroin are at increased risk of miscarriage or preterm delivery; treatment with methadone (a safer, synthetic form of heroin) for the remainder of the pregnancy is recommended instead (National Institute on Drug Abuse, 2002). Evidence about the effects of prenatal exposure to marijuana are less clear, but heavy use has been linked to birth defects, low birthweight, and neurological disturbances (Dreher, Nugent, & Hudgins, 1994).

Babies born to drug-addicted mothers are often addicted themselves and suffer withdrawal symptoms at birth. Women who inject drugs are at risk of becoming infected with the HIV virus and, as we will soon see, may pass the virus on to their babies.

Medication.   Many women become ill at some point during their pregnancy and are faced with questions about whether and how to relieve the symptoms of colds and other short-lived illnesses. Aspirin and ibuprofen should be avoided in the last 3 months of pregnancy because they may cause problems in the fetus or complications during delivery (Koren, Pastuszak, & Ito, 1998; Meadows, 2001). Pregnant women also need to be concerned about the potentially harmful effects of herbal treatments and dietary supplements, which may not be safe for the developing fetus, despite being "natural" products.

Up until the 1960s, some women took a tranquilizer called thalidomide to treat morning sickness. Sadly, thalidomide—even as little as one tablet—caused numerous birth defects in more than 7,000 infants. The drug's specific effects varied as a function of when in the critical period it was taken (teratogenic effects were produced only during days 34 to 50 after the mother's last menstruation). The mechanisms through which thalidomide causes birth defects are not well understood, and research is hampered because the only animal models for the drug are primates. After the drug's teratogenic effects were documented, it was withdrawn from the market. It is beginning to be prescribed again, however, to treat tumors, autoimmune problems, and leprosy (Gilbert, 2000; Raje & Anderson, 1999).

The dangers of prescription medication are not always apparent during the prenatal period and may not be known for many years. In the 1940s and 1950s, millions of women were prescribed a synthetic estrogen called diethylstilbestrol (DES) to prevent miscarriage. Babies—boys as well as girls—born to these women experienced a high rate of genital-tract structural abnormalities and cancers as they reached adulthood. Many DES daughters have had reproductive problems, including a higher incidence of infertility, miscarriage, and preterm delivery (Goldberg & Falcone, 1999; Kaufman, 1982; Robboy et al., 1984; Swan, 2000; Trimble, 2001).

For women who have chronic health conditions, not related to pregnancy per se, questions about the safety of prescription medications that treat those conditions can be a significant source of concern. According to current guidelines, medical conditions such as diabetes, epilepsy, and high blood pressure should continue to be treated and kept under control during pregnancy. Women taking psychoactive drugs to modify mood and behavior in the treatment of psychiatric illnesses, such as schizophrenia, depression, and obsessive-compulsive disorder, should also keep those conditions under control. Changes in the woman's physiology during pregnancy can influence the effectiveness of the pre-pregnancy dose, however, requiring either an increase or a decrease. Studies of how the body absorbs, distributes, metabolizes, and excretes drugs may help doctors determine the optimal doses of medications to help pregnant women stay physically and mentally healthy (Meadows, 2001).

The effects of medication on the developing fetus are often unclear or unknown, and ethical issues limit the experimental testing of medications on pregnant women (American

Academy of Pediatrics, 2000e; Brent, 2004; Meadows, 2001). What options are available, then, to women who must take medication during pregnancy? If there are concerns about a new drug's safety, an older version of the drug can be prescribed, since an absence of safety concerns in a long-used drug can provide some reassurance. Some drugs that are known to be harmful only during a particular stage of prenatal development can be withheld until the vulnerable period has passed. This has been done with the antibiotic tetracycline, which can cause permanent staining of a baby's teeth if taken before 24 weeks. The psychoactive drug lithium carries a small risk of heart defects, so women who use lithium may be advised to stop taking it during the time when the baby's heart is forming. Third trimester use of anti-depressant medication carries an increased risk of preterm birth and other adverse birth outcomes (Källen, 2004). Clearer labeling being developed by the Food and Drug Administration may also help women and their doctors make decisions about the risks and benefits of using various medications during pregnancy (American Academy of Pediatrics, 2000e; Meadows, 2001).

Nicotine.   Tobacco use during pregnancy has declined since 1989, but it has not disappeared. In 2004, approximately 10 percent of pregnant women in the United States smoked cigarettes. Younger women (those under age 25), women with lower levels of education, and women with lower incomes are more likely than other groups of women to smoke during pregnancy (Beck et al., 2002; Centers for Disease Control & Prevention, 2000e; Department of Health and Human Services, 2001; Hamilton et al., 2005).

Cigarette smoke contains more than 2,500 chemicals, and the effects of these substances on prenatal development are not known, so pregnant women who smoke are putting their unborn children at significant risk. Cigarette smoking during pregnancy tends to result in low-birthweight babies (weighing less than 5.5 pounds) because nicotine depresses the mother's appetite at the same time that it reduces her ability to supply oxygen to the fetus (Martin et al., 2005; Ventura et al., 2003). If women stop smoking by the 16th week of pregnancy, however, they are no more likely to have a low-birthweight baby than women who never smoked. Even women who stop smoking only in the third trimester of pregnancy can improve their baby's growth. Nicotine has also been associated with infertility, miscarriages, ectopic pregnancies, infant mortality, preterm delivery, child morbidity, and an increased incidence of asthma and ear infections (Centers for Disease Control & Prevention, 2002; Lieu & Feinstein, 2002). One review of 17 large-scale studies found that maternal smoking during pregnancy was associated with intellectual and behavioral problems during childhood (Eskenazi & Castorina, 1999). As we will discuss when we consider paternal influences shortly, secondhand smoke also appears to be harmful to pregnant women and their fetuses, suggesting that all smokers in the home should try to quit or stop smoking around the mother.

Caffeine.   One legal stimulant that is frequently consumed before pregnancy is caffeine, which is found in coffee, tea, colas, and chocolate. Many women curtail their consumption of caffeine during pregnancy, but it appears that a moderate level (fewer than 5 cups per day) is not teratogenic (Hinds et al., 1996; Santos et al., 1998). An archival study of more than 25,000 children in Denmark found that low to moderate consumption of coffee during pregnancy did not appear to compromise brain development or place children at an elevated risk for seizures (Vestergaard et al., 2005).

Disease

Fetal development can be adversely affected by diseases carried by the mother. Some of these diseases can be treated before birth, but others cause permanent defects and disabilities or even lead to miscarriage or stillbirth.

HIV and Other Infections. Between 6,000 and 7,000 U.S. women infected with HIV give birth each year. Perinatal HIV infection occurs when women infected with HIV pass the virus on to their babies during pregnancy, delivery, or breastfeeding. Drug treatment during pregnancy can dramatically reduce the risk that the virus will be passed on if women with HIV take zidovudine (ZDV, also known as AZT) during the second and third trimesters of pregnancy and during labor and delivery. Guidelines from the U.S. Public Health Service also recommend giving ZDV to newborns for the first 6 weeks of life, even if the newborn has not yet been diagnosed with HIV (medication is stopped when tests show that the baby does not have HIV (Centers for Disease Control & Prevention, 2000d, 2002). Worldwide, however, many HIV-infected women who give birth do not receive these drugs. As a result, perinatal HIV and pediatric AIDS continue to be a significant threat in many developing countries (Lindegren et al., 1999; March of Dimes, 2002).

Whether ZDV is available or not, HIV-infected women can reduce the risk for their babies by having a cesarean delivery before labor begins and their membranes have ruptured. The American College of Obstetricians and Gynecologists (1999) recommends that women with HIV be offered this delivery option, unless there are very low or undetectable amounts of the virus in their blood.

Cytomegalovirus infection (CMV), a member of the herpes virus family, is the most common congenital infection in the United States, affecting approximately 40,000 babies each year. CMV infection is so common that as many as half of all adults are thought to have been infected by age 30. Most infected babies are not harmed by the virus, but about 8,000 babies each year develop permanent disabilities from CMV. CMV is spread from person-to-person contact with infected body fluids, such as saliva, urine, blood and mucus. It may also be transmitted sexually or from infected blood products. The most serious neurological effects and mental retardation are seen among babies whose mothers become infected in the first 20 weeks. Pregnant women with CMV can have their fetuses tested for the virus with amniocentesis and ultrasound, but routine testing is not recommended for women who developed CMV before becoming pregnant.

The diseases we have considered so far, especially HIV, can be prevented if women avoid sexual intercourse with infected partners. Another infection, toxoplasmosis, is caused by a parasite that can be avoided by eating only cooked meat, peeling or washing all raw fruits and vegetables before eating, and avoiding contact with cat or rabbit feces that may contain the parasite. Pregnant women who own cats or rabbits should have someone else empty and clean the litter boxes. They should also avoid uncovered children's sandboxes, which may be used by cats as litter boxes, and they should wear gloves when gardening to avoid contact with soil that may contain the parasite. If a woman develops toxoplasmosis during pregnancy, prenatal tests can determine whether the fetus is infected as well. Fetuses that are infected can be treated by giving medication to the mother. The most serious effects include miscarriage or stillbirth, severely impaired eyesight, cerebral palsy, and seizures. As with CMV, these effects tend to be observed when the mother becomes infected early in the pregnancy (American College of Obstetricians and Gynecologists, 2000).

Women who contract rubella (German measles) during pregnancy, especially during the first trimester, have an increased risk of giving birth to babies with congenital rubella syndrome—a collection of birth defects that includes eye defects, hearing loss, heart defects, mental retardation, and sometimes movement disorders. Congenital rubella syndrome is rarely seen when infection occurs after 20 weeks of pregnancy because the development of nearly all vulnerable organs is complete by that time (Shonkoff & Phillips, 2000). Some infected babies have short-term health problems, while others may not develop noticeable problems with vision, hearing, learning, and behavior until childhood. More than 30,000 babies were born with birth defects in an outbreak of the disease in 1963 to 1965 that also resulted in thousands of miscarriages and stillbirths (Gilbert, 2000). Major outbreaks of rubella no longer occur in the United States, thanks to routine vaccination in childhood (Advisory Committee on Immunization Practices, 2001).

Preexisting Chronic Diseases. As we noted earlier, it is generally recommended that women with preexisting chronic diseases continue treating and controlling their symptoms after they become pregnant. The chance of having a chronic disease or developing a medical condition during pregnancy increases as a woman's age goes up (Centers for Disease Control & Prevention, 2005; Martin et al., 2005). With proper medical care, however, including early prenatal care, most women with chronic diseases can expect to have healthy babies.

About 1 percent of women of childbearing age have diabetes before pregnancy, and another 3 to 5 percent develop gestational diabetes (diabetes that develops during pregnancy). If left untreated, diabetes can damage organs, including blood vessels, nerves, eyes, and kidneys. Daily insulin injections can prevent these complications. Diet and exercise can also help control blood sugar levels (Brankston et al., 2004). Women with poorly controlled diabetes prior to pregnancy are more likely than nondiabetic women to have a baby with neural tube defects or heart defects. They are also at greater risk of miscarriage and stillbirth (Wren, Birrell, & Hawthorne, 2003). Gestational diabetes tends to develop relatively late in pregnancy, and women with this form of the disease usually do not have an increased risk of giving birth to a baby with birth defects. Most women are routinely screened for gestational diabetes between the 24th and 28th week of pregnancy.

Because extra sugar in the mother's blood crosses the placenta and goes to the fetus, women with poorly controlled diabetes of either type tend to give birth to babies who are very large, perhaps 10 pounds or more, and may require a cesarean delivery. The most serious birth defects related to diabetes occur in the early weeks of pregnancy, so it is essential that women with preexisting diabetes consult their doctor before pregnancy. Some oral diabetes medications have been associated with birth defects, and these medications need to be replaced by insulin before and during pregnancy. Close monitoring is also important because physiological changes in the woman's body during pregnancy may change the dose of insulin that is needed. Women with gestational diabetes usually do not need to take insulin; their symptoms can often be treated with diet and exercise (Kjos, 1999).

Some women have chronic hypertension (high blood pressure) before they become pregnant and many develop hypertension during pregnancy (pregnancy-induced hypertension).

Although hypertension usually causes no obvious symptoms in the mother, it can slow fetal growth by constricting the blood vessels that supply oxygen and nutrients. Hypertension is also a risk factor for conditions that place the mother and fetus at risk, including placental abruption (separation of the placenta from the uterine wall), preeclampsia (high blood pressure accompanied by protein in the urine), and eclampsia (a rare but life-threatening condition that causes convulsions and coma). Most women with chronic hypertension have healthy babies, but it is important to seek medical advice about whether the form and dose of medication that they usually take to control their blood pressure is safe to continue taking during pregnancy.

Rh Disease.   Some diseases, like Rh disease, do not develop until a woman becomes pregnant. Rh disease is defined as an incompatibility between the blood of the mother and her fetus. Without treatment, the incompatibility causes destruction of fetal red blood cells and can lead to stillbirth. In newborns, Rh disease can cause jaundice, anemia, brain damage, heart failure, and death. The mother's health is not affected.

Most people have Rh-positive blood and produce Rh factor, a protein found in their red blood cells. Rh-negative individuals lack the Rh factor but are just as healthy as those who are Rh-positive. A baby conceived by a mother who is Rh-negative and a father who is Rh-positive may inherit the father's Rh-positive blood type. As we noted earlier, the fetus and mother have separate circulatory systems. During labor and delivery, and sometimes during pregnancy, however, some of the baby's Rh-positive blood cells may enter the mother's bloodstream, triggering an immune system response and production of antibodies. In a first pregnancy, Rh-positive babies are at little risk, but subsequent Rh-positive fetuses are endangered by the mother's Rh antibodies, which can cross the placenta and destroy fetal blood cells. (Babies conceived by two Rh-negative parents are not at risk for Rh disease.) A simple maternal blood test prior to pregnancy can reveal whether a woman is Rh-negative and whether she has been sensitized to Rh factor in a previous pregnancy. All babies born to Rh-negative women are tested for their Rh type at birth or, in some cases, with amniocentesis, but a maternal blood test is being developed to determine fetal Rh status (Lo et al., 1998).

Before 1968, approximately 20,000 babies in the U.S. were born with Rh disease each year. With the development of a purified blood product called Rh immune globulin (RhIg), that number has fallen to approximately 4,000 babies each year. When Rh-negative mothers receive an injection of RhIg within 72 hours of delivery, the production of antibodies can be prevented in nearly all cases. Because some women develop antibodies during pregnancy, RhIg injections are also given at about 28 weeks of pregnancy. RhIg prevents the production of Rh factor antibodies by destroying any Rh-positive fetal cells in the mother's bloodstream. Treatment with RhIg must be repeated with each pregnancy and in any situations in which fetal blood cells might mix with the mother's blood, including miscarriage, ectopic pregnancy, and amniocentesis. Fetuses that are known to have Rh disease can be treated with blood transfusions as early as the 18th week of pregnancy (Grab et al., 1999). These treatments are usually successful, and most treated babies with severe Rh disease survive.

Stress

Prenatal exposure to stress has been linked to complications during pregnancy as well as behavioral abnormalities after birth (DiPietro, 2004; Kofman, 2002; Kurki et al., 2000;

Mulder et al., 2002). When animals and humans perceive threats or other aversive environmental events, there are rapid changes in heart rate and blood pressure. Stress also activates the hypothalamic-pituitary-adrenal (HPA) axis, producing higher levels of adrenalin and stress hormones, such as cortisol. The placenta buffers the developing fetus to a degree, but increased levels of these hormones in the mother's body are known to increase fetal exposure.

The attack on the World Trade Center on September 11, 2001, induced high levels of stress in residents of New York City, including those who were in utero at the time. To examine the effects of this stressful prenatal event on fetal growth and subsequent health and development, researchers compared birth outcomes for infants born to 300 women who were pregnant on September 11. They found that infants whose mothers were in the first trimester of pregnancy at the time of the World Trade Center event and lived within a 2-mile radius of the World Trade Center had significantly briefer gestations, lower birth weights, and shorter birth lengths than infants whose mothers were in the second or third trimester when the attack occurred (Lederman et al., 2004). Although these findings indicate that the effects were greatest during the earliest period of prenatal development, it is not clear that they were the result of stress alone. It is possible, for example, that they were produced by exposure to pollution in the air during the days and weeks following the event. As we will discuss shortly, there is substantial evidence that prenatal exposure to environmental pollutants negatively affects fetal development and growth (Brent & Weitzman, 2004; Perera et al., 2002).

Studies with animals show that fetuses that are exposed to high levels of stress hormones tend to develop fewer receptors in the brain for those hormones. This deficit may explain later behavioral and emotional difficulties that are observed after birth, including problems coping with and recovering from stress (Huizink, Mulder, & Buitelaar, 2004; Huizink et al., 2002; Shonkoff & Phillips, 2000). One review of more than 250 animal and human studies of the effects of maternal stress found that the most common consequences in offspring were impairments in learning, motor development, and emotional reactivity (Huizink et al., 2004).

It is difficult to know whether the findings from studies of animals, such as rats and monkeys, can be directly generalized to humans (Brent, 2004). Whereas maternal stress in humans is typically investigated by assessing levels of self-reported psychological stress and anxiety encountered on a daily basis, in studies of animals, stress is usually induced by exposing them to environmental events, such as prolonged or repeated periods of loud noise. Given significant differences in the types of stressors that are used in human versus animal studies, some researchers assert that caution must be used in drawing inferences about the effects of prenatal stress in humans.

Research focusing solely on humans is also challenging to interpret, in part because of the tendency to use maternal reports rather than independent measures both to measure anxiety during pregnancy and to rate infants' behavior after birth (DiPietro, 2004). One recent study with humans addressed this issue by creating stressful experiences in the laboratory. The researchers asked pregnant women to complete a challenging cognitive task and also showed them graphic scenes from a video about labor and delivery (DiPietro, Hilton, Hawkins, Costigan, & Pressman et al., 2002). Surprisingly, women who experienced higher levels of stress during these tasks had infants who had better scores on assessments of their development. These results suggest that relatively mild prenatal stress is not necessarily harmful and may even be beneficial for later development—a finding that has also been observed in animal studies involving mild stress (DiPietro, 2004; Fujioka et al., 2001). More studies are needed, but it appears that it may be as unnecessary as it is impossible for pregnant women to eliminate stress completely.

Environmental Hazards

While some potential hazards come from within, others exist in the external world. Pregnant women should avoid exposure to environmental hazards such as radiation and paint fumes, since these agents are known to be teratogenic. Dental X rays should be skipped during pregnancy, and another adult should complete any home improvement projects, including painting the baby's room. If there are hazards in the mother's workplace, such as paint fumes, she should try to find a different, less risky assignment or another job entirely, if possible.

A noisy work environment, in which the mother is exposed for hours at a time to loud machinery, for example, is also regarded as a potential hazard for the fetus. As we have already discussed, the sensory organs that permit hearing develop by the 24th week of gestation, and fetuses respond to sounds in the environment outside of the womb. Studies of women who reported that they were exposed consistently to workplace noise during pregnancy have found that their offspring may be at increased risk for high-frequency hearing loss. In addition, although the evidence is mixed, prenatal noise exposure may be associated with preterm birth and intrauterine growth retardation. This is an area in which well-controlled, randomized human experiments are not possible, but studies with animals suggest that the risks of prenatal noise exposure should not be overlooked (American Academy of Pediatrics Committee on Environmental Health, 1997; Brent & Weitzman, 2004).

Environmental hazards in the places where food is raised can also have teratogenic effects. Fish is a good source of low-fat protein, but during pregnancy it is a good idea to limit the type of fish that is consumed. Babies who are exposed prenatally to chemical pollutants such as polychlorinated biphenyls (PCBs) or large amounts of mercury may suffer brain damage resulting in developmental delays or even cerebral palsy, seizures, and mental retardation (Grandjean et al. 1997; Hubbs-Tait et al., 2005; Jacobson & Jacobson, 1996). Generally, it is thought that fish from grocery stores and in restaurants are safe for pregnant women to eat, and ocean fish are less likely to be contaminated than river and lake dwellers. Some fish are known to pose a greater risk than others, however, and, to be safe, experts recommend that pregnant women avoid eating bluefish, striped bass, and freshwater fish from contaminated sources. Consumption of swordfish, shark, tuna, and halibut should also be limited during pregnancy, since these fish tend to contain the highest concentrations of mercury (Oken et al., 2005).

Pesticide regulations vary from one country to another, so it is a good idea to choose fruits and vegetables carefully during pregnancy. In the United States, two pesticides that were previously approved for household use—chlorpyrifos and diazinon—were banned by the federal government in 2000 after animal studies showed that exposure during pregnancy impaired growth and brain development in offspring. Additional supporting evidence of the potential harm caused by these pesticides came from The Mothers & Children Study in New York City, which was initiated in 1998 to study health effects of exposure to air pollutants, tobacco smoke, pesticides, and allergens. Analysis of data associated with approximately 400 births suggested that higher levels of prenatal exposure to chlorpyrifos were associated with smaller head circumferences. Given that small head circumference tends to predict delays and other problems with cognitive development, this finding suggests that the pesticide probably affects brain development in humans as well as in other animals (Berkowitz et al., 2004). Fortunately, the beneficial effects of the ban on these pesticides may already be evident. A study of approximately 300 infants born in New York City showed that whereas infants born before the ban had higher levels of exposure and weighed an average of half a pound less than infants with no detectable pesticide levels, exposure levels decreased after the ban and were no longer associated with growth problems (Whyatt et al., 2004). Continuing and expanded monitoring of children's exposure to environmental contaminants may lead to other bans and the prevention of many childhood health and developmental problems that begin before birth (Goldman et al., 2004; Hubbs-Tait et al., 2005).

In many regions of the world, pregnant women may not be aware of or able to avoid toxic chemicals and pollutants that permeate the food, water, and air around them. In regions of the former Soviet Union, such as Kazakhstan, where industrial production was unregulated for years, high concentrations of lead, mercury, and zinc in drinking water, vegetables, and air appear to be responsible for a twofold increase in the incidence of birth defects since 1980 (Edwards, 1999; Gilbert, 2000). Radioactive fallout from the Chernobyl nuclear power plant disaster of 1982 has also been implicated in an increase in the rate of anemia and birth defects in regions of the former Soviet Union where exposure was the highest (Petrova et al., 1997). Researchers are concerned about environmental pollution in Eastern Europe and in China as its industrial economy surges forward, but even in cities in the United States, there is evidence that fetal development and growth are adversely affected by exposure to environmental contaminants (Adibi et al., 2003; Jedrychowski et al., 2004; Perera, et al., 2004b).

Paternal Influences

Pregnant women are not the only ones who need to be concerned about the teratogenic effects of environmental hazards, including those that exist in the workplace. There is increasing evidence that a number of agents, such as lead and radiation, can affect men's reproductive health by lowering the number of sperm or producing abnormally shaped sperm that have trouble swimming or lack the ability to fertilize the egg (Bellinger, 2005; Parker et al., 1999). Researchers are beginning to understand the risks posed by these chemicals and the potentially harmful effects on the health of family members who are exposed to chemicals brought home on the worker's skin, hair, clothes, shoes, tool box, or car (Klemmt & Scialli, 2005). Lead that is brought home in this way, for example, can cause severe lead poisoning among family members and neurobehavioral and growth effects in fetuses (National Institute on Occupational Safety and Health, 2002).

Men who use cocaine are also putting their offspring at higher risk for birth defects, since the drug appears to interfere with the production of normal sperm (George et al., 1997; Li et al., 1997; Yazigi, Odem, & Polakoski, 1991). Paternal use of certain medications, such as amphetamines and diet pills, has been linked to mutations that increase the risk of leukemia in children (Shu et al., 2004). Infants born to fathers who use marijuana during conception, pregnancy, and after birth have also been found to have a higher risk of dying before the age of 1 year (Klonoff-Cohen & Lam-Kruglick, 2001).

Men who smoke cigarettes in the home create a hazardous environment for their wives and children, including those not yet born. Babies whose fathers smoke tend to be lower birthweight than those without prenatal exposure to secondhand smoke, and they have a higher rate of childhood cancer (Ji et al., 1997). Effects of prenatal exposure to secondhand smoke on birthweight and head circumference are amplified for children with prenatal exposure to other environmental pollutants, such as those often found in cities (Perera et al., 2004a).

These findings indicate that both expectant parents can be involved in giving their baby a healthy start in life. As we will see in Chapter 4, fathers as well as mothers have a role to play at their child's birth and during the newborn period.

WRAPPING IT UP: Summary and Conclusion

As a result of recent scientific breakthroughs, we know more than ever before about the genetic basis for many hereditary conditions, including those that may compromise prenatal development and the chance for a healthy birth and childhood. Most diseases and complex characteristics are influenced by multiple genes interacting with each other and with environmental influences that are not yet completely understood.

The genetic basis of conception and prenatal development are becoming more clearly understood, and researchers using animal models have discovered genes that determine the development of specialized body structures and parts of the brain. Some of these discoveries may help couples experiencing infertility by offering new options to help them conceive a child. Assisted reproductive technologies tend to be associated with a higher rate of multiple births and the complications those births entail.

The basic stages of prenatal development are the same, regardless of how conception is achieved. The germinal stage (0 to 2 weeks postconception), embryonic stage (2 to 8 weeks postconception), and fetal stage (8 weeks to birth, or approximately 38 weeks) differ in terms of their duration as well as the key events taking place. With intensive care, a fetus born at 24 weeks may survive. Brain development begins during the embryonic stage, but the most rapid prenatal period of brain development is during the last 2 months. Unlike other major organs, the brain is not completely developed at birth.

Birth defects are less common today than in the past but they continue to be the leading cause of infant death. Neural tube defects in the United States have been reduced through folic acid fortification of cereal grain products. Congenital heart defects range in severity but even children with the most serious defects are more likely to survive as a result of new diagnostic and treatment options.

A number of options exist for prenatal diagnosis and treatment. Low-risk ultrasound images and maternal blood screening are used routinely on most pregnant women. Chorionic villus screening and amniocentesis are used only in specific circumstances to diagnose or rule out defects and chromosomal abnormalities. Couples with a known high risk of having a child with a serious genetic disorder may consider using preimplantation genetic diagnosis (PGD).

Fetal therapy options are expanding, and many fetal problems already are treated or prevented by giving drugs to the mother or by choosing a cesarean delivery. Fetal surgery has been perfected for some defects but is still considered experimental for most other conditions.

With early prenatal care, women are more likely to consume a healthy, nutritious diet during pregnancy. Alcohol and drugs damage the developing child by crossing the cell membranes of the placenta. Prescription medications, like illicit drugs, may have permanent teratogenic effects on the fetus, so alterations in the specific amount or type of medication may be necessary.

Fetal development can be adversely affected by preexisting chronic conditions and by infectious diseases carried by the mother. Environmental hazards may exist in the mother's or the father's workplace and are sometimes found in the foods the mother eats. Parents, as well as prospective parents, who are aware of these potential risks can take steps to avoid them or minimize their impact. As a result, most pregnancies in the United States and other developed countries end with the birth of a healthy, full-term baby—the focus of our next chapter.

THINK ABOUT IT: Questions for Reading and Discussion

1. How would you respond to the advertisement at the beginning of the chapter for an egg donor? Based on the information in this chapter, would you encourage or discourage the couple?

2. Would you want to know if you, your parents, or your future spouse carried genetic mutations for disease? Why or why not? If so, when would you want to have this information and how would you use it?

3. Discuss the assisted reproductive technology (ART) options available to couples facing infertility. If friends of yours were considering ART or other methods of becoming parents, what advice and information would you give them?

4. Many prohibitions placed on pregnant women in the past are now known to be unnecessary. Besides those discussed in the chapter, what other "old wives tales" have you heard about things women should avoid during pregnancy? Did you find any support in this chapter for those ideas?

5. Compare the three stages of the prenatal period in terms of length, major events, and vulnerability to teratogens.

6. If you were asked to make a Top Ten list of steps that expectant parents could (or should) take to help their baby have a healthy start in life, what would be on that list and why?

7. Compare the relative importance of nutrition, alcohol and drugs, disease, and environmental hazards on prenatal development. If you could focus on only one of these influences, which would it be and why?

8. What assessment, diagnostic, and treatment options are available for expectant parents today? Which options would you want to take advantage of if you and your spouse were expecting a child? If there are some options that you would avoid, what are they and why would you avoid them?

KEY WORDS

Amniocentesis (90)	A procedure for prenatal diagnosis in which a small sample of fluid is taken from the amniotic sac and used to detect any genetic or chromosomal abnormalities
Assisted reproductive technology (ART) (74)	Fertility treatments in which both egg and sperm are handled
Autosomes (67)	Any of the chromosomes other than the sex-determining chromosomes
Blastocyst (77)	The hollow, spherical structure comprised of approximately 100 identical cells formed through mitosis during the first week after conception
Cephalocaudal principle (79)	The pattern of growth in which development begins in the anterior (head) and later occurs in the posterior (tail) of the organism
Chorionic villus sampling (CVS) (90)	A procedure for prenatal diagnosis in which cells are collected from the chorion, the fetal membrane that gives rise to the placenta
Chromosomes (67)	Physical structures consisting of DNA and supporting proteins
Deoxyribonucleic acid (DNA) (67)	Strands of molecules that carry the genetic code of a cell
Dizygotic twins (74)	Siblings resulting from two different eggs, also known as fraternal (DZ) twins
Down syndrome (70)	A congenital syndrome, also referred to as trisomy 21, in which there is an extra chromosome 21; individuals with Down syndrome have distinctive facial features and other physical characteristics and have mild to severe mental retardation
Ectoderm (81)	The upper layer of the inner cell mass, which gives rise to the brain and spinal cord, sensory organs, and skin, nails, hair, and teeth
Embryonic stage (79)	The second prenatal stage, lasting from 2 weeks to 8 weeks
Endoderm (81)	The lower layer of the inner cell mass, from which the respiratory and digestive systems develop
Fetal alcohol syndrome (FAS) (95)	A constellation of physical, behavioral, and cognitive abnormalities caused by prenatal exposure to alcohol
Fetal stage (82)	The third prenatal stage, lasting from 8 weeks until birth
Genes (67)	Units of hereditary information; each gene is a segment of DNA in a specific location on a chromosome
Germinal stage (77)	The first prenatal stage, beginning at conception and ending at approximately 2 weeks
Maternal serum alpha fetoprotein (MSAFP) test (89)	A screening test in which the level of alpha fetoprotein in the mother's bloodstream is measured; also known as the triple screen because it measures the amount of estriol and HCG present in the mother's blood
Meiosis (73)	The process through which sex cells divide at conception
Mesoderm (81)	The middle layer of the inner cell mass, from which the circulatory and excretory systems, muscles, and skeleton develop
Mitosis (67)	The life-long process of cell division in which a cell divides into two identical cells

Monozygotic twins (74)	Siblings resulting from a single egg, also known as identical (MZ) twins
Multifactorial transmission (71)	The interaction of genes and the environment that produces most complex human characteristics
Neural tube defects (85)	Birth defects that involve abnormal development of the neural tube during the first few weeks of the prenatal period
Neurons (83)	Nerve cells in the brain, comprised of a cell body, axons, and dendrites
Ovum (72)	Female sex cell
Placenta (79)	A network of blood vessels, formed from cells in the trophoblast and from cells in the uterine lining, the function of which is to convey oxygen and nutrients to the embryo and carry away waste products
Preimplantation genetic diagnosis (PGD) (88)	A procedure in which a biopsy is performed on blastocysts resulting from in vitro fertilization, with the purpose of selecting blastocysts that are not carriers of genetic mutations for disease for transfer to the woman's uterus
Proximodistal principle (79)	The pattern of growth in which development begins in the center of the body and moves toward the extremities of the organism
Sex-linked inheritance (69)	Transmission of characteristics via the mother's X chromosome; sons but not daughters inherit the trait
Sex chromosomes (67)	The pair of sex-determining chromosomes that each human possesses: XX in females and XY in males
Sperm (72)	Male sex cell
Teratogens (77)	Substances, such as alcohol, drugs, nicotine, and radiation, that are known to cause harm to the developing fetus
Ultrasound (89)	A prenatal diagnostic tool, also referred to as ultrasonography, that uses sound waves to create moving images of the fetus and detect any structural abnormalities
Umbilical cord (81)	The structure through which the embryo is connected to the placenta
Zygote (73)	The cell that results when an ovum is fertilized by a sperm cell

Birth and the Newborn

The children's book *On the Day You Were Born* describes the late 1980s world into which a baby named Calla is born (Frasier, 1991). Through colorful paper collages and poetic prose, the book illustrates the joyful anticipation with which Calla's family, along with animals, trees, the oceans, the sun, the moon, and the Earth itself, awaits her arrival. Reading this book with their parents, young children often ask about the day *they* were born and the family and community into which they were welcomed. The story that they hear is a special one because it is their story, unlike anyone else's. Even twins and other multiples have their own unique birth experiences and are usually aware of distinctive details such as which sibling was born first, even if it was by just a few minutes.

In many families, children's birth stories are accompanied by pictures showing the moments after, and sometimes during, their birth. For children born at home—a rare event in the United States but a relatively common occurrence in other parts of the world—the pictures are likely to show surroundings that are familiar and people they recognize. For all children, the pictures are also likely to reflect how their parents viewed their birth—as a public act; an event for which siblings, other relatives, and even close friends should be present; or as a more private experience, something to be shared with others only after the baby was born.

Underlying this uniqueness, all birth stories share a common plot. That is, childbirth, like prenatal development, is a physiological process with predictable, universal stages. We begin this chapter, then, by considering the fundamental aspects of the story of human birth that we all share. In doing so, we will examine the typical birth experience for healthy, full-term infants and explore the normal variability that exists in the birth process. We will also consider some of the complications associated with childbirth and the sorts of measures that are used to gauge newborn infants' health. In addition, because childbirth is an event that occurs within a particular context, we will examine childbirth practices from a number of historical and cultural perspectives and consider the options that are available to expectant mothers and fathers today.

The Birth Process: Stages of Childbirth

Before the events that trigger the birth process were understood, they inspired a great variety of practices and folk theories concerning pregnancy, labor, and delivery. Women in seventeenth- and eighteenth-century Europe, for example, appealed to saints to initiate and ensure a safe delivery. They also relied upon childbirth sachets, which they tied onto or placed upon their bellies in the days or hours before labor began. These sachets, filled with medallions, rosary beads, and tiny parchments covered with religious writings and magic formulas, were often handed down from one generation to the next. To coax a reluctant baby from the womb, birth assistants often untied all knots in the home. They also tried to stimulate labor by shaking or frightening the mother, or putting pepper in her nostrils to cause sneezing and contractions (Fontanel & d'Harcourt, 1997).

Traditional views in Bali, by contrast, held that the onset of labor is the result of actions taken by four "sibling spirits" of the fetus. These "siblings," believed to be present in the blood, the amniotic fluid, the placenta and umbilical cord, and the waxy vernix caseosa covering the infant at birth, were said to open the cervix and even push the infant from behind (DeLoache & Gottlieb, 2000). In some respects, this view was fairly accurate. As we discuss next, one of the "sibling spirits" (the placenta) does in fact play a significant role in initiating labor.

The First Stage: Contractions, Dilatation, and Effacement

Approximately 266 days after conception, hormones produced by the placenta, including corticotropin releasing hormone (CRH), trigger the first stage of labor (Grammatopoulos & Hillhouse, 1999). The first stage consists of regular, progressive uterine contractions and **dilatation**, or widening, of the cervix from its normal, closed position to a full 10 centimeters. Not all women experience labor in the same way. For some women, dilatation occurs over a period of 1 or 2 days, but for others it is accomplished within 1 or 2 hours.

One common sign that labor is imminent is the loss of the mucous plug that sealed the cervix during pregnancy. The "bloody show" that results when the mucous plug is lost is an imprecise indicator, however, and the first contractions could still be days or weeks away. In about 2 to 3 percent of pregnancies, the mother's "water" breaks before contractions begin, a phenomenon referred to as **premature rupture of the membranes, or PROM** (Martin et al., 2005). When this happens, the membranes surrounding the amniotic sac break open, and amniotic fluid is released, sometimes in a dramatic gush and other times as a slow, steady leak (the fluid continues to be replenished even after the membranes rupture). In most cases, contractions begin within 12 to 24 hours. Most women experiencing PROM give birth within 72 hours. If labor does not progress after the membranes rupture, both mother and baby may be vulnerable to infection caused by bacteria that are normally present in the vagina. Depending on the perceived risk, and the

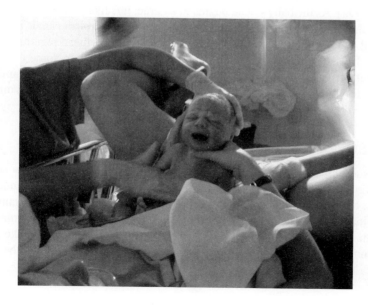

In a normal vertex delivery, the baby's head emerges first.

birth setting, steps may be taken to hasten delivery in order to prevent infection. As we will discuss shortly, some research suggests that stimulating or inducing labor in this situation is not necessary and may even lead to complications and a more difficult delivery (Feinbloom, 1993).

The first stage of labor consists of a latent phase and an active phase. In first labors, the **latent phase** usually lasts less than 20 hours, fewer hours in subsequent pregnancies. Uterine contractions during the latent phase often begin 5 to 30 minutes apart and last between 15 and 40 seconds. These contractions typically are not painful for the mother, and she is able to rest between them. In the **active phase**, contractions come closer together, perhaps 2 to 5 minutes apart, and they last approximately 45 to 60 seconds. In addition to the more intense and frequent contractions, the rapid opening of the cervix in the active phase makes it the most difficult and painful part of labor (Feinbloom, 1993).

As the cervix widens, it also begins to thin out—a process known as **effacement**— preparing for the next stage of labor, in which the baby begins to enter the birth canal. As the baby descends, the mother often feels increased pressure and the urge to push. If her cervix is adequately dilated, she will be allowed to follow these urges, if she wishes. Although it is commonly believed that the mother's pushing is essential to delivery, the real work is performed by uterine contractions and, depending on the mother's position, the force of gravity (Feinbloom, 1993).

The Second Stage: Delivery of the Infant

The second stage of labor typically lasts less than 2 hours in a first birth and is even briefer in subsequent births. During this stage, the baby is gradually pushed out, usually in the head-first **vertex position**. The shape and contours of the birth canal are not uniform along its length, and some babies may need to be turned or guided during labor (Feinbloom, 1993). As the baby's head begins to emerge, it is likely to show signs of compression and molding as a result of being squeezed through the birth canal. This elongation is normal and occurs because the skull bones have not yet fused together; it is only temporary and usually diminishes within a few days after birth. In some cultures, the birth attendant actively shapes and smooths the newborn's head with her hands rather than waiting for this to occur on its own (DeLoache & Gottlieb, 2000; Fontanel & d'Harcourt, 1997).

The Third Stage: Placental Expulsion

In the third stage of childbirth, uterine contractions expel the placenta, now separated from the uterine wall. The delivery of the placenta usually takes only a few minutes. During this time, the attendant clamps and cuts the baby's umbilical cord and examines the mother's vagina for any tears or bleeding. Although most attention from this point on will be given to the baby and mother, the placenta itself is inspected in order to make sure that it has been completely expelled; any tissue that remained in the uterus could be a source of bleeding.

Complications of Childbirth

Each year, approximately 4 million babies are born in the United States (Hamilton et al., 2005; Martin et al., 2002, 2005). Unlike the past, when maternal and neonatal mortality rates were high, and many women spent their entire pregnancy preparing to fight for their lives during childbirth, most newborns and their mothers now survive the experience. This does not mean, however, that all births proceed smoothly or as the parents had envisioned the process. Fortunately, with the development of obstetrical medicine, new procedures have been developed to respond to complications of childbirth when they arise, though there is not complete agreement about whether and when to use these procedures.

Failure to Progress

For some women who reach term (37 weeks gestation) and experience premature rupture of the membranes (PROM), labor begins and then fails to progress (Sheiner et al., 2002). When this happens, both expectant parents may feel impatient, disappointed, or discouraged. They may even become concerned that something has gone wrong or that their baby is in jeopardy. Labor contractions sometimes subside in response to pain medication that is administered to the mother, but the reasons labor fails to progress during the first stage are not always known.

According to some childbirth experts, failure to progress is simply a reflection of normal variability, not a sign of pathology. As long as neither the fetus nor the mother is in danger, they argue, the labor should be allowed to follow its own natural time course (Feinbloom, 1993; Kennedy & Shannon, 2004; Rooks, 1997). Many hospitals, however, have a policy of using synthetic hormones to induce labor if spontaneous contractions have not begun within 12 hours. (We will discuss labor induction in more detail in the section on medical interventions.) This practice is followed even though there is equivocal evidence of links between labor induction following PROM and better neonatal and maternal outcomes. Some studies suggest, for example, that labor that is induced is more likely to end in a cesarean (surgical) delivery than is labor that starts on its own (Alexander, McIntire, & Leveno, 2001; Cammu et al., 2002; Rayburn & Zhang, 2002; Rooks, 1997; Sheiner et al., 2002).

Prolonged labor during the second stage is also viewed in different ways by different childbirth experts. In one study of 1,200 vaginal deliveries, comparing women whose second stage of labor had lasted less than 2 hours with women who had labored in the second stage for more than 4 hours, there was no significant difference in the health of their newborns. In the absence of evidence that prolonged second stage labor is disadvantageous for the baby, these researchers recommend that the condition of mother and baby—rather than the amount of time that has passed since full cervical dilatation was achieved—determine whether the pace of the labor should be accelerated (Janni et al., et al., 2002). Additional studies of neonatal outcomes following prolonged labor are needed to provide useful guidelines for determining when intervention should occur and when it is not necessary (Kawasaki et al., 2002).

Breech Presentation

During the last weeks of the prenatal period, most fetuses settle into an inverted position, which allows for a head-first birth. In approximately 3 to 4 percent of singleton pregnancies, however, the fetus assumes a **breech presentation**, with the feet or buttocks emerging first in a vaginal delivery (Martin et al., 2005). A breech presentation can usually be detected in advance of labor through a combination of manual exploration of the mother's belly and ultrasound imaging.

Babies born preterm are more likely to be in a breech position, as are twins and other multiple pregnancies. Vaginal deliveries of breech babies are generally regarded as dangerous because of the risk that the umbilical cord will be compressed, robbing the infant of oxygen during delivery (Uygur et al., 2002). Current guidelines direct obstetricians and midwives to attempt to turn the fetus in utero at about 37 weeks gestation in a procedure known as external cephalic version (American College of Obstetricians & Gynecologists Committee on Obstetric Practice, 2002; Feinbloom, 1993; Rooks, 1997). This procedure is most successful when drugs are administered to relax the mother's uterus (Hofmeyr, 2002). Even when external cephalic version is successful, the pregnancy continues to be high risk, with a greater likelihood of fetal distress, failure to progress in labor, and frequently cesarean delivery (Chan et al., 2002). If the fetus's position cannot be changed, the preferred option is a cesarean delivery (Hutton, Hannah, & Barrett, 2002).

Preterm Birth

As worrisome as labor that does not progress quickly may be, a more serious concern is labor that begins before the end of normal gestation. In the year 2004, 12.5 percent of all babies—the

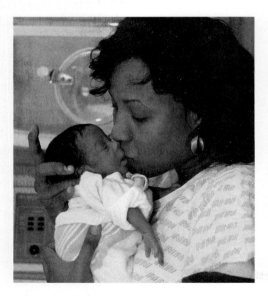

Preterm birth rates have continued to rise in the United States, but survival rates have also increased, thanks to the development of neonatal intensive care units.

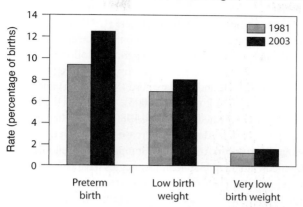

FIGURE 4.1 Rates of preterm birth, low birthweight, and very low birthweight have increased since the early 1980s.

Source: Based on Martin, Hamilton, Sutton, Ventura, Menacker, & Munson, 2005.

highest number ever reported in the United States—were born **preterm** (before 37 weeks gestation). A smaller proprotion, approximately 4 percent, were born **very preterm** (before 32 weeks gestation) (Hamilton et al., 2005). As shown in Figure 4.1, the proportion of infants born preterm or very preterm has increased in recent years (Hamilton et al., 2005). Progress at reducing the incidence of preterm birth has been hampered by lack of full understanding of the causes (Behrman & Butler 2006; Holzman et al., 2001; Howse, 2001; Johnston et al., 2001).

Preterm birth is the leading cause of neonatal mortality in the United States and in other industrialized countries (Kramer et al., 2001). There is widespread agreement, therefore, that preterm labor should be stopped, if possible, in order to give the fetus the greatest chance of continuing to develop and be supported in utero (Howse, 2001). Preterm labor may be quieted by giving the mother steroids or other drugs that temporarily end uterine muscle contractions (Feinbloom, 1993). Efforts to identify which women will have a preterm delivery have not been successful to date. In one study of portable uterine monitors, women who gave birth preterm had a slightly greater frequency of early contractions than women who gave birth after the 35th week, but researchers were unable to use this information to make accurate predictions about preterm delivery (Iams et al., 2002).

The likelihood of preterm birth increases for twins and other multiple pregnancies. Preterm birth is associated with PROM and with medical induction of labor (Martin et al., 2002, 2005). Preterm labor and birth may also occur when there are maternal infections or abnormalities of the placenta or uterus (Feinbloom, 1993; Goldenberg & Jobe, 2001; Romeroet al., 2001). Many people believe that sexual activity late in pregnancy may cause preterm delivery, because the contraction-inducing hormone oxytocin is released during orgasm. Researchers studying patients in prenatal clinics, however, found that frequency of intercourse or orgasm during late pregnancy was not associated with an increased risk of preterm delivery (Sayle et al. 2001).

There is a greater incidence of preterm birth among mothers living in poverty, and some researchers are exploring whether chronic and acute exposure to psychological stress may lead to increased secretion of corticotropin-releasing hormone (CRH) by the placenta (Kramer et al., 2001). The rate of preterm birth varies as a function of race/ethnicity, with the highest rate is observed among African American infants (17.9 percent), followed by American Indian (13.7 percent), Hispanic/Latino (12.0 percent) and non-Hispanic white (11.5 percent) infants. The lowest rates of preterm birth are found for Japanese (8.3 percent) and Chinese (7.3 percent) babies (Martin et al., 2002; Hamilton et al., 2005). Some racial/ethnic differences in preterm birthrates for singletons diminished during the 1980s and 1990s, primarily because of an increase among non-Hispanic whites (due to an increase in the birth rate of twins and other multiples) and a decrease among African Americans (Branum & Schoendorf, 2002). Across all groups, however, existing medical and public health strategies have been relatively ineffectual in reducing preterm birth (Goldenberg & Jobe, 2001; Johnston et al., 2001).

Unlike the prevention rate, the *survival* rate for preterm infants has improved dramatically since the 1970s (from 10 percent to 45 percent for babies weighing 2 lb. or less), thanks to the development of **neonatal intensive care units (NICUs)** (see Table 4.1). New methods that were introduced, especially in the 1970s and 1980s, include improved delivery room care and resuscitation, assisted ventilation, monitoring of blood oxygenation and heart rate, intravenous nutrition, and drugs to improve the functioning of preterm infants' immature lungs (Hack, Klein, & Taylor, 1995; Horbar & Lucey, 1995). In 1989, the Centers for Disease Control and Prevention began collecting data on a subset of neonatal intensive care practices. These data show that the rate for assisted ventilation, a treatment for respiratory distress syndrome in preterm infants, increased from approximately 11 out of every 1,000 births in 1989 to 22 per 1,000 births in the year 2000 (Martin et al., 2002).

Despite this progress and an improved chance of survival, extremely preterm infants are still at greater risk of developing life-threatening infections, respiratory distress syndrome, and brain hemorrhages than are full-term infants (Feinbloom, 1993; Mouradian, Als, & Coster, 2000). Survival rates increase with infant age. One Canadian study found that only 56 percent of babies born at 24 weeks survived until discharge from an NICU, as compared with nearly 70 percent of babies born at 25 weeks (Effer et al., 2002). Infants born very preterm (before 32 weeks) are more likely to die during the first year of life than are infants born either moderately preterm (32 to 36 weeks) or at term (37 to 41 weeks). Treatment with glucocorticoids prior to preterm delivery diminishes some of these risks by causing fetal tissues to mature, but treatment must be brief enough to avoid potentially undesirable side effects, including impairment of fetal growth (Goldenberg & Jobe, 2001).

Every effort is made to extend pregnancy as close as possible to full term because development within the uterine environment has measurable advantages. Preterm infants, even when they are healthy, show less mature sucking and feeding behaviors at 40 weeks than full-term (same chronological age) infants at birth (Medoff-Cooper, McGrath, & Shults, 2002; Mouradian et al., 2000). Smaller and less mature infants have the most profound complications (Feinbloom, 1993), but research examining children up to 2 years of age indicates that even infants who are born between 1 and 4 weeks preterm are at increased risk of a delay in some developmental milestones, such as crawling and combining words (Hediger et al., 2002).

TABLE 4.1   Technologies and Procedures in the Neonatal Intensive Care Unit[a]

Vital Signs Are Monitored
    Blood pressure
    Heart rate
    Lung function
    Respiration
    Temperature
The Environment Is Optimized
    Ambient noise and light are reduced
    Continuous positive airway pressure keeps lungs functioning
    Feeding and nutrition are provided through intubation or an IV line
    Mechanical ventilation is provided via an endotracheal tube and respirator
    Pain relief is administered through an IV line
    Parents are encouraged to be involved in care and to provide skin-to-skin contact
    Phototherapy is used to treat jaundice
    Supplemental oxygenation is administered through an oxygen hood or nasal tube
    Temperature is controlled through an overhead warmer or in an isolette chamber
Tests Are Performed
    Blood sample analysis
    CT scanning
    Electrocardiogram (EKG)
    Electroencephalogram (EEG)
    Eye and retinal exam
    Genetic analysis
    Hearing screening
    MRI imaging
    Spinal fluid analysis
    Ultrasound
    X rays

Note: (a) Not all infants will experience all of these technologies and procedures.

Source: Some information is adapted from Horbar and Lucey, 1995, p. 141.

Preterm infants who survive have a higher rate of neurological impairments, including cerebral palsy, and the effects of these impairments may be long lasting (Hack, et al., 1995). One review of research showed that children born preterm had lower cognitive test scores and a higher incidence of attention-deficit hyperactivity disorder (ADHD) and other problem behaviors at age 5 compared to full-term children (Bhutta et al., 2002).

The most serious developmental outcomes and neurological impairments are seen among very low birth weight infants (those weighing less than 3 1/4 lb.) who grow up in a deprived environment (Hack et al., 1992; Hack et al., 1995; Leonard et al., 1990), but intervention research suggests that some of these problems may be treatable. The Infant Health and Development (IHD) Program (1990), a controlled intervention study that we will discuss further in Chapter 11, provided educational enrichment and parental support for approximately

1,000 preterm, low-birthweight infants and their families. The IHD Program, which used random assignment to either an enrichment program or pediatric follow-up care, found that children in the enrichment group had higher IQ scores at age 3 than their matched counterparts in the control group. The intervention made the greatest difference—at least in the short term— for infants whose mothers had the fewest years of education (Hack et al., 1995).

Some researchers suggest that it may be possible to produce even more positive and longer lasting outcomes for preterm infants by making individualized modifications in the NICU and at home (Als et al., 2003; Mouradian et al., 2000). The Newborn Individualized Developmental Care and Assessment Program (NIDCAP) was designed to address one of the most important differences between extremely preterm infants and full-term infants— preterm infants' brains have not yet undergone the rapid growth that normally occurs during the last trimester of pregnancy. As a result of their brain's greater immaturity, preterm infants tend to respond more dramatically to external stimuli, such as noises and bright lights, and they become more easily fatigued because they have more difficulty calming themselves after they become stimulated. A number of studies have found that preterm infants benefit from NIDCAP individualized care that recognizes these fragile infants' need for interactions that are calmer, slower, and quieter than those that typically occur in traditional NICUs (Als et al., 2003; Mouradian & Als, 1994). NIDCAP care also uses specialized accessories, such as natural sheepskins for babies to lie on and extra-soft pacifiers. While many studies have produced promising results, more research is needed before NIDCAP individualized care can be recommended as the preferred method of caring for all preterm infants (Jacobs, Sokol, & Ohlsson, 2002).

Low Birthweight

The median birth weight for infants born in the United States in the year 2003 was 7 lb. 5 oz., or 3,325 grams (Martin et al., 2005). Approximately 8 percent of all babies born each year are considered **low birthweight (LBW)** because they weigh less than 5 1/2 lb., or 2,500 grams. Approximately 1.5 percent are **very low birthweight (VLBW)**, weighing less than 3 1/4 lb., or 1,500 grams, at birth (Martin et al., 2005). (Figure 4.1 shows recent trends in LBW and VLBW.) Low birthweight in a full-term infant may be the result of maternal illness during pregnancy, especially conditions that interfere with circulation in the uterus and placenta. Some forms of fetal growth disturbance are caused by fetal genetic or chromosomal abnormalities, and still others occur, as we discussed in Chapter 3, when the fetus is exposed to teratogens such as alcohol and cocaine. In many cases, the cause of fetal growth impairment is unknown (Feinbloom, 1993).

The incidence of LBW, like the incidence of preterm birth, varies as a function of race/ethnicity. The rate of LBW in the United States is significantly higher among African American infants (13.7 percent) than among non-Hispanic white infants (7.2 percent) and Hispanic/Latino (6.8 percent) infants. The highest rate of VLBW (3.1 percent) is also found among African American infants (Hamilton et al., 2005).

Women carrying multiple fetuses are more likely to give birth preterm, and their babies have a higher incidence of LBW and VLBW. In the year 2003, 58.2 percent of all LBW births were twins or higher multiples (Martin et al., 2005). Because older women are more likely to have multiple pregnancies, the risk of LBW and VLBW increases with maternal age. In the year 2000, approximately 55 percent of all LBW babies born to mothers 45 years of age or older were twins or a higher multiple (Martin et al., 2002, 2005; Martin, MacDorman, & Mathews, 1997).

Mortality rates are strongly influenced by infants' birth weight. Around the world, 98 percent of all neonatal deaths occur in developing countries, often as a consequence of preterm birth and low birthweight (Moss et al., 2002). In the United States, the majority of VLBW infants (weighing less than 1,500 g) survive, but approximately 25 percent die before the age of 1 year, as compared with 2 percent of LBW infants (weighing between 1,500 grams and 2,499 grams) and only 0.03 percent of infants weighing 2,500 grams or more at birth (Martin et al., 2002, 2005). In comparison with normal birthweight children, LBW and VLBW children are at greater risk for mental retardation, cerebral palsy, blindness, deafness, psychomotor problems, school failure, subnormal growth, and health problems (Hack et al., 1995; Martin et al., 2002). As we noted earlier in our discussion of preterm infants, some of these problems respond to intervention that includes parental support and environmental enrichment, so there is more hope than ever before for preterm, LBW, and even VLBW infants.

Postdate Birth

Some babies are born past their due date and weigh considerably more than average. At the upper end of the range are **macrosomic births**, the term used for babies weighing more than 8 lb. 13 oz., or 4,000 grams, at birth. Approximately 9 percent of births in the year 2003 were macrosomic. Of these infants, only a tiny number (1.5 percent) weighed more than 11 lb., or 5,000 grams (Martin et al., 2005).

In 2003, approximately 36 percent of all births occurred at 40 weeks and later, as compared with 48 percent in 1990. During the same period, the proportion of births taking place between 37 and 39 weeks increased from 41 percent to 52 percent. These figures reflect an increase during that period in the proportion of managed deliveries and the use of induction and cesarean deliveries (Martin et al., 2005).

When labor has not begun by 40 weeks gestation, the expectant parents may become impatient and ask that labor be induced. If they are planning to give birth in a hospital, where the standard practice typically is to induce labor after 41 weeks gestation, they are likely to have their request granted. Given some estimates that as many as 70 percent of postdate pregnancies (pregnancies extending beyond 41 weeks gestation) are actually normal term pregnancies for which there was an error in estimating the date of conception, the decision to induce is considered in conjunction with other measures of the fetus's age (Rooks, 1997).

How do postdate babies fare, in comparison with babies born "on time"? Some postdate babies have malformations and others suffer from malnutrition and asphyxia as the aging placenta begins to function less effectively and the level of amniotic fluid begins to drop (Caughey & Musci, 2004). Post-term, or postdate, infants tend to be longer than full-term babies, and they tend to have drier, looser skin and longer fingernails and body hair (Feinbloom, 1993). National studies comparing mortality rates for postdate and full-term **neonates**

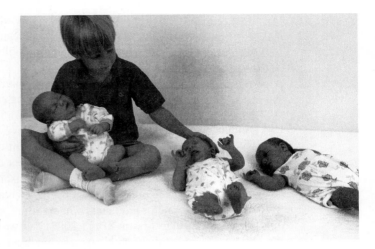

For a variety of reasons, the number of births of twins or higher multiples has increased dramatically since the 1970s and 1980s.

(newborns and infants younger than 1 month of age) also suggest that postdate births carry a higher risk of infant death (Caughey & Musci, 2004). It is not clear, however, that all babies should be delivered by 41 weeks. According to one study in which postdate pregnancies were randomly assigned to be induced at 41 weeks or to continue until labor began on its own, there was no difference in the health of babies in the two groups (Hannah et al., 1992). On the other hand, a review of 16 studies using randomized controlled trials showed that the rate of cesarean delivery was higher for post-term pregnancies that were not induced at 41 weeks, possibly due to their large size (Sanchez-Ramos et al., 2003). Despite these potentially serious complications, the majority of post-term babies are normal and healthy at birth.

Twins and Other Multiple Births

The number of births of twins or higher multiples has increased dramatically since the 1970s and 1980s. The rate of twin births increased from 19 per 1,000 total births in 1980 to approximately 32 per 1,000 births in the year 2003 (Martin et al., 2005). The rate of triplet and other higher order multiple births increased from 37 per 100,000 live births in 1980 to approximately 193 per 100,000 births in 1998 and to 187 per 100,000 births in 2003 (Martin et al., 2002, 2005). More triplets were born between 1990 and 1995 than during the entire decade of the 1980s (Martin et al., 1997).

What accounts for these trends? One strong influence is the increasing availability and successful utilization of new assisted reproductive technologies (ART). Almost one-half of all triplets born in 1998, for example, were born to parents who had used ART (Centers for Disease Control and Prevention, 2002).

Another factor contributing to the increased rate of twin and multiple births is the older age of childbearing in the United States. Birth rates for women in their late thirties and older have increased dramatically since 1980 (Martin et al., 2002, 2005). As shown in Figure 4.2, women in their 30s and 40s are more likely than women in their 20s to have a

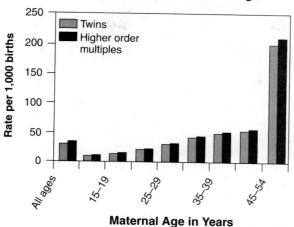

FIGURE 4.2 The rate of twin and higher order multiple births (more than twins) increase as a function of maternal age.

Source: Based on Martin, Hamilton, Sutton, Ventura, Menacker, & Munson, 2005.

multiple pregnancy, even without the use of ART or fertility-enhancing drugs. In fact, in the year 2000, approximately 40 percent of all births to women 50 years of age and over were twin or other multiple births (Martin et al., 2002). As we noted in Chapter 3, parents using ART are strongly encouraged to try to achieve pregnancies involving no more than two fetuses, primarily because twins and multiple pregnancies tend to be higher risk than singleton pregnancies. The recent decline in the proportion of triplet and higher order births is a reflection of this awareness and of improved ART procedures that allow a smaller number of embryos to be implanted and survive (Martin et al., 2005).

The twin birth rate has increased for each of the three largest racial/ethnic groups in the United States. There are differences across these racial/ethnic groups, however, with the highest rates of twin births occurring among African American women (34.7 per 1,000 births) and non-Hispanic white women (35.2 per 1,000 births) and the lowest rate among Hispanic/Latina women (21.3 per 1,000 births, Martin et al., 2005). For reasons that are not well understood, Asian women are less likely to give birth to twins and other multiples.

Twin and other multiple pregnancies are more likely to be complicated than singleton pregnancies, and the birth process itself is more likely to be difficult for mother and infants. As we have already discussed, twins and other multiples have an elevated risk of preterm birth, low birthweight, and other complications, such as breech position. Twins and other multiples also face a higher risk of death during infancy than do singleton births (Martin et al., 1997; Mathews, MacDorman, & Menacker, 2001).

Singleton infants born to mothers older than 35 tend to have an elevated risk of preterm birth, low birthweight, and mortality. This risk is not seen, however, among twins and other multiples born to older mothers. One likely reason is that older mothers with twin and triplet pregnancies tend to benefit from having more resources, including better access to early prenatal care. These women are also more likely to have used ART or other fertility treatments to achieve conception, a trend that entails several potential benefits for the infants (Zhang et al., 2002). First, multiple-gestation pregnancies produced using ART are less likely than their naturally achieved counterparts to share a placenta or amniotic sac, reducing the risk of complications involving these structures. Second, older women who use ART and donor eggs to achieve conception are usually using eggs that are younger because they were donated by a younger woman. Third, many older women who use ART to conceive have more financial resources than women whose multiple-gestation pregnancies occur without intervention.

The degree of potential control entailed with ART and other fertility treatments is unprecedented in human history and raises new ethical and technological questions for prospective parents to consider. The array of childbirth options that are now available in most developed countries has expanded as well, and expectant parents have numerous options to consider regarding the setting, participants, and obstetrical procedures.

Childbirth Options

Where and how does childbirth take place, and who provides support and advice during labor and delivery? More often than not, throughout history and across diverse cultures, birth has taken place in a woman's own home, and other, more experienced women have served as birth attendants (Fontanel & d'Harcourt, 1997; Rooks, 1997). In the mid–twentieth century, however, especially in the United States and other Western cultures, childbirth and pregnancy began to be treated by many in the medical community as a disease to be cured rather than a natural, healthy process (Cosans, 2004; Hausman, 2005; Kennedy & Shannon, 2004). Despite the obligatory presence of the mother during labor and delivery, childbirth came to be regarded as a process with which only doctors were qualified to assist. For a time, as this view became predominant in Western culture, midwives were chastised and even prosecuted for practicing medicine without a license (Borst, 1995; Rooks, 1997).

Today, trained nurse midwives are part of the obstetrical team in many hospitals in developed countries. Obstetricians predominate at births in the United States, but as we will discuss, there is a trend toward greater use of midwives and non-medical birth assistants. In developing countries, traditional childbirth practices still exist but are increasingly augmented by Western obstetrical procedures (DeLoache & Gottlieb, 2000). Moreover, it is now assumed that fathers will not only be present but will play an important role in their child's birth. Expectant couples often take childbirth classes and read books about specific childbirth techniques (Bradley & Montagu, 1996). These trends indicate that the experience of childbirth varies not only across but also within cultures.

Medical Interventions

Expectant parents today have a range of obstetrical procedures to consider and play an important role in writing their child's birth story. Ideally, they will have a chance to learn about these procedures well in advance of their baby's birth and will be aware of potential advantages and disadvantages for baby and mother. (Figure 4.3 shows recent trends in obstetric procedures.)

Obstetric Procedures, 1989–2003

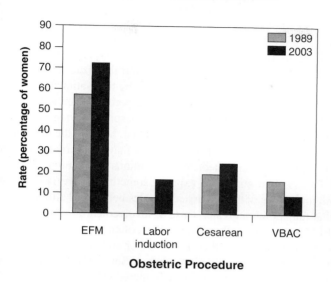

FIGURE 4.3 Rates of EFM, labor induction, and cesarean delivery have increased, while VBAC has decreased in recent years.

Source: Based on Martin, Hamilton, Sutton, Ventura, Menacker, & Munson, 2005.

Induction of Labor. As we discussed earlier, if labor fails to progress in a full-term pregnancy or fails to begin in a postdate pregnancy, the expectant parents and their obstetrical team may consider **labor induction**. If this choice is made, labor can be initiated by intravenously administering a synthetic form of oxytocin, a hormone normally released by the pituitary gland and a stimulant for uterine muscles. (Naturally secreted oxytocin is also involved in the production of breastmilk.) In the year 2003, labor was induced in 21 percent of all U.S. births, a rate that is more than double the rate of 9 percent in 1989 (Martin et al., 2002, 2005).

Analysis of the reasons for the rise in inductions suggests that not all of these inductions met the criteria to be considered medically necessary (Rayburn & Zhang, 2002). Because spontaneous labors tend to have fewer complications than those that are induced, induction that is not medically necessary is strongly discouraged (Martin et al., 2002). The association between induced labor and childbirth complications was demonstrated in a study involving more than 15,000 live births in Belgium (Cammu et al., 2002). In comparison with women whose labor began spontaneously, women with elective induced labor had a higher rate of cesarean delivery, delivery using instruments such as forceps, and pain medication. Babies born to mothers with electively induced labor were also slightly more likely than comparison babies to be transferred to a neonatal hospital ward for special care.

Elective induction—inducing labor at a "convenient" time—is not recommended. If the gestational age has been miscalculated, the infant could be born preterm (Feinbloom, 1993). Another consideration is that induction of labor does not always work, especially if the woman's cervix is not ready. Approximately 20 percent of women who are induced fail to go into labor within 24 hours and ultimately require a cesarean delivery (Pandis et al., 2001).

Electronic Fetal Monitoring.   If contractions have begun, continuous **electronic fetal monitoring (EFM)** may be used to monitor the contractions and the infant's heart rate. External sensors, attached to a belt placed across the mother's abdomen, may be used in EFM, but a more sensitive procedure involves introducing a wire into the mother's vagina and placing a sensor on the infant's scalp. If the mother's labor has failed to progress or if there are concerns about possible complications, internal EFM can alert the obstetrician to fetal distress (Feinbloom, 1993). According to data collected in 2003 by the National Center for Health Statistics, the majority of births in the United States (85 percent) used at least one form of electronic fetal monitoring (EFM) (Martin et al., 2005). Despite the widespread use of EFM, critics of the procedure question its value. They assert that, because the meaning of certain fetal heart-rate patterns is not always clear, fetal distress may be overdiagnosed and subsequently responded to with unnecessary medical interventions (Feinbloom, 1993).

Mothers and fathers, like childbirth experts, sometimes have conflicting feelings about EFM. In-depth interviews with 15 married couples before and after the birth of their first child showed that fathers felt a greater sense of involvement in and control over labor and delivery when EFM was used. Mothers, by contrast, often reported feeling that the EFM information and technology minimized their role in labor and delivery and diminished the importance of their active participation and awareness. Some women resented their husband's fascination with the EFM readings or were bothered by the restrictions EFM equipment placed on their ability to move freely during labor (Williams & Umberson, 1999). These findings suggest that it may be important for expectant parents to discuss with each other their feelings about medical interventions well in advance of actual labor and delivery.

Pain Relief.   Pain is a normal part of childbirth, and labor and delivery last merely hours out of an entire lifetime. Knowledge of these facts may be of little comfort to a woman in labor, however, as the pain becomes stronger and contractions intensify and accelerate. There are a number of options available to help women cope with pain during childbirth.

One option that has been in use throughout history and across cultures is to have the woman change position, as often as is necessary and helpful. A woman who is lying on her back may find relief by turning on her side, getting on all fours, squatting, or standing up and walking around. Massage and pressure applied to her back may also provide some relief (Feinbloom, 1993; Rooks, 1997).

Women who take childbirth education classes may learn about a second option—relaxation and breathing techniques to alleviate pain. A major goal of these techniques, based on approaches pioneered in the 1940s by Grantly Dick-Read in England, Ivan Pavlov in Russia, and Ferdinand Lamaze in France, is to short-circuit the links between a laboring woman's fear, tension, and pain by teaching her a distracting pattern of controlled breathing. Childbirth educators today do not universally endorse these breathing patterns, and many now argue that breathing normally in response to the body's own needs is preferable. Some experts note that shallow, controlled breathing may result in hyperventilation, reducing the amount of oxygen in the blood, which may affect the baby. These experts also recommend that women not hold their breath while pushing the baby out during labor. Instead, they suggest that gentle breathing be combined with pushing (Feinbloom, 1993).

A third option is to use medication to manage pain during childbirth. As early as the mid-1800s, physicians began experimenting with chloroform and other substances. By the early 1900s, injections of narcotics were being used, with harmful side effects occurring for some mothers and infants (Walker & O'Brien, 1999). The medication options available to women in labor today are less dangerous, but they still introduce risks that are not entailed by massage, change of position, or controlled breathing. Statistics indicate that the majority of women in the United States are willing to assume these risks. Approximately two-thirds receive medication to help manage the pain of childbirth (Beilin, 2002).

Analgesic medication can be used to reduce pain without eliminating it. These drugs are usually injected and take effect quickly. Side effects may include drowsiness and euphoria. Analgesics pass through the placenta to the fetus and can interfere with the infant's responsiveness and feeding for hours after birth. To minimize these effects, analgesics are usually given during the first stage of labor, when birth is still hours away (Feinbloom, 1993).

In contrast to analgesics, **anesthetic medication** works by eliminating pain entirely. In the past, general anesthesia was often used to enable the obstetrician to deliver the baby while the mother "slept." Although women were spared the pain of childbirth, they also missed out on positive aspects of the experience, such as seeing the baby emerge and holding their newborn child in the moments after birth. General anesthesia also complicates recovery after childbirth because it affects the mother's entire system. With the exception of emergencies, general anesthesia is no longer used in labor and delivery (Feinbloom, 1993).

Women in labor who choose anesthetics may instead select a drug that blocks the nerves that send pain messages to the brain. The most widely used of these anesthetics are spinals and epidurals. Spinal anesthetics temporarily block the sensory and motor nerves in the mother's pelvic area and legs. As a result, the woman is unable to feel or move. Her ability to push during contractions is eliminated, and the contractions themselves often decrease in force. Additional interventions (which we will discuss shortly) may be required to deliver the baby.

Spinal blocks cannot be given for vaginal deliveries until the cervix is fully dilated. This means that they provide no relief during the most painful and intense stage of labor (Feinbloom, 1993). For this reason, and because spinal anesthesia may be risky for the mother's health, some childbirth experts recommend that spinal anesthesia not be used (Rooks, 1997).

Epidural anesthetics are a popular alternative to spinal blocks. Epidurals numb the woman's pelvis and legs but do not eliminate her ability to move. In addition, in contrast to spinal blocks, epidurals can be given during the active phase of the first stage of labor. A catheter is left in place in the woman's back so that more anesthesia can be administered as needed. Epidural blocks are not without risk. Epidurals that are started too early may stop labor. Like spinal blocks, epidurals tend to decrease uterine contractions, possibly leading to the use of interventions such as forceps to deliver the baby (Feinbloom, 1993; Sharma et al., 2002; Walker & O'Brien, 1999).

One relatively new form of spinally administered analgesia, intrathecal opioids, has gained some popularity. In this case, narcotics are injected into the fluid of the spinal canal early in labor. Intrathecal analgesics offer pain reduction for up to 10 hours with almost no impairment of muscle control (Feinbloom, 1993). A review of clinical trials found that intrathecal opioids provide early labor analgesia that is comparable to epidural blocks (Bucklin, Chestnut, & Hawkins, 2002). However, another study in which women chose the type of pain medication they wanted to use revealed that intrathecal injections provided less effective, briefer pain relief than continuous epidural blocks. Intrathecal injections appear to work most effectively for women who give birth within 2 to 3 hours of the injection (Fontaine, Adam, & Svendsen, 2002). Some investigations of intrathecal opioids have found that they are associated with fetal heart rate abnormalities, although these "nonreassuring" patterns do not result in a greater number of cesarean deliveries or neonatal problems (Van de Velde, Vercauteren, & Vandermeersch, 2001). Taken together, it is clear that more research is needed to clarify the risks and benefits of this approach to pain relief.

Forceps and Vacuum Extraction.   As we noted in our discussion of pain medication, uterine contractions sometimes decrease in force during delivery, becoming less effective at pushing the baby out of the birth canal. When this happens, if the baby has descended far enough, the obstetrician may use instruments, such as forceps or a vacuum extractor, to help with delivery. Forceps are metal instruments that reach into the birth canal, grasp the infant's head, and pull the infant out. The vacuum extractor, by contrast, is a plastic cup with which the obstetrician applies suction to the baby's scalp (Feinbloom, 1993). Review of a large childbirth database revealed that vacuum extraction is an acceptable replacement for forceps. Babies delivered with the assistance of vacuum extraction are more likely than babies delivered with forceps to exhibit bruising of the scalp and retinal bleeding, but serious injury is unlikely (Johanson & Menon, 2000). With vacuum extraction, there is also less damage to the mother, a lower need for anesthesia, and a lower incidence of cesarean delivery. Nevertheless, as the cesarean rate has increased, the combined rate of forceps and vaccum extraction has declined from 9.5 percent in 1994 to 5.6 percent in 2003 (Martin et al., 2005).

Episiotomy.   When it appears that the mother's vaginal opening may not be large enough to accommodate the infant without tearing, many obstetricians perform an **episiotomy**. In an episiotomy, an incision between the vagina and the anus widens the opening before the baby's head emerges. Critics of this procedure point out that women with episiotomies tend to have worse outcomes than those without them; one randomized study reported that women with vaginal tears healed better than women who had had episiotomies (Klein et al., 1992; Feinbloom, 1993).

In light of controversy about the necessity and value of the procedure, overall episiotomy rates declined between 1983, when they were 70 percent, and 2000, when they dropped to 20 percent. Episiotomies are most likely to be performed in deliveries using forceps (Goldberg et al., 2002). They are also more frequently performed for non-Hispanic white women and for women with private health insurance (Weeks & Kozak, 2001).

To minimize the need for an episiotomy, childbirth educators recommend that women give birth in an upright position, since tearing seems to occur more frequently among women giving birth while lying on their back. It is also helpful to avoid pushing too strenuously. Instead, uterine contractions can be allowed to do most of the "heavy lifting" during delivery. Allowing the birth to proceed at its own pace, as long as mother and child are doing well, may also guard against the temptation of performing an episiotomy in order to hasten the delivery (Feinbloom, 1993).

Cesarean Delivery.   **Cesarean delivery** is a surgical delivery, performed with the mother under spinal or epidural anesthesia. General anesthesia is used in emergencies, when other forms of anesthesia would take too long to begin working (Feinbloom, 1993). Cesarean deliveries (also referred to as cesarean births, or C-sections) are performed when there is reason to believe that a vaginal delivery would be too dangerous for mother, baby, or both. Some cesareans occur in response to an unexpected medical emergency, but others are scheduled before labor ever begins. As we have noted already in this chapter, cesarean deliveries are often performed when labor fails to progress, when the baby is in a breech position, when there are twins or higher multiples, and when the baby is too large to pass safely through the birth canal. There is also a greater likelihood of cesarean delivery following induction of labor.

Cesarean delivery rates in the United States have increased significantly since 1970, when only 5.5 percent of all births were cesarean. By the year 1988, rates had soared to 25 percent of all births (Martin et al., 2002) and critics expressed alarm, questioning whether all cesareans were medically necessary. Rates then began to decline, before rising again in the 1990s. Since 1996, the rate of primary cesarean deliveries (first-time surgical deliveries) and the rate of repeat cesarean deliveries have increased. As a result, in 2004, the rate climbed to 29.1 percent of all births, an all-time high (Hamilton et al., 2005).

At the same time that cesarean rates were increasing, the rate of vaginal births after cesarean (VBAC) fell markedly, from 28.3 percent in 1996 to 9.2 percent in 2004 (Hamilton et al., 2005). This trend reflects changes in medical advice after a large, population-based observation study indicated that women attempting VBAC were three times as likely to experience a uterine rupture during spontaneous labor and 15 times as likely to suffer this life-threatening complication if labor was induced. Infants in these VBAC cases were 10 times as likely to die as infants delivered by cesarean (Martin et al., 2005; Smith et al., 2002).

Cesarean rates overall increased in the year 2003 for all racial/ethnic groups (Martin et al., 2005). In that same year, as in previous years, there was a higher total rate of cesarean deliveries among older women than among younger women (42.5 percent for those between 40 and 54 years of age versus 22.6 percent for those ages 20 to 24) (Martin et al., 2005). One reason older women have more cesareans is that they have higher rates of induced labor, including elective induction. In addition, older women are more likely than younger women to have a cesarean when there is failure to progress and when the fetus is in distress (Ecker et al., 2001).

Cesarean deliveries are generally safe for mother and baby, but there are some risks involved. Infants delivered by elective cesarean section are nearly five times more likely to experience respiratory distress than infants delivered vaginally (Levine et al., 2001). Women who give birth via cesarean are more likely to develop infections and complications of anesthesia, and they are slightly more likely to die than are women who give birth vaginally. Some experts suggest, however, that women who die following a cesarean are more likely to have preexisting health conditions that are the real reason for their higher mortality rate. Even without life-threatening complications, cesarean delivery is a major surgical procedure. In addition to being more expensive than vaginal delivery, a cesarean adds at least 1 week of recovery time for the mother following the birth (Feinbloom, 1993).

In light of the high, increasing rate of cesarean deliveries, childbirth educators work with all expectant parents, not just those considered high risk, to prepare them for the possibility of a cesarean birth and the more complicated recovery it entails. The goal, especially when the cesarean is a scheduled rather than an emergency procedure, is to help both

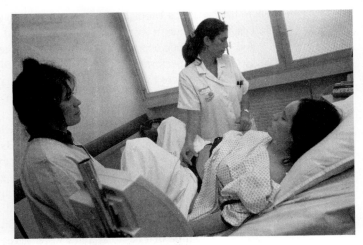

Although doulas perform no medical procedures during childbirth, they play an important role as the mother's advocate and provide her with guidance, encouragement, and reassurance.

parents experience the birth as fully and joyfully as possible, even though the story will have a different ending than the one they had initially anticipated.

Whether parents experience childbirth as joyful depends, in part, on the context and setting in which their child is born. Parents in the twenty-first century have a range of experiences, often as a consequence of choices that they make about the setting for and participants in their child's birth.

Hospital, Home, or Birth Center?

Until the middle of the twentieth century, most women chose to give birth at home (Fontanel & d'Harcourt, 1997). In fact, the earliest maternity hospitals functioned primarily as charities, and only the very youngest, most destitute, and socially isolated women delivered their babies in them (Meier, 1999). Most births occurring at home before the middle of the twentieth century were attended by women from the community. In the southeastern United States, these women were sometimes referred to as granny midwives. Granny midwives were typically trained through apprenticeship to older midwives, but some received additional training from state health departments. In Texas and the southwestern United States, *parteras* from the community assisted Latina women in childbirth, just as Native American women usually were assisted by experienced—but not medically trained—Native American women (Rooks, 1997).

Birth Attendants and Settings.   Today, 99 percent of all U.S. births take place in a hospital, with a physician—usually an **obstetrician**, a physician trained to assist and perform procedures during labor and delivery—in attendance in the vast majority of births (91.4 percent in 2003). In 1975, only 1.0 percent of all births were attended by a **certified nurse-midwife (CNM)**. This figure increased to 7.7 percent in 2003 (Martin et al., 2002, 2005). Certified nurse-midwives are registered nurses who have completed nurse-midwifery education programs and met criteria for certification by the American College of Nurse-Midwives. They are licensed to practice throughout the United States and attend births in all settings, but most work exclusively in hospitals. Almost half (46 percent) of all midwives in industrialized countries are nurses (Rooks, 1997).

Some expectant parents, including those who opt for a hospital delivery with an obstetrician, choose to have the additional assistance of a **birth doula**, a trained layperson who guides, encourages, praises, and reassures the woman but performs no medical procedures during childbirth (Rooks, 1997). Some doulas are professionally trained in postpartum care for the family. Postpartum doulas offer breastfeeding support and advice, cook meals, provide child care, and run errands (Doulas of North America, 2002).

Hospital versus Home Birth.   In many parts of the world, especially in developing countries, children still are born at home, and the mother is assisted and supported by experienced female relatives and women from the community. Increasingly, these births are a blend of traditional and modern medical practices, and fathers are finding new roles to play (DeLoache & Gottlieb, 2000; Kay, 1982).

As the birth process became medicalized and centralized during most of the twentieth century, the number of home births in developed countries declined. Home births have begun to increase recently in some developed countries, however, including Denmark, England, Germany, and New Zealand. Among developed countries, the Netherlands has the largest number of home births—approximately 30 percent. These home births are attended by trained and regulated midwives who provide continuous support during labor, delivery, and the infant's first week. Home births in the Netherlands are generally safe for mother and baby; there is a low incidence of complications and consequently a low rate (less than 5 percent) of cesarean deliveries (Feinbloom, 1993; Rooks, 1997; Tew & Damstra-Wijmenga, 1991). Studies of home birth safety in a number of other countries, including England, Wales, Australia, and Canada, provide similar results (Rooks, 1997).

In the United States, there is mixed evidence about the safety of planned home births. Studies of home births are hampered by the fact that, for both practical and ethical reasons, random assignment of pregnant women to a home versus a hospital birth setting cannot be done. Unlike in the Netherlands, there is often variation in the United States from one home birth to another, in terms of the attendant's experience, adding another challenge to researchers comparing home and hospital births.

Some research using birth and death certificates has shown higher infant mortality rates during labor and in the neonatal period for births occurring in hospitals than in homes. This pattern, however, probably reflects the greater tendency for high-risk pregnancies to be directed to hospitals (Rooks, 1997). Among infants born at home, deaths during labor or in the neonatal period occur most frequently when there are undiagnosed congenital abnormalities, such as heart defects, or when there are known risks, such as breech presentation, twins or other multiples, or postdate birth. When women with these risks are excluded from data analysis, some studies report mortality rates for home births that resemble those associated with low-risk hospital births, approximately 2 to 3 deaths per 1,000 live births (Rooks, 1997).

The safety of home births appears to be affected by the level of training of the attendant, with greater risk associated with lower levels of training. Physicians and certified nurse-midwives are rarely present at home births, however, and lay midwives are not allowed to be the primary attendant at hospital births. As a result, direct comparisons of birth attendants with different levels of training in the same settings are not possible (Pang et al., 2002).

Unlike the situation 100 years ago, only 1 percent of all U.S. births today take place at home, a tiny proportion that would not necessarily be predicted by the number of studies suggesting that home births for low-risk pregnancies are generally as safe as births that take place in hospitals. Why, then, don't more expectant parents choose home birth? One reason may be lack of information about birth outcomes and safety. In addition, in the United States, the health care system is based on the assumption of a hospital birth, and a woman's health care insurance may not cover birth that is planned to take place in another setting or with an attendant other than a physician or certified nurse. Expectant parents may also worry about potential complications, even in a low-risk pregnancy, and choose to have the latest medical technology available nearby in the event that an emergency arises.

For women without adequate health care insurance, cost may be a factor that motivates them to choose a home birth. The total cost of a home birth attended by a midwife may be as much as 30 percent less than the cost of a hospital birth attended by an obstetrician (Rooks, 1997). Women living in remote rural areas may lack transportation to a hospital and choose to give birth at home instead. Some women have had prior negative experiences with hospital births or desire to have a birth experience that is "natural" and under their control, occurring without medical interventions (Davis-Floyd, 1994). Finally, the familiar, private home environment appeals to some women because it makes them feel more relaxed and secure (Rooks, 1997).

In recognition of the desire to give birth in a relaxed, private setting, many hospitals in the United States and in other developed countries now offer expectant parents a homelike atmosphere, with labor and delivery occurring in the same room. Analysis of labor and birth outcomes for almost 9,000 women who gave birth either in a homelike setting or in a conventional hospital maternity ward showed that women in the homelike setting used less pain medication, were less likely to have a cesarean delivery, and expressed greater satisfaction with their care (Hodnett, 2001).

In some hospitals, certified nurse-midwives support the woman throughout labor and delivery. Studies of this kind of continuous care, including randomized controlled studies of thousands of women in Australia, Canada, and the United States, indicate that it provides mothers (and fathers) with support and technical expertise that results in a greater sense of control and a more positive birth experience than labor and delivery attended by a series of nurses they have not met before (Hodnett et al., 2002; Homer et al., 2002).

Women who receive continuous care from an attendant who is known to them also tend to require less pain medication and have fewer medical interventions performed, including cesarean deliveries (Klaus & Kennell, 1997). These benefits appear to accrue even when continuous care is provided by a doula, rather than a nurse-midwife (Keenan, 2000; Langer et al., 1998; Nolan, 1995; Scott, Berkowitz, & Klaus, 1999; Scott, Klaus, & Klaus, 1999; Zhang et al., 1996). In addition to providing a continuous physical presence, doulas help women in labor try a variety of nonpharmacological pain-relief techniques, including controlled breathing, relaxation, massage, and changing position (Doulas of North America, 2002).

As we have already noted, many hospitals have responded in recent years to expectant parents' preferences by offering homelike birthing rooms and greater choice in terms of birth attendants, pain medication, and obstetrical procedures. Many hospitals have also responded to their patients' interest in natural and alternative treatments by exploring acupuncture and herbal treatments during pregnancy, labor, and delivery. The medical community in the United States has drawn the line, however, at a controversial practice known as water birth (American Academy of Pediatrics Committee on Fetus and Newborn, 2005). Proponents of water birth, which is more common in Switzerland and other European countries, assert that women who submerge themselves during labor are able to achieve pain relief without using medication. Advocates of water birth also report that women who deliver their children underwater require fewer medical-surgical interventions, use less pain medication, and have a lower rate of cesarean section (Eberhard & Geissbuhler, 2000; Geissbuhler & Eberhard, 2000, 2005; Geissbuhler, Stein, & Eberhard, 2004; McCraw, 1989).

These claims have been challenged by medical experts who question the methodological rigor of existing studies of water births (Nikodem, 2004; Rush et al., 1996; Woodward & Kelly, 2004). Even if the purported positive effects for laboring mothers were substantiated through randomized control trials (the "gold standard" for evaluating the efficacy and safety of new health and mental health treatments), there would still be a lack of evidence that water births are better for babies (Gilbert, 2002). In fact, there are many questions about whether water births are even as safe as traditional "land births." Documented complications ensuing from water births include drowning and near drowning, asphyxiation, seizures caused by water intoxication, respiratory distress syndrome, pneumonia, and other infections (Bowden et al., 2003; American Academy of Pediatrics Committee on Fetus and Newborn, 2005; Gilbert & Tookey, 1999; Nguyen, Kushel, & Teele, 2002; Zimmerman, Huch, & Huch, 1993). Expectant parents should be aware, therefore, that there does not appear to be sufficient evidence that the alleged benefits of water births outweigh the potential dangers (American Academy of Pediatrics Committee on Fetus and Newborn, 2005).

Birth Centers. An increasing number of expectant parents in the United States and in many other countries, including Australia, France, Germany, Japan, and Switzerland, are choosing to give birth in a birth center, a freestanding site that may be affiliated with a hospital. In the United States, birth centers are typically licensed and regulated by the states in which they operate, and a set of national standards has been developed to allow for accreditation and comparability in terms of quality of care, birth outcomes, and cost (National Association of Childbearing Centers, 2002).

Giving birth in a birth center is generally less costly than in a hospital (Stone et al., 2000). Birth center costs are lower, in part, because lay midwives, rather than more expensive CNMs or obstetricians, typically attend the birth. In addition, different obstetrical procedures are followed in birth centers and in hospitals. Midwives in birth centers generally wait for labor to begin on its own, avoid the use of pain medication, and perform intermittent rather than continuous electronic fetal monitoring, which leaves the woman free to move about throughout labor. Episiotomies are performed in only about 12 percent of birth center deliveries, as compared with 20 percent of hospital births (Lubic, 2002).

Comparisons of birth outcomes for low-risk pregnancies delivered in birth centers and hospitals in countries with low overall rates of medical interventions have typically found little difference between the two settings. A recent 2-year study in Norway of more than 1,200 women who started labor in birth centers found that they generally fared well; only 4.5 percent of the women had to be transferred to a hospital, five infants showed distress within the first 5 minutes of their birth, and two infants died (Schmidt, Abelsen, & OIan, 2002). Similarly, a comparison of birth outcomes in Australia showed no significant difference in the cesarean rate for women in birth centers (3.5 percent) and women in hospitals (4.3 percent) (Homer et al., 2000). Another Australian study of 200 women who were randomly assigned either to a birth center or a hospital found no differences in birth outcomes, but women in the birth center group had higher levels of satisfaction with their birth experience and felt greater encouragement to breastfeed immediately after birth (Byrne, Crowther, & Moss, 2000).

Even larger differences have been found in the United States. One study of nearly 18,000 women who delivered in U.S. birth centers showed that neonatal mortality was low (1.3 deaths out of 1,000 births), maternal mortality nonexistent, and cesarean delivery rates strikingly low (4.4 percent in 1989, when the national rate was approximately 9 percent). Nearly all of the women using a birth center were satisfied with their experience and said that they would recommend it to others or return in the future (Rooks et al., 1989).

Neonatal Assessment

As we have seen, the experience of childbirth varies across birth settings and, increasingly, reflects parents' preferences. Newborn infants, of course, are unaware of these preferences.

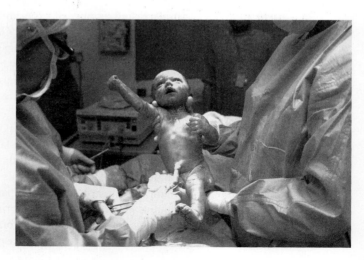

Some first-time parents may be shocked to see how red, wrinkled, and misshapen their newborn infant looks. They may also be surprised to see how alert their baby is in the moments after birth.

They come into the world without any notion of where they are or who was present at their birth, but they arrive ready to interact with and respond to that world in numerous ways, often to the surprise and amazement of their parents.

Assessment at Birth

The first question that many new parents ask (if they do not already know the answer) is whether their child is a boy or girl. The second question, for all parents, is how their baby is doing. Some first-time parents may be shocked at how red, wrinkled, and misshapen their baby looks. Fluid and mucous may need to be suctioned out of the infant's nose and mouth. The infant's body is usually covered in vernix caseosa, an unappealing waxy coating that protects the skin from exposure to amniotic fluid in utero. The baby may have a thick head of hair or appear to be bald at birth, and the genitals and breasts of newborns, both boys and girls, tend to be swollen as a result of stimulation by the mother's hormones (Eisenberg, Murkoff, & Hathaway, 1991; Feinbloom, 1993). Taken together, these attributes may give the newborn a face and body that only a parent could love.

Birth attendants also want to know how the baby is doing. They find out by using a quick screening procedure that is named after the doctor who developed it in the early 1950s—Virginia Apgar (1953). The **Apgar Score** provides an immediate profile of the infant's physical health at 1 and 5 minutes after birth. As shown in Table 4.2, the scale measures five dimensions that are a convenient mnemonic for the name of the assessment—*A*ppearance (color), *P*ulse (heart rate), *G*rimace (reflex irritability), *A*ctivity (muscle tone), and *R*espiration (breathing). The infant receives a score of 0, 1, or 2 for each dimension, with a total possible Apgar score ranging from 0 to 10. Scores from 7 to 10 are considered normal, scores of 4 to 6 are intermediate, and scores between 0 and 3 indicate that the infant is in need of medical attention or even resuscitation.

TABLE 4.2 Apgar Components and Scores

	Scores		
Components	**0**	**1**	**2**
Appearance (Color of arms, legs, and body)	Blue	Blue limbs, pink body	Pink
Pulse (Heart rate in beats per min.)	None	Slow (under 100 bpm)	Rapid (100 to 140 bpm)
Grimace (Coughing, sneezing)	None	Weak	Strong
Activity (Muscle tone, arm and leg movements)	None	Weak	Strong
Respiration (Breathing)	None	Irregular	Strong, regular

Source: Adapted from Apgar, 1953.

. The Apgar score at 5 minutes after birth is a useful indicator of the effectiveness of resuscitation, particularly if the score is different than the 1-minute Apgar score (Martin et al., 2002, 2005). Apgar scores are useful when used for their intended purpose, but they do not provide specific, reliable information about the child's future neurological functioning or indicate the cause of congenital conditions such as cerebral palsy. The Apgar is valid with newborns irrespective of race/ethnicity; the score for the color component is based on the color of mucous membranes of the mouth, of the whites of the eyes, and of the lips, palms, hands, and soles of the feet (Eisenberg et al., 1991). Apgar scores may be affected by maternal medications and infant conditions, including preterm birth and low birth weight, and thus need to be interpreted in conjunction with other available information about the pregnancy, labor, and delivery (American Academy of Pediatrics Committee on Fetus and Newborn, 1996; American Academy of Pediatrics, Committee on Fetus and Newborn, American College of Obstetricians and Gynecologists, & Committee on Obstetric Practice, 2006).

Of the 48 states reporting Apgar scores in the year 2000, only 1.4 percent of U.S. newborns had Apgar scores below 7 at 5 minutes after birth, a statistic that has not changed significantly since 1990. The stability of this statistic, in the context of an increasing number of preterm and LBW infants, is evidence of the success of most neonatal resuscitation efforts (Martin, et al., 2002, 2005).

Reflexes

Newborn infants come equipped to respond to their environment. Touch is the first sense to develop prenatally, and a number of preadapted **reflexes** can be stimulated through touch. Some of these reflexes are described in Table 4.3 and include rooting, sucking, grasping, stepping, and the Babinski. As shown in the table, other reflexes, such as the Moro, are stimulated when the infant's vestibular sense responds to the loss of physical support. Some of these reflexes, such as rooting (which prepares the infant to nurse), are of obvious survival value, but others, such as stepping, have no immediately useful function.

Many of the reflexes that are present at birth diminish over the next few months and then disappear. This is evidence of maturation of centers in the brain that control voluntary movements. Other reflexes, such as blinking in response to an object approaching the eyes, continue to function throughout the life span. As we will discuss in Chapter 6, at least one reflex that seems to disappear—stepping—can actually be activated at later ages than was once thought possible.

Sensory Abilities

Infants are able to use all of their senses at birth, but not all of their senses are equally well developed. Newborns are able to distinguish between different tastes. They have a built-in preference for sweet tastes (a preadaptation that makes breastmilk, which is naturally sweet, especially appealing) and an innate aversion to bitter tastes. The sense of smell is also very well developed at birth. Newborns quickly learn their mother's scent and can even

TABLE 4.3   Examples of Reflexes Present at Birth

Reflex	How It Works
Babinski response	The infant's big toe flexes and all of the other toes spread out when the sole of the foot is stroked lengthwise.
Incurvation (Gallant response)	When held horizontally and facing down so that the arms and legs are free, the infant's lower body swings to the side when a finger runs along the spine.
Moro reflex	A startle response in which the infant's arms and legs extend and then are pulled in toward the body after a sudden bump to the infant's crib or a slight loss of support (as might happen when a short parent or babysitter is unable to reach all the way over the crib rail when placing the sleeping baby in his/her crib).
Palmar grasp	The infant grasps a finger that is placed into his/her hand, pressing on the palms.
Rooting Response	The infant's head turns and the mouth opens when the cheek or corner of the mouth are touched by a finger or nipple.
Stepping or walking reflex	When held upright, the infant's feet make stepping movements if they are placed on a table or other solid surface.
Sucking response	The infant begins to suck when a finger, nipple, or pacifier is placed in the mouth.

Source: Based on information in Brazelton & Nugent, 1995.

discern the difference between the smell of their own amniotic fluid and the amniotic fluid from another newborn (Marlier, Schaal, & Soussignan, 1998; Schaal, Marlier, & Soussignan, 1998). As we discussed in Chapter 3, the sense of hearing is functioning well before birth. Newborns are able to distinguish between their mother's voice and the voice of another woman and, as we will see in Chapter 8, they recognize the contours of the language their mother speaks and notice differences between that language and other languages to which they were not exposed in utero.

The least well-developed sense at birth is vision, but newborns do respond to different levels of brightness. They look away from light that is very bright and toward areas of dark-light contrast. We will discuss the development of vision, as well as sensation and perception, in greater detail in Chapter 6.

Adaptations during the Neonatal Period

In the moments following birth, infants need to adjust to a number of sudden changes. For the first time, they move in a light-filled, nonaqueous environment, begin to regulate their own body temperature, and breathe air into their lungs. Having never experienced hunger before, they must also adapt to sucking and swallowing as they nurse or drink from a bottle. Sounds that previously were muffled through the filter of the uterine wall are now heard more clearly and at greater volume. Newborns who have a chance to receive "kangaroo care" (skin-to-skin contact achieved by placing the infant directly on the mother's chest or abdomen) shortly after delivery appear to adapt to these changes more quickly than newborns who receive standard care. Babies randomly assigned to kangaroo care in one experiment slept longer, in a quieter sleep state, and exhibited more relaxed movements and postures than babies randomly assigned to a no-treatment standard care group (Ferber & Makhoul, 2004).

Within a day or two, newborn infants begin to show regularities of behavior, including **states of arousal**, or distinct levels of alertness within which behaviors occur (Ingersoll & Thoman, 1999). Even before birth, as early as 29 weeks into the prenatal period, there are predictable patterns of activity and relative inactivity, corresponding roughly to active sleep, quiet sleep, and wakefulness (Mirmiran et al., 1992). In the newborn period, infants' time awake can be further differentiated into drowsy or semi-dozing, quiet alert, active alert (which can include fussing), and crying (Brazelton & Nugent, 1995). When asleep, the typical newborn alternates between active and quiet sleep every 15 minutes, waking up every 1 to 6 hours (Feinbloom, 1993).

States are one measure of an infant's central nervous system maturation. Newborns initially spend more than two-thirds of their time asleep or drowsy, and much of their time awake is spent fussing, crying, or moving between states. Over the course of the subsequent weeks and months, infants spend an increasing amount of their time awake in a quiet alert state, providing parents and other caregivers with new opportunities for interaction.

States provide parents with information about infants' needs, including their receptivity to interaction. It is not always easy, however, for new parents to differentiate between their newborn's changing states. One tool that can be helpful is the **Brazelton Neonatal Behavioral Assessment Scale (NBAS)** (Brazelton & Nugent, 1995), a structured interactive examination that is used with infants until the end of the second month of life. According to its developer, Dr. T. Berry Brazelton, the third day after birth is the optimal day for conducting the first assessment, but it may be used at any time, provided that the infant is midway between feedings and has recovered from any painful medical procedures or other influences that could affect responses to items of the NBAS. The goal, overall, is to elicit from infants their best performance possible. Interpretation of the results is thus done in conjunction with the examiner's notes about the infant's predominant state during the exam.

The NBAS consists of 28 behavioral items and 18 reflex items that are "packaged" into sets of related items and administered in a particular sequence. The exam begins with a 2-minute observation of the infant in a sleep state. The examiner notes the sleeping baby's reactions to auditory, visual, and tactile stimulation. When parents are present for the assessment, they may be surprised to see that their infant startles in response to the sound of a ringing bell but quickly becomes habituated to the stimulus and is able to continue sleeping. The examiner subsequently tests the infant's reflexes, responses to being undressed, and social interactive behaviors. Crying or fussing during the exam is not unusual and provides an opportunity to assess the infant's consolability, including self-consolability.

A single assessment with the NBAS is useful as a screening instrument for gross neurological or behavioral dysfunction. When several consecutive assessments are made, the NBAS can be used to study the effects over time of maternal substance use and other risk factors. The NBAS has additional value as a teaching and intervention tool for parents. As noted above, the examiner can help parents see that their infant has many capabilities for both shutting out and interacting with people and objects in the world. The examiner can highlight changes in the baby's motor movements as a function of state changes. Parents can be invited to test the infant's reflexes and to help console the baby. Seeing the infant relax when the sucking reflex is stimulated helps parents understand the importance of oral comfort for very young infants (Brazelton & Nugent, 1995).

Infants who are born preterm often respond differently to caregivers and the environment than full-term infants. In order to measure these differences more precisely, and in order to differentiate among low- and high-risk preterm infants, researchers developed the **Assessment of Preterm Infants' Behavior (APIB)** by modifying items from the NBAS (Als et al., 1982, 2005). The APIB has been used in many studies of preterm infants and is a useful tool for gauging the effects of interventions and treatments on motor, state, and other neurobehavioral responses (Als et al., 2003; Mouradian & Als, 1994; Mouradian et al., 2000).

Other researchers working with at-risk infants, primarily those believed to have been exposed prenatally to cocaine or other harmful substances, developed the **Neonatal Intensive Care Unit Network Neurobehavioral Scale (NNNS)** to assess their functioning (Lester et al., 1994). The NNNS is similar to the NBAS in that it measures a range of neonatal behaviors sometimes referred to as the "four As of infant behavior": arousal, attention, affect (including social interaction), and action (motor patterning) (Lester et al., 2004). Using the NNNS, researchers associated with the Maternal Lifestyle Study of neonatal and long-term health and developmental outcomes have been able to assess the immediate and subsequent effects of cocaine and opiate use during pregnancy (Lester, et al., 2002, 2004).

WRAPPING IT UP: Summary and Conclusion

Childbirth is much safer today in the United States and other developed countries than at any previous time. New options and more participatory models enable parents to help write their child's unique story. Childbirth experts disagree about some issues, such as whether delivery should be hastened when there is failure to progress, but they agree about many others, including the value of educating expectant parents about childbirth and including them in the entire process.

Preterm birth rates have remained high despite efforts to reduce them, and more research is needed to clarify the reasons for racial/ethnic differences in the rate of preterm birth. Advances in neonatal intensive care have led to better survival rates for these tiny, fragile babies. Some preterm infants are twins and other multiples. The rate of twin and multiple-infant births has increased dramatically, as a result of increased use of fertility treatments and increases in maternal age. Pregnancy, labor, and delivery are riskier when twins or other multiples are involved.

Many births in the United States use medical and surgical interventions during labor and delivery. The incidence of cesarean delivery has continued to increase and occurs in approximately one-third of all births in the United States. Unlike in many other parts of the world, nearly all births in the United States take place in a hospital with a physician or certified nurse-midwife in attendance. Other, less frequently chosen options include giving birth at home or in a birth center. Lay midwives and doulas assist some women during labor, delivery, and the postpartum period.

The Apgar Score reflects the newborn's condition immediately after birth. Most infants have a score indicative of good health by 5 minutes. Neonates possess innate reflexes, many of which disappear within the first few months of life. Newborns' senses are functional at birth, enabling them to feel, taste, smell, and hear with surprising precision. Vision is the least well developed sense at birth.

Newborns make many adaptations to the external world. States of arousal, including sleep-wake states, change during the first months after birth. These changes affect infants' ability to interact with parents and other caregivers and to learn from the environment.

The Brazelton Neonatal Behavioral Assessment Scale (NBAS) assesses newborn infants' capabilities, showing parents how well they are preadapted to interact and learn. Other neonatal assessments have been developed to assess preterm infants (APIB) and infants whose prenatal exposure to drugs places them at developmental risk (NNNS). All of these assessments can help pediatricians understand infants' needs and provide them with the most appropriate care and treatment during the neonatal period and beyond. The NBAS and other neonatal assessments are not a substitute, of course, for other assessments of infant health and well-being, and they cannot be administered reliably beyond the first months of life. In the next chapter, we'll consider measures that can be used in this way— aspects of health, nutrition, and physical growth that constitute the milestones and targets for development from birth to age 3.

THINK ABOUT IT: Questions for Reading and Discussion

1. If an expectant couple wanted to know what their child's birth is likely to be like, what would you tell them? Which aspects of labor and delivery do you think they would be most surprised to learn about?

2. What options are available for alleviating the pain of childbirth? Consider the advantages and disadvantages of these options and rank them in order from most to least preferred.

3. How have rates of preterm birth and low birthweight changed since the 1970s? What seem to be the principal reasons for these changes? What are the short- and long-term outcomes of preterm birth and low birthweight?

4. How might the recent increase in the rate of twins and other multiple births affect our society?

5. Why has the cesarean delivery rate increased so dramatically in the United States?

6. Compare the relative risks of giving birth in a hospital, at home, and in a birth center. Where would you choose to give birth? Explain.

7. Explain how the Brazelton Neonatal Behavioral Assessment Scale (NBAS) can be used with new parents.

8. What do you think is the most important neonatal characteristic for new parents to understand? How might you help them learn about this characteristic?

KEY WORDS

Active phase (112)	The second phase of labor, with increasingly painful contractions coming more frequently as the cervix opens
Analgesic medication (125)	Drugs that reduce pain without eliminating it
Anesthetic medication (125)	Drugs that eliminate pain by blocking nerves that send pain signals to the brain
Apgar Score (133)	An assessment used at 1 and 5 minutes after birth to provide a profile of the infant's physical health
Assessment of Preterm Infants' Behavior (APIB) (137)	A modification of the NBAS that is designed to gauge the effects of interventions and treatments on preterm infants' motor, state, and other neurobehavioral responses (see Brazelton Neonatal Behavioral Assessment Scale)
Birth doula (129)	A trained layperson who provides nonmedical assistance during labor and delivery
Brazelton Neonatal Behavioral Assessment Scale (NBAS) (136)	A structured examination that is used with infants from birth until the age of 2 months to assess reflexes and social interactive behaviors
Breech presentation (114)	A birth in which the infant emerges feet or buttocks first
Certified nurse-midwife (CNM) (128)	Registered nurses who are trained to assist during labor and delivery
cesarean delivery (126)	A surgical procedure performed when a vaginal delivery would be too dangerous for mother, baby, or both
Dilatation (111)	Widening and opening of the cervix during labor
Effacement (112)	The thinning out of the cervix during labor
Electronic fetal monitoring (EFM) (124)	The use of external or internal sensors to monitor contractions and detect signs of fetal distress
Episiotomy (126)	A procedure in which an incision is made to widen the vaginal opening
Labor induction (123)	A procedure in which a hormone is administered in order to initiate uterine contractions leading to labor and delivery
Latent phase (112)	The initial phase of the first stage of labor, marked by widely spaced contractions that are not painful
Low birth weight (LBW) (118)	A birthweight of less than $5\frac{1}{2}$ lb., or 2,500 grams
Macrosomic birth (119)	A birthweight of more than 8 lb. 13 oz., or 4,000 grams
Neonate (119)	Newborns and infants younger than 1 month of age

Neonatal Intensive Care Unit (116)	A specialized hospital setting for the care of medically vulnerable infants, including those born preterm and very preterm
Neonatal Intensive Care Unit Network Neurobehavioral Scale (NNNS) (137)	A measure designed to assess the functioning of at-risk infants, primarily those believed to have been exposed prenatally to alcohol, cocaine, or other teratogens
Obstetrician (128)	A physician trained to assist and perform procedures during labor and delivery
Premature rupture of membranes (PROM) (111)	Condition occurring when the amniotic sac breaks open before contractions begin
Preterm (115)	A birth that occurs before 37 weeks gestation
Reflexes (134)	Involuntary responses to stimuli, present at birth and gradually diminishing during the first few months of life
States of arousal (136)	Distinct levels of alertness within the general behavioral categories of active sleep, quiet sleep, and wakefulness
Very preterm (115)	A birth that occurs before 32 weeks gestation
Very low birth weight (VLBW) (118)	A birth weight of less than $3\frac{1}{4}$ lb., or 1,500 grams
Vertex position (112)	A birth in which the infant is delivered head first

CHAPTER 5

Physical Growth, Health, and Nutrition

When Baby Nadia was adopted from an austere Russian orphanage at the age of 15 months, she weighed only 13 pounds and her head fit into a cap intended for 3- to 6-month-olds. Nadia's adoptive parents also noted that she couldn't sit up on her own, didn't know how to feed herself, and didn't play with the toys they had bought for her. After being spoon-fed and cared for in her new home, Nadia began to gain weight and her head circumference increased. She also learned to pick up small pieces of food with her fingers and eventually fed herself with a spoon. By the age of 3 years, Nadia was still smaller than most children her age, but she was a healthy, energetic child—a little girl who most people would not have guessed began life facing great adversity and deprivation.

As they marveled at her progress, Nadia's parents also had some special concerns about her experience before she joined their family. How atypical was her development prior to her adoption? Would her catch-up growth have happened more quickly if it had been possible for them to adopt her at an earlier age? What sort of caregiving environment and nutrition should have been provided in the orphanage in order to put Nadia on a course for normal growth and development from the start? In addition, like most parents of infants, they wanted to learn about the topics that we'll focus on in this chapter—how to keep infants safe and healthy.

Physical Growth

Growth during the first 3 years is faster than at any other point after birth (Behrman, Kliegman, & Jenson, 2000). Most infants lose about 10 percent of their birthweight during the first week, which may worry first-time parents, but this weight is usually regained by the time the baby is about 10 days old. Growth occurs in spurts, rather than at a steady rate (Lampl, Johnson, & Frongillo, 2001; Lampl, Veldhuis, & Johnson, 1992). By the age of 1 month, the average infant weighs about 9 pounds. Birthweight typically doubles by about 5 months and triples by 12 months. If the child's weight continued to triple each year, the average

Three-year-olds may seem like giants next to their younger siblings.

3-year-old would weigh approximately 200 pounds! Fortunately, the rate of weight gain decreases after the first year and does not increase again until adolescence.

Infants also grow in length, increasing by about 1 inch during the first month. By the end of the first year, most infants are about 10 inches longer than they were at birth. Increases in length slow down by one-half during the second year and by one-third by the age of 3 years (American Academy of Pediatrics, Shelov, & Hannemann, 1998).

As we will discuss shortly, significant brain growth and development occur after infants are born. The newborn's skull grows rapidly too, increasing more during the first 4 months than at any other time in life. During the first month, the average newborn's head grows 1 inch—from $13\frac{3}{4}$ inches to $14\frac{3}{4}$ inches around (American Academy of Pediatrics, Shelov, & Hannemann, 1998). Head circumference correlates well with postnatal brain growth in infants and is one of several measures available to track early physical growth and development (Johnson, 2000).

Measuring and Predicting Growth

Pediatricians—and many new parents—use growth charts to compare individual infants' weight, length, and head circumference with the measurements of other children of the same age. These charts—first constructed by the National Center for Health Statistics (NCHS) in 1977—are a series of percentile curves (covering the range from the third to the 97th percentile) showing the distribution of selected body measurements in children in the United States. Commonly used growth charts for infants up to 36 months track length-and-weight-for-age, head-circumference-for-age, and weight-for-length. Separate charts are used for boys and girls because boys tend to be slightly longer and heavier.

The original set of growth charts for infants was based on a sample of Caucasian, formula-fed, middle-class infants from southwestern Ohio in the 1970s and did not accurately reflect the cultural and racial diversity of the United States. In addition, the infants in the sample, which was part of the Fels Longitudinal Study, were measured at 3-month intervals from 3 through 12 months, limiting the ability of the infant growth charts to track development at 1-month intervals (Kuczmarski et al., 2000).

The newest growth charts were derived from the National Health and Nutrition Examination Survey (NHANES), a national health survey that collects data based on actual physical examinations of a cross-section of the U.S. population (Kuczmarski et al., 2000). The growth charts covering ages 2 and older were revised at the same time as the infant charts, with newer NHANES data being used in place of data that was collected between 1963 and 1974. Because height can be reliably measured after age 2, there are separate sets of charts for preschoolers (ages 2 to 5), and for children between 2 and 20 years of age, tracking stature-for-age, weight-for-stature, and weight-for-age.

The new charts also contain information about body-mass-index-for-age for ages 2 to 20 years. **Body mass index (BMI)** is a measure of weight in relation to height and is calculated for adults by dividing an individual's weight in pounds by the square of their height in inches and multiplying the result by 703. To determine if children are overweight, the Centers for Disease Control and Prevention uses age- and gender-specific BMI at the 95th percentile or above. Overweight and obesity are an increasingly prevalent problem in the United States, affecting children as well as adults. An estimated 15 percent of children aged 6 to 11 years are overweight, approximately twice the percentage (7 percent) of 20 years ago. To reverse this trend, greater emphasis will need to be placed on ensuring that even toddlers and very young children engage in healthy levels of activity and consume a nutritious diet (Federal Interagency Forum on Child and Family Statistics, 2005; U.S. Department of Health and Human Services, 2001).

As infants grow, their body proportions change. Whereas the newborn infant's head is approximately one-fourth of the overall body length, the typical 3-year-old child is less top-heavy and has a slimmer build. Growth rates vary across children, however, and many 3-year-olds still have a big tummy even if their arms and legs have begun to slim down. Changes in body proportions, along with increases in strength and coordination, have implications for motor development, a topic that we will consider in depth in Chapter 6.

What do researchers know about the factors that influence gains in weight and height? Individual infants' physical growth is affected by genetics, and taller-than-average parents are likely to have taller-than-average children, whereas shorter-than-average parents typically have shorter-than-average children. In addition, as we will see later in this chapter, health and nutrition also play important roles in physical growth and determine whether and how genetic potentials are expressed. We turn now to a psychosocial factor that is another critical determinant of growth—the quality of caregiving that infants receive.

Failure to Thrive

It has long been known that infants deprived of physical contact, like Nadia and other infants in orphanages or other institutional settings, tend to grow slowly, even if they are fed an adequate diet—a condition referred to as **failure to thrive** (Alanese et al., 1994; Gardner, 1972; Gohlke et al., 1998; Skuse, 1985; Spitz, 1945; Widdowson, 1951). Consistent with previous research, numerous studies have recently documented a high incidence of growth failure among institutionalized children in Eastern Europe. Like Baby Nadia, when these children are adopted, most frequently by families in the United States, the United Kingdom, and Canada, the majority are below normal weight and height, and more than one-third are below the third percentile for length, weight, and head circumference. Analysis of growth data from orphanages in Eastern Europe and China indicate that children lose 1 month of linear growth for every 3 months spent in an institutional setting. Growth stunting in these children is influenced to some degree by their prenatal experience and postnatal diet, but it is also thought to be the result of a psychosocially induced factor—abnormal growth hormone secretion due to stress and poor quality of care (Johnson, 2000).

Recent studies of preterm infants born in the United States may shed light on the abnormal production of growth hormone among institutionalized infants and children. These studies show that infants benefit from skin-to-skin "kangaroo care" and gain more weight when they experience and receive a special form of tactile/kinesthetic stimulation known as infant massage (Field, 1995; Field, Hernandez-Reif, & Freedman, 2004). In one study, massaged preterm infants gained 47 percent more weight than unmassaged comparison infants who received the same number of calories (Field et al., 1986). The mechanisms underlying the growth-stimulating effects of touch are not completely understood, but preliminary research suggests that touch may increase the release of gastrointestinal food absorption hormones or activate growth genes, just as lack of caring touch may interfere with the normal action of these hormones and genes (Field, 1995). Also relevant, as we will see shortly, there is evidence that threats to physical or psychological safety change the brain's neurochemistry, interfering with the normal function of the hypothalamus and brainstem, areas that regulate food intake, digestion, growth, and respiration (Shonkoff & Phillips, 2000).

Classic studies of children with failure to thrive report that there is almost always a dramatic growth spurt when they are moved to a new, caring environment, a surge that is most likely due to improvements in diet and in growth hormone secretion (Widdowson, 1951). This pattern has also been observed among infants adopted from orphanages in Eastern Europe. In one study of institutionalized Romanian adoptees younger than 18 months of age, nearly 80 percent of previously growth-stunted children were in the normal range for height-length within 9 months of their adoption (Johnson et al., 1993). Catch-up growth in head circumference is also typical among previously institutionalized adoptees (Johnson, 2000; Rutter, 1998).

There are limits in the extent to which previously deprived children can recover from the effects of earlier institutionalization. The greatest catch-up growth is usually observed among children who were adopted before the age of about 6 to 8 months. Experiments with rodents and nonhuman primates have shown that adequate caregiving reverses or reduces the effects of early adversity on infants' physiological stress responses. In humans, deprivation early in the lives of institutionalized infants has been linked to elevated stress hormones years after adoption by a caring family (Gunnar, 2000). It is possible, therefore, that catch-up growth in children adopted at later ages is impeded by the lingering effects of inadequate caregiving on their physiological response to stress.

Tooth Development

Primary teeth develop in the fetal jaw during the prenatal period but, with very few exceptions, do not emerge through the gums until after birth. The eruption of the first tooth typically occurs between the ages of 5 and 9 months but can be as early as 3 months or as late as 12 months. As the teeth push their way through, the gums become swollen and red. In response to this discomfort, some infants temporarily change their nursing behavior, cry more, and have difficulty sleeping. In previous centuries, teething was believed to be potentially fatal (Fontanel & d'Harcourt, 1997). Even today, many parents believe that teething causes fevers and other illnesses. These other problems are actually unrelated to teething, but the coincidental timing makes it tempting to assume that there is a causal relationship.

Some parents may be surprised to learn that a more serious problem is premature loss of primary teeth due to decay—the most common chronic disease of childhood, especially among lower-income children whose families do not have dental insurance or who are unaware of the importance of preventing oral diseases (Mouradian, Wehr, & Crall, 2000). Given the clear links between oral health and overall health throughout the lifespan, following oral health practices beginning in infancy can make a difference (Satcher, 2000).

As soon as the first tooth erupts, parents can use a soft cloth or baby toothbrush to keep it clean. After the age of 2 years, a pea-sized amount of fluoridated children's toothpaste may be used. Some infants have primary teeth pulled as a result of early decay, but this can usually be prevented by making sure that they do not take bottles of milk, formula,

Infants' first teeth typically erupt between the ages of 5 and 9 months, contributing to a gradual transformation from "baby" to "child".

or juice to bed during a nap or at night. The problem with this common practice is that the liquid tends to pool around the baby's teeth, bathing them in sugar, and leading to baby-bottle caries (Lott, 2002).

Infant nutrition can also affect development and health of the primary teeth. Results of one prospective, 4-year longitudinal study of children in Peru showed that a single episode of malnutrition before the age of 1 year led to delayed eruption of the primary teeth and a higher incidence of dental caries during the first 4 years of life. The most pronounced effects were found in children whose malnutrition had resulted in the most extreme degree of stunted growth (Alvarez et al., 1993). As we'll see shortly, nutrition also plays an important role in the development of the infant brain.

Brain Development

Like other aspects of physical growth, brain development occurs rapidly after birth. A new-born's brain is approximately one-quarter the size of an adult's but grows to about 80 percent by 3 years of age and 90 percent by age 5 (Johnson, 1997a; Shonkoff & Phillips, 2000).

Unlike other fundamental aspects of physical growth during infancy, such as changes in weight and length or the appearance of teeth, the developing brain cannot be seen by the casual observer—or interested parent. Yet, with the assistance of **electroencephalograms** (**EEGs**, which measure the brain's activity through external electrodes placed on the scalp) and imaging tools, such as **positron emission tomography** (**PET**, which shows the amount of activity, such as glucose uptake, in the brain), or **magnetic resonance imaging** (**MRI**, which reveals the brain's structure), researchers have documented the profound changes occurring in the months and years after birth.

Milestones of Brain Development.   As we learned in Chapter 3, brain development begins during the prenatal period with the generation of nerve cells called neurons. By birth, most of these neurons have migrated to regions of the brain where they will perform specialized functions, such as those involved in processing sensory information and controlling motor movements. In order to perform these functions, neurons must become interconnected to a network of other neurons by forming **synapses**, or connections. With the generation and migration of most neurons taking place before birth, the brain's growth after birth is primarily the result of new projections from each neuron—the axons and dendrites that form synapses with other neurons' axons and dendrites. As shown in Figure 5.1, **axons** carry electrical messages away from the neuron cell body and **dendrites** bring those signals to the cell body. In the space between one neuron's axon and the next neuron's dendrites, biochemicals called **neurotransmitters** are released from **vesicles** (or storage spaces) at the end of the axon and taken up by the next neuron's dendrite.

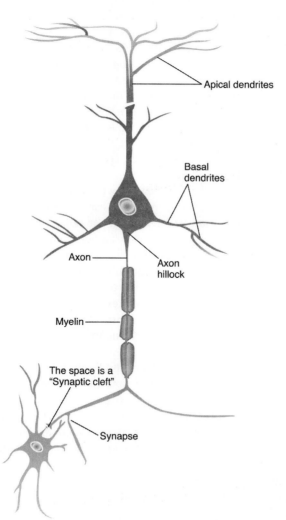

Apical dendrites

Basal dendrites

Axon

Axon hillock

Myelin

The space is a "Synaptic cleft"

Synapse

FIGURE 5.1   Axons and dendrites connect neurons together in a network.

There is regional variation in **synaptogenesis** (the formation of synapses), with the most rapid increase of synapse formation and the peak density of synapses occurring at different ages in different areas (Johnson, 2001; Shonkoff & Phillips, 2000). Before 5 weeks of age, the most active areas of the brain appear to be in the sensorimotor cortex, thalamus, brainstem, and parts of the cerebellum. The highest activity levels at 3 months of age, are in other regions, such as the parietal, temporal, and occipital cortices. Between 3 and 4 months, there is a rapid increase in the number and density of synapses in the visual cortex, resulting in the peak density between 4 and 12 months. The prefrontal cortex, by contrast, is slower to develop and does not reach its peak until after the first year (Johnson, 2001). During the most active period of its development, 2 million new synapses are created every second in the cerebral cortex, and by 2 years of age more than 100 trillion synapses have been formed in this region of the brain (Shonkoff & Phillips, 2000).

The brain's development is more like sculpting a block of marble than it is like building a snowman. This is because many more neurons are produced than will actually become part of an established network, and some of the originally generated material is "carved away." Beginning at the end of the first year, many of the synapses in the developing brain cease functioning. The "pruning" of these synapses occurs at different ages in different regions of the brain. In the primary visual cortex, the number of synapses per neuron begins to drop at the end of the first year, but synapses in areas involved in higher forms of learning and reasoning may not be eliminated until adolescence, or even into adulthood (Johnson, 2001; Thompson, 2001). Pruning helps make the child's brain work more efficiently and quickly by ultimately removing about one-third of the synapses between early childhood and adolescence (Shonkoff & Phillips, 2000).

Axons in the synapses that remain become covered with **myelin** (a dense, fatty sheath that enhances the speed with which electrical messages can be sent between neurons). Myelination has been documented as late as 30 years of age but begins during the first 2 years of life and is complete in many areas of the brain by the age of 4 years (Johnson, 2001).

Early survival and control of the most basic bodily functions, including respiration, heartbeat, circulation, sleeping, and reflexes depends on the lower brain. This part of the brain consists of the spinal cord and brain stem and is well developed at birth. The higher regions of the brain—the limbic system and cerebral cortex—are immature at birth and relatively slow to develop. As we discuss next, this timing provides ample opportunity for the influence of experience on the brain's architecture and functioning.

The Role of Experience.   "Human brain development closely follows the sequence of events observed in other primates, albeit on a slower timescale" (Johnson, 2001, p. 475). Many experts have pointed out that in comparison to more precocious species, the extended timetable gives human brains a relatively longer period in which to be shaped by early experience. Experience activates neurons, and repeated experiences strengthen neural networks, but the role of experience is not always the same for different aspects of brain development. The majority of neural connections in the visual cortex and auditory cortex are made within the first several months after birth, for example, whereas the majority of connections in the areas of the brain responsible for certain aspects of language are formed during the second half of the first year. By contrast, the prefrontal cortex, the center for higher cognitive functions, continues to develop and remains open to experience (Shonkoff & Phillips, 2000).

Some aspects of brain development are **experience-expectant**; these structures seem to "expect" to have certain kinds of stimulation and are ready to develop once they receive it. The visual cortex, for example, "expects" to receive signals from both eyes, but it depends on receiving that early visual stimulation to develop normally—with equal representation of visual input from both eyes. Infants born with a congenital cataract in one eye (an opaque covering that blocks light from reaching the retina) do not provide their visual cortex with input from both eyes. They need to have corrective surgery as soon as possible, ideally before the age of 2 months. Without it, and subsequent patching of the normal eye during the infant's waking hours, the input from the normal eye will stimulate and take over the regions of the visual cortex that would ordinarily process input from the previously occluded eye.

Many other aspects of brain development function differently and are **experience-dependent**. These structures and systems develop as a result of each person's experiences, such as musical training. It is these experiences that determine whether or not particular brain functions are developed and reinforced. Unlike experience-expectant aspects of brain development, experience-dependent abilities are generally open to the effects of experience throughout an individual's lifetime, enabling new skills to be learned at any age (Shonkoff & Phillips, 2000; Thompson, 2001).

Effects of Early Adversity. Not all experiences exert a positive influence on brain development. In Chapter 3, we considered the effects of prenatal exposure to a variety of influences, including drugs, alcohol, environmental toxins, and maternal illness and nutrition. We noted then that the amount and type of damage produced depends on the timing, amount, and duration of exposure, as well as each child's genetically determined vulnerability. The developing brain is equally vulnerable to harmful influences after birth, and the same lessons about timing and context of exposure are applicable.

As we saw in our earlier discussion of failure to thrive, there is evidence that the experience of early physical and psychological stress produces abnormal functioning in areas of the brain (the hypothalamus and brainstem) that regulate fundamental aspects of healthy growth and development. The extent of the abnormalities is influenced by the length of exposure to inadequate caregiving. In addition to suffering from neglect of many basic interpersonal needs, there is no doubt that some infants living in institutional settings suffer from intentional abuse as well (Johnson, 2000). How do abuse and neglect affect the brain's development? Sadly, this question is equally relevant for hundreds of thousands of noninstitutionalized maltreated children every year.

Maltreatment and the Brain

Maltreatment, defined by the National Child Abuse and Neglect Data System (NCANDS) as neglect, medical neglect, physical abuse, sexual abuse, or psychological maltreatment, affects large numbers of children in the United States annually. Data collected by NCANDS show that in 2003, approximately 906,000 children were identified as victims of child abuse or neglect. The highest incidence of maltreatment (16.4 per 1,000 children) was found among the youngest children, those younger than 3 years. Children younger than 1 year comprised approximately 10 percent of all victims of maltreatment. Of the estimated 1,500 children who died in 2003 due to abuse or neglect, approximately 80 percent were younger than 4 years of age. The highest rate of fatalities was found among infant boys younger than 1 year of age. The leading cause in 2003, responsible for about one-third of child fatalities, was neglect (36 percent), followed by physical abuse (29 percent) and multiple maltreatment types (28 percent). The majority of perpetrators were parents, relatives, or unmarried partners of parents (National Child Abuse and Neglect Data System, 2004; Schnitzer, & Ewigman, 2005). For children who survive maltreatment, what are the effects on the developing brain?

The amygdala, the area of the brain that registers and responds to fear and anxiety, is relatively mature at birth and is thought to be fully functional by the age of 1 year. One implication of this is that infants are capable of experiencing fear, anxiety, and psychological stress (Shonkoff & Phillips, 2000). Relatively little direct evidence exists regarding the effects of early abuse and neglect on brain structures and brain functioning. What is known comes primarily from studies of animals.

Experiments with rodents and nonhuman primates show that in the absence of adequate maternal care, overstimulation of the amygdala early in life results in an animal version of posttraumatic stress disorder that lasts into adulthood. Rat pups, for example, that experience a high level of stress in the absence of comforting maternal care later have difficulty modulating their fear responses. Rat pups reared with adequate maternal care, by contrast, seem to develop the ability to respond to the same stressors with less anxiety and fear. As another example, infant rhesus monkeys deprived of normal maternal care become fearful, anxious adult animals that show exaggerated physiological stress responses. These animals produce higher levels of stress hormones and anxiety-related brain neurochemicals than monkeys reared with adequate maternal care (Shonkoff & Phillips, 2000; Suomi, 1991).

Are the findings from experiments with rodents and other animals applicable to humans? Clinical studies of children severely neglected or abused in early childhood document profound disturbances of normal development, including delays and abnormalities in cognitive, emotional, social, and physical development. In a classic study of institutionalized children, Spitz (1945) showed that children who were placed in foster care and received more sensitive, nurturing care had better developmental outcomes. Clinical reports do not reveal the effects of early adversity on the developing brain, but new evidence from developmental neuroscientists is beginning to provide some of the answers.

One study using MRI scans found that maltreated children suffering from post-traumatic stress disorder had significantly smaller brains than children who had not been abused. The researchers also found that brain volume decreased as duration of abuse increased, with the areas of the brain most closely involved in the physiological stress response more affected than other areas of the brain (Beers & De Bellis, 2002; De Bellis et al., 1999).

Brain abnormalities were also found in another study using MRI scans to study children who were severely neglected. Children who experienced the most global neglect, involving minimal exposure to language, touch, and social interaction, fared the worst. In these children, head circumference and brain size were smaller (below the eighth percentile, on average) than in children who had not been neglected (Perry & Pollard, 1998). Although much additional research is needed, these pioneering studies suggest that findings from animal models are relevant to humans. Across the species that have been investigated, early adversity and deprivation leave their mark on the developing brain.

Shaken Baby Syndrome

The infant's brain is vulnerable to sudden injury when a child is the victim of **shaken baby syndrome (SBS)**. Many cases of SBS occur when a parent or caregiver reacts out of frustration to a crying baby, violently shaking the child. Some adults shake babies in the mistaken belief that it is less damaging than spanking or hitting an infant (Silverman & Ollendick, 1999). In fact, whiplash motions are especially harmful because infants' heads are heavy and large, but their neck muscles are relatively weak; their brain and blood vessels are fragile and easily damaged (Carty & Ratcliffe, 1995; Palmer, 1998).

During shaking, parts of the brain—which has been compared to a bowl of gelatin—may separate as the brain slams into the front and then the back of the skull. When an angry adult shakes a child, the force is five to 10 times greater than if the child had simply tripped and fallen (Wiggins, 2000). Physicians diagnose SBS when they find bleeding in the retina of the infant's eyes, blood on the brain, and increased head size caused by fluid build-up in the brain. There may also be damage to the spinal cord and broken ribs (American Academy of Pediatrics Committee on Child Abuse and Neglect, 1993; Palmer, 1998). Shaken infants are often brought for medical attention after losing consciousness, having difficulty breathing, or developing seizures, and some caregivers report to medical authorities that the baby was shaken during resuscitation efforts (Palmer, 1998).

Approximately 50,000 cases of SBS occur in the United States each year, and 25 percent of all shaken babies die (Wiggins, 2000). Some experts believe that many milder cases of SBS go undetected or are misdiagnosed. Infants who do not die from the abuse nearly always sustain permanent damage that may include partial or complete loss of vision, hearing impairments, seizures, or cerebral palsy, as well as cognitive impairments and behavior problems (Palmer, 1998).

In 65 to 90 percent of cases of SBS, the perpetrator is an adult male in his early 20s—usually the baby's father or the mother's boyfriend. Female perpetrators of SBS are more likely to be a babysitter or child care provider rather than the infant's mother (Sinal et al., 2000).

Because it is known that brain damage occurs with shaking that lasts as little as 20 seconds, some parents worry that they might unintentionally damage their infant's brain during active, physical play. Experts caution against rough play that is age-inappropriate, but adults twirling, spinning, tossing, or bouncing infants are unlikely to cause SBS injuries. A more likely danger is that infants will be injured if the adult accidentally drops them (National Center on Shaken Baby Syndrome, 2002).

Health and Safety

In Chapter 4, we saw that nearly all newborns are screened in the minutes after birth, yielding an Apgar Score, while assessments, such as the Brazelton NBAS, check the newborn's reflexes and other abilities during the first days and weeks after birth. Newborns' health is also screened in all 50 states and the District of Columbia, although the number of disorders and conditions assessed varies from state to state.

Newborn Screening

Mandatory screening exists nationwide for just three conditions: PKU (an inherited metabolic disorder leading to accumulation of the amino acid phenylalanine, developmental delay, mental retardation, and autistic-like behavior), congenital hypothyroidism (an inadequate production of thyroid hormone that can lead to mental retardation and a growth disorder), and galactosemia (a metabolic disorder that can result in failure to thrive, mental retardation, and death). Several states screen for 20 or more other conditions (American Academy of Pediatrics Committee on Genetics, 1996; Mitka, 2000). Newborn screening is usually accomplished within 24 hours of the infant's birth by analyzing a blood sample obtained by pricking the baby's heel.

As the study of genetics continues to advance, and as new equipment and new techniques are developed, the debate grows over how many and which disorders to include in newborn screening. Tests are currently available for about 30 conditions, and some groups, such as the March of Dimes, advocate screening for any condition for which a test and treatment are available, even rare diseases, if the information would make a difference to the child. Critics argue that enthusiasm for screening needs to be tempered by an assessment of the availability of resources for treatment (Mitka, 2000).

In many congenital disorders, early diagnosis enables intervention to begin earlier, usually leading to better outcomes (American Academy of Pediatrics Committee on Children with Disabilities, 2001). This is often true for hearing loss, which is now part of newborn screening in about 25 states. As many as 5,000 infants born in the U.S. each year have hearing deficiencies at birth. Significant hearing loss affects approximately 1 to 3 per 1,000 healthy newborn infants and 2 to 4 per 100 infants in intensive care units. Without newborn screening, the average age of detection of hearing loss is at approximately 14 months, and family history alone identifies only about 50 percent of infants with hearing loss (American Academy of Pediatrics Task Force on Newborn and Infant Hearing, 1999; Yoshinaga-Itano et al., 1998).

Hearing loss in infants is most frequently assessed through otoacoustic emissions (OAE), which involves placing a miniature microphone in the infant's ear and measuring sound waves produced in the cochlea (inner ear) in response to clicks or tones. Another technique, auditory brainstem response (ABR), involves pasting electrodes on the infant's scalp in order to measure electroencephalographic (EEG) waves in response to clicks or other sounds. The American Academy of Pediatrics recommends that all newborns be screened for congenital hearing loss, with identification occurring for 100 percent of infants by 3 months of age and treatment beginning by 6 months (American Academy of Pediatrics Task Force on Newborn and Infant Hearing, 1999).

Screening for Lead Poisoning

Children living in homes built before 1978, especially if the paint is deteriorating or if remodeling is being carried out, should be assessed for an additional threat to their health and development—lead poisoning. Lead is a highly toxic metal that causes brain damage, behavioral problems, learning disabilities, seizures, and even death. In 1978, lead-based paints were banned for use in housing, but the Centers for Disease Control and Prevention estimates that more than 4 million homes of young children currently have deteriorated lead paint or elevated levels of lead-contaminated house dust (Centers for Disease Control and Prevention, 2002b).

The effects of lead exposure are cumulative but initially cause no obvious symptoms, although children may be lethargic or complain of abdominal pain. It is imperative, therefore, that children at risk be evaluated through a simple test that checks the level of lead in their blood. Approximately 900,000 U.S. children under the age of 6 years have blood lead levels that exceed the recommended limit (Centers for Disease Control & Prevention, 2000; Centers for Disease Control & Prevention, 2002b). Lead affects every system in the body, and infants and very young children are at greatest risk because they tend to put their fingers, toys, and other objects—and any lead dust on them—into their mouths. Lead also finds its way into children's blood when they eat lead-based paint chips. Children younger than 3 years of age are especially vulnerable to the effects of lead because they are growing rapidly and their bodies absorb more lead than the bodies of adults with the same exposure (Children's Environmental Health Initiative, 2002).

Given that the prevalence of elevated blood lead levels is low among children in general (about 4 percent), the Centers for Disease Control and Prevention recommends that screening be targeted rather than universal (American Academy of Pediatrics Committee on Environmental Health, 1998). Children with the greatest exposure to older, poorly maintained housing—low-income urban children—have the highest rates of lead poisoning. Children from low-income families are eight times more likely to have elevated blood lead levels than children from high-income families (Centers for Disease Control & Prevention, 2002b; Hubbs-Tait et al., 2005).

The effects of lead on cognitive functioning may be only partly reversible (Hubbs-Tait et al., 2005; Tong et al., 1998). It is best, therefore, to prevent ingestion of lead in the first place. Lead-based paint that is peeling or flaking should be removed, but improper removal of lead-based paint can actually increase the risk to children by spreading paint chips and dust. In many instances, the safest way to prevent lead poisoning is by covering and containing the painted areas. Another way to minimize the spread of lead dust in the environment is to clean floors and window sills in potentially contaminated areas with damp mops and cloths rather than with brooms or vacuum cleaners. Children at play need to be supervised, and their hands and toys should be washed frequently. Toys themselves may be a source of lead, especially if they are imported from countries where lead-based paints are still in use, so parents need to be aware of this possible threat.

Exposure to lead can also be reduced by making sure that food is not prepared or served in pottery that may be glazed with a lead-based finish. Using cold water for food preparation is helpful, too, since hot water is more likely to carry lead from plumbing in older houses in which lead pipes have not been replaced with copper or other safe alternatives.

What can be done to help children with elevated blood lead levels? Besides educating parents and caregivers about ways to minimize further environmental exposure, nutritional interventions are usually recommended. Iron and calcium supplements, for example, are known to reduce absorption of ingested lead, as is a low-fat diet. (American Academy of Pediatrics Committee on Environmental Health, 1998; Hubbs-Tait et al., 2005).

The prevalence of lead poisoning in the United States has declined over the past 20 years as a result of the reduction or elimination of lead in paint, gasoline, food cans, and other consumer products (Alliance to End Childhood Lead Poisoning, 2002). With increased awareness and efforts to prevent contamination in high-risk communities, it may be possible to vanquish this serious threat to children's physical and intellectual well-being.

Infant Mortality

In most parts of the industrialized world, **infant mortality rates** (**IMRs**, the number of infants who die before reaching the age of 1 year) are significantly lower today than ever before. Since 1950, IMRs in the United States have dropped more than 75 percent (National Center for Health Statistics, 2002, 2003). Even during the period from 1980 to 2001, infant mortality in the United States declined from 12.6 deaths per 1,000 live births to 6.8 deaths per 1,000 live births (Centers for Disease Control & Prevention, 2002c, 2005d). Rates increased slightly in 2002, principally as the result of an increase in the number of infants who were born at extremely low birthweights (Centers for Disease Control & Prevention, 2005d).

Although IMRs dropped between 1995 and 2000, as shown in Figure 5.2, they still vary by race and ethnicity. The highest rate (13.5) is found for infants of African American mothers and the lowest rate (3.5) for infants of Chinese mothers. Mortality rates for infants of non-Hispanic white mothers (5.7) and Native American mothers (8.3) are between these extremes, as are rates for Hispanic subgroups (ranging from 4.6 to 8.2). Rates also vary by state and region, with the highest rates for states in the South and lowest rates for states in the West and Northeast (Mathews, MacDorman, & Menacker, 2002). One recent study of IMRs in the 60 largest U.S. cities between 1995 and 1998 documented wide differences both within and among racial/ethnic groups. This finding suggests that it may be possible to

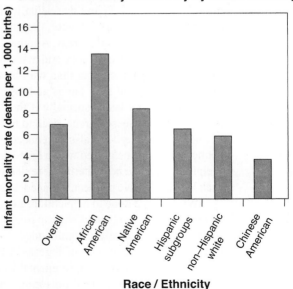

U.S. Infant Mortality Rates Vary by Race / Ethnicity

FIGURE 5.2   Infant mortality rates vary by race and ethnicity.

Source: Based on Centers for Disease Control & Prevention, 2002.

reduce IMRs further even among groups that currently have the highest rates (Centers for Disease Control & Prevention, 2002c). Significant advances will be required in order to move closer to the national health objective called Healthy People 2010, which targets an overall rate of 4.5 infant deaths per 1,000 live births and a reduction in disparities among racial and ethnic populations (Centers for Disease Control & Prevention, 2005d; U.S. Department of Health and Human Services, 2000).

The three most common causes of infant deaths are congenital malformations, disorders related to preterm birth and low birthweight, and sudden infant death syndrome (SIDS), which we will discuss shortly. The next most frequent causes of infant deaths are maternal complications of pregnancy and complications of the placenta, umbilical cord, or membranes. Infant death in the United States is more likely to occur for infants whose mothers had no prenatal care, were teenagers, had less than 12 years of education, were unmarried, or smoked during pregnancy (Phipps, Blume, & DeMonner, 2002). Male infants are at greater risk than are female infants, and, as we saw in Chapter 4, there is a higher mortality rate for multiple births (Mathews et al., 2002).

How do these findings compare with IMRs in other parts of the world? As shown in Table 5.1, the lowest reported rates tend to be found in industrialized countries. (Sweden, for example, had a rate of just 3 deaths per 1,000 live births in 2000.) Some nations currently listed in the top ten achieved significant improvement in this statistic during the last half of the twentieth century. Infant mortality rates continue to be significantly higher in

TABLE 5.1   International Rankings for Infant Mortality Rates in Selected Countries, 1960–2002

Country	1960	2002
Australia	5	17
Austria	5	17
Denmark	8	12
England and Wales	9	21
Finland	4	10
France	15	8
Hong Kong	26	1
Japan	18	4
New Zealand	10	26
Norway	3	7
Singapore	21	3
Spain	28	6
Sweden	1	2
Switzerland	7	13
United States	11	28

Note: Rankings are from lowest to highest. Countries with the same IMR receive the same rank.

Source: Based on National Center for Health Statistics, 2005.

developing countries (Bhutta et al., 2005). According to UNICEF (2002), the highest IMRs in the year 2000 were found in Sierre Leone (180 deaths per 1,000 live births), Angola (172 deaths per 1,000 live births), Afghanistan (165 deaths per 1,000 live births), Niger (159 deaths per 1,000 live births), and Liberia (157 deaths per 1,000 live births). Across these settings, infant mortality is linked to the same basic factors—poverty, inadequate prenatal care, and complications of pregnancy, exacerbated by health-compromising conditions such as malnutrition and scarcity of clean drinking water. Low rates of immunization are also found in the countries with the highest rates of infant mortality (Bhutta et al., 2005; UNICEF, 2006). As we will discuss shortly, where there is a high rate of immunization, childhood illnesses and diseases that were once viewed as inevitable have been reduced or even eliminated for most children.

Common Illnesses

The most common reason for rehospitalization during the first 2 weeks of life is physiologic jaundice (Lee et al., 1995). Approximately 60 percent of U.S. newborns become clinically jaundiced, meaning that the infant's immature liver is unable to contribute to the normal breakdown of oxygen-carrying red blood cells. As a result, the baby's skin and whites of the eyes begin to turn yellow, usually by the second or third day of life. This condition, which is more common in preterm infants, begins to subside within 10 days. Jaundice also occurs more frequently among infants who are breastfed and may last a bit longer than among bottle-fed babies but is rarely cause for concern. A more serious condition, pathologic jaundice, is rare but extremely dangerous because it develops quickly (within 24 hours after birth) and may lead to brain damage or even death if not treated. Mild cases of normal jaundice are often left untreated, but infants with more serious cases receive phototherapy under special ultraviolet lamps (American Academy of Pediatrics Subcommittee on Hyperbilirubinemia, 1994, 2004; Ip et al., 2004; Porter, & Dennis, 2002).

Fortunately, most illnesses affecting infants and toddlers do not result in hospitalization. Most children get their first cold around the age of 6 months and have an average of seven or eight colds per year until the age of about 5 years. As their immune systems develop, children have fewer colds each year until adolescence, when they reach an adult level of about four colds annually. Infants with colds frequently develop a fever as high as 100 to 104 degrees, and many parents worry when they see their child's elevated temperature, especially when it lingers for a few days. Fever is a sign that the body's immune system is functioning, however, and most fevers under 105 degrees are not harmful. Exceptions would be a child who is having convulsions or who otherwise acts or looks very sick. After the age of 2 months, acetaminophen can be given to reduce a fever, but only if the child is very uncomfortable. Pediatricians caution that aspirin should never be given to a child with a fever, because it may cause a severe brain infection known as Reye's syndrome (Schmitt, 1991).

Compared with infants cared for at home, infants in group child care may have between two and four times more infectious illnesses (Thacker et al., 1992). The risk of transmission is affected by the hygiene practices in place. Infants and toddlers, like older children and adults, become ill through person-to-person transmission or through airborne exposure, and infection rates can be decreased when child care providers are conscientious about hand washing and disinfection of surfaces and toys. Because these precautions cannot prevent all infections, parents may be heartened to know of correlational evidence suggesting that infants who develop infections may have fewer allergies later in childhood than infants with fewer early illnesses (Johnston & Openshaw, 2001).

In addition to having an immature immune system, infants and toddlers are especially susceptible to contagious illnesses because they tend to have poor personal hygiene and frequently place their hands, toys, and other objects in their mouths. Viruses, bacteria, and parasites are responsible for the most common contagious illnesses that develop in infancy and early childhood. These illnesses include skin infections (e.g., chicken pox, fifth disease, impetigo, and lice), respiratory infections (e.g., bronchitis, croup, strep throat, and whooping cough), intestinal infections (e.g., diarrhea and hepatitis A), and other infections (e.g., pinkeye).

Immunization against Childhood Diseases.   Some contagious diseases, such as whooping cough, mumps, measles, and hepatitis can be prevented through immunization. As Table 5.2 shows, infants in the United States currently receive a combined series of vaccines, with the first dose for most of these vaccines given at the age of 2 months. As a result, vaccine-preventable childhood diseases—and the disabilities and deaths that are caused by these diseases—are at record lows in the United States and in countries with similar rates of immunization (Centers for Disease Control & Prevention, 2002d, 2005a; UNICEF, 2002, 2006). Infants and children in licensed child care programs have high rates of immunization because children enrolled in these settings are required to provide proof of immunization before they may attend (Thacker et al., 1992).

New vaccines have been added to the recommended schedule in recent years, including a vaccine for varicella (chicken pox) in 1995. Some parents may wonder whether their infant's immune system can safely assimilate multiple vaccines or whether there might be negative effects on their infant's development. Recent studies, however, have shown that these concerns are largely unfounded (Offit et al., 2002). Even in rare cases where children develop high fevers or seizures as a reaction to vaccines, there is no evidence of later speech delay, developmental problems, or autism when compared with children who did not have seizures following immunization (Barlow et al., 2001). Nor, according to recent evaluations of more than 2,000 studies of millions of children, is there any evidence to support some parents' fears that the measles-mumps-rubella (MMR) vaccine causes autism or other diseases and disabilities (Donald & Muthu, 2002; Fombonne & Chakrabarti, 2001; Institute of Medicine Immunization Safety Review Committee, 2004).

Overall immunization rates in the United States today are higher than in past years, with rates for some individual vaccines as high as 93 percent (National Center for Health Statistics, 2003). One paradoxical outcome of the development and widespread use of vaccines is that some parents balk at having their children immunized, since there is no apparent threat of contracting polio or other once-prevalent childhood diseases. Many vaccine-preventable diseases exist in other parts of the world, however, and may be carried to the United States by travelers, including infants who come to the United States through international adoption (Centers for Disease Control & Prevention, 2005c). Without vaccines, epidemics could return and pose a threat once again, causing serious illness, disability, and death, as in years past (Centers for Disease Control & Prevention, 2002d; Gawande, 2004). Even with high immunization rates in the United States, there are still outbreaks of vaccine-preventable childhood diseases, such as pertussis (whooping cough) and chicken pox,

TABLE 5.2   Recommended Immunization Schedule: Birth to 3 Years[*]

Immunization	Age
Hepatitis B (HepB)	
Dose #1	0–2 months
Dose #2	1–4 months
Dose #3	6–18 months
Diphtheria, Tetanus, Pertussis (DTaP)	
Dose #1	2 months
Dose #2	4 months
Dose #3	6 months
Dose #4	12 months
Haemophilus influenzae Type b (Hib)	
Dose #1	2 months
Dose #2	4 months
Dose #3	6 months
Dose #4	12–15 months
Inactivated Poliovirus (IPV)	
Dose #1	2 months
Dose #2	4 months
Dose #3	6–18 months
Measles, Mumps, Rubella (MMR)	
Dose #1	12–15 months
Varicella (Chicken Pox)	12–18 months
Pneumococcal (PCV)	
Dose #1	2 months
Dose #2	4 months
Dose #3	6 months
Dose #4	12–15 months

Note: [*]Some vaccines require additional doses after 3 years of age.

Source: Adapted from Centers for Disease Control & Prevention, 2005b.

which can prove fatal among nonimmunized children, especially infants younger than 6 months (Centers for Disease Control & Prevention, 2005b, 2005f).

Ear Infections.   With the advent of vaccines and the virtual elimination of many childhood illnesses, infections of the middle ear (otitis media) have become one of the most common problems associated with respiratory infections, especially among infants. Most ear infections respond to treatment with antibiotics because they are caused by bacteria accumulating in the eustachian tube of the ear. For about 40 percent of children with ear infections, fluid collects in the ear and reduces their ability to hear. To ensure that this temporary hearing problem does not interfere with language acquisition, infants and toddlers who have frequent ear infections may have tiny plastic ventilation tubes surgically inserted through the ear drum. Ventilation tubes allow fluid to drain out of the middle ear and reduce the likelihood of subsequent ear infections. The tubes often fall out on their own after about 1 year but sometimes need to be surgically removed (Schmitt, 1991).

Parents can help reduce the number of ear infections their infants experience by making sure that they are not exposed to tobacco smoke in the home or child care setting. Secondhand smoke is known to be associated with a higher rate of ear infections as well as sore throats, sinus infections, colds, respiratory infections, asthma, and sudden infant death syndrome, which we will discuss shortly (Lieu & Feinstein, 2002; Richter & Richter, 2001; Schmitt, 1991).

Accidental Injuries

As a result of widespread immunization in the United States, infants less than 1 year of age are now unlikely to die from childhood illnesses. Instead, the major causes of early childhood death are from injury, approximately one-fourth of which are ruled to be homicides. Of the remaining infant deaths due to unintentional injury, the leading causes are suffocation, motor vehicle accidents, fire, drowning, choking on food, and choking on objects (Overpeck et al., 1999).

Most unintentional injuries in childhood can be prevented through education, changes in the environment or in products, and legislation or regulation (The Future of Children, 2000). Child car seats are required by law in all 50 states for infants and children younger than 4 years of age, preventing many accident-related deaths. To be effective, child car seats need to be installed properly and have child-proof buckles. Whereas nearly all children from birth to 2 years of age are protected through appropriate child restraints, more than half of children aged 4 to 8 are incorrectly restrained with seat belts intended for adult passengers (Winston et al., 2004). Federal Motor Vehicle Safety Standards, affecting all passenger vehicles made after September 1, 2002, make protecting children riding in car seats even easier through the LATCH system—a permanent three-point anchor system to which car seats can be secured (National Highway Traffic Safety Administration, 2002).

Most states do not have bicycle helmet laws, but helmets protect children—including those riding tricycles or being pulled in a bicycle trailer behind an adult's bicycle—from brain injuries. Children who are required to wear a helmet from the first time they engage in these activities learn that protective equipment is part of having fun, just as buckling up is part of riding in a car. As with car seats, to be effective, helmets need to be the right size for the child's head and used as intended.

Deaths due to fire can be prevented through adult supervision and by never allowing children to play with matches, lighters, or lighted candles. Open flames should be kept out of children's reach, and sleepwear should be flame-retardant. Child-proof covers can be used to prevent young children from starting a fire by turning the controls on stoves.

Drowning and near-drowning are significant causes of childhood death and injury before the age of 4 years, especially in states where there are many pools or bodies of water (Hwang et al., 2003). Children should always be supervised in these situations, and pools should be fenced in with child-proof locks on gates. For infants and very young children, whose proportionately large heads make them top heavy, even a shallow bath or bucket of

The safest place for an infant or toddler inside a car or van is in a car seat that is properly installed in the back seat.

water may pose a danger, since they may not have the strength to lift their head and move into a safer position. Infants should never be left alone in a bathtub. Those who are able to sit upright in a special bathtub chair can slip through the harness and into the water, and even babies who sit well on their own may lose their balance and be unable to right themselves (American Academy of Pediatrics Committee on Injury and Poison Prevention, 1993).

As infants' fine and gross motor abilities improve (a topic we will take up in greater detail in Chapter 6), new hazards must be considered and eliminated. The ability to use a pincer grip to pick up tiny objects, such as pieces of dry cereal, between thumb and finger develops in most infants between 8 and 10 months of age. Infants of this age learn through oral exploration, so objects that are picked up usually are carried to the mouth, enabling infants to experience the joy of feeding themselves. Because infants' windpipes are quite narrow, parents need to ensure that pieces of food are small enough to be swallowed without blocking the child's airway or causing them to choke (e.g., grapes should be cut into two to four pieces). Any object that fits inside a circle 1.7 inches in diameter should be considered a choking hazard (U.S. Consumer Product Safety Commission, no date). In addition, because infants use this new manipulative skill to learn about the world beyond their high chair, parents need to be vigilant about picking up small objects—including older siblings' toys—and keeping them away from infants and toddlers.

Despite clear messages about the dangers of baby walkers (wheeled devices that hold pre-walking infants upright with their feet in contact with the floor), many parents continue to use them, often in the mistaken belief that the practice "walking" in the walker will accelerate their infant's independent walking. In fact, infants in walkers have a high rate of injury, most commonly from falling down stairs in the walker (20,000 children under the age of 15 months were injured in walkers in 1995 alone). These falls are especially harmful because the walker's wheels actually accelerate the speed at which the infant falls. New standards for baby walkers, along with parent education about them, have led to a decrease in the number of walker-related injuries (there were "only" 8,800 in 1999). New baby walkers are wider than a standard 36-inch-wide doorway, and some have features that stop them at the top of stairs (American Academy of Pediatrics Committee on Injury and Poison

Prevention, 2001b; Brown, 2000). These improvements will not prevent all walker-related accidents, since some injuries occur when infants have access to hazards they would not otherwise be able to reach from a crawling or sitting position on the floor.

Around the age of about 4 months, many infants are able to roll over. With practice, they can use this skill to cross a room, even before they learn to crawl. Many infants begin to pull themselves up to a standing position around the age of 7 or 8 months. From this position, infants are able to reach new levels of danger on their own, creating the need to reevaluate the safety of the environment. Are there small appliances, such as irons, with dangling cords that infants are able to pull on? Are cups of coffee or other hot liquids close to the edge of a table? Could a tablecloth be pulled off, bringing heavy or potentially harmful objects down onto the infant's head? By getting down on the floor, parents can see these potential hazards from their child's perspective.

Another concern that needs to be addressed with these developmental milestones is the danger of falling. The top of any stairs in the child's home needs to have a child-proof safety gate installed. Consideration must be given as well to other new hazards, such as balconies, porches, or decks. Building codes throughout the United States now require that all new construction include railings that are at least 36 inches high and spaced no more than 4 inches apart (American Academy of Pediatrics Committee on Injury and Poison Prevention, 2001a). In older homes, it is up to parents and caregivers to check to make sure that these features are present.

Falls from low heights, such as a low deck or even down a staircase, may cause injury but usually are not fatal. In fact, experts suggest that child abuse be considered in children with serious injuries from unwitnessed falls that were reportedly from low levels. Falls from heights of two stories or more are a significant cause of fatalities in children younger than 15 years of age. Falls from great heights are an especially serious problem for children living in urban areas in older, multistory housing.

Infants and young children are more likely than older children to fall from windows, and boys are more likely to fall than girls. Children who live in the riskiest types of housing have the greatest incidence of falling from heights. Falls from windows tend to occur most in warm climates and in summer months, when windows are open in homes without air conditioning (American Academy of Pediatrics Committee on Injury and Poison Prevention, 2001a).

Prevention efforts include close supervision and modification of the environment. In addition to railings on balconies, decks, and porches, window guards can be installed on all windows. In cities where window guards are required by law, there have been sizable reductions in the number of injuries and fatalities caused by falls. In many other urban areas, window guards are not mandatory, which means that prevention efforts are the responsibility of parents and caregivers rather than landlords. Education about potential problems and solutions, such as moving the child's crib and other furniture away from windows, can help parents become more aware of ways to keep their young children safe from falls at home.

Not all falls and injuries occur at home, of course, and parents may wonder about the safety of their infant's child care setting. They may be both surprised and relieved to discover that research shows lower rates of injury for children in group child care than for children who are cared for at home (Thacker et al., 1992). In child care settings, the highest rates of injury tend to occur in warmer months, with the playground being the most frequent site of injury. As with other sources of unintentional injuries that we have discussed, changes to the environment are an effective way to protect children. Softer play surfaces; distinct, age-appropriate play areas for older and younger children; and fences to separate play areas from bicycle and vehicle traffic have resulted in fewer injuries on the playground, both in child care settings and in public parks.

Many parents may prefer not to think about the potential hazards facing their infants and toddlers. With a little effort, however, they can assess the settings in which their children spend time, anticipate potential problems, and act to remove them. If they do, they can celebrate and support their children's development, knowing that they have created a safe environment for playing, eating, bathing, and exploring. As we will see next, parents and caregivers can also take steps to protect their infants while they sleep.

Sudden Infant Death Syndrome

The American Academy of Pediatrics recommends that all healthy babies be placed on their back to sleep. The reason for this policy is a clear association between prone (facedown) stomach-sleeping and **sudden infant death syndrome (SIDS)**. SIDS, the leading cause of death in infants between 1 month and 1 year of age, is the diagnosis given when an infant younger than 1 year dies and a complete investigation is unable to identify a specific cause (National SIDS Resource Center, 2002). The American Academy of Pediatrics also advises parents to avoid other identified risk factors for SIDS, such as soft bedding, bed-sharing, and exposure to secondhand cigarette smoke. Infants sleeping in an overheated room or wearing two or more layers of clothing while they sleep also face an increased risk of SIDS (American Academy of Pediatrics, 2000; Iyasu et al., 2002; Malloy & Freeman, 2004; Task Force on Sudden Infant Death Syndrome, 2005). It is possible that pacifier use may also reduce the risk of SIDS, but the evidence is correlational and not universally accepted among infant health experts and researchers (Fleming et al., 1999; Hauck, Omojokun, & Siadaty, 2005; Task Force on Sudden Infant Death Syndrome, 2005).

Some cases of suffocation have been documented for infants sleeping on surfaces other than those designed for infants, and one study concluded that infants sleeping in adult beds are approximately 20 times more likely to suffocate, compared with infants sleeping in cribs (Scheers, Rutherford, & Kemp, 2003). Bed-sharing among parents and infants in the United States is on the rise in the general population, increasing from 5.5 percent in 1993 to 12.8 percent in 2000, and is especially prevalent (48 percent) among unmarried, low-income African American mothers living in urban areas (Brenner, Simons-Morton, Bhaskar, Revenis, Das, & Clemens, 2003; Willinger et al., 2003). Proponents of bed-sharing assert that it leads to more and longer periods of breastfeeding, which is known to be beneficial to infant health and development (Chen & Rogan, 2004). Opponents highlight the increased risk of suffocation and note further that bed-sharing is associated with a greater incidence of SIDS when it occurs along with maternal cigarette smoking, recent parental alcohol consumption, and parental exhaustion. The American Academy of Pediatrics advises parents to breastfeed their infants and keep them close at night, sharing the same room but avoiding co-sleeping (Task Force on Sudden Infant Death Syndrome, 2005).

The peak age for SIDS is between 2 and 4 months. Boys are more likely to be victims of SIDS than are girls, and most deaths occur in the fall or winter, when infants are most likely to be dressed in multiple layers or to be covered with blankets and comforters. There is a higher incidence of SIDS among infants whose mothers were less than 20 years old at the time of their first pregnancy as well as among infants whose mothers received late or no pre-natal care (Iyasu et al., 2002; Phipps, Blume, & DeMonner, 2002). Preterm and low birth-weight infants are also at heightened risk for SIDS. Among African Americans, rates of SIDS are two to three times higher than the rates among white babies in the United States. The rate among Native American babies is also two to three times higher than the rate among white infants.

A public health campaign, Back to Sleep, was launched by the National Institute of Child Health and Human Development (NICHD) in 1994 to inform parents, caregivers, and health professionals of the risks associated with stomach-sleeping for infants. This campaign, as well as advocacy by the American Academy of Pediatrics, has led to a reduc-tion in the number of SIDS deaths by about 40 percent, from about 6,000 each year during 1983 to 1992 to approximately 2,300 in the year 2002 (American Academy of Pediatrics, 2000; Kochanek et al., 2004). Figure 5.3 shows the decrease in SIDS since 1988.

Parents and caregivers are more likely to place infants on their back to sleep when their infant's doctor makes an explicit recommendation to do so. According to the National Infant Sleep Position Study (NISP), about 80 percent of those surveyed in 1997 to 1998 said that they had received this advice from a physician or nurse or had learned of the rec-ommendation from reading materials or radio and television. Caregivers who said that they had received this advice from all four sources were six times more likely to follow the rec-ommendation (Willinger et al., 2000).

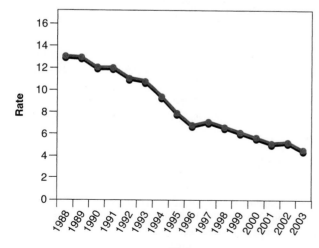

FIGURE 5.3 Since 1988, rates for SIDS have decreased.

Source: Based on Kochanek, Murphy, Anderson, & Scott, 2004; and National Center for Health Statistics, 2005.

Differences exist in sleep position choice, with approximately 30 percent of African American parents placing their infants on their stomach to sleep, as compared with about 17 percent of white parents (National SIDS Resource Center, 2002). One study in Chicago, covering the years from 1993 to 1996, found that a higher percentage of African American babies were placed on their stomach to sleep than were babies from all other ethnic/racial groups included in the study (43 percent versus 12 percent). The study confirmed previous findings that African American parents were less likely than white parents to have been told by health care providers to avoid placing their babies on their stomach to sleep. The link between back-sleeping and SIDS was also confirmed by the finding that 75 percent of SIDS cases were African American, whereas only 13 percent were white Hispanic and 12 percent white, non-Hispanic (Hauck et al., 2002). In response to these trends, the National Black Child Development Institute joined forces with NICHD and other organizations to spread the important message of the Back to Sleep campaign and to help all parents and caregivers become aware of the power that they have to prevent SIDS (see Table 5.3).

Many young infants are cared for by people other than their parents, and it is vital that parents ensure that those caregivers place their baby in the familiar back position to sleep because cases of SIDS have occurred in child care settings when infants were placed in the unfamiliar prone position (Moon, Patel, & Shaefer, 2000). One study found that young infants who were placed in the unaccustomed stomach position by a nonparental caregiver were nearly 20 times more likely to succumb to SIDS than were infants placed in the familiar back-sleeping position. The importance of discussing back-sleeping when child care arrangements are first being made is highlighted by the study's finding that approximately 30 percent of SIDS-related deaths in child care occurred in the first week, with half of those deaths occurring on the first day (Mitchell et al., 1999).

TABLE 5.3   Recommendations to Reduce the Risk of SIDS

Place infants on their backs every time they go to sleep.

Use a firm sleep surface and do not place soft materials or objects under a sleeping infant.

Keep soft materials or objects such as pillows, quilts, comforters, sheepskins, and stuffed toys out of the infant's crib.

Do not smoke during pregnancy and avoid exposing infants to secondhand smoke.

Avoid bed-sharing but provide a crib or other separate sleeping environment in the same room as the parents.

Consider using a pacifier at nap time and bedtime.

Avoid overheating by dressing infants lightly for sleeping and keeping the bedroom temperature comfortable.

Avoid commercial devices that claim to reduce the risk of SIDS.

Do not use home monitors as a strategy for reducing the risk of SIDS in otherwise healthy infants.

Minimize positional plagiocephaly (flattening of the back of the head) by encouraging "tummy time" when infants are awake and being observed by a caregiver.

Support the Back to Sleep campaign and share these recommendations with all caregivers of infants, including child care providers, grandparents, foster parents, and babysitters.

Source: Based on Task Force on Sudden Infant Death Syndrome, 2005.

We know more than ever about specific actions to take and practices to avoid, but it is also becoming clear that even the best outreach programs and the most conscientious caregiving are unlikely to prevent all SIDS deaths. This is because some cases of SIDS may be linked to conditions that are beyond the control of parents. For some infants, the problem may be a brain abnormality, such as a defect in a portion of the brain that is involved in controlling breathing and waking during sleep (Kinney et al., 2003). These abnormalities alone probably do not cause SIDS, but they may make infants with the defects less able to cope with a lack of oxygen and elevated levels of carbon dioxide, possible outcomes of respiratory infections or rebreathing air that is trapped in soft bedding during stomach-sleeping. Other SIDS deaths may be the result of underlying metabolic disorders that eventually lead to a disruption in breathing and heart functioning. Some researchers believe that prenatal exposure to cigarette smoke or alcohol may contribute to the brainstem abnormalities involved in SIDS (Kinney et al., 2003). Research is underway to determine whether and how these underlying conditions might be detected and treated (National Institute of Child Health and Human Development, 1997b).

Nutrition and Feeding

In Chapter 3, we saw that maternal nutrition during pregnancy has profound consequences for the developing fetus. Nutrition continues to be critical after the child is born. There are differences across cultures, however, in beliefs about the foods that are most life-sustaining for newborns and about the age at which solid foods should be introduced. In some cultures, infants are fed traditional herbal preparations or pre-chewed solid foods almost from birth, whereas in other cultures, breast milk is the only food given until the infant is several months old. Cultures differ in whether they value the mother's first milk for its unique health-giving properties or discard it because it is regarded as undigestible or even harmful to the infant. There are also differences in beliefs about whether infants should be fed on demand (i.e., whenever the infant shows signs of hunger or cries) or according to a set schedule (DeLoache & Gottlieb, 2000). In addition, when caregivers from older generations disagree with parents, or when cultural traditions and beliefs differ from current research-based recommendations, it may not always be easy to determine which practices to follow.

In the remainder of this chapter, we will discuss nutritional requirements of infants and very young children and the unique contributions of breast milk to infant development. In addition to focusing on the benefits of good nutrition, we will examine the devastating effects of malnutrition early in life. Throughout our discussion, we will see that when parents feed their infants and young children, they are influencing important aspects of cognitive, social, and emotional development at the same time they are providing the necessary nutrients to support physical growth and development.

Nutritional Requirements in Infancy

Good nutrition is important throughout the life span, but different amounts of nutrients are required at different stages of development. Infants require the greatest amount of energy per pound of body weight, and children under the age of 2 years need more fat in their diets than any other age group. In addition, because infants' brains, bones, and other body structures and systems are developing rapidly, malnutrition in infancy or early childhood has different—and more damaging—effects than malnutrition at other points in the life span (Napier & Meister, 2000; Pollitt et al., 1993).

Feeding Newborn Infants.   Before infants are born, parents often make choices about how they plan to feed their newborn. Mother's milk is the most natural and least expensive way to provide nourishment for human infants. Commercially produced infant formulas have improved dramatically in recent years, however, and now offer parents a safe, nutritionally acceptable alternative to breast milk (Napier & Meister, 2000). The decision to breast- or bottle-feed is a personal one, and parents should be supported in their choice once it is made. We will discuss shortly the evidence that parents should consider when making their decision, but for now we will focus on something else that parents need to consider—how they will know when it is time to feed their infant and when it is time to stop.

The typical newborn wakes up between 10 and 12 times during every 24-hour period, ready to be fed. Regular feeding is so important during the first 2 weeks of life that newborns should be awakened for feeding if they sleep more than 4 hours at a time. After a feeding and diaper change, most newborn babies fall back to sleep. As infants begin to spend more time awake in the first weeks and months after birth, however, parents no longer need to assume that time awake should be used primarily for feeding. Instead, they can learn to read their infant's cues for signs of hunger, signs that include bringing the hands to the mouth, rooting or pressing the face against the adult's body, and facial grimacing. Feeding is likely to proceed more smoothly if parents can feed their infant when these signs appear, before fussing and crying—the last indicators of hunger—begin (American Academy of Pediatrics/Work Group on Breastfeeding, 1997; National Center for Education in Maternal and Child Health, 2002). Responding to these cues is a good idea because hungry infants can become exhausted from prolonged crying. As we will see in Chapter 9, responsive parenting also builds a sense of trust between babies and their caregivers.

Signs of fullness are also evident, if parents know what to look for: turning the head away from the nipple, closing the mouth, and showing interest in things other than eating (National Center for Education in Maternal and Child Health, 2002). Experts advise against coaxing infants to finish a bottle, since this behavior may set up a pattern of overfeeding and unhealthy weight gain that could predispose the child to overweight or obesity later in life (Napier & Meister, 2000). Parents can feel confident about their infant's milk consumption as long as the infant is swallowing, producing between six and eight wet diapers daily, and gaining weight (National Center for Education in Maternal and Child Health, 2002).

Nutritional Requirements from Birth to 6 Months.   During the first year of life, infants require the same basic nutrients that are part of a healthy diet for older children and adults—energy, protein, calcium, iron, vitamins, and other micronutrients. Until the age of about 4 to 6 months, they can get all of these nutritional requirements through breast milk or infant formula. In fact, because newborns have a gag reflex that causes them to push solids out of their mouth with their tongue, and because infants do not develop the ability to chew and swallow until the second half of the first year, a liquid diet is ideal for young infants (Napier & Meister, 2000). According to most experts, including the American

Academy of Pediatrics, human milk is the preferred form of feeding for infants, even those who are preterm or ill (Furman et al., 2003).

Breast Milk. Human milk fulfills infants' nutritional needs, just as the milk of all other mammals is ideally suited to meet the nutritional needs of their offspring. Cow's milk, evaporated milk, or any substitutes other than commercially made infant formula are not easily digested and may cause health problems.

For mothers who choose to breastfeed, nursing should begin as soon as possible after birth (American Academy of Pediatrics/Work Group on Breastfeeding, 1997). The mother's first milk, **colostrum**, is a thick, yellowish fluid, richer in protein and protective antibodies than the milk that is produced a few days later. Colostrum satisfies the newborn's health needs until the milk comes in and helps newborns fight infections.

Both colostrum and breast milk contain disease-preventing proteins—lactoferrin and lysozyme—that help fight bacteria and promote growth and maturation of the intestinal tract (Napier & Meister, 2000). Research shows that human milk reduces the risk of many diseases and lowers the risk and severity of diarrhea and a number of infections, including those of the lower respiratory system, middle ear, and urinary tract. In addition, breastfeeding may protect infants against SIDS, diabetes, allergies, asthma, digestive diseases, and even high cholesterol levels in adolescence (American Academy of Pediatrics/Work Group on Breastfeeding, 1997; Chen & Rogan, 2004; Owen et al., 2002; Singhal et al., 2004).

There is also evidence from studies in countries where mothers breastfeed their infants for longer durations than U.S. mothers that breastfeeding may enhance cognitive development. Researchers in Denmark found an association between duration of infant breastfeeding and intelligence in young adulthood (Mortensen et al., 2002). Researchers in Norway and Sweden reported that full-term, small-for-gestational-age (SGA) infants

Mother's milk contains disease-preventing substances and is the most natural and least expensive way to provide nourishment for human infants.

(those weighing 6 pounds or less) scored an average of 11 points higher on IQ tests if they were exclusively breastfed for the first 6 months, in comparison to SGA infants who were fed formula or solid food before the age of 6 months (Rao et al., 2002). Studies of normal-size, full-term infants have reported similar trends, although the advantage for breastfed infants at 5 years of age was an average of only three IQ points.

Mothers, too, benefit from breastfeeding, both during the postpartum period and across their adult years. In the hours and days following birth, breastfeeding triggers the release of the hormone oxytocin, which helps the uterus return to its original size and reduces postpartum bleeding. Breastfeeding burns up approximately 500 calories per day, helping new mothers return more quickly to their pre-pregnancy weight. There is also evidence of benefits for nursing mothers' bones, including a reduction in hip fractures in the postmenopausal period, and a reduced risk of ovarian cancer and premenopausal breast cancer (American Academy of Pediatrics/Work Group on Breastfeeding, 1997).

Ideally, infants should be breastfed exclusively for the first 6 months after birth. If this is not possible, pediatricians recommend that mothers breastfeed as long as they can in order to maximize the health benefits for both infant and mother (American Academy of Pediatrics/Work Group on Breastfeeding, 1997). The American Academy of Pediatrics also recommends that infants who are weaned from breast-milk before the age of 12 months should be switched to a commercially prepared infant formula, with cow's milk given after the age of 1 year.

In the United States, the popularity of breastfeeding declined during the twentieth century until about 1970. Rates began to rise at that point until the mid-1980s, slipped again, but then began to increase (American Academy of Pediatrics/Work Group on Breastfeeding, 1997; Wright & Schanler, 2001). Data from the 2005 National Immunization Survey indicate that approximately 73 percent of new mothers had ever breastfed at the time of hospital discharge. Oonly 39 percent of infants were still being breastfed at 6 months, however, and only 20 percent until 1 year (Centers for Disease Control & Prevention, 2005h). These data show that initial breastfeeding rates have moved closer to the target of 75 percent set by the national health initiative known as Healthy People 2010. They fall short, however, of the goal of having at least 50 percent of mothers continuing to breastfeed for 5 to 6 months and 25 percent for 1 year (U.S. Department of Health and Human Services, 2000).

The highest rates of breastfeeding in the United States are found among higher-income, college-educated women who are at least 30 years of age (American Academy of Pediatrics/Work Group on Breastfeeding, 1997; Centers for Disease Control & Prevention, 2005h) and among women who were born outside of the United States. Educating younger mothers about the benefits of breastfeeding is both important and challenging (Guise et al., 2003). One study of mothers in Women, Infants, and Children Supplemental Nutrition Program, better known as WIC (a nationwide nutrition program for women, infants, and children), found that 50 percent of mothers younger than 20 years of age stopped breastfeeding by 19 days after their infant's birth. Cultural beliefs also play a role in decisions about infant feeding (Baydar et al., 1997).

Given that human milk is the ideal form of nutrition for infants, why do some mothers choose not to breastfeed? In some cases, the benefits of breastfeeding would be outweighed by putting the infant at risk of contracting infectious diseases the mother carries, such as HIV/AIDS, tuberculosis, or West Nile virus (American Academy of Pediatrics

Committee on Pediatric AIDS, 1995; Centers for Disease Control & Prevention, 2002d; Miotti et al., 1999). These risks are not present, however, for most of the mothers who either decide not to breastfeed in the first place or begin breastfeeding in the hospital but discontinue before their child has reached 6 months of age.

Some women get discouraged and switch to formula within weeks or even days of their child's birth when they have more difficulty establishing breastfeeding than they had anticipated. Mothers who combine formula with breast milk have a high likelihood of discontinuing breastfeeding when they notice their milk supply beginning to decrease. They may lose confidence in their ability to sustain the infant on their own, despite the fact that the mother's body responds readily to the infant's needs. If several feedings each day begin to use formula in place of breast milk, the supply will decrease, but it will increase again if the mother nurses her child more frequently. Many hospitals have lactation consultants on their staff who can educate new mothers in the hours after their baby is born and provide assistance later as questions arise, such as how to continue breastfeeding after returning to work and how to wean their child later (Guise et al., 2003).

Women who return to work full time can continue to provide breast milk for their infant's caregiver to give their baby. Fathers, as well as other family members, can also participate by feeding the infant from bottles containing the mother's milk. Employers in some states are required to provide adequate, private facilities for the mother to express milk a few times a day and refrigeration to keep it cold until it can be taken home. Concerns about the inconvenience of expressing milk in the workplace, however, combined with co-workers' or employers' negative attitudes, may discourage some mothers from continuing to breastfeed. Employers who are unmoved by the many health benefits of breastfeeding might be persuaded by studies showing that employees who are supported in continuing to breastfeed are less likely to miss work, in part because their infants are less likely to become ill (Cohen, Mrtek, & Mrtek, 1995).

Away from work, mothers may find embarrassment, negative attitudes, and even hostile reactions if they breastfeed in public. Many people in the United States are not well informed about the value of breastfeeding for at least 6 months and may question or actively discourage women who continue nursing rather than switch to formula and bottle-feeding. Some mothers nursing in public have even been charged with indecent exposure. To ensure that a woman's right to breastfeed is not infringed upon, most states have passed legislation to clarify the differences between indecent exposure and breastfeeding (Baldwin, 2001; Vance, 2006).

The World Health Organization (WHO) has studied breastfeeding rates and practices in 94 countries around the world. In regions where water is unsanitary and other hygiene risks exist, it is safer for mothers to breastfeed their infants than to use bottles and formula, provided that the mothers themselves do not carry infectious diseases. According to the WHO (2000) Global Data Bank on Breastfeeding, however, only 35 percent of infants worldwide are exclusively breastfed until 4 months of age.

Campaigns publicizing the benefits of breastfeeding, and the Baby-Friendly Hospital Initiative (begun by WHO and UNICEF in 1992) have increased breastfeeding rates wherever these efforts have occurred, suggesting that further increases are possible (Kramer et al., 2001). As of the end of 1999, more than 16,000 baby-friendly hospitals had been designated in nearly 200 countries. The Initiative helps mothers begin breastfeeding soon after birth, keep their babies with them around the clock, and refrain from giving them any food or drink other than breast milk, unless it is medically necessary (Merten et al., 2005; Merewood et al., 2005; World Health Organization, 2000).

Infant Formula.   The infant formula available today is the best alternative to breast milk that has ever existed. Parents who choose to give their babies formula can feel confident that no other substance (besides breast milk) would be safer or healthier, in part because infant formula is monitored and regulated by the U.S. Food and Drug Administration (Birch et al., 2000).

Most formula is made from modified cow's milk, but there are also soy-based alternatives available. Some parents switch to soy formulas when they believe their infant is allergic to formula made from cow's milk, while parents who are vegetarians may choose a soy-based formula for its compatibility with a non–animal-based diet. Regardless of the base, a formula that is enriched with iron will ensure that infants do not become iron deficient (American Academy of Pediatrics Committee on Nutrition, 1999b; Napier & Meister, 2000).

The same feelings of warmth and physical closeness that are experienced through breastfeeding can be approximated by holding infants being fed with formula rather than having the bottle propped up. Close contact also makes it easier to pay attention and respond to the infant's signals.

Nutritional Requirements from 6 Months to 1 Year.   The end of exclusive breastfeeding or formula-feeding marks the beginning of **complementary feeding**, a transition that occurs gradually from 6 to 18 or 24 months. In the United States, the first solid food is often iron-fortified baby cereal, made from rice or another single grain and mixed with breast milk or formula. At first, the consistency is quite thin; as they get older, and their digestive systems become more mature, infants can tolerate increasingly thicker cereal and other pureed foods (National Center for Education in Maternal and Child Health, 2002).

Infant cereal can be followed by simple, single-ingredient foods, such as pureed fruits and vegetables. Pureed meats are a good source of iron at this age. By choosing fruits and vegetables that are rich in vitamin C, parents can help their infant's body absorb the iron in their diet. It is not necessary to sweeten or otherwise season these foods in order to make them more enticing Most foods need to have multiple introductions, perhaps as many as 15 to 20, before they are accepted by infants (National Center for Education in Maternal and Child Health, 2002).

By introducing one new food at a time, parents can determine whether their infant is allergic to it. Foods that are most likely to cause an allergic reaction are wheat, eggs, nuts, and citrus fruits. Infants should not be given honey before the age of 1 year because it may contain harmful bacteria (Napier & Meister, 2000).

The balance between breast milk or formula and solid foods begins to shift toward solid foods around the age of 6 months. A small amount of fruit juice can be offered, but breast milk or formula should still be the main sources of liquid food. To provide sufficient energy, snacks should be given in midmorning and afternoon (National Center for Education in Maternal and Child Health, 2002).

In the second half of the first year, babies can tolerate thicker foods and foods containing a mixture of ingredients. They often begin to participate more actively in feeding by reaching for the spoon, and they show interest in the food being eaten by the rest of the family.

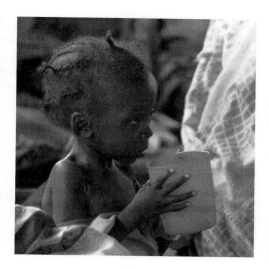

This young girl, suffering from malnutrition, is receiving medical treatment in a refugee camp in Darfur.

To enhance the infant's social and language development, meals should be relaxing occasions in which parents and other family members enjoy food and conversation together. Unless the main meal is very spicy or presents choking hazards, small pieces of each dish should be shared with the infant. As fine motor skills and hand-eye coordination improve, small pieces of soft finger foods can be given to infants to encourage self-feeding. Foods to be avoided for their choking potential include nuts, hot dogs, raisins, raw carrots, whole grapes, popcorn, and peanut butter or any other thick, sticky foods (Fox et al., 2004; Napier & Meister, 2000).

Nutritional Requirements in Toddlerhood and Early Childhood

During the second year of life, growth slows down, but toddlers still need energy to support their increasing levels of activity. Toddlers can feed themselves with increasing success, brought about by improvements in fine motor skills and by the appearance of more teeth. They have smaller and less consistent appetites than infants, which some parents find worrisome. Parents can be assured, though, as long as a healthy variety of foods are offered, and provided that the child continues to grow, gain weight, and develop normally. Nutrition experts suggest that 1- to 2-year-olds be given serving sizes of approximately 1 tablespoon for each year of age (Fox et al., 2004; Napier & Meister, 2000).

Children ages 2 to 3 years generally have healthier diets than children between the ages of 4 and 9 years, and only 4 percent have a diet that the USDA Healthy Eating Index (HEI) would rate as poor. Even so, only 36 percent of 2- to 3-year-olds have a diet that is considered good according to the (HEI), and the majority (60 percent) have a diet that needs improvement. According to a recent dietary "report card" the percentage of 2- to 3-year-olds consuming recommended amounts of each of the major food groups—grains, vegetables, fruit, milk, meat, and total fat—is too low (Carlson et al., 2001; Fox et al., 2004).

The nutrients that are most frequently missing from U.S. toddlers' diets at the recommended daily levels are iron, zinc, and calcium. Unless iron deficiencies are severe and exacerbated by other illnesses, however, they can be addressed by giving toddlers more iron-rich foods, including meat, and combining them with foods that are rich in vitamin C.

Meat is also a good source of zinc, as are dairy products, eggs, and whole-grain cereals. Without adequate amounts of zinc, the immune system does not function properly and growth may be delayed. Zinc deficiencies also cause impairments in attention and learning (Hubbs-Tait et al., 2005; Rao & Georgieff, 2000).

As many as one-third of U.S. toddlers fail to consume enough calcium (Fox et al., 2004; Napier & Meister, 2000). Children who drink too much juice or other beverages rather than milk are at greatest risk of not having adequate calcium intake. Calcium is essential for the development of healthy bones, skin, and teeth. Besides milk, other good sources of dietary calcium are dairy products such as yogurt and cheese, broccoli, tofu, and dried beans and peas. These foods are especially important for children with lactose intolerance who have difficulty digesting milk (American Academy of Pediatrics/Committee on Nutrition, 1999a).

The Problem of Malnutrition

At the beginning of this chapter, we noted that overweight and obesity are health problems affecting an increasing number of children in the United States. Worldwide, however, many more children (perhaps as many as 40 percent of those under the age of 5 years) suffer from problems related to an insufficient amount of food or an inadequate intake of essential nutrients (World Health Organization, 2002). Many children first become malnourished as they make the transition to complementary feeding. For infants whose mothers do not have access to a healthy diet during their pregnancy, malnutrition is part of their lives even before birth.

Researchers working with rodents and other animal models are beginning to learn more about the effects of isolated nutrient deficiencies on the development and functioning of the brain (deUngria et al., 2000; Hubbs-Tait et al., 2005; Johnson, 2005; Rao & Georgieff, 2000). It is becoming clear that the timing of deprivation or supplementation of nutrients affects the influence of those substances on the developing brain. In addition, whereas the very same micronutrients promote normal development at recommended levels, higher levels produce toxic effects (Hubbs-Tait et al., 2005; Rao & Georgieff, 2000). As informative as these findings are, as we consider some of the major problems of malnutrition affecting infants and young children, we should remember that nutrient deficiencies rarely occur in isolation. Instead, they are usually compounded by environmental hazards and stressors such as poverty, poor prenatal care, and nonoptimal caregiving (Hubbs-Tait et al., 2005).

Protein-Energy Malnutrition. The most common form of malnutrition, **protein-energy malnutrition (PEM),** affects children who do not consume enough protein and calories. Children with PEM are susceptible to marasmus (a wasting disease in which fat and muscle are depleted) and kwashiorkor (a disease that occurs in response to a sudden deprivation of food, marked by apathy and swelling of the extremities, torso, and face). According to the World Health Organization (2002), PEM is responsible for half of all child deaths and affects approximately 25 percent of children worldwide. The majority of children suffering from PEM live in Asia and Africa.

Infants and young children are more susceptible to PEM-caused growth impairment than are older children because of their high energy and protein needs and their vulnerability to infection. Infants who experience PEM have reduced IQ scores and lower verbal and spatial abilities (Rao & Georgieff, 2000). Nutritional supplementation appears to reverse some of the cognitive impairments associated with PEM, with beneficial results lasting even several years after supplementation (Pollit et al., 1993, 1996).

Micronutrient Deficiences. To be healthy, all humans need enough protein and calories, as well as a number of micronutrients, such as vitamins, iron, and zinc. The effects of **micronutrient deficiencies** on the brain and body include damage to cell structure and impairment in cell metabolism that affects fundamental processes such as DNA and RNA synthesis, myelination, and neurotransmission (Johnson, 2005; Rao & Gerogieff, 2000). In this section we will focus on two particularly serious forms of malnutrition, deficiencies of the micronutrients iron and vitamin A.

Worldwide, iron deficiency is the most common nutritional disorder after PEM. Iron deficiency anemia affects as many as 40 percent of children under age 5 around the world, mostly in developing countries. In many developing countries, the effects of iron deficiency anemia are magnified by malaria and worm infections that lead to blood loss (World Health Organization, 2002). Iron-deficiency anemia causes fatigue, restlessness, irritability, and a poor attention span—problems that contribute to delays and abnormalities in cognitive and social development. It also interferes with the development of motor skills, such as standing and walking (Guesry, 1998; Hubbs-Tait et al., 2005; Napier & Meister, 2000; Rao & Georgieff, 2000, 2001).

Children with vitamin A deficiencies develop severe visual impairment and blindness as well as life-threatening illnesses and infections (Rao & Georgieff, 2000). Because breast milk is a natural source of vitamin A, one of the best ways to combat vitamin A deficiency is through breastfeeding. High doses of vitamin A can also be given to children in liquid or capsule form, but the effects last only 4 to 6 months. The best approach, therefore, is to promote and provide a diet that is rich in vitamin A foods, such as carrots, sweet potatoes, and fruit (World Health Organization, 2001b).

Preventing and Reducing Malnutrition. In the United States, the federally funded WIC nutrition program protects and improves the health and nutritional status of low-income women, infants, and children by offering supplemental nutritious foods as well as nutrition education and counseling. The WIC program also screens participants and makes referrals to other health, welfare, and social services. Studies of WIC outcomes since the program's inception in 1974 indicate that pregnant women who participate have longer, healthier pregnancies, with fewer preterm births, fewer infant deaths, and higher rates of breastfeeding. Children participating in WIC programs have better diets overall, as well as a higher intake of iron and other key nutrients, than comparable nonparticipants (U.S. Department of Agriculture, 2002).

In other parts of the world, programs to end malnutrition are administered by a variety of governmental and nongovernmental organizations, including UNICEF and WHO. The greatest needs are in countries suffering from food shortages or famine due to emergencies, war, or agricultural problems caused by extreme drought or flooding. In addition to working to ensure that there is enough healthy food available, successful childhood malnutrition programs focus on supporting prenatal nutrition, promoting breastfeeding, and educating parents about appropriate nutrition for infants and children. The problems are daunting, but community-based interventions in many parts of the world have proven effective at reducing malnutrition (Pollitt et al., 1996; Santos, Victora et al., 2001; World Health Organization, 2001). These aid efforts are critical because, as we have seen in this chapter, developing infants and young children cannot wait.

WRAPPING IT UP: Summary and Conclusion

Growth during the first 3 years is faster than at any other point after birth. Like Baby Nadia, whom we met at the opening of this chapter, infants who are deprived of physical contact, such as those living in orphanages, may show failure to thrive and grow slowly, even if they are fed an adequate diet. When these children are moved to a new, caring environment, a dramatic growth spurt typically occurs.

Brain development begins prenatally with the production and migration of neurons. Postnatal brain growth primarily consists of the interconnection of neurons and the formation of synapses involving axons and dendrites. Different regions of the brain develop most rapidly at different ages. Pruning of synapses begins at the end of the first year and helps make the child's brain work more efficiently and quickly.

Experience activates neurons, and repeated experiences strengthen neural networks. Findings from experiments using animal models suggest that early adversity, stress, and deprivation leave their mark on the developing brain. The infant's brain is especially vulnerable to injury caused by shaken baby syndrome (SBS).

Mandatory newborn health screening exists nationwide for three conditions, and states vary in the number of additional diseases included in newborn screening. All newborns should be screened for congenital hearing loss. Early detection of hearing loss makes it more likely that treatment can begin early, usually leading to better outcomes than treatment that begins later.

The effects of lead poisoning are cumulative and if untreated can result in brain damage, behavior problems, learning disabilities, seizures, and even death. Low-income, urban, and African American children have the highest rates of lead poisoning.

In most parts of the developed world, infant mortality rates are significantly lower today than ever before. As with many environmental influences on health, infant mortality rates in the United States vary by race and ethnicity. Across the world, infant mortality is linked to poverty, inadequate prenatal care, complications of pregnancy, malnutrition, lack of clean drinking water, and low rates of immunization against childhood illnesses and diseases. The major causes of early childhood death are from unintentional injuries, most of which can be prevented.

Sudden infant death syndrome (SIDS) is the leading cause of death in infants between 1 month and 1 year of age. The risk of SIDS can be reduced by placing all healthy babies on their back to sleep and by avoiding the use of soft bedding. Other environmental risks have been identified, including maternal smoking, sleeping in an overheated room, and bed-sharing. Some cases of SIDS may be caused by an abnormality in the portion of the brain that is involved in controlling breathing and waking during sleep.

Different amounts of nutrients are required at different stages of development. Children under the age of 2 years need more fat in their diet than any other age group. Until the age of about 4 to 6 months, infants can get all of their nutritional requirements through breast milk or formula. According to most experts, human milk is the preferred form of feeding for infants. Overweight and obesity are growing concerns in the United States. Worldwide, however, infants and young children are more likely to suffer from problems related to an insufficient amount of food or of essential nutrients due to a diet low in protein and calorie content. Infants and young children are more susceptible than older children to growth impairment caused by protein-energy malnutrition (PEM).

As we have seen so far, setting infants on a course for healthy development begins with experiences during the prenatal period and continues when the caregiving environment is nurturing and safe. In our next chapter, we will see that infants also benefit from an environment that stimulates all of their sense and allows them to explore freely.

THINK ABOUT IT: Questions for Reading and Discussion

1. Identify two potential advantages and two potential disadvantages of using growth charts.

2. Explain the ways in which the brain is an incompletely formed organ at birth. What are some of the factors that shape its postnatal development?

3. Infant mortality rates in the United States, as in most other industrialized countries, are lower than ever before. What do you think is the most significant reason for the decline in infant mortality rates?

4. What would you need to do in order to make your own home, apartment, or dormitory room safe for an infant? What would you have to do to make it safe for a toddler? For a preschooler? Which age do you believe faces the greatest risk from accidental injuries? Explain.

5. What instructions can parents give their infant's caregivers to prevent shaken baby syndrome? Sudden infant death syndrome?

6. What are the benefits of breastfeeding? Why don't all parents breastfeed their infants as long as the experts recommend? What could be done to increase the rate of breastfeeding?

7. When does complementary feeding begin? What steps should be taken to ensure that children continue to have all of their nutritional needs met during this important transition?

8. What are the most serious problems of malnutrition affecting infants and young children? What can be done to reduce the prevalence of malnutrition?

KEY WORDS

Axon (147)
A branchlike structure that conveys electrical messages outward from a neuron's cell body and toward the synapse

Body mass index (BMI) (143)
A measure of weight in relation to height

Colostrum (167)
A thick, yellowish fluid, richer in protein and protective antibodies than the breast milk that is produced a few days after birth

Complementary feeding (170)   The transition from exclusive breastfeeding or formula-feeding to the inclusion of solid food in an infant's diet

Dendrites (147)   Branchlike structures that convey electrical messages from the synapse and toward a neuron's cell body

Electroencephalogram (EEG) (146)   A measure of the brain's activity that uses external electrodes placed on the scalp

Experience-dependent (149)   Aspects of brain development that develop solely as a result of a person's experiences

Experience-expectant (149)   Aspects of brain development that "expect" to have certain kinds of stimulation and are ready to develop once they receive it

Failure to thrive (144)   Growth stunting that is caused by deprivation of physical contact

Infant mortality rates (154)   Statistics representing the number of infants who die before reaching the age of 1 year

Magnetic resonance imaging (MRI) (146)   An imaging technology that reveals the brain's structure

Maltreatment (149)   Neglect, medical neglect, physical abuse, sexual abuse, or psychological abuse

Micronutrient deficiency (173)   A form of malnutrition that occurs when insufficient amounts of minerals and vitamins are consumed in the diet

Myelin (148)   A fatty covering that insulates axons and increases the efficiency of neural functioning

Neurotransmitters (147)   Biochemical substances that transmit information between neurons through release and uptake at synapses

Positron emission tomography (PET) (146)   An imaging technology that shows the amount of activity in the brain

Protein-energy malnutrition (PEM) (172)   A form of malnutrition that occurs when insufficient amounts of protein and calories are consumed in the diet

Shaken baby syndrome (SBS) (151)   A form of maltreatment in which an angry or frustrated adult shakes an infant violently, resulting in brain damage or even death

Sudden infant death syndrome (SIDS) (162)   The diagnosis given when an infant younger than 1 year dies and a complete investigation is unable to identify a specific cause

Synapses (147)   Spaces between neurons, in which biochemical messages are released and absorbed

Synaptogenesis (148)   Formation of synapses in a network of neurons

Vesicles (147)   Neurotransmitter storage spaces at the end of the axon

CHAPTER **6**

Sensation, Perception, and Motor Development

Across cultures, the majority of infants take their first independent steps around the age of 12 months. Those steps are typically halting and tentative, and infants continue to rely on crawling when they want to cover ground quickly. It is striking, therefore, that at about the same age that Tiger Woods was learning to walk, he picked up a golf club and successfully copied his father's swing, which he had been watching for months from a high chair in his father's practice space in the family garage. Tiger's ability to swing and putt continued to develop during his toddler years (and beyond), and there are few who would deny that his perceptual and motor development—as reflected in his precocious golf skills—were extraordinarily advanced (Owen, 2000). Most parents do not have children who become legendary professional golfers, but they would be fully justified in being amazed at the remarkable changes in sensation, perception, and action that occur during their children's first 3 years of life.

Initially immobile infants learn to coordinate their limbs and maintain balance to roll over, sit upright, stand, and begin to walk, often in time for their first birthday party. The toddler and preschool years see many other achievements, including the ability to run, hop, and walk up and down steps independently. There is also significant improvement in the ability to pick up and manipulate small objects, with the result that very young children become able to use tools found in their culture, such as crayons, zippers, and chopsticks. The predictable progression of these abilities suggests that there is an underlying maturational timetable directing development. We will see in this chapter, however, that motor and perceptual abilities are also influenced by experience.

Perceptual experience is one important influence on motor skill development, seen not only in the example of Tiger Woods learning to swing a golf club simply by observing his father's efforts, but also in studies of infants blind from birth whose lack of sight contributes to delays in postural control, basic manual skills, and motor development (Bertenthal & Clifton, 1998; Tröster & Brambring, 1993, 1994). We begin by considering the normal range of development of sensory and perceptual abilities, including those supporting the perception-action system that contributes to maintaining balance, reaching for and manipulating objects, moving through space, and for some children, swinging a golf club.

Sensory Abilities and Perceptual Development

At birth, infants are able to see, hear, feel, taste, and smell. As shown in Table 6.1, these abilities are not equally well developed, but they all provide newborns with important information about the people and objects in their world. Some of these senses, such as hearing, are activated during the prenatal period. Other senses, such as vision, receive their first stimulation only after birth. Although the senses are interconnected at birth—newborns turn their head in the direction of a sound, especially if the sound is their mother's voice—we will focus our discussion on one sense at a time. The vast majority of research in infant perception has investigated the development of vision, which will be the focus of this chapter as well. We will consider evidence regarding the development of two widely studied aspects of the sense of hearing—speech perception and music perception—elsewhere in this book (Chapters 8 and 12, respectively).

Research conducted over the last few decades has provided a picture of infants as relatively competent perceivers who are able to detect and respond to sights, sounds, tastes,

TABLE 6.1   Infants' Sensory and Perceptual Abilities

Sense	Examples of Abilities
Vision	Newborns notice objects and people in motion. Between 8 and 14 weeks, infants improve in their ability to use smooth eye movements to track moving targets. Newborns prefer looking at patterns with high contrast. They appear to find the human face particularly attractive. Infants younger than the age of 4 weeks have a very limited ability to distinguish between different colors and initially perceive the difference only between red and white. By 8 weeks, color vision is still not mature, but most infants are able to discriminate between white and a number of other colors. Newborns can perceive objects and surfaces around them, but their visual acuity is estimated to be 20/400. By about 8 months, visual acuity is nearly as good as it would be in an adult with "perfect" 20/20 vision. The visual cortex is immature at birth, and accurate vision depends on unimpeded stimulation and visual experience.
Hearing	Newborns and young infants turn toward the source of a sound, but they have more difficulty than older children and adults in locating the precise origins of sounds, especially when they are very brief. Newborns pay special attention to the sound of the human voice. They prefer listening to their own mother's voice and the language that they heard her speaking before they were born. Newborns are not able to hear the full pitch range that adults perceive, but this perceptual ability improves significantly by the age of 6 months. Infants tend to become interested and attentive when they hear high-pitched sounds and voices. Low-pitched sounds, by contrast, tend to have a soothing and calming effect.
Touch	Infants need touch and physical contact with caregivers in order to grow and thrive. Most of the neonatal reflexes are triggered by the sense of touch. Newborn infants are able to feel pain, although they may not always cry or move in ways that clearly reflect their discomfort. Swaddling is effective because it affects newborns' sense of touch. Skin-to-skin contact with a parent or other caregiver is another reliable way to comfort newborns. Many parents use massage with younger infants, but it can also be used with older infants and toddlers to provide an important emotional connection.
Taste	Newborns are able to differentiate between sweet, salty, sour, and bitter tasting substances. They prefer sweet flavors but dislike sour and bitter flavors. Salty substances rarely elicit negative reactions. Prenatal and postnatal exposure to flavors influences infants' acceptance and enjoyment of those flavors.
Smell	Newborns appear to have a preference for sweet aromas and a dislike of odors that older children and adults find unpleasant. Olfactory learning begins during the prenatal period and continues from the moment of birth.
Other Senses	The vestibular sense as well as the proprioceptive and kinesthetic senses provide infants with information about the body's position and movement. This feedback contributes to motor development and motor learning.

aromas, and textures. As we will see, infants are prepared at birth to use their senses to learn about the world and to interact with the people in it. For many, many years before valid and reliable research procedures were developed, however, the accuracy of infant perception was questioned.

Theories of Infant Perception

Debates about infant perception began long before developmental psychology and child development emerged in the twentieth century. As shown in Table 6.2, philosophers pondering adults' knowledge about the world probed the origins of this knowledge in the newborn

TABLE 6.2   Theoretical Views of Infant Perception

Theoretical View	Key Theorist	Assumptions
Empiricist	Berkeley	Knowledge about the world must be constructed because sensory receptors, such as the retina, do not provide direct, accurate information about the properties of objects in the world. Infants are not able to perceive the world in three dimensions until they have learned to associate different eye muscle movements with the act of focusing on objects that are near versus far.
Nativist	Kant	Accurate perception of the world is possible from birth or with only a limited amount of experience because knowledge about objects and their properties is innate. Infants are able to perceive the world in three dimensions because they are born with the ability to interpret information for depth and distance.
Gestalt	Koffka	The world is perceived accurately from early in life because the human brain is designed to enhance and interpret information that it receives from the sensory receptors. Perception of depth and three-dimensionality is the result of the brain's inherent ability to transform and organize the limited information conveyed to it by the flat retina.
Ecological	Gibson	The perceptual system perceives information about the world directly and accurately, without any intervening interpretive steps, because it has evolved to extract regularities from the organized patterns that exist in all settings. Infants are able to perceive depth and distance in the world because they are sensitive to a rich array of cues in the environment, such as the receding texture of a floor pattern from near to far, or different views of the same object as they move around it.

Source: Based on Kellman & Arterberry, 1998, 2006.

child. From the perspective of late seventeenth- and early eighteenth-century British empiricist philosophers, such as Berkeley (1709/1901), this knowledge had to be constructed since it was not contained in the information picked up by the sensory receptors. Only through experience, and by piecing together the individual bits of information conveyed by those specialized receptors, could meaning be imposed on and perceived in the meaningless sensations (Kellman & Arterberry, 1998, 2006; Spelke & Newport, 1998).

A contrasting viewpoint came from thinkers who favored nativist explanations. Philosophers like Kant (1781/1924), writing in the late eighteenth century, refuted the notion that accurate associations and meanings could be built up during infancy with only a limited amount of sensory experience. Instead, nativists asserted, the ability to perceive the world must be innate.

A particularly problematic issue for many early theorists was the development of **depth perception**—the ability to perceive the world in three dimensions. The logical problem with which they grappled was how the retina, which is flat, could convey the world in 3-D. From an empiricist point of view, philosophers asserted that infants could only perceive depth after they had accrued enough experience with different two-dimensional views to be able to combine and interpret them as different aspects of the same view. Empiricists also thought that indirect perception—learning through association—occurred as infants became aware of the different eye muscle movements involved when they focused at near versus far distances (Kellman & Arterberry, 1998, 2006).

Other theorists hypothesized that the capacity for three-dimensional perception was present from birth and did not require a period of learning. Gestalt psychologists, for example, who were most active from the 1930s until the 1950s, believed that the brain is designed to perceive information from the flat retinal image in three dimensions (e.g., Koffka, 1935). To the extent that they asserted that two-dimensional information is inherently meaningless and needs to be translated and organized into accurate three-dimensional representations, Gestalt views were congruent with other theories in existence at that time (Kellman & Arterberry, 1998, 2006).

Beginning in the 1960s, psychologists endorsing a new perspective—the **ecological theory of perception**—proposed something quite different, the idea that the visual system perceives meaningful information directly, without any intermediate steps to interpret it. The best known proponents of this ecological view, J. J. Gibson (1966, 1979) and E. J. Gibson (1969, 1984), held that information in the world is organized in meaningful ways and that humans, like all other animals, have evolved the ability to perceive and make use of this organization. According to the ecological view, the ability to discern the available information may improve with experience, and increasingly subtle differences may be detected, but infants do not need to learn to impose meaning per se.

How does the ecological perspective explain the development of the ability to see the world in 3-D? One answer is that humans, like other animals, move about the world and, as they do, they perceive the boundaries of objects and are able to determine the relative locations of a set of objects by noticing how their views of those objects change. In this way, for example, as infants crawl around a playroom, they are able to perceive that toys that are closer to them cover up more of the view of toys that are farther away. Even without moving around the entire set of toys, infants—like all perceivers—are able to gain a changing array of meaningful views of the toys by simply adjusting their posture and moving their head.

Where does the theoretical debate about the development of perception stand now, in the twenty-first century? As we will see, while some aspects of the debate between the empiricists and the nativists continue today, experiments are actively exploring—and often validating—predictions of ecological theory. In addition, although the specific neurophysiological mechanisms that the Gestalt psychologists posited are viewed as implausible by today's experts, the general notion that unlearned organizational tendencies may underlie many aspects of infant perception is still influential (Kellman & Arterberry, 1998; Spelke & Newport, 1998).

Vision

Vision is the most studied but least well-developed sense at birth. The study of infants' visual abilities relies on measures and methods that we discussed in Chapter 2. Researchers make inferences about infants' ability to perceive a range of visual stimuli (objects or projected images) based on changes in their rate and pattern of sucking, the length and direction of their gaze, their heart rate, and patterns of brain activity. Several decades of sophisticated experiments have produced a clear description of visual abilities during infancy.

Newborns notice and pay attention to objects and people in motion. By the age of 8 weeks, infants are able to distinguish between moving and stationary objects, even while they themselves are in motion (Kellman & von Hofsten, 1992). They have difficulty before the age of 2 months using smooth eye movements to track objects, especially if the object is moving swiftly (Aslin, 1981). Instead of keeping up with a toy as it moves, infants younger than 2 months tend to lag behind or make a series of jerky eye movements (saccades) that fall short of where the moving target is positioned. The accuracy of these saccadic eye movements improves significantly by the age of 11 to 14 weeks (Kellman & Arterberrry, 1998; Shea & Aslin, 1990).

As we will discuss at greater length shortly, newborns prefer some patterns more than others. Areas of high contrast, such as a person's hairline or dark wood trim at the edge of a light-colored ceiling, draw their attention from an early age. Research on pattern perception has shown consistently that newborns find the human face particularly attractive (Kellman & Arterberry, 2006; Slater & Butterworth, 1997). It has been well documented, for example, that newborns prefer to look at a drawing of a face rather than at a sample of newsprint (Fantz, 1963; Fantz, Fagan, & Miranda, 1975) or a drawing of a rectangular grid (Kellman & Banks, 1998; Kleiner, 1987; Kleiner & Banks, 1987).

Certain patterns, such as black-and-white checked mobiles and toys, seem to be especially attractive to *parents*, who may buy them because they have heard that newborns cannot perceive color. Is this belief supported by research? Before we can answer that question, it is important to understand that "color" is actually comprised of three attributes: brightness (the light intensity of an object), hue (the wavelength of an object), and saturation (the distribution of wavelengths of an object). Early studies of infant color perception were often inconclusive because the stimuli that were used varied in more than one of these attributes. As a result, infants who appeared to respond differentially to different hues, such as red and green, might actually have noticed and responded to differences in brightness. More recent research has been able to match levels of brightness while varying the hues of paired stimuli (Kellman & Arterberry, 2006).

Some of these experiments have reported that infants younger than 4 weeks of age are able to distinguish between red and white but do not distinguish between white and other hues (Adams, Courage, & Mercer, 1994). By the age of 8 weeks, many infants are able to discriminate between white and a number of colors, specifically, red, orange, blue, certain greens, and certain purples but not between white and yellow or yellow-green (Teller, Peeples, & Sekel, 1978). This pattern of discrimination suggests that some form of early color vision exists, but it is markedly different from adult color vision. Researchers are still working to determine whether failures to discriminate between hues are due to a lack of **cones** (photoreceptors in the eye that respond to specific hues, or wavelengths of light) or are the result of other immaturities in the visual system (Kellman & Arterberry, 2006; Kellman & Banks, 1998). Regardless of the reasons, color vision continues to develop over the first year of life. By about 4 months of age, however, parents and their infants have a fairly similar ability to perceive a spectrum of distinct colors (Adams, Courage, & Mercer, 1991; Kellman & Arterberry, 2006).

How clearly can newborns see? **Visual acuity** (the smallest spacing that can be perceived between parts of a pattern) is significantly worse at birth than "perfect" 20/20 vision. In adults, visual acuity is typically measured with the Snellen scale, which compares how well a person sees letters on an eye chart at 20 feet to the distance at which a person with good vision would see the letters with the same degree of clarity. An adult whose vision is said to be 20/60 thus sees at 20 feet what a person with good vision is able to see at 60 feet. To study visual acuity in infants, researchers replace eye charts displaying letters of the alphabet with gratings (patterns of stripes spaced at varying distances) or other high-contrast patterns, such as those shown in Figure 6.1. Because infants tend to look at the more complex

FIGURE 6.1   In studies of visual acuity, infants are shown pairs of stimuli of varying complexity.

of two visual stimuli, researchers present two gratings and measure the amount of time the infant looks at each.

In a variation on this procedure, called **forced-choice preferential looking**, infants are shown two targets—a screen displaying a grating with a particular spacing between the stripes and another screen that is uniformly blank. Infants who are able to perceive the grating prefer looking at it, but infants who are unable to detect the pattern perceive it as another uniform field and show no clear preference (Kellman & Banks, 1998).

Some researchers have used electrophysiological measures, such as the visual evoked potential, to study visual acuity and a related ability known as contrast sensitivity. Contrast sensitivity is the ability to perceive differences among the elements of an image or pattern under varying degrees of contrast between the pattern and its background (e.g., black patterns on a white background versus a grayish background). For both visual acuity and contrast sensitivity, high-tech measures tend to be more sensitive than behavioral measures in estimating infants' abilities (Kellman & Arterberry, 2006).

Based on numerous studies, newborn visual acuity is estimated to be approximately 20/400. Practically speaking, newborns' poor visual acuity means that they are able to perceive objects and surfaces in their environment, but they miss many of the finer details, such as texture and intricate patterns. Nevertheless, even without the ability to perceive these details, infants can perceive the world quite accurately; in fact, some researchers have compared young infants' acuity to that of an adult cat (Kellman & Arterberry, 1998; von Hofsten, 1983).

By the age of about $5\frac{1}{2}$ months, visual acuity improves to approximately 20/100 and to nearly adult levels by the age of about 8 months. At the same time that visual acuity improves, a related ability, contrast sensitivity. also develops. One reason for these improvements is the eyeball's rapid growth during the first year of life. As the size of the eye increases, the greater distance from the front of the eye to the retina at the back creates a larger, clearer image on the retina (Kellman & Banks, 1998). In comparison with adult vision, visual acuity and contrast sensitivity are initially particularly poor in the **fovea** (the center of the eye). One reason is that newborns' foveal photoreceptors, which transmit light signals to the optic nerve, are spaced about four times farther apart than those of adults. Peripheral vision, by contrast, is not significantly different for infants and adults; at all ages, acuity and contrast sensitivity are relatively poor at the periphery and under conditions of low illumination (Kellman & Arterberry, 1998; Kellman & Banks, 1998).

Another reason for newborns' initially poor vision lies in the brain. The **visual cortex**, which processes visual information, is immature at birth. Whereas in the mature visual system, the optic nerve sends messages first to the lateral geniculate nucleus and then to the visual cortex, visual processing during the first several weeks after birth relies primarily on a subcortical visual system that provides information from the periphery rather than the fovea. Recent studies suggest that many future brain pathways are partially activated in very young infants, but there is debate about whether initial processing occurs throughout the brain or progresses from posterior to anterior regions. Subcortical pathways dominate visual processing until higher cortical areas become specialized and more efficient (Johnson, 2000; Kellman & Arterberry, 1998).

Vision problems are relatively rare among infants, although some groups, such as those born preterm, those with developmental delays, and those with a family history of eye problems, are at greater risk (American Academy of Pediatrics Committee on Practice and Ambulatory Medicine and Section on Ophthalmology, 2002a; American Academy of Pediatrics Section on Ophthalmology, 2002b). When problems do exist, early detection and treatment are essential because the visual cortex depends on stimulation in order to develop normally. With unimpeded **binocular vision** (input from two eyes that are aligned and move together), signals are received from both the left and right visual fields. These signals stimulate the development of columns of neurons that respond specifically to the signals received from either the left or the right eye. The integration of the slightly different view that each eye sees underlies the ability to perceive a three-dimensional world. The visual system responds to other cues for depth that we will discuss shortly, and, as we will see, infants are also able to use this information to perceive the environment accurately.

When the visual system does not function correctly during infancy and early childhood, the allocation of neurons in the visual cortex changes to reflect the child's visual experience. If, for example, one of an infant's eyes is crossed (as occurs in conditions known as amblyopia and strabismus), areas of the visual cortex that normally would register signals from the misaligned eye are taken over and respond to stimulation that the other, uncrossed eye receives. Children with amblyopia or strabismus often have normal (20/20) vision in one eye but vision that is significantly worse (20/200) in the other eye. Amblyopia and strabismus are usually treated by covering the stronger eye with a patch during the child's waking hours and using glasses to strengthen the weaker eye. Treatment regimens traditionally specified that the normal eye should be patched for 6 hours each day, but new research shows that patching for only 2 hours a day may be just as effective for most children (Repka et al., 2003). As another treatment alternative, special eyedrops can be used to blur vision temporarily in the normal eye, with results that are comparable to patching (Repka, 2002). These new options are easier to comply with, and parents using them report less concern about the potential stigma of patching.

Infants with congenital cataracts, a condition that we discussed in Chapter 5, are also at risk for vision problems, if the cataract is not surgically removed (Ellemberg et al., 2000). Follow-up care for these children typically involves patching the normal eye and correcting the vision in the eye that was operated on (Maurer et al., 1999). If vision problems are not corrected at an early age, the brain's ability to receive signals from the weaker or occluded eye diminishes and eventually ceases.

Only 20 percent of preschool-aged children are screened for visual problems, often not until just before entering kindergarten. Parents of young children with vision problems may notice delays in motor skill development or lack of coordination, and their child may fall down or bump into objects on one side, but many cases go undetected. In light of the necessity of early treatment, experts recommend that all infants have their vision checked at the age of 6 months and again at 3 years. Vision screening during infancy can be performed with a simple red reflex exam that checks for asymmetries in the amount and pattern of light reflected from the back of the eyes (American Academy of Pediatrics Committee on Practice and Ambulatory Medicine and Section on Ophthalmology, 2002a; American Academy of Pediatrics Section on Ophthalmology, 2002b).

Perception of Objects.   As infants look at objects around them, such as a ball on the floor or a cup on the tray of their high chair, how do they know where each object begins and ends? Researchers studying object perception note that this seemingly simple ability is actually comprised of several steps. Infants need to be able to detect the edges of each object, determining whether ambiguous markings (such as shadows) are edges of an object, and assigning each apparent boundary or edge to a specific object or surface. In addition, infants need to be able to solve the problem of object unity—perceiving entire three-dimensional objects, rather than a set of separate elements (Johnson, 1997b; Kellman & Arterberry, 1998, 2006). This may sound like a complex analytical problem, but some evidence suggests that these tasks are less formidable than they seem at first.

One way in which infants may be helped is that most objects are composed of homogeneous substances. Balls, for example, tend to be made out of rubber, or plastic, or metal, but not all three substances. The substance of an object, such as a woven basket, may also help infants distinguish that object from the table on which it rests, especially if that surface is made from a very different substance, such as smooth wood. Another potential aid in edge detection (and thus object perception) comes from the way in which object properties, such as texture, color, or pattern, tend to be consistent across an object but "disappear" abruptly at an object's edges. Finally, keeping in mind that infants do not usually see static views of the world, it is plausible that differences in the properties of objects and their surroundings may become even more salient as objects and infants move around. For example, it seems likely that infants watching a ball roll across a floor have information about object boundaries and properties that infants watching a motionless ball do not have. Even a slight change in posture and head position may highlight the fact that the surface of a plastic laundry basket responds differently to changes in the reflected ceiling light than does the texture of the tiled floor on which it sits (Kellman & Banks, 1998).

How well can infants use this sort of information to perceive objects as entities that are separate from their surroundings? As it turns out, very little developmental research has addressed this question directly (Kellman & Arterberry, 1998, 2006), but some inferences can be drawn. First, as we noted earlier, it is well documented that infants are able to detect patterns and areas of high contrast from a very early age (Fantz, Fagan, & Miranda, 1975). From birth, they also seem to recognize objects, even when they are displayed from different angles, an ability that implies perception of the edges of those objects (Slater & Morison, 1985). Although these findings do not prove that newborns perceive the entire object to which edges belong, it does suggest that they are able to perform the first step in object perception—edge detection—from the earliest weeks of life (Kellman & Arterberry, 1998, 2006).

At what age can infants use information about texture, color, and other properties of objects and their surroundings in order to perceive discrete objects? One set of experiments suggests that this ability may appear later than the ability to detect edges, perhaps not until after the age of 5 months. Infants aged 3, 5, and 9 months were shown either a homogeneous display (in which an object and the surface on which it rested were identical in color, texture, and other visible properties) or a heterogeneous display (in which an object and the supporting surface were different in color, texture, and other visible properties). The homogeneous display showed a clear boundary between the object and surface, whereas the heterogeneous display did not. Following the homogeneous or heterogeneous display, infants saw either an event in which the object and its surface moved together or an event in which the object moved independent of its surface. The researchers hypothesized that infants would look longer at the event that they perceived as being novel—different from the display that they had seen initially. They found that 3-month-olds looked longer at the independent-movement event, suggesting that they had perceived the initial display as a single, unified object. This looking preference was found whether the initial display had been homogeneous or heterogeneous, which the researchers interpreted as evidence that 3-month-olds did not use the color, texture, and other visible properties of the object and its supporting surface as information for object boundaries. The 5- and 9-month-olds in the study, by contrast, showed some rudimentary use of this information (Spelke et al., 1993). These findings suggest that several months of perceptual experience may be necessary before properties such as color and texture assist infants in object perception.

What about movement as a source of information in the perception of objects? When elements in a display move, infants appear to be able to use this information as a basis for perceiving object boundaries. In a number of studies, infants have been habituated to displays in which two linear vertical arrangements of elements on a video screen move back and forth in opposite directions. The **accretion and deletion** of these elements creates a display that adults judge to show distinct edges. In other studies, the accretion and deletion of elements in the display creates the appearance of an object moving against a stationary background. In these studies, infants as young as 2 to 3 months dishabituate and show renewed visual interest when they see other patterns of elements moving in different ways. These findings suggest that movement helps infants perceive edges and objects, and that infants are able to make use of this information earlier than information about object properties, such as color and texture (Granrud et al., 1984; Johnson & Mason, 2002; Kaufmann-Hayoz, Kaufmann, & Stucki, 1986; Kellman & Arterberry, 1998, 2006).

Movement is such an effective source of information that it even helps infants perceive object unity, as has been shown in numerous experiments with partially occluded objects. Infants in these studies are habituated to a display that adults perceive as a single, partially hidden object moving behind a stationary rectangle (display A, shown in Figure 6.2). If infants show dishabituation to (renewed interest in) display B, researchers conclude that they perceived two separate objects behind the occluder in display A. Dishabituation to display C, by contrast, is regarded as evidence that infants perceived a unitary object behind the occluder in display A. Results from experiments using this procedure indicate that newborn infants do not perceive the initial display as a single, unified object; this ability has been found in infants as young as 2 months, however, as long as the occluder is not too wide (Johnson & Aslin, 1995, 1996; Kellman & Spelke, 1983; Slater et al., 1996).

Movement is also a source of information about the continuity of an object's trajectory, such as when an object moves completely behind and then reappears at the other side of an occluding object. Perception of the continuous path of an object moving behind an occluding screen develops slightly later, however, than the ability to perceive the unity of a moving, partially hidden object. In one recent set of experiments involving 2-, 4-, and 6-month-olds, researchers varied the width of the occluding screen, which affected how long the object was out of sight (Johnson et al., 2003). Under all occlusion conditions tested, 6-month-olds perceived the continuous path of a ball that disappeared on one side of a screen and reappeared on the other side. Four-month-olds perceived the continuity of the ball's trajectory at brief and intermediate durations, but not when it disappeared for a longer

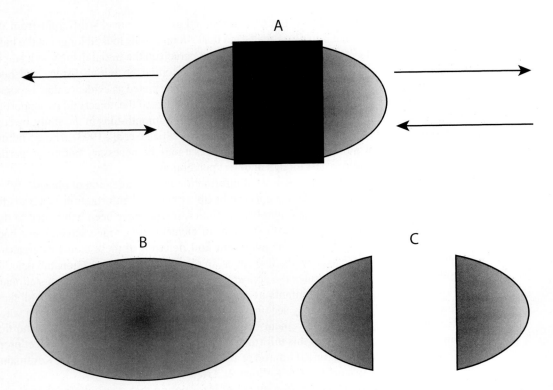

FIGURE 6.2   In studies of object perception, infants are habituated to an object moving behind a screen (A). In test trials, they are shown either an image of a whole object (B) or an image of that object with the middle missing (C). Dishabituation to C suggests that infants perceived A as showing a single, coherent object.

interval, suggesting that this ability was not well established. Two-month-olds' looking behavior, by contrast, suggested that they did not perceive the ball moving behind one edge of the occluding screen as being on a continuous path that emerged at the other edge of the screen. These findings suggest that experience over the first few months of life watching objects and people as they move in and out of sight contributes to the ability to perceive them accurately. This study also appears to contradict other researchers' assertions that the ability to perceive the unity of objects and the continuity of their path of movement behind a screen is innate (Baillargeon, 1995; Spelke, 1990). Although infants' attention is attracted to moving objects from birth, their ability to use movement as a basis for perceptual inferences about those objects is initially relatively limited.

When do infants accomplish the final step in perceiving objects—perceiving them as three-dimensional forms? This question has been investigated by studying infants' responses to transformations, such as their ability to recognize a three-dimensional object from more than one viewpoint. One researcher developed a procedure in which infants were habituated to a three-dimensional object as it rotated in one direction and were then shown either a different object rotating in the same orientation or the same object rotating in a different orientation. Four-month-old infants who saw a dynamic display, showing continuous transformations of the three-dimensional object, recognized that object when they saw it later from a different orientation, but infants who saw only static "snapshots" of the same display did not recognize the object when they saw a different view of it (Kellman, 1984). Subsequent research showed that dynamic displays are also informative when the transformation is the result of the infant's changing position relative to a stationary object (Kellman & Short, 1987). The superiority of dynamic information over static information from an early age has been shown in numerous studies of infant object perception and has led some researchers to conclude that the perceptual system has evolved to notice and respond to motion-carried information (Kellman & Banks, 1998).

Another aspect of object perception that functions early in life, perhaps from birth, is **size constancy**—the ability to perceive an object's actual size correctly, even when it is viewed from different distances (creating a retinal image of varying size). In one experiment with neonates, researchers showed infants a cube, familiarizing them to either a large or a small cube presented at different distances. In test trials, the large cube was always placed farther away than the small cube, but the cubes were placed at distances from which they would produce retinal images of the same size. Infants looked longer at the new cube, whose actual size was different from the cube that they had seen during the familiarization phase. This result suggests that they perceived size constancy and recognized that the initial cube continued to be the same object at varying distances (Slater, Mattock, & Brown, 1990).

Perception of Depth.   Taken together, there is strong evidence that infants are able to perceive information about objects from an early age. Certain information, specifically information carried by motion, is especially salient. As we have just seen, infants perceive three-dimensional objects from a very young age and may even perceive size constancy from birth. Do these findings indicate that infants perceive the world around them in 3-D? Do they perceive the spatial location of objects and people in relation to their own location? The answer to both questions is yes, although (as shown in Table 6.3) infants initially rely on just a subset of the information that older children and adults can use to perceive depth.

The information that infants use earliest to perceive depth is carried by motion, and researchers refer to it as **kinematic depth cues**. One type of kinematic depth cue that came up in our earlier discussion of edge detection, accretion and deletion of texture, may also provide information about which of two edges is closer. Five- and seven-month-old infants in one experiment with computer displays of moving dot patterns reached more frequently to the display that adults judged to appear closer (Granrud et al., 1984). Another type of kinematic depth cue is **optical expansion and contraction**—the increase and decrease of the size of an object's image on the retina. When older children and adults see a two-dimensional image, such as a shadow, increase in size symmetrically (in all directions), they perceive the approach of an object. By contrast, when the size of a shadow form decreases, older children and adults perceive an object that is moving away from them. What do infants perceive? As early as 1 month of age, infants who are shown rapidly symmetrically expanding two-dimensional forms blink their eyes in a defensive response, much as they would if a three-dimensional object approached at the same rate. They do not show this response

TABLE 6.3   **Development of Sensitivity to Depth Cues**

Depth Cue	Age	Examples
Kinematic	1 month	A two-dimensional shadow form increases and decreases in size, producing optical expansion and contraction. The viewer perceives a three-dimensional form moving toward and then away from them.
	5–7 months	Two random-dot patterns move on a video monitor, producing systematic, unified accretion and deletion of the dots. The viewer perceives the dots as belonging to two separate shapes, with the leading edge of one shape moving in front of the other shape.
Stereoscopic	2–4 months	Two slightly different two-dimensional images of the same picture create binocular disparity. The viewer perceives a single, three-dimensional image.
Pictorial	5–7 months	Relative size: a smaller-looking, more distant stroller is judged to be the same size as a larger-looking stroller that is closer to the viewer.
	5–7 months	Linear perspective: railroad tracks converge toward the horizon, suggesting distance and depth.
	5–7 months	Texture gradient: floor tiles gradually appear to get smaller toward the horizon.
	5–7 months	Interposition: a nearby shoe covers part of the view of a ball that is farther away from the viewer.

Source: Adapted from Kellman & Arterberry, 1998, 2006.

when the two-dimensional forms expand asymmetrically (in just one direction) or when the two-dimensional forms contract (Nanez, 1988; Nanez & Yonas, 1994). These findings suggest that optical expansion and contraction convey information about the position of objects relative to the self from the first weeks of life.

Between the ages of 2 and 4 months, infants begin to use another source of information—**stereoscopic depth information**—to perceive depth. Stereoscopic information is produced by **binocular disparity**, which is the difference between the image on each retina. In experiments using preferential looking as the response measure, 4-month-olds looked longer at displays containing disparity that adults judged to show depth (Held, Birch, & Gwiazda, 1980). Other experiments using a range of response measures have found corroborating evidence for the development of stereoscopic sensitivity by about 4 months of age (Kellman & Arterberry, 1998, 2006; Kellman & Banks, 1998). The underlying change that makes stereoscopic perception possible is believed to be the maturation of disparity-sensitive cells in the visual cortex. The maturation of alternating columns of cells that receive stimulation from either the left or the right eye occurs during the period from birth to 6 months (Kellman & Banks, 1998). As we discussed earlier, the timetable for this maturation is the reason that visual problems that interfere with the input from either eye should be detected and treated as early as possible.

Infants become sensitive to a third source of depth information—**pictorial depth cues**—between 5 and 7 months of age. Pictorial depth cues make it possible for artists to convey information for a three-dimensional scene on a two-dimensional surface. These cues include relative size (showing two same-sized objects at different sizes and distances from the viewer), linear perspective (showing parallel lines converging toward the horizon), texture gradients (showing surface elements gradually getting smaller toward the horizon), and interposition (showing closer objects in front of objects that are farther away).

In experiments exploring the development of sensitivity to pictorial depth cues, researchers typically eliminate depth information that might be carried via binocular disparity by covering one eye with a patch. Most researchers use a preferential reaching procedure and interpret infants' reaching toward objects or displays as evidence that they perceive those objects as being closer (Kellman & Banks, 1998). The results of numerous experiments with a range of pictorial depth cues indicate that sensitivity to these cues emerges between 5 and 7 months of age. Macaque monkeys develop sensitivity to pictorial depth cues at an age that is approximately equivalent to the age at which sensitivity emerges in human infants (Gunderson et al., 1993). In light of the consistency with which this age has been identified, many researchers believe that the ability to perceive pictorial depth cues is the result of maturation of the visual system as well as experience with the cues.

Hearing

Fetuses are able to hear as early as the 24th gestational week and often move or even startle in response to sudden loud noises. As we noted earlier, from birth, infants turn in the direction of sounds, as if searching for the source. **Auditory localization**—the ability to detect the location of sound sources—appears to undergo a U-shaped developmental change. Whereas newborns respond reliably, turning their heads toward the sound of a rattle that is shaken to one side, 1- to 3-month-olds respond less strongly and less frequently. By the age of 4 to 5 months, infants once again respond consistently and correctly. This pattern is thought to be the result of a shift in control of the response from subcortical to cortical brain structures (Muir et al., 1979; Muir, Clifton, & Clarkson, 1989; Muir & Hains, 2004).

When newborns and young infants turn toward a sound, they are nearly as accurate as older children and adults in a general sense, but they are significantly less able to locate the precise origins of sounds, especially if the sounds are very brief (Clarkson & Montgomery, 2000). One study with 2- to 7-month-olds compared their ability to reach in the dark toward one of four conditions: an invisible noise-making object, a glowing visible object, a single object that could be both seen and heard, and two objects (one visible and the other audible) in different locations. At all ages tested, infants were slower and less accurate in reaching for unseen objects that they could hear than for visible-but-silent objects (Stack et al., 1989). These findings indicate that pinpoint localization develops more gradually than other aspects of audition.

Newborns pay special attention to the human voice and seem to prefer it to other sounds. They are particularly attuned to the sound of their mother's voice and, as a result of experience while still in utero, are able to discriminate between her voice and the voices of other women (DeCasper, & Fifer, 1980; DeCasper, & Spence, 1986; DeCasper et al., 1994; Kisilevsky et al., 2003; Saffran, Werker, & Werner, 2006). They are even able, at just 2 days after birth, to detect the difference between their native language (the language that they have heard their mother speaking in utero) and other languages (Moon, Cooper, & Fifer, 1993).

Mothers, as well as fathers and other caregivers, usually speak to infants in a high-pitched voice. This modification, and others that we will discuss in Chapter 8, draws infants' attention to the speaker and may even facilitate language learning. As we will see in Chapter 12, many parents and caregivers know that low-pitched sounds, such as those found in most lullabies, tend to have the opposite effect—soothing and quieting infants, rather than arousing their attention and interest. Newborns are not able to hear the full pitch range that adults perceive, but over the first 6 months of life, they become more skilled in their ability to detect differences between a wider variety of pitches (Clarkson, 1996; Clarkson, Martin, & Miciek, 1996; Montgomery & Clarkson, 1997; Saffran, Werker, & Werner, 2006).

To protect hearing, the American Academy of Pediatrics Committee on Environmental Health (1997) recommends shielding infants, and children of all ages, from extremely loud noises. In addition to obvious sources of noise, such as lawnmowers and loud music, parents need to consider their children's toys as a potential source of damaging noise. Toys that make sounds are attractive to infants, but the volume needs to be checked and set at a low level. If there is not an adjustable volume setting, a piece of clear tape can be placed over the speaker in order to mute sounds that are too loud. As we saw in Chapter 4, children's hearing should be screened during visits to the pediatrician, beginning in the newborn period (Cunningham et al., 2003; Yoshinaga-Itano et al., 1998).

Touch

As we have discussed previously, infants need touch and physical contact with caregivers in order to grow and thrive, and they are born prepared to respond to stimulation of this sense. One clear sign of their readiness is the set of neonatal reflexes, which are triggered by the sense of touch. Stroking the sole of a newborn's foot elicits the Babinski reflex, in which the foot flexes and the toes fan out. Touching the infant's cheek elicits the rooting reflex, in which the head turns and the mouth opens, as if searching for a source of food. Supporting the infant and placing the feet on a flat surface produces a stepping reflex.

Researchers have long wondered about the connection between reflexes, such as the stepping reflex, and later motor patterns, such as walking. Early views were that the reflexes disappeared as a result of development of the motor cortex. Contemporary research shows, however, that this assumption must be questioned (Bertenthal & Clifton, 1998). Taking into account the rapid growth and weight gain during the first months after birth, researchers instead proposed that reflexes such as the stepping reflex diminish in response to biomechanical constraints, such as the increasing weight of the infant's leg and muscle strength that is no longer adequate to perform the stepping movement. They tested this hypothesis in one well-known experiment by putting weights on the legs of infants who were still exhibiting the stepping reflex at a high rate. With the added weight, the reflex "disappeared." They also partially immersed babies who had stopped exhibiting the stepping reflex on dry land. With the effects of gravity reduced in the water, the reflex reappeared (Thelen, Fisher, & Ridley-Johnson, 1984).

Another sign of newborns' sense of touch is their ability to feel pain. Although it was formerly thought by some neurologists (e.g., Beales, 1982; Owens, 1984) that newborns could not feel pain, pediatricians now routinely use local anesthetics and other forms of pain medication to lessen stress and physical discomfort for infants undergoing surgery as well as procedures that are relatively more routine, such as circumcision (American Academy of Pediatrics Committee on Fetus and Newborn, Committee on Drugs, 2000; Simons et al., 2003). Contrary to earlier views, it is now recognized that a lack of crying or movement cannot be assumed to indicate an absence of pain (American Academy of Pediatrics, 2000d; Peters et al., 2003). Relying on facial expressions alone may not be sufficient because these responses to pain may change with age. In one longitudinal study of infants' responses to an event that elicits acute pain—the DPT inoculation—2-month-olds cried and showed facial expressions of "emergency pain." As the sample of infants returned for DTaP booster shots at 4, 6, and 18 months of age, they continued to cry and show facial expressions of pain, but their reactions became mixed with expressions of fear and anger, as their increasing cognitive abilities enabled them to anticipate the inoculation (Izard, Hembree, & Huebner, 1987).

Infants who are held and comforted by their parents during inoculations may recover more quickly from these painful but necessary medical procedures. Skin-to-skin contact, as well as swaddling, are also simple but effective ways to comfort newborns by affecting their sense of touch (Gray, Watt, & Blass, 2000). Giving breast milk or formula may help comfort infants who are experiencing mild pain; in one experiment, newborns who were given a sweet solution following a routine heel prick (to obtain a blood sample for health screening) cried less and showed less physiological distress than infants who were not given sucrose to drink (Blass & Hoffmeyer, 1991; Smith & Blass, 1996). Newborns who need significant pain relief are not easily comforted, however, and may be more distressed by subsequent painful events than infants who have not experienced similar levels of neonatal pain (American Academy of Pediatrics, 2000; Ruda et al., 2000; Taddio et al., 1995, 1997).

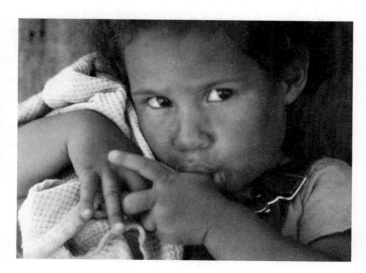

This toddler is comforted when she sucks her thumb and feels the familiar texture of her favorite blanket.

The sense of touch continues to be important for older infants and toddlers, many of whom find emotional comfort when they stroke a special corner of a favorite blanket, hug a stuffed animal, suck their thumb, or twirl their hair. In addition, while many parents use massage with younger infants to soothe them and create an emotional connection, this contact and other forms of touch, such as back rubs, can also be used with toddlers and older children for similar purposes.

Taste

In comparison with studies of vision, hearing, and touch, relatively little research has been directed at understanding infants' sense of taste. The first stimulation of this sense occurs during the prenatal period, when flavors of food the mother consumes may be passed on to the fetus in the amniotic fluid, which is a salty liquid. After birth newborns' sense of taste contributes to their survival; they seem to have an innate preference for high-energy, sweet-tasting substances, such as breast milk. Infants who are breastfed are exposed to flavors of food their mother eats, and some researchers have found that this early exposure—and the pairing with the sweetness of the breast milk—increases the likelihood that those other flavors will be received favorably when solid foods are introduced (Harris, 1997; Harris, Thomas, & Booth, 1990; Mennella & Beauchamp, 1991, 1999; Mennella, Jagnow, & Beauchamp, 2001). Infants who are formula fed also develop taste preferences as a result of their early postnatal exposure. Infants in one study who had been fed soy formulas, for example, were more likely as preschoolers to prefer broccoli and bitter-flavored apple juice compared with children who had been fed milk-based formulas (Mennella & Beauchamp, 2002).

Controlled studies of infants' sense of taste up to the age of about 4 months usually involve giving water or another liquid to which flavoring has been added, while older infants may be given either flavored liquid or flavored solid food, such as bland rice cereal. Infants' responses to tastes are most frequently determined through their facial expressions, sucking rates, or the quantity of liquid or solid food that is ingested (Harris, 1997). The intensity of infants' responses depends, in part, on the strength of the solution—*how* sweet, salty, sour, or bitter it is. A very dilute solution generally produces a less extreme response than a solution that is more concentrated. The results of numerous experiments indicate that newborns are able to differentiate between sweet, salty, sour, and bitter tasting substances. They dislike sour and bitter flavors, as shown in their negative facial expressions and limited consumption of substances with these flavors. Sweet tasting substances, by contrast, typically produce placid facial expressions, and infants suck faster and more steadily, consuming relatively large quantities. Infants tend to have moderate responses to salty solutions and begin to prefer them between the age of 3 and 6 months (Beauchamp et al., 1994). Even at birth, salty substances rarely elicit negative facial expressions, and infants usually do not refrain from ingesting them, perhaps a reflection of their in utero exposure to amniotic fluid (Crook, 1978; Harris, 1997; Harris, Thomas, & Booth, 1990; Steiner, 1979).

In an experiment that tested the specificity of flavor learning, one (prenatal exposure) group of pregnant women drank carrot juice during pregnancy and water while breastfeeding, a second (early postnatal exposure) group drank water during pregnancy and carrot juice while breastfeeding, and a third (control) group drank water during pregnancy and while breastfeeding. Later, when infants began complementary feeding, and before they had ever been fed foods or juices containing the flavor of carrots, they were given cereal prepared with carrot juice as well as cereal prepared with water. Videotapes of the infants' facial expressions were consistent with mothers' ratings indicating that, unlike the control group, infants who were exposed prenatally to the flavor of carrots enjoyed the carrot-flavored cereal more than plain cereal. Infants who had been exposed to the flavor of carrots only through breastfeeding showed fewer negative facial expressions when eating carrot-flavored cereal than infants who had never tasted carrots before. These findings demonstrate that prenatal and early postnatal exposure to flavors may enhance infants' subsequent acceptance and enjoyment of those flavors (Mennella, Jagnow, & Beauchamp, 2001).

Infants continue to change their taste preferences as a result of experience. When 6-month-olds in one experiment were given salted and unsalted rice cereal, they preferred the salted version. Interestingly, the magnitude of their preference for the salted cereal correlated positively with the number of times they had eaten salted foods during the previous week. After the age of about 12 months, infants and toddlers showed a preference in new foods for salted over unsalted versions. For familiar foods, however, they preferred versions that were similar to the way they usually had experienced those foods, whether that was with or without salt (Harris, 1997).

With age, cognitive factors play an increasingly important role in children's taste preferences. In the second year of life, children tend to eat more of foods that they have watched others eating or foods with which they have positive emotional associations. In addition, over time, food that is presented in a way that emphasizes its instrumental role tends to become less preferred (Harris, 1997). Parents can minimize this tendency by being careful not to create the impression that broccoli is primarily a tool for getting a cookie.

Infants' temperaments may also affect the degree to which they accept or reject new tastes. As we will discuss in Chapter 10, infants differ in their response to novelty, such as unfamiliar toys or unusual sights. Just as some infants have strong negative emotional reactions to these stimuli, while other infants show interest and positive emotions, new flavors, textures, and aromas may elicit different responses—negative, neutral, or positive—in different infants as a function of whether they are "conservative" or "sensation-seeking" eaters (Harris, 1997).

Smell

The ability to taste also depends, in part, on the ability to smell, a sense that is well developed at birth. Without direct prior exposure, infants appear to have a preference for sweet aromas, such as vanilla, and a dislike of odors that older children and adults find unpleasant, such as fish and ammonia. They wrinkle their nose and even cry when exposed to the latter but not the former (Wilson & Sullivan, 1994). Studies using EEG recordings have also found that infants and adults respond similarly to lavender and rosemary, aromas that adults find pleasing (Sanders et al., 2002).

Although there are innate reactions to specific aromas, it is also clear that olfactory learning begins during the prenatal period and continues from the moment of birth. As a result, newborn infants are able to recognize the smell of their own amniotic fluid (Schaal, Marlier, & Soussignan, 1998, 2000). In addition, when they are just days old, they are able to detect the difference between breast milk produced by their own mother and breast milk from another lactating woman, an ability that may contribute to the development of the infant-parent relationship (Makin & Porter, 1989; Marlier & Schaal, 2005; Porter et al., 1992; Porter & Winberg, 1999). Two- and four-day-old infants who are being bottle-fed, however, show a preference for the prenatal odor of amniotic fluid rather than the postnatal odor of the formula they are being fed (Marlier, Schaal, & Soussignan, 1998). The specificity of prenatal olfactory learning was demonstrated in one study in which infants whose mothers consumed licorice while pregnant subsequently showed a postnatal preference for the odor of anise, whereas infants without prenatal exposure showed aversive or neutral responses (Schaal, Marlier, & Soussignan, 2000).

Pleasant and familiar odors appear to have a soothing effect on infants' behavioral states. Newborns in one experiment, for example, were significantly less distressed following a heel-stick procedure required for a routine blood test if they were presented with either their mother's breast milk or the smell of vanilla (Rattaz, Goubet, & Bullinger, 2005). Newborns in another study cried significantly less if they were exposed to the smell of amniotic fluid (Varendi et al., 1998). Many nonhuman animals show a similar sensitivity to biological odors, including their mother's milk. Some researchers suggest, therefore, that parents and caregivers should avoid using products that mask these potentially important cues (Varendi, Porter & Winberg, 1992). These findings also suggest that infants' olfactory sense and the aromatic properties of the environment should not be overlooked as potentially important influences on behavior and mood during infancy and even beyond. It is not unusual, for example, for children who develop a special attachment to a favorite blanket or stuffed animal to derive just as much comfort from its unique, soothing odor as they do from the way it feels.

Most of the experiments that we have discussed so far have focused on perception without considering whether and how the senses might work together. We turn now to examine infants' ability to integrate multiple simultaneous sources of sensory information—**intermodal perception**. We will also discuss evidence for **cross-modal perception**, the ability to transfer information about an object from one sense, such as vision, and use it when encountering the object later using a different sense, such as touch.

Intermodal and Cross-Modal Perception

An infant watching her bathtub being filled with water from a shower hose is witnessing a multisensory event. She sees the spray of water at the same time that she hears it hit the plastic tub. If her mother holds her near the tub, the infant may also feel the water spraying on her hand and notice its warmth. If she puts her fingers in her mouth, she may notice that the water tastes different than the milk and rice cereal she just finished eating. The infant's mother experiences bath time as a unified sensory event, one in which the sight and sound of the water, along with its other properties, not only coincide but unmistakably belong together. Does the infant perceive this event in the same way as her mother?

Intermodal Abilities.   It is well known that newborn infants orient visually toward sounds, suggesting that visual-auditory integration exists from birth. Some researchers have suggested that this response is simply a reflex, but there is compelling evidence from studies in which the source of the sound was moved from one location to another and infants oriented toward the new location (Morrongiello et al., 1994).

The classical empiricist view of multisensory perception is based on the observation that sensory receptors are specialized to pick up only one kind of input, such as visual or auditory, but not both. According to this view, the information that the receptors convey is separate at birth and only becomes associated and integrated through experience. As we will see, the empiricist view has not been supported by recent research. Instead, it appears that cells in certain areas in the brain respond to more than one sensory modality (Stein, Meredith, & Wallace, 1994). Moreover, current evidence strongly suggests that some degree of sensory integration is present from birth (Lewkowicz, 2000). The prevailing view about the development of sensory integration emphasizes infants' ability to use **amodal properties**, such as the temporal relationship between simultaneous sights and sounds. In the bathtime example, the sound of each spurt of water hitting the plastic tub corresponds exactly to the sight of each spurt of water, and this amodal property unifies the multisensory information (Kellman & Arterberry, 1998). In addition to synchrony, research has shown that infants' intermodal perception is facilitated by other amodal properties, including rate, rhythm, and duration (Lickliter & Bahrick, 2000).

From an early age, infants are also able to match video displays of events and soundtracks. The typical experimental procedure involves showing infants two different videotaped events side by side, while a single, centrally located recorded soundtrack is played. Infants who look longer at the display that matches the soundtrack are believed to notice the correspondence between the information provided by each sensory modality. Using this procedure, researchers have documented infants' ability to match faces and voices on the basis of age and gender of the speaker (Bahrick, Netto, & Hernandez-Reif, 1998). Infants are also able to perceive intermodal displays of happy and angry expressive behaviors and musical events (Pick et al., 1994; Soken & Pick, 1992). Other experiments have shown that infants can use synchrony to coordinate visual and auditory information about events. For example, when infants see two displays—several small marbles being shaken inside a plastic tube and a single large marble being shaken inside an identical plastic tube—they look longer at the display that matches the collision soundtrack that they hear (Bahrick, 1987).

Infants are also able to integrate simultaneously presented information from the visual and proprioceptive systems. In one experiment testing this ability, 5- and 7-month-old infants saw two side-by-side video monitors, each showing a "point-light display" of an infant's legs moving. (In each display, the infant wore long black socks painted with dots of florescent paint, and special lighting and filming conditions made only the dots appear in the video.) The two displays that each infant saw were a live (contingent) display of their own legs moving and a recorded (noncontingent) display of another infant's legs. (Infants were seated with their legs extending underneath a table, so the videotaped display was their only source of visual information about their legs.) Infants of both ages looked longer at the noncontingent display, suggesting that they noticed that it did not match the proprioceptive information about their own legs' movements (Schmuckler & Fairhall, 2001). A similar study that employed ordinary video displays found that infants as young as 5 months also looked longer at noncontingent displays that showed recordings of either their own or another infant's legs instead of a live, contingent display of their own legs (Bahrick & Watson, 1985). Coordination of visual and proprioceptive information clearly supports infants' perception of the world and it may contribute to their developing awareness of a coherent, enduring physical self, a topic that we will take up in Chapter 10.

Cross-Modal Abilities. Examples of cross-modal perception are nearly as prevalent as intermodal events, as we will see as we continue with our bath-time scenario. If the infant's mother reaches deep into her baby's diaper bag to find a favorite pacifier, she is likely to be able to locate it by feeling around, ignoring other items in the bag—a package of baby wipes, teething toys, and diapers—until she finds it. If, during her groping, she encounters another infant's rattle, mistakenly dropped into the bag during a play date with other mothers and babies, she may notice—through her sense of touch alone—that it is not one of her child's belongings. Would her infant be able to perceive properties of a novel object in one modality and then transfer this perception to another modality?

Studies of cross-modal abilities indicate that infants are, in fact, able to coordinate visual information with **haptic information**—exploratory mouth or hand movements that go well beyond mere tactile contact with an object. In one well-known study, 1-month-old infants haptically explored a pacifier that was either bumpy or smooth by sucking on it. The researchers made sure not to allow the infants to see the pacifier as it was being placed in and later removed from their mouth. When the infants later saw two pacifiers—one bumpy, the other smooth—they looked longer at the pacifier that matched the one on which they had previously sucked, suggesting that they were able to transfer haptically derived texture information to the visual modality (Meltzoff & Borton, 1979).

Investigations of cross-modal transfer involving visual and manual exploration have yielded less consistent results. In some studies, infants as young as 2 months who explored an object only with their hands have perceived that object as familiar in a later visual test, but transfer in the other direction—from visual familiarization to manual recognition—has not been found. This pattern and other inconsistencies may reflect young infants' limited ability to explore objects systematically with their hands (Kellman & Arterberry, 1998; Rochat, 1989; Streri, 1987; Streri & Molina, 1993). Taken together, however, these findings suggest that some degree of visual-haptic coordination is present early in life. As we will see shortly, the ability to explore the world through reaching, grasping, and manipulating undergoes significant change during infancy, enabling children to act in new ways, expanding their play repertoire, and developing self-care skills that include eating and dressing.

Other Senses

Some of the neonatal reflexes that we discussed in Chapter 4 are stimulated by other senses, including the **vestibular sense**, which conveys information about balance and support. One example of how this sense works is the Moro reflex, activated when neonates feel a loss of support and fling their arms and legs out quickly before drawing them in toward the center of the body. As infants become mobile, and throughout the rest of the life span, the vestibular sense provides important feedback that helps maintain equilibrium.

The **proprioceptive** and **kinesthetic senses** provide information from muscles, tendons, and joints about the body's position and movement. This information contributes to the ability to reach toward an object, adjust the speed and direction of the arm as it is extended, and grasp the object with the appropriate amount of force while bringing it back toward the body. As we will see in the remainder of this chapter, sensory and perceptual abilities interact with physical growth and change (which we discussed in Chapter 4) to contribute to major milestones of motor development from birth to age 3.

Motor Development

Researchers investigating the onset and development of a range of motor skills, from reaching and manual exploration to crawling and walking, have documented an intimate link between perception and action. This link was seen in a classic experiment using a "visual cliff" (an apparatus that, observed under specific lighting conditions, creates the illusion of a drop-off beneath an "invisible" Plexiglas tabletop). Infants felt the Plexiglas with their hands and looked closely at the surface as they hesitated to crawl across it (Gibson & Walk, 1960). The more crawling experience that infants had gained, the more likely they were to draw back from the virtual "edge." In addition, when the "drop-off" was adjusted to appear to be about the distance from one step to the next, infants with stair-crawling experience sometimes turned around and attempted to descend backwards down the illusory staircase. As we will discuss shortly, more recent studies have provided further support for the notion of a dynamic perception-action system.

Major motor milestones typically appear in a predictable fashion during the first 3 years (as shown in Table 6.4). For this reason, although there is variation in specific test content and administration, motor milestones are usually assessed in developmental inventories, such as the Denver Developmental Screening Test II (DDST-2) and the Minnesota Child Developmental Inventory (MCDI). One of the most widely used developmental assessments, designed for use with infants from birth to 42 months of age, is the **Bayley Scales of Infant Development-Second Edition (BSID-II)** (Bayley, 1993). Researchers have recently developed a briefer version of the BSID-II called the Bayley Short Form-Research Edition (BSF-R) and have used it successfully in a large-scale, longitudinal study of infancy and early childhood (Flanagan & Park, 2005). The BSID-II does not correlate well with children's later scores on intelligence tests, a point to which we will return in Chapter 7. However, both the BSID-II and the BSF-R allow researchers and practitioners to compare individual children's abilities to a set of normative ages for the development of a range of **fine motor skills**, such as grasping objects between finger and thumb, and **gross motor skills**, including the achievement of balance and postural control that enables infants to sit alone, stand without support, and move on to even more advanced skills, such as walking up stairs and jumping. The timing of these motor skills highlights the cephalocaudal direction (from the head to the trunk and lower body), in which infants typically develop the ability to control and stabilize body movements. As we will see next, researchers now recognize that these predictable motor skills are part of a dynamic perception-action system, one that must adapt to properties of the environment and changes in the infant's own body.

Even before infants are able to move around well on their own, they adjust their posture in response to visual information. Sometimes, however, the visual system overrides other information about the stability and supportability of surfaces. This was demonstrated in a classic study that presented 13- to 16-month-old infants with conflicting information about postural sway and balance. The researchers designed a room that moved around a standing infant, creating the illusion of movement in the absence of kinesthetic information for movement (similar to the phenomenon created when a person sitting in a parked car experiences the sensation of moving as cars on either side begin to move). The majority of infants lost their balance or moved to compensate for the apparent movement indicated by the moving walls (Lee & Aronson, 1974). Several other experiments have found similar

TABLE 6.4 Approximate Ages for the Appearance of Fine and Gross Motor Milestones

Milestones	Age	Examples
Fine Motor Skills		
Prereaching	Present at birth	Neonates extend their arms in the direction of nearby objects.
Coordinated reaching	3–4 months	Infants hold objects and examine them visually before bringing them to their mouth.
Smooth reaching	5–6 months	Infants now are able to make one or two targeted movements, instead of several jerky movements, as they reach for objects. They are able to pass objects back and forth from one hand to the other.
Adjusting hand position	6–8 months	Infants make adjustments in their hands in order to grasp different types of objects and objects in different orientations. Visual feed back from their own hands is not necessary at this age.
Increasing specificity	8–9 months	Infants are able to grasp objects and explore them manually with increasing specificity. Whole-hand grasping is replaced by a finger-tip grasp involving opposition of the thumb to the other fingers.
Handedness	11 months	Infants show a clear preference for using one hand or the other in activities such as self-feeding.
Manipulating objects	10–20 months	Fine motor skills are used to perform a variety of increasingly complex activities, including scribbling and "drawing" with markers, painting with paintbrushes, and building with blocks.
Gross Motor Skills		
Head control	3 weeks–4 months	Infants are able to hold their head steady when their body is supported and held upright.
Upper body control	3 weeks–2 months	When placed on their stomach, infants are able to raises their head and use their arms to push their upper body off of the surface on which they are lying.
Rolling	3 weeks–5 months	Infants are able to change position, rolling from their side to their back.
Rolling over	2–7 months	Infants are able to roll over when placed on their back.
Independent sitting	5–9 months	Infants are able to sit upright by themselves.
Crawling	5–11 months	Infants begin to crawl, using a variety of postures and approaches as they learn about balance and coordination.
Pulling up	5–12 months	Infants are able to grab onto furniture and pull themselves up to a standing position, at first using their arms and later relying on their legs to push themselves up from the floor.

TABLE 6.4 Continued

Milestones	Age	Examples
Independent walking	9–17 months	Infants are able to take steps in an upright position. With experience, they adjust their body posture and leg position and learn to maintain their balance while in motion.
Running	18–24 months	Children possess sufficient balance and coordination to run.
Galloping and hopping	24–36 months	As leg muscles become stronger and balance becomes better controlled, children are able to perform other locomotor skills.

Source: Based on Adolph & Berger, 2006; Bayley, 1993.

results, including a study of prewalking infants who adjusted their posture while seated in a moving room (Butterworth & Hicks, 1977), and a study of young walkers whose movement was affected by their passage through a moving hallway (Schmuckler & Gibson, 1989). These findings, and others that we will discuss shortly, clearly illustrate the fundamental integration of the perception and action systems, whether the action involves the whole body or just the hands and arms.

Reaching, Grasping, and Manipulating Objects

The ability to reach for an object, hold it, and explore it manually is an important motor skill that develops over the first year of life. Neonates display prereaching movements, extending their arms in the direction of nearby objects (Ennouri & Bloch, 1996; Rönnqvist & von Hofsten, 1994), suggesting that the foundation for this skill is present at birth. In one experiment, newborns who saw their own arm movements displayed on a video monitor were able to use this visual feedback to pull their arm back against a small weight; when they were unable to see their own limbs, they did not direct their arm movements in this way (van der Meer, van der Weel, & Lee, 1995). This innate ability is believed to help infants coordinate visual and proprioceptive information and contribute to the further refinement of controlled reaching (Bertenthal & Clifton, 1998).

Coordination of reaching, grasping, and mouthing develops rapidly over the first 6 months of life. Infants are able to bring their hands to their mouth from a very early age, and objects that infants grasp are usually carried to the mouth. By the age of about 4 months, infants typically study objects visually before bringing them to their mouth (Bertenthal & Clifton, 1998; Rochat & Senders, 1991). Reaching at around 4 to 5 months of age tends to be less smooth and direct than the reaching of infants 6 months of age and older. Younger infants' reaches tend to be comprised of several movements as they reach toward an object, rather than the one or two targeted movements that are observed in older infants' reaches (von Hofsten, 1991). The number of movements varies, however, as a function of the type of action. When infants are trying to bat at an object, rather than grasp it, they are able to make smooth, relatively accurate arm movements (Berthier, 1996). Reaching is also affected by infants' postural control and support, as shown in one experiment with 6-month-olds who were not yet able to sit independently. When placed in a specially modified infant seat that facilitated postural control, infants made smoother reaching movements than when they did not have this support (Hopkins & Rönnqvist, 2002).

By the second half of the first year of life, infants can make adjustments in their hands in order to grasp objects in different orientations, and they can do so even when they do not have visual feedback from their own hands (Clifton et al., 1991, 1993, 1994). In one experiment with 7-month-olds, infants who saw lighted rods in a dark room adjusted their hand orientation as they reached for the rod (McCarty, 1993, cited in Bertenthal & Clifton, 1998). Infants are also able to catch moving objects at various speeds and lighting conditions, adjusting their reach in anticipation of the object's trajectory (von Hofsten, 1983; Robin, Berthier, & Clifton, 1996). These findings indicate that proprioceptive information alone can be used to guide arm movements from a very early age.

Early studies of infants' grasping and manual exploration (Halverson, 1931, 1932) led to the identification of three distinct stages: a whole-hand grasping stage from 20 to 28 weeks of age, an intermediate stage involving the thumb's opposition to the palm from 28 to 32 weeks of age, and beginning at 32 weeks of age, a finger-tip grasp involving opposition of the thumb to the other fingers. More recent research has validated the notion of a general developmental progression for various grips during infancy (Siddiqui, 1995), but it is also clear that even infants as young as 6 months are able to adjust their grasp in response to the properties of objects, including their size, shape, weight, substance, and noise-making propensity (Gibson & Walker, 1984; Palmer, 1989). Visual information guides grasping and manual exploration with increasing specificity; by the age of 8 to 9 months, infants are able to anticipate object shape and size, adjusting their finger and

By the age of about 11 months, most infants have developed a clear hand preference for self-feeding.

thumb positioning well in advance of contact with the object (Bertenthal & Clifton, 1998). As infants begin walking, around the age of 12 months, their reaching is perturbed, and they tend to return to two-handed reaching. This decline is only temporary, however, and coordinated reaching with one hand resumes once a stable walking gait is established (Corbetta & Bojczyk, 2002).

Toward the end of the first year of life, infants begin using tools that they encounter, the most obvious of which may be a spoon. By the age of about 11 months, most infants have developed a clear hand preference for self-feeding. One longitudinal study that focused on the development of this skill between 11 and 17 months of age found that infants initially tried a variety of grips before settling on the most successful approaches (Connolly & Dalgleish, 1989). Longitudinal studies like this one have shed light on early tool use, indicating that it is a gradual development that shares many characteristics with other skills arising from infants' perception-action system (Lockman, 2000).

Crawling and Walking

When the systematic study of locomotor development was in its own infancy in the 1930s and 1940s, researchers produced detailed, normative descriptions of apparently obligatory substages in the development of crawling, as well as other motor abilities. These descriptions led to the prevailing view that changes in these skills were the direct result of the maturation of neural structures. Differences in the rate of development were thought to reflect genetic differences in the timing of cortical control of movements previously under reflexive control, rather than variations in experience (Gesell, 1946; McGraw, 1935, 1940). More recent studies have challenged this assumption, documenting a variety of ways in which independent locomotion develops and highlighting the contributions made by infants' own adaptive responses as they move through the environment (Adolph & Berger, 2006).

One longitudinal study of 28 infants, for example, started with their first attempts at crawling (between the ages of approximately 7 to 8 months) and continued until they began independent walking (at approximately 12 months). A variety of crawling postures were observed, but there was no evidence of a strict sequence of stagewise development. Approximately half of the infants crawled on their bellies before crawling on hands and knees, while the other half of the sample began with hands-and-knees crawling (Adolph, Vereijken, & Denny, 1998).

As infants become more expert at crawling, some time between the ages of 7 and 12 months, they pull themselves up to stand and begin cruising—walking, usually stepping sideways, with support. Initially, infants hold onto furniture, moving just one limb at a time, but later they develop a more complex pattern of movement involving two or three limbs simultaneously. One 10-week-long study focusing on five infants cruising as they held onto a chest-high metal bar showed that they became more stable—less wobbly—over time. They continued to use several distinct patterns of limb and body movements, however, rather than settle on just one combination. As the researchers point out, this is an adaptive solution that allows for greater flexibility when cruising in a range of settings requiring different degrees of involvement by the trunk and arms relative to the legs (Haehl, Vardaxis, & Ulrich, 2000). In this way, infants can adjust and cruise successfully whether they are holding onto a soft couch, a wooden dining room table, or a parent's legs.

When infants begin to walk without support, they tend to fall down frequently, in part because there is great variability in their gait. From one moment to the next, their legs may be close together or far apart; their leading foot may be followed more or less quickly by their other foot. To compensate for this variability, infants initially achieve stability by raising their arms and taking slow steps that are placed relatively wide apart—a "Frankenstein-style of walking." After two to three months of practice, leg muscles become stronger and the limbs are better coordinated; infants' gait becomes much more stable and consistent. Whereas beginning walkers have both feet planted on the ground for as much as 60 percent of the time (for adults, the comparable figure is 20 percent), experienced walkers become better able to maintain their balance as their weight shifts from one foot to the other (Adolph & Berger, 2006; Adolph, Vereijken, & Shrout, 2003; Bertenthal & Clifton, 1998; Clark & Phillips, 1993).

Between the ages of 18 and 24 months, balance and coordination improve enough to enable children to run—a form of locomotion in which part of the time neither foot is touching the ground. Running is based on the same pattern of coordinated limb movements as walking but requires the additional ability to produce enough force to leap into the air. By the age of about 3 years, nearly all children are able to perform two other locomotor skills, galloping and hopping. These skills undergo further refinement during childhood, improving as leg muscles get stronger and balance becomes better controlled (Bertenthal & Clifton, 1998).

Children also become more adept at using visual input to guide their locomotion, adjusting to information about whether the terrain surrounding them is rigid enough to support walking or would be better negotiated by crawling (Gibson et al., 1987; Stoffregen et al., 1997). Infants and toddlers also adjust their crawling and walking in response to their perception of the slope of an incline, the support offered by a handrail, and the width of a platform (Berger, Adolph, & Lobo, 2005). Surprisingly, infants are not always able to transfer learning from one posture, such as sitting, to another posture, such as crawling (Adolph, 2000). Other evidence also indicates that, although experience affects performance in locomotor tasks, lessons learned while crawling in specific settings are not necessarily

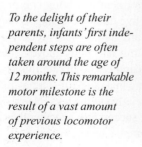

To the delight of their parents, infants' first independent steps are often taken around the age of 12 months. This remarkable motor milestone is the result of a vast amount of previous locomotor experience.

carried over to walking and may need to be re-learned. (Adolph, 1997; Adolph, Vereijken, & Shrout, 2003; Berger & Adolph, 2003).

Walking experience helps infants and toddlers learn about their own physical abilities and the suitability of those skills for particular settings. In one experiment with 12- to 30-month-olds, walking experience was strongly related to whether children attempted to climb over barriers of varying heights; with experience, walkers were more discriminating and more accurate in judging which barriers to attempt climbing over (Schmuckler, 1996). Other studies have reported links between walking experience and the ability to move through doorways of varying widths (Adolph, 1997). In all of these studies, children's locomotor experience—but not their height, weight, or other body-size characteristics—has been found to be associated with accurate perceptions of their ability to climb over barriers, squeeze through openings, and negotiate variable terrain.

The Role of Experience: Implications for Parents and Caregivers

Across cultures, there is considerable variation in how prewalking infants are handled and in the role that parents play in encouraging locomotor development (Gardiner, Mutter, & Kosmitzki, 2002; Hewlett et al., 1998; Hopkins & Westra, 1990; Rogoff & Morelli, 1989). In many parts of the world, infants are carried on the mother's back, secured in place with a blanket or strips of cloth, leaving the mother's hands free to cook, weave, tend to crops, or perform other daily tasks (Pretorius, Naude, & Van Vuuren, 2002; DeLoache & Gottlieb, 2000). In the United States and in most developed countries, by contrast, infants are more likely to be strapped into strollers and wheeled, rather than carried. In addition, in cultures in which there are concerns about sanitation, crawling may be discouraged or even forbidden; whereas in other cultural contexts, parents give their infants "tummy time" on a blanket on the floor and baby-proof the home to enable their children to crawl and explore in safety. Finally, in some cultures, infants are discouraged from walking before the age of 1 year, whereas in other cultures, including the United States, many infants spend time in devices that parents hope will encourage early independent walking (DeLoache & Gottlieb, 2000).

Do these different caregiving practices result in different patterns of locomotor development? The answer is that there is mixed evidence, depending on the type of early experience and the specific locomotor ability in question (Gardiner, Mutter, & Kosmitzki, 2002; Super, 1976). Infants in traditional cultures who are strapped onto their mother's back, for example, do not appear to crawl or walk later than infants who are not confined in this way (Gardiner, Mutter, & Kosmitzki, 2002). Infants who spend time in walkers, however, appear to begin walking later than infants who are not placed in walkers—the opposite result that parents using walkers are often trying to achieve (Siegel & Burton, 1999). If, as many researchers have found, infants explore and test out a variety of crawling, cruising, and walking postures on their way to becoming more skilled in these forms of locomotion, it is possible that infants confined in walkers are actually missing out on opportunities to develop a flexible repertoire of relevant skills (Adolph & Berger, 2006).

Infants who are assisted in performing specific locomotor skills may benefit from the practice. In one study of Jamaican infants who were assisted in sitting upright from an early age, independent sitting appeared earlier than among a comparison group of English infants

This Mexican mother carries one child on her back while she sorts tomatillos with her other child.

who were not given early assistance with this skill. Jamaican infants in this study also walked slightly earlier, on average, than the English infants, but there were no differences in the onset of crawling (Hopkins & Westra, 1990). In another study, researchers who systematically activated 2-month-old infants' stepping reflex over a period of weeks reported that these infants began to walk approximately two months earlier than a comparison group of infants who did not receive this extra stimulation (Zelazo, Zelazo, & Kolb, 1972).

What are the implications of these findings for parents and caregivers? As we have discussed, motor abilities—even "automatic" motor milestones, such as crawling and walking—develop gradually as a result of repeated experience. Before learning to roll over by themselves, for example, infants benefit from practice coordinating their limbs with the movements of their head and body. Structured infant exercise programs and equipment are not necessary, however, for the development of healthy infants (American Academy of Pediatrics Committee on Sports Medicine, 1988). Instead, infants should be in a safe environment that stimulates all of the senses and enables them to participate actively. While parents can make occasional use of infant "containers," such as bouncy seats, playpens, and strollers, they should be sure to give their babies significant chances every day to move and explore. There should be a range of toys and other child-safe objects made out of a variety of substances with different noise-making capabilities.

For toddlers and preschoolers, experts recommend that, during waking hours, children should not be sedentary for more than 1 hour at a time (National Association for Sport and Physical Education, 2002). Beginning in the toddler years, children benefit from both structured physical activity and unstructured free play and should have time for both kinds of activities every day. The ideal environment at these ages is one that gives children objects to ride, push, pull, throw, and catch, and structures that they can climb through and on. Above all, these activities should be fun for the children involved and provide them with a foundation for lifelong physical activity, even if they cannot guarantee a successful career as a professional athlete, like Tiger Woods.

WRAPPING IT UP: Summary and Conclusion

Infants are able to see, hear, feel, taste, and smell at birth. Some of these senses are activated during the prenatal period, but others receive their first stimulation only after birth. Traditional empiricist theories assumed that infants are initially unable to perceive the world accurately, whereas nativist theories challenged the empiricist notion that initially meaningless sensory information could become meaningful as a result of experience during infancy. Gestalt theories asserted that the brain is designed to translate and organize sensory information that would otherwise be meaningless. According to the more recently developed ecological theory, the perceptual system perceives information about the environment accurately and directly. Although perceptual abilities may improve with experience, infants do not need to learn to impose meaning per se.

Vision is the least well developed sense at birth. Newborns notice and pay attention to objects and people in motion. Their attention is drawn to areas of high contrast, and they prefer some patterns more than others. Visual acuity is poor at birth but improves to nearly adult levels by the age of about 8 months as the size of the eyeball increases and as cortical pathways become involved in visual processing. Visual problems are relatively rare among infants but can be detected with early screening. Early treatment is necessary to prevent permanent impairment and promote normal development of the visual cortex.

In order to perceive objects, infants need to be able to detect the edges and boundaries of each object as well as perceive objects in 3-D. Movement provides more useful information about object properties and object unity than texture, color, or substance. During the first 6 months of life, infants become able to use an increasing number of cues for the perception of depth.

Newborns pay special attention to the human voice and seem to prefer it to other sounds. Infants are aroused by high-pitched speech and soothed by low-pitched sounds. Beginning at birth, children's hearing should be screened during visits to the pediatrician.

Infants need touch and physical contact with caregivers in order to grow and thrive. Most neonatal reflexes are activated through the sense of touch. Responses to pain change as infants' cognitive abilities increase and enable them to recognize and anticipate previously encountered sources of discomfort, such as inoculations.

Infants have an innate preference for high-energy, sweet tasting substances but dislike sour and bitter flavors. The foods that pregnant women consume have an influence on newborns' reaction to flavors and odors during the early postnatal period, possibly predisposing them to respond favorably to their culture's cuisine. Infants respond to aromas in ways that are similar to adults' responses. Like adults, infants appear to find sweet smells pleasant and odors of fish and ammonia unpleasant. Newborns are able to recognize salient biological odors, such as amniotic fluid or their own mother's breast milk.

Intermodal perception of events is facilitated by infants' ability to perceive amodal properties of those events, and cross-modal perception is possible soon after birth, as shown by studies of visual-haptic transfer. Infants' vestibular sense conveys information about balance and support, and some neonatal reflexes are activated by stimulation of this sense. The proprioceptive and kinesthetic senses provide information from muscles, tendons, and joints about the body's position and movement.

Fine and gross motor skills develop in a predictable order and are part of a dynamic perception-action system that enables infants to adapt to their environment. Coordination of reaching, grasping, and mouthing objects develops rapidly over the first 6 months of life. Infants develop a variety of crawling, cruising, and walking postures, but not all infants pass through the same substages of locomotor development. Visual information guides infants' locomotion, and locomotor experience helps them learn about their own physical capabilities. Across cultures, there is variation in how prewalking infants are handled and in the role that parents play in encouraging locomotor development. Infants who are assisted in specific locomotor skills may benefit from that practice. Structured exercise programs are not necessary, however, for healthy infant development. Beginning from infancy, children need opportunities every day to move, explore, and develop their perceptual and motor abilities.

THINK ABOUT IT: Questions for Reading and Discussion

1. What are newborn infants able to see, hear, feel, taste, and smell?

2. Based on your knowledge of infants' sensory abilities, how would you decorate a room for an infant in order to optimally stimulate all five senses?

3. In what ways is motor development part of a perception-action system?

4. How do researchers determine whether infants are able to perceive objects? Can you think of any other research techniques that could be used to explore object perception?

5. Why do you think that movement is such a salient source of information for infants? Compare the potential value of knowing an object's location or trajectory with the potential value of knowing its color, shape, or size.

6. How does independent mobility affect infants' lives? What impact does it have on their parents?

7. Describe the ideal environment for supporting and stimulating locomotor development during infancy.

8. What could be gained by studying sensation, perception, and motor development across a range of cultural contexts? Suggest a specific topic or question that could be studied in this way, and outline how it might be investigated.

KEY WORDS

Accretion and deletion (187)	The apparent appearance and disappearance of elements of a visual stimulus, such as its texture or pattern
Amodal properties (197)	Properties of events that are not specific to a particular sensory modality, such as the synchrony of a sight and its accompanying sound
Auditory localization (191)	The ability to detect the location of sound sources
Bayley Scales of Infant Development-Second Edition (BSID-II) (199)	A widely use assessment that includes scales for measuring motor development from birth to 42 months of age

Binocular disparity (190)	Slightly different retinal images that are produced when a viewer looks at a single object or visual stimulus
Binocular vision (185)	Visual input from two eyes that are aligned and move together
Cones (183)	Photoreceptors in the eye that respond to specific hues, or wavelengths of light
Cross-modal perception (196)	The ability to transfer information about an object from one sense, such as vision, and use it when encountering the object later using a different sense, such as touch
Depth perception (181)	The ability to perceive a three-dimensional world
Ecological theory of perception (181)	A theory that assumes that the visual system perceives meaningful information directly from the properties of the environment
Fine motor skills (199)	Skills, such as grasping small objects, that involve movements of the fingers and hands
Forced-choice preferential looking (184)	A research procedure in which infants are shown two visual stimuli simultaneously and the total amount of time they spend looking at each display is compared
Fovea (184)	The center of the eye
Gross motor skills (199)	Skills, such as crawling and walking, that involve movements of the whole body and large muscle groups
Haptic information (198)	Exploratory mouth or hand movements that go well beyond mere tactile contact with an object
Intermodal perception (196)	The ability to integrate multiple simultaneous sources of sensory information, such as sights and sounds produced by a single object or event
Kinematic depth cues (189)	Information about perceptual depth that is carried by motion
Kinesthetic sense (198)	A sense that conveys information about the body's position and movement
Optical expansion and contraction (189)	The increase and decrease in the size of an object's image on the retina
Pictorial depth cues (191)	Information about perceptual depth that is used in two-dimensional representations of the three-dimensional world, including relative size, linear perspective, texture gradients, and interposition
Proprioceptive sense (198)	A sense that conveys information from muscles, tendons, and joints about the body's position and movement
Size constancy (189)	The ability to perceive an object's actual size correctly, even when it is viewed from different distances
Stereoscopic depth information (190)	Information about perceptual depth that is produced by binocular disparity
Vestibular sense (198)	A sense that conveys information about physical balance and support
Visual acuity (183)	The smallest spacing that can be perceived between parts of a pattern
Visual cortex (184)	The area of the brain that processes visual information

Cognition, Learning, and Intelligence

Defining and Testing Intelligence in Infancy
Traditional Tests of Infant Intelligence
Information Processing Assessments of Infant Intelligence

Wrapping It Up: Summary and Conclusion

Between 6 and 12 months of age, infants become able to use a spoon to help feed themselves, showing increasing skill and a consistent hand preference by the age of about 11 months. As thrilled as parents are by this achievement, in the second year of life something even more amazing happens—very young children begin to use spoons to *pretend* to feed themselves. Approaching their second birthday, children become increasingly adept at employing familiar objects and realistic props to simulate a range of familiar actions, such as giving a doll a bath or putting their teddy bear to sleep. If the ability to feed oneself depends on perceptual-motor development, what underlies the ability to act *as if* imaginary food is being eaten?

Children pretending to feed a stuffed animal follow a sequence of steps that is similar to the routine they have observed their parents enacting: picking up a spoon, moving it toward the "baby's" mouth, and offering an encouraging commentary about the delicious food. At a minimum, the ability to engage in pretense depends on being able to pay attention to an ongoing event, notice and remember its components, and perform the same actions in a different context. As we will see in this chapter, these are all cognitive abilities that emerge during the first 3 years of life. They are advances that enable children to learn, remember, and organize knowledge about the world, in short, to behave intelligently. In this chapter we will review these aspects of cognitive development, as well as efforts to define and measure intelligence in infancy and to use those measures to predict intelligence later

This young boy's pretend conversation might not occur without the presence of such a realistic prop.

in childhood. We begin with an examination of the development of play—a pervasive childhood activity that both depends upon and contributes to cognitive development.

The Development of Play

Play is an aspect of infancy and childhood that is both familiar and ambiguous (Sutton-Smith, 1997). When infants and very young children play, how is their behavior different from other activities? How do we know, for example, that a child putting a doll to sleep is playing—pretending that it is bedtime—rather than acting on the belief that the doll is actually tired? In contrast to other activities, play is intrinsically motivated, characterized by attention to means rather than ends, and distinguished from purely exploratory behavior. In addition, play is often characterized by pretending and unlike games is free from externally applied rules (Rubin, Fein, and Vandenberg, 1983).

Children pretending that it is naptime for their doll often initiate this activity on their own, rather than have it suggested or set up for them by an adult. (Even very young children pretend about scenarios that no adult would suggest, such as unrolling a toilet-paper "snake" into the toilet or "vacuuming" the kitchen table with an apple slice.) To the extent that children have noticed and remembered the elements associated with their own naptime or bedtime experiences, they are likely to give the doll a snack or a drink before taking off the doll's shoes, laying the doll down with a pillow and blanket, and finally reading a story or singing a lullaby to the doll.

Play with Objects

Young children's play is influenced by the materials and opportunities that are available. Children in developed countries are typically provided with toys that are designed to be safe, attractive, developmentally appropriate, and educational. Toys for today's infants tend to be colorful, made of plastic, and increasingly, activated by a tiny computer chip. While these features make toys attractive to adults who buy them, infants may not even notice that their toys are expensive and smart. As many studies have shown, infants' play behavior is chiefly a function of their evolving motor, cognitive, and social skills. Table 7.1 shows the progression of types of object play over the first 3 years of life.

Until the age of about 4 months, infants engage in **exploratory play**, which tends to consist of the repetition of motor movements. Even if a vast array of toys is available, infants' focus during this period is on their own body. Toys and other objects may be grasped and manipulated, especially if an object is placed in the infant's hands or if the infant's car seat has toys that are within reach, but a significant amount of attention is given to the self. Between 4 and 12 months of age, infants become increasingly attracted by the external world and are better able to reach for and grasp objects that interest them. The tendency seen at this age is to engage in **relational play**, simultaneously touching or manipulating two unrelated objects, such as a piece of paper and a bucket. When infants between 12 and 18 months of age play with objects, they are increasingly likely to engage in **functional play**, in which they discover how their own actions create reactions, and their play with objects becomes more intentional. They also engage in **functional-relational play** at this

TABLE 7.1 Types of Object Play from Birth to Age 3

Type of Play	Ages	Characteristics and Examples
Exploratory	Birth to 4 months	Repetitive motor movements, focused on the infant's own body: kicking their legs, reaching for and sucking on their toes, practicing moving and rolling over.
Relational	4 to 12 months	Bringing together and manipulating objects that are not related to each other, such as a piece of silky fabric and a plastic measuring cup. Repeatedly banging objects or putting them into containers and dumping them out are favorite activities.
Functional	12 to 18 months	Infants discover how their own actions create reactions, and play with objects becomes more intentional. After discovering that a toy can be activated by pushing a button or pulling a string, infants repeat this action.
Functional-relational	12 to 18 months	Objects are increasingly used in ways that show understanding of their intended use: children roll objects with wheels, pretend to drink out of empty cups, and "talk" on toy telephones. They bring together related objects, such as a bowl and spoon or a doll and the doll's bed.
Gross motor play	12 to 24 months	As gross motor skills develop, children use them to push toys such as small carts or pull toys that have strings. Children also enjoy play that involves climbing, sliding, swinging, spinning, or moving their whole body through containers such as play tunnels, gigantic cardboard boxes, and ball crawls (shallow vats of large plastic balls).
Fine motor play	24 to 36 months	As children's fine motor skills develop, they are able to play with fingerpaint and Play-Doh®. They also enjoy filling and emptying containers with dried beans, uncooked pasta, sand, and water. Fine motor skills can also be used to string beads, put together simple puzzles with large pieces, and build towers and other structures with wooden blocks or age-appropriate Legos®.

Source: Based on information in Garner, 1998.

age, as shown by their increasing tendency to bring together related objects, such as a bowl and spoon or a doll and the doll's bed.

Babies develop expectations about the world as a result of their exploratory play with objects. This was shown in one experiment in which children first played with new toys and then were given a chance to play with the same toys after they had been altered by the researchers. For some of the toys, the researchers removed noise makers, while for other toys they changed only the appearance. Although the 13- and 14-month-old infants in this experiment were given just 30 seconds to play with the toys before they were altered, this turned out to be enough time for them to develop expectations about the toys' properties. Given the chance to pick up a toy that had previously made noise, for example, infants tried to reproduce that sound with the altered toy and persisted when their initial attempts were not successful (Baldwin, Markman, & Melartin, 1989). This study indicates that exploratory play makes important contributions to very young children's understanding of the world and the objects and people in it.

As children become more skilled at walking, between the ages of 12 and 24 months, a significant amount of play uses gross motor skills. Between the ages of 2 to 3 years, children are less likely to put objects automatically in their mouth and now enjoy using their fine motor skills to play with a variety of materials. As they near the age of 3 years, children can use scissors, glue sticks, and paint brushes with increasing control, although the focus of these activities still tends to be on playful manipulation and exploration.

Social Play

With an increasing array of computer software being developed for children as young as 2 or 3 years of age, play during the first years of life now may also include moving a computer mouse and playing with characters and objects in a virtual world. The best "object" to interact with, however, is still a responsive human playmate. In many parts of the world, parents and adult caregivers play games with young infants, eliciting and responding to their smiles, coos, and changes in visual attention (Fernald & O'Neill, 1993). Adult-infant play tends to consist of pat-a-cake and other singing games with hand and arm movements, give-and-take games (trading toys or other objects back and forth), pointing-and-naming games, and peek-aboo. As they get older, infants play an increasingly active role, initiating play as well as responding to adults' behaviors (Fogel, Nwokah, & Karns, 1993). Adult-infant play is not universal, however. In some cultures, adults do not regularly play with infants and young children, and play is regarded as unimportant or appropriate only for child participants, such as the infant's older siblings and peers (Bornstein et al., 1999; Farver & Howes, 1993; Farver, Kim, & Lee, 1995; Roopnarine et al., 1998; Tamis-LeMonda & Bornstein, 1996).

Where adult-infant play is common, parents often perceive their involvement as an extension of their role as their child's teacher. Mothers are more likely than fathers to use play as an opportunity for teaching infants about words and routines, whereas fathers tend to play in a way that is more physical and "just for fun" (Barnard & Solchany, 2002; Parke, 2002). The ways in which mothers and fathers interact and play with their infants vary, however, and even within the same culture, may be affected by factors such as the parents' employment status, knowledge of child development, and involvement in their infant's daily care (Pedersen, Cain, & Zaslow, 1982; Tamis-LeMonda, Chen, & Bornstein, 1997).

Culture's influence is seen not only in whether parents view themselves as partners in their children's play but also in the content of the "lessons" that parents teach through playful interactions. Cross-cultural research with young children has shown that mothers who view play as contributing to cognitive development are more likely to provide props and specific suggestions than are mothers who regard play as a primarily social or entertaining activity (Farver & Howes, 1993; Farver, Kim, & Lee, 1995; Farver & Wimbarti, 1995; Tudge, Lee, & Putnam, 1998). There is also evidence that children in collectivist (group-oriented) cultures are guided in mother-child play to use toys to promote social interaction, whereas children in individualist cultures (like the United States) are more often prompted to focus on the toys themselves. In one study comparing Argentine and U.S. mothers, Argentine mothers (who are part of a collectivist culture) encouraged their 20-month-olds to pretend to perform social routines, such as feeding or sharing with others, but U.S. mothers encouraged their children to use the same set of toys in functionally appropriate ways, such as nesting cups or dialing a toy telephone (Bornstein et al., 1999).

Studies comparing other cultures have found that Japanese mothers tend to emphasize social routines during play ("Feed the teddy" or "Say thank you"), whereas American mothers more frequently use play as an opportunity to teach infants about objects' names and functions ("That's a dump truck" or "Push the car"). Given that Japanese culture is built on a foundation of interdependence and mutual empathy, whereas U.S. culture tends to emphasize independence and individual achievement, these different patterns suggest that parents use play as one means of socializing infants and young children, teaching them about the prevailing beliefs and practices of their culture (Fernald & Morikawa, 1993; Tamis-LeMonda et al., 1992).

Although there are cultural variations in the extent to which adults play with children, play with peers and siblings is apparently universal and begins at a very early age. There appears to be little need to teach infants to play. They typically respond with great interest and enthusiasm whenever there is a chance to interact with other infants or young children (Howes, 1996). Initially, infants demonstrate their interest through visual gaze at the other child, excited vocalizations, and reaching or other movements of the hands, arms, and body—a behavioral repertoire that some parents describe as "species recognition." If they are close enough, precrawling infants may reach toward each other, examining the other child or fingering toys as they lie or sit side by side. With independent mobility, infants crawl toward each other and in the direction of toys and objects that draw their attention. Toddlers can carry toys and objects as they seek out each other. Their give-and-take play focuses on these items as part of their social interaction. Infants and toddlers who spend time together on a regular basis show clear preferences for specific play partners within a larger group of children. Experience with coordinated, complementary play activities, like chasing games and give-and-take games, during the early toddler years may serve as a foundation for more complex forms of social pretend play during the third year of life and beyond (Garner, 1998; Howes, 1996).

Pretend/Symbolic Play

Pretend/symbolic play usually emerges after the first birthday, when children behave in a nonliteral way, acting *as if* they were performing familiar routines, such as eating, going to sleep, or washing their face. The earliest pretend actions tend to be brief and unrelated to children's other ongoing behavior. They may, for example, add sound effects ("vroom, vroom") and motions that transform a piece of toast into a car just before eating it. As they get older, several pretend actions may be combined, strung together as part of a coherent sequence, such as washing a doll's face, brushing her hair, and then feeding her lunch.

Children's pretend play is initially dependent on the presence of realistic props, such as a toy telephone, and children have difficulty substituting objects that have little resemblance to the real object, such as a wooden block, until they are nearly 3 years of age. Children younger than the age of 3 years also avoid using objects that already have specific functions, such as a shoe, to symbolize other objects, such as a telephone (Garner, 1998).

At first, children's pretend play is focused on the self, but it gradually expands to include other participants. A 13-month-old who places a bowl on his head, for example, pretending that it is a hat, is unlikely to place the bowl/hat on a parent's head unless asked to do so. By the age of about 15 months, children begin to engage in parallel pretend play—sitting near each other, making eye contact from time to time, as both children rock their own baby doll or push their own small train engine along a wooden track.

Pretend play becomes more social between 2 and 3 years of age, and children begin to coordinate their pretend actions with those of their playmates, whether they are peers or adults. Between the ages of 16 and 32 months, children first coordinate their actions through nonverbal imitation, such as pretending to drink from a cup after seeing playmates pretending to drink from their own cups. Children also begin to respond by verbally imitating their play partners and by producing their own play-related speech (Eckerman & Didow, 1989). The ability to comprehend pretend play in others advances significantly after the second birthday (Harris & Kavanaugh, 1993). As a result, a child whose play partner knocks over an empty cup and exclaims over the "spilled milk" now may respond by pretending to dry off the table or refill the cup from an empty pitcher.

Between the ages of 2 and 3 years, children begin to construct narratives about their play, often drawing on past experiences (Kavanaugh & Engel, 1998). Children's developing verbal skills enable them to comment on their own actions and coordinate them with others as part of a larger play theme (Cohen & Tomlinson-Keasey, 1980; Howes, 1985; Lloyd & Goodwin, 1995). They use words to specify the setting ("This is a bus"), their roles ("I drive the bus"), and those of their play partners ("You ride the bus"). Children's shared, cooperative pretend play (also known as **sociodramatic play**) reveals their understanding of the world, including everyday scenes (e.g., family life at home), less frequent events (e.g., a checkup at the doctor's office), and relatively rare experiences (e.g., flying on an airplane).

Parents do not explicitly teach their children how to pretend, but they do provide inspiration through the materials and experiences they provide and in the way that they respond to their children's play. Many parents contribute by engaging directly in pretense with their young children, using unique verbal and nonverbal behaviors, such as higher pitched speech, exaggerated actions, and a greater incidence and duration of sound effects, smiling, and direct eye contact (Lillard & Witherington, 2004; Reissland & Snow, 1996). In one recent experiment, mothers of 18-month-olds both pretended to have a snack with their child and ate a real snack together. Mothers pretending to eat Cheerios® and drink juice talked more about those actions than when they were actually eating and drinking, and they made more sound effects (e.g., "mmmm"), a combination of behaviors that may help very young children understand the pretend mode (Lillard & Witherington, 2004).

Studies of children between the ages of approximately 18 months and 3 years, comparing solitary pretend play and joint pretend play with their mother, consistently have shown that the duration and quality of play increase when parents join in (Bornstein et al., 1996; Cohen & Tomlinson-Keasey, 1980; Harris & Kavanaugh, 1993; Kavanaugh & Engel, 1998). In comparison with solitary pretend play when the mother is present (in the same room but not participating), mother-child pretend play lasts longer and occurs more frequently. In addition, when mothers become involved, more time is spent setting up make-believe episodes by clarifying roles, finding props, and specifying the sociodramatic play theme. Once pretend play is under way, mothers ask questions, make suggestions, and give demonstrations. These behaviors appear to facilitate children's play, as long as the mother's involvement is not intrusive or insensitive to children's interests (Garner, 1998; Harris & Kavanaugh, 1993; Stilson & Harding, 1997).

Joint make-believe with older siblings has also been shown to enhance young children's pretend play. Some studies have found that young children playing with an older sibling engage in more role-playing than when they play alone or even with their mother and sibling together. The explicit discussion of each sibling's role is thought to contribute to young children's understanding of others' feelings and beliefs (Youngblade & Dunn, 1995). The ability to appreciate others' states of mind, including their feelings and beliefs, is a significant cognitive achievement called **theory of mind**, usually observed for the first time around the age of 3 years. There is some intriguing evidence that preschoolers who frequently engage in make-believe role playing are more advanced on tests of mental representation than are children who seldom engage in role playing (Kavanaugh & Engel, 1998). We turn now to examine the theory and legacy of Jean Piaget—one of the first scientists to study the development of children's play and children's minds.

Piaget's Theory of Cognitive Development

According to Piaget (1896–1980), a pioneering Swiss researcher and theorist who observed his own three children beginning at birth, the capacity for pretense depends on the emergence of specific cognitive abilities, including **mental representation**—the ability to remember and think about objects and events, even when those objects and events are not present. Piaget asserted that the capacity for mental representation develops during the last half of the second year of life as the culmination of a series of invariant stages.

Piaget (1936/1952, 1937/1971, 1946/1962) developed a theory of cognitive development that described four discrete periods of intelligence. Infancy (birth to 2 years) is the period of **sensorimotor intelligence**, early childhood (2 to 6 years) the period of preoperational thought, middle childhood (6 to 12 years) the period of concrete operations, and adolescence (12 years and older) the period of formal operations. At each stage, according to Piaget, the child thinks about the world in a qualitatively unique way, eventually developing the capacity for logical, abstract reasoning. Our focus in this chapter is on the sensorimotor period.

Sensorimotor Intelligence: Constructing Knowledge through Action

Piaget is known as a constructivist. Departing from the well-known dichotomy of nativism versus empiricism, his theory proposes that knowledge is neither innately given nor provided through passive experience. Instead, knowledge is said to be constructed and derived from children's own actions, specifically, their efforts to adapt to the environment. As we saw in Chapter 6, when infants encounter new objects and surfaces in the environment, they explore them and pick up useful information, such as which toys can be grasped and which surfaces are suitable for walking across. Given a new object that looks like a ball, they may use actions—which Piaget termed **schemes**—that are similar to those they have used previously to touch or push other balls. If the new ball has a jingle bell inside that makes noise as the ball is touched or pushed, however, they may explore it further by using a different scheme, such as a shaking motion.

In Piaget's view, infants engage in **assimilation** when they employ previously used actions to explore an object, whereas they use **accommodation** when they adjust their exploratory actions to an object's novel characteristics. An example of assimilation would be when an infant rolls a new ball in the same manner as other balls that have previously been encountered. In accommodation, by contrast, the infant might shake a new ball if doing so produces a jingling noise. Piaget noted that assimilation and accommodation are always simultaneously in use, although one process typically predominates. Through the complementary processes of assimilation and accommodation, Piaget asserted, schemes are modified as a result of experience. During the sensorimotor period, schemes are primarily physical—based on sensory and motor acts—but during the later three periods, schemes may also be conceptual, as when ideas are either reinforced or modified by experience.

Six Stages of Sensorimotor Development

Piaget (1937/1971) believed that the foundation for all knowledge begins in infancy, during the period of sensorimotor intelligence. In his view, infants are **egocentric**, meaning that they initially understand the world in a way that is filtered through their own sensory and motor acts. Across the first 2 years of life, infants gradually become more aware of other perspectives, but egocentrism continues to affect children's thinking into early childhood. The incremental nature of cognitive development can be seen in the six distinct stages (shown in Table 7.2) into which Piaget divided the sensorimotor period.

Stage 1: Birth to 1 Month.   In Stage 1, **reflex schemes** provide infants with a set of initial responses to the world. Learning during this stage is limited, however, because reflex schemes are unchanging across different sources of stimulation, showing little accommodation or modification. That is, the same rooting reflex is elicited whether the infant's cheek is touched by the stroke of a finger, a nipple, or a rubber pacifier. Piaget asserted that reflex schemes, as well as the separate senses, are independent and isolated from one another. More recent research has challenged this theoretical assumption. As we saw in Chapter 6, it is now clear that intermodal and cross-modal perception occur as early as the first weeks of life.

TABLE 7.2   Piaget's Six Stages of Sensorimotor Intelligence

Stage	Ages	Characteristics and Examples
1. Reflex schemes	Birth to 1 month	Infants respond reflexively to sensory stimulation. Grasping, sucking, and other reflexes provide infants with a set of schemes for initial learning.
2. Primary Circular Reactions	1 to 4 months	Infants learn about the world through chance activation of schemes. Grasping or sucking on toes initially occurs as a result of random movements but is subsequently repeated "just for fun."
3. Secondary Circular Reactions	4 to 8 months	Infants intentionally use schemes to repeat actions and achieve specific outcomes. Pushing a button occurs repeatedly and intentionally in order to activate a musical toy.
4. Coordination of Secondary Schemes	8 to 12 months	Infants coordinate two separate schemes in order to produce a specific outcome. An obstacle in front of a toy is moved before the toy is picked up and manipulated.
5. Tertiary Circular Reactions	12 to 18 months	Infants "experiment" with schemes to discover how they work. Banging on a toy xylophone with a small mallet makes "music," whereas using fingers or a plastic cup produces a different sound.
6. Mental Combinations	18 to 24 months	Toddlers are able to think about and select schemes to achieve desired out comes. After looking at vertical crib bars, the child modifies his grasp on a toy in order to pull it through the first time.

Source: Based on information in Piaget, 1937/1971.

Stage 2: 1 to 4 Months.   In Stage 2, infants exhibit **primary circular reactions**, and sensory and motor schemes occur by chance. Examples of primary circular reactions include infants grasping and releasing objects just for the "fun" of it, or sucking on their own fingers after they happen to put them in their mouth. In the stage of primary circular reactions, schemes are discovered by chance, and infants work hard to recreate those schemes, intentionally moving their hand to their mouth and then sucking on their fingers. Infants' repeated (circular) actions could be described as being used for "entertainment" rather than to provide information about the world, however, and, in Piaget's view, this shows that infants are still egocentric and focused inward.

Stage 3: 4 to 8 Months.   In Stage 3, **secondary circular reactions**, schemes are less egocentric and infants focus on repeating actions to achieve specific outcomes. Examples of secondary circular reactions include infants dropping Cheerios® over the side of their high chair and watching them land on the floor or pushing a button on a toy to activate recorded music. The events that infants initiate and repeat in this stage often produce laughter or other signs of enjoyment. Piaget's daughter Lucienne reportedly squealed with laughter each time she kicked her legs and made a mobile over her crib move (Crain, 2000).

Stage 4: 8 to 12 Months.   Stage 4 infants show **coordination of secondary schemes** when they carry out two separate schemes in order to produce an interesting outcome. Piaget observed his son, Laurent, move an obstacle (Piaget's hand) out of the way in order to reach a matchbox. Laurent's coordination of two schemes (moving and grabbing) was not the first solution he tried as he attempted to grab the matchbox, but it was the most successful one (Crain, 2000). Piaget inferred from this behavior that his son had begun to develop a basic understanding of spatial relationships—the notion that some objects are in front of others—as well as the relevance of the order in which the two schemes were used, since grabbing the matchbox could not occur until the hand had been moved out of the way. In Piaget's view, however, infants' conception of space is still egocentric at this stage, and infants are unaware of the spatial relations among objects in the world, independent of their direct contact with those objects.

Stage 5: 12 to 18 Months.   At Stage 5, **tertiary circular reactions**, infants try out different schemes to discover the effects of those actions. Piaget noted that his son used different banging actions, some hard and others soft, to explore a new table (Crain, 2000). Infants in this stage are like little scientists, performing "experiments" on the world around them.

Stage 6: 18 to 24 Months.   In the last stage, **mental combinations**, children are able to think about their actions and select schemes to achieve an outcome. Piaget's example of this ability was his daughter Lucienne's discovery of a solution for retrieving a small chain from a matchbox in which her father had placed it. Piaget noted that Lucienne first tried turning the box over and then attempted to squeeze her finger into the closed box. When these schemes failed, she reportedly opened and closed her mouth, while looking intently at the matchbox, and then quickly slid back the cover to make the opening of the matchbox wide enough to retrieve the chain (Crain, 2000).

According to Piaget, mental representation enables children to perform **deferred imitation**, repeating actions that have been observed earlier, in the absence of a model for those actions. One well-known example comes from Piaget's daughter Jacqueline, who had a temper tantrum in her playpen that exactly mimicked a temper tantrum she had witnessed in another child the previous day. Fortunately, children also show deferred imitation of behaviors that parents find desirable, including hugging and sharing.

Mental representation is evident in many other achievements at this age. It underlies the use of gestures, words, and signs to communicate ideas, as well as the use of numbers to count. Mental representational ability also contributes to children's emerging self-concept, and as we noted previously, their ability to engage in pretend play. In Stage 6, Piaget credited infants with the ability to comprehend space as an independent environment that exists around them, in which they are just one of numerous people and objects.

According to Piaget, whereas the first symbols appearing at the end of the sensorimotor period are representations of actions, the symbols that children use in the preoperational period (2 to 6 years) may be either action-based or linguistic. Around the age of 2 years, children begin to use language to represent and talk about past and present experiences, as well as desires for the future. A child giving his stuffed animal a turn on his riding toy, for example, may narrate the activity, saying, "ride, bear." A child who accompanies her grandmother to the airport at the end of a visit together may tell her babysitter the next day, "Nanny go bye-bye." As we will see in Chapter 8, in which we discuss language development in much greater detail, 2- and 3-year-old children's early vocabulary provides a window into their cognitive abilities.

The Development of Object Permanence.   One of the best-known components of Piaget's theory of sensorimotor intelligence is his notion of **object permanence**, Piaget's term for infants' gradually developing understanding that objects continue to exist even when they are not in sensory or motor contact with them. If infants younger than 4 months drop a toy that they have grasped in their hand, for example, they do not actively look for it. Piaget asserted further that, although infants older than 4 months of age (Stage 3) look for toys and other objects that they have dropped, their searches are short-lived, suggesting that they are not sure that the objects still exist. Piaget tested object permanence by placing an ordinary object (his pocketwatch) under a blanket. He noted that, unless some part of the watch remained visible, Stage 3 infants typically failed to lift up the blanket and retrieve the hidden object.

In Piaget's theory, object permanence begins to develop around 8 months of age (Stage 4). At this stage, infants who watch a toy being hidden under a cloth or inside a container successfully search for and retrieve it, but their understanding of object permanence is not yet complete. Piaget noted that Stage 4 infants tend to make the **A-not-B error**, an error that occurs when infants watch an object being hidden repeatedly in one location (A) and successfully retrieve it from that location, but continue to search for the object there even after they have seen it being hidden at a different location (B). According to Piaget, the A-not-B error reflects infants' belief that their own actions will cause the object to appear at the location where those actions were previously successful.

In Stage 5, Piaget noted that infants are able to search for and retrieve an object at any location, regardless of whether they have previously searched at that spot. This new flexibility in search behavior depends, however, on the child having observed the object being moved and hidden in its final location. Piaget granted 18- to 24-month-olds (Stage 6) full object permanence. At this stage, he reported, children search flexibly and are able to continue searching in potential hiding spots until they find the object.

Taken together, Piaget's observations and theory painted a picture of sensorimotor intelligence that highlights infants' cognitive deficits and shortcomings. As we will see next, that picture has faded over the years, as the results of more recent research have shown that many cognitive abilities emerge earlier than Piaget reported.

Evaluating Piaget's Theory of Sensorimotor Intelligence

When we evaluate Piaget's theory of sensorimotor intelligence, it is important to remember that he used different methods to explore infants' abilities than subsequent researchers have

TABLE 7.3   **A Variety of Procedures Have Been Used to Study Object Permanence**

Procedure	Researcher	Principal Findings
An object is hidden underneath a cloth or inside one of two opaque containers.	Piaget	Full object permanence, without the A-not-B error, develops between 18 and 24 months.
An object is "hidden" by darkness.	Goubet & Clifton	Infants search for objects in the correct location, based on an auditory cue, by 6 1/2 months.
An object is involved in an look "impossible" event, such as disappearing after being placed behind an occluding screen.	Baillargeon	Infants as young as $2\frac{1}{2}$ to $3\frac{1}{2}$ months "surprised" because their expectations about object existence and object properties such as solidity are violated.

employed. (Several examples of the variety of procedures used are shown in Table 7.3.) As a result, most psychologists now agree, Piaget underestimated infants' cognitive abilities.

Object Permanence.   In studying the development of object permanence, Piaget used a task that depends on infants' motor abilities. To perform successfully, infants need to remember that the hidden object still exists and they have to remember its location, but they must also be able to lift the blanket or remove the cover of a container before they can retrieve the object. Unless they are given weeks of practice, infants younger than 12 months have difficulty coordinating and sequencing their movements in this way (Bojczyk & Corbetta, 2004). It is possible, therefore, that infants might know that a hidden object continues to exist but fail to search for it because they do not have the necessary motor skills to retrieve hidden objects from containers (Baillargeon, Spelke, & Wasserman, 1985).

One recent experiment modified the task in order to test the conditions under which infants search successfully for an object that they have observed being hidden. In this study, 14-month-old infants saw an object hidden in a container but were prevented from searching for it for 24 hours. Some infants returned to the same room and searched correctly for the object, but infants who were brought to a different room tended not to search, even though the original container with the object inside it had been moved to the new setting. These findings suggest that infants of this age may be guided by the notion that objects have a unique identity. Like older children and adults, they search for a particular object that they saw disappear in a specific setting and do not assume that they will find that object in an identical container in a different location (Moore & Meltzoff, 2004). This account could be tested further by allowing infants to observe the original container being moved from one room to another or by bringing them back to the first room to see if they would search upon finding the original container there.

Other experiments have tested infants' ability to search for an object that is hidden by darkness, rather than a blanket or a container (Clifton et al., 1991; Goubet & Clifton, 1998; Hood & Willatts, 1986). In one such study, $6\frac{1}{2}$-month-old infants first watched a ball drop down a tube a number of times and learned that it would emerge from the tube in one of two locations, each of which made a distinctive sound when the ball landed there. During the next phase of the experiment, which was carried out in darkness, the ball was dropped and infants heard one of the two auditory cues. Although they were unable to see the ball, they reached for it in the correct location, suggesting that they remembered its existence even when they could not maintain visual contact with it (Goubet & Clifton, 1998).

Some researchers have eliminated manual search and a reaching response entirely, using looking time as the measure of infants' understanding of object properties. They have asked, for example whether infants understand that objects are both solid and continuous (in other words, whether they recognize that one solid object cannot pass through another solid object or that objects exist despite changes in location and, if unimpeded, move without interruption or changing direction). In these studies, infants watch events that are either possible, such as a ball rolling freely down a track, or impossible, such as a ball rolling down a track despite the presence of a visible barrier in its path (Baillargeon, 1993, 1994b; Spelke et al., 1992). If infants look longer at the impossible event than at the possible event, it is assumed that they are noticing and responding to the novelty of a violation of physical laws. Numerous studies using this **violation-of-expectation procedure** have shown that infants as young as $2\frac{1}{2}$ to $3\frac{1}{2}$ months of age look longer at impossible events, suggesting that they possess more sophisticated knowledge about objects than Piaget ascribed to them.

Studies using the violation-of-expectation procedure suggest that infants possess some understanding of object properties before they are able to succeed on Piaget's original manual search tasks, but research has also revealed that not all object properties are understood at the same age. It is not until infants are $4\frac{1}{2}$ to $6\frac{1}{2}$ months, for example, that they show surprise when their expectations about object support are violated, as when a box appears not to fall, despite being pushed almost all the way off of a platform. Infants of this age also begin to look surprised about impossible collisions, as when a wheeled toy moves farther after being bumped by a small object than by a bigger object. Around the same age, infants also look longer when they see a toy that they observed being hidden in one spot in a sandbox emerge from a different spot (Baillargeon, 1994; Nwecombe & Huttenlocher, 2006; Newcombe, Sluzenski, & Huttenlocher, 2005).

Infants may understand another aspect of objects, namely, their numerosity and transformations of addition and subtraction. Using the violation-of-expectation procedure, Wynn (1992) found that 5-month-old infants who watched dolls being placed behind a screen, and then saw the occluded set being deleted or increased by the removal or addition of one doll, looked longer at impossible than at possible events. In this experiment, the impossible events were those in which the screen was removed and revealed the wrong number of dolls after the subtraction or addition of a doll. For example, if a set of two dolls had been increased by the addition of one more doll, infants looked longer when the screen lifted to show a set of two rather than three dolls (see Figure 7.1). These findings have been replicated and extended by Wynn (1996, 2000) and other researchers (e.g., Simon, Hespos, & Rochat, 1995; Uller et al., 1999). There is debate, however, about whether infants' looking behavior actually reflects an early understanding of number concepts and addition and subtraction. Some critics, for example, argue that infants in these studies may simply be surprised not to see a doll that they saw placed behind the screen, while others suggest that infants are responding to more general

First, all infants see three toys being placed behind a screen:

Step 1. One toy is placed on a stage, then covered with a screen.

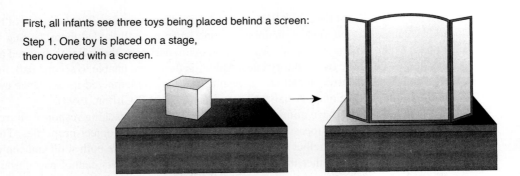

Step 2. Two or more identical toys are placed behind the screen, one at a time (1 + 1 + 1 =   )

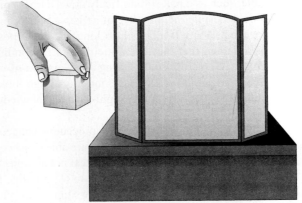

Next, one group of infants is shown a "possible" event (1 + 1 + 1 = 3)

Step 3a. When the screen is removed, three identical toys are visible.

A second group of infants is shown an "impossible" event (1 + 1 + 1 = 2)

Step 3b. When the screen is removed, only two identical toys are visible.

FIGURE 7.1   Some experiments with 5-month-olds test their understanding of numerosity, addition, and subtraction.

Source: Based on Wynn, 1992, 1996, 2000.

differences between an initial set of objects and a subsequent collection (Haith & Benson, 1998; Mix, Huttenlocher, & Levine, 2002; Wakeley, Rivera, & Langer, 2000a, 2000b)

Interpreting the findings of violation-of-expectation studies, some researchers have asserted that infants possess innate beliefs about objects and object properties, while others have hypothesized that infants possess innate learning mechanisms that help them accurately interpret their experience with objects from an early age. According to the innate-belief account, infants are born with a core set of principles about the physical world, principles upon which they subsequently build a more complete understanding (Spelke et al., 1992; Van de Walle & Spelke, 1996; Wynn, 2000). Advocates of the innate-learning-mechanism explanation, by contrast, propose that infants find certain kinds of experiences particularly salient and pay attention to them, learning about the physical world as they observe toys, food, and other objects being supported or falling, rolling freely or bumping into obstacles, being given to them or taken away, and disappearing under a couch or reappearing on the other side (Baillargeon, 1994). Debate about these interpretations and the meaning of infants' increased attention to impossible events continues, with some new experiments focusing on specifying the factors that influence infants' responses to different types of events (Casasola, Cohen, & Chiarello, 2003). Critics, meanwhile, question the basic claim that infants in violation-of-expectation studies are in fact expressing "surprise" when they look longer at impossible events (Haith & Benson, 1998). Regardless of the interpretation that is favored, there is a growing body of evidence that many of Piaget's claims about infants' incompetence with objects must be reexamined.

The A-not-B Error.   In contrast with subsequent studies of object permanence, Piaget's observation of the A-not-B error has been replicated by many other researchers, even when the containers at both locations are transparent (Marcovitch & Zelazo, 1999; Munakata, McClelland, Johnson, & Siegler, 1997; Newcombe & Huttenlocher, 2006; Wellman, Cross, & Bartsch, 1986). According to some accounts, infants make the A-not-B error, despite being able to see the "hidden" toy inside the transparent container, because they are confused by the contradiction between their ability to see the toy and tactile information that a barrier is in the way (Diamond, 1991). Harder to explain, however, is infants' tendency to make the A-not-B error when the object is "hidden" in plain view at location B—without any cover at all (Willatts, 1997).

Some researchers think that infants may know that a toy is hidden at location B but have difficulty restraining themselves from performing a previously successful motor act at location A (Diamond, 1991; Newcombe & Huttenlocher, 2006; Zelazo, Reznick, & Spinazzola, 1998). One way to test this explanation would be to see whether infants show, through facial expressions or other behaviors, that they know they are making an erroneous reach (Willatts, 1997). During the first year of life, the ability to inhibit reaching to previous locations over longer delays develops as connections form between the prefrontal cortex and areas of the brain that control motor movements (Diamond, 1991; Diamond, Werker, & Lalonde, 1994).

Other researchers have asserted that infants make the A-not-B error because they are inexperienced with the motor skills required to use both hands to lift the cover of a container and then retrieve a toy (Bojczyk & Corbetta, 2004; Munakata, 1998; Munakata et al., 1997; Newcombe & Huttenlocher, 2006). In one microgenetic study, $6\frac{1}{2}$-month-old infants were given weekly exposure to a task that required coordinated, two-handed movements to retrieve a toy from a box. Half of the infants were given an opaque box and could not see the toy, whereas the other half were given a semi-transparent box that provided consistent visual and tactile information about the existence of a barrier, while still allowing them to see the "hidden" toy. During the study, infants in both conditions explored the boxes manually—scratching, banging, and pushing on them—and eventually discovered how to retrieve the toy. Infants with the semi-transparent box, however, made this discovery 1 month sooner than infants with the opaque box. This finding indicates that sustained visual contact with the toy was an important aid to infants' exploration of the box (Bojczyk & Corbetta, 2004).

Other studies have found that repeated exposure to the A-not-B task, even over a brief period of time, is helpful. The more opportunities infants have to find a toy when it is hidden at the second location, the less likely they are to make the A-not-B error (Spencer, Smith, & Thelen, 2001). In addition, marginally preterm infants in one experiment outper-formed full-term infants in two different versions of the A-not-B task. Infants from both groups were studied from 28 to 60 weeks and were tested at the same age since conception. According to the researchers, preterm infants' superior performance may have resulted from their greater experience (due to being born earlier) watching objects being placed into and removed from containers and performing those actions themselves (Matthews, Ellis, & Nelson, 1996). Taken together, the association between infants' exploratory actions and success on the A-not-B task lends some support to Piaget's claims that infants' own sensori-motor activities contribute to the development of means-end behavior and other aspects of cognitive functioning.

The A-not-B error is more prevalent when there is a delay (even as little as 3 to 5 seconds) between the time when the object is hidden at location B and the time when the infant is allowed to search for it (Diamond, 1991; Diamond, Werker, & Lalonde, 1994; Wellman, Cross, & Bartsch, 1986). As memory ability improves, the length of delay that infants can tolerate before making the A-not-B error increases. Although the A-not-B error becomes less frequent with age, search errors continue into the early preschool years when children look for objects that are placed in or have moved through containers, including those with transparent walls (Berthier et al., 2000; Butler, Berthier, & Clifton, 2002; Hood, Cole-Davies, & Dias, 2003; Newcombe & Huttenlocher, 2006). This is perhaps to be expected, given that even cognitively mature adults looking for a set of keys or some other misplaced item sometimes return to a previous location where an object was found, despite having searched in that spot unsuccessfully. Apparently, even when logic and accurate memory are available to guide our search behavior, we do not always use that information.

The Representation of Space.   Even very young infants perceive a three-dimensional world in which objects vary in distance from one another, with some objects within reach-ing distance and others beyond their grasp. According to Piaget, however, infants do not *understand* that objects exist independent of their own physical presence until the end of the sensorimotor period. As we discuss next, subsequent studies have not uniformly supported this view.

Many studies of infant's ability to keep track of their position in relation to a location in space have used a procedure in which infants are trained to expect to see a particular toy or a person's face in a specific location whenever they hear an auditory signal. Following training, infants are moved in the room and the auditory signal is presented without any event occurring. If infants use an **egocentric framework** (relying on the direction in which they previously turned their body or head to see the event), they end up looking in a different location during the test phase. If, on the other hand, they use an **allocentric framework** (using cues in the room, such as a distinctive color or pattern in the original location), they look at the same spot as they did during the training phase (Acredolo, 1978).

A number of studies using this procedure have found that the ability to use landmarks (distinctive features in a room) as cues about spatial relationships begins to develop at the end of the first year of life (Acredolo, 1990; Bushnell et al., 1995; LePecq & Lafaite, 1989; Newcombe & Huttenlocher, 2006; Rieser, 1979). When there is a single "direct" landmark, infants as young as 8 and even 6 months of age are able to use that external cue to locate the target after their own position in the room has changed (Keating, McKenzie, & Day, 1986; Rieser, 1979). If there is more than one landmark, or if a landmark is "indirect" (occupies a spot other than the target location), however, infants typically have difficulty using the information in the environment before the age of 11 months.

Some researchers have hypothesized that infants' ability to use landmarks may be aided by locomotor development (Bai & Bertenthal, 1992). According to this view, self-generated movement may help children learn that certain features of the environment do not move and may even serve as guideposts (Acredolo, 1978; Newcombe & Huttenlocher, 2006; Newcombe et al., 1998). This explanation does not explain infants' difficulty using indirect landmarks, however, which remain just as stable in the environment as direct landmarks. Moreover, not all studies have found a link between the onset of independent locomotion and spatial orientation abilities (McComas & Field, 1984).

Some studies have found that the ability to use indirect landmarks in tasks requiring active search for objects, rather than simple visual location of targets, may not develop until as late as 24 to 26 months of age (DeLoache & Brown, 1983), long after infants have become independently mobile. These findings suggest that locomotor development and independent movement in the environment are not the only route to knowledge about spatial relationships. In one series of experiments investigating the use of direct and indirect landmarks, 12-month-olds searched for toys that they saw being hidden either beneath or near cushions that varied in their distinctiveness (Bushnell et al., 1995). As expected, infants benefited from the presence of a direct landmark (when the toy was hidden under a unique-looking pillow) but actually performed worse when there was an indirect landmark (when the toy was hidden near an equally distinctive pillow) than when there was no landmark at all. Infants' greater difficulty with indirect landmarks may reflect the greater cognitive challenge involved in keeping track of a two-step solution for finding the hidden toy. Remembering to use the distinctive pillow is the first step, but once they arrive at that spot, infants must also remember where, in relation to that location, they will find the hidden toy.

It is possible that the ability to use indirect landmarks depends on maturation of the hippocampus—a part of the brain that underlies the spatial memory system (Diamond, Werker, Lalonde, 1994; Mangan et al., 1994). One study with infants and toddlers ranging in age from 16 to 36 months is consistent with this explanation (Newcombe et al., 1998). Children watched as researchers hid toys by burying them in a sandbox filled with sand. In some conditions, the sandbox was completely surrounded by a plain curtain, eliminating the use of indirect landmarks in the room as the basis for finding the hidden toys. In other conditions, the curtain was opened, and children could make use of features in the room to guide their search (as shown in Figure 7.2, p. 229). Before children were allowed to search for the hidden toys, their parents turned them around and walked with them to the other end of the sandbox, changing their perspective by 180 degrees.

When this infant uncovers the hidden toy, he is showing his understanding that objects continue to exist even when they are not visible.

When the curtain was drawn, children of all ages had difficulty but still performed above chance levels when retrieving the hidden toys. When the curtain was not present, however, children older than 21 months of age searched more accurately, presumably because they were able to use the indirect landmarks in the room; younger children, by contrast, did not benefit from being able to see those features. Improvement in the use of indirect cues was dramatic and abrupt—absent at 16 months but present at 21 months. According to the researchers, these findings suggest that infants' spatial memory ability develops through neurological maturation as well as experience with upright locomotion. Although this account awaits further exploration, it is compatible with evidence from studies of young rats learning to use indirect landmarks to find their way through a maze; the ability to use external cues (those outside of the maze) appears to depend on maturation of the hippocampus (Seress, 2001).

Understanding and Using Representations of Space.   Children gradually become more skilled at using and understanding information about spatial relationships, including representations such as photographs, video images, and scale models. At 24 months, for example, children show clearer awareness than at 18 months that objects shown in photographs are two-dimensional and cannot be grasped (DeLoache et al., 1998). Children as young as 24 months understand as well that a photograph or a video image can be a symbol for something else, such as a particular space. When shown a photograph or video image of a room and given a description of a toy's hiding place in that room, children of this age are able to retrieve the toy when they are allowed to search in the actual room (Suddendorf, 2003).

Some studies have reported a low level of performance overall among 24-month-olds because they tend to have a high level of success on first searches but not on subsequent trials when the same toy is hidden in different locations in the same room (DeLoache & Burns, 1994; Sharon & DeLoache, 2003). Reminiscent of the A-not-B error, 24-month-olds in those studies tended to search in previous hiding spots in the room, rather than in the most recent location. When these sorts of incorrect searches are prevented, however, by

FIGURE 7.2 This room can be modified to compare younger and older infants' ability to use indirect cues to find a hidden toy.

using four different toys hidden in four different, distinctively furnished rooms, performance levels are significantly better, suggesting that they were able to understand the relation between a photograph of each space and the space itself (Suddendorf, 2003).

Representational insight (awareness of the relation between a space and a symbol for that space) is still uneven at 30 months. Children of this age have greater difficulty using three-dimensional symbols, such as a scale model of a room, than two-dimensional representations, such as a photograph or video image of the same space. It is not until the age of about 36 months that children are consistently able to use scale models to find hidden toys in the spaces that the models represent (DeLoache, 1987, 1991, 1995, 2000; Newcombe & Huttenlocher, 2006).

The processes that contribute to the development of representational insight, which eventually enables older children to understand and learn from abstract representations, such as maps and globes, are not well understood and continue to be the focus of research. According to some hypotheses, children's failures at younger ages may be the result of an inability to shift their attention from one initial representation (e.g., the toy is under the orange pillow) to another, more recent representation (e.g., the toy is in the drawer), suggesting that the problem is due to the interference of competing memories. This hypothesis raises the question of how infant attention and memory develop, topics we consider later in this chapter.

We turn now to an influential theory articulated by Lev Vygotsky that places cognitive development and learning in the context of social interactions. As widely accepted as this perspective is now, it was overshadowed for many years by Piaget's theory. Unlike Piaget's emphasis on the child's own developing mind, Vygotsky regarded cognitive development as the result of social interaction and the child's internalization of their culture's organization and communication of knowledge.

Vygotsky's Sociocultural Theory

Lev Vygotsky (1896–1934) was a Russian psychologist who built his theory on the assumption that cognitive abilities develop in and are shaped by children's **sociocultural contexts**—home, school, and other settings in which they spend time. From his perspective, knowledge is created through children's interactions with others, primarily parents and teachers, rather than being innate or discovered through their own actions or introspection. In Vygotsky's theory, the most significant psychological tool for children's acquisition of knowledge is the speech of those around them. According to this view, the 18-month-old child whose mother makes up a song to narrate the steps involved in putting on his shirt (e.g., "right arm, left arm, over the head, and pull it down") becomes a 3-year-old who sings the same song aloud as he tries to dress himself. Vygotsky (1934/1986) described the child's verbal behavior at the later age as **egocentric speech**, speech that is directed to himself or herself rather than to others, with the purpose of enhancing their own concentration on goals and strategies while performing a task or solving a problem. Eventually, through the process of internalization, the child no longer needs to utter the words out loud; he retains the narrative as inner speech that represents the steps involved in getting dressed. In this way, young children whose parents provide a rich speech environment are laying an important foundation for the subsequent development of skills and understanding of the world.

The Zone of Proximal Development

As a psychologist who focused primarily on school-age children's learning, Vygotsky was interested in enhancing each child's potential. After observing the effects of teachers on

When this girl's mother offers helpful hints and encouragement, she is able to complete a puzzle that was too challenging to complete on her own.

children's performance, he described the concept of the **zone of proximal development (ZPD)**, the distance between a child's actual developmental level—the ability to solve a problem alone—and the level of potential development—how much better the child can solve the problem when assisted or guided by a more capable individual. Vygotsky did not provide a full account of the ZPD or explain the process through which internalization occurs, but more recent researchers have adapted and expanded upon these ideas (Wertsch, 1979, 1985). Some of these applications of his theory might surprise Vygotsky, who generally ascribed very little importance to young children's play. Moreover, he asserted that imaginary (pretend/symbolic) play was essentially impossible before the age of 3 years (Lambert & Clyde, 2003; Vygotsky, 1933/1978). Nevertheless, the profound roles of social interaction and the child's sociocultural context have been incorporated into many current investigations of play and learning during the first 3 years of life.

The concept of the ZPD has been extended, for example, to describe parent-child interactions during problem solving, as when a 3-year-old girl guided by her father is able to complete a 20-piece puzzle that she would not be able to put together on her own. Building on Vygotsky's notion of the ZPD, Wood, Bruner, and Ross (1976) coined the term **scaffolding** to describe the process through which tutors structure tasks to boost children's performance. During scaffolding, tutors "remove" the parts of the task that are beyond the child's ability, leaving only those elements that are within range. The critical steps in the process of scaffolding are recruiting the child's interest in the task, simplifying the task to enable the child to recognize the parts that he or she can perform, maintaining the child's interest, highlighting relevant aspects of the child's response so that he or she can judge its accuracy, and demonstrating correct solutions to the task (Wood, Bruner, & Ross, 1976). The father scaffolding his young daughter's puzzle play may thus show her the front of the puzzle box (e.g., "Look at this picture of Big Bird. After we put this puzzle together, we'll have the same picture") or put aside the more complicated middle pieces of the puzzle and ask her to begin by finding the four corner pieces. He may also draw her attention to the part of the picture that can be seen on each piece of the puzzle, asking her to find specific pieces (e.g., "I see one of Big Bird's feet. Can you find it?"). To maintain his daughter's interest in the puzzle, he may provide encouraging feedback about her performance (e.g., "You did it! Now can you find his other foot?").

Many researchers have extended Vygotsky's theory—and the concept of scaffolding—to describe the contributions that parents and older siblings make to young children's play (Bodrova & Leong, 1996, 1998). Mothers of 21-month-olds in one study, for example, successfully scaffolded their children's play as a function of their knowledge about how play typically develops during infancy and toddlerhood; those who were the most knowledge-able about the development of play provided their children with the most developmentally appropriate structure, guidance, and verbal commentary (Tamis-LeMonda, Damast, & Bornstein, 1994). As we will see next, parents' assumptions about the goals and process of effective scaffolding also reflect the characteristics of the culture in which they live (Bornstein et al., 1999).

Guided Participation: Learning as a Social Activity

In the Vygotskian tradition, learning is regarded as a social activity, yet around the world cultures vary in terms of how much time children and parents spend together and the types of activities they engage in during the course of a typical day. In the United States and other developed countries, children of employed parents almost never accompany their parents to their place of work, and they rarely see their parents engaged in the work for which they are paid. When adults—parents or paid caregivers—interact with them, they tend to focus on child-centered activities, such as playing, reading, eating, and cleaning up. In many other cultures, however, infants are carried on their mother's back and observe her while she works in the home or in the fields. Toddlers in these cultures are often cared for by older siblings, and they are more likely than most U.S. children to spend the day near their mother, observing and even assisting her as she engages in tasks such as cooking, cleaning, sewing, weaving on a loom, or making baskets (Maynard, 2002; Rogoff, 1998; Tomasello, Kruger, & Ratner, 1993).

Despite the obvious differences, children across these cultures all learn through social interaction and structured activities, a process that has been referred to as **guided participation** (Rogoff et al., 1993, Rogoff, 1998). In guided participation, an extension of Vygotsky's ZPD, "individual development is regarded as occurring during joint problem solving with people who are more skilled in the use of cultural tools, including inventions such as literacy, mathematics, mnemonic skills, and approaches to problem solving and reasoning" (Rogoff et al., 1993, p. 6). Guided participation occurs in all cultures and encompasses explicit and implicit instruction as well as nonverbal demonstrations provided by more skilled members of a community. In this way, the concept of guided participation goes beyond Vygotsky's emphasis on verbal instruction as the foundation of learning.

Support for the notion that guided participation reflects the goals and beliefs of child-drearing in particular cultural contexts comes from a multitude of cross-cultural studies of mother-child interaction (Bornstein et al., 1999; LeVine et al., 1994). This variation was documented in an observational study of parents and toddlers ranging in age from 12 to 25 months in Guatemala, India, Turkey, and the United States (Rogoff et al., 1993). In this in-depth study, the researchers interviewed parents about their child's development, behavior, and daily routines, including feeding, dressing, and sleeping. They also asked about the kinds of play and social games the child enjoyed, and they asked the parent to present a set of novel objects to their child, with the goal of having the child use the objects. The objects included a pencil box with a sliding lid, a jumping-jack doll, a metal embroidery hoop, a clear plastic jar covered with a lid and containing a small toy, and a peek-a-boo puppet.

As anticipated, there were differences in guided participation (shown in Table 7.4). In communities in which children were usually kept apart from their parents' daily work activities (the United States and Turkey), parents tended to take charge of the interaction with each novel object, providing verbal commentary and joining in the exploration with their child. In communities in which children were integrated into adults' daily social and work activities (Guatemala and India), by comparison, parents tended to support toddlers' inclination to explore without specific prompting and instruction. In both types of communities, parents guide young children to explore and learn about the world in ways that are consistent with the institutions and structures of that community. In the case of the middle-class communities, guided participation prepares children for the world of school, which emphasizes decontextualized learning, verbal communication, and following spoken or written instructions given by an adult leader/teacher. In the non–middle-class communities, guided participation is more compatible with a world of learning in the context of doing, in which children learn and gradually take on adult roles through hands-on apprenticeships (Rogoff et al., 1993).

Evaluating Vygotsky's Sociocultural Theory

Taken together, the research literature provides support for the Vygotskian notion that children learn from parents and other knowledgeable members of their culture. Learning in a social

TABLE 7.4   Differences Observed In Guided Participation Across Four Communities

Community	Guided Participation
Middle-class United States and Turkey	Parent gives specific verbal instructions to child. Parent motivates child during structured, playful interactions. Parent engages child in conversation as a peer.
Non–Middle-Class Guatemala and India	Parent uses nonverbal communication (gestures, shared visual attention) with child. Parent stands to the side, ready to help the child, if needed, during exploration. Parent remains in adult role rather than becoming engaged with child as a peer.

Source: Based on information in Rogoff, Mistry, Göncü, & Mosier, 1993.

After electrodes are attached to this special cap, the researchers will study this infant's brain activity in response to visual stimuli.

context begins in infancy, however, long before the school years on which Vygotsky focused his attention. The findings also support Vygotsky's concept of the ZPD, the position that children's learning is enhanced by social interaction that takes into account their developmental level and the culture in which they are living. Depending on the cultural context and goals, specific verbal instruction is not always a necessary feature of learning in a social context; there are many ways in which young children can gain valuable knowledge that prepares them to function well in their community.

Cognitive Science Perspectives on Early Learning and Memory

In contrast with the Vygotskian and Piagetian traditions, contemporary studies of early learning and memory place infants' development within the framework of cognitive science, an approach that combines traditional questions about cognitive development with newer information processing and neuroscience methodology. Like Piaget's pioneering research, these newer approaches investigate cognitive functioning at the behavioral level, but they also incorporate physiological and neurological variables, such as changes in heart rate and brain wave activity. The emerging picture is one of a surprisingly competent infant, equipped with cognitive abilities that provide a foundation for learning.

The Development of Attention

As we have previously discussed, infants' looking behavior—the amount of attention they pay to a stimulus—has been used in habituation and violation-of-expectation procedures to answer questions about early sensory, perceptual, and cognitive functioning (Canfield et al., 1997). In recent years attention itself has become the subject of research. These studies have shed new light on the development, determinants, and consequences of infant visual attention.

One fundamental initial discovery was the finding that duration of looking in the standard habituation procedure declines with age. The average 3- or 4-month-old, for example, fixates longer on visual stimuli than does the average 7- or 8-month-old (Colombo & Mitchell, 1990). Infants' looking time at a visual stimulus declines, research has shown, because infants become more efficient at scanning and taking in the features of the stimulus (Colombo, 2001, 2002).

Toward the end of the first year of life, infants often allocate their looking behavior as a function of the behavior of adults with whom they are interacting. As they gain increasing control over their own attention, infants notice and respond to the direction of adults' gaze by looking and pointing in the same direction. They also learn when *not* to attend. By approximately 10 months of age, they are less likely to look or point in the same direction that an adult turns his or her head if that adult's eyes are closed or covered by a blindfold (Brooks & Meltzoff, 2002, 2005). These aspects of the development of attention support infants' ability to engage in **joint attention** (shared perceptual exploration with another person), a phenomenon that contributes to the development of language, object knowledge, and emotional communication (Bornstein, 1985; Brooks & Meltzoff, 2005; Flom & Pick, 2003).

Studies of infant attention have revealed that the duration of looking varies among same-age infants and that these individual differences tend to be stable over time (Colombo & Mitchell, 1990). In addition, infants with shorter, more efficient looking patterns typically perform better on other tasks tapping visual recognition memory than infants with more prolonged looking patterns. According to some views, rather than being more involved in active information processing of the stimulus, infants with prolonged looking during habituation are actually "stuck" and have difficulty disengaging their attention from the stimulus (Colombo, 2002). An experiment with 3- and 4-month-olds provided some support for this explanation (Frick, Colombo, & Saxon, 1999). The researchers first assessed infants' look duration using a visual habituation procedure and then tested infants' ability to shift their attention from a centrally located display to one on the periphery of their visual field. The stimulus in the center of their visual field continued to be illuminated, which required that infants disengage their attention in order to focus on the new stimulus on the periphery. Infants who had more quickly habituated to the visual stimuli in the first task were also faster at shifting their attention in the second task than were infants with longer habituation times. As we will discuss shortly, there is some evidence that the efficiency of infants' information processing, including speed of habituation, may predict their subsequent performance on intelligence tests (Colombo, 1993; Colombo & Janowsky, 1998; McCall & Carriger, 1993; Rose & Feldman, 1995, 1997; Rose et al., 2005).

Differences between infants who show shorter versus longer looking times during habituation have also been found when patterns of change in heart rate are compared. When a visual stimulus is first presented, infants typically show a deceleration of heart rate, which coincides with greater and more active engagement in examining and processing the stimulus. Infants with longer looking times during habituation tend to show an initial heart rate deceleration, but while their gaze remains fixated on the stimulus, their heart rate then returns to levels that reflect the end of attention. These findings support the hypothesis that longer duration of looking does not necessarily indicate more thorough processing of a stimulus (Colombo et al., 2001; Colombo, 2002).

Researchers using another psychophysiological measure that we discussed in Chapter 2—**event-related potential (ERP)** recordings of brain activity—have also investigated attention, charting the development of a waveform that represents attention to stimuli. To study ERPs in infants, researchers use a special lightweight helmet to place dozens of small electrodes (sometimes more than 100) on the surface of the baby's scalp. After an initial baseline phase, a visual or auditory stimulus is presented and a record is made of the brain's activity while the infant attends to the sight or sound. In the future, measures of these waveforms may be used to identify attention-related deficits early in life (Nelson & Monk, 2001).

Some researchers believe that infants who are less able to shift their attention away from a stimulus may fail to do so because of differences in the frontal or parietal areas of the brain (Colombo, 2002). Does this mean that these infants cannot learn to become more efficient and achieve greater control over their looking behavior? Not necessarily. In one recent experiment, researchers showed that 5-month-old infants with longer look durations could be assisted in shifting their attention to different parts of a stimulus (Jankowski, Rose, & Feldman, 2001). Current research efforts are focused on exploring the malleability of visual information processing in infancy and in determining whether and how individual differences in attention in infancy may be related to higher-order cognitive skills during the preschool years and beyond (Colombo, 2002).

The Development of Memory

Most adults report that their earliest memories extend back only as far as the age of approximately 3 years, a phenomenon referred to as **infantile amnesia**. For many years, researchers inferred from the existence of infantile amnesia that infant memory operated differently than memory in older children and adults and that the onset of language was the key event that enabled infants to create and retrieve representations of past events (Bauer, 2002, 2006). More recent research has shown, however, that the organization of the memory system is, in many ways, highly similar in infants, older children, and adults (Bauer, 2002, 2006; Rovee-Collier, 1999). Aspects of both **explicit memory** (conscious awareness of specific information, such as events and facts) and **implicit memory** (unconscious learning, including conditioning and aspects of motor learning) exist early in life, but the majority of research on infant memory has focused on the development of explicit memory (Nelson, 1998).

Long-term Memory.   We cannot ask infants and toddlers to provide verbal answers to questions about their **long-term memory** (information that is stored and available to be retrieved repeatedly over time), but we can determine whether children of this age are able to recall past experiences by using techniques of habituation and novelty preference. Infants who are habituated to a display (e.g., a drawing of a checkerboard) until they no longer show a high level of visual interest in it are inferred to have a memory for that display if they look longer at a different display (e.g., a drawing of a maze). The type of memory that is tested in these studies is known as **recognition memory**; infants either recognize a previously seen display or fail to recognize it when it is presented.

Infants' long-term memory has also been explored using the technique of conditioning. In one well-known procedure used primarily with 2- to 6-month-old infants, researchers tie a ribbon onto the infant's leg and connect it to an overhead mobile; when the infant kicks, the mobile moves (see Figure 7.3). Later, the infant is placed in the same situation with the mobile, but this time without the connecting ribbon in place. Even so, infants kick their legs at a high rate when they see the mobile, suggesting that they recognize the situation and remember the effect of their kicking during the previous session. To test memory in older infants and toddlers (between 6 and 18 months of age), researchers use a different task, in which pressing on a lever makes a toy train move around a track. Memory is tested

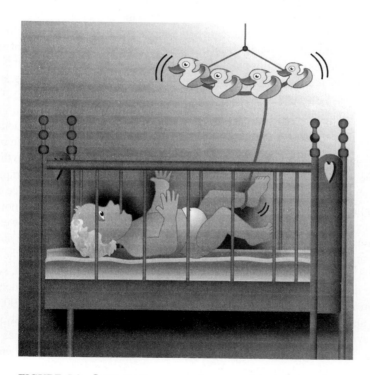

FIGURE 7.3   Long-term memory is assessed in infants younger than 6 months by tying a ribbon onto their leg and connecting it to an overhead mobile so that when the infant kicks, the mobile moves. Infants who return to the laboratory show that they remember this contingency by kicking their legs even when the ribbon is not attached to the mobile. By varying the characteristics of the laboratory setting, researchers can test the strength of this memory.

Source: Based on Rovee-Collier, 1999.

in this age group by deactivating the lever; infants and toddlers who continue pressing the lever at a high rate are credited with memory for the task (Rovee-Collier, 1999).

Numerous studies using these procedures have shown that long-term memory is functioning from birth. Newborns are able to create a memory for visually presented information and retrieve it, even when tested a few days later. The period of time over which memories can be retrieved increases with age, however, from just a few days in newborns to a few months in 18-month-olds. Retrieval of the memory is better if infants are tested in the same setting. In fact, at the youngest ages, even small changes in the setting (such as the color or pattern of the mobile), can inhibit memory retrieval. Durability of the memory can be enhanced, however, if infants are given brief glimpses of the display periodically (Rose, 1981; Rose, Feldman, & Jankowski, 2001, 2002; Rovee-Collier, Hartshorn, & DiRubbo, 1999; Schneider, & Bjorklund, 1998; Slater & Morison, 1991). In showing the beneficial effects of practice and familiarity, these studies indicate that infant memory is affected by the same factors as memory at later ages (Hayne, Barr, & Herbert, 2003; Rovee-Collier, 1999).

Studies using ERP measures have found that, by 6 months of age, infants have neural representations for familiar sights. Different brain activity and different ERP waveforms occur in response to pictures of the mother's face compared with pictures of different strangers' faces, and even pictures of a similar looking stranger. Moreover, the pattern that is found in 6-month-old infants is consistent with the pattern that is found in adults looking at familiar and unfamiliar faces (de Haan & Nelson, 1997; Nelson, 1998; Nelson & Monk, 2001).

Researchers studying older infants and toddlers have explored their long-term memory abilities in imitation tasks by first demonstrating novel, multistep sequences (e.g., building and playing a small gong) during an initial laboratory session and then observing their spontaneous performance with the same props during a subsequent visit to the laboratory. In some studies, a verbal description of the objects and actions accompanies the experimenter's demonstration and the infant is then given a chance to practice the same actions. In other studies no verbal labels are provided and the infant does not have an opportunity to practice the actions until their return visit. Children who are allowed to practice the actions immediately are better able to imitate the actions later and are aided more by verbal reminders than are children who are not allowed to practice (Hayne, Barr, & Herbert, 2003). Because the props used in the sequences are completely novel, successful performance depends on deferred imitation—the ability to reproduce the sequence based on long-term memory for the order of events (Bauer, 1996, 2002, 2005, 2006). These experiments also test **recall memory**, which is the ability to remember a previously presented stimulus or event in the absence of current, ongoing perceptual support (such as visual or tactile contact). Although infants might be expected to recognize the props when they are given to them during the testing session, the previously demonstrated multistep sequence can only be enacted with those props if it is recalled and recreated from memory.

As is true for older children and adults, infant memory is enhanced if there are **enabling relations**—a logically or practically necessary order among the steps in a sequence— rather than **arbitrary relations**—a sequence that may be performed in any order because the steps are not logically or practically linked (Bauer, 2002). It is easier, therefore, for infants and toddlers to recall how to build a gong (a sequence in which the gong must be hung up before striking it) than it is for them to remember the exact order in which blocks were previously placed into a container (a sequence in which the outcome is unaffected by the order in which red, yellow, and blue blocks are selected). Although Piaget asserted that deferred imitation did not develop until 18 to 24 months of age, more recent experiments suggest that it emerges during the last half of the first year of life, perhaps as early as 9 months of age (Bauer, 2002, 2005, 2006; Klein & Meltzoff, 1999; Meltzoff, 1988a, 1988b). Deferred imitation before the age of 12 months is relatively fragile, however, and is affected by the type of sequence and infants' exposure to it. Only about half of 9-month-old infants in one experiment reproduced the correct sequence of steps after a 1-month delay, and then only if they had had multiple exposures to the sequence before they attempted to reproduce it (Bauer et al., 2001). By the age of 13 months, by contrast, the majority of children in another study were able to reproduce a sequence of steps after a 1-month delay. By the age of 20 months, they could reproduce the sequence after a 12-month delay (Bauer et al., 2000).

One recent experiment with 9-month-olds helps explain why 9- and 13-month-olds perform at such different levels (Bauer et al., 2003). In the experiment, a researcher demonstrated three different two-step sequences (e.g., turning on a light by first placing a toy car in a specially designed apparatus and then pushing a rod to create a ramp for the car). These sequences were demonstrated at each of three sessions $1\frac{1}{2}$ days apart. Approximately 1 month later, infants' memory for the sequences was tested, using the deferred imitation task. Despite repeated exposure to the sequences over three sessions, less than half of the infants (46 percent) reproduced at least one sequence in the correct order.

Measures of brain activity offer a clue about the difference between infants who performed accurately and the other infants (54 percent) who did not. Immediately after the third demonstration session and again 1 week later, infants were shown digital photos of the steps in the sequence. ERP recordings made when infants first saw the photos showed that infants who were able to recall the sequences correctly 1 month later showed evidence of greater functional maturity of parts of the hippocampus involved in long-term recall memory (Bauer et al., 2003). Although portions of the hippocampus are active from birth and enable infants to be conditioned to suck in response to an auditory stimulus or kick their legs in response to a visual display, the full neural network does not begin to function until the end of the first year of life (Nelson, 1995, 1997). It is plausible, therefore, that individual differences in the maturation of the network were reflected in the difficulty or ease with which infants were able to encode information during the three demonstration sessions and draw upon it later during the deferred imitation task.

Short-term Memory.   Information that is stored in long-term memory was once active in **short-term memory**—a limited storage system that holds information for only a few seconds if the information is not actively rehearsed (Baddeley, 1986, 1992). The existence of long-term memory in infants thus implies that they also possess short-term memory, a conclusion that has been verified in a number of experiments (Rose, Feldman, & Jankowski, 2001; Ross-Sheehy, Oakes, & Luck, 2003).

In one recent study of short-term memory (Ross-Sheehy, Oakes, & Luck, 2003), 4- to 13-month-old infants were shown two brief simultaneous displays of colored squares (ranging in number from one to six squares) on side-by-side video monitors (depicted in Figure 7.4 as a change in one square's pattern). The squares blinked on and off throughout the testing session. On one of the screens, the colors remained the same, but on the other screen, one square changed

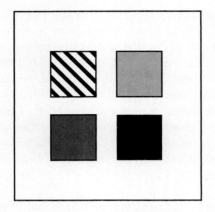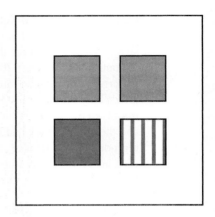

Initial display of blinking squares.

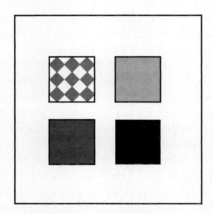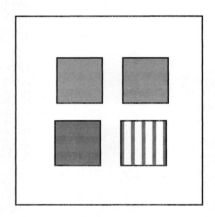

Subsequent display with one square's color changed.

FIGURE 7.4 Infants' short-term memory is tested by presenting visual displays in which elements change rapidly. Researchers measure infants' looking time to see if they are able to notice the difference between a previous display and the variation that follows it.

Source: Based on Ross-Sheehy, Oakes, & Luck, 2003.

color each time the display blinked off and then on again. The researchers compared the amount of time infants looked at the changing and unchanging displays and hypothesized that infants whose short-term memory capacity was greater than or equal to the number of squares in the display would be able to detect the color changes and show a preference for the (novel) changing display. If the number of squares exceeded their memory capacity, by contrast, the researchers expected that infants would look equally long at the unchanging and changing displays. Results showed that visual memory capacity increased over the first year of life. Whereas 4- and 6 $\frac{1}{2}$-

Selecting several blocks to play with, while ignoring the other toys nearby, suggests that this baby possesses an early ability to categorize objects.

month-old infants were able to retain short-term memory only for displays of one square, 10- and 13-month-old infants were able to notice changes in displays with as many as four squares, a level that was similar to adults' performance when tested using the same procedure.

Improvement in short-term memory for spatial location of objects at this age has also been documented. As we discussed earlier, in studies in which infants watch as an object is hidden at one of two or more locations and are then allowed to search for the object after a brief delay, the number of locations that infants can remember and use to search accurately increases between 6 and 10 months (Diamond, 1998; Diamond, Werker, & Lalonde, 1994; Reznick, Fueser, & Bosquet, 1998). These findings are consistent with a number of other studies showing that short-term memory capacity improves dramatically during the last half of the first year of life. As with the improvement in long-term memory, development of short-term memory is supported by neurological maturation. Studies using ERP measures suggest that even newborn infants are able to detect changes in stimuli and, within a few months of life, produce wave-forms that are increasingly similar to patterns of brain activity seen in adults. Cognitive scientists hope to incorporate noninvasive ERP measures into future longitudinal research, perhaps in conjunction with other imaging methods, such as MRI scans. The resulting studies should shed new light on the origins and development of memory and other cognitive abilities (Nelson, 1995; Nelson & Monk, 2001; Nelson & Webb, 2002; Van der Molen & Molenaar, 1994).

Categorization

In Piaget's view, **categorization**—the ability to group objects, people, or events into similar categories based on shared attributes—does not develop until infants achieve mental representation, at approximately 18 to 24 months. More recent researchers employing visual fixation procedures have reported that even infants as young as 3 and 4 months of age respond differently to exemplars from different categories. In some of these studies, infants are habituated with examples from one category and then tested to see if they increase their visual attention (show dishabituation) when shown an example from a different category. In other studies, a familiarization/novelty preference procedure is used, in which infants are first shown examples from one category and then given two displays to look at simultaneously, one a new example from the category and the other an example from a different category. In one experiment, for example, 3- and 4-month-olds were shown photographs of cats. After the infants had been presented with many different images of cats, the researchers showed them two new photographs, one of a cat and the other of a dog. Infants looked longer at the photograph of the dog, suggesting that they had formed the category of "cat" based on their exposure to the set of photographs (Quinn, Eimas, & Rosenkranz, 1993).

Other researchers have used an object manipulation task to infer infants' categorization. In these studies, infants old enough to handle objects effectively (6 months and older) are presented with a diverse set of small objects, such as a collection of toy animals and doll house furniture. The researchers then observe the order in which the intermingled objects are manipulated. Infants who display sequential, within-category touching—manipulating first a pig, then a sheep, and finally a horse before touching a chair, a table, and a bed—are said to possess distinct categories, in this example, for animals and furniture (Mandler, 1998). In some studies, 6- to 7-month-olds have discriminated between categories at the global level (e.g., animals versus vehicles) but not between categories at a more basic level (e.g., dogs versus rabbits); basic-level discriminations within the category of animals did not appear until the end of the first year of life (Mandler & McDonough, 1993, 1998). Based on the results of these and similar experiments, some researchers have concluded that infants develop basic-level categories later than they develop categories at the global level, perhaps as a result of learning to notice correlations among features both between and within members of categories (Rakison & Poulin-Dubois, 2002).

Considered together, the findings we have discussed so far appear to be in conflict. That is, the finding of cat-dog differentiation in 3- to 4-month-olds appears to contradict the observation that infants younger than 12 months have difficulty making distinctions within the category of animals. One explanation for this difference may lie in the different methods that were used; even the same experimenters do not always find converging evidence when they use different procedures (Oakes & Madole, 2000). Some researchers have speculated that different tasks may tap different levels of processing, with visual familiarization tasks involving low-level perceptual categorization and object manipulation tasks requiring higher-level conceptual categorization (e.g., Mandler, 1988, 1992). A related account holds that infants who are allowed to manipulate objects, rather than simply inspect them visually, are more likely to form categories based on the functional possibilities of those objects, such as whether they make noise when they are shaken or roll when they are pushed (Cohen & Cashon, 2006; Horst, Oakes, & Madole, 2005; Madole, Oakes, & Cohen, 1993).

Another explanation, however, is that infant categorization reflects learning about specific pictures or objects that are presented during an experiment (Oakes & Madole, 2000). Support for this account comes from a number of studies in which infants intentionally have been presented with different examples of stimuli in order to determine whether and how their categorization might be affected (Oakes, Coppage, & Dingel, 1997; Younger, 1985). When 10-month-olds in one experiment were presented with a series of perceptually similar items within the category of "land animals" (e.g., horse, dog, and cow), they subsequently differentiated that category from the category of "sea animals." When the items within the category of "land animals" were more perceptually variable (e.g., rabbit, bear, ram), however, they did not make the same distinction and treated all of the items as examples of the category of "animals" (Oakes, Coppage, & Dingel, 1997).

Demonstrations that the amount of within-category perceptual variability affects infants' categorization have led researchers to give greater attention to investigating how the characteristics and the context of experiments affect on-line processing in infant categorization tasks (Cohen & Cashon, 2006; Gelman & Kalish, 2006; Oakes & Madole, 2000). The contribution of changes in attention, motor abilities, and memory are also being explored, however, since it is clear that older infants are more sensitive than younger infants to functional characteristics shared by a set of objects (Horst, Oakes, & Madole, 2005).

Researchers are also exploring the possibility that, with age, infants may be more likely to use preexisting, real-world knowledge to group objects, responding to features other than perceptual similarity. This was demonstrated in a series of experiments with 10- and 11-month-olds (Pauen, 2002), in which infants examined sets of toy animals and miniature furniture that varied in the type of perceptual similarities they shared. For some groups of infants, special versions of animals and furniture were designed so that they shared the same color (e.g., both a giraffe and an arm chair were yellow and brown), pattern (e.g., both a zebra and a side chair were striped), or shape (e.g., both a crocodile and a bed were flat and elongated). Infants were presented with a series of manipulable objects from the same category (e.g., animals), one after the other, and the amount of time they spent examining each object was measured. After infants had been familiarized with these examples of the category, they were given a new object from that category, and their examination time was measured. Finally, infants were presented with a new object from a different category (e.g., furniture), and their examination time was again measured.

It was hypothesized that infants would spend more time examining objects that they regarded as coming from a new category than they would spend examining objects that they viewed as belonging to the initial category, and this is in fact what occurred, regardless of the degree of perceptual similarity between objects in the initial category and the new one. Although infants presumably noticed similarities in color, pattern, or shape, those features were relatively unimportant and not sufficient to lead infants to treat a striped chair as just another example of a zebra. These results suggest that by the end of the first year of life, infant categorization is affected by preexisting knowledge of distinct categories. These findings do not, however, identify the specific basis for categorization, and researchers continue to explore the mechanisms involved in this fundamental cognitive ability (Cohen & Cashon, 2006; Gelman & Kalish, 2006; Oakes & Madole, 2000; Pauen, 2002).

Defining and Testing Intelligence in Infancy

The majority of intelligence tests, whether designed for adults or children, include questions designed to tap memory, quantitative abilities, logical reasoning, pattern recognition, analogical reasoning, vocabulary knowledge, and verbal comprehension. Standardized achievement and aptitude testing, using a written format, is now a nearly universal childhood experience in the United States, and in many other developed countries, beginning in the early elementary school years. The assessment of cognitive abilities and intellectual potential begins even earlier, however, and different, nonverbal tests have been constructed to assess intelligence in the first 3 years of life. In the following section, we will consider how intelligence is defined and measured in these tests, whether these tests are valid and reliable measures of infant and toddler intelligence, and whether the results of these tests enable researchers to predict later performance on traditional intelligence tests. We will also examine newer information processing approaches to the assessment of intelligence early in life.

Traditional Tests of Infant Intelligence

At the same time that adult intelligence tests were being developed, there were also researchers who began to construct tests for infants. Some of these researchers were known for their groundbreaking studies in other areas, such as Arnold Gesell (1954), who pioneered systematic research in locomotor development. Other researchers developed assessments based on influential theories about infant development, such as the Uzgiris–Hunt Ordinal Scales of Psychological Development (1975), which assess infants' progress through stages that correspond roughly to Piaget's substages of sensorimotor development.

One of the best-known measures of intelligence over the first 3 years of life, however, is the **Bayley Scales of Infant Development** (Bayley, 1969, 1993). Developed by Nancy Bayley, who began studying infant intelligence in the early decades of the twentieth century, the BSID assesses sensation, perception, motor, cognitive, memory, language, and social abilities from 1 month to 42 months of age. The BSID items are grouped into three major scales: a motor scale (tapping sensorimotor coordination and fine and gross motor skills), a mental scale (measuring perception, memory, and vocal/verbal behavior), and a behavior rating scale (based on information provided to the examiner by the parent).

Although the BSID provides a profile of infants' current functioning, scores often vary considerably from one testing time to another. This variability in performance may reflect variations in individual infants' states of arousal and motivation, or as some researchers have suggested, it may indicate that intelligence itself is variable during infancy (Bornstein et al., 1997). The BSID is also notoriously poor at predicting later performance on traditional intelligence tests, a limitation that Bayley herself reported in an early longitudinal study comparing infants' and children's test performance with their intelligence scores at age 18 years (Bayley, 1949; Bornstein et al., 1997). As Bayley and many others have noted, items on the BSID mental scales measure perceptual and motor development (e.g., "uses eye-hand coordination in reaching"), whereas intelligence tests for older children and adults do not assess these abilities (Bornstein et al., 1997). It should not be surprising, therefore, that infant measures do not predict later performance. In fact, as Bayley and many others have found, it is not until the age of about 5 years that intelligence test scores are significantly associated with later test scores.

Information Processing Assessments of Infant Intelligence

Growing awareness of the limitations of traditional tests of infant intelligence led researchers to reconsider assumptions about the measurement of early cognitive abilities. The resulting assessments focus on specific information processing components, chiefly, the visual-perceptual skills involved in attending to and examining stimuli so that information about those stimuli may be stored in and later retrieved from memory. As we noted earlier in this chapter, studies of infant attention, habituation, and visual recognition memory have shown that information processing varies as a function of the complexity of stimuli and generally becomes more efficient with age (Colombo, 2002). We also know that there are individual differences in infants' information processing skills (e.g., some infants are "short lookers" in habituation procedures, whereas others are "long lookers") and that infants who are at risk for cognitive delay tend to process information less efficiently than normally developing infants (Bornstein et al., 1997; Colombo, 2002; Rose et al., 2005).

Subsequent studies have shown that information processing measures tend to be fairly reliable, especially when measures are taken close together in time (days or weeks apart, rather than months apart) (Bornstein, 1988). These measures have also been reported to be moderately successful as predictors of later intelligence. That is, the efficiency of infants' information processing during the first 6 months of life appears to be linked to their subsequent performance on tests of cognitive abilities and intelligence between 2 and 12 years of age—"short lookers" tend to have higher scores in childhood than do "long lookers" (Bornstein, 1985; Bornstein & Tamis-LeMonda, 1994; Colombo, 1993; Colombo & Janowsky, 1998; McCall & Carriger, 1993; Rose & Feldman, 1995, 1997; Rose et al., 2005).

Taken together, many researchers regard these findings as evidence that there are inherent, possibly genetic, individual differences in the neurological substrate for information processing (Bornstein et al., 1997; Colombo & Janowsky, 1998; Reznick, Corley, & Robinson, 1997). The findings do not indicate, however, how information processing efficiency is affected by other factors, such as infants' reaction to the novel laboratory setting; it is possible, for example, that "easy" babies may settle more quickly and perform more efficiently than babies who are "slow to warm up" or even "difficult." It should also be emphasized that findings of early individual differences do not negate the importance of environmental influences on cognitive performance and development (Reznick, Corley, & Robinson, 1997) nor preclude the possibility of modifying infants' information processing behavior (Jankowski, Rose, & Feldman, 2001; Colombo, 2002). Indeed, as we will see in Chapter 11, there is compelling evidence that early interventions, as well as everyday interactions with parents and caregivers, have significant short- and long-term impacts on infants' cognitive development.

WRAPPING THINGS UP: Summary and Conclusion

The first 3 years of life are a time of rapid growth and development in the areas of cognition, learning, and intelligence. Today's researchers are indebted to both Piaget and Vygotsky for framing fundamental issues and providing a foundation of detailed, systematic observations, but there are still many unanswered questions about development in these domains. New technology and knowledge about the brain offer the possibility of addressing many of these questions by augmenting behavioral measures with new levels of analysis. In addition, researchers today are less likely to be guided by grand theories that attempt to explain numerous aspects of development than they are by "mini-theories" and the desire to understand specific developmental phenomena as they unfold over time and in different contexts (Haith & Benson, 1998). Even as these new approaches emerge, however, it is possible to reflect on and be impressed by how much has been learned so far.

The development of play during the first 3 years of life depends on the development of motor, cognitive, and social skills. Play also helps develop skills in these domains by enabling infants and toddlers to learn about themselves, other people, objects, and events. We know that the participants, materials, and content of play are affected by the social and cultural context in which it occurs.

Piaget's theory asserts that infants operate at the level of sensorimotor intelligence until the age of about 2 years. His theory emphasizes limitations over achievements at this stage. Key ideas are the incremental development of understanding of object permanence, spatial relationships, and categorization.

Vygotsky's sociocultural theory is built on the assumption that cognitive abilities develop in and are shaped by children's sociocultural contexts. Interactions with more advanced individuals help children learn within their own zones of proximal development. Contemporary researchers have adapted Vygotsky's concepts and introduced the notions of scaffolding and guided participation to describe the process through which young children learn during interactions with parents, caregivers, and others.

Cognitive science perspectives on development during the first 3 years of life offer new levels of analysis that may be fruitfully combined with traditional behavioral measures. It is now clear that infants' information processing abilities function from an early age and undergo important changes during the first year of life. Measures of the allocation of attention, speed of habituation, and visual recognition memory provide new insights into individual differences in these abilities.

Infants' memory system functions from birth and is influenced by many of the same factors that affect memory in older children and adults. Significant neurological development beginning during the end of the first year of life supports increasing efficiency and flexibility in the infant's memory system.

Traditional measures of infant intelligence tend not to yield stable profiles of infants' cognitive abilities, nor do they predict later performance on tests of intelligence. Information processing tasks, by comparison, provide fairly stable and predictive measures of infant intelligence and intelligence later in childhood, but they do not negate the importance of early environmental and experiential influences.

The research that we have discussed in this chapter shows that, long before infants are able to produce and comprehend language, they notice and remember a surprising amount of information about the people, objects, and events they encounter. This information is not "lost," nor does it become inaccessible, when infants become verbal, as was once thought; instead, it continues to influence their behavior and interactions on a daily basis and over time. The acquisition of language is a significant development during the first 3 years of life, of course, and provides a fascinating and useful window into young children's past, present, and future experience. We will examine the profound changes that occur in the domain of language in our next chapter.

THINK ABOUT IT: Questions for Reading and Discussion

1. What are the different kinds of play that develop during the first 3 years of life?

2. In order for pretend/symbolic play to develop, what sorts of developmental changes need to occur?

3. What sorts of toys would you recommend that parents provide for their infant at each of the following ages: 6 months, 12 months, 18 months, 24 months, 30 months, 36 months? Explain the basis for your recommendations.

4. If new parents wanted to know if they should join their child in play during infancy, the toddler years, and beyond, what would you recommend? How would you explain the evidence for and against adult-child play?

5. How would parents who endorse Piaget's theory of cognitive development interact with their child, as compared with parents who support Vygotsky's theory? What sorts of behaviors and situations might they create (or avoid)?

6. Piaget's theory has had a significant influence on the study of cognitive development during the first 3 years of life. Does it matter that many of his views have not been supported by more recent research? Explain.

7. What can we do with the new findings about infant cognitive abilities? What are the implications for parents and caregivers?

8. Should infant intelligence be assessed? Why or why not? Assuming that you did want to assess intelligence in an infant or toddler, which measure(s) would you use? Explain.

KEY WORDS

Accommodation (218)	Piaget's term for adjusting exploratory actions in response to an object's novel characteristics
Allocentric framework (226)	Spatial orientation that is based on external cues in the environment
A-not-B error (221)	Piaget's term for the tendency, first seen around 8 months of age, for infants to search for objects at locations from which they previously successfully retrieved objects, even thought they saw the object being hidden at a different location
Arbitrary relations (238)	Steps in a sequence that may be performed in any order because they are not logically or practically linked
Assimilation (218)	Piaget's term for employing previously used actions to explore an object
Bayley Scales of Infant Development (BSID) (244)	A measure that is used to assess infant intelligence through motor, mental, and behavior rating scales
Categorization (241)	The ability to group aspects of the world according to shared attributes
Coordination of secondary schemes (220)	Piaget's fourth substage of the sensorimotor period, in which infants perform two separate schemes in order to produce a desired outcome
Deferred imitation (220)	The ability to remember and repeat an action that was observed earlier, in the absence of a model for those actions

Egocentric (218)	Piaget's term for infants' tendency to understand the world through their own sensory and motor acts
Egocentric framework (226)	Spatial orientation that is based on one's own body and physical actions
Egocentric speech (230)	Verbal behavior that is directed toward oneself rather than others, with the purpose of enhancing concentration and performance during an activity
Enabling relations (238)	A logically or practically necessary order between steps in a sequence
Event-related potentials (ERPs) (236)	Recordings of brain activity from a network of electrodes placed on the scalp's surface
Explicit memory (236)	Conscious awareness of specific information, such as events and facts
Exploratory play (212)	Play commonly seen in the first year of life, consisting of repetition of motor movements
Functional play (212)	Play observed beginning at 12 to 18 months of age that reflects children's understanding of objects' intended uses
Functional-relational play (212)	Play observed beginning between 12 and 18 months of age that involves bringing together related objects
Guided participation (232)	Patterns of social interaction and structured activity during joint problem solving involving people with different levels of skills and knowledge
Implicit memory (236)	Unconscious learning, including conditioning and aspects of motor learning
Infantile amnesia (236)	The inability that most adults have to recall events that happened before they were about 3 years old
Joint attention (235)	Shared perceptual exploration with another person
Long-term memory (236)	Information that is stored and available to be retrieved repeatedly over time
Mental combinations (220)	Piaget's sixth substage of the sensorimotor period, in which infants are able to think about their actions and select schemes in order to achieve a desired outcome
Mental representation (217)	The ability to remember and think about objects and events, even when those objects and events are not physically present
Object permanence (221)	Piaget's term for infants' gradually developing understanding that objects continue to exist even when they are not in sensory or motor contact with them
Play (212)	Activity that is intrinsically motivated, focused on means rather than ends, different from purely exploratory behavior, nonliteral, and free from externally applied rules
Pretend/symbolic play (215)	Play that emerges after 12 months of age, in which children behave in a nonliteral way
Primary circular reactions (219)	Piaget's second substage of the sensorimotor period, in which sensory and motor schemes are activated by chance
Recall memory (238)	The ability to remember a previously presented stimulus or event in the absence of ongoing perceptual support
Recognition memory (237)	The ability to remember a previously presented stimulus or event when it is presented at a later time
Reflex schemes (218)	Piaget's first substage of the sensorimotor period, in which infants respond to the world with a limited set of preadapted behaviors

Relational play (212)	Play before the age of 12 months that involves unrelated objects
Representational insight (229)	Awareness of the relation between a space and a symbol for that space
Scaffolding (231)	The process through which more capable individuals structure tasks to boost less capable individuals' performance
Schemes (218)	Piaget's term for actions used to explore and interact with the physical environment
Secondary circular reactions (220)	Piaget's third substage of the sensorimotor period, in which infants repeat schemes in order to achieve specific outcomes
Sensorimotor intelligence (217)	Piaget's first stage of cognitive development, from birth to 24 months of age
Short-term memory (239)	A limited storage system that holds information for only a few seconds if the information is not actively rehearsed
Sociocultural contexts (230)	Settings in which children spend time, including home, child care, and school
Sociodramatic play (216)	Cooperative pretend play emerging between 2 and 3 years of age, in which children use verbal skills to coordinate their own actions with those of other children as part of a larger play theme
Tertiary circular reactions (220)	Piaget's fifth substage of the sensorimotor period, in which infants try different schemes to discover the effects of those actions
Theory of mind (217)	A cognitive achievement that emerges around the age of 3 years, enabling children to understand others' feelings and beliefs
Violation-of-expectation procedure (223)	A procedure in which infants are shown possible and impossible events in order to test their understanding of physical phenomena and object properties
Zone of proximal development (ZPD) (231)	Vygotsky's term for the distance between a child's ability to solve a problem alone and how much better the child can solve the problem when guided or assisted by a more capable individual

Language and Communication

I t is just another day in the Tiny Tugboat room, the childcare setting for a group of children between 20 and 30 months of age. Simon, who is $2\frac{1}{2}$ years old, responds quickly and directly to a younger child who has just bitten his friend, Andrew, in a struggle over a toy. While the teacher is making her way over to intervene and comfort Andrew, who still clutches the toy in his hands, Simon emphatically tells the perpetrator, "We don't bite our friends! That's not okay!" When the teacher arrives, just moments later, she utters a nearly identical statement, to which Simon and the other children listen intently. Then, tears are dried, a band-aid is applied, the dispute is discussed, and snack-time begins, soon to be followed by story time and an art project. Just another day in which the Tiny Tugs will hear language used by teachers to comfort, question, read to, and guide them. Just another day in which they will be encouraged to "use their words"—instead of their teeth—to share their thoughts and feelings.

Simon's verbal response shows that he has been paying attention in the Tiny Tugboats room. As a result, he not only has acquired particular vocabulary words, but he also has learned how and when to use them. Two years earlier, when Simon was in the Sunshine room, he also heard lots of language and learned from it, but it would have been more difficult for him to produce evidence of his developing language skills. Still, Simon's caregivers knew that the words he heard every day, and their responses to his earliest efforts to communicate, would have an impact on his subsequent ability to understand and use language. Researchers who study first language acquisition know this as well and have designed clever studies to illuminate the factors that influence development in this important domain. Before we examine this evidence, however, let's consider some of the reasons that language is such an important aspect of development from birth to age 3.

Why Language Matters

Language matters because it is a multipurpose tool that promotes learning as well as social and emotional development. Parents and caregivers use words and signs to draw infants' attention

These 2-year-olds are learning about literacy, a valued skill in their culture.

to specific objects, people, and events. The repetition of consistent labels also provides infants with symbols with which to refer to aspects of their experience, including internal states. A positive emotional tone encourages infants to pay attention to and participate in ongoing activities, whereas a harsh or negative tone discourages them from doing so (Fernald, 1993). Children who engage in conversations about others' feelings, beliefs, and desires gain insight into those perspectives, which supports the development of theory-of-mind knowledge (Dunn, 1998). Early exposure appears to be critical, and the more experience children have with language and verbal interaction during the first 2 years of life, the more advanced their language skills are when they reach school age (Hart & Risley, 1995; Huttenlocher, 1998).

Language also matters because it contributes to young children's developing sense of self by providing descriptions and evaluations of children's characteristics and abilities (Harter, 1998; Neisser, 1991, 1993; Nelson, 1993). Parental rules and standards are conveyed through language, and adults' comments about children's compliance with these standards support the development of self-regulation and an early sense of morality (Emde et al., 1991). Language also offers very young children a means of specifying and negotiating play activities, as well as relating to peers in other situations. As early as the third year of life, children use language to insert themselves into family conversations, even turning the topic of conversation from others to themselves (Dunn & Shatz, 1989; Howes, 1996). Like other aspects of parent-child interaction, patterns of conversation vary across cultures, revealing a range of parental beliefs and expectations about child development. For these reasons and others that we will discuss in this chapter, language matters.

Studying Language Development

Traditionally, researchers have subdivided language into separate systems or modules corresponding to the sound patterns of language (**phonology**), the meanings of words (**semantics**), rules for combining words (**grammar**), and the practical uses of language (**pragmatics**). As the following brief overview shows, a wide array of creative measures has been used to study both the production and comprehension of elements of these systems.

Studies of phonological development often use methods that we first learned about in Chapter 2, such as habituation or preferential looking. Infants' ability to perceive different speech sounds is inferred by measuring changes in their attention and interest in those sounds. Some researchers condition infants to turn their head when they hear a change in an auditory stimulus; once this behavior has been established, researchers can ask infants to "tell" them if they notice differences between subsequent speech samples. In other experiments, infants are familiarized to a set of speech sounds. Then, in a test phase, their visual attention is drawn to a loudspeaker, and researchers compare the amount of time that infants look at the loudspeaker when familiar versus novel speech sounds are played over it. Some researchers have used "sentences" combining invented "words" like *boga, giku, kuga*, and *gapi* in order to determine how rapidly infants learn to recognize different kinds of recurring patterns. By manipulating the phonological characteristics and word order in those sentences and presenting them repeatedly, researchers can then measure infants' interest in looking at loudspeakers playing familiar samples as well as samples that violate the patterns they have learned. Some studies of phonological awareness have begun to use event-related potential (ERP) technology to measure infants' brain activity in response to a variety of speech sounds. These measures can be especially informative when infants fail to show an overt behavioral response, such as preferential looking. Although the focus has been on infants' *responses* to auditory stimuli, some researchers have explored infants' ability to *produce* speech sounds and signs by recording samples of cooing, crying, and babbling, as well as recognizable words and signs.

Semantic development has often been studied by researchers who audiotape infants' spontaneous speech in order to document their first words, noting whether they refer to objects, people, actions, or internal states. Other researchers have created controlled laboratory situations in which they use an invented word, such as *zop* or *dax*, to determine how very young children learn its meaning. In testing competing hypotheses, some researchers focus on the nonlinguistic and contextual aspects of word learning, such as joint attention with adults.

At the level of grammar, there is a vast range of phenomena to explore, from the grammatical markers that create the past tense of a verb to the order of words in a sentence. Like other language researchers, those studying grammar have used a variety of methods. In some studies, children are asked to judge which words or phrases in a set of utterances are correct (e.g., "feet" versus "foots"). In other studies, infants and toddlers are shown side-by-side videotaped displays that are accompanied by a single narration describing one of the displays. Researchers in these experiments measure children's looking time in order to gauge their comprehension of the phrases or sentences that they hear (e.g., "the elephant bumped the ball" versus "the ball was bumped by the elephant"). Other researchers have examined children's spontaneous production of grammatical errors by recording conversations in the child's home and in other naturalistic settings.

When children understand the pragmatic uses of language, they know that it can be used for a variety of purposes. Simon's comments to his biting classmate suggest that he understands which words to utter, as well as the circumstances and manner in which to state them, in order to reprimand a misbehaving child. Before long, he will also learn how to use language in conversation and to perform other functions, such as entertaining, persuading, or comforting other people. A number of studies in both laboratory and naturalistic settings have shown that children younger than 3, like Simon, begin to use certain kinds of utterances selectively and appropriately to achieve specific social goals. Other kinds of pragmatic awareness develop much later, such as the ability to understand figurative language (e.g. "she was a soft-hearted person") or respond to a request that is implicit in a statement (e.g., "that open window is making it cold in here").

Until recently, the study of language acquisition was a debate between theorists favoring a learning explanation of language and those advocating a nativist account. A key proponent of learning theories was B. F. Skinner, while Noam Chomsky came to be associated with the nativist perspective. In Skinner's (1957) view, children learn language in much the same way that they learn other behaviors—through imitation and reinforcement. Table 8.1 shows some of the evidence that may be viewed as consistent with Skinner's learning theory of language acquisition. He asserted that children acquiring language are actually learning to produce specific modeled and reinforced combinations of words, while suppressing other combinations that are neither modeled nor reinforced. Simon's

TABLE 8.1   Evidence Supporting Learning and Nativist Views of Language Acquisition

Evidence Supporting Learning Views	Evidence Supporting Nativist Views
Children learn the language that is spoken around them, including a particular dialect and vocabulary.	Children progress through the same series of prelinguistic stages as they learn language.
The amount and variety of early exposure to language is predictive of children's later acquisition of both semantics and grammar.	The rate of acquisition varies across children, but there is a similar order for the acquisition of grammar.
Children learn about pragmatics as a result of language experience.	Children make errors they have never heard in adult speech.
Parents frequently modify their speech, simplifying the infant's language processing task.	Children are able to apply rules of grammar to words they have never heard before, including invented words.
Parents often create and take advantage of naturally occurring opportunities to label objects and actions for their infants and to expand their young children's earliest utterances.	Deaf children being reared without exposure to formal sign language invent their own rule-governed, gestural systems of communication.
Parents correct their children's language errors in an effort to teach them to produce grammatically acceptable speech.	

word-for-word imitation of his teacher's responses in previous biting incidents suggests that imitation does play a role in language acquisition.

Chomsky (1958), however, might have noted that Simon also utters many novel sentences that no one has produced before, indicating that there must be more than simple imitation involved. In fact, Chomsky pointed out that naturally occurring language tends to be complex, making it impossible for very young children to keep track of all of the reinforcement probabilities for different words and word orders as a basis for determining which words can be used as verbs as opposed to nouns and adjectives. Moreover, if the frequency of words in the language that children heard predicted their acquisition, then often used parts of speech like articles ("a" and "the") would be expected to be acquired early. As we will see shortly, these are not among most children's first words. Chomsky and others also responded to Skinner by noting that adult language is not always a good model; parents and caregivers do not always produce complete, grammatical sentences. In addition, even when their own speech is grammatically correct, parents do not always react to their young children's grammatical errors. Instead, they seem to see past those errors and focus on the content and meaning (Brown & Hanlon, 1970; Hirsh-Pasek, Trieman, & Schneiderman, 1984).

Given that children are able to acquire much of the grammar in the language they are learning by the age of about 2 years, Chomsky initially asserted that infants are born possessing a universal set of grammatical rules for learning to understand and produce speech (Chomsky, 1965, 1980, 1986). Compelling support for this argument was found in studies of deaf children who developed their own sign language in the absence of an adult model in the environment (Goldin-Meadow, 2006; Goldin-Meadow & Mylander, 1983, 1998; Senghas & Coppola, 2001; Senghas, Kita, & Özyurek, 2004.) Table 8.1 summarizes observations that may be viewed as supporting Chomsky's nativist assertions.

For years, researchers amassed evidence in favor of one side or the other, but today the learning-nativist debate is over, and no one would dispute the key role of learning and experience with language input. At the same time, it is clear that there are built-in constraints and abilities that hasten the process of acquiring a first language (Kuhl, 2000, 2004). We also know that the apparently separate systems of language are not entirely independent modules (Bates & Goodman, 2001). Instead, there are intimate connections between the sounds, meanings, forms, and uses of words (Saffran, 2003). The picture that emerges is thus a complex one, but as we will see, this complexity does not deter babies from embarking on and succeeding at the task of language acquisition.

Prelinguistic Communication

Infants "listen" long before they can understand words, responding from birth to the human voice and, within just a few months, coordinating their vocal activity and body movements in response to another person's verbal and nonverbal rhythmic patterns (Feldman, 2006; Jaffe et al., 2001). During the first year of life, infants learn how to take turns in routines and games, such as peek-a-boo, preparing them for later turn-taking in conversations (Rochat, Querido, & Striano, 1999).

Infants also "send messages" long before they can speak. The earliest messages—newborns' cries—convey information about hunger, pain, and other internal states, although these messages are sent without any intent to communicate. Infants also produce nondistress vocalizations, which serve as social signals that elicit contingent responses from parents and promote further interaction (Hsu & Fogel, 2003a). Intentional communication emerges by about 10 months of age but is still more likely to be nonverbal than verbal (Bates et al., 1979). One-year-olds make the most of the few words they have, embellishing their "requests" for food, toys, or particular people with pointing and gestures, as well as visual gaze and variations of vocal tone, such as whining. Taken together, these forms of prelinguistic communication lay a foundation for later language development.

Receptivity to Language

Like young birds and other animals, human infants are most responsive to the sounds produced by members of their own species (Aslin, Jusczyk, & Pisoni, 1998). Speech directed to infants is an especially attractive signal, even for babies just a few days or weeks old (Cooper & Aslin, 1990; Fernald, 1984, 1985; Fernald & Simon, 1984; Werker & McLeod, 1989; Pegg, Werker, & McLeod, 1992). Known as **infant-directed (ID) speech** (formerly "motherese"), this form of language differs from adult-directed (AD) speech in that ID utterances are shorter, more repetitive, higher-pitched, more variable in pitch, and less complex in vocabulary and grammar (Aslin, Jusczyk, & Pisoni, 1998; Snow, 1972). Speech directed to infants also tends to be more focused on emotional communication than AD speech, which may ultimately explain why infants prefer listening to ID speech (Trainor, Austin, & Desjardins, 2000).

Parents in some nonwestern cultures believe that it is either unwise or unnecessary to speak to infants, and they are thus unlikely to use ID speech (DeLoache & Gottlieb, 2000; Ochs & Schieffelin, 1984; Schieffelin, 1990). ID speech has been found in so many languages and cultures, however, that some researchers regard it as practically universal (Kuhl et al., 1997). Infant-directed communication also appears to be universal in another way. Just like parents who use spoken language, parents who use sign language modify their signs when addressing an infant, using exaggerated hand and arm movements, displaying more emotional facial expressions, slowing down the rate of signing, and repeating signs more than they would when addressing an adult. Not surprisingly, deaf infants show a preference for ID over AD sign language (Erting, Prezioso & O'Grandy Hynes, 1990; Masataka, 1992, 1996).

Some researchers have suggested that a preference for ID speech develops as a result of learning during the first few months after birth, but infants respond to ID speech even when it is in an unfamiliar language (Cooper & Aslin, 1994). This was found in one study in which $4\frac{1}{2}$ and 9-month-old English-learning infants who listened to Cantonese showed a preference for ID samples (Werker, Pegg, & McLeod, 1994). A cross-linguistic preference for ID language has also been found in other studies, including one in which 6-month-old hearing infants, who had not previously been exposed to sign language, showed a preference for the slower, more exaggerated and repetitive motions of ID sign language (Masataka, 1998).

ID speech may function like a set of introductory language lessons for young infants. This is because ID speech exaggerates information about the sound system of the infant's native language, more effectively separating sounds into categories and providing a more distinctive basis for the child's imitation. In a study in the United States, Russia, and Sweden, mothers of 2- to 5-month-old infants produced more extreme vowels when speaking to their infant than when they addressed an adult. One effect of ID speech, therefore, may be that it "stretches" the vowel space, providing information about the sounds that are the foundation for words (Kuhl, 2004; Kuhl et al., 1997; Liu, Kuhl, & Tsao, 2003). ID speech may also assist young language learners by more clearly segmenting the ongoing speech stream into words and phrases (Kemler et al., 1989; Thiessen, Hill, & Saffran, 2005).

In addition to simplifying language for infants, what other functions might ID speech play in language development? One role may be to engage and maintain infants' attention, since they are more likely to notice and attend to a speaker whose language has a sing-song, rising and falling intonation pattern (Fernald & Kuhl, 1987; Fernald & Mazzie, 1991; Kaplan et al., 1995). Infants who are paying closer attention are also more likely to be able to learn from the language that they hear (Thiessen, Hill, Saffran, 2005). In what may be one of its most important functions, ID speech also carries information about a caregiver's emotions (Fernald, 1992, 1993; Trainor, Austin, Desjardins, 2000). Consider the very different acoustic information that infants hear when they are being praised ("good!") and when they are being warned ("stop!" or "no!"). Even though young infants do not understand the difference in the *meaning* of the words "good" and "stop," the short, sharp exclamation normally accompanying the word "stop" is effective at keeping them from touching a forbidden or dangerous object.

Of all the sounds surrounding infants every day, they respond to and eventually imitate language, rather than doorbells or the sounds that their pets make. What is the basis for this imitative behavior? Does a specialized speech mode exist from birth? Are humans unique in the way we process speech sounds? What is the role of experience in the development of infants' speech and auditory processing abilities? Since the early 1970s, researchers around the world have worked to find answers to these questions. As a result, many aspects of this fascinating process have become clearer.

Speech Perception

In all spoken languages, there are variations of sound that function as speech units called phonemes. **Phonemes** are linguistically meaningful categories that signal differences in words through combinations of vowels and consonants. In English, for example, the difference between the words *back* and *pack* is a function of which of two phonemes, /b/ or /p/, is present. The **phonetics**, or set of vowels and consonants, that a particular language uses is only a subset of all possible speech sounds. The sounds that speakers produce may be phonetically different while still being perceived as belonging to the same phonemic category. That is, when analyzed in terms of acoustical physical energy, the /p/ in *pin* is not objectively identical to the /p/ in *spin*. Nevertheless, English speakers listening to these words report hearing the same phoneme /p/.

Speech perception is a complex task for first language learners. One challenge is that most utterances are actually continuous streams of speech, without obvious pauses and markers between words and phrases. Considered in objective terms, infants hear sentences like *hilittlebabyareyouawake?* but they must learn to perceive them as distinct words and phrases. At the same time, infants need to learn to ignore differences in the speech stream, such as the phonetic differences between the /p/ in *pin* and *spin*, in order to perceive these words as containing two instances of the same phoneme /p/. They also need to be able to perceive multiple examples of a phoneme as the same phoneme, despite differences between speakers in dimensions such as pitch, intonation, and speed. For example, although there are objective acoustical differences in the way that parents, older siblings, and grandparents pronounce an infant's name, the infant needs to be able to ignore these variations and hear these utterances as the same name. Fortunately, this ability is well developed by 4 to 6 months of age and may even be present in 1-month-olds (Kuhl, 1979, 1987; Kuhl & Miller, 1982; Saffran, Werker & Werner, 2006). If this were not the case, the task of learning to produce speech sounds would be difficult, if not impossible, since infants would need to try to match the infinite number of variations produced by different speakers uttering the same speech sounds.

Adding a final layer of complexity, languages differ in the phonemic distinctions that they make. Native speakers of Japanese, for example, produce sounds that approximate /r/ and /l/ in English, but the Japanese language does not make a phonemic distinction in that range of speech sounds. As a result, native speakers of Japanese have great difficulty *hearing* /r/ and /l/ as two distinct phonemes (Iverson et al., 2003; Zhang et al., 2005). As another example, native speakers of English are not sensitive to a contrast in Hindi between /Da/ and /da/; instead of two functionally different phonemes, they perceive only one—/da/ (Werker & Tees, 1984).

From birth, infants are able to perceive speech sounds categorically. Like adults, they discriminate between phonetic categories, such as /ba/ and /pa/ (Eimas et al., 1971). Unlike adults, infants are able to perceive phonemic categories from all human languages that have been tested. Categorical perception of human speech samples also has been documented in nonhuman animals, including chinchillas, monkeys, and quail (Kuhl, 1981, 2004; Newport & Aslin, 2000; Ramus et al., 2001; Saffran, Werker, & Werner, 2006). Taken together, these findings indicate that language is a highly salient signal for infants, but that categorical perception of phonemes may be "merely" a general auditory processing ability and not a special speech processing mode (Aslin, Jusczyk, & Pisoni, 1998; Kuhl, 2004; Saffran, Werker, & Werner, 2006).

As we have already noted, the phonemes that languages use are only a subset of all possible speech sounds that could be used. In the course of acquisition, language learners become specialists at perceiving and producing that subset of phonemes, and it becomes more difficult to discriminate between phonetic contrasts that are not linguistically meaningful in one's native language. A significant benefit of this specialization is that it appears to make it easier to learn the native language. When infants in one study were tested at 7, 14, 18, 24, and 30 months of age, those who were better at discriminating native-language phonemes at 7 months showed accelerated language ability at later ages, whereas those who were better at nonnative-language discrimination at 7 months showed reduced later language abilities (Kuhl et al., 2005b; Tsao, Liu, & Kuhl, 2004).

When do infants become phonemic specialists, and how does experience with language affect this process? At 6 months of age, infants are able to discriminate native as well as nonnative consonant contrasts, but by 10 to 12 months, the ability to perceive nonnative phonemes is significantly worse (Aslin, Jusczyk, & Pisoni, 1998; Kuhl, 2000, 2004; Saffran, Werker, & Werner, 2006; Werker & Lalonde, 1988; Werker & Tees, 1984). Change in sensitivity to nonnative vowel contrasts occurs slightly earlier, possibly because vowels tend to be longer and louder than consonants (Iverson & Kuhl, 1995; Kuhl et al., 1992; Polka & Bohn, 1996; Polka & Werker, 1994).

Researchers initially thought that these declines in sensitivity were an example of the "use it or lose it" principle. Phonetic feature detectors for all human languages were thought to be present from birth but to atrophy without stimulation from language input (Eimas & Corbit, 1973). This view was later undermined by experiments showing that adults can regain the ability to distinguish nonnative contrasts, if they have sufficient training (Flege, 1989; Lively, Logan, & Pisoni, 1993; Lively et al., 1994; Logan, Lively, & Pisoni, 1991). There is also evidence that even in the absence of language exposure, some nonnative phonemes can be perceived into adulthood (Best, McRoberts, & Sithole, 1988). In addition, recent experiments, including some using ERP measures, have shown that language exposure affects auditory processing through neural commitment to frequently occurring patterns in the native language (Iverson et al., 2003; Zhang et al., 2005). These findings show that, with cumulative exposure to native language, perceptual sensitivity to nonnative contrasts is not lost. Instead, in a phenomenon known as the **perceptual magnet effect**, sensitivity shifts to favor phonemes in the native language, "pulling in" acoustically more distant phonemes that were initially perceived as more peripheral examples of that phoneme (Kuhl, 1991; Kuhl et al., 1992). Exposure to native language is best thought of, therefore, as warping and contouring the initial acoustic space. The resulting pattern of neural commitment is evident in most infants before the age of 12 months (Kuhl, 2000, 2004; Rivera-Gaxiola, Silva-Pereyra, & Kuhl, 2005; Saffran, Werker, & Werner, 2006).

Native-language specialization can be modified as a result of experience with another language. This was demonstrated in an experiment with 9-month-old English-learning infants who were exposed to native Mandarin Chinese speakers. After 12 laboratory sessions, amounting to approximately five hours of exposure, infants showed a reverse of the usual decline in sensitivity to Mandarin phonemes, whereas a control group of infants who were not exposed to Mandarin continued to lose their sensitivity to the nonnative language. The performance of infants who were exposed to Mandarin was comparable to the level that was found in infants living in Taiwan, indicating that even short-term exposure is effective at this age (Kuhl, Tsao, & Liu, 2003). Further studies are needed to explain how infants who live in bilingual or multilingual homes and communities maintain sensitivity to different sets of phonetic contrasts.

Recent experiments also suggest that experience with language is important in another way. According to the **constrained statistical learning framework**, infants possess the ability to perform a sort of statistical analysis that enables them to extract recurring patterns. In these studies, 7- to 9-month-old infants hear continuous sequences of syllables containing words from an invented language. After being familiarized with multiple repetitions of a sequence from that language, such as *golabupabikututibubabupugolabupabikututibubabupu . . .* , researchers play individual words that were part of the sequence, such as *gola* or *bupa*. They compare infants' looking time at a loudspeaker playing one of those words with their looking time at a loudspeaker playing a word that was not part of the original sequence, such as *bugo* or *kubi*. If the looking times are different, researchers infer that infants were able to discriminate between the words being played and that they were able to use phonological regularities in the original sequence to extract word boundaries.

According to this account, infants perform the same sort of analysis on real language. After months of experience, for example, infants are able to extract the words *pretty* and *baby* (but not *tyba*) from the continuous speech stream *prettybaby*. This is because they have previously encountered the combination of *pre* and *tty* in other speech streams, such as *prettybig* and *prettygirl*, and the combination of *ba* and *by* in utterances such as *goodbaby* and *that'smybaby*. By comparison, they have less frequently heard the combination *ty* and *ba*. A number of studies have now documented this statistical ability, suggesting that infants are able to use their cumulative language experience to *find* words in a continuous speech stream before they begin to learn their meaning (Kuhl, 2000; Saffran, 2003; Saffran, Aslin, & Newport, 1996; Saffran & Thiessen, 2003; Saffran, Werker, & Werner, 2006). As with categorical speech perception, constrained statistical learning has been found in monkeys, suggesting that it may also be a more general learning ability (Hauser, Newport, & Aslin, 2001). Experiments are under way to shed further light on the learning mechanisms that infants use in these tasks and to determine how infants contend with multiple, sometimes conflicting cues for word boundaries that exist in real language samples (Marcus et al., 1999; Thiessen & Saffran, 2003).

The capacity to notice a variety of properties of language thus appears to be present at birth, but experience with the native language shapes infants' attention to those properties as they learn its specific features. Awareness of these features supports infants' ability to perform detailed analyses of the native language, more effectively processing and segmenting the speech they hear (Nazzi, Jusczyk, & Johnson, 2000; Saffran, 2003; Saffran, Werker, & Werner, 2006). These findings have led a number of researchers to speculate that languages themselves may have evolved to match these perceptual-learning abilities. According to this view, this may explain why language is acquired easily by most infants (Kuhl, 2004; Saffran, 2003).

Early Production: Babbling

For the first few months of life, infants coo and vocalize randomly. Around 3 to 4 months of age, infants' vocalizing begins to approximate the contours of **syllables**, combinations of consonants and vowels, such as *baba* and *mama* (Bloom, 1998). Infants' vocalizing resembles mature speech sounds more if an adult vocalizes just after the infant does (Bloom, Russell, & Wassenberg, 1987). These experiences support infants' ability to notice the similarities between the sounds they produce and the sounds they hear and may be important in guiding the development of connections in the brain for the eventual approximation of speech sound categories (Bloom, 1998; Kent & Miolo, 1995).

Between 6 and 9 months of age, the frequency of vocalizing increases as infants engage in **babbling**, patterned but meaningless sequences of reduplicated sounds, such as *babababa* and *mamamama* (Bloom, 1998; Taylor, 1990). The most frequent sounds in infants' babbling repertoires (/b/, /d/, /g/, /p/, /t/, /k/, /m/, and /n/) are those that tend to occur frequently in the language they hear and that reflect the infants' developing speech system (Bloom, 1998).

Initially, babies everywhere produce babbling patterns that are highly similar, regardless of the language spoken by those around them (Blake & de Boysson-Bardies, 1992; Locke, 1983). Even deaf babies begin to babble at approximately the same age as hearing babies (Lenneberg, Rebelsky, & Nichols, 1965; Smith, 1982). Continuation and elaboration of vocal babbling depends, however, on infants hearing the speech sounds that they and others around them produce (Oller & Eilers, 1988).

For deaf infants born to deaf parents, manual babbling begins around the same age as vocal babbling in hearing infants (Petitto & Marentette, 1991). With exposure to sign language, deaf infants babble with their hands and fingers and show hand movements that are the manual equivalent of the phonetic and syllabic patterning in hearing children's vocal babbling. Hearing infants whose parents are profoundly deaf and thus communicate with them only in sign language also exhibit silent manual babbling (Petitto et al., 2001, 2004). Both vocal babbling and manual babbling are controlled by the brain's left hemisphere (Holowka & Petitto, 2002; Petitto et al., 2000). These findings are compelling evidence that infants are able to extract visual and well as auditory patterns from the environment and, moreover, that speech is only one of the possible forms of language.

Gestural Communication

Ask parents about their infant's early language development, and they will likely describe the first time their child consistently used a word to stand for a person, object, or experience, even if their pronunciation was not completely correct, such as *ba* for ball. For many years, language researchers would have focused on vocal language too, but recent studies of children's gestures have expanded the definition of language development to include early manual communication.

Beginning at birth and continuing into the second half-year, infants cry, coo, and use their face and body in an unintentional way, although caregivers often interpret these behaviors as reflecting communicative intentions (e.g., "Do you need a new diaper?" and "You sound hungry"). At approximately 8 to 10 months of age, infants begin to use gestures in an intentional way to signal their desires and to indicate their interests to those around them (Bates et al., 1979; Goldin-Meadow, 2006; Messinger & Fogel, 1998). In this stage, babies raise their arms to indicate that they wish to be picked up, and they reach toward objects that they want, even when those objects are not close enough to be touched. These early gestures are closely tied to the context and may be interpretable only if the viewer follows the gesture's path to its target (Goodwyn, Acredolo, & Brown, 2000). As caregivers respond to infants' pointing and reaching by fulfilling their nonverbal requests, routines involving sharing and trading of objects frequently emerge. The communicative nature of these gestures and routines is reflected in infants' tendency to vocalize and visually check with the caregiver. Although gestures initially appear without vocalizations, consistent vocal patterns (e.g., *wa* for water) gradually begin to accompany gestures (Carpenter, Nagell, & Tomasello, 1998; Dore et al., 1976; Goldin-Meadow, 2006).

During the period between the onset of gestures (around 10 months) and the point in development when spoken words are plentiful (about 24 months), infants use symbolic gestures, such as bringing the thumb to the mouth for *bottle*, to represent objects and events. These gestures are often modeled by adults who use them as tools for communication and as visual accompaniment to children's songs, such as "Twinkle Twinkle Little Star" or "The Itsy Bitsy Spider." Even when parents and children use the same gestures, they do not always use them in the same way. One recent analysis of child-parent interactions from 14 to 22 months of age, for example, showed that children were more likely than parents to use gestures such as pointing to reinforce (*bike* + point at bike), disambiguate (*that one* + point at bike), and supplement (*ride* + point at bike) their words (Özcaliskan & Goldin-Meadow, 2005a, 2005b).

Symbolic gestures alleviate the frustration that may arise before children have the ability to produce many words, and they may also promote verbal development. The more symbolic gestures children have in their communication repertoires by 19 months, the larger their verbal vocabularies at both 19 and 24 months. Comparisons to national norms show that children using symbolic gestures progress faster than average in verbal development, although this progress may also reflect a tendency for their parents to speak more to them (Acredolo & Goodwyn, 1988, 1990).

In one study of symbolic gestures, parents of 11-month-old infants were instructed to promote symbolic gesturing to accompany spoken words, using any physical motions that made sense to them (e.g., "Birdie!" [FLAP ARMS] "See the birdie!"). Infants' language acquisition was measured beginning at 15 months, and a clear advantage emerged for the sign training (ST) group over two control groups, especially early on. Although ST children were not significantly ahead of children in the control groups by the 36-month comparison, the early benefits for the ST group included easier and more positive communicative interactions. Children used symbolic gestures to request specific foods and activities, to share their feelings, and to elicit parental clarification of words. These results suggest

When this infant and his mother engage in joint attention—looking at and pointing to the same picture on the wall—they are communicating through words, actions, and emotions.

that infants are receptive to symbolic gesturing and that this form of nonverbal communication does not hamper verbal development but may even facilitate it (Goldin-Meadow, 2006; Goldin-Meadow & Mylander, 1983; Goodwyn & Acredolo, 1998; Goodwyn, Acredolo, & Brown, 2000).

Semantic Development

Whether infants are exposed to spoken language, sign language, or both, they become aware that patterns of speech sounds or signs have consistent meanings and contexts for use. Out of this awareness, children's first words emerge, augmenting their prelinguistic and nonverbal repertoire with new tools for learning and communication.

Milestones in the Acquisition of Meaning

The milestones of semantic development—the acquisition of vocabulary and word meaning—are well documented. Children's first words appear around the age of 12 months. Word learning begins gradually and then accelerates as children approach the end of the second year. During the second year, infants acquire words in the context of interactions with particular people and objects, guided by the perceptual qualities of those people and objects, such as their size, shape, texture, and color (Bloom, 1998). Infants and toddlers display their comprehension of words before they can produce them, responding with excitement, for example, to parents' conversations about their favorite foods long before they can name those foods or ask for them with words (Hirsh-Pasek & Golinkoff, 1991, 1996; Oviatt, 1982). Language production is relatively straightforward to measure because it is directly observable. Researchers interested in language *comprehension*, however, face the challenge of studying a mental event that must be inferred from overt behavior and the context in which it occurs (Fernald et al., 1998).

In some studies, researchers have assessed infants' speech comprehension by asking parents to provide reports about the words they believe their child knows. In the MacArthur Communicative Development Inventories, for example, which we will discuss later in the chapter, parents use lengthy vocabulary checklists to indicate the words that they believe their children comprehend (Fenson et al., 1994). This indirect measure is only informative if parents are aware of and give accurate reports about the words their infants know.

In other studies, infants' own behavior has provided information about their receptive vocabulary. In these studies children are asked to choose a named object from among a number of alternatives (Woodward, Markman, & Fitzsimmons, 1994). Although this is a relatively direct measure, there are also practical and motivational limitations to using this procedure because infants may become fatigued, bored, or distracted.

Another limitation of both parent-report and object-choice measures is that they do not provide information about the process of word recognition or how that process changes with age and experience. To address this limitation, some researchers study word recognition in infants ages 15 to 24 months by tracking their eye movements as they look at pictures in response to familiar spoken words—*doggie, baby, ball,* and *shoe.* Infants see pictures of two of these objects at a time and hear ID-speech–style sentences ("Where's the ___? See the ___?"), and the researchers measure how long it takes infants to look at the picture matching the spoken target word. Speed and efficiency of verbal processing increase dramatically over the second year. Whereas 15-month-olds usually do not seek out the correct picture until after the target word is spoken, 24-month-olds tend to shift their gaze to the correct picture before the word has been completely uttered, much as adults do in similar tests of word recognition. Infants are nearly as fast as adults at shifting their gaze by about 3 months of age. Age-related differences in response time found in this kind of experiment, therefore, probably reflect differences in speed of linguistic processing rather than maturation of the visual-motor system (Fernald, Perfors, & Marchman, 2006; Fernald et al., 1998; Golinkoff et al., 1987).

When this infant is shown two different images, will he look at the image matching the word for the object that is shown–the ball instead of the shoe?

Many parents report that their babies understand words as young as 8 months of age (Bates, Dale, & Thal., 1995; Bloom, 1993, 1998). One study even found that, as early as the age of $4\frac{1}{2}$ months, infants are able to recognize highly frequent words, such as their own name (Mandel, Jusczyk, & Pisoni, 1995). The researchers in this study also tested infants' responses to names of similar length and stress pattern, but they were not able to control for differences in the amount of previous exposure that infants had had to their own name. In other studies, researchers have known precisely how much prior exposure infants had to particular words (Jusczyk et al., 1993; Jusczyk & Hohne, 1997). One team of investigators visited 8-month-olds in their homes 10 times and played recordings of children's stories. After 2 weeks, infants heard lists of words that either occurred frequently or did not occur in the stories. Infants listened longer to the lists of story words, whereas a control group of infants, with no exposure to the stories, did not show a preference (Jusczyk & Hohne, 1997). These findings indicate that 8-month-olds engage in long-term storage of information (for a period of at least 2 weeks) about words that they have heard, even when there is no visible referent for the words (Aslin, Jusczyk, & Pisoni, 1998).

Children's first words typically do refer to visible objects and people, however, and parents as well as researchers are likely to credit infants with knowledge of a word when their vocalization meets specific criteria, including "its phonetic shape, consistency, frequency, and meaningfulness in relation to something going on in the situation" (Bloom, 1998, p. 321). Thus infants who consistently utter *da* whenever a dog appears (but never make this sound when they see any other object or animal) are likely to be granted the word *dog* as part of their productive vocabulary.

Most children experience a vocabulary spurt, becoming "vacuum cleaners" for words (Pinker, 1994). By the age of 18 to 19 months, most infants have learned about 50 new words (Bates, Dale, & Thal, 1995; Bloom, 1993, 1998). The rate of productive vocabulary growth increases so rapidly beginning at about 18 months of age that some researchers have referred to it as a "naming explosion" (Bloom, 1973; Goldfield & Reznick, 1990). During this time, some children are reported to learn as many as 40 new words per week, and many go from having only 10 to 20 words to having well over 100 within a month or two (Dromi, 1986; Goldfield & Reznick, 1990; Woodward & Markman, 1998). Among young deaf infants learning sign language, first referential signs and a naming (signing) explosion occur at approximately the same ages as spoken vocabulary growth in hearing infants (Bloom, 1998; Folven, & Bonvillian, 1991). Contrary to some popular beliefs, bilingual infants follow a similar timetable, whether they are acquiring two spoken languages, such as French and English, or one spoken and one manual language, such as French and Langue des Signes Québécoise (Holowka, Brosseau-Lapré, & Petitto, 2002; Petitto & Kovelman, 2003).

One-Word Utterances

Children's first words often refer to animals, vehicles, food, clothing, toys, body parts, people, household items, places to go, things outside, actions, games, and routines (Bloom, 1998; Nelson, Hampson, & Shaw, 1993; Waxman & Lidz, 2006). For many years, researchers sought to categorize these first words as if they were parts of speech in sentences produced by older children and adults. Although it is true that many of children's first words could be described as nouns—names for objects, like *ball, cookie, bottle*, and *dog*—there are a number of reasons to use caution when applying abstract grammatical categories to children's earliest utterances.

This 2-year-old girl and her mother communicate through American Sign Language. Research has shown that children learning sign language progress through the same stages as children learning a spoken language.

Focusing on the nouns in children's early language production may be misleading because children are also learning many other kinds of words, like *more, down, pretty*, and *open*. In fact, in one well-known study of 1-year-olds, object names made up only about one-third of the words children uttered (Bloom, Tinker, & Margulis, 1993). Even in a classic study reporting that more than half of some children's first words were nouns, some of the words named events like *lunch*, or transient "objects" like *lap* (Bloom, 1998; Nelson, 1973; Nelson, Hampson, & Shaw, 1993).

Assigning children's first words to formal speech categories is also difficult because names for objects are often used to communicate other meanings (Bloom, 1994; Bloom et al, 1988; Waxman & Lidz, 2006). These **holophrases** allow children who can produce only one word at a time to use each word in a more flexible way (Flavell, Miller, & Miller, 2002). The word *cookie*, therefore, might mean "That's a cookie," but it might also mean "I want a cookie," "I want another cookie," or even "I dropped my cookie," depending on the context in which it is uttered and the accompanying emotion.

Another problem is that, when children first learn new words, they do not always use them in the same way that older children and adults do. One common error is **overextension**, which occurs when children use a word, such as *dog*, to refer to other objects, such as cats or rabbits, that may be perceptually or functionally similar to the word's correct referent (Anglin, 1977; Flavell, Miller, & Miller, 2002; Rescorla, 1980). In one now famous example of creative overextension, the young son of two language researchers overextended the name of their English sheepdog, Nunu, to a variety of objects, including other dogs, fuzzy slippers, and even a salad garnished with two large black olives that resembled their dog's nose (de Villiers & de Villiers, 1978). Although it is more difficult to detect, children sometimes make the opposite error of **underextension**—applying a word only to a specific instance, such as using the word *dog* for the family collie but not applying it to poodles, Dalmatians, or dogs in general.

Individual Differences: The Role of Language Experience

Children differ in when they produce their first words and in the rate at which they acquire subsequent words (Smith, 2000). In one study, the range in age for first words was from

10 to 17 months, and the range for the vocabulary spurt was from 13 to 25 months (Bloom, 1993). What are some of the reasons for this variability? One factor may be differences in infants' ability to analyze the sound patterns of the speech they hear and compare them to their own early vocalizations (Bloom, 1998). As we have seen already, development of speech perception depends on both the maturation of infants' auditory and linguistic capacities and exposure to language.

Another important factor in early language development is the amount and variety of language that infants hear every day. Consistent associations have been found between the quantity and quality of language input and infants' socioeconomic background (Bates, Bretherton, & Snyder, 1988; Bates, Dale, & Thal, 1995). In one longitudinal study that began when infants were 7 to 9 months old, researchers made observations in the home. They found that parents in lower-income families talked less often to their children than parents in higher-income families; they also made fewer efforts to engage their children in conversation and gave verbal feedback that was more frequently corrective or critical than affirmative or encouraging. Children in lower-income families received less than one-half the language experience of children in middle-income families (616 versus 1,251 words per hour) and less than one-third that of children in higher-income families (2,153 words per hour). Based on these averages, in a 100-hour week, the researchers noted that the average child in a lower-income family would amass 62,000 words of language experience, the average child in a middle-income family 125,000 words, and the average child in a higher-income family 215,000 words. When they were 30 months old, children in lower-income families had smaller vocabularies than children in higher-income families (an average of 357 versus 766 words), suggesting that language input may have been a contributing factor (Hart & Risley, 1995, 1999).

Other studies have also found support for the relation between naturally occurring variations in infants' early language environments and their later language skills (Hoff, 2003; Hoff-Ginsberg, 1997). Even within middle-class samples, some studies have found a wide range in the amount that mothers talk to their 16-month-olds (from 700 to 7,000 words per hour) and, correspondingly, in children's vocabulary at age 26 months (from 200 to 800 words) (Huttenlocher, 1998; Huttenlocher et al., 1991, 2002; Huttenlocher, Levine, & Vevea, 1998).

In addition to the amount and variety of speech that children hear, maternal responsiveness influences the timing of milestones in children's early expressive language (LeMonda, Bornstein, & Baumwell, 2001). Researchers in one study videotaped mother-child free play at 9 and 13 months and coded the interactions for maternal responsiveness when their children vocalized, called to or looked at them, or played with/explored an object or toy. Focusing on two early occurring language milestones (first imitations and first words) and three later language milestones (50 words in expressive language, combining words, and the use of language to talk about the past), the researchers found that maternal responsiveness predicted all five. Mothers' affirmations (e.g., "Nice job") and descriptions (e.g., "That's your Big Bird") at 9 months predicted the two early language milestones. Mothers' vocal imitations (e.g., saying "doll" after the child said "da") and expansions (e.g., saying "Where did the ball go?" after the child said "ba?") at 13 months were predictive of the three later language milestones.

These findings suggest that infants benefit most when mothers are responsive in ways that are relevant to their attention focus at different developmental stages. As 9-month-olds begin to explore and learn about the environment, their ability to imitate words and produce their own first words is supported and stimulated by mothers who attend and respond verbally to their children's explorations, providing labels for objects and events that their child has noticed. Later, however, at 13 months of age, children's language development seems to benefit more when mothers respond by imitating their child's vocalizations, asking questions related to the topic of their child's communicative efforts, or offering suggestions and prompts that are relevant to that topic—in short, responding to their children as more advanced communicative partners.

Cultural and Linguistic Influences

Efforts to generalize about children's first words may not fully succeed, because there is great diversity in the words in young children's early productive vocabularies. Out of 11,000 words that one researcher recorded from 14 children, for example, only five words appeared in the vocabularies of all the children (*baby, ball, down, juice,* and *more*). This diversity reflects the different sorts of topics that attract different children's attention. It also reflects the specific words that parents use in conversation, the goals that they have for different kinds of conversations, and their expectations about conversations with sons versus daughters (Bloom et al., 1993; Fivush et al., 2000; Smith, 2000). When talking about the past, some mothers ask their child many questions and provide a large amount of information about specific events, whereas other mothers ask fewer questions and provide less information, or even focus more on the child's feelings during the events than on objective facts about the experience. These styles contribute to differences in children's ability to remember past events as well as the content of those memories (Fivush & Fromhoff, 1988).

Across cultures, parents also differ in the sorts of topics they talk about with their children and how they use language to socialize them. Beng parents in the West African nation of Ivory Coast, for example, emphasize teaching infants appropriate greetings and words for all of their relatives as early as possible. After learning to greet politely, however, the Beng believe that it is also important for babies to learn how to tease and even playfully insult their relatives (Gottlieb, 2000).

Cross-cultural comparisons of parent-child conversations about past events have found that American parents tend to focus on building self-esteem and supporting their young children's developing sense of themselves as unique individuals. Chinese parents, by contrast, tend to use these conversations as opportunities to reinforce children's awareness of standards for appropriate behavior as well as their obligations and connectedness to the family (Miller et al., 1997; Wang, 2004).

Cultures also vary in the extent to which they encourage talkativeness in children. Japanese mothers in one study used both verbal and nonverbal cues to shorten their preschool-age children's personal narratives, creating minimally descriptive reminiscences that the researchers compared to haiku poetry. These interjections were used to teach children that empathy and shared understanding with listeners are valued more than detailed recitations in which one person holds the floor to a significantly greater degree than another. Talkativeness is considered especially undesirable for males in Japan, which may explain why Japanese mothers responded differently to boys than girls, interjecting more often in an effort to discourage their sons from speaking too much. English-speaking Canadian

Infants learn through joint attention and instruction from a more skilled person. After this infant's father demonstrates and talks about how to use the hammer, he will give his son a chance to try it out.

mothers, by contrast, tended to ask a greater number of questions, encouraging sons and daughters alike to speak more and to provide additional descriptive details in their personal narratives. These distinctive approaches reflect the different value that each culture places on individual self-expression in dyadic conversation (Minami & McCabe, 1995).

Cross-cultural studies also indicate that not all parents engage their infants in the reciprocal vocalizing and object labeling that is so characteristic of mother-infant interactions in middle-class western societies (Bloom, 1998; Crago, Annahatak, & Ningiuruvik, 1993; Pye, 1986; Smith-Hefner, 1988). Given the evidence we've already considered about the role of language experience and a rich language environment, it would be reasonable to ask how infants in some non-Western cultures acquire language. One answer seems to be that, unlike many western cultures in which infants spend much of their first months or even years in mother-child dyadic interaction, infants in non-Western cultures are often raised in multifamily, multiparticipant conversational contexts in which they are exposed to language. From the very beginning, therefore, infants in these cultures are surrounded by and overhear adults' speech to older children of various ages and stages of language acquisition. Further study is needed, but the success with which children in these cultures acquire language suggests that overheard speech can serve as an important resource in first language acquisition (Akhtar & Tomasello, 2000; Oshima-Takane, Goodz, & Derevensky, 1996). Another potentially helpful form of language modeling occurs in some non-Western cultures in which parents "speak for" their infants by holding them up and answering for them, for example, saying, "I'm fine" in response to the question "How are you?" (Gottlieb, 2000).

Many children around the world grow up in bilingual or multilingual families and communities. Research indicates that bilingual children acquire new words from both languages and usually use their first words in ways that show their awareness of different contexts for use (Holowka, Brosseau-Lapré, Petitto, 2002 ; Petitto & Kovelman, 2003). A child addressing his English-speaking childcare provider, for example, would tend to use the word *milk*, but when communicating with his Spanish-speaking grandmother, would be more likely to use the Spanish word for milk—*leche* (Yavas, 1995). Just like monolingual children, bilingual children begin to put together two words sometime after the age of 18 months (Bhatia & Ritchie, 1999).

Explaining Early Word Learning

How readily do young children learn new words? In one controlled study, a few minutes of training by an unfamiliar experimenter in a laboratory setting was sufficient to enable 18- and even 13-month-olds to recognize novel labels for novel objects (Woodward, Markman, & Fitzsimmons, 1994). This finding suggests that children make significant progress in word learning long before the naming explosion occurs, but how do infants solve the problem of matching individual words with the objects, people, events, and feelings to which they refer? As we discuss next, a number of theories have been proposed for the acquisition of children's first words. Table 8.2 shows that some explanations focus on adjustments that parents use when communicating with infants, whereas other accounts emphasize contributions made by infants themselves. Laboratory studies of word learning tend to explore carefully controlled language input that enables researchers to test specific assertions of competing theories. It is important to remember, however, that most early language learning environments are considerably richer, with multiple cues available (Bloom, 2000; Carpenter, Nagell, & Tomasello, 1998; Hollich et al., 2000; Tomasello, 2006; Waxman & Lidz, 2006; Woodward & Markman, 1998). For semantic development, then, like the development of other aspects of language, there may not be any ". . . 'smoking gun' arguments that settle the interesting particulars of many current hypotheses" (Maratsos, 1998, p. 461).

Social and Pragmatic Cues. Social/pragmatic theories begin with the observation that language learning occurs in a social context, typically a dyadic interaction between an infant and caregiver. According to this view, infants' primary motivation for language learning is to achieve emotional sharing with the caregiver, locating the self in a social world (Akhtar & Tomasello, 2000; Bloom, 1993, 1998). Through **joint attention**—achieved through nonverbal adjustments in posture, gaze, and head orientation—infants and caregivers share understanding and examine objects or events. Eventually, their shared emotional communication becomes shared in speech (Bloom, 1998).

Many parents use "follow-in" labeling, providing names for the objects to which their babies are attending (Masur, 1982). Some researchers have found that children whose parents use follow-in labeling have more advanced vocabularies than children who do not experience this kind of language input (Akhtar, Dunham, & Dunham, 1991; Tomasello & Farrar, 1986). Parents are not always aware of what their babies are looking at or interested in, however, and some studies suggest that they may engage in this form of labeling only 50 to 70 percent of the time (Baldwin, 1991). How, then, do infants avoid making semantic errors when parents do not establish joint attention with them?

One possibility is that infants might be able to use other information provided by the speaker to determine which words and referents belong together. This kind of information, known as **referential cues**, consists of verbal and nonverbal behaviors, such as gaze, facial expression, and head orientation, that reflect an individual's attentional focus, intentions, or expectations. One researcher taught 16- to 19-month-old infants a novel object label under two conditions, a follow-in labeling condition and a condition in which the experimenter provided an object label only when the baby and experimenter were looking at different objects. As expected, babies at both ages learned the label in the follow-in condition. When the experimenter uttered the label in the absence of joint attention, 16-month-olds failed to

TABLE 8.2   Theories of Early Word Learning

Theory	Assumptions	Examples
Social/Pragmatic	Infants learn language in order to communicate with other people, share emotions, and locate the self in a social world.	Infants learn when they and their caregivers give joint attention to objects, people, or events. Infants use speakers' referenial cues to learn which words and referents go together.
Constraints/Principles	Infants are able to build their vocabulary with relative ease because they are guided by a set of assumptions about the possible meanings of new words.	The whole object assumption biases infants to assume that new words refer to whole objects rather than actions, spatial location, or parts or features of objects. The taxonomic assumption biases infants to extend a new word for one kind of object to other examples of that kind of object.
Mutual Exclusivity	Infants assume that objects have only one name.	Infants map new words onto new objects whose names they do not know. They avoid using a new word for an object whose name they already know.
Grammatical Cues	Children use grammatical cues in utterances they hear to narrow down the possible meanings of new words.	Children use the presence or absence of an indefinite article ("a") to infer whether a new word refers to a specific, unique object or all objects of that type.
Semantic Contrast	Children learn the meaning of new words by contrasting them with known words from the same domain.	Children who are asked to bring the "navy" pants, not the "green" ones, are able to guess the meaning of the word "navy."

learn the new word but they did not make mistakes by mapping the new word onto the object they had been playing with and looking at (Baldwin, 1991).

These findings and those from subsequent studies suggest that infants do not follow a simple rule of association (Baldwin, 1993a; Baldwin et al., 1996; Baldwin & Tomasello, 1998). Instead, they are able to monitor a speaker's attentional cues and use that information as a basis for mapping words to the objects of the speaker's attention. Another series of experiments showed that 2-year-olds are able to use cues about a speaker's referential intent to learn new words. Children of this age assume, for example, that a speaker who says that he is looking for a *crug* has found it if he shows a gleeful expression, looks wide-eyed, and says "Ah!" upon encountering an object. If the speaker displays signs of unhappiness or disappointment, by contrast, 2-year-olds conclude that the object that was located is not a *crug*. Two-year-olds are also able to use speakers' nonverbal behavior to determine whether an intended action, described by a novel verb, such as *dax*, has occurred (Tomasello, 2000; Tomasello & Barton, 1994).

In addition to noticing a speaker's referential intent, young children are also capable of monitoring the success of their own communicative efforts. In one study, 30-month-old children requested particular toys. When these requests were (deliberately) misunderstood by an experimenter, children clarified their requests, indicating that they were keeping track of the experimenter's comprehension (Shwe & Markman, 1997).

In summary, the research literature provides some support for the social/pragmatic view of word learning. Many parents of infants, at least those in middle-class western cultures, monitor their infants' attentional and nonverbal cues, providing opportunities for "teaching" their infants new words for the objects and actions in which they are interested. These adjustments simplify the task of word learning for infants so that "children are not plagued with too many options for word-to-world mappings. Rather, the cooperating adult limits the hypothesis space" (Hollich, Hirsh-Pasek, & Golinkoff, 2000, p. 12). For their part, children seem able by about 18 months of age to "read" social situations and notice even quite subtle referential cues.

Constraints and Principles. When children hear a new word, such as *gerbil*, how do they learn the meaning of that word? How do they decide that gerbil refers to the entire animal in front of them and that it does not mean feet, tail, furry, scamper, or any of the other things they might see at the moment they hear someone utter the word gerbil? One answer to these questions is that the human mind must be equipped with constraints or principles to eliminate at least some of the possible meanings. In fact, according to the constraints/principles view, children are guided by a set of default assumptions, of which the whole object, taxonomic, and mutual exclusivity assumptions are the best known (Hollich, Hirsh-Pasek, & Golinkoff, 2000; Waxman & Lidz, 2006; Woodward, 2000).

The **whole object assumption**, sometimes referred to as the principle of object scope (Hollich et al., 2000), guides children to assume that new words refer to whole objects rather than actions, spatial location, or parts or features of objects. Evidence offered in support of the whole object assumption includes the finding that young language learners, even 1- and 2-year-olds, tend to regard a new word, such as *bix*, as if it refers to an object as a whole, as opposed to its substance, color, or parts (Golinkoff, Mervis, & Hirsh-Pasek, 1994; Markman, 1989). The characteristics of an object influence the tendency to focus on a whole object or its features. For complex objects, like certain kinds of kitchen utensils, 2-year-olds tend to assume that a new word refers to the entire object, but they are much less likely to make this inference for less complex objects and nonsolid substances, such as a foamy pile of shaving cream (Imai & Gentner, 1997).

Some researchers have asserted that object labels may be easier for children to learn because objects are more perceptually obvious than actions or relations between objects (Gentner, 1982, 2000). When 1- to $1\frac{1}{2}$-year-olds in one study were given significant exposure to eight new object labels and eight new action words, for example, they learned and produced the object labels more quickly than the action words (Schwartz & Leonard, 1980).

The notion that objects are inherently more perceptually obvious than other aspects of infants' experience is not universally accepted, however, and some researchers have instead investigated the possibility that objects may be more salient to infants because parents tend to emphasize objects more than actions in their speech. The evidence about this kind of influence is mixed. One line of inquiry has focused on the structural properties of language, such as word order, which may result in certain kinds of words being highlighted. English-speaking parents, for example, tend to end utterances with nouns because English tends to follow a subject-verb-object structure, as in the sentence "the girl read the book." Languages like Korean and Japanese, however, have a verb-final sentence structure that leads parents to end utterances with verbs. One study of 15- to 24-month-old infants interacting with their parents confirmed that Korean-speaking parents tended to end utterances with verbs, whereas English-speaking parents tended to end utterances with nouns. Despite this difference, there was little evidence of a difference in the *proportions* of nouns and verbs in English versus Korean parental speech, and both groups of children had many more nouns than verbs in their vocabularies (Au, Dapretto, & Song, 1994). In contrast, a similar study of Korean- and English-speaking parents interacting with their 12- to 26-month-old infants found that English-learning infants produced many more nouns than verbs, whereas Korean-learning infants produced nearly equal numbers of labels for objects and actions (Choi & Gopnik, 1995).

Taking a different approach, some researchers have wondered whether object labels might be more salient to young children whose parents tend to highlight objects in their conversations (Goldfield, 1993; Messer, 1981). In one laboratory investigation with 6-, 12-, and 19-month-olds, for example, English-speaking mothers tended to focus on teaching their children object names, whereas Japanese-speaking mothers tended to talk more about ongoing actions and to use language to involve children in social routines (Fernald & Morikawa, 1993). These conversational differences appeared not to be the most important factor, however, because there was no difference between the Japanese- and English-learning children at 12 and 19 months of age in the proportion of object labels that they produced. Children in both groups produced about twice as many nouns as verbs.

Studies examining children's first 50 words raise questions about the relative prominence of nouns and verbs in children's speech. These studies show that children learn words for whole objects, of course, but they also acquire words that are adjectives, action terms, and prepositions. In one longitudinal study of 14 children, for example, monthly observations showed that object words comprised as few as 10 percent for some children and, at most, 50 percent for other children (Bloom, 2000; Bloom, Tinker, & Margulis, 1993; Nelson, Hampson, & Shaw, 1993).

The **taxonomic assumption**, sometimes referred to as the principle of categorical scope (Hollich et al., 2000) or the principle of extendibility (Behrend, Scofield, & Kleinknecht, 2001), guides children to assume that new words should be extended to objects that are related to the category of the originally named object rather than "thematic associates" (Markman & Hutchinson, 1984). According to this view, the taxonomic assumption is at work when young children are taught a word for one kind of bird (e.g., calling a purple bird a *sud*) and then extend that new word to other kinds of birds but not to a bird's nest. The research literature provides support for this constraint on preschool children's word learning (Golinkoff et al., 1995). Studies of 9- to 20-month-olds suggest that this constraining assumption is operating at even earlier ages (Huttenlocher & Smiley, 1987; Waxman & Hall, 1993; Waxman & Markow, 1995; Waxman & Senghas, 1992).

The **mutual exclusivity assumption** leads children to assume that objects will have only one name. It also guides them to search for a nameless object referent as soon as they hear a novel word. In studies of this assumption, researchers typically present children with a familiar object, such as a ball, and an unfamiliar object, such as a shoe horn. The experimenter then uses a novel label, such as *glorp*, to ask the child for one of the objects. Children who follow the mutual exclusivity assumption select the novel, unnamed object rather than the ball when asked for the *glorp*. Beginning after the age of 2 years, children map novel labels to novel objects and novel actions (Behrend, 1995; Golinkoff et al., 1992, 1995; Merriman & Bowman, 1989; Merriman & Schuster, 1991).

One version of the mutual exclusivity assumption predicts further that children should resist learning second labels for objects that already have names. In controlled word learning experiments, monolingual children typically resist redundant labeling well before their second birthday. Researchers in one experiment taught 16-month-old infants a novel label either for an object with a name that they already knew or for an object whose name they did not know. In keeping with the mutual exclusivity prediction, infants applied the labels only when they were presented for previously unnamed objects (Liittschwager & Markman, 1994). Arguments against this point, however, include the fact that children can and do learn more than one word for the same object. Bilingual children, for example, are willing to use a novel label to refer to an object for which they already know the name, if they believe that the two labels are from different languages. Consistent with the mutual exclusivity assumption, they resist applying a novel label to an already labeled object if they believe that the two labels come from the same language (Au & Glusman, 1990).

Grammatical Cues.   At the same time that children acquire vocabulary, they are also learning about the rules of grammar for the language they are acquiring. Is it possible that children's emerging understanding of grammar provides cues about the meaning of new words? As a classic study showed many years ago, preschool-age children use grammatical cues, such as word endings, to interpret unfamiliar words (Brown, 1957). Using these cues, they might guess, for example, that *wugging* refers to an activity, whereas *wug* refers to an object. These findings have been replicated in numerous studies of preschoolers, and a growing body of research shows that children as young as 2 years of age are also able to use grammatical cues to narrow down the possible meanings of new words (Gelman & Taylor, 1984; Gleitman, 1990; Hall, Lee, & Belanger, 2001; Katz, Baker, & Macnamara, 1974; Macnamara, 1982; Naigles, 1990, 1996; Soja, 1992; Waxman & Kosowski, 1990).

In one series of experiments, toddlers aged 20 to 37 months learned a novel label for a doll. For some children, the doll was presented using a proper noun—"This is ZAV"—and for other children the doll was presented using a count noun—"This is *a* ZAV." A second identical doll was then placed nearby and the children's task was to choose one of the two dolls as a referent for the novel word, responding to one of two questions, either "Where is ZAV?" or "Where is a ZAV?" By the age of 24 months, children were more likely to select the first, labeled doll if they heard a proper name than if they heard a count noun (Hall, Lee, & Belanger, 2001).

Contrasting Semantic Relations.   If grammatical cues do not adequately explain how children learn new words, what other information might they use? As children's vocabularies increase, one source of information might be the words they already know and the phenomenon known as **lexical contrast** (Carey & Bartlett, 1978). As a result of lexical contrast, children who hear adults ask for "the khaki pants, not the blue ones" might become aware of the color to which the word *khaki* refers. This hypothesis was tested in one study by using a lexical contrast approach to teach 3- and 4-year-old children a novel color word—*chromium*—to describe the color olive. The researchers found, after just a single session and a one-week delay, that about one-half of the children showed some learning of the term *chromium* (Carey & Bartlett, 1978).

Subsequent research has used more sensitive measures, including a larger array of color choices and additional domains, such as shape and texture, to investigate young children's ability to learn from lexical contrast. Two-year-olds in one experiment, for example, were able to learn novel words, such as *granular*, on the basis of hearing them contrasted with known words, such as *smooth*, from the same domain (Heibeck & Markman, 1987).

After decades of studying semantic development, researchers now understand the need to consider the multiple cues and sources of information that infants use to learn new words (Hall & Waxman, 2004; Hollich, Hirsh-Pasek, & Golinkoff, 2000; Woodward & Markman, 1998). Infants have a surprisingly early sensitivity to social and pragmatic cues about communicative intentions. There also appear to be constraints on early word learning that make the task simpler than was previously assumed. By the age of 2 years, children are able to use their awareness of some aspects of another developing language system—grammar—to interpret new words.

The Acquisition of Grammar

Languages differ in word order and in whether and how they mark concepts such as the past, gender, and relationship status. As an English-learning child, Simon can simply refer to his *brother*, but if he were learning Mandarin Chinese, he would need to choose between two different words—*didi* (younger brother) and *gege* (older brother). How early do children become aware of the rules of the language that is spoken around them? How does experience interact with innate constraints to guide young children's acquisition of grammar?

Multiword Utterances

Long before children are able to put two or more words together, they are able to infer meaning from word order. This has been shown in studies with infants as young as 17 months of age, who have not yet moved beyond the one-word level of production. When researchers showed infants of this age two simultaneous video displays of different actions (e.g., Ernie washing Cookie Monster versus Cookie Monster washing Ernie) and played an audiotaped sentence that described one of the two actions (e.g., "Look! Ernie is washing Cookie Monster!"), they found that infants tended to look at the display that matched the sentence (Hirsh-Pasek & Golinkoff, 1996). These findings show that infants of this age have already learned to use one grammatical marker—word order—to interpret sentences they hear.

More obvious evidence of the acquisition of grammar appears around 18 to 24 months of age, when children begin to produce two-word utterances, using words they have already learned to say individually (Bloom, 1998). Children now say things like "mommy sock," "more juice," and "give me shoe," leaving out the little grammatical markers, like articles, plural endings, prepositions, and auxiliary verbs. Because of their economy of expression, children's utterances at this stage are often referred to as **telegraphic speech** (Brown, 1973).

Children's early two-word utterances communicate a range of meanings, including agent + action (e.g., "Daddy eat"), action + object (e.g., "Eat cookie" and "Throw hat"), agent + object (e.g., "Mommy car"), object + attribute (e.g., "Big doggie"), recurrence (e.g., "More juice"), and nonexistence (e.g., "No cookie"). The order of the words in these phrases is usually fixed, reflecting the order in which children hear the words combined with other words in adult speech (Bloom, 1973, 1998; Brown, 1973). As a result, children almost never say things like "Cookie eat" or "Hat throw."

Grammatical Morphemes

Some of children's early two-word utterances, such as "all gone" or "go byebye," are derived from familiar activities and routines, and researchers believe that these phrases are actually learned as single units or formulas. Their existence does not indicate that children have learned how the order of the individual words determines the meaning relationships between them (Bloom, 1998). They also point to an important fact about tracking children's grammatical development—simply counting words is not always a useful index. Instead, language researchers compute the **mean length of utterance (MLU)**, a measure based on the number of morphemes in children's speech. **Morphemes** are the minimal meaningful units in speech and they come in two varieties, free and bound. Free morphemes are words or parts of words that can function on their own, such as *boy, girl, walk, ocean*, and *call*. By contrast, bound morphemes are grammatical tags or markers that cannot stand alone; these include word endings like *-est, -s, -ing*, and *-ed*. When attached to free morphemes, bound morphemes modify the meaning. That is, in English, adding *-ed* to *walk* changes the meaning to the past tense. To compute the MLU for a particular child, researchers count up the number of morphemes (both bound and free) per utterance in a sample of the child's speech and divide that total by the number of utterances in the sample.

To illustrate, the utterance "Mommy sock" has two morphemes, whereas "Mommy's sock" has three; "Kitty eat" has two morphemes, whereas "Kitty is eat-ing" has four. As MLU increases, the number of words in an utterance increases, but even more importantly, the presence of more morphemes makes the child's speech seem more adultlike, less telegraphic (Flavell, Miller, & Miller, 2002).

As shown in Figure 8.1, several distinct stages of early language development have been described in terms of MLU. In the 1970s, researchers began to pay special attention to Stage II, when children first produce morphemes with which they can fine-tune the meaning of their speech. In what was to become groundbreaking research, the researchers focused on

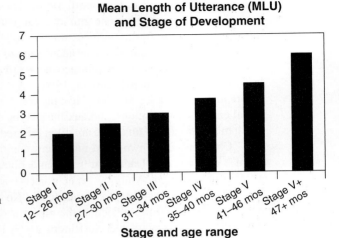

FIGURE 8.1 Early language development can be described in terms of the mean length of utterance (MLU).

Source: Adapted from Owen, 1984.

three children's acquisition of 14 grammatical morphemes, including the present progressive ending *-ing* (driv*ing*), prepositions *in* and *on*, the regular plural *–s* (birdie*s*), past tenses of irregular verbs (*came, fell, broke, sat, went*), possessive *'s* (baby*'s*), articles *a* and *the*, past tense of regular verbs *–ed* (push*ed*), regular third person *–s* (jump*s*), irregular third person (*does, has*). Beginning at the age of about 2 years, spontaneous language samples were recorded in the children's homes approximately every 2 weeks as they interacted with their mothers and, sometimes, with the researchers. Although the three children acquired the 14 morphemes at different rates, they followed a nearly identical order (Brown, 1973). A follow-up cross-sectional study of the same morphemes with 21 English-speaking children confirmed the order of acquisition (de Villiers & de Villiers, 1973).

After these results became known, linguists wanted to know why children acquire these morphemes in essentially the same order. If some of the morphemes were phonologically easier, that could explain the pattern of acquisition. Arguing against this sort of account, however, is the finding that children showed a different order of acquisition for three *-s* morphemes that sound alike but are grammatically different. Across the studies of these morphemes, the plural (*pigs*) almost always preceded the possessive (*pig's*), and these, in turn, were followed by the third-person singular verb ending (*jumps*) (Flavell, Miller, & Miller, 2002).

Another possible explanation is that the frequency with which morphemes occur in adult speech determines the order of acquisition. Analysis of parental speech showed, however, that although articles (e.g., *the* and *a*) were among the most frequently produced morphemes, they were not among the first morphemes children acquired (Brown, 1973).

The most widely accepted explanation for the nearly invariant order of morpheme acquisition is that the complexity of the morpheme itself determines the ease with which children acquire it. As linguists define complexity, it refers both to semantic and grammatical characteristics, including the amount of information children must keep in mind in order to produce a correct utterance. To use the past tense verb *were*, for example, it is necessary to consider the subject, the number of the subject, and when the event occurred. The ending for regular plurals -*s*, by contrast, requires only that the child keep track of number. The difference in complexity, therefore, is one plausible explanation for the finding that the regular plural -*s* is acquired in Stage II, whereas the past tense plural verb form *were* is not acquired until Stage V.

Overregularization

Once young children acquire rules of grammar, they are able to use them to modify new words. This was first shown in the *wug* test, a classic experiment in which children heard and completed fill-in-the-blank statements like, "I know a man who likes to *bod*. He did the same thing yesterday. Yesterday he _____." Children who reliably mark the past tense in their own speech by adding the morpheme -*ed* to verbs readily supply the word *bodded*, demonstrating that they have learned a rule for generating new utterances, rather than simply memorizing verbs as they encounter them (Berko, 1958).

In English, most verbs apply the suffix -*ed* to form the past tense, but there are approximately 180 irregular verbs, exceptions to the -*ed* rule, which form the past tense in idiosyncratic ways (Marcus et al., 1992). As young children begin learning these words, they show a U-shaped pattern in which they initially produce a high proportion of them correctly. Subsequently, they begin to make **overregularization** errors, applying grammatical morphemes to words for which English makes an exception. As they make this error, they produce forms that they never hear adults utter, such as *mouses, foots, falled*, and *goed*. Eventually, children once again correctly produce a large proportion of irregular verb forms and irregular plurals.

These well-known errors were explored in an analysis of more than 11,000 irregular past tense utterances in the spontaneous speech of 83 children whose transcribed language samples are part of an archive known as the Child Language Data Exchange System (ChiLDES) (MacWhinney & Snow, 1985, 1990). Although the study confirmed previous reports of a U-shaped pattern of acquisition, it also produced some unexpected results. Despite the salience of overregularization in young children's speech, the errors turned out to be relatively rare, occurring in approximately 2.5 percent of irregular past tense forms produced. The study also revealed that overregularization remained at roughly the same low rate from the age of 2 years into the school-age years. In addition, it was found that the more often a parent correctly used an irregular form (e.g., *came*), the less often the child overregularized it (e.g., *comed*).

Individual Differences in Early Grammar

When study after study showed striking similarity in the order of acquisition of English morphemes, despite variations in children's language experience, many language researchers concluded that children learn grammatical rules in similar ways. This assumption of universality has been tempered, however, by studies showing that there are some differences in the routes children take on their way to acquiring grammar (Bates, Dale, & Thal, 1995; Bates et al., 1994; Bloom, 1998). In one early study of three children (Bloom, 1970), for example, two children's utterances combined verbs with nouns and used nouns to mark possession (e.g., *eat meat, throw ball*, and *mommy sock*).

By contrast, the third child in this study combined verbs with pronouns (e.g., *eat it* and *do this one*).

Whether children begin by combining verbs or objects of possession with nouns (e.g., *ride on the bus*) or start by combining these parts of speech with pronouns (e.g., *ride on it*) may be related to variation in children's single-word vocabularies or to differences in caregivers' speech to children (Goldfield, 1987; Hampson & Nelson, 1993; Nelson, 1975; Shore, 1995). Regardless of which pattern children use initially, their use of nouns and pronouns tends to become more similar by the end of the second year (Bloom, 1998).

Cross-Linguistic Studies of the Acquisition of Grammar

Until fairly recently, child language researchers focused most of their attention on the acquisition of English grammar (Slobin, 1985, 1992). As one linguist noted, "There is nothing wrong with early English as an example of aspects of grammar. But the normal range of languages also includes many languages in which basic sentence structure presents quite different grammatical problems" (Maratsos, 1998, p. 426). In this section, we consider briefly the contributions of cross-linguistic studies of early acquisition by examining the evidence for one aspect of grammar—agent-action-patient relations.

In English, active sentences follow a basic pattern: agent-action-patient (sometimes labeled subject-verb-object). This pattern seems "natural" to English speakers, since it "directly" refers to agents acting upon patients (e.g., *The girl drank the milk*). Moreover, children learning English both comprehend and produce sentences possessing this pattern by the age of about 24 months. Not all languages use this pattern, however, so children learning languages that do not use fixed word order need to learn other ways to communicate about agents and patients (Maratsos, 1998).

Children learning Turkish, for example, hear agents, patients, and actions in all possible orders (Slobin, 1982). To express the idea that *Simon hugged Andrew*, the words may appear in any order, but the noun for the patient must have the suffix *-/u/* attached: *Andrew-u hugged Simon* (Maratsos, 1998). Children learning Turkish as their first language are not given explicit instructions about this system, but they hear older children and adults around them speaking and they acquire the relevant rule. Although this may seem like a complex system, at least to English speakers, Turkish children use it correctly by or before the age of 2 years (Aksoy & Slobin, 1985). In addition, just as children learning English almost never make word-order errors (e.g., saying *Cookie eat baby* instead of *Baby eat cookie*), children learning Turkish rarely make errors in suffixation (e.g., adding *-/u/* to the agent instead of to the patient).

Other languages communicate agent-patient relations in other ways. Again, although English speakers regard these as more difficult systems to learn, young children have little difficulty acquiring these rules and usually do so with very few errors by 2 years of age. Based on these and similar findings from other cross-linguistic studies, language researchers need to "give up the assumption that what is complicated for adults to think about is necessarily complicated for children to acquire" (Maratsos, 1998, p. 434).

Atypical Language Development

As we have already noted, children of the same age may understand and produce different numbers of words. Given the wide range for first words, the naming explosion, and other milestones of language development, parents of infants and toddlers who seem to be slower than their peers may wonder if their child's development is still on track. In this final section we'll consider several tools available for measuring whether a child's early language development is progressing normally. We'll also briefly explore new evidence about language development that is different enough to be considered atypical, focusing on two examples—early language delay and autism.

Measuring Language Development

Of the more than 40 language-screening instruments available, only a small number are designed specifically to assess children younger than 2 years of age (Sturner et al., 1994). These instruments differ from one another in a number of ways and entail different advantages and disadvantages. Assessments based on parental report are subject to criticism, for example, since some parents may misunderstand instructions or fail to give accurate reports about their children's language development. Parental reports are less time-consuming and less expensive than evaluations performed by clinicians, however, so reliable, valid measures that can be used with young children are needed in order to achieve the earliest diagnosis and follow-up treatment possible.

The Language Development Survey (LDS) (Rescorla, 1989) is a parent-report instrument, intended for use with children between 12 and 24 months of age. In the LDS, parents write out three of the child's longest recent sentences or phrases and respond to a 310-word expressive vocabulary checklist. Evaluations of the LDS show that it is a valid and reliable screening device (Fenson et al., 1994; Rescorla & Alley, 2001).

Several standardized tests have been developed, including the Sequenced Inventory of Communication Development-Revised (SICD-R) (Hedrick, Prather, & Tobin, 1984), the Reynell Developmental Language Scales-U.S. Edition (Reynell & Gruber, 1990), and the Preschool Language Scale-3 (PLS-3) (Zimmerman, Steiner, & Pond, 1991). These tests are limited, however, in that they sample only a small set of language behaviors and need to be administered by highly trained examiners following a specific and fairly inflexible procedure (Fenson et al., 1994).

Assessment of children's language in naturalistic settings, such as the home, presents different sorts of problems. These samples may be more likely than a standardized assessment to yield a representative language profile for a particular child, if the child is motivated to interact and speak. However, transcription and analysis require special skills and a significant investment of time—it can take from 3 to 10 hours just to transcribe a 30-minute language sample (Fenson et al., 1994).

Some general developmental screening instruments include scales for assessing language. These tests include the Denver Developmental Screening Test (DDST) (Frankenburg, Dodds, & Archer, 1990) and the Minnesota Child Development Inventory (MCDI) (Ireton & Thwing, 1974). The DDST provides very little information about language development, based on a small number of items at each age level. The MCDI, by contrast, is more comprehensive, with 64 expressive language items and 67 receptive language items (Fenson et al., 1994).

One widely used tool for assessing both expressive and receptive abilities—the MacArthur Communicative Development Inventories (CDI)—shares many of the positive features of the tests previously mentioned while also providing a detailed, representative sample of language in approximately 30 minutes (Fenson et al., 1994). The CDI is based on parent reports and checklists. As shown in Table 8.3, there is one form for infants between 8 and 16 months of age and another for toddlers between 16 and 30 months of age.

Researchers in one study used the CDI to describe language growth trends in 1,800 children between the ages of 8 and 30 months (Fenson et al., 1994). They found wide variability across children in the time of onset and course of acquisition of language and communication skills. Individual children, however, showed significant stability in the rate of language development. The predictive power of the CDI is low for infants between 8 and 16 months, but increases sharply when used with children 16 months of age and older (Fenson et al., 2000).

Early Language Delay

Parents whose children do not progress through the expected milestones, such as a naming explosion at 18 months, followed by the beginning of two-word and multiword utterances, are likely to become concerned about their language development and follow up by discussing the situation during a visit with their child's pediatrician. One response that they might be relieved to hear is that the majority of 2-year-olds with language delay have normal language abilities by the age of 3 or 4 years. In those cases, children may simply be at the extreme low end of the normal range of development. Another well-established finding

TABLE 8.3   Comparison of the Infant and Toddler Forms of the MacArthur CDI

Infant Form	Toddler Form
396-word vocabulary checklist Assesses understanding and production of early words, sound effects, and animal sounds.	680-word vocabulary checklist Assesses production of specific words, sound effects, and animal sounds.
Checks infant's understanding of familiar words, such as their own name, and phrases, such as "no no" and "there's mommy/daddy." One section focuses on actions and gestures; parents indicate whether their child plays patty cake, points to interesting objects or events, and engages in pretend play.	Checks frequency of child's multiword utterances/ sentences, as well as use of grammatical morphemes, such as word endings used to form the plural –s and past tense of regular verbs –ed. Parents list three of the longest sentences that they have heard their child say recently.

Source: Based on Fenson et al., 1994.

may prove less comforting, however; nearly all children who have language impairments in later years had some sort of prior language delay (Dale et al., 1998, 2003).

Studies of more than 3,000 pairs of 2-year-old twins have shown that there is a strong genetic influence in some cases of early language delay. In one investigation, when one twin in a pair had a CDI vocabulary score in the lowest 5 percent, the other twin was also very likely to have a similar degree of language impairment. The strength of the association was stronger for monozygotic than for dizygotic twins. As CDI vocabulary scores increased, there was a lower concordance rate. Taken together, these findings support the conclusion that children with a significant degree of impairment have a genetically distinct language disorder, whereas those with even modestly higher scores—at the 10th rather than the 5th percentile—may be more influenced by environmental factors (Dale et al., 1998). Further study may enable parents and pediatricians to use CDI measures and other parent reports to differentiate between and respond appropriately to transient and persistent language impairment (Bishop et al., 2003).

Recent studies of clinical syndromes have yielded potentially important information about the representation of language in the brain. Although there is not complete agreement about the meaning of these findings, researchers have uncovered compelling data that now must be incorporated into any explanation of mind-brain relations. As we conclude our exploration of language and communication, we will consider evidence concerning one of the most widely studied developmental syndromes, in which there is impairment of one language ability at the same time that other aspects of language appear to remain intact.

Language and Communication in Children with Autism

Autism is a syndrome characterized by disordered social interactions and problems with language and communication. Affecting as many as one in 500 children, autism is a genetically based brain disorder that is believed to develop during the first few weeks of fetal growth (Rapin, 1997; U.S. Department of Health and Human Services, 2000).

Although autism exists from birth, it is often not diagnosed until 18 to 36 months of age. One reason for the relatively late diagnosis is that appropriate screening tools for autism have not always been widely available (Filipek et al., 2000). This is changing, however, as a result of new studies, including some that involved retrospective analyses of early home videos of infants who were later diagnosed with autism (Dawson et al., 1998; Osterling & Dawson, 1994; Werner et al., 2000). These and other studies showed that as early as 8 to 10 months of age, infants with autism display fewer social and joint attention behaviors than normally developing infants. In particular, infants with autism rarely point in order to show objects to others, look at others, or respond to their own name (Baron-Cohen, 1989; Loveland & Landry, 1986; Mundy et al., 1986). These findings suggest that clinicians might be able to achieve earlier diagnosis by looking for signs of atypical prelinguistic development. Other research suggests that diagnosis might benefit as well from examining early parent-infant interactions, not as a causal factor, but because there is evidence that even prior to a time that parents report autistic symptoms, they tend to use compensatory strategies to engage their infants and attract their attention (Baranek, 1999).

Another reason for the relatively late diagnosis of autism may be that there are actually five diagnoses possible under **autism spectrum disorder (ASD)**: Autistic Disorder,

TABLE 8.4   Autism Spectrum Disorder (ASD) Comprises Five Possible Diagnoses

Diagnosis	Characteristics
Autistic Disorder	Children exhibit poor language skills, withdrawn behavior, repetitive patterns of behavior, and the inability to engage in imaginative play.
Asperger's Syndrome	Children display similar general symptoms as children with Autistic Disorder but usually have well-developed language skills and normal or near-normal IQ.
Pervasive Developmental Disorder, Not Otherwise Specified	Children do not fall within the realm of other ASDs but show signs of a severe developmental disorder with autistic symptoms.
Rett's Syndrome	Affects only girls; development appears normal until approximately 6 to 18 months of age, when children lose language and motor abilities.
Childhood Disintegrative Disorder	Children show normal development until 2 years of age, then rapidly lose acquired skills, usually between 36 and 48 months of age.

Source: Based on information in U.S. Department of Health and Human Services, 2000.

Asperger's Syndrome, Pervasive Developmental Disorder Not Otherwise Specified, Rett's Syndrome, and Childhood Disintegrative Disorder (U.S. Department of Health and Human Services, 2000). As shown in Table 8.4, these syndromes vary in terms of the severity of language skill deficits, children's measured IQ level, and the appearance and course of symptoms. The heterogeneity of these diagnoses posed a problem for early studies because the same criteria were not always used for including children in an autistic sample. To ensure that comparisons between different studies will be appropriate and interpretable, researchers now use two valid and reliable diagnostic tools: the Autism Diagnostic Interview-Revised (ADI-R) (Lord, Rutter, & LeCouteur, 1994) and the Autsim Diagnostic Observation Schedule-Generic (Lord et al., 2000; Tager-Flusberg, 2004).

Approximately half of children with autism never develop functional language. This is because the development of language is correlated with normal or near-normal IQ and the majority of children with autism have some degree of mental retardation as well (Travis & Sigman, 2000). Some children with autism produce words, but their speech may include echolalia (repetition of speech that they have heard) and reversal of pronouns, such as *I* and *you*. When children with autism do acquire language, acquisition of vocabulary and grammar tends to proceed normally (Tager-Flusberg, 1993; Travis & Sigman, 2000). One longitudinal study of grammatical morpheme acquisition, for example, found that the order of acquisition for autistic children was similar to the order reported for typically developing children (Tager-Flusberg, 1993; Tomasello, 2006). In addition to relatively normal development in the domains of semantics and grammar, children with autism also tend to show relatively normal ability to articulate language sounds. Their use of stress and intonation may be unusual, however, and their speech may sound harsh, shrill, or hollow.

For autistic individuals who are verbal and at least produce phrases, if not entire sentences, the major language deficit is in the realm of pragmatics (Hale & Tager-Flusberg, 2005; Travis & Sigman, 2000). Children (and adults) with autism often have awkward conversations, in which they may transmit and receive facts accurately while failing to achieve the smooth exchange of information that is found in most normal conversations (Travis & Sigman, 2000). Rigid, stereotyped patterns of expression may be used, as well as invented or idiosyncratic words and phrases (Volden & Lord, 1991). Maintaining a topic and responding contingently to another person during a conversation may also be problematic for children with autism (Hale & Tager-Flusberg, 2005).

The deficit in pragmatic development has been interpreted by some researchers as evidence that individuals with autism suffer from a specific inability to understand mental states in themselves and in others (Leslie, 1987; Leslie & Roth, 1993; Hale & Tager-Flusberg, 2005). Lacking a "theory of mind"—awareness of the relation between mental states and behavior—children with autism fail to notice the emotional signals of others and are unable to share joint attention, engage in pretend play, entertain false beliefs, or use rules of politeness and contingency in conversation (Kasari et al., 1990; Sigman & Ruskin, 1999).

This interpretation is not universally accepted by researchers studying autism (Klin, Volkmar, & Sparrow, 1992). Among other objections, critics note that identifying a deficit in theory of mind does not indicate a causal connection with autism. Some researchers have responded to criticisms of theory of mind research by using brain imaging and ERP measures to gain greater insight into the neurocognitive basis of social and linguistic behavior in autism (Dawson et al., 2002; Hadjikhani et al., 2004). Initial intriguing findings indicate that the brains of children with ASD process social and linguistic stimuli differently from comparison samples that are matched in terms of chronological age or IQ. Children with ASD, for example, show a preference for nonspeech signals rather than speech samples. They also differ from comparison children in failing to show ERP changes in response to changes in syllables (Kuhl et al., 2005). Future studies employing longitudinal designs, beginning when infants are first diagnosed with ASD, are needed in order to advance our understanding of autsim and links between genetics, cognitive abilities, social behavior, language, and brain development.

WRAPPING IT UP: Summary and Conclusion

Young children's communication and language skills are an important foundation for learning, development, and social interaction. Infants' early experience listening to or, in the case of deaf infants, watching their native language sensitizes them to the phonemes and rhythmic patterns in that language.

Children's first spoken words appear around the age of 12 months. Most children experience a vocabulary spurt at about 18 months of age. The rate of children's semantic development is influenced, in part, by the amount and variety of language that is addressed to them. Language that is responsive and attuned to children's interests and abilities is especially helpful. Infants use multiple cues and sources of information to expand their vocabulary.

Social and pragmatic factors play an important role, but infants also appear to benefit from a set of guiding constraints as they learn new words.

Children's earliest multiword utterances reflect their acquisition of grammatical rules, including word order. There seems to be an essentially invariant order of acquisition of grammatical morphemes. Cross-linguistic studies show that children are able to acquire grammatical rules for their native language—regardless of how complex those rules may seem to adults who are not native speakers of that language—and usually do so with very few errors by 2 years of age.

Children's language development can be assessed and compared to normative growth trends. Recent studies have led to greater understanding of genetic influences on language delay in young children. Investigation of autism has yielded potentially important information about the representation of language in the brain and the relation between language development and cognitive ability.

As we have seen in this chapter, language develops rapidly during infancy. Assuming that there are no genetic conditions predisposing infants to language delay or impairment and assuming that they are interested, responsive adults present every day, babies make the most of information in the environment. Playing a CD of ID speech for infants or showing them a DVD—even if it shows face-to-face interactions or adults using ID speech—does not have the same effects. It is essential that verbal and nonverbal information are experienced in the context of face-to-face interactions, ideally in familiar relationships.

In our next chapter, we will see that relationships also develop rapidly during infancy. As Simon's experience in the Tiny Tugboat room and his defense of his friend Andrew showed, relationships can provide the words, motive, and opportunity to learn and use language. In addition to being the principal vehicle for language development, however, we will see that they are important in their own right.

THINK ABOUT IT: Questions for Reading and Discussion

1. What recommendations would you give new parents who want to help their newborn acquire language? How would your advice change as their baby becomes a toddler and then a young child?

2. Although it is possible to learn the vocabulary and grammar of many languages other than one's first language, it is often difficult to sound like a "native speaker" of those languages. How do studies of infants' speech perception help explain this difficulty?

3. If you were going to design a language assessment for the first 3 years of life, which abilities would you include and how would you assess these abilities?

4. How does the acquisition of language affect children and their families, especially parent-child interactions?

5. What can be learned by studying the acquisition of languages other than English? If you know more than one language, how do they differ in grammatical rules?

6. Should language researchers use parental reports? Discuss the advantages and limitations of this measure of language development.

7. Consider a hypothetical baby or toddler whose most frequent source of exposure to speech is provided by people on television. In what ways would this baby's ability to learn language be affected?

KEY WORDS

Autism (281)	A syndrome characterized by disordered social interactions and problems with language and communication
Autism spectrum disorder (ASD) (281)	A cluster of five related syndromes that vary in terms of language skill deficits, children's IQ, and the appearance and course of symptoms
Babbling (260)	Patterned but meaningless sequences of reduplicated sounds, such as strings of syllables
Constrained statistical learning framework (259)	The ability to extract recurring patterns from repeated experience with stimuli
Grammar (252)	Systems of rules for combining words or signs
Holophrase (265)	Infants' first one-word utterances that name objects but also communicate other meanings
Infant-directed speech (255)	Modifications that adults make when speaking (or signing) to infants, producing language that is shorter, more repetitive, higher-pitched, more variable in pitch, and less semantically and grammatically complex than language addressed to adults
Joint attention (269)	Nonverbal adjustments in posture, gaze, and head orientation that enable infant-adult dyads to focus their attention together on objects or events
Lexical contrast (274)	The ability to learn a new word's meaning by comparing it to words that are already known
Mean length of utterance (MLU) (275)	A measure of grammatical development that is based on the number of morphemes in speech
Morphemes (275)	Minimal meaningful units in speech, such as words, parts of words, or word endings
Mutual exclusivity assumption (273)	A constraint on learning that guides children to assume that objects will have only one name and to look for a nameless object when they hear a new word
Overextension (265)	A common error in which children use a word to refer to other objects that may be perceptually or functionally similar to the word's correct referent
Overregularization (277)	An error in which children apply grammatical morphemes to words for which a language makes an exception to the rule
Perceptual magnet effect (258)	A phenomenon in which acoustic space is altered as a result of increasing sensitivity to native language phonemes and declining sensitivity to nonnative language phonemes
Phonemes (257)	Linguistically meaningful phonetic categories that signal differences in words through combinations of vowels and consonants
Phonetics (257)	A set of vowels and consonants that a particular language uses
Phonology (252)	Sound patterns of language

Pragmatics (252)   Using language for particular purposes in specific social contexts

Referential cues (269)   Verbal and nonverbal behaviors, such as gaze, facial expression, and head orientation, that reflect an individual's attentional focus, intentions, or expectations

Semantics (252)   Meanings of words or signs

Syllables (260)   Combinations of consonants and vowels, such as *baba* and *mama*

Taxonomic assumption (272)   A constraint on learning that guides children to assume that new words should be extended to objects within the same category rather than thematic associates

Telegraphic speech (275)   Early two-word and multiword utterances that sound like telegrams because they lack grammatical markers and extra words, such as articles, plural endings, prepositions, and auxiliary verbs

Underextension (266)   An error in which children apply a word only to a specific instance or fail to use it to refer to other referents for which the word would be correct

Whole object assumption (271)   A constraint on learning that guides children to assume that new words refer to whole objects rather than actions, spatial location, or parts or features of objects

Relationships and Social Development

If you were invited to a baby shower, what sort of gift would you bring? If you are like most people, you would select an item that reflects your ideas about the things every infant needs: clothing, toys, blankets, or perhaps a device with which the new parents can rock, roll, or carry their newborn. If you selected a gift from a registry compiled by the expectant parents, you would have a glimpse into their beliefs about the things their child needs most, a wish list that is influenced by culture, climate, historical period, and even the child's sex if they know it in advance.

The things that all babies need most, however, are never found on gift registry lists for the simple reason that they are not "things" but experiences that come from relationships between infants and those who care for and interact with them. According to one list of Ten Things Every Child Needs (Robert R. McCormick Foundation, 1997), the top three needs—interaction, touch, and a stable relationship—come directly from infants' social world. The remaining needs—a safe/healthy environment, self-esteem, quality child care/preschool, communication, play, music, and reading—are difficult, in infancy, to experience outside of a social context.

Relationships are important in infancy and across the lifespan. They influence development and functioning in social, cognitive, and emotional domains. From an evolutionary perspective, relationships are adaptive and even affect physical health and well being through their influence on basic biological processes (Reis & Collins, 2004). Relationships affect children's development, and children's development, in turn, transforms their relationships (Hartup, 1989, 1996).

In this chapter we will consider "vertical" relationships—those involving children and adults, in which there is an asymmetry of social power, skills, and experience. Vertical relationships serve important functions of protecting children when they are young and fostering the development of basic physical, social, and cognitive skills. The most important vertical relationship is the early infant-caregiver relationship, which has an impact on infants' and toddlers' development as well as contributing to development in early childhood and beyond. We will also explore "horizontal" relationships—those characterized by partners (siblings, peers, and friends) who are similar in terms of their roles, abilities, and knowledge. In horizontal relationships, children refine and apply basic skills, learn about cooperation and competition, and eventually achieve psychological intimacy (Hartup, 1989, 1996). We begin with a look at the foundation for infant-caregiver relationships—caregivers' beliefs about infants as social beings.

Infant-Caregiver Relationships

In most Western societies, the infant-parent relationship is regarded as the primary social bond, augmented by a small number of familial relationships, but this view is not universal. In many parts of the world, entire villages are involved in childrearing, and each household's connection to the newest member of the community is reinforced by a visit to the newborn's home within hours of the birth. In some societies, infants are raised by a large group of extended kin or are adopted by other families in the village and develop close, open relationships with both their adoptive and their biological kin (DeLoache & Gottlieb, 2000; Nsamenang, 1992).

In the United States in 2002, approximately 70 percent of all children under the age of 3 years lived in a household with two parents. Children's living arrangements differed, however, across categories of race/ethnicity and socioeconomic status. Whereas 23 percent of all children lived with a single mother, nearly one-half (48 percent) of all African American children lived in such households. In the same year, Census Bureau data show that African American children also were more likely than other children to live with a grandparent (Fields, 2003; Wakschlag, Chase-Lansdale, & Brooks-Gunn, 1996). Regardless of the makeup of a child's household, infants and toddlers develop most optimally when they grow up in a "village" of some sort—when their parents have support from three or more other adults, ask for help when it is needed, and live in a community in which there are caring, involved neighbors who monitor and supervise all children, not just those to whom they are related (Search Institute 2000a, 200b).

In many cultures, parents first begin to relate to their child before birth when they choose a name for their baby. The names that they consider may link him or her to previous generations, as when parents decide to give a firstborn son the same name as his father or grandfather. Potential names may embody qualities that parents hope their child will have; girls are sometimes named after delicate flowers, whereas boys may be given names that sound strong or masculine. In some cultures, children are not named until they reach a significant milestone, such as the age of 100 days, and grandparents or even unrelated elders in the community—not the child's parents—may have the responsibility of bestowing names. Regardless of the variation in naming practices, parents everywhere anticipate what their child will be like and how their lives will be interconnected. They develop beliefs about their unborn child and envision his or her future role in the family and community (DeLoache & Gottlieb, 2000).

Patterns of Care and Interaction: Beliefs about Infants

Goals of socialization and expectations about behavior differ across cultures (Bornstein, 2006; Bornstein & Cote, 2004; Bugental & Grusec, 2006; Harwood et al., 1996; Shweder et al., 2006). In some cultures, very young children are taught the names of all members of the community—a sign that social relationships outside of the immediate family are important (DeLoache & Gottlieb (2000).

Parents' goals can also affect how much arousing stimulation infants receive during the first postnatal months of life. In one study comparing parents' beliefs and practices in the United States and the Netherlands, Dutch parents were significantly more concerned with providing their newborns with rest and regularity, whereas U.S. parents focused on providing stimulating interaction. These concerns were reflected in different patterns of care; at 6 months of age, Dutch babies went to bed earlier than U.S. babies (7:00 p.m. versus 8:30 p.m.) and received an average of 2 hours more sleep per day. The U.S. mothers also spent more time talking to their babies and touching them. This may be the reason the U.S. infants spent more time in an active alert state, whereas the Dutch infants spent more time in a state of quiet arousal (Super et al., 1996).

A different cross-cultural study of parental management of young children's sleep in the United States, Italy, and Japan also found links between parents' beliefs and sleeping practices. Italian and Japanese families and African American families in the United States were much more likely to report co-sleeping regularly with their children. Italian and Japanese parents were sympathetic to their children's sleep problems and tended to view sleep difficulties as evidence of the child's legitimate need to be with the mother. White non-Hispanic parents, by contrast, more frequently reported trying to ignore their child's cries and protests during the night so that self-comforting could be established during infancy. Taken together, these patterns suggest that minority and non–North American families tend to emphasize interpersonal relatedness through close physical contact, whereas White non-Hispanic families more often reinforce notions of early independence and individuality (Wolf, Lozoff, Latz, & Paludetto, 1996).

Researchers observing Central African foragers and farmers reported finding distinctive patterns of childcare among neighboring groups, patterns that may reflect different socialization goals (Hewlett et al., 1998). The foragers—nomadic Aka pygmies—lived in community groups that were interdependent as well as physically close together. Aka babies were usually carried in a sling on their mother's left side, whereas infants of the Ngandu people—farmers who tend to remain in the same dwellings year after year and to work the same fields for several years in a row—were more often put down and were usually strapped to their mother's back when they were carried. During observations at the age of 3 to 4 months and again at 9 to 10 months, Aka infants were more likely to be held, fed, and asleep or drowsy. They were also more likely to be in close physical contact with their caregivers. Ngandu infants, by contrast, were more likely to be left alone and to fuss or cry, smile, vocalize, and play. Ngandu parents seemed to socialize their infants to become more independent by interacting with them at a greater distance and allowing a greater period of time to pass before comforting them. Aka infants, on the other hand,

Patterns of caregiving reflect socialization goals. This infant is growing up in a culture that values interdependence, which his mother promotes by keeping him physically close to her during much of each day.

were usually surrounded by others and attended to more quickly. They were also more likely to observe adults sharing caregiving responsibilities as well as food and other physical resources. These findings indicate that parenting strategies reflect socialization goals and social values and may vary significantly, even among traditional non-Western cultures living in relatively close proximity to one another (Hewlett et al., 1998; Keller et al., 2004a).

Given the variability in parents' beliefs about infants, is it possible to identify any universal caregiving practices and patterns of face-to-face interaction? Is there a typical or optimal way that parents and infants interact? Are fathers different from mothers and, if so, what are their unique contributions to infants' development? We'll consider these issues next.

As we discuss parents' caregiving behaviors, we need to remember that infants themselves influence the kinds of interactions they experience. Even in the earliest days and weeks, social interaction is **bidirectional**—involving reciprocal behaviors and responses. Newborn infants who sleep for several hours in a row elicit a different type of care than those who spend more time awake or who are fussier. Whereas one infant may be soothed by rocking, another may find singing and vocalizing more effective. In addition, although there is often stability in individual infants' behavior patterns and cycles, there is also change and even day-to-day fluctuation, necessitating a flexible, sensitive approach to caregiving and interaction (St. James-Roberts & Plewis, 1996). Mothers and fathers who look to their infants for signals about whether their caregiving efforts are successful learn about their children's preferences, become aware of their developing capabilities, and use their evolving understanding to provide effective care.

Caregivers and infants develop their own style of interaction, often leading to a phenomenon known as **dyadic synchrony**—caregiver-infant interactions that are characterized by mutual attention and affective matching or regulation (Harrist & Waugh, 2002). One example of dyadic synchrony is the back-and-forth sharing of emotions or vocalizations. An infant coos or gurgles and gazes at the mother, who returns her child's visual gaze and responds with words or sounds that seem to mirror the infant's behavior. Dyadic synchrony would also be seen in an interaction in which an infant looks away from the mother, who responds by pulling back or reducing the intensity of her speech or physical contact with the infant until the infant looks back at or vocalizes to her.

Most parents learn to read and respond to their infant's signals as they gain experience with him or her over the first days and weeks after birth. This learning process can also be facilitated through parent education. A study carried out in Brazil found that mothers of newborns who saw a video based on the Neonatal Behavioral Assessment Scale (NBAS) (Brazelton & Nugent, 1995), emphasizing infants' competencies and the importance of sensitive, face-to-face interaction, showed more dyadic synchrony involving vocal exchanges, looking to the partner, and physical contact during home observations one month later than did mothers of newborns who saw a video describing basic caregiving practices for infants. Mothers who saw the NBAS video were also more responsive to their infant's crying and involuntary responses (Wendland-Carro, Piccinini, & Millar, 1999). It is not known whether there were any long-term differences in this particular sample, but many other studies suggest that caregivers who are responsive and engage in synchronous interactions are more likely to set the stage for a good infant-caregiver relationship.

One review of the literature found that most interactions between children and their caregivers are not synchronous; in fact, the typical rate of synchronous interactions is probably well below 50 percent of all interaction time (Harrist & Waugh, 2002). This does not mean that dyadic synchrony is unimportant. Indeed, dyadic synchrony is believed to serve several main functions in infancy. It provides opportunities for infants to experience and process multisensory input. The infant waving his arms, for example, has the chance to notice the corresponding rhythm and patterning of his mother's voice. Dyadic synchrony is also thought to help infants develop the capacity for self-regulation; by responding to the infant's level of arousal and activity, caregivers may assist infants in learning to move from one state to another in the earliest months of life.

A third function of dyadic synchrony that has been proposed is helping the infant experience **effectance**—the feeling of moving between different states, including from a state of nonsynchrony to a state of synchrony (Gianino & Tronick, 1988). Finally, dyadic synchrony provides a foundation for the evolving relationship between infant and caregiver. Infants who experience a sense of effectance and come to expect that their caregiver will respond to them in positive, predictable ways are likely to develop a sense of trust in that caregiver.

The structure and function of dyadic synchrony change from infancy through toddlerhood. During infancy, dyadic synchrony consists of a maintained, shared focus of attention, coordination of the timing or rhythm of body movements, and linked behaviors. Caregivers, rather than infants, achieve these three aspects of synchrony by noticing and responding to signals from their baby. As many studies have reported, caregiver responses are not mere imitation; the intensity and rhythm of an infant's arm movements, for example, may be matched by the mother's tone of voice and rate of speech instead of being reflected in her arm movements.

Infants notice the contingency between their own actions and those of their mother. This was demonstrated in a study in which 2- and 3-month-olds first interacted with their mothers through closed-circuit video and then saw a recording of their mother's behavior from the first session. Infants responded with interest during the first session, when their mother's behavior was actually in response to their own behavior. They turned away from the video during the second session, suggesting that they were sensitive to the lack of contingency in the recording (Murray & Trevarthen, 1985).

Dyadic synchrony continues to be relevant in toddler-caregiver interactions. Many observational studies of toddler-caregiver interactions show that caregivers continue to bear the primary responsibility for facilitating synchrony, although children begin to play a greater role. During the toddler years, dyadic synchrony supports new aspects of child-parent interactions, namely, children's increasing communicative competence and their growing autonomy and self-control (Harrist & Waugh, 2002). Parents and children who are attuned to one another may thus have more conversations about objects and events that are the focus of shared attention. Dyadic synchrony at this age may also make it easier for parents to keep track of children as they become increasingly interested in exploring and testing their own abilities and limits. With dyadic synchrony present in a relationship, parents who pay attention to their toddler's actions are likely to have children who notice if their parents approve of their independent efforts. As we will discuss in more depth in Chapter 10, this sort of shared attention and coordination of behavior may also underlie the development of conscience and compliance with parents' requests and expectations (Kochanska, 2002).

Infants and their parents achieve dyadic synchrony when they share attention and communicate similar emotions at the same time.

As we have already noted, in achieving dyadic synchrony, especially at the youngest ages, caregivers need to observe the infant for signals and then interpret and respond to those signals. The degree to which caregivers are attentive, accurate in their perceptions, and responsive has also been described as sensitivity (Ainsworth, Bell, & Stayton, 1974). Caregivers who are sensitive are able to detect signs of distress and hunger and thereby promote infants' survival by protecting them from harm and providing nutrition.

Parental sensitivity may vary across settings and across different points in development, and it is influenced by parents' beliefs, childrearing goals, and culturally specific practices. Parents can be sensitive when trying to comfort a child who is upset, and they can be sensitive when trying to engage a child in play or other dyadic activities. Parental sensitivity is affected by parents' social stress and support (De Wolff & van IJzendoorn, 1997; Thompson, 1998; Valenzuela, 1997). Sensitivity may be enhanced through parent education, however, as was demonstrated in a study of low-income mothers of irritable newborns. In this study, mothers were randomly assigned to either an intervention program that focused on maternal sensitivity and responsiveness or a control program. Nine months later, mothers in the intervention group were significantly more responsive and stimulating than mothers in the control group; mothers in the intervention group were also more likely to have more harmonious and effective relationships with their infants (van den Boom, 1994).

Studies of maternal sensitivity in countries as diverse as Chile, Colombia, Kenya, Mexico, and the United States have shown that sensitive responsiveness may vary across cultures in terms of whether it is predominantly physical, verbal, or visual (Posada et al., 2004; Richman, Miller, & LeVine, 1992). One study of the Gusii people of Kenya, for example, showed that they were physically responsive, touching and holding their 9- and 10-month-old infants when they cried, whereas mothers in Boston tended to use visual and verbal—but not physical—responses when their same-age infants showed distress (Richman, Miller, & LeVine, 1992). The researchers noted that the Boston mothers, with higher than average levels of education, had been socialized to employ verbal methods that would engage their infants in emotionally arousing conversational interactions. The Gusii mothers, by contrast, used methods that were consistent with their culture's tendency to define competent parenting in terms of the ability to soothe and comfort infants and with the Gusii notion that it is unnecessary to speak to preverbal infants. Despite these differences, the researchers saw "no indication in this evidence that one group of mothers is more responsive than the other, only that they are responsive in different ways to their infants' signals" (Richman, Miller, & LeVine, 1992, p. 620). These findings suggest that, despite cross-cultural variations, competent caregivers use socially valued behaviors to respond to their infants. Failure to do so is associated with less than optimal physical growth and perhaps psychological harm (Valenzuela, 1997). Although there appear to be universal aspects of parental sensitivity, cross-cultural variations in caregiving behavior do exist and are fascinating to explore, as we will see next.

Cross-Cultural Differences in Mothers' Involvement

Many comparisons between White non-Hispanic mothers and Latina mothers have found that Latina mothers tend to emphasize politeness, control, and obedience in their children, whereas Anglo mothers more typically focus on their children's individuality and independence (Harwood et al., 1996, 2002). When researchers videotaped mothers interacting with their 12- to 15-month-old children in four everyday settings—feeding, social play (mother-child play without toys), free play (mother-child play using toys), and in three teaching tasks—they observed that Puerto Rican mothers tended to direct and structure their infants' activities and to physically position and restrain them more than Anglo mothers did. Anglo mothers, by contrast, were more likely to use verbal praise and to make suggestions in order to influence their children's behavior. Cross-cultural differences were also found in mothers' comments about their socialization goals and strategies; whereas Puerto Rican mothers indicated a preference for direct teaching and control of their children in order to instill a sense of proper demeanor, Anglo mothers said that they would attempt to structure the teaching situation so that the child's autonomy and sense of personal accomplishment would be maximized (Harwood et al., 1999).

Cultural patterns of interaction and caregiving beliefs are derived from parents' culture of origin, but they also tend to reflect influences of the mainstream culture if it is different from the culture of origin. Mothers' tendency to respond verbally during interactions with infants, for example, reflects their previous experience in school and other "institutionalized systems of communication and education" (Richman, Miller, & LeVine, 1992, p. 614). A number of researchers have thus explored the influence of acculturation on parenting beliefs and strategies. In one recent study, more and less acculturated Mexican American families, as well as European American and African American infant-mother dyads, were observed when the infants were 15 months old and again at the age of 25 months (Ispa et al., 2004). Acculturation status was determined by generational status (mothers born in the United States to U.S.-born parents were the most acculturated, followed by mothers born in the United States to Mexican-born parents and then mothers born in Mexico) and language usage (greater acculturation was ascribed to mothers who spoke English rather than Spanish at home). European American mothers displayed high levels of warmth and relatively low levels of control over their infants' actions, whereas less acculturated Mexican American mothers showed lower levels of warmth and higher levels of control. When more acculturated Mexican American mothers played and read with their toddlers, they showed a combination of warmth and control that was intermediate between these two patterns. These findings are consistent with other studies of immigrant parents that have demonstrated the cumulative effects of exposure to mainstream dominant culture on immigrants' parenting behaviors (Buriel, 1993; Hill, Bush, & Roosa, 2003; Parke & Buriel, 2006).

Experience caring for a firstborn may affect parents' interactions with later-born children. In one study involving mothers and their first- and second-born infants at 2 months of age, mothers showed more positive emotion with second-born infants than they had with their firstborn infants (Moore, Cohn, & Campbell, 1997). The difference in these mothers' behavior may reflect greater confidence interacting with their second-born infants. As a result, siblings in the same family are likely to experience unique emotional interactions with their mother from a very early age.

In two-parent families, all children experience unique interactions with caregivers to some degree because parents differ in terms of experience with and knowledge about infants. Mothers and fathers may also provide different types of care as a result of gender-related expectations about caregiving roles. As we discuss next, although there are numerous similarities in mothers' and fathers' behavior and goals, they also play complementary roles in their children's lives (Lamb, 1997; Lamb & Lewis, 2004; Lewis, 1997).

Father-Infant Caregiving and Interaction

Researchers who study father involvement have specified several dimensions of involvement in order to reflect the multiple ways in which fathers are involved in their children's lives. These dimensions include **accessibility** (the father's presence and availability), **engagement** (the father's direct contact and interaction with his children), and **responsibility** (the father's participation in tasks such as taking his children to the doctor, arranging play dates, and monitoring their activities). On all of these dimensions, father involvement in the United States increased during the last half of the twentieth century (Pleck, 1997; Pleck & Masciadrelli, 2004; Pruett, 1987), but many current studies have found that fathers still interact with their young infants less than mothers do. According to one survey, fathers in two-parent households spent 67 percent as much time with their children as mothers did on weekdays and 87 percent as much time on weekends (Yeung et al., 2001). Mothers tend to spend more time than fathers engaged in basic routines and daily caregiving activities, including feeding, bathing, and soothing (Hossain & Roopnarine, 1994; Lamb, 1997). It was not unusual in the United States and other Western countries for fathers of young infants to spend a mere 45 to 50 minutes in direct interaction and to perform only one caregiving task per day (Lamb, 1997). Based on these patterns, some researchers have concluded that "research has yet to identify any child-care task for which fathers have primary responsibility" (Pleck, 1997, p.73). The major exception to this conclusion is in single-father households, which have increased since the late 1990s and now comprise approximately one-sixth of all single-parent households (U.S. Bureau of the Census, 1999).

Whereas single fathers are compelled to be accessible, engaged, and responsible by necessity, observational studies suggest that fathers in two-parent families are able to perform caregiving tasks as well as mothers when they are asked to do so, but often defer under other circumstances, leaving primary responsibility to the child's mother. When both parents are employed outside of the home, fathers tend to be more engaged in childcare tasks, but the proportion of interactions that are playful typically remains higher among working fathers than among working mothers (Lamb, 1997; Marsiglio, 1993, 1994; Radin, 1994). Fathers are also more likely to interact in more physically stimulating and unpredictable ways than mothers do. As a result of these different interaction styles, it should not be surprising that some infants and toddlers prefer their fathers as play partners (Lamb, 1997).

As children grow older, fathers tend to become more involved in daily care, but it is still the case that most fathers of infants and very young children are more active as playmates than as caregivers (Lamb & Lewis, 2004). Fathers in one 4-year study of children in infancy and again at age 5 years, for example, showed that fathers were more involved in social interaction than in caregiving at both ages. Caregiving was typically provided by the mother, but paternal caregiving increased over time. Fathers in this longitudinal study became more engaged as mothers' employment outside of the home increased (Bailey, 1995). These findings are in keeping with other studies showing that fathers become more directly involved in childcare the greater their wives' income is relative to their own (Casper & O'Connell, 1998). Fathers also provide a greater amount of childcare for infants when their work hours are different from their wife's than when their work schedules overlap (Brayfield, 1995).

Early analyses of fathers' and mothers' interactions with sons and daughters suggested that there were numerous significant differences in the ways that parents behave with boys and girls, particularly during the toddler and early preschool years (Block, 1976; Fagot & Hagan, 1991). Some researchers reported, for example, that fathers were more likely than mothers to tease or play roughly with their children (Hossain & Roopnarine, 1994; Labrell, 1994). A number of more recent studies, however, have come to a different conclusion; although fathers often engage in more physical play with sons than with daughters and are slightly more likely than mothers to encourage sex-typed activities (e.g., urging boys to play with trucks rather than dolls), fathers and mothers tend to be highly similar in the behaviors they use to nurture, discipline, and teach very young children (Lamb & Lewis, 2004; Lewis, 1997; Lytton & Romney, 1991). In summary, studies of two-parent, middle-class families suggest that there is only limited support for gender-linked patterns of parent-child interaction, especially during the transition from infancy to toddlerhood and the preschool years. As a result, new attention has been directed to the study of culture as an influence on fathers' patterns of caregiving and interaction (Cabrera et al., 2000; Sun & Roopnarine, 1996; Tamis-LeMonda et al., 2004).

Cross-Cultural Differences in Fathers' Involvement

One fundamental finding from cross-cultural studies of fathers' involvement is that a wide range of family structures exists. In most regions of the world, including the United States, the percentage of children living in a female-headed household increased during the end of the twentieth century. In many of these families, the reasons for the growth in father-absent households is thought to be the underemployment of men and the increased employment of women; when mothers provide resources that fathers are unable to bring into the family, the father's role may change (Engle & Breaux, 1998).

In some countries and cultures, father-absence is the norm, and fathers typically do not live in the same house as their children. This is the case in the African country of Botswana, where mothers and their children traditionally live in the maternal household of origin and do not form a separate household until well after the mother and father have reached middle age (Townsend, 1997). Similarly, in parts of West Africa, fathers have multiple wives, and children traditionally are regarded as belonging to the extended kin group. Fathers confer social status on their children but are not responsible for feeding or nurturing them; there are even taboos against fathers having contact with infants. The father's primary role is one of disciplinarian and authority figure in the clan (Nsamenang, 1992). Urbanization and new work roles may lead to changes in the father-child relationship in these countries (Engle & Breaux, 1998).

Comparatively high proportions of children in African American families are raised in a nonmarital household or grow up living apart from their father (Roopnarine, 2004). Despite these trends, it is difficult to generalize about father-child relationships in the African American population, due to the great variety that exists. Among African American families, especially those with lower levels of education and economic resources, it is not unusual for household membership to change or for children to experience multigenerational family life, with assistance and support being given by grandparents, other relatives, and unrelated father figures. In one recent review of the literature, father involvement was described as ranging from infrequent, intermittent visits to "daily contacts with appreciable time investment" (Roopnarine, 2004, p. 65). To date, there has been only a small amount of data gathered about African American fathers in married and two-parent households, and many of the existing studies of both married and unmarried fathers have used self-report measures rather than observing father-child interactions directly. The existing research clearly indicates that across socioeconomic classes, age categories, and family structures, high percentages of African American fathers show interest in, care for, and support their children, beginning in infancy.

It is also important to recognize that even fathers who do not reside with their children may have a positive impact on their development and well-being. Some studies have found that children who have contact with their father have fewer behavioral problems, more self-confidence, and higher self-esteem. Children of unmarried parents have even been found to perform better in school and to show more advanced cognitive development when they carry their father's name (Engle & Breaux, 1998).

Latino fathers traditionally were responsible for providing discipline and economic resources, while mothers played the primary role in caring for and nurturing infants and young children. As with other examples that we have considered, there is evidence that the traditional Latino father role may be changing with increasing urbanization and acculturation (Engle & Breaux, 1998; Mirande, 1988). At the same time, it is important to remember that there is inherent variation in Latino parenting in the United States as a function of socioeconomic status, country of family origin, and acculturation to mainstream U.S. society (Buriel, 1993; Cabrera & Garcia Coll, 2004; Halgunseth, 2004; Harwood et al., 2002; Ispa et al., 2004).

In China, the father's traditional role was to serve as a stern disciplinarian and breadwinner, whereas the mother provided care and nurturance (Ho, 1987). Elements of these complementary roles were observed in one naturalistic study of father-infant interaction in public parks in Inner Mongolia (Jankowiak, 1992). Fathers in this sample rarely held their young infants or interacted with them before the age of 6 months, and both men and women said that they doubted that men could care competently for infants. These views appear to be changing, especially in urban areas of China, where parents are likely to have a higher level of education and the one-child policy has been more strictly enforced. New expectations for fathers of infants in China today may thus be taking hold, reflecting the higher value that is placed on fathers' contributions to their only child's development (Engle & Breaux, 1998; Shwalb et al., 2004).

Fathers in Japan traditionally have not been closely involved in caring for infants and young children. Even today, despite higher levels of urbanization and education and fewer offspring, they may be relatively remote figures in their children's lives. In recent years, the Japanese government has implemented new policies and slogans ("A man who does not participate in child rearing is not a father") to promote greater father involvement, and more Japanese fathers are present at their child's birth than in the past. Nevertheless, the majority of Japanese fathers today are not actively involved with their children. This is due, in part, to the long distances that many fathers in urban Japan commute to work each day. Complementary parental roles are reinforced in Japan because many women leave the paid workforce when they become mothers and devote themselves to nurturing and educating their children, beginning in infancy (Allison, 1996; Shwalb et al., 2004; Shwalb, Shwalb, & Shoji, 1996; Tobin, Wu, & Davidson, 1989).

Among the Aka pygmies of Central Africa, whom we discussed earlier in this chapter, the traditional role for fathers provides a striking contrast with fathers' roles in many other parts of the world. Described as "the most nurturant fathers yet observed," (Engle & Breaux, 1998, p. 5), Aka fathers tend to hold their infants and nurture them at higher rates (20 percent versus 4 percent) than in other hunter-gatherer cultures that have been observed (Hewlett, 1987, 2004; Hewlett et al., 1998). Aka fathers' style of interaction is also less physically stimulating than fathers' play in other cultures. As a result, from birth, Aka children experience care from two nurturing, attentive parents who play generally reinforcing rather than complementary roles (Engle & Breaux, 1998).

As we conclude our discussion of father-infant involvement, it is clear that many questions are still unanswered, in part because family life is evolving in many parts of the world, often as a result of changes in economic systems, including new patterns of maternal employment. As societies undergo change, the most important things that infants need remain unchanged—stable, caring relationships and predictable, sensitive interactions. Sadly, as we discuss next, not all infants have these things.

Disturbances in Infant-Caregiver Relationships

Our discussion of infant-caregiver interaction thus far has made it clear that there is no single right way for parents to care for their infants. Across a broad range of patterns, informed by different belief systems, parents act to nurture their children and promote healthy development. Some infant-caregiver relationships and patterns of interaction are unequivocally harmful to early development, however, and we turn now to consider three significant examples of disturbances in the infant-caregiver relationship: maternal depression, maltreatment, and early institutionalization.

Maternal Depression

Being the parent of a newborn can be an exhausting and overwhelming experience, both physically and emotionally. Although both parents suffer from the effects of sleep deprivation and new daily routines, new mothers in particular may feel ambivalent about the demands of their new role. Many women worry because they do not feel an immediate, positive emotional connection to their child. As many as 50 to 80 percent of new mothers even experience a sadness that is so well known it is referred to as the "baby blues" (Seifer & Dickstein, 2000). Some new mothers feel anxious and unprepared to care for such a tiny, seemingly fragile creature. Others feel guilty about missing their former role as half of a carefree, childless couple. These are all normal feelings in the days and weeks after a child is born, and they usually diminish as the new parents recover physically, become more confident in their caregiving ability, and have time to get to know their baby. For some women, however, negative feelings predominate and do not dissipate with time. These women, 15 percent of all new mothers (Seifer & Dickstein, 2000), experience **postpartum depression**— a sense of despair and sadness so pervasive that it affects their ability to care for and interact effectively with their baby.

Any woman may be susceptible to postpartum depression, but mothers of sick newborns and mothers without economic or emotional support appear to be especially vulnerable (Petterson & Albers, 2001; Shonkoff & Phillips, 2000). Many depressed mothers with supportive, nondepressed husbands who are involved in caregiving are able to interact positively and sensitively with their children (Cummings & Davies, 1999; Goodman & Gotlib, 1999). Nevertheless, even in low-risk, married, middle-class samples, depressed mothers interact differently with their infants than do nondepressed mothers. In one study of women who were not socioeconomically disadvantaged, depressed mothers showed less sensitivity to their 2-month-old infants and were less affirming and more negating of their behavior (Murray et al., 1996). Evidence from many other studies indicates that mothers suffering from depression tend to interact less with their babies and are less likely to look at, smile at, touch, or talk to them. Some depressed mothers show a different pattern and are physically intrusive with their infants (poking or prodding them, sometimes roughly), rather than withdrawn (Field, 1998b; Field et al., 2003; Tronick & Weinberg, 1997; Zeanah, Boris, & Larrieu, 1997).

How does interaction with a depressed mother affect children's early social development? Earlier in this chapter, we discussed an experiment that demonstrated infants' preference for interactions that are contingent and responsive to their own behavior (Murray & Trevarthen, 1985). To explore the effect of behavior that resembles the behavior of depressed mothers, researchers instructed nondepressed mothers of 3-month-old infants to adopt a withdrawn depressed expression for 3 minutes during face-to-face interactions, either before or after a 3-minute session of normal behavior. Infants responded to their mother's simulated depressed state by showing higher proportions of negative behaviors (protests, wariness, and looking away) than during a 3-minute session of normal interaction. Infants whose mothers simulated depression prior to the normal-behavior session tended to carry their negativity into the normal episode (Cohn & Tronick, 1983).

Similar effects were found in a study of 18- to 36-month-old children whose mothers simulated withdrawn depression for 10 minutes, either before or after a 10-minute episode of normal behavior (Seiner & Gelfand, 1995). Given their age and relatively greater maturity, children in this experiment had more ways of responding than the infants in previous studies (Cohn & Tronick, 1983). They responded by withdrawing from their mothers, making more negative physical bids for attention (e.g., attacking toys or throwing them at their mother), and becoming more unfocused (e.g., staring vacantly or failing to become engaged in play or other activities). These results may indicate that younger infants have fewer means of coping and are thus more vulnerable than toddlers to the negative effects of maternal depression and withdrawal.

What do studies of mothers who actually are depressed tell us about the impact on their infants? One important finding is that the effects appear to depend on the duration of the mother's depression. This was shown in a study involving married, middle-class women (all first-time mothers) who were diagnosed as being depressed when their infants were 2 months old (Campbell, Cohn, & Meyers, 1995). Mothers and their infants were videotaped as they interacted at home when the infants were 2, 4, and 6 months of age. In comparison with a group of nondepressed mothers and their infants, mothers whose depression lasted through 6 months were less positive during feeding, face-to-face interaction, and toy play. Women whose depression ended before 6 months, by contrast, were more positive with their infants even at times when they met criteria for depression. Consistent with this pattern, negative effects on infants (less positive infant behavior) were seen only for infants whose mothers were more chronically, persistently depressed.

Infants who experience maternal depression show negative, "depressed" behavior themselves, even when interacting with nondepressed adults (Field et al., 1988). This finding, from a study of 3- to 6-month-olds, suggests that infants generalize interaction styles, especially patterns of visual attention and gaze, at a very early age. Unexpectedly, the nondepressed adults who participated in this study were negatively affected by their interactions with the "depressed" infants and showed less optimal interactive behavior with them than with infants of nondepressed mothers, despite being unaware of their mothers' depression.

If infants of depressed mothers elicit different, less optimal behavior from other adult caregivers, those caregivers may need to work harder to attract the infant's attention and maintain positive engagement. Overcoming "depressed" infants' behavioral tendencies may be challenging, however, because their brains appear to process emotional information differently than the brains of nondepressed infants. A number of studies using EEG measures have shown that as early as 11 months of age, infants of depressed mothers show unusual frontal brain electrical activity when they are interacting with their mothers and even when they are interacting with other adults in emotionally positive ways. In contrast to infants of nondepressed mothers, who show more activity in the left versus the right frontal region of the brain in response to negative emotions, infants of depressed mothers show reduced left frontal activity. This atypical pattern suggests that interacting with a depressed mother may modify infants' processing and experience of positive as well as negative emotions (Dawson, 1994; Dawson & Ashman, 2000; Dawson et al., 1997; Dawson, Frey, Panagiotides, Yamada, Hessl, & Osterling, 1999; Shonkoff & Phillips, 2000).

Other evidence, however, suggests that this brain asymmetry is present considerably earlier, perhaps even during the neonatal period (Field, 1998a, 1998b; Field et al., 1995; Jones et al., 1997). These findings suggest that other explanations for EEG asymmetry need to be considered, including the possibility that at least some infants of depressed mothers are born predisposed to respond to emotions in unusual ways. Additional studies are needed to disentangle the relative contributions of prenatal factors and postnatal environmental influences (Shonkoff & Phillips, 2000).

It is also important to determine how to intervene most effectively in order to help depressed mothers and their infants. Without intervention, depression-related disturbances in early infant-mother interactions are associated with poorer cognitive outcomes at 18 months (Murray et al., 1996) and less secure parent-child relationships in infancy and early childhood (Carter et al., 2001; Teti et al., 1995). There is also evidence that, without intervention, children whose mothers experienced depression when they were younger than 3 years of age are at increased risk at ages 5 to 11 years for attention-deficit/hyperactivity disorder and anger management problems that may result in aggressive and antisocial behavior (Hay et al., 2003; Wright et al., 2000).

Fortunately, several promising interventions offer hope for depressed mothers and their infants. The first comes out of the observation that infants of depressed mothers who are cared for by a nondepressed parent or caregiver are more likely to be able to engage in positive interactions. This finding suggests that it is essential to have the father, grandparents, or other nondepressed caregivers involved in daily care in order to support the mother and provide the infant with at least one emotionally sensitive and responsive interaction partner (Field, 1998a, 1998b; Hossain et al., 1994; Peláez-Nogueras et al., 1995). Second, a study of 1- to 3-month-old infants born to depressed adolescent mothers showed that infants who experienced massage therapy two days a week for six weeks spent more time in active alert and active awake states, cried less, and had lower stress hormone (cortisol) levels than infants who were simply rocked for the same amount of time. Infants in the massage therapy group also gained more weight and showed greater improvement on measures of emotional arousal, sociability, and soothability (Field et al., 1996).

A third approach that has also achieved success involves coaching depressed mothers and showing them how to touch their infants during face-to-face interactions, a technique that can be tailored to the specific problematic behaviors displayed by withdrawn mothers as opposed to those exhibited by intrusive mothers. Withdrawn mothers, for example, are encouraged to touch their infants more often, whereas intrusive mothers are coached to slow down and imitate their infant's behaviors (Malphurs et al., 1996; Peláez-Nogueras et al., 1996). Finally, interventions that directly target mothers' mood states may also benefit their infants. Toward this end, researchers have successfully treated mothers with massage therapy as well as music therapy (Field et al. 1996; Field, 1998a, 1998b). While these interventions alleviate mothers' symptoms, at least short term, they do not necessarily enhance mother-infant interaction (Hay et al., 2003), reminding us that, above all else, interventions need to provide infants of depressed mothers with sensitive and emotionally responsive face-to-face interaction.

Maltreatment: Abuse and Neglect

There is no doubt that maternal depression places infants at developmental risk, but it is rarely as life-threatening as a second group of disturbed infant-caregiver relationships, those involving child **maltreatment**, which we also considered in Chapter 5. For infants and children who survive maltreatment, there are negative effects in all developmental domains. Prolonged maltreatment is linked to higher levels of stress hormones than briefer exposure to abuse and neglect (De Bellis et al., 1999; Shonkoff & Phillips, 2000). In infancy, the quality of the infant-caregiver attachment relationship, which we will discuss shortly, tends to be poor and subsequently jeopardizes other relationships in which children participate (Barnett, Ganiban, & Cicchetti, 1999; Cicchetti & Toth, 2006). As toddlers, children who are physically abused are more likely to be more aggressive and to have less awareness of and empathy toward others' emotions. They are also more likely to have learning and behavior problems in school. Less is known about the effects of neglect, but negative outcomes have also been reported for that form of maltreatment (Erickson & Egeland, 1996; Shonkoff & Phillips, 2000).

Maltreatment has the most serious consequences when children and their families are faced with multiple stressful life circumstances. The effects of child maltreatment can be buffered, however, by the presence of a nonabusive caregiver or another emotionally supportive adult upon whom the child can rely (Rutter, 2000; Werner, 2000).

Can child abuse and neglect be prevented? Nurse home visitation programs have had promising results by targeting parents before their child is born and offering parent education (Eckenrode et al., 2000; Olds et al., 1999). Other interventions focus on connecting at-risk parents with community resources and support groups. Breaking the cycle of maltreatment can be done and is well worth the effort for all concerned (Cicchetti & Toth, 2006; Egeland, Jacobvitz, & Sroufe, 1988; Reynolds & Robertson, 2003).

When interventions do not succeed or cannot be implemented rapidly enough to protect children in abusive or neglectful homes, one option is to remove them from that setting. When this action is taken, they may be placed with relatives or in foster care provided by an unrelated family. These arrangements are generally preferable to group care in institutional settings, such as orphanages, which are associated with a number of poor developmental outcomes, at least in the short term.

Early Institutionalization and Social Deprivation

In the 1930s to 1940s, René Spitz documented the physical, cognitive, and social-emotional harm that institutionalization caused infants and young children (Emde, 1992). Interest in the effects of early institutionalization has increased in recent years, however, as the result of a growing trend since 1989 for parents in the United States and other countries to adopt children who have spent months, and sometimes years, living in orphanages (Immigration and Naturalization Service, 1998; Selman, 2002).

In the United States, approximately 23,000 foreign-born children of all ages were adopted in 2004. The vast majority were either infants under 1 year (40 percent) or children between the ages of 1 and 4 years (45 percent). The most common source of foreign-born adoptees in 2004 was Asia (43 percent), followed by Europe (36 percent) and Central America (15 percent). The largest percentage of infants under the age of 1 year came from China (30 percent), followed by Guatemala (23 percent), Russia (19 percent), and Korea (18 percent) (Yearbook of Immigration Statistics, 2004).

Overall, more foreign-born girls than boys were adopted in 2004 (65 percent versus 35 percent, respectively). In some countries, such as Russia, nearly equal numbers of girls and boys were adopted by U.S. families. In other countries, especially in China, where there is a strong cultural preference for sons, more daughters were given away by their biological parents, with the result that 95 percent of all children who were adopted from that country were girls (Yearbook of Immigration Statistics, 2004). Foreign-born adoptees are often referred to as orphans, but most of these children have parents who are still living but gave up their children due to severe economic hardship and an inability to care for them. In China, the traditional preference for boys and a government policy that limits parents to one child are the main reasons that so many infant girls are surrendered soon after birth (Johnson, 2000; Kreider, 2003).

The Eastern European country of Romania was a major source of young orphans during the 1990s, and it is those adoptees who have been studied most intensively in recent years. Between 1991 and 1998, approximately 40,000 Romanian children were adopted by U.S. families. Many others found families in Canada, England, and Western European countries (Immigration and Naturalization Service, 1998; Johnson, 2000; Zeanah et al., 2003). In 2004, by contrast, fewer than 100 Romanian children were adopted in the United States. This dramatic reduction is, in part, a sign of the lessening of the crisis caused by ousted Romanian dictator Nicolae Ceausescu's efforts to engineer the conception and rearing of more than 100,000 children (Johnson, 2000; Yearbook of Immigration Statistics, 2004). For many of the families who adopted these children, the consequences of their early experience have been carried into the present.

Caregivers in Romanian orphanages, like those in many traditional Baby Homes in Russia today, provided care that placed children at risk in all developmental domains. Typically, each caregiver was charged with the care of between 10 and 20 infants, a daunting task that they managed by keeping infants in their cribs as much as possible and limiting the attention that they paid to each one. They propped bottles rather than holding them for younger infants and spoon-fed older infants as efficiently as they could. Children received a restricted diet that did not always provide enough or the right types of food, and most received few if any immunizations. Care groups were separated by age, and there was little or no time spent engaged in stimulating free play. As a result of these experiences, there were delays in children's language, cognition, and motor skills. Many of the children failed to grow at normal rates before being adopted. The greater the amount of time children lived in the orphanage, the more severely stunted they were. In addition to neglect, many children suffered physical and sexual abuse, which left its own emotional and developmental scars (Johnson, 2000).

Not all previously institutionalized children experienced negative consequences to the same degree, and in many cases marked improvement occurred after they were adopted and cared for in a family setting. Researchers in Canada compared two groups of adoptees when they were 4 to 5 years of age: those who were adopted within 4 months of birth (Early Adopted, EA) and those who were adopted after 8 months or more of being cared for in an orphanage (Romanian Orphanage, RO). Median age at adoption in the RO group was 18.5 months, and time in the orphanage ranged from 8 to 53 months. These children were also compared with a group of Canadian born (CB) children who were living with their families of origin. Across several studies, the EA and CB groups were found to be very similar to each other on most measures, whereas the RO group was more likely to have significant cognitive and emotional problems (Ames, 1997; Fisher et al., 1997; Morison, Ames, & Chisholm, 1995).

Other comparisons of these groups have found that many of the Romanian adoptees tended to show **indiscriminate friendliness**—"behavior that was affectionate and friendly toward all adults (including strangers) without the fear or caution characteristic of normal children. In these cases, a child's behavior toward other adults could not be discriminated from his or her behavior toward caregivers" (Chisholm, 1998, p. 1094; Chisholm et al., 1995). In keeping with other studies of these samples, children in the RO group were more likely to show indiscriminately friendly behavior than were Canadian-born children and children in the EA group. This pattern was found even though the children were between 4 1/2 and 9 years of age and had thus been in their adoptive homes for years. Parents of RO children reported that they were "overly friendly" and had shown no improvement in this behavior over time. There was also a higher incidence of behavior problems among RO children who had not formed an emotionally close relationship with their parents. These parents reported higher levels of parenting stress than did parents of RO children who had established a special, preferential relationship with them. Indiscriminate friendliness, which may garner children special attention from caregivers and visitors in an orphanage setting, contributes to parenting stress in a family setting, in part because of safety-related concerns that children may wander away or leave with a stranger without noticing or becoming distressed.

Other researchers studied the cortisol (stress-hormone) responses of children in the Canadian sample approximately 7 years after they had been adopted (Gunnar, 2000). Early adopted (EA) children and Canadian born (CB) children showed similar, normal cortisol levels, highest in the morning and then decreasing during the day. Children in the RO group, by contrast, had higher levels of cortisol throughout the day and especially in the evening, a pattern that is associated with higher levels of cognitive and physical developmental delays (Carlson et al., 1995; Carlson & Earls, 1997). The amount by which cortisol levels were different from the normal pattern corresponded to the amount of time the children had spent in an orphanage. These findings suggest that the RO children's early experience of social and physical adversity had lasting effects on their physiological stress-response system, perhaps making them react more strongly than other children to challenges or stressors (Gunnar, 2000).

The findings from the sample of Romanian adoptees in Canada are consistent with a number of studies of similar children who were adopted in other countries. Over and over, these studies show that children who were adopted early and who received reliable, sensitive, and responsive care in a family setting before the age of 1 year, often escape many of the negative consequences of institutionalized care (O'Connor et al., 1999, 2000; Rutter & the English & Romanian Adoptees (ERA) Study Team, 1998; Rutter et al., 1999; Rutter, Kreppner, & O'Connor, 2001; Zeanah, 2000). Studies of the effects of institutionalization in Russia have also shown similar results in terms of the effects of early deprivation and adversity and differences between early adopted and later adopted children's subsequent development (Johnson, 2000; Juffer & Rosenboom, 1997; Juffer & van IJzendoorn, 2005). Taken together, these studies indicate that parents who adopt previously institutionalized children need to be as concerned about their children's social and emotional well being as they are about their cognitive and physical development (Shonkoff & Phillips, 2000). They also clearly support what Spitz showed so many years ago—early placement with adoptive families needs to be a priority (Emde, 1992; Gunnar & Van Dulman, 2003).

Given the reality that not all children will be placed with new families at an early age, can anything be done to improve their early experience while living in an institutional setting?

New studies suggest that there are a number of concrete changes that can be made which will result in physically and emotionally healthier infants and children. These modifications include reducing the child-caregiver ratio (e.g., from 20:1 to 4:1) and assigning caregivers to specific children in order to provide the greatest stability and continuity possible. Caregivers can also be trained to stimulate infants with toys and through face-to-face communication (Carlson & Earls, 1997). In some interventions that have been carried out in Russian Baby Homes, children are housed in homelike living quarters with children of different ages, as would be found in an actual family. In these institutions, children also participate in enriched daily activities that may include massage, music classes, swimming, and dance (Groark et al., 2003, 2005; Gunnar, 2000).

One recent intervention in Baby Homes in St. Petersburg, Russia, compared developmental outcomes in three kinds of institutions: those in which caregivers had received training but no other changes had been made (Training Only), homes in which caregivers had been trained and structural changes in the living arrangements were put in place (Training and Structure), and Baby Homes in which no changes were made (Control). Initial findings from this controlled study echo those from other interventions; infants in the Training and Structure group grew better and showed fewer developmental delays than infants being reared in traditional Baby Homes (Chugani et al., 2001; Groark et al., 2003, 2005; Zeanah et al., 2003). These findings provide hope that fewer children adopted from orphanages will experience the perturbations caused by early adversity and social deprivation, with the result that they and their new families will have a better chance of forming trusting, secure relationships.

Developing Trust, Becoming Attached

In Erik Erikson's classic theory, the initial task in infancy is to establish a sense of basic trust. Infants conclude this stage around the age of 18 months. At that time, if their care has been consistently nurturing and sensitive, they emerge with a sense of hope and a feeling that the world is a safe and supportive place. According to Erikson (1950), although a sense of trust is desirable, infants also need to retain an element of mistrust—a self-protective ability to differentiate between caregivers and all other individuals. These ideas were developed further in another influential theory about infant-parent relationships that we will consider next.

Bowlby's Theory of Infant-Caregiver Attachment

John Bowlby's (1969/1982) theory of the infant-caregiver **attachment relationship** incorporated elements of several different perspectives. From psychosocial and psychoanalytic theories of his day, including Erikson's, Bowlby embraced the assumption that early experiences in a person's life may have a profound effect on the subsequent course of development. Bowlby asserted that human infants—like the young of many other mammals—possess a built-in repertoire of **attachment behaviors** that attract attention and elicit care from caregivers. He noted, for example, that infants cry, coo, smile, look at, reach for, and eventually crawl or walk toward their caregivers—behaviors that most caregivers are unlikely to ignore.

Bowlby also noted that, over the course of the first year of life, infants' cognitive abilities increase and these new abilities enable infants to form a representation of their relationship with their caregiver, based on specific memories of their experiences with him or her. Bowlby called these representations **internal working models**. He reasoned that infants with a working model of a relationship with a caregiver who is consistently sensitive and effective would come to rely on that caregiver for comfort and assistance in novel or distressing situations. By contrast, infants whose caregivers had been insensitive, unpredictable, and ineffective would not necessarily seek out the caregiver when uncertain or distressed. If they did, the response that they received would not necessarily be effective at comforting and reassuring them (Bowlby, 1969/1982, 1973, 1980, 1988).

In Bowlby's view (shown in Table 9.1), attachment develops gradually, beginning in the first 2 months with a stage in which there is no clear preference for familiar caregivers. Infants display attachment behaviors, including crying, cooing, and smiling, to known and unknown individuals equally and can be comforted by a wide range of people who respond to those behaviors.

From 2 to 7 months, infants begin to differentiate between their usual caregiver and a stranger. They may smile more at the caregiver and stare uncertainly at a stranger. When they are upset, the caregiver's actions are likely to be more soothing than the same response by a stranger. Infants in this stage join their caregiver in face-to-face games like peek-a-boo but may not participate if the play partner is a stranger. These behaviors show that infants have developed specific expectations about specific individuals, based on their experience with those individuals.

TABLE 9.1   Bowlby's Stages of the Development of Attachment

Age/Stage	Characteristics
Birth–2 months/ Indiscriminate Sociability	Attachment behaviors are displayed to both familiar and unfamiliar individuals. Infants are comforted equally well by primary caregivers and unfamiliar persons.
2–7 months/ Discriminating Sociability	Infants possess expectations about caregivers' behavior and respond differently to them than to unfamiliar persons. Caregivers' efforts to soothe and comfort infants tend to be more effective than other persons' attempts.
7–24 months/	Attachment behaviors are directed toward primary caregivers and are intended to maintain proximity to those caregivers.
Directed Attachment Behaviors	Primary caregivers are more effective than other persons at comforting distressed infants.
24 months+/ Goal-Corrected Partnerships	Children's improving verbal abilities enable them to talk with caregivers about their relationship. Their growing awareness of others' thoughts and feelings also helps them understand caregivers' behavior and desires.

Source: Adapted from Bowlby (1969/1982).

The third stage, from 7 to 24 months, coincides with infants' increasing mobility, which gives them a new way to show their preference for a particular caregiver by moving toward him or her. Infants try to be near their preferred caregiver when they are distressed or in ambiguous settings, such as an unfamiliar room in which there are unfamiliar people. They also protest separations from their caregiver by displaying attachment behaviors such as crying, vocalizing, and crawling or toddling after them.

Finally, beginning at 24 months, children's improving verbal abilities enable them to talk with caregivers about their relationship. A growing awareness of others' thoughts and feelings helps them understand caregivers' behavior and desires at the same time that it helps them reflect on their own actions and wishes.

As these stages indicate, attachment relationships emerge gradually over time and begin to be discernible in infants' behavioral preferences sometime between the ages of 6 and 9 months. Bowlby's theory thus makes it clear that infants do not become attached to their parents at birth.

Assessing Attachment Relationships

Bowlby's theoretical predictions were first tested by Mary Ainsworth, a researcher who carried out studies of infant-caregiver interaction in Uganda as well as in the United States. Ainsworth observed that infants who experienced sensitive mother-infant interactions (such as those characterized by dyadic synchrony) were likely to have effective, positive attachment relationships (Ainsworth & Bell, 1969; Ainsworth, Bell, & Stayton, 1972; Ainsworth et al., 1978; Blehar, Lieberman, & Ainsworth, 1977). The most sensitive mothers—those who responded quickly and effectively when their infants cried—were most likely to have children who showed a pattern of attachment behavior at the age of 12 months that reflected a **secure attachment relationship**. Numerous studies, including a meta-analysis of 66 studies, have subsequently supported Ainsworth's observations that maternal sensitivity is linked to security of attachment. These studies also indicate, however, that sensitivity is affected by environmental factors, such as changes in family structure and other life circumstances (De Wolff & van IJzendoorn, 1997; Harrist & Waugh, 2002; Posada et al., 2004; Susman-Stillman et al., 1996).

Attachment relationships from 12 months to 5 years of age can be assessed using a rating system known as the **Attachment Q-Sort (AQS)** (Waters, 1995; Waters & Deane, 1985). The majority of studies of attachment, however, tend to make use of the **Strange Situation**, a laboratory procedure that Ainsworth developed for assessing attachment relationships at ages 12 to 24 months. As shown in Table 9.2, researchers observe how the infant behaves in a series of episodes and the degree to which the caregiver is used as an effective source of comfort when the infant is distressed. Through a variety of behaviors, securely attached infants (also referred to as Type B) use the caregiver as a secure base during the Strange Situation. During the first three episodes, some secure infants may make eye contact with the caregiver and "check in" from time to time while playing on their own; other secure infants may vocalize or seek physical contact with the caregiver intermittently while they play. During the reunion portions of the Strange Situation (Episodes 5 and 8 in the table), some securely attached infants may seek contact with the caregiver by vocalizing,

TABLE 9.2   Ainsworth's Strange Situation Procedure

Episode	Activity and Participants in Original Procedure	Episode	Activity and Participants in Sibling Procedure
1	Introduction to playroom (30 secs)	1	Mother and siblings play together (3 mins)
2	Parent and infant alone (3 mins)	2	Mother plays with only one sibling (3 mins)
3	Stranger enters, plays with infant	3	Mother plays with only the other sibling (3 mins)
4	Parent leaves room, baby and stranger remain	4	Mother leaves room, siblings remain together
5	Parent returns and stranger departs	5	Stranger enters room
6	Parent leaves room, baby remains alone	6	Stranger leaves room with older sibling, younger sibling remains alone
7	Stranger returns	7	Older sibling returns to room
8	Parent returns and stranger departs	8	Mother returns to room

Source: Based on information in Ainsworth et al., 1978; and Teti & Ablard, 1989.

whereas others may move close to him or her for a hug or other physical comforting. Regardless of the specific behaviors they display during these episodes, securely attached infants show that they are happy to see the caregiver return and do not withhold contact from him or her. According to attachment theory, these positive feelings are based on months of interactions in which the caregiver responded to the infant's attachment behavior with sensitive, predictable, and effective actions.

Infants who are not securely attached may be insecurely attached in one of several ways. Infants with **insecure-avoidant attachment** (Type A) tend to avoid the caregiver by failing to greet him or her or by delaying their response to the caregiver's return. Infants with **insecure-resistant attachment** (Type C, sometimes referred to as ambivalent), on the other hand, display contradictory behavior—despite appearing preoccupied with the caregiver during the Strange Situation, they may resist making contact or even show anger and distress when he or she returns. Many attachment researchers believe that infants who are classified as insecure (either Type A or Type C) behave as they do because their caregivers have been unpredictable in their mood and reactions. To cope with this uncertainty, infants develop internal working models that make them alert and vigilant to their caregiver's current state, prepared to change their own behavior accordingly (Vondra & Barnett, 1999).

Insecure-avoidant attachment may develop when infants are overstimulated by caregivers who are intrusive. Insecure-resistant attachment, on the other hand, may develop when caregivers are rejecting or withdrawn, depressed, and unresponsive to infants' needs (Isabella & Belsky, 1991; Teti et al., 1995).

TABLE 9.3   Attachment Classification in Relation to Characteristics of Infants, Mothers, and the Childrearing Environment

Attachment Classification	Sample	Incidence
Secure (Type B)	Middle-class, North American	60–75%
Insecure-Avoidant (Type A)	Middle-class, North American	15–25%
Insecure-Resistant (Type C)	Middle-class, North American	10–15%
Disorganized/Disoriented (Type D)	Middle-class	15%
	Lower income	25%
	Teen mother	25%
	Abused/neglected child	48%
	Maternal alcohol/drug abuse	43%
	Maternal depression	19%
	Children in clinical samples (autism, Down syndrome, neurological problems)	35%

Source: Based on information in van IJzendoorn, Schuengel, & Bakermans-Kranenburg, 1999; and Thompson, 1998.

Higher levels of insecure attachment are found in low-income samples, in which parents experience high levels of stress that may impede their ability to provide sensitive, responsive care in a consistent manner (Thompson, 1998, 2006; Vondra, Hommerding, & Shaw, 1999). Higher rates of insecure attachment have also been found among infants who were adopted after spending at least 8 months in a Romanian orphanage. Infants who were adopted at an earlier age, by contrast, do not appear to have an elevated rate of insecure attachment to their adoptive parents (Chisholm, 1998).

As shown in Table 9.3, attachment classifications vary as a function of characteristics of infants, mothers, and the childrearing environment. In typical middle-class samples in North America, the majority of 12- to 18-month-old infants observed in the Strange Situation are classified as securely attached (Type B). Comparatively smaller proportions of infants in typical samples are classified as insecure-avoidant (Type A) or insecure-resistant (Type C) (Thompson, 1998; Vondra & Barnett, 1999).

Not all infants, however, can be classified into attachment types A, B, or C. To address this problem, a fourth classification, **disorganized/disoriented attachment** (Type D), has been identified and confirmed in a number of studies (Main & Solomon, 1986, 1990; van IJzendoorn, Schuengel, & Bakermans-Kranenburg, 1999). These infants may simultaneously display contradictory behavior, such as a mixture of anger and apparently calm play. They also may show unusual behaviors, such as "freezing" in midmovement or showing fear when the caregiver returns. In typical middle-class samples, a relatively small proportion of infants are classified as Type D, but the percentages are significantly higher among lower income samples, children of teen mothers, abused and neglected children, and children whose mothers abuse alcohol and drugs or who report higher levels of depression or other psychiatric symptoms. Children in clinical samples, such as those with autism, Down syndrome, and neurological problems, tend to have a higher incidence of Type D attachment. This pattern is believed to be a reflection of these children's unusual social and cognitive abilities, however, and is not caused by mothers' behavior (Barnett, Ganiban, & Cicchetti, 1999; Carlson, 1998; Hildyard & Wolfe, 2002; Macfie, Cicchetti, & Toth, 2001; van IJzendoorn, Schuengel, & Bakermans-Kranenburg, 1999).

Mothers of Type D infants may show unusual or disrupted emotional communication during the Strange Situation. They may not greet the infant during the reunion episodes, or they may give contradictory cues, such as calling the infant to them but then moving away or holding them at arm's length. Some mothers of Type D infants fail to respond when the infant becomes distressed or behave inappropriately by mocking or teasing the infant. Pulling the infant roughly by the wrist is another behavior displayed by some mothers of Type D infants. Appearing confused, frightened, or disoriented during the interaction has been observed, as has evidence of role confusion and trying to elicit comforting from the infant. Helping these mothers resolve their feelings of trauma or loss is seen as an important step to fostering a healthy relationship with their child (Adam, Gunnar, & Tanaka, 2004; Erickson, Korfmacher, & Egeland, 1992; Lieberman & Zeanah, 1995; Lyons-Ruth, Bronfman, & Parsons, 1999; Seifer et al., 2004; Vondra & Barnett, 1999).

Another classification, **reactive attachment disorder**, has recently been proposed for maltreated and institutionalized children (Zeanah & Boris, 2000; Zeanah & Emde, 1994; Zeanah & Fox, 2004). These children tend to show unusual patterns of behavior, either emotionally withdrawn-inhibited or indiscriminately social-disinhibited. Additional studies of attachment disorders are needed in order to validate more fully this new classification and illuminate its relation to other attachment phenomena.

Attachment to Other Caregivers.   Infants may become attached to any caregivers, provided that those caregivers interact with them on a regular basis, provide physical and emotional care, and are emotionally invested in the child (Howes, 1999; Wakschlag, Chase-Lansdale, & Brooks-Gunn, 1996). Infants may be securely attached to one parent but insecurely attached to the other parent or another caregiver (Shonkoff & Phillips, 2000). Attachment to multiple caregivers tends to be similar when those adults cooperate in providing care, demonstrate and reinforce caregiving behaviors for each other, and discuss the child's behavior and personality, reinforcing a shared view (Sagi et al., 1995).

As with mothers, fathers who are highly stressed or who respond insensitively are more likely to have infants who are insecurely attached to them. Finally, reflecting the importance of the triadic infant-mother-father relationship, many researchers have found that the quality of the marital relationship and the degree of emotional support that the father provides to the mother in her role as caregiver are linked to the security of infant-caregiver attachment relationships (Belsky, 1996; Lamb & Lewis, 2004).

Infants' Influence on Attachment.   Thinking of the family as a system raises questions about the infant's own contributions to the attachment relationship. Is attachment security influenced by how easy or difficult infants are to take care of? Do fussier babies tend to develop insecure forms of attachment? A number of researchers have found that it is more challenging to provide sensitive, responsive care for some infants than for others (Atkinson et al., 1995, 1999; Capps, Sigman, & Mundy, 1994).

The effect of most infant characteristics, however, is generally thought to be less important than the way that parents respond to those characteristics (Bokhorst et al., 2003; van IJzendoorn et al., 1992, 2000). Put another way, attachment security is a product of both infant and maternal characteristics. Where there is a match between the baby's behaviors and the expectations or understanding of the caregiver, a phenomenon known as **goodness-of-fit**, there is a greater likelihood that sensitive-yet-effective care can be provided (Chess & Thomas, 1996).

In one study, mothers' sensitivity to infants who tended to show distress or respond in negative ways to the environment was shown to be the primary factor related to the quality of the attachment relationship. Mothers who were more sensitive and effective at soothing their irritable 6-month-old infants were more likely to have securely attached 12-month-olds than were mothers who were less sensitive and less effective (Susman-Stillman et al., 1996). Similar findings were reported in a study in which security of attachment was predicted by maternal personality. Infants who had a tendency to become distressed were more likely to be insecurely attached at 13 months if they had mothers who had relatively rigid and constraining personalities. Distress-prone infants whose mothers were more flexible, by contrast, were more likely to be securely attached (Mangelsdorf et al., 1990). Parent education may help new parents recognize their infant's behavioral tendencies and learn to adjust their caregiving to meet their child's needs, leading to more harmonious, effective interactions.

The majority of studies of low-risk preterm infants indicate an equal prevalence of secure and insecure attachment among preterm and full-term infants (van IJzendoorn et al., 1992). For very low birth weight (VLBW) preterm infants, however, the risks may be elevated. Infants born more than 4 weeks early and weighing, on average, less than 1,000 grams were assessed at 14 and 19 months. By 19 months, VLBW infants were more likely to be insecurely attached, possibly because the caregiving system was under significant stress (Mangelsdorf et al., 1996). Parents of these infants may actually experience increasing psychological distress as their children fall behind their full-term peers in achieving developmental milestones. The increase in insecure attachment in the VLBW group may also reflect diminishing social support provided to parents of preterm infants beyond the first birthday. These results, and similar findings from a recent study of families with triplets, suggest that parents of VLBW infants are likely to benefit from sustained support for the multiple challenges entailed in parenting high-risk children during infancy and beyond (Feldman, Eidelman, & Rotenberg 2004; Mangelsdorf et al., 1996).

Culture and Attachment. Cross-cultural research examining parents' ideas about attachment behavior has shown that both differences and similarities exist. In one study comparing lower-income Puerto Rican mothers with lower- and middle-income European American mothers, the secure pattern in the Strange Situation was overwhelmingly preferred across cultures and socioeconomic groups. Mothers' judgments about insecure patterns, however, varied as a function of culture. Puerto Rican mothers gave negative ratings to the independent behavior of insecure-avoidant infants, whereas European American mothers responded negatively to the clinging, dependent behavior of insecure-resistant infants (Harwood, Miller, & Irizarry, 1995).

Mothers of 2- to 3-year-old children in six diverse cultures (China, Colombia, Germany, Israel, Japan, and the United States) also tended to agree about behaviors that are characteristic of an "ideally secure" child—namely, using the mother as a base for exploration (Posada et al., 1995). There were cross-cultural differences in mothers' views about the importance of their children maintaining physical contact with them, showing positive emotions when complying with their requests, and being willing to interact with other adults.

Even with the apparently universal appeal of secure-base behavior, it is important to remember that there may also be variability *within* cultures (Bugental & Grusec, 2006; Ianzito, 2004; Shweder et al., 2006; Thompson, 1998, 2006). A good example of this comes from studies of Israeli kibbutz-reared infants (Sagi et al., 1985, 1995). When kibbutz-dwelling infants who experienced traditional communal sleeping arrangements apart from their parents were compared with infants also living in kibbutzes who slept at home, infants in the traditional group showed higher levels of insecure-resistant attachment (Sagi et al., 1994).

Attachment and Subsequent Development

According to attachment theory, security of attachment affects children's expectations— their internal working models—about relational partners, and children interact with new individuals in ways that reflect and confirm their beliefs about social roles and relationships. Securely attached children are thus more likely to have positive expectations and to behave in ways with others that elicit positive behaviors from them. Insecurely attached children, on the other hand, tend to have negative expectations and are more likely to enact roles that they are familiar with, displaying dependency, hostility, or indifference, which negatively influences the behavior of new social partners (Sroufe, 1979; Sroufe, Carlson, & Schulman, 1993; Sroufe & Fleeson, 1986; Thompson, 1998).

Attachment theory also predicts that securely attached children will tend to have positive models of the self that make them curious and confident about exploring their environment, motivated to persevere when faced with challenges, and resilient enough to adapt to new situations and ask for assistance when they perceive the need for it. Insecurely attached children, by contrast, are believed to have incorporated their caregivers' negative views and reactions into their model of the self. At an early age, these children may be less likely to explore their immediate environment, more likely to give up when confronted with challenges, and less able to monitor their own capabilities and seek help accordingly (Sroufe, 1979; Sroufe, Carlson, & Schulman, 1993; Teti & Teti, 1996; Thompson, 1998; Verschueren, Marcoen, & Schoefs, 1996).

In the short-term, secure attachment relationships appear to protect children from the physiological effects of stress. When infants become distressed, fearful, or anxious, levels of the stress hormone cortisol tend to increase, just as they do in human adults and in nonhuman primates. In some stressful situations that have been investigated, however, including the Strange Situation, securely attached infants and young children do not experience increases in the amount of cortisol, even though they appear distressed, afraid, and worried, as long as their parent is nearby. By contrast, for insecurely attached children and especially for disorganized/disoriented children, the parent's presence does not have the same buffering effect on the child's stress-hormone system (Hertsgaard, Gunnar, Erickson, & Nachmias, 1995; Nachmias et al., 1996; Spangler & Grossmann, 1993).

Infants' attachment relationships may also help them cope with the stress of adjusting to a new child care arrangement. At 15 months of age, securely attached infants in one study had lower physiological stress responses than insecurely attached infants during the transition to nonparental child care. Children's feelings of security were also enhanced when their mothers were sensitive to their feelings and spent time helping them adapt to the new arrangement (Ahnert et al., 2004). These findings also support another facet of attachment theory, the notion that securely attached children may continue to thrive to a greater extent than insecurely attached children because securely attached children are more likely to continue receiving sensitive, warm, responsive care from their primary caregivers as they move into new settings and negotiate new tasks (Lamb, 1987; Thompson, 1998).

One meta-analysis of links between attachment security and cognitive development found that basic intelligence did not differ between secure and insecure attachment groups, but there was a strong association between attachment and language, with securely attached children showing more competence than insecurely attached children. The researchers speculate that language development may be more optimally stimulated in secure attachment relationships because parents are better "teachers" and children are better motivated "students" (van IJzendoorn, Dijkstra, & Bus, 1995, p. 115). Put another way, secure children tend to be "more receptive to the parent's instruction, guidance, and teaching" (Shonkoff & Phillips, 2000, p. 238).

To the extent that securely attached children are receptive to other adults' instruction, guidance, and teaching, they would be predicted to adjust more easily to school and to receive more positive evaluations from teachers. These findings have been reported in longitudinal research comparing attachment classifications from infancy with measures (shown in Table 9.4) in early childhood and into late adolescence (Carlson, Sroufe, & Egeland, 2004;

TABLE 9.4   Measures Used in the Mother-Child Longitudinal Study

Child Age	Measure
Prenatal	Maternal medical history
Birth–10 days	Infant medical history, Neonatal Behavioral Assessment Scale
	Maternal history of abuse and psychological problems, relationship status, risk status
3 months	Home observation of a feeding session
	Maternal rating of child's "personality" and behavioral tendencies (e.g., intensity, mood, adaptability, distractibility, persistence)
6 months	Home observation of play and teaching
12 & 18 months	Strange Situation
24 months	Laboratory problem-solving task with mother
42 months	Laboratory teaching task with mother
$4\frac{1}{2}$–5 years	Teacher and peer assessments of behavior grades 1, 2, 3, 6, and high school
10 & 15 years	Observation in four-week summer camp
13 years	Laboratory tasks with mother
$17\frac{1}{2}$ years	Self-assessment of affective disorders and schizophrenia
19 years	Self-assessment of dissociative disorders

Source: Based on information in Carlson, 1998; and Carlson et al., 2004.

Erickson, Sroufe, & Egeland, 1985; Grossmann, Grossmann, & Zimmermann, 1999; Sroufe, 1983). In fact, as a result of a comprehensive study begun in 1975, researchers are now able to examine long-term effects of attachment in adolescence and will eventually report data from young adulthood (Carlson, Sroufe, & Egeland, 2004). The study, known as the Mother-Child Interaction Project, recruited a large sample of lower income mothers while they were receiving prenatal care at public health clinics.

At 12 and 18 months of age, infants and their mothers were observed in the Strange Situation. A laboratory task was used at 24 months to assess mother-child interaction as they encountered a series of problems of increasing difficulty. When children were 42 months old, mothers were asked to teach them how to build specific types of block towers, name things with wheels, match colors and shapes, and follow a pattern on an Etch-a-Sketch® maze toy. Additional observations were carried out and information was gathered from teachers and peers from preschool through high school.

Taken together, the results have generally shown that children who were identified in infancy as securely attached receive higher ratings than insecurely attached children on a variety of measures of social skills and behaviors as well as measures of self-confidence and emotional health (, 1998; Carlson, Sroufe, & Egeland, 2004; Sroufe, Egeland, & Carlson, 1999; Thompson, 1998). Securely attached children also tend to have more positive relationships with peers and friends than insecurely attached children. In adolescence, a history of insecure attachment, especially disorganized/disoriented attachment, is associated with a higher risk of psychopathology (Carlson, 1998; van IJzendoorn et al., 1999). This finding is consistent with a meta-analysis of approximately 80 studies showing that disorganized/disoriented attachment is strongly predictive of a greater susceptibility to the effects of stress, more behavior problems, and a higher risk of dissociative behavior (van IJzendoorn et al., 1999).

Other types of infant attachment are not always a reliable predictor of later behavior and relationships (Belsky et al., 1996; van IJzendoorn et al., 1999). Not all insecurely attached infants, for example, have more behavior problems or interpersonal difficulties in childhood than securely attached infants. At least some of these patterns reflect sampling and other methodological issues (Belsky et al., 1996). Lack of stability may also be due to changes in the quality of the parent-child relationship over time. The specific contribution of a number of key influences—maternal characteristics and behavior, social support, and infant characteristics—is still not well understood but deserves further investigation (Shonkoff & Phillips, 2000; Thompson, 1998; Vondra et al., 1999). The possibility that attachment relationships may change on their own or improve through intervention provides hope for infants who experience adversity and instability early in life.

Sibling Relationships

We move now from "vertical" relationships involving infants and caregivers to relationships that are more "horizontal," specifically sibling relationships and relationships with peers and friends (Hartup, 1989). Relationships with siblings, peers, and friends vary along three basic dimensions—symmetry, closeness, and voluntariness (DeHart, 1999; Laursen, Hartup, & Koplas, 1996). Some brothers and sisters, such as twins, triplets, and other multiples, enter the family and grow up together, experiencing major milestones of development, including the development of attachment relationships, at the same time. Most siblings, however, do not experience development that is so closely synchronized.

On the dimension of symmetry, sibling relationships are more similar than parent-child relationships but more dissimilar than peer relationships. Compared to sibling relationships, relationships between same-age peers have fewer differences in physical, cognitive, and social development. As one researcher put it, sibling relationships are actually "*diagonal* relationships, with steepness of slope depending on age gap and individual characteristics and gradually changing from nearly vertical in early childhood to nearly horizontal by the end of adolescence" (DeHart, 1999, p. 282, italics in original).

The dimension of closeness refers to emotional intimacy and the number and type of interactions that are experienced. Siblings know each other extremely well and, especially in early childhood, tend to be closer physically and emotionally than they are with peers (a pattern that reverses itself by adolescence). Sibling relationships also tend to be more emotionally intense than peer relationships, in both positive and negative ways.

In terms of voluntariness, siblings do not create their own relationships, whereas peers and friends typically do so. Friendships and peer relationships are based on mutually positive interactions; they need to be managed if they are to continue, but this is not generally a prominent concern for siblings. As a result, siblings tend to play together more and have more conflicts than do peers and friends. Children tend to be more cooperative and flexible when interacting with friends than with siblings (DeHart, 1999).

Becoming a Sibling

It is not uncommon for firstborn children to experience the birth of a sibling negatively. Some preschool children become increasingly clingy, withdrawn, or aggressive or develop problems sleeping or using the toilet (Baydar, Greek, & Brooks-Gunn, 1997; Baydar, Hyle, & Brooks-Gunn, 1997; Brody, 1998; Dunn, Kendrick, & MacNamee, 1981).

Not all firstborns react negatively. Children who are younger than 18 months tend to show little disruption and negativity in comparison with preschool-age firstborns. Whether the firstborn is a boy or girl may also make a difference in firstborns' reactions. Preschool-age boys, in particular, have been reported to react more negatively than preschool-age girls to the baby's birth (Dunn, Kendrick, & MacNamee, 1981).

Firstborn children's friendships may help buffer negative effects of the birth of a sibling, as was found in one study of 3- to 5-year-old firstborn children whose families were expecting a second child. Firstborns responded more positively to the birth of their sibling if they and their friends were able to manage conflicts when they arose and if they engaged in fantasy play, including pretense that involved sibling-related themes (Kramer & Gottman, 1992). This finding suggests that parents can ease firstborns' adjustment to siblinghood by supporting their relationships with peers and friends.

Firstborns may also experience the arrival of a new baby more positively if their mother reinforces the existing parent-child bond before the new sibling is born (Gottlieb & Mendelson, 1990; Teti et al., 1996). Mothers who consistently behave in positive, helpful, and emotionally supportive ways not only tend to form a secure attachment relationship with their firstborns, but they are also more likely to create a similarly secure relationship with their second-borns (Ward, Vaughn, & Robb, 1988). A securely attached older sibling is less likely than an insecurely attached older sibling to show hostility when the mother shows attention only to the younger child. In addition, in the mother's absence, securely attached older siblings are more likely to respond to younger siblings' distress by trying to soothe and comfort them. These results were found in studies using a variation of the Strange Situation (shown in Table 9.2), in which interactions, separations, and reunions involved the mother and both siblings (Stewart, 1983; Stewart & Marvin, 1984; Teti & Ablard, 1989).

Like parents, older siblings may provide a secure base for infants and toddlers in new settings. When 2-year-olds and their mothers were observed with and without 4-year-old siblings in the backyard of an unfamiliar home, even during their first visit, younger siblings traveled greater distances from their mothers when older siblings were present. Older siblings provided emotional comfort and security. Very few younger siblings showed distress when the older sibling was present, but some younger siblings cried or indicated that they wanted to leave in the sibling-absent condition. The mere presence of older siblings also led to greater exploration of the space and the toys and other objects in it (Samuels, 1980).

When a second child is born, the existing family system evolves. The new sibling subsystem creates different issues for parents to consider, especially after the second child becomes more independently mobile and the possibility of conflicts over space and possessions increases (Dunn & Kendrick, 1982; Kojima, 1999; Kreppner, 1988; Parke & Buriel, 2006; Teti, 2002). Mothers adapt to this new system by using a variety of means to influence their children's interactions and tailoring those methods to each child's developmental level. Mothers' regulating behaviors affect the quality of sibling interactions. If mothers refer to infant siblings' emotions or actions, for example, older siblings are more likely to direct positive behaviors toward them (Howe & Ross, 1990). Talking about and interpreting family members' feelings and actions also help link the existing mother-child relationship to the newer sibling relationship (Dunn, 1998, 2002).

How Siblings Contribute to Development

In many parts of the world, older siblings contribute directly to their younger siblings' development by serving as their primary caregivers when parents are working or caring for a newborn infant (Zukow-Goldring, 2002). Even where this is not a typical arrangement, siblings affect each other through their daily interactions. These interactions change over time, as the diagonal "slope" between siblings becomes less steep, and initially large differences in siblings' abilities begin to diminish (Abramovitch et al., 1986; Dunn & Brown, 1996).

Sibling interactions are both intensely positive and intensely negative, and some of the most revealing studies have focused on conflicts between brothers and sisters in their own homes. One study began when the second-born child in each family was 14 months old and ended when that child was 24 months old. Sibling conflicts became more physically aggressive over time, with younger siblings increasingly joining their older siblings in initiating conflicts. By 18 months, younger siblings also showed increasing understanding of

This girl's mother reinforces their relationship at the same time that she encourages her to form a positive relationship with her baby brother.

how to annoy the older sibling, especially through teasing. Younger siblings became aware of their mother's reactions to conflicts and learned to appeal to them for help when the older child had started the conflict but not when they themselves had been the aggressor (Dunn & Munn, 1985).

Children's early experience in family conflicts contributes to their understanding of others' feelings, thoughts, and actions. Sibling interactions are also linked to children's experience and competence in peer relationships (DeHart, 1999; Herrera & Dunn, 1997). Although siblings typically play complementary roles, in which the older child is more often the initiator and the younger child is more frequently the imitator and submitter, peer relationships can also be complementary when one child has the "home field advantage" (Abramovitch et al., 1986, p. 228). Rather than consistently playing the subordinate role, therefore, younger siblings learn both parts and can "step into a dominant role when the situation permits" (p. 228).

Peer Relationships and Friendship

Many interactions with peers and friends from birth to age 3 take place in what might be considered neutral territory, childcare settings and preschool classrooms. What do we know about infants' and very young children's capacity to interact with one another in the absence of either child's mother? Until relatively recently, many people—including experts in child development—believed that peer relationships and friendships among children younger than 2 years of age either did not exist or could not be studied. When researchers began to use reports from adults who spend time caring for infants and toddlers, as well as direct observations of young children's interactions, it became possible to explore children's earliest friendships and peer relationships (Howes, 1996; Rubin, Bukowski, & Parker, 1998, 2006; Shonkoff & Phillips, 2000).

Peer Interactions

An important finding from studies of interactions involving 12- to 18-month-old children is that groups of unacquainted peers behave differently with one another than do groups of peers who are well acquainted. Toddlers who know each other well have even been observed participating in unexpectedly advanced activities, such as coordinated games and cooperative fantasy play (Howes, 1985, 1988, 1996; Howes & Matheson, 1992; Howes & Unger, 1989). In one observation of groups of toddlers attending the same childcare centers, the youngest children (16 to 17 months of age) engaged in simple social play involving taking turns interacting with toys. A surprisingly advanced form of play—cooperative social pretend play—was observed in all of the children over 30 months of age and in half of the children just under the age of 24 months. Although other researchers had found that this form of play usually does not appear until at least 3 years of age, children's familiarity with one another may have supported its earlier emergence in this sample (Howes, 1985).

In numerous ways, mothers and fathers influence children's peer relationships and social competence. High quality play with fathers helps young children, especially boys, learn about the regulation of negative emotions that may arise during play that is physical and competitive. Fathers as well as mothers influence children's peer interactions by serving as advisors, social guides, and rule providers, giving advice, supervising play, and making or enforcing standards during play with peers. Like mothers, fathers are often managers of children's social opportunities, arranging play dates and choosing specific social activities (Parke et al., 2004).

Friendship

A large body of evidence now exists to suggest that very young children should be credited with the capacity to form true friendships that involve companionship, mutual affection, intimacy, and closeness (Rubin et al., 1998, 2006). By approximately 12 months of age, toddlers who spend time together prefer some of their peers to others and seek them out. Children show their compatibility and mutual preference by spending significant amounts of time together and by frequently achieving a high level of interaction whenever social contact is made. Parents and other caregivers are often aware of their children's social preferences, especially when verbal skills advance enough to enable children to talk about their friends (Howes, 1996). There is also evidence that very young children's peer preferences tend to be stable. Many preschool children's friendships begin when they are toddlers, and they show the special connection that they feel through consistent efforts to play together and stay close to one another (Rubin et al., 2006; Shonkoff & Phillips, 2000).

Toddlers who are friends, like older children who are friends, tend to be similar in their activity levels, interaction styles, and social skills. Children show a preference for same-sex peers as early as 30 to 36 months of age and are thus more likely to become friends with same-sex peers (Serbin et al., 1994). Children who are friends often play familiar games and engage in favorite routines. As they develop the ability for social imitation, cooperation, and role reversal during play, young children who are friends build on their shared social skills and are able to play together at a more complex level than children who are not friends (Howes, 1983, 1996).

These girls have been friends for most of their young lives. Their interactions involve mutual affection, sharing, and a strong preference to play together.

Young children's mutual affection and intimacy with friends is reflected in a number of ways. Children who are friends tend to share emotions frequently, smiling or laughing together while looking at each other. The emotional significance of early friendships is also seen in the finding that children who are friends and move up to the next age grouping in a child care setting together tend to adjust better than if they are moved alone (Howes, 1988). In addition, toddlers tend to respond to friends' emotional distress by attempting to comfort or help them, but they are less likely to do so if a nonfriend is distressed (Howes & Farver, 1987).

WRAPPING IT UP: Summary and Conclusion

Relationships are important in infancy and across the life span. Socialization goals and practices vary widely across cultures, however, as does the number and type of relationships beyond the infant-parent relationship. Some relationships, like the infant-parent relationship, are "vertical" and are characterized by an asymmetry of social power, skills, and experience. Other relationships, such as those between siblings, peers, and friends, are "horizontal" in the sense that they involve partners who are similar in terms of roles, abilities, and knowledge.

As our exploration of the vast literature on early social interactions has shown, the first 3 years of life are a critical time for the development of both types of relationships. Children are born prepared to form relationships with those who care for them, and those early experiences influence the relationships that they develop within the family and in the greater world outside of the home. Out of those relationships, children learn to differentiate and respond appropriately to the demands of different partners.

One of the greatest social challenges that very young children face is learning to control their emotional responses across different settings and with different partners. Parents, siblings, and peers all play a role in the socialization of emotion, a topic that we will explore in our next chapter. We will also consider when and how children develop a sense of themselves as coherent individuals who continue to exist despite situational variations in their behavior and feelings.

THINK ABOUT IT: Questions for Reading and Discussion

1. Compare the importance of "vertical" and "horizontal" relationships. Are they equally important across the first 3 years of life? If not, how does their influence change?

2. A number of universal aspects of infant-caregiver relationships have been identified, but there are also many cross-cultural differences. What do these patterns tell you about social development from birth to age 3?

3. Compare the influence of mothers and fathers on babies during the first 3 years of life. To the extent that differences in these roles exist, how do they influence development in infancy and toddlerhood?

4. How do disturbances in the infant-caregiver relationship, such as maternal depression or maltreatment, affect infants' development?

5. If you knew a couple considering adopting an infant from an orphanage, what advice would you give them? What sort of information would you suggest that they gather about the infant or the institution? How would that information be useful?

6. How does the attachment relationship affect physical, cognitive, and social development? Are there other aspects of development that might also be affected by the attachment relationship? How might you study those effects?

7. Compare the importance of the attachment relationship with the influence of sibling and peer relationships from birth to age 3.

8. What are some of the things that parents can do to help their firstborn child adjust well to the birth or adoption of a younger infant sibling?

KEY WORDS

Accessibility (295)	A dimension of parental involvement that reflects presence and availability to the child
Attachment behaviors (305)	Infants' built-in behaviors, such as crying, cooing, smiling, looking at, and reaching for caregivers, that attract attention and elicit care
Attachment Q-Sort (AQS) (307)	A rating system that can be used outside of a laboratory setting to assess individual differences in infant-caregiver attachment relationships
Attachment relationship (305)	The special relationship that develops over the first year of life between infants and the adults who care for them
Bidirectional (291)	Interactions that involve reciprocal behaviors and responses between social partners

Disorganized/disoriented attachment (309)	An infant-caregiver relationship that may develop when caregivers show contradictory, disrupted, or otherwise unusual emotional communication with their infants; also referred to as Type D
Dyadic synchrony (291)	Interactions between infants and caregivers that are characterized by mutual attention and affective matching or regulation
Effectance (292)	The feeling of moving between different states, including from a state of nonsynchrony to a state of synchrony
Engagement (295)	A dimension of parental involvement that reflects direct contact and interaction with the child
Goodness-of-fit (311)	A match between an infant's behaviors and the caregiver's expectations and understanding of those behaviors
Indiscriminate friendliness (303)	Behavior that is affectionate and friendly toward all adults, including strangers, without the fear or caution characteristic of normal children; often observed in children adopted from orphanages or other institutional settings
Insecure-avoidant attachment (308)	An infant-caregiver relationship that may develop when caregivers are overstimulating and intrusive when interacting with their infants; also referred to as Type A
Insecure-resistant attachment (308)	An infant-caregiver relationship that may develop when caregivers are rejecting or withdrawn, depressed, and unresponsive to infants' needs and attachment behaviors; also referred to as Type C
Internal working model (306)	Infants' mental representations of their relationship with their primary caregiver(s)
Maltreatment (301)	Neglect, medical neglect, physical abuse, sexual abuse, or psychological abuse
Postpartum depression (299)	A sense of despair and sadness so pervasive that it affects a mother's ability to care for and interact effectively with her baby; approximately 15 percent of new mothers are affected in this way
Reactive attachment disorder (310)	A recently proposed type of attachment that may develop in institutionalized infants who are severely maltreated
Responsibility (295)	A dimension of parental involvement that reflects participation in tasks such as taking the child to the doctor, arranging play dates, and monitoring activities
Secure attachment relationship (307)	An infant-caregiver relationship that develops when caregivers respond quickly and sensitively to their infant's signs of distress and other attachment behaviors; also referred to as Type B
Strange Situation (307)	A laboratory procedure that Ainsworth developed to assess individual differences in infant-caregiver attachment relationships

Temperament, Emotions, and the Self

In the United States in 2005, the three most popular names given to baby boys were Jacob, Michael, and Joshua, while the three most popular names for girls were Emily, Emma, and Madison (Social Security Administration, 2006). As shown in Table 10.1, many thousands of parents chose these names for their babies, yet none of the 25,347 Jacobs or 23,544 Emilys will grow up to be the *same* Jacob or Emily. Each will be shaped by a unique interaction of biologically based tendencies and environmental influences. In this chapter, we examine infants' early behavioral and emotional responses to the people and events they encounter. We also consider how infants' behaviors, and the responses those behaviors evoke, contribute to the development of a unique self.

If it had been possible in 2006 to gather together in an enormous playroom all of the Jacobs and all of the Emilys who were born in just one month in 2005, we would have noticed differences in their responses to the large crowd. Some infants would have been moving around, wide eyed with interest, joyfully taking in all of the different sights and sounds, while other infants would have been looking timid, perhaps even crying. There would also have been differences in infants' ability to adjust to the unusual circumstances, with some children quickly appearing comfortable and happy, and others taking more time

TABLE 10.1   Top Ten Baby Names for Boys and Girls, 2005

	Name	Number of Infants
Boys		
1	Jacob	25,347
2	Michael	23,324
3	Joshua	22,775
4	Matthew	21,045
5	Ethan	21,039
6	Andrew	20,323
7	Daniel	19,776
8	Anthony	19,016
9	Christopher	18,871
10	Joseph	18,737
Girls		
1	Emily	23,544
2	Emma	19,976
3	Madison	19,240
4	Abigail	15,492
5	Olivia	15,453
6	Isabella	14,908
7	Hannah	14,553
8	Samantha	13,436
9	Ava	13,411
10	Ashley	13,092

Source: Based on Social Security Administration, 2006.

From birth, infants show differences in their emotional reactions to the people and situations they encounter. Some babies are drawn to novelty, whereas others are inhibited by it.

to become accustomed to being surrounded by so many unfamiliar peers. These diverse responses reflect variations in temperament, a theoretical construct about which there has been vigorous and sustained research as well intense debate and disagreement. In many ways, as we will see, the study of temperament is still in its own infancy.

Temperament

The first source of disagreement in the study of temperament concerns how to define and measure it. At a basic level, there is agreement that **temperament** consists of qualities which parents as well as researchers are able to discern, including irritability, soothability, motor activity, sociability, attentiveness, adaptability, response to novelty, arousal, and regulation of states (Kagan, 1994; Wachs & Bates, 2001). Temperament has also been defined as "constitutionally based individual differences in emotional, motor, and attentional reactivity and self-regulation" (Rothbart & Bates, 1998, p. 109). Beyond these descriptions, there is no clear consensus about how many dimensions of temperament exist or how to measure them. We will first consider the predominant ways in which researchers have defined and measured temperament in infancy. Then, because children's temperament influences their interactions with caregivers, we will explore links between temperament and attachment and, finally, discuss evidence of continuity between temperament in infancy and personality in childhood and beyond.

Defining and Measuring Temperament

It is clear that there are individual differences in infants' patterns of sleeping, waking, feeding, fussing, and crying (St. James-Roberts & Plewis, 1996), patterns that can be predicted from differences in fetal activity (DiPietro et al., 1996). There is also little debate that there are innate differences between infants in their reactions to new situations, people, and objects, but there is disagreement among researchers about how to conceptualize these

TABLE 10.2   Models of Infant and Toddler Temperament

Key Proponent(s)	Dimensions	Assessment Instrument
Thomas & Chess (1977)/Carey & McDevitt (1978)	Activity level Approach-withdrawal Adaptability Quality of mood Attention span/persistence Distractibility Rhythmicity/regularity Intensity of reactions Threshold of responsiveness	Revised Infant Temperament Questionnaire (RITQ)
Bates, Freeland, & Lounsbury (1979)	Fussy-difficult Unadaptable Dull Unpredictable	Infant Characteristics Questionnaire (ICQ)
Rothbart (1981)	Activity level Fear Distress to limitations Smiling and laughter Soothability Duration of orienting	Infant Behavior Questionnaire (IBQ)
Rothbart (2004)	Surgency/extraversion Negative affectivity Orienting/Regulation	
Buss & Plomin (1984)	Activity level Negative emotionality Sociability	Emotionality Activity Sociability Questionnaire (EAS)
Goldsmith (1996)	Anger proneness Pleasure Interest-persistence Activity level Social fearfulness	Toddler Behavior Assessment Questionnaire (TBAQ)

Source: Based on Bates, Freeland, & Lounsbury, 1979; Buss and Plomin, 1984; Carey and McDevitt, 1978; Goldsmith, 1996; Goldsmith et al., 1987; Rothbart, 1981, 2004; Rothbart & Bates, 1998, 2006; Thomas & Chess, 1977.

tendencies. As shown in Table 10.2, all definitions of temperament include basic dimensions of infants' activity level and emotional responsiveness, but some go on to make additional behavioral distinctions that others do not address (Goldsmith et al., 1987; Rothbart & Bates, 1998, 2006). These different approaches can make it difficult to make comparisons across studies of temperament, especially given the tendency for similar phenomena to be labeled differently by different researchers (Frick, 2004; Rothbart, 2004; Wachs & Bates, 2001). Although several models have been proposed, four views of temperament have dominated research in this area.

Thomas and Chess's Model of Temperament.   The first approach comes from the New York Longitudinal Study (NYLS) by Thomas, Chess, and their colleagues (Chess & Thomas, 1996; Thomas, Chess, & Birch, 1968; Thomas et al., 1963). As shown in Table 10.2, they assessed infants in terms of nine dimensions. Approximately 35 percent of the infants in the NYLS sample could not be categorized and were thus described as "average." Based on their observations of the remaining infants, however, the researchers identified three major temperament classifications comprised of ratings on the set of nine dimensions: "easy," "difficult," and "slow to warm up."

Thinking about our hypothetical baby party, Jacobs and Emilys who are "easy" babies (approximately 40 percent of the NYLS sample) would tend to show positive emotions, adapt well to the new situation and unfamiliar people, and react at a low or moderately intense level. "Difficult" Jacobs and Emilys, by contrast (approximately 10 percent of the NYLS sample), would be more likely to display negative moods, such as irritability; adjust slowly to the new situation and people; and show a high level of intensity in their reactions. Slow-to-warm-up babies (approximately 15 percent of the NYLS sample) would be likely to show negative emotions, and adjust slowly to the new situation but would be only moderately intense in their reactions and low in activity level.

Bates, Freeland, and Lounsbury (1979) developed the Infant Characteristics Questionnaire (ICQ) to explore the dimension of "difficultness," which is conceptualized as four dimensions that are shown in Table 10.2. Questions in the ICQ include "How much does your baby fuss in general?" and "When your baby gets upset, how vigorously does he/she cry and fuss?" Not all temperament researchers agree with the "difficultness" classification system. Rothbart (1984), for example, whose system we discuss next, does not measure a dimension of "difficulty" and has questioned whether the term "difficult" is useful or even desirable when studying temperament. Behavior that is difficult in one setting, she points out, may not be problematic in other settings, and behavior that some researchers define as difficult may not be perceived in the same way by caregivers or even by other researchers (Goldsmith et al., 1987).

Thomas and Chess advocate assessing children's temperament by observing them in a variety of naturalistic settings for an extended period of time. One temperament rating that incorporates the Thomas and Chess dimensions is the Revised Infant Temperament Questionnaire (RITQ) (Carey & McDevitt, 1978). The value of carrying out an accurate temperament assessment, Thomas and Chess argue, is that it makes it possible to determine whether a child's behavior problems are primarily the result of caregiving practices or actually reflect behavioral styles that are inherently part of the child's responsiveness to the world. In the Thomas and Chess account, temperament reflects innate, genetic aspects of the "wiring" of the newborn's brain, but these early traits evolve over time as the child develops cognitively and as the family and other caregiving environments influence the child. As a result, temperament is viewed as being only relatively stable over time (Goldsmith et al., 1987). One implication of this view is that parents and caregivers can respond to children's temperamentally based behaviors and preferences—as well as their own tendencies—and strive to achieve goodness-of-fit. As we discussed briefly in Chapter 9, goodness-of-fit is correlated with security of attachment and occurs when there is a match between the child's temperament and characteristics of the environment. Seen in this way, an infant with a high level of activity may be a good match for a parent who also has a high activity level but may require adjustments for a parent who usually prefers to be less active.

Rothbart's Framework. In the second major approach, Rothbart defines temperament as relatively stable, biologically based "individual differences in reactivity and self-regulation, observed in the domains of emotionality, motor activity, and attention" (Rothbart, 2004, p. 82; Rothbart & Derryberry, 1981). Unlike some other temperament theorists, Rothbart believes that "temperament can be observed at all ages as individual differences in patterns of emotionality, activity, and attention" (Goldsmith et al., 1987, p. 510). In her view, "temperament and personality are seen as broadly overlapping domains of study, with temperament providing the primarily biological basis for the developing personality" (Goldsmith et al., 1987, p. 510). As shown in Table 10.2, Rothbart initially developed the Infant Behavior Questionnaire (IBQ) to assess Duration of Orienting as well as five behavioral dimensions (Rothbart, 1981). Questions on the IBQ ask parents to rate the frequency with which particular behaviors occur, such as how often their infants cry loudly while waiting to be fed.

The dimensions represented in the IBQ are regarded as being present from birth but may not be observable until several months later or even toward the end of the first year of life. Different dimensions may also become salient at different points in early development. Rothbart notes, for example, that there is a biobehavioral shift at 2 to 3 months of age in which all infants show sharp increases in attending to people around them, smiling, and laughing; thereafter, individual differences in smiling and laughing tend to become more stable. Levels of distress, by contrast, appear to show distinctive patterns within individuals after approximately 6 months of age (Goldsmith et al., 1987).

Rothbart's model emphasizes stability of temperament over time, but it also includes a role for caregiver sensitivity (Rothbart, Derryberry, & Hershey, 2000). This perspective recognizes, for example, that some highly unreactive infants may require more conscious stimulation in order to become engaged in face-to-face interaction and that infants who cry with greater intensity may need different amounts and types of comforting (Jahromi, Putnam, & Stifter, 2004).

Recently, Rothbart's model has been revised to contain just three factors, shown in Table 10.2 (Rothbart, 2004). According to this model, infants who are high on surgency-extraversion show a high degree of positive emotions, seek out high-intensity activities, have a high activity level, tend to be impulsive, and are rarely shy. High scores on negative affectivity include a tendency to feel shy, to have difficulty being soothed, and to experience discomfort, fear, anger-frustration, and sadness. Scores for orienting/regulation reflect infants' perception and attention to the immediate setting and activities as well as the ease with which negative emotions can be influenced by cuddling and soothing (Derryberry & Rothbart, 1997; Rothbart, 2004; Rothbart et al., 2001; Rothbart & Bates, 1998, 2006). Additional exploration of these three factors may prove fruitful in bringing together the diverse set of models and terms that has been generated thus far in the study of temperament.

Buss and Plomin's Approach. A third major framework, proposed by Buss (1995; Buss & Plomin 1984; Goldsmith et al., 1987), focuses on three core dimensions that are included in the items on Buss and Plomin's (1984) Emotionality Activity Sociability (EAS) questionnaire. Within this system, the activity level dimension ranges from lethargy to extreme rapidity of vocalizing or speaking and moving. Emotionality ranges from barely discernible reactions to intense reactions that are out of control; emotionality is initially defined as strong arousal in response to events in the environment but becomes differentiated into fear and anger by 12 months of age. The sociability dimension varies from a preference for being alone to a strong tendency to seek out others with whom to interact and share activities.

According to Buss, temperament is a set of genetically based personality traits that appear during the first 2 years of life, traits that are distinct from those that are acquired or appear later in life. The focus is on only those traits that have a lasting effect on later personality and the model excludes traits that are regarded as irrelevant, such as rhythmicity (regularity in infants' eating and sleeping). In this view, although there may be temporary environmental effects, such as an illness that makes a normally active child less so, temperamental traits are generally stable over time and experience.

Goldsmith's Model.   A fourth perspective, contributed by Goldsmith (1996; Goldsmith & Campos, 1990), defines temperament as early individual differences in five dimensions of emotionality. Goldsmith developed the Toddler Behavior Assessment Questionnaire (TBAQ) to measure these dimensions of temperament in children aged 16 to 36 months. The TBAQ (shown in Table 10.2) is intended to extend upward Rothbart's IBQ, and several of the dimensions are the toddler version of an infant dimension: Distress to Limitations/Anger Proneness; Smiling and Laughter/Pleasure; and Duration of Orienting/Interest-Persistence.

Parents complete the TBAQ by rating their child in terms of the frequency with which behaviors are exhibited. Anger Proneness is assessed with questions such as "When you do not allow your child to do something for her/himself, for example, dressing or getting into the car seat, how often does our child try to push you away?" Pleasure is gauged with questions such as "When in the bathtub, how often does your child babble or talk happily?" Interest-Persistence is measured with questions such as "How often did your child play alone with his/her favorite toy for 30 minutes or longer?" Questions such as "When playing with a movable toy, how often does your child attempt to go as fast as s/he could?" measure Activity Level, while "When your child is being approached by an unfamiliar adult while shopping or out walking, how often does your child show distress or cry?" assess Social Fearfulness.

The Influence of Parental Report in Temperament Assessment.   Most studies of temperament use parental report questionnaires, a practice with both strengths and limitations (Kagan, 1998; Rothbart & Bates, 1998, 2006; Wachs & Bates, 2001). The main advantage of this approach is that parents have a vast amount of experience with their infants across a wide range of settings. Only parents and other caregivers would know, for example, that a researcher observing an infant for the first time in a new setting is seeing behaviors that are not typical of that child in other settings. Parental reports and questionnaires are also less expensive to use than other methods of assessing temperament, such as observations in the laboratory or the home.

Disadvantages of using parental reports include low to moderate levels of agreement between mothers and fathers as well as low to moderate levels of agreement between parents and researchers (Atella et al., 2003; Bornstein, Gaughran, & Segui, 1991). Lack of agreement between parents suggests that reports about temperament may contain a subjective element or bias; this possibility is also reflected in correlations that have been found in some studies between parental characteristics, such as parental preconceptions and maternal depression, and ratings of infant difficultness (Clarke-Stewart et al., 2000). In as much as temperament ratings are affected to some degree by parental perceptions, psychological functioning, experience, and preferences, they are cultural and personal constructions and may or may not resemble more objective descriptions (Kagan, 1998; Kiang, Moreno, & Robinson, 2004; Shwalb, Shwalb, & Shoji, 1996).

To address these concerns, some researchers have added parental diaries in which patterns of sleeping, crying, and fussing are recorded over several days (Atella et al., 2003; St. James-Roberts & Plewis, 1996). One study of parents' reports of difficultness in their 6-week-old infants used a multimethod approach combining maternal and paternal ICQ ratings, diary records of infants' state behaviors, and laboratory observations. Although mothers and fathers interpreted some infant behaviors differently, for mothers, reports of difficult temperament appeared to correspond to other measures of infants' crying and fussing behaviors (Atella et al., 2003).

In a study of 8- to 10-month-olds, researchers compared parental reports about infants' temperament with their responses during a laboratory procedure designed to elicit the emotions of joy, fear, anger, and distress (discomfort to aversive stimulation). They also observed infants' emotional tone during naturalistic interactions with their mothers. Elicited emotions in the laboratory were consistent with fathers' temperament ratings and with infants' emotional tone during interactions with mothers, providing support for the validity of parent reports (Kochanska et al., 1998).

Temperament and Neurophysiological Responses

A number of theorists have posited the existence of neurobehavioral characteristics that differentiate among temperaments, and there is some evidence of such markers from studies in controlled laboratory settings. Advances in instrumentation have enabled researchers to ask new questions about infant temperament and offer an attractive supplement to parent reports.

Heart Rate.   Greater variability in fetal heart rate has been correlated with greater emotional reactivity, as well as more irritability and difficulty in infancy (Porges, Doussard-Roosevelt, & Maiti, 1994). Other studies have reported links between fetal neurobehavior and temperament; more active fetuses tend to be rated by their mothers as being more difficult, less predictable, less adaptable, and more active in infancy (DiPietro et al., 1996). Kagan and his colleagues have reported that extremely shy children tend to have higher and less variable heart-rate responses to unfamiliar people and events than do extremely bold children (Kagan & Fox, 2006; Kagan, Reznick, & Snidman, 1988).

The Stress-Response System.   Other researchers have focused on links between temperamental differences and activation of the stress-response system. Gunnar and her colleagues, for example, have found correlations between 9-month-old infants' tendency to be distressed and measured levels of salivary cortisol (Gunnar, 1994; Gunnar et al., 1989, 1992; Gunnar, Malone, and Fisch, 1985; Nachmias et al., 1996; Stansbury & Gunnar,

1994). Interestingly, these studies show that cortisol responses differ in familiar and unfamiliar settings and are buffered when sensitive, responsive caregivers are available. Additional study of the role of cortisol is needed, however, since some studies have found that children who are rated as bold, outgoing, and even risk-taking also tend to show elevations of cortisol in novel settings when they are experiencing positive rather than negative emotions (Buss et al., 2004; Donzella et al., 2000).

Reactivity and Inhibition.   In studies of 1- and 2-year-old children, Kagan and Snidman (1991a, 1991b; Kagan, 1994) explored individual differences in responses to novel situations that they created in the laboratory. Their studies, which provide additional evidence of neurophysiological differences in temperament, focused on two extreme groups of children. They referred to one group as **inhibited to novelty** because they responded to unfamiliar people and places by consistently becoming "quiet, vigilant, restrained, and avoidant while they assess the situation and their resources before acting" (Kagan, 1994, p. 16). The second group of children, those who were **uninhibited to novelty**, consistently responded to equally unfamiliar situations with spontaneous engagement and interest.

These groups were explored further in a longitudinal study of infants at 2, 4, 9, 14, and 21 months of age (Kagan & Snidman, 1991a, 1991b). Two extreme patterns of response to novel visual, auditory, and olfactory stimuli were identified, patterns that predicted which infants would be inhibited and which uninhibited at the age of 2 years. At 4 months, infants were presented with a series of novel stimuli, including mobiles, toys, the sound of an unfamiliar woman's voice, and a sample of dilute butyl alcohol presented on a cotton swab. Some of the infants in this study were termed **high-reactive** and others were classified as **low-reactive**. High-reactive infants showed "extreme degrees of motor activity, combined with fretting or crying" (Kagan, 1994, p. 17). These infants moved their arms and legs vigorously, arched their backs, and sometimes cried in response to the unfamiliar sights, sounds, and smells. Low-reactive infants, by contrast, showed low levels of motor activity and rarely cried or fussed. Both groups of infants were tested again at 14 and 21 months of age, when stimuli included toys that moved, a blood pressure cuff, electrodes, a noisy spinning bingo wheel, an unfamiliar woman who tried to get children to taste an unidentified liquid from a medicine dropper, an unfamiliar woman whose face was obscured from the child's view by a gas mask, and an unfamiliar woman with a black cloth over her head and shoulders. A small proportion of the high-reactive infants (about 15 percent of the total sample) were extremely fearful and inhibited at 14 and 21 months, whereas a slightly larger subsample of infants who had been low reactive (approximately 25 percent of the total sample) responded with a degree of positive emotion and interest that led them to be classified as uninhibited.

In addition to behavioral responses, the researchers measured heart rates of children in their longitudinal study and found that high-reactive (but not low-reactive) 4-month-olds had had higher heart rates both before birth and 2 weeks after birth. There were also group differences in the rate at which children's heart rates increased in response to novel events during the laboratory sessions. Moreover, inhibited (as compared with uninhibited children) also showed greater pupillary dilation and larger changes in blood pressure in response to stimuli. Kagan interpreted these findings as evidence that high-reactive infants were genetically predisposed to have a lower threshold for activation of the sympathetic nervous system—the source of the "fight or flight" response—whereas low-reactive infants inherited a higher threshold (Kagan 1994; Kagan, Snidman, & Arcus, 1998). Subsequent findings of continuity between inhibition at age 2 years and social anxiety at age 13 years have supported Kagan's conclusions, at least for the extreme groups in his studies (Biederman et al., 2001; Kagan & Fox, 2006; Kagan & Snidman, 1999; Schwartz, Snidman, & Kagan, 1999).

One longitudinal study examined early inhibition in children whose mothers were depressed and in a comparison group of children whose mothers were not depressed. When the children were toddlers, the researchers assessed their inhibition to novel social and nonsocial events and at the age of 5 years, children were observed interacting with an unfamiliar peer. Those who had been extremely socially inhibited as toddlers were more shy and inhibited with the peer, especially during the initial interaction, and they sought to be closer to their mothers than children who had not been inhibited at the first assessment. No differences in behavior were found as a function of maternal depression, suggesting that children's temperamental reaction to novelty played a more significant role in their behavior at age 5 (Kochanska & Radke-Yarrow, 1992).

Kagan's procedures were also used to study infants whose mothers had clinically diagnosed panic disorder. The researchers videotaped these infants and a comparison group as they encountered Kagan's stimuli at 4 and 14 months of age. Mothers in this study also completed the IBQ temperament subscale to rate their infants' responses to sudden or novel stimuli at both 4 and 14 months. Infant salivary cortisol samples were also obtained at both ages. No behavioral differences between infants of mothers with panic disorder and comparison infants were observed in response to Kagan's stimuli. Infants of mothers with panic disorder had higher cortisol levels than comparison infants at both ages, however, suggesting that they were more distressed. Mothers with panic disorder appeared to be aware of their infants' susceptibility to distress and, despite the absence of behavioral differences, rated their 4-month-olds significantly higher on this dimension of the temperament questionnaire. Given that infants whose mothers have panic disorder may themselves be at higher risk for anxiety disorders, measures of cortisol response may offer a promising method for early detection and therapy (Warren et al., 2003).

Other studies of neurophysiological responses, fear, and temperament using less extreme or nonclinical samples have not uniformly supported Kagan's conclusions (Buss et al., 2003; Schmidt et al., 1997; Schmidt et al., 1999). Additional research using more similar measures and comparable samples is needed to understand these connections (Buss et al., 2004). For now, it seems reasonable to conclude that even initial predispositions may be altered by subsequent experience, since not all high-reactive infants in Kagan's study became extremely inhibited 2-year-olds or socially anxious 13-year-olds.

Temperament and Attachment

In Chapter 9, we noted that some attachment theorists explain similarity in children's attachment to different caregivers as the result of the caregivers' shared goals and co-constructed views of the child, which then produce similar caregiving behavior. As might be expected, temperament researchers offer a different explanation. Pointing to modest but significant concordances between children's attachment classifications to mothers and fathers, they emphasize that the infant's temperament elicits similar responses from different caregivers during the Strange Situation and across many other settings, thereby contributing to similarity in attachment security (Fox, Kimmerly, & Schafer, 1991). In this account, infants who are distressed by separation from their mothers are also distressed by separation from their fathers, and it is their consistent distress that evokes similar responses from both parents.

Given that infants with a difficult temperament place greater demands on caregivers than do infants with an "easy" temperament, parents' sensitivity and responsiveness is thought to have a significant influence on security of attachment. The research literature on links between attachment and temperament indicates that it is possible for infants who are temperamentally difficult, irritable, or prone to distress to become securely attached to their caregivers, provided that those caregivers are sensitive, responsive, and emotionally warm (Belsky & Rovine, 1987; Mangelsdorf et al., 1990; Mangelsdorf & Frosch, 1999; Susman-Stillman et al., 1996; Vaughn & Bost, 1999). Parents of irritable newborns who do not respond consistently to their infants' crying, by contrast, are more likely to have insecurely attached infants (van den Boom, 1989, 1994, 2001).

In one study, infants who showed higher levels of irritability in the Neonatal Behavioral Assessment Scale were significantly more likely than nonirritable newborns to be insecurely attached when assessed in the Strange Situation at 12 months (van den Boom, 1989). There is also limited evidence of links between parent reports of dimensions of temperament (e.g., distress) and specific behaviors during the Strange Situation (e.g., fussiness or resistance), but links between temperament measures and Strange Situation attachment classification per se have seldom been found (Rothbart & Bates, 1998, 2006; Shaw & Vondra, 1995). When attachment has been assessed using the Attachment Q-Set (AQS), however, stronger correlations have emerged, especially for toddlers and children as old as 3 years (Seifer & Schiller, 1995; Seifer et al., 1996; Vaughn et al., 1992). In general, children who are rated higher on temperamental measures of negative emotional reactivity tend to be rated lower for attachment security in the AQS.

Temperamental "difficultness" has been linked to less optimal outcomes later in childhood. One study of infants adopted by Dutch families before the age of 6 months followed them until they were 7 years old. Attachment security was assessed in the Strange Situation at 12 months of age, and a Dutch version of the ICQ was used to measure temperament at 12, 18, and 30 months. Maternal sensitivity was assessed at 12, 18, and 30 months and once more at 7 years. Several additional measures of socioemotional and cognitive development were used at 7 years. Higher levels of maternal sensitivity and secure attachment led to better outcomes, suggesting that early caregiving interactions influenced subsequent development. There were still influences of temperament, however. Easy temperament was associated with better outcomes for cognitive, social, and personality development at age 7, whereas infants who were temperamentally difficult had poorer childhood outcomes. The combination of disorganized attachment and difficult temperament was associated with less optimal cognitive and personality development (Stams, Juffer, & van IJzendoorn, 2002).

A difficult temperament may also interact with quality of care to produce unexpectedly positive outcomes. In one investigation, 12-month-old infants whose mothers rated them on the IBQ as more likely to show distress to novelty had higher IQ scores on the Stanford–Binet Intelligence Scale at 36 months of age, but only if the infants had been classified as insecurely attached in the Strange Situation (Karrass & Braungart-Rieker, 2004). The researchers speculate that infants who are temperamentally fearful and who live in caregiving environments that are insufficiently sensitive and responsive may have heightened wariness and, in the absence of predictable caregiver behavior, learn to depend on their own attention to the environment. This increased attention, they suggest, may promote cognitive growth that is reflected in IQ scores, an effect that has also been reported in other studies of temperament-linked attentiveness and language and cognitive development (Karrass et al., 2002).

Interventions to help parents of irritable, difficult infants become more skilled in noticing, interpreting, and responding to their infants' cries have proved effective in enhancing the development of secure attachment. This was found in one study with lower-income mothers whose infants were extremely irritable from birth. When mothers were instructed to read and respond promptly to their infants' cues at 6 and 9 months of age, security of attachment in the Strange Situation was higher than among a group of control mothers and infants. Infants in the intervention group were also more sociable in their interactions with their mothers and had higher levels of exploration (van den Boom, 1989, 1994, 2001).

Some researchers have begun to explore whether certain positive or adaptable "easy" temperaments may provide protection from the effects of nonoptimal early caregiving in settings such as orphanages. Investigators involved in the Bucharest Early Intervention Project (a study of Romanian orphanages which we discussed in Chapter 9), for example, note that not all infants who experience serious maltreatment and environmental adversity in institutional settings develop reactive attachment disorder or other forms of psychopathology (Cicchetti & Toth, 2006; Zeanah & Fox, 2004). As developmental psychologists and clinicians begin to collaborate, there are many important questions to pursue, and answers may be forthcoming if differences in definitions and methods can be overcome (Frick, 2004; Lahey, 2004).

Temperament and Personality

To varying degrees, the major models of temperament propose that infant temperament is related to later personality and behavior. Temperamental qualities related to irritability, negative affective, and difficultness are generally expected to predict behavior problems that include internalizing (e.g., withdrawal) and externalizing (e.g., aggression). Temperamental fearfulness in response to novelty, by contrast, is conceptually linked principally with internalizing and social anxiety. Positive affect, sociability, activity level, and surgency/extraversion are thought to be linked to lower levels of behavior problems (Rothbart & Bates, 1998, 2006).

Continuity from infancy into childhood has been reported for a variety of measures and dimensions of temperament. The results of numerous studies suggest that the longer the time between comparisons, and the older the ages being compared, the greater the degree of continuity (Bates et al., 1991; Buss, 1995; Carey & McDevitt, 1978; Caspi, 2000; Hubert et al., 1982; Korn, 1984; Lee & Bates, 1985; Lemery et al., 1999; Thomas & Chess, 1982).

As we have already seen, there is evidence that high-reactive infants who show extremely negative (fearful) reactions to novel objects are also more likely than low-reactive infants to become inhibited and distressed in response to novel objects and situations during childhood and early adolescence (Kagan, 1998). Theoretically compatible findings were reported in a different study using parental ratings rather than direct observations of behavior. Toddlers who were rated lower on sociability (higher on shyness) in Buss and Plomin's (1984) EAS questionnaire were more likely to be rated as socially withdrawn at 4 years of age (Hagekull, 1994).

Recently, researchers in Sweden used a sample of 85 families to examine links between infant temperament, attachment, and personality traits in middle childhood (approximately 8 to 9 years of age) (Hagekull & Bohlin, 2003). Attachment to mother was assessed in the Strange Situation at 15 months, and parents used the EAS to rate their child's temperament at 20 months of age. Personality in middle childhood was rated by mothers and teachers using the Five Factor Model (FFM), a widely recognized system for studying the structure of personality (Rothbart, Ahadi, & Evans, 2000). Infant temperament and attachment security predicted the FFM factor of Extraversion/Surgency in middle childhood. As expected, infants who were rated higher on the Activity and Sociability dimensions were later rated higher in Extraversion/Surgency. Attachment security was also related to several FFM factors: securely attached infants were rated in childhood as being more extraverted, more open to experience, and more emotionally stable than children who had been insecurely attached as infants. The researchers interpret their findings in terms of attachment theory, which holds that security of attachment produces internal working models promoting positive interactions and exploration.

A longitudinal study of 1,300 children from Finland provides additional relevant evidence, although the first temperament ratings were not made until children ranged from 3 to 12 years of age (Pesonen et al., 2002). Mothers completed Buss and Plomin's (1984) EAS questionnaire at the initial measurement, and 17 years later the now-adult children used the EAS to provide self-ratings. There was significant but weak evidence of continuity between childhood ratings and those provided in adulthood. Children who had been rated low in sociability (indicating perceived social maladjustment) tended to rate themselves higher on items measuring anger (irritability, aggressiveness, and impatience) in adulthood. A measure of difficult temperament in infancy (not part of the EAS per se) showed slightly stronger continuity with an adult measure of difficult temperament (conceptualized as a combination of high activity-tempo, high anger, and low sociability).

In keeping with these findings, other comparisons of early temperament ratings at age 3 and self-reported personality traits in adulthood have found that children who were more impulsive and showed less self-control tended to be less likely as adults to report avoiding harm and more likely to be socially alienated. In addition, children who were inhibited were more likely as adults to avoid harm, less likely to be aggressive, and less likely to be socially powerful (Caspi & Silva, 1995).

Taken together, these results generally indicate the long-term predictive value of early temperament measures. At the same time, however, the evidence for continuity has not always been strong, and there is not agreement about how to interpret the findings. Although the evidence points to a relatively direct link between infant temperament and subsequent behavior and personality, many questions still exist about the process through which early constitutional qualities exert their influence. Many temperament researchers favor an explanation in which temperament is seen as providing a context for subsequent development. In this way, a difficult temperament makes a child more vulnerable for later problems but does not inevitably lead to poorer behavior and outcomes (Rothbart & Bates, 1998, 2006). Given the intriguing findings thus far, it is clear that there is still a need for studies using larger samples, longitudinal designs, and multiple measures of temperament and personality (Caspi, 1998; Caspi & Shiner, 2006).

Emotions

All of the temperament measures that we have discussed include at least one dimension of infants' emotionality. Questions about infants' typical emotional reactions and mood imply that parents and other caregivers who spend time with particular infants are able to discern and differentiate between their displays of emotions such as fear, anger, and distress. Considering that temperament assessments have been carried out as early as 6 weeks of age, on what do parents base their ratings? As we begin our examination of emotional life during the first 3 years of life, we will answer this question by exploring a slightly different one; namely, on what do *researchers* base their ratings of infants' emotional expressions? We will also consider whether infants' observable expressions of emotion correspond to their subjective emotional experiences.

Expressing Emotions

If we wanted to know how the infants in our hypothetical Jacob-and-Emily playgroup were feeling, how could we find out? Given their preverbal status, asking them to tell us in words obviously would be of limited value, but a reasonable approach would be to study the expressions on their faces, perhaps noting what they and those around them were doing. We might also try smiling at them or showing them a toy in order to see how their facial expressions change in response. As we discuss next, this is in fact the basic approach that many researchers have taken.

According to some theories of emotional development, infants are either born with or very quickly develop a set of **primary emotions**. Primary emotions are relatively easy for most adult caregivers to notice and interpret correctly. At least some of these emotions may have survival value because they occur, for example, when infants are in distress due to pain or hunger (Witherington, Campos, & Hertenstein, 2001). Infants who are in distress not only cry, but they also show a configuration of facial muscular activity that has been shown to correspond to the subjective feeling of emotional distress (Izard, 1979; Oster, Hegley, & Nagel, 1992).

How many primary emotions are there? One pioneering infant emotion researcher, Carroll Izard (1977; Izard & Malatesta, 1987), asserted that there are eleven: interest, joy, surprise, sadness, anger, disgust, contempt, fear, shame, guilt, and shyness. Lewis (1995, 2000), by contrast, proposed that infants have just three primary emotions at birth: distress, interest, and pleasure. As shown in Table 10.3, additional primary emotions emerge as these initial responses are differentiated: distress gives rise to sadness, disgust, anger, and fear. Interest evolves into surprise, and pleasure is transformed into joy.

TABLE 10.3   Proposed Timeline for the Development of Emotions (Birth to 3 Years)

Birth	By 6 months	By 18 months	By 24 months
Distress	Sadness	Embarrassment	Guilt
	Disgust	Jealousy	Shame
	Anger		
	Fear		
Interest	Surprise		Pride
Pleasure	Joy		

Source: Based on Lewis, 1995.

Is there any evidence of emotional experience at birth or in the first months of life? Researchers exploring this question have relied on infants' facial expressions. As we learned in Chapter 6, newborns who are given sweet-tasting liquids smile with apparent pleasure, a facial expression that is not displayed when unpleasant smelling and bad tasting substances are presented. Observers in one study who did not know what infants had just tasted or smelled were able to judge their emotional reactions accurately (Ganchrow, Steiner, & Daher, 1983; Steiner, 1979).

In addition, when 1- to 9-month-old infants were videotaped in a wide range of settings, including playing with their mothers and receiving a shot in a doctor's office, adults who saw the videotapes were able to use infants' facial expressions to identify a range of corresponding discrete emotions, such as happiness, interest, fear, and anger (Izard et al., 1980). Other studies have confirmed what parents already know, namely, that young infants being given routine immunizations are in emotional distress, as their facial expressions indicate (Izard et al., 1983).

Infants begin to communicate anger, distinct from distress caused by pain, at a young age (Coie & Dodge, 1998; Dodge, Coie, & Lynam, 2006). This was shown in a study in which 1-, 4-, and 7-month-olds' forearms were restrained and held in front of them for a few minutes (Stenberg & Campos, 1990). One-month-olds showed a variety of negative facial expressions, none of which matched widely recognized criteria for the emotion of anger (Izard, 1979; Oster, Hegley, & Nagel, 1992). By 4 months of age, however, nearly half of infants studied displayed facial expressions that unequivocally showed anger. In a different study, 7-month-old infants consistently showed angry facial expressions when a desired object (a teething biscuit that they were eating) was removed against their wishes (Stenberg, Campos, & Emde, 1983).

As we saw in Chapter 9, infants of depressed mothers show expressions of sadness in early infancy, by 2 to 3 months of age. Sad facial expressions have also been observed in young infants whose mothers are not depressed but who suddenly "freeze" with their faces expressing no emotion at all—a well-known laboratory procedure referred to as the **still-face paradigm**, which we will discuss in greater detail shortly (Cohn & Tronick, 1983, 1987).

Infants show expressions of fear after the age of about 6 months. This is reflected in their increasing wariness around unfamiliar adults (Mangelsdorf, 1992) and in their

This baby's attachment to his father is evident in his initial wariness toward his father's co-worker.

reactions in laboratory situations intended to induce fear, such as those involving toys that make sudden, unexpected movements toward them (Buss & Goldsmith, 1998; Hiatt Campos, & Emde, 1979).

Raised eyebrows and wide eyes with an open mouth are key criteria for facial expressions of surprise (Izard, 1979). Facial expressions matching these criteria have been seen in 5- to 7-month-old infants, but they may also be displayed when infants are engaged in exploring toys (Camras, Lambrecht & Michel, 1996).

Infants begin to show joyful facial expressions and smiling between 2 and 3 months of age (Izard et al., 1995). Parents and other caregivers not only notice these signs of joy but they also work hard to elicit smiling and laughter through face-to-face playful interactions and tickling (Fogel et al., 1997). Infants' first laughs usually appear after the age of $2\frac{1}{2}$ months and then become a frequent part of face-to-face interactions (Nwokah & Fogel, 1993; Nwokah et al., 1999).

Beyond the first year, how do emotions develop? According to Lewis (1995, 2000), a set of **secondary emotions**—embarrassment, envy, empathy, pride, shame, and guilt— emerge in the second and third years of life as a result of cognitive development and the capacity for mental representation. These emotions are also referred to as **self-conscious emotions** (also called social emotions) because they require the ability to engage in self-reflective thought and to compare oneself or one's actions to standards and expectations that others hold. Each of the self-conscious emotions is associated with a unique set of body postures (Barret & Nelson-Goens, 1997; Stipek, Recchia, & McClintic, 1992). Children feeling shame, for example, seem to be trying to hide or disappear as they look downward and their body appears to collapse inward. Children who feel guilty, on the other hand, may move around as if trying to repair or undo specific mistakes that they have made. When feeling embarrassed, children tend to smile while alternately looking away from and then looking at people who are nearby. Feelings of pride seem to be expressed by smiling

This girl's attempts to hide her face as she looks downward suggest that she is experiencing a negative self-conscious emotion, such as shame.

broadly, "puffing up," and even raising the arms triumphantly. We will examine evidence for the development of these emotions later in this chapter as we consider how they contribute to children's capacity for self-regulation and prosocial behavior. We turn now to consider infants' ability to recognize emotions in others.

Perceiving Emotions

Just as the ability to express emotions appears to be functioning almost from birth, infants also appear to be able to notice and respond differentially to expressions of emotion in others from an early age, although perhaps not from birth. Initial studies with infants as young as 2 or 3 days old led some researchers to conclude that newborns are able to recognize and imitate specific facial expressions (Field et al., 1982, 1983; Meltzoff & Moore, 1983). Subsequent research revealed that neonates' responses were not specific to facial expressions. Tongue protrusion, it turned out, could be triggered by an adult sticking out his or her tongue at the infant but also by other interesting sights, such as a pencil moving toward and then away from them. These newer studies suggest that, rather than a reflection of efforts to match facial expressions modeled by adults, newborns' oral "matching" behaviors (which diminish after the age of about 2 months) may actually be a component of early exploratory behavior (Anisfeld, 1996; Jones, 1996).

Even though neonates may not be able to engage in expression-specific matching, there is still evidence that they are sensitive to others' emotions. This has been shown in numerous studies of infants' perception of facial expressions. Most of these studies have used either habituation procedures or paired comparisons (both of which we first discussed in Chapter 2). In habituation studies, infants are shown the same facial expression repeatedly until they are no longer interested in it. If the initial facial expression is replaced with a different face, researchers check to see whether infants show renewed interest, which is interpreted as evidence that they can discriminate between the two faces. In paired comparison studies, infants see two different facial expressions and researchers compare the total amount of time that they spend looking at each one. If there is a difference in looking time, it is interpreted as evidence that infants have noticed a difference between the two faces. As we discussed in Chapter 2, there are limitations to using looking time as a measure of infants' face perception, including knowing how to interpret infants' failure to respond differently to two given stimuli. It is also difficult to know whether infants understand the meaning of the faces that they are shown.

Results of many studies indicate that 2-month-old infants can discriminate between facial expressions of different emotions, such as happy versus sad or angry faces (Nelson & Horowitz, 1983). The ability to discriminate visually between faces is limited before the age of 2 to 3 months because neonates tend to scan only the edges of faces—the boundary between the forehead and hairline—rather than look at both internal and external features—the eyes, nose, and mouth. The ability to discriminate among variations within emotional categories, such as a closed-mouth smile versus an open-mouth smile, appears to develop at approximately 7 months of age (Nelson, 1987).

A number of studies have shown that infants are also able to engage in intermodal perception—matching expressions of emotion that they both see and hear. In these studies, infants are seated in front of two side-by-side video monitors showing two different facial expressions of emotion, such as happiness and anger. A single verbal or vocal soundtrack, corresponding to just one of the video displays, is played from a central location and researchers measure the amount of time infants spend looking at each facial expression. Across many different emotions, 7-month-olds tested in this procedure tend to look longer at faces matching the soundtrack, suggesting that they recognize, for example, that happy faces and voices go together, just as angry faces and voices do (Walker-Andrews, 1986). The capacity for intermodal perception of emotion has been found even when the soundtrack does not match the videotaped display in any way except in its emotional valence and even when the visual information is extremely limited, as in studies in which only small white dots attached to the actor's face are visible in the videotape (Soken & Pick, 1992, 1999).

Studies adopting a different approach have investigated the impact of emotional stimuli on infants' own emotional experience. These studies indicate that even newborns show **emotional contagion**, a phenomenon in which facial, vocal, or gestural cues of one person give rise to a similar or related state in another person (Saarni, Mumme, & Campos, 1998). Neonates in one study who heard another neonate's tape recorded cry tended to cry as well, a response that occurred significantly less often when they heard recordings of their own cry, an older infant's cry, or a chimpanzee's cry (Martin & Clark, 1982). Other studies have shown that 10-week-old infants respond differentially to their mothers' happy, sad, and angry facial and vocal expressions; infants in one study looked happier when their mothers expressed happiness, for example, than when they expressed sadness or anger (Haviland & Lelwica, 1987). These findings are consistent with evidence from studies of infants of depressed mothers, which we discussed in Chapter 9, showing that infants themselves appear to be "depressed" at an early age, apparently as a consequence of weeks and months of face-to-face interactions with a sad caregiver.

The emotional contagion response has also been observed when infants hear verbal and vocal messages, even if they cannot understand them. This was shown in a study of 5-month-old infants who responded differentially to tape recordings of adults' expressions of approval and disapproval, whether they were presented in a familiar or unfamiliar language (Fernald, 1993). This finding suggests that infants are sensitive to information about emotion that is not presented in the visual modality. It also helps explain why parents who offer comforting words to distressed infants who have awakened in the middle of the night are often able to soothe them and alter their emotional state without turning on a light, especially if they offer a soothing touch or body contact as well.

Often when parents convey information with emotional cues, they hope to influence children's behavior as well as change their emotional state. This happens, for example, when parents change their emotional tone of voice in order to stop their infants from crawling toward a household hazard, such as the top of the stairs or a fireplace. Parents who want to help their infants feel comfortable with a new babysitter may use a warm, friendly tone of voice and smile while talking to the unfamiliar caregiver in front of their child. When do infants perceive the meaning of these emotional expressions and when are they able to use them to modify their own behavior?

Communicating with Emotions

Infants' early ability to both express emotions and perceive them in others enables them to engage in emotional communication with those around them. Current functionalist theories of emotional development assert that emotions are relational rather than residing within the individual, meaning that emotional experiences occur in the context of some other person, object, or stimulus (Barrett & Campos, 1987; Campos, Campos, & Barrett, 1989; Campos et al., 1994; Fogel et al., 1997). In Chapter 9, we learned about dyadic synchrony, the coordination of attention and behavior that may include communication through emotional expression. Here, we consider studies of infants' ability to comprehend and respond to messages that caregivers and others convey through emotional communication.

The still-face paradigm (Cohn & Tronick, 1983, 1987), which we described earlier in this chapter, has been used to study emotional communication between infants and caregivers. Close study of parents' and infants' behavior during normal face-to-face interactions has shown that infants notice and respond to parents' emotions from an early age. From birth to 3 months of age, infants become capable of doing much more than simply attending to their parents and are increasingly able to show emotionally positive forms of attention to them (Lavelli, & Fogel, 2005). Parents, for their part, usually adjust their behaviors in response to their infants' signals in order to achieve and maintain an emotionally positive interaction. When mothers or fathers show an expressionless, unresponsive "still face" in the midst of normal interactions, therefore, infants as young as 2 to 3 months respond to the absence of a clear "message" with negative emotions and physiological signs of distress, such as increased heart rate (Braungart-Rieker et al., 1998; Moore & Calkins, 2004; Moore, Cohn, & Campbell, 2001).

Studies of infants between the ages of 2 to 9 months show that most infants respond to their parents' still face by showing less positive and more negative emotions themselves. They may attempt to reengage their parents by brief intervals of smiling and eye contact,

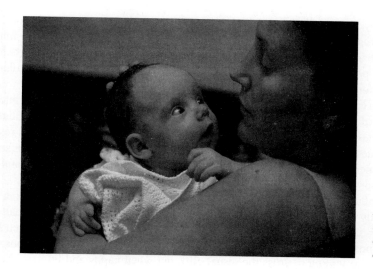

Even very young infants notice and respond to caregivers' facial expressions of emotion.

alternating with averted gaze and self-comforting behaviors, such as thumb sucking. The emotional effects of a 3-minute still-face episode are not thought to cause lasting harm to the parent-infant relationship, but their short-term impact may be seen in subsequent interactions, even after parents have resumed their normal style of interaction (Moore, Cohn, & Campbell, 2001; Weinberg, & Tronick, 1994, 1996; Weinberg et al., 1999).

Observations in many different cultures have shown that, during typical interactions, parents touch their infants at least 50 percent of the time (Keller et al., 2004a; Stack & Muir, 1990). When Canadian researchers in one study with 5-month-olds varied the still-face episode by allowing parents to continue touching their infants as usual, they found that infants were significantly less upset by their parent's silence and neutral facial expression (Stack & Muir, 1992). This finding suggests that some of the distress that infants experience during the still-face episode may be the result of the absence of normal tactile contact. It also suggests that tactile stimulation not only reinforces the emotional message that is conveyed through parents' vocal, verbal, and visual contact but may contribute in its own way to infant-parent emotional communication. For parent-infant dyads in which one or both participants are deaf, the combination of visual and tactile channels may be even more important ways of achieving and maintaining effective emotional communication (Koester, 1995; Koester et al., 2004).

Across cultures, face-to-face interactions involving mutual eye contact occur at different rates (Bornstein, 2006; Bugental & Grusec, 2006; Shweder et al., 2006). One recent study compared free play between 3-month-old infants and their mothers in West Africa, India, Costa Rica, Greece, and Germany. The researchers found that the highest percentages of mutual eye contact and face-to-face interactions occurred in Greece and Germany, cultures in which parents tend to view infants as equal communication partners and give them numerous opportunities to be the "leader" of their shared "conversation." Higher percentages of close body contact and stimulation, by contrast, were seen in the other cultures, which tend to follow a hierarchically structured apprentice model in which infants learn principally by maintaining close physical proximity and imitating examples that parents and other caregivers provide (Keller et al., 2004b). These differences in typical interaction patterns raise the intriguing possibility that the standard still-face paradigm might have different effects on infants as a function of their culture's implicit model of optimal infant-parent communication.

Infants communicate with their parents in settings other than face-to-face interaction, of course, and emotional signals are sent and received in a wide range of settings. Many studies have explored the phenomenon of **social referencing**, in which infants respond to emotional cues from parents and other adults. A commonly used procedure in studies of social referencing involves placing infants in unfamiliar or ambiguous settings and observing whether or not their parents' emotional expressions influence their behavior.

In an often cited study using the visual cliff (originally developed by Walk & Gibson, 1961, to study depth perception), 12-month-old infants were placed on the "shallow" end of the apparatus while their mothers stood on the other side, near the "deep" end (Sorce, Emde, Campos, & Klinnert, 1985). When mothers displayed fearful expressions, none of the infants were willing to cross the visual cliff, but when happy and interested emotions were expressed, the majority of infants crawled across. The visual information for support was equally ambiguous in both instances, but infants used mothers' facial expressions to impose either a "safe" or "dangerous" interpretation on it and then act accordingly.

In other studies, reminiscent of the Strange Situation, an unfamiliar adult enters a room. When mothers greet the stranger positively, 10-month-old infants are more likely to behave positively toward the stranger than when the stranger receives a negative response or no response at all from the mother (Boccia & Campos, 1989). These findings suggest that parents may be able to help their infants feel more comfortable when they meet strangers by expressing the emotions that they would like their infants to display.

The majority of social referencing studies have observed infants and parents in laboratory settings in which a novel object, usually a noisy or moving toy, is introduced. In many cases, parents are instructed to show either positive or negative emotions about the object, and researchers watch to see whether infants approach or avoid it. In a variation on this popular social referencing procedure, researchers showed 10- and 12-month-old infants a videotape in which an unfamiliar woman looked directly at one of two objects and expressed facial and vocal signals that were positive, negative, or neutral. Infants were then presented with the two objects and researchers observed how they interacted with each one. Ten-month-olds' behavior with the objects was not influenced by the emotional content of the videotape, but 12-month-old infants avoided objects about which the speaker in the videotape had expressed negative emotions. Positive emotions, by contrast, did not elicit more positive interactions with objects than did neutral emotions (Mumme & Fernald, 2003). These findings are consistent with previous studies showing that the capacity to use emotional cues as a guide to behavior in potentially ambiguous settings emerges sometime between 10 and 12 months of age (Hornik, Risenhoover, & Gunnar, 1987; Moses et al., 2001; Mumme, Fernald, & Herrera, 1996).

By approximately 18 months of age, children become aware that emotions are not inextricably linked with objects but reflect particular individuals' feelings about those objects. An object that one person dislikes, therefore, might very well be liked by someone else. An experimenter in one study expressed disgust about a kind of food that the child liked and joy about a kind of food that the child did not like. Eighteen-, but not 14-month-olds, were more likely to give the experimenter the food about which she had expressed delight rather than disgust, even though they did not personally prefer it (Repacholi & Gopnik, 1997). These results are consistent with the findings of many studies of early understanding of emotions (Wellman & Wooley, 1990; Wellman et al., 1995). Recognizing that different people like different kinds of food or toys indicates that even very young children understand that emotions are subjective, internal states that are linked to specific people, objects, and events.

Regulating Emotions

When parents attempt to change their infants' emotions and behavior, they may only hope to have an impact at that precise moment. They may, for example, want to end a tired child's temper tantrum, reassure a timid infant about entering a new playgroup, or entertain and distract a lively toddler while waiting in line at the grocery store. As children get older, parents also tend to be guided by longer-term goals when they attempt to influence their children's emotions and behavior. The toddler years are notorious for being a period of increasingly negative, oppositional behavior—the so-called "terrible twos." According to Erik Erikson, and many other developmental researchers, this is a normal part of development in which children strive for autonomy and self-directed behavior at the same time that parents try to introduce and reinforce societal expectations and standards. As children get older, then, parents may articulate new expectations and demand greater compliance than before. They may also try to reinforce and encourage the emotions that prompt prosocial behavior, such as sharing and helping others, and reduce undesirable emotions and behavior, such as jealousy and aggression. How do parents intervene to modify their infants' emotional experience? At what age do children become capable of regulating their own emotions and behavior? A number of studies have addressed these questions and offer fascinating glimpses into the socialization of emotion.

There is debate about how to define and study emotion regulation (Bridges, Denham, & Ganiban, 2004; Cole, Martin, & Dennis, 2004; Eisenberg & Spinrad, 2004). Some researchers working with older children have used brain-imaging techniques to explore how the development of the prefrontal cortex during adolescence affects the processing and regulation of emotion (Lewis & Stieben, 2004). Other researchers have recently begun to study brain and behavior responses when 5- and 10-month-old infants experience distress and negative emotions. The initial phase of an ongoing longitudinal study, this investigation will shed light on changes in infants' emotional reactivity as a result of the developing attention system and caregiver behaviors (Bell & Wolfe, 2004). Taken together, these new lines of inquiry have the potential to provide multiple, converging measures that will illuminate the development of emotions and emotion regulation (Eisenberg, Fabes, & Spinrad, 2006; Goldsmith & Davidson, 2004).

For now, the most commonly used definition of **emotion regulation** states that it is both an internal and external process through which emotions are monitored, appraised, and modified in relation to goals (Campos, Frankel, & Camras, 2004; Campos et al., 1994; Kopp, 1989; Thompson 1994). The emotions that are involved may be positive or negative, including joy, pleasure, distress, anger, and fear, but most research to date has explored the regulation of negative emotions. In keeping with the notion of emotions as relationship-based phenomena, successful self-regulation of emotion is typically defined by external criteria and standards for expressing emotion in particular situations or in particular cultures (Friedlmeier & Trommsdorff, 1999; Kopp, 1989). Children need to learn, for example, that a critical difference between "outside" and "inside" voices is not necessarily the emotion that they experience, which may be positive in both settings, but the degree of arousal that is expressed.

According to one influential theoretical analysis (Kopp, 1989), self-regulation of emotion during the first 3 years of life develops gradually and depends on three factors: possessing a set of behaviors that can be used in emotion-arousing situations, developing a repertoire of internal skills in domains such as memory and language, and receiving external support from caregivers for regulating emotions. Initially, the behaviors that are used in response to negative emotional arousal are more reflexive than voluntary. Young, immobile infants cry and experience physiological changes when they become sad or distressed, whereas toddlers and more cognitively advanced children are able to reflect on past experience and choose from an array of possible behaviors, such as sucking their thumb, running to their mother, or searching for their favorite stuffed animal to make themselves feel better.

By the end of the first year of life, infants are able to shift their attention and use their emerging motor, social-emotional, and cognitive skills to regulate their feelings of wariness or to indicate that they want specific kinds of responses from caregivers. It is not unusual, for example, to see toddlers hide behind their parents' legs when a stranger pays attention to them, peeking out at the unfamiliar adult to the degree that they feel comfortable. Some of the strategies that infants and toddlers use, such as looking quickly to their mothers, are quite brief, but other reactions, such as turning away from an overwhelming fireworks display and covering one's ears, may be maintained for a longer period of time (Mangelsdorf, Shapiro, & Marzolf, 1995). These strategies may not always succeed in eliminating or even reducing strong negative emotions. One study of 6-, 12-, and 18-month-old infants in fear-eliciting laboratory episodes (involving a large, remote-controlled spider and an unpredictable mechanical dog) indicated that infants as young as 6 months of age tried to withdraw from the approaching objects and looked to their mothers when they were afraid, but these behaviors only prevented the fear from growing stronger rather than diminishing it (Buss & Goldsmith, 1998). As language develops, especially between 18 and 30 months, young children are able to use words to refer to their emotions and to have conversations with others about their feelings (Bretherton et al., 1986). Discussions with parents and other family members about emotions support children's growing awareness of others' feelings and thoughts as well as their own (Brown & Dunn, 1996; Bugental & Grusec, 2006; Dunn, Brown, & Beardsall, 1991; Parke & Buriel, 2006).

Caregivers intervene in different ways as children develop. They may respond to young infants' signals of emotional distress simply in an effort to change that negative emotion. Later, they embed socialization goals and lessons about self-regulation in their responses, for example, insisting that children use a pleasant-sounding voice instead of whining when they ask for something to eat. Parents and other caregivers socialize young children toward self-regulation by instituting rules and increasing the number and kind of rules as children get older. Early rules for 13-month-olds tend to emphasize safety and moral issues—climbing onto the coffee table, hitting other people. In addition to those rules, 3-year-old children are also expected to follow rules that encompass social conventions—eating in appropriate areas of the home, putting away toys, using good manners—and self-care—washing one's own hands, getting dressed by oneself (Gralinski & Kopp, 1993).

Children's growing awareness of these rules is reflected in their increasing levels of compliance and in their reactions to peers who violate caregivers' rules. Younger toddlers (approximately 20 months of age) notice and respond to peers' violations of moral rules but tend to disregard violations of social conventional rules, whereas older toddlers (approximately 30 months of age) notice and respond to both types of transgressions (Lamb & Zakhireh, 1997; Smetana, 1984).

Parents may intervene in different ways with different children. One study of jealousy in sibling pairs in which the younger sibling was 16 months of age and the older sibling was a preschool-age child showed that older siblings were generally better able than younger siblings to wait for their turn to play with a new toy. Younger siblings who were rated as being more temperamentally negative and angry were especially likely to experience feelings of jealousy as they watched their older sibling play with the toy, if they had not yet had their own turn with it. Parents who recognize differences between their children and take their individual temperaments and cognitive maturity into account may be more successful at helping their children manage negative feelings (Volling, McElwain, & Miller, 2002). In this example, parents could decide to let their younger child have the first turn in order to make it easier for them to watch their older sibling having his or her turn.

Differences in the regulation and socialization of emotion are seen across cultures, and the actions that caregivers take vary across caregiver belief systems (Bornstein, 2006; Bugental & Grusec, 2006; Friedlmeier & Tromsdorff, 1999; Hastings & Rubin, 1999; Kopp, 1989; Parke & Buriel, 2006; Shonkoff & Phillips, 2000). As we noted in Chapter 9, parents in different cultures do not always have similar childrearing objectives and expectations about desirable or appropriate child behavior. Dutch parents, for example, appear to have different goals than U.S. parents in terms of achieving and maintaining particular states of infant arousal and alertness (Super et al., 1996). In Japan, mothers tend to use soft, quiet vocalizations and physical contact to soothe infants and minimize crying and distress. Parents in the United States, by contrast, are more likely to follow a "let-them-cry-it-out" approach. To a greater degree than is typically seen in the United States, therefore, Japanese parents attempt to regulate infants' expressions of negative emotion (Miyake et al., 1986; Saarni, Mumme, & Campos, 1998; Shwalb, Shwalb, & Shoji, 1996). In a study of $2\frac{1}{2}$-year-olds, Chinese parents were more likely than European American parents to remind children of the negative consequences and negative emotions associated with past violations of standards for behavior. European American parents, by contrast, tended to transform discussions about children's previous transgressions into emotionally positive, entertaining stories of affirmation in an effort to preserve their child's self-esteem (Miller et al., 1997). Across cultures, parent-child discourse and reminiscing occur about children's past emotional and moral experiences (Laible, 2004a, 2004b). It is clear, however, that there are cross-cultural differences in parents' socialization strategies—highlighting versus minimizing negative emotions in the context of discussions about behavioral standards and expectations for the regulation of future behavior (Miller, Fung, & Mintz, 1996; Miller et al., 1997; Shweder et al., 2006).

Even within cultures, there are differences in parents' responsiveness to infants' emotional signals. Some studies have found that mothers tend to smile more and be more emotionally expressive when interacting with daughters than with sons (Karraker & Coleman, 2002; Malatesta & Haviland, 1982). In one longitudinal study, infant daughters, but not sons, became more emotionally expressive over time (Malatesta et al., 1989).

A number of researchers have explored links between emotion regulation and attachment (Cassidy, 1994) or maternal depression (Field, 1994). These investigations indicate that individual differences in parents' responsiveness influence infants' subsequent emotional expressiveness. This was shown in a study of infants who were observed between $2\frac{1}{2}$ and 22 months of age (Malatesta et al., 1989). Some mothers smiled when their infants were distressed or ignored their infants' sadness. Over time, these infants tended to express less joy than infants whose mothers had responded when they cried and looked sad.

Mothers' responses to infants' emotions and behavior may have long-lasting effects on their children's self-regulation and subsequent behavior. In one longitudinal study of 565 pairs of genetically identical twins, one twin in each pair received more maternal negativity and less emotional warmth, often beginning at birth, than the other twin. By the age of 5 years, twins who had been the target of mothers' negative emotions had more problems regulating their own emotions, as reflected in a greater number of antisocial behavior problems (Caspi et al., 2004).

Developing and Using Social Emotions

When young children engage in antisocial behavior, such as biting another child in order to obtain a desired toy, parents, caregivers, and peers typically respond in ways that let them know that they have violated expectations and standards. As we noted earlier, even toddlers are aware of rules (e.g., "We don't bite our friends"), and, by the age of 2 to 3 years, most children have begun to develop a moral code or **conscience**—an internal set of standards that guide behavior (Emde et al., 1991; Kochanska, 2002; Thompson, 2006). By the age of 2 years, most children show emotional distress and signs of guilt when they are responsible for a mishap that results in damage to objects or harm to other people. Informative results have been obtained in studies observing 2-year-olds' emotional responses when they believed that they had broken a doll or spilled some juice. In actuality, the experimenters had rigged the dolls and the cups to make sure that these "accidents" would occur. Most of the 2-year-olds in one study showed signs of guilt through tension and frustration, and most tried to repair the damage, attempting to fix the doll or clean up the juice (Cole, Barrett, & Zahn-Waxler, 1992).

How does parents' emotional expressiveness help children's social emotions become established? One possibility is that parents communicate their feelings about their children's social successes and failures, and these verbal and nonverbal emotional messages influence children's own emotional experience (Barrett & Nelson-Goens, 1997). When children share their toys, for example, parents tend to show positive emotions and possibly compliment them for their behavior, but when children throw their toys or take away other children's toys, parents show clear disapproval. Studies of 17-month-olds have documented these kinds of parental responses and their contributions to children's own emotional reactions to success and failure in a variety of settings. These studies also suggest that parents' positive emotional reactions may have a more significant impact than their negative emotional reactions. As evidence, children whose parents show more positive reactions to desirable behavior subsequently show more feelings of guilt when they think that they have damaged an object (Barrett & Nelson-Goens, 1997).

Kochanska and her colleagues have reported similar findings, namely, that parents' emotional responsiveness and positive emotional tone contribute to the development of social emotions, which in turn support the development of conscience (Aksan, & Kochanska, 2005; Kochanska, 2002; Kochanska, Coy, & Murray, 2001; Kochanska & Murray, 2000). Between 12 and 36 months of age, children become increasingly capable of complying with parents' requests and adjusting their behavior when asked to do so. Empathic parents who establish a **mutually responsive orientation (MRO)**—a "positive, close, mutually binding, cooperative, and affectively positive" relationship (Kochanska, 2002, p. 192)—increase the likelihood that their children will not only become aware of their standards and rules but will also internalize and comply with them even when parents are not present.

Two forms of compliance, committed and situational, have been identified. **Committed compliance** is seen when children "embrace the maternal agenda, accept it as their own, and eagerly follow maternal directives in a self-regulated way" (Kochanska, Coy, & Murray, 2001, p. 1092). When asked to help clean up toys, children exhibiting committed compliance are likely to pick up toys throughout the play area without having to be prompted to move from one pile to another. They may also clap their hands when finished and show nonverbal signs of pride in their accomplishment. **Situational compliance**, by contrast, "describes instances when children, although essentially cooperative, do not appear to embrace wholeheartedly the maternal agenda" (Kochanska, Coy, & Murray, 2001, p. 1092). Children displaying situational compliance in a toy cleanup task are likely to pick up only a small number of toys or only those that they have been asked to pick up; they may even begin playing instead of putting the toys away.

Children with MRO relationships tend to display committed compliance, whereas children without a history of MRO are more likely to exhibit situational compliance. The link between MRO and committed compliance borrows the concept of the working model from Bowlby's attachment theory (Kochanska, 2002). According to this view, an MRO contributes to children's developing representations of their relationship with their parents as a "cooperative, reciprocal, mutually accommodating relationship in which partners naturally do things for one another" (p. 194). Parents and children construct an MRO through "willing, sensitive, supportive, and developmentally appropriate response to one another's signals of distress, unhappiness, needs, bids for attention, or attempts to exert influence" (p. 192). An MRO is also built on a foundation of "pleasurable, harmonious, smoothly flowing interactions infused with positive emotions experienced by both" (p. 192).

A number of laboratory tasks have been used to explore the hypothesized links between children's MRO relationships, compliance, social emotions, and conscience. In one longitudinal study, children were observed at 14 and 22 months as mothers tried to enlist them in acting out three pretend sequences (Clean the Table, Tea Party, and Feed the Bear). Conscience was assessed when children were 33 and 45 months of age by examining their ability to resist playing with a set of prohibited toys and to resist cheating in an unwinnable game. The social emotion of guilt was also assessed at these ages, using rigged objects in tasks like those developed by Cole and her colleagues (Cole, Barrett, & Zahn-Waxler, 1992). In support of the MRO model, toddlers who were more willing and eager to comply with their mothers during the imitation-of-pretense task showed more developed conscience (greater resistance to temptation) and higher levels of guilt as preschoolers (Forman, Aksan, & Kochanska, 2004).

In another longitudinal study, children's behavior in "Do contexts" at 14, 22, 33, and 45 months of age was compared with their compliance in "Don't contexts" at the same ages (Kochanska, Coy, & Murray, 2001). Do contexts are those in which children are asked to perform an action, such as cleaning up a play area and putting toys away, whereas Don't contexts require children to inhibit actions, such as resisting an attractive set of toys. Children in this study were also observed longitudinally for their emotional reactions when they encountered an experimenter wearing different masks and when they entered a Risk Room filled with odd-looking objects (e.g., toys wearing masks) in which an unfamiliar adult encouraged them to perform mildly stressful risky acts (e.g., putting their hand in a mask's mouth or falling backward onto a trampoline). At 33 and 45 months, mothers used the Child Behavior Questionnaire (CBQ) (Rothbart, Ahadi, & Hershey, 1994) to rate their children's shyness and effortful control (the ability to delay or suppress behaviors). Children were also observed at 22, 33, and 45 months when they were asked to delay or suppress behaviors (e.g., waiting before retrieving a piece of candy that had been placed under a cup, or playing games like Simon Says and Red Light, Green Light). Children's compliance and cooperation with an unfamiliar adult was also assessed at 33 months of age.

Results of this large, complex study showed that the Do contexts—which require that children persist in a tedious activity—were more challenging and elicited lower levels of committed compliance than the Don't contexts—which require children to resist performing a desired activity (Kochanska, Coy, & Murray, 2001). As had been reported in other studies, girls displayed more committed compliance than boys at every age in the Don't contexts. Children who showed higher levels of committed compliance in their mothers' presence were also more likely to comply with requests when they were not monitored by their mothers or any other adult. This finding supports the link between committed compliance, internalization of rules, and self-regulation.

There was also evidence of the influence of individual differences on children's compliance. Children who were temperamentally more inhibited (i.e., as rated in the CBQ and reflected in more fearful behavior in the Risk Room) showed a higher rate of committed compliance in the Don't contexts than children who were less inhibited. Temperamental ability to delay or suppress behaviors (both rated in the CBQ and observed in the laboratory) was also related to children's behavior in the Don't contexts. Committed compliance was observed more frequently among children who were able to delay or suppress their behavior in other settings.

Children who showed committed compliance with their mothers did not necessarily show greater levels of cooperation with the unfamiliar adult, suggesting that MRO is a reflection of a particular relationship history, rather than being a characteristic of the child per se. It remains to be seen whether children who show committed compliance with their mothers also show committed compliance with their fathers and other caregivers with whom they have an existing relationship (Kochanska, Coy, & Murray, 2001).

In sum, in several longitudinal studies covering the ages 7 to 66 months, it appears that a responsive parental relationship in infancy sets the stage for the development of social emotions, internalization of parental standards, conscience, and self-regulation (Kochanska, 2002; Kochanska & Murray, 2000). Other researchers have reported similar findings in separate studies (Laible & Thompson, 2000; Thompson, 2006). Taken together, these results reinforce the notion that parents' emotional communication with infants and toddlers plays a central role in the development of social emotions and conscience, motivating children to follow an internalized set of standards for moral behavior as if it were their own. When parents' standards are internalized, children are able to experience compliance and cooperation as self-generated regulation, which reduces the oppositional behavior that is so often observed during the toddler years (Kochanska, Coy, & Murray, 2001; Thompson, 1998, 2006).

The Self

Thinking about our hypothetical Jacob and Emily party, if we called out "Jacob! Emily!" at what age would we expect large numbers of infants to swivel their heads to see who had called their name? As it turns out, the ability to recognize one's own name develops relatively early, during the middle of the first year of life. It is so atypical for infants of this age not to respond when they hear their names, in fact, that those who do not show this reaction by 9 to 12 months of age may need to be seen by a pediatrician or infant mental health specialist to determine the extent and cause of this developmental delay. Although there may be other explanations, one study of home movies of infants later diagnosed with an autism spectrum disorder showed that these infants tended not to respond to their names, showed poor social attention, and lack of social smiling and appropriate facial expressions (Dawson et al., 2004; Werner et al., 2000). Assuming that all of the Jacobs and Emilys on hand oriented to the sound of their own name, would it be accurate to infer that they had a clear concept of themselves as objective, coherent individuals? As we will see, the development of a sense of self is a gradual achievement that takes place over the first 3 years of life (Harter, 1998, 2006; Thompson, 1998, 2006).

Recognizing the Self

Few researchers would conclude that a 7-month-old infant who consistently turns when her name is called understands that she is Emily. Over the course of the first year of life, however, infants gradually build a subjective sense of self. They do this by becoming aware of their ability to affect parents and other people through their daily interactions. In a sensitive and responsive caregiving environment, when infants cry, someone attends to their needs; when they roll over or sit up by themselves, someone exclaims enthusiastically about their achievement of a motor milestone. In games of peek-a-boo and other give-and-take activities, infants play a specific role that is inherently linked to their partners' actions. Infants also act upon objects in their environment, moving their hands, reaching toward objects, and bringing those objects to their mouths for oral exploration. All of these experiences, as well as a consistent subjective frame of reference, provide feedback to infants that they are distinct from others (Harter, 1998, 2006). By the age of about 12 months, they display social referencing and other forms of shared communication that many researchers assert signify a "dawning awareness of others (and oneself) as subjective entities with different and potentially shareable viewpoints" (Thompson, 1998, p. 76).

Objective awareness of the self—understanding of one's own characteristics and traits—does not emerge until later in the second year of life. To assess children's objective awareness of the physical self, Lewis and Brooks-Gunn (1979) developed a test of **visual self-recognition**, the rouge test. In this well-known laboratory procedure, a dot of rouge is surreptitiously applied to the child's nose and then they are placed in front of a mirror. If children touch the spot of rouge after seeing their reflection (as opposed to merely pointing at their reflection), they are credited with visual self-recognition. This reaction is seen reliably in most children by 18 months of age but may appear as early as 15 to 16 months or as late as 24 months (Asendorpf, & Baudonniere, 1993; Courage, Edison, & Howe, 2004; Lewis & Ramsay, 1997).

Soon after children show objective self-recognition, they begin to refer to themselves as specific individuals and comment on their own emotions and internal states. They also begin to use their own names as well as personal pronouns such as "me" and "mine" (Bertenthal & Fischer, 1978; Pipp, Fischer, & Jennings, 1987). As we noted earlier, children become increasingly motivated to behave autonomously, rejecting offers of help with the often heard assertion that they want to "do it myself." Around this same age, children also begin to engage in pretend play, which (as we discussed in Chapter 7) depends on the

This toddler's sense of self is still developing, but her reaction to her own reflection shows that she knows that she is looking at herself.

ability to think of objects and, at more advanced levels, the objective self as something other than what it really is (Kavanaugh, Eizenman, & Harris, 1997). One recent longitudinal study of children at 15, 18, and 21 months found that children who showed self-recognition in the rouge test used more personal pronouns and engaged in more advanced forms of pretend play than those who had not yet developed visual self-recognition. According to the researchers, the nearly simultaneous emergence of these three measures suggests that they are linked to the development of an underlying objective representation of the self (Lewis & Ramsay, 2004).

It is likely that links between self-representational awareness, **self-referential language**, social emotions, and socially desirable behavior are complex and multidirectional (Courage, Edison, & Howe, 2004). Investigations of early parent-child relationships appear to be a promising developmental context to explore (Bugental & Grusec, 2006; Parke & Buriel, 2006; Shweder et al., 2006; Thompson, 2006). One recent cross-cultural investigation, for example, found evidence that differences in caregiving experience at the age of 3 months influence children's self-recognition and self-regulation at 18 to 20 months (Keller et al., 2004a, 2004b). In this study, infants of Nso farmers in Cameroon, who experience a proximal caregiving style that emphasizes body contact and body stimulation, were compared with infants in urban Greek families, who experience a distal caregiving style in which interactions tend to involve face-to-face contact and object stimulation. These groups were compared with a third group of infants, from middle-class Costa Rican families, in which caregiving blends aspects of proximal and distal styles. As shown in Table 10.4, infants in the Cameroon sample developed self-regulation (compliance with parents' requests to either perform particular actions or refrain from particular actions) earlier than infants in the other groups, whereas infants in the Greek sample developed self-recognition (assessed in the rouge test) earlier. As expected, infants in the Costa Rican sample were intermediate between the other groups of infants on both measures.

Taken together, these findings suggest that early infant-caregiver interactions that emphasize shared feelings and physical interdependence (the proximal style) tend to result in the formation of a self that is viewed as "a communal agent who is basically interconnected

TABLE 10.4   Links between Caregiving Style, Self-Regulation, and Self-Recognition

| | | Age at Assessment | |
| | | *3 months* | *18–20 months* |
Sample	**Caregiving Style**	**Frequency of Self-regulation**	**Frequency of Self-recognition**
Cameroon	Proximal	72%	3%
Costa Rica	Proximal and Distal	42%	50%
Greece	Distal	2%	68%

Source: Based on Keller et al., 2004b.

with others, role oriented, and compliant" (Keller et al., 2004b, p. 1745). Infant-caregiver interactions that emphasize interpersonal distance and separateness, by contrast (the distal style), appear to lead children to an earlier awareness of the self as "an individual agent who is bounded, self contained, unique, and separate from others" (Keller et al., 2004b, p. 1745).

It seems reasonable to conclude that the objective self is itself a reflection, a mirror image of children's social and emotional experience. Parents' statements to and about their infants, as well as their emotional communication and actions, play a central role in the self that is constructed throughout infancy and childhood (Brown & Dunn, 1996; Harter, 1998, 2006; Laible, 2004a; Miller et al., 1992, 1997; Shweder et al., 2006).

Evaluating the Self

As we noted earlier, at 2 and 3 years of age, children increasingly respond to and look for evaluative feedback about their actions from parents and other adults. In one study involving 13- to 39-month-old children, an experimenter introduced several new toys and demonstrated how they worked (Stipek et al., 1992). Children were then invited to take their turn and see if they could do it too. Children of all ages tended to smile both after the experimenter's demonstration and after their own performance, deriving pleasure directly from their actions. After the age of 21 months, however, and especially after 30 months of age, children were more likely to look up at the experimenter after they themselves had produced the outcome with the toy than after the effect had been produced by the experimenter. This pattern suggests that younger children do not anticipate or seek out adults' reactions to their performance, whereas at 22 months and beyond, children increasingly look for acknowledgement when they have performed a task correctly and may even be expecting praise for their performance.

In a follow-up study of 24- to 60-month-old children, researchers compared reactions of children who succeeded at a task with reactions of children who failed (Stipek et al., 1992). The tasks in this study consisted of puzzles as well as nesting cups that could be stacked from largest to smallest to form a tower. In the failure condition of each task, one puzzle piece was replaced with a piece from a different puzzle, and two same-sized cups were included in the set, making it impossible to stack them on top of each other in descending size as the experimenter had requested.

Children of all ages smiled more and were more emotionally positive in the success condition than in the failure condition. Many 2-, 3-, and 4-year-olds who succeeded showed "open" body postures consistent with feelings of pride. Following success, children were also more likely to look at the experimenter and call attention to their completion with comments such as "I did it" or "Done." Approximately half of the children in the success condition were praised for their performance, whereas the other half simply received a neutral comment noting that they had completed the task. Even without praise, children who succeeded showed positive emotions, but these emotions were heightened when praise was given following success.

Following failure, children of all ages tended to avoid eye or face-to-face contact with the experimenter by turning their heads or bodies in the opposite direction. "Closed" body postures indicative of negative self-consciousness or embarrassment were observed more frequently among children in the failure condition than in the success condition. When they encountered difficulty in the failure condition, older children tended to continue studying and working on the task, whereas younger children were more likely to lose interest and stop trying. After 32 months of age, children who failed were increasingly likely to express negative emotions by pouting or frowning. Together, these findings indicate that children as young as 2 years of age reacted with negative emotion to failure in social settings, possibly because they equated failing at the tasks with failing to comply with the experimenter's instructions. Considering that 2-year-olds acted as if failure to complete the tasks was equivalent to failing to comply with a behavioral standard, the researchers caution that parents who are critical or demanding in one arena may inadvertently create anxiety in young children about evaluation in another arena. "If our analysis is correct, even parents who are careful not to criticize their young children's achievement 'failures' could contribute to achievement anxiety by expressing disapproval of behavior in other domains" (Stipek et al., 1992, p.74).

Children who hear comments like "Good girl!" or "Nice job picking up your toys!" show feelings of pride that are incorporated into the developing representation of the self. Parents who denigrate their children's efforts, by contrast, are more likely to induce feelings of shame or embarrassment that become incorporated into their self-representations. Children whose mothers praised them frequently during free play were more likely than children who were less frequently praised to call attention to their own achievements during free play. This observation led the investigators to assert that "[a] certain amount of praise may be essential for children to develop a sense of themselves as competent . . ." (Stipek et al., 1992, p. 59).

This conclusion is also consistent with the findings of an important review of early intervention programs, which identified six psychosocial mechanisms that have repeatedly been associated with positive cognitive, social, and emotional outcomes. These mechanisms are 1) encouragement to explore the environment, 2) celebrating new skills, 3) protection from inappropriate punishment or ridicule for developmental advances, 4) mentoring in basic cognitive and social skills, 5) stimulation in language and symbolic communication, and 6) rehearsing and expanding new skills (Ramey & Ramey, 1998a, 1998b). When these experiences occur in children's lives on a daily basis, they and their parents co-construct self-representations that prepare them for subsequent developmental challenges and opportunities, whether they're named Jacob or Emily.

WRAPPING IT UP: Summary and Conclusion

As we have seen in this chapter, it is not children's names that make them unique but rather the dynamic interplay between their inherent temperament and the sensitivity that their parents and other caregivers show in trying to understand and respond to those qualities. Although researchers still do not agree about how to define and measure temperament, there is a general consensus that it consists of infants' characteristic responses, such as irritability, soothability, motor activity, attentiveness, adaptability, response to novelty, arousal, and regulation of states. Continuity from infancy into later childhood has been reported for a variety of measures and dimensions of temperament, including activity and sociability. Some studies have also reported finding links between early temperamental "difficultness" and less optimal relationships and development at later ages. Social and cognitive development appear to be buffered, however, when parents of "difficult" infants learn how to adjust their caregiving behaviors to their child's characteristics and behavioral tendencies.

Most major theories of emotional development suggest that infants are born with, or very quickly develop, a set of primary emotions. Researchers do not agree about how many primary emotions exist. At a minimum, some researchers assert that there are three—distress, interest, and pleasure—and that this initial set subsequently becomes differentiated into multiple emotions, including sadness, anger, fear, surprise, and joy. Secondary emotions emerge in the second and third years of life as a result of cognitive development and the capacity for mental representation. These emotions are also referred to as self-conscious or social emotions because they require the ability to engage in self-reflective thought and to compare oneself or one's actions to external standards and expectations. Examples of secondary emotions are embarrassment, envy, empathy, pride, shame, and guilt.

Infants' ability to both express emotions and perceive them in others enables them to engage in emotional communication with those around them. Current theories emphasize that emotions are relational rather than residing within the individual, meaning that emotional experiences occur in the context of some other person, object, or event. Infants notice and respond to parents' emotions from an early age and are increasingly able to engage in an emotional "dialogue" with them. Across infancy and the toddler period, parents raise their expectations for their children's behavior and emotion regulation. As they do, they are increasingly likely to encourage and reinforce emotions that prompt prosocial behavior and reduce emotions and behavior that are undesirable, aggressive, or antisocial.

The development of a sense of self is a gradual achievement that takes place over the first 3 years of life. Beginning in the first year of life, infants develop a subjective sense of self through daily interactions with parents and other caregivers. Objective self-recognition and awareness of the physical self emerges late in the second year of life, typically by the age of about 18 months. Other signs of children's growing sense of self are the appearance of self-referential language, social emotions, and socially desirable, self-regulated behavior. Cross-cultural studies suggest that early infant-caregiver interactions influence the developing sense of self.

Just as no two infants or toddlers are interchangeable, neither are all parents alike. Some, for example, are more likely than others to provide sensitive, responsive care for their infants and toddlers, at least initially. As we will see in the next chapter, all caregivers can benefit from education about children's needs from birth to age 3, and all children benefit from quality care.

THINK ABOUT IT: Questions for Reading and Discussion

1. How might parents and other caregivers differ in their behavior toward infants and toddlers if they believe that temperament is largely unchangeable, as opposed to believing that temperament can be modified by experience?

2. What are the advantages and disadvantages of using parent reports to study temperament? How would you increase the usefulness of parent reports if *you* were going to conduct a study of temperament?

3. How does temperament influence early relationships with family members, other care-givers, and peers? How does it affect infants' and toddlers' developing sense of self?

4. How does early dyadic emotional communication affect infants' and toddlers' functioning in other developmental domains? Put another way, what sorts of skill deficits would you expect to find in infants and toddlers who did not experience early dyadic emotional communication?

5. How do infants and toddlers learn to regulate their emotions?

6. How might the development and differentiation of emotions during the first 3 years of life coincide with or even contribute to the development of milestones in other domains? Consider examples as diverse as learning to walk, uttering first words, and forming an attachment relationship in developing your answer.

7. Which developmental milestones must be achieved before a child is capable of experiencing self-conscious (social) emotions?

8. How is development of the self related to development in other domains, such as cognition and language?

KEY WORDS

Committed compliance (347)	Children's tendency to follow parents' directives and requests with a minimum of prompting and reminding
Conscience (346)	An internal set of standards that guide behavior
Emotional contagion (339)	A phenomenon in which facial, vocal, or gestural cues of one person give rise to a similar or related state in another person
Emotion regulation (343)	A process through which emotions are monitored, appraised, and modified in relation to goals
High-reactive (330)	Infants who respond to novelty by showing extreme degrees of motor activity, fretting, and crying
Inhibited to novelty (330)	A constitutionally based tendency to respond to unfamiliar people and places by becoming quiet, vigilant, restrained, and avoidant
Low-reactive (330)	Infants who respond to novelty by showing low levels of motor activity and a general absence of crying and fussing
Mutually responsive orientation (MRO) (347)	A relationship quality that consists of positive emotions and close cooperative interactions
Primary emotions (335)	A set of emotions—distress, interest, and pleasure—present at birth and differentiating into other emotions during infancy
Secondary emotions (337)	A set of emotions—embarrassment, envy, empathy, pride, shame, and guilt—that emerges during the second and third years of life

Self-conscious emotions (337)	Emotions that involve the comparison of oneself or one's actions to standards and expectations that others hold; also called social emotions
Self-referential language (351)	An aspect of the self, seen in children's use of their own name, as well as personal pronouns, such as "me" and "mine"
Situational compliance (347)	Children's tendency to require prompting and reminding in order to follow parents' directives and requests
Social referencing (342)	Attention that is focused on another person in order to gauge his/her emotional and behavioral response to an ambiguous situation
Still-face paradigm (336)	A procedure for studying emotional communication and regulation by disrupting the normal verbal and nonverbal signals that parents and infants use to communicate
Temperament (324)	A theoretical construct consisting of constitutionally based individual differences in emotionality, motor activity, attentiveness, adaptability, and self-regulation
Uninhibited to novelty (330)	A constitutionally based tendency to respond to unfamiliar people and places by showing spontaneous engagement and active interest
Visual self-recognition (350)	An early aspect of the self, measured by children's understanding that when they look in a mirror, the reflection that they see is their own

CHAPTER 11

Building Better Babies: Child Care and Early Intervention

Around the world, when women and men become mothers and fathers, they look forward to spending time recovering from their infant's birth, caring for their child, and getting to know him or her. In most European and Scandinavian countries, as well as in Canada, new parents know that they will do these things while using a paid leave from their place of employment. In fact, using a combination of paid and unpaid leaves, some working mothers do not return to their jobs until their children are 1 or even 2 years old. As a result, families in these countries tend not to use nonparental child care when their infants are still very young.

In the United States, by contrast, one of the most significant and emotional decisions that new parents make concerns who will care for their infants. The vast majority of Americans believe that parents, especially mothers, should be the primary caregivers (Sylvester, 2001). Alternative arrangements are often needed, however, because 55 percent of all mothers of infants in the United States now return to work before their children are 1 year old, 40 percent by 4 months after birth (Downs, 2003; Hofferth & Curtin, 2003). According to one survey of 324 new mothers, 83 percent stated a preference for child care provided by a family member, but most (78 percent) were not able to achieve that type of arrangement (Riley & Glass, 2002). Deciding among feasible child care options often becomes increasingly urgent as infants near the age of 3 months and mothers reach the end of their maternity leave. Besides the time limits imposed by maternity leave policies, what are the factors that influence new mothers' decisions about whether and when to return to work? How do parents of infants resolve these issues, and how different is their experience from the experience of parents in earlier years?

In this chapter we will consider these questions by examining parental leave options in the United States and comparing them to policies available to parents in other parts of the world. As we will see, parents who have access to relatively lengthy paid leaves tend to make different decisions about returning to work and using nonparental child care. Given that child care for infants and toddlers has become increasingly common in the United States, there is now evidence from numerous studies of its impact on physical, cognitive, and social and emotional development early in life. We also have a good understanding of the hallmarks of high-quality child care—characteristics that parents should look for when choosing child care arrangements. Among the questions we will address are whether nonparental child care is ever equivalent to care provided by a child's parents and whether it has an impact on the parent-infant relationship. Finally, we will consider studies of early intervention—a form of child care that is designed either to compensate for or prevent developmental delays and deficits that may occur as a result of exposure to nonoptimal caregiving and high-risk environments.

Child Care

The age at which children enter child care is related to their mother's employment before birth and decisions about whether and when to begin working after birth. In the United States, the proportion of employed women with children under 3 years of age increased from 34 percent in 1975 to 57 percent in 2004, after reaching a peak of 62 percent in 1997 and 1998 (U.S. Department of Labor/Bureau of Labor Statistics, 2005). The largest increase in participation in the labor force during this time was among mothers of infants younger than 1 year (Downs, 2003). Before we explore the range of child care arrangements from which parents make choices, let's take a look at the types of parental leaves that enable working women—and sometimes men—to take time off from work in the first place. As we will see, employees in the United States generally have a different set of options than workers in other countries. Even within the United States, there are significant differences in the amount of support that new parents receive and in the factors that influence their decisions about whether and when to return to work.

Parental Leave Policies

Several types of parental leaves exist in developed, industrialized countries. **Maternity leaves** are job-protected leaves from work for employed women during the weeks after (and sometimes before) childbirth. For fathers, **paternity leaves** are job-protected leaves for employed men and are typically taken after childbirth, albeit for a much shorter time than maternity leaves. **Parental leaves** are job-protected leaves that are open to mothers or fathers and are typically available as a supplement to maternity and paternity leaves; they may extend to cover children until they reach the age of 2 or even 3 years. **Family leaves** enable parents to take job-protected time off from work for a variety of reasons other than the birth of a child. Depending on the country and the employer, these leaves may be paid or unpaid (Kamerman, 2000; Lamb & Ahnert, 2006).

In the United States, paid maternity leaves were once uncommon but have become more widespread, especially for women with higher levels of education (see Table 11.1). The largest increase in paid maternity leaves occurred between the early 1970s and the early 1980s, years straddling the **Pregnancy Discrimination Act of 1978**, which prohibited employment discrimination on the basis of pregnancy or childbirth (O'Connell, 1990; Smith & Bachu, 1999; Smith, Downs, & O'Connell, 2001).

Parental Leave Policies in the United States. The most uniform leave policy in the United States is the **Family and Medical Leave Act (FMLA)**, which enables public and private workers to take up to 12 weeks of unpaid leave without risking the loss of their job.

TABLE 11.1 Proportion of Women Taking Paid Maternity Leaves, 1960s—Early 1990s.

	Early 1990s		
All Women* (1961–1965)	*All Women* (1986–1990)*	*College Graduates*	*Less than High School Education*
16%	43%	63%	18%

*These data are not disaggregated based on education.

Source: Based on information in Smith, Downs, & O'Connell, 2001.

The law entitles them to return to their previous job or its equivalent with the same pay, benefits, and other work conditions. It covers mothers or fathers who wish to care for a newborn infant, but any eligible worker can use an FMLA leave to care for a newly adopted child or a foster child, as well as a spouse or parent with a serious health condition. It can also be used by employees to take time off from work due to their own serious health condition or maternity-related disability.

Coverage by the FMLA is not universal. Private employers with fewer than 50 employees working within a 75-mile radius of their worksite are not required to provide FMLA leaves, and workers in eligible businesses must have worked for their employer for at least one year and for at least 1,250 hours (an average of 25 hours per week) during that year. In the end, approximately 55 percent of the workforce is covered by the FMLA. Those who are ineligible are more likely to be lower income, part-time workers, and new employees, including single women moving from welfare to work (Asher & Lenhoff, 2001; Kamerman, 2000). Eleven states—California, Connecticut, Hawaii, Maine, Minnesota, New Jersey, Oregon, Rhode Island, Vermont, Washington, and Wisconsin—and the District of Columbia have expanded the FMLA to cover part-time employees or employees in smaller businesses (Asher & Lenhoff, 2001; U.S. Department of Labor, 2005).

Before the FMLA was passed in 1993, the majority of employed women did not receive paid maternity leaves, and new parents used other leave time instead, including paid sick leave, vacation leave, and short-term disability leave (Hofferth et al., 1991; Hofferth & Curtin, 2003). The proportion of women who return to work in the first 24 months after the birth of their child is higher now than before the FMLA. In addition, since 1993, women who take a leave after the birth of a child have been more likely to return to the same employer than was the case before the FMLA existed. These findings suggest that the FMLA has not been detrimental to most eligible employers and may even be associated with greater employee retention.

One reason for its minimal impact on employers may be that use of the unpaid FMLA leave is actually quite low. In 2000, only 17 percent of all employees took a leave for family or medical reasons. Out of those leaves, approximately 8 percent were taken as maternity leave, and 18 percent were used to care for a newborn, newly adopted, or newly placed foster child. Most employees do not use the entire 12-week period allowed; in 2000, the median leave length was only 10 days. The majority of employees who needed a leave but chose not to take it made their decision based on their need for continued income. Unsurprisingly, workers who have access to other forms of paid leave time are more likely to use those options and thus forego the opportunity to take an additional 12 weeks off from work without their usual income (Asher & Lenhoff, 2001; Cantor et al., 2001; Hofferth & Curtin, 2003; Waldfogel, 2001).

Employed women tend to return to work sooner now than they did before the FMLA was enacted. Table 11.2 shows that in the early 1960s, only a small proportion of all mothers with newborns had returned to work by the time their child was 6 months old, and only slightly more had returned by the time their child turned 1 year old. By the mid-1990s, by contrast, more than half of new mothers returned to work by the sixth month (Smith, Downs, & O'Connell, 2001). Is the FMLA the reason for these trends? Not necessarily. Most of the available evidence suggests that other factors have played a more significant role.

TABLE 11.2   Proportion of Women Returning to Work as a Function of Child Age, 1960s—Early 1990s.

1960s		Early 1990s	
6 months	*1 year*	*6 months*	*1 year*
14%	17%	52%	60%

Source: Based on information in Smith, Downs, & O'Connell, 2001.

One factor is the proportion of women who worked during their pregnancy, especially during the last trimester, and thus have prior work settings to which they can return after childbirth. As shown in Table 11.3, in the early 1960s, fewer than half of women worked during their pregnancy and less than one-fourth worked during the month before the birth of their first child. By the early 1990s, two-thirds of women worked during their pregnancy, and more than half continued until less than 1 month before giving birth (Smith, Downs, & O'Connell, 2001).

Some of the other factors that determine how soon new mothers return to work after childbirth are women's wages, marital status, and family structure. Women with higher incomes tend to return to work sooner than women with lower paying jobs. Women whose spouses have high paying jobs, however, tend to return less quickly because their own income is less critical to their family's economic well-being. Women with only one child return to work more quickly than women with more children, possibly because the cost of child care for multiple children would be a greater economic drain on the family. Although

The proportion of women who work during the last month of pregnancy has increased dramatically.

TABLE 11.3   Proportion of Women Working During Pregnancy, Early 1960s—Early 1990s.

Early 1960s		Early 1990s	
During pregnancy	Within 1 month of birth	During pregnancy	Within 1 month of birth
44%	23%	67%	53%

Source: Based on information in Smith, Downs, & O'Connell, 2001.

single mothers may depend to a greater extent on the income from their jobs, married mothers tend to return to work more quickly than unmarried mothers. The presence of a spouse provides the opportunity for shared parental child care, and a spouse's income can also help the couple pay for child care more easily than a single mother's income (Hofferth & Curtin, 2003; Lamb & Ahnert, 2006).

Race/ethnicity are also related to new mothers' return to work. In the early 1990s, white non-Hispanic women and Asian women (33 percent for each) were slightly more likely to return to work within 3 months after the birth of their first child than African American women (25 percent) and even more likely to do so than Hispanic/Latina women (20 percent) (Smith, Downs, & O'Connell, 2001).

Women's earlier return to work after childbirth may also be related to demographic changes in postsecondary education and the age at which women become first-time mothers. During the second half of the twentieth century, growing numbers of women completed undergraduate degrees (NCES, 2004). Women with higher levels of education, especially women with a college degree, are significantly more likely to return to the same job than mothers with lower levels of education. Education is also related to how quickly mothers return to work. Women with at least a bachelor's degree are more likely to return within 3 months than women with less than a high school education. A related finding is that older mothers tend to return to work sooner than younger mothers. Women aged 25 years and older at the time their first child was born are more likely to return within 3 months than women who are younger than 25. The increase in the proportion of first-time mothers who are age 30 or older may thus be another reason that women have tended to return to work earlier in the years since the FMLA was passed (Hofferth & Curtin, 2003; Smith, Downs, & O'Connell, 2001).

As we have seen, the FMLA does not cover all employees in the United States, and many eligible employees choose not to use it either, because they cannot afford to give up their income or because their employers provide them with more attractive paid leave options. The majority of women who work during pregnancy return to work within 1 year after their child's birth, with most mothers who return to work doing so by the time their child is 6 months old (Smith, Downs, & O'Connell, 2001). These patterns result in large numbers of infants and toddlers in nonparental child care. Would these trends be different if the FMLA were a paid leave?

In the late 1990s, there was growing interest in and public support for proposals that would strengthen the FMLA in this way (Walker, 1996). One survey of 3,000 adults in the

United States showed that 88 percent of parents of young children and 80 percent of all adults supported some form of paid parental leave. Forty percent of those surveyed supported a paid leave of 3 months or less for mothers, 25 percent supported 4 to 11 months, and almost 33 percent favored 1 year or more (Sylvester, 2001). Legislatures in a number of states have considered proposals to offer paid leaves for parents, but as of 2005, only California had enacted a paid family leave policy.

The California law, which went into effect in 2004, allows all workers to take a partially paid family leave for up to 6 weeks to care for a newborn infant, a newly adopted child, or an ill family member. Employees may receive 55 percent of their usual wages during their absence (with a maximum of $728 per week). Unlike the unpaid FMLA, businesses with fewer than 50 employees are not required to protect the job of an employee who goes on paid family leave (U.S. Department of Labor, 2005). Without job protection, it remains to be seen whether California's paid leave policy will result in more parents of newborns taking time off from work and whether it will be significantly better than the original FMLA at supporting working parents so that they can serve as their infants' primary caregivers. Given its brevity, it is possible that the 6-week leave will be used primarily by mothers recovering from childbirth, perhaps in combination with other existing paid leaves, such as vacation time and sick leave.

Parental Leave Policies in Other Countries. Women's rates of participation in the labor force in European and Scandinavian countries increased in parallel with rates in the United States; however, using a combination of paid and unpaid leaves, working mothers in many of these countries return to their jobs much later after the birth of a child (Kamerman, 2000). Maternity leave providing at least 50 percent (and sometimes 100 percent) of the mother's regular wages is offered in Austria, Belgium, the Czech Republic, Denmark, Finland, France, Germany, Greece, Hungary, Ireland, Italy, Luxembourg, the Netherlands, Norway, Poland, Portugal, Spain, Sweden, Switzerland, Turkey, and the United Kingdom. It is also found in Canada, Israel, Japan, and Mexico. Depending on the country, the length of maternity leave ranges from 4 to 16 weeks. Out of all the advanced industrialized countries known as the Organization for Economic Cooperation and Development (OECD), only the United States, Australia, and New Zealand have no paid maternity leave (Kamerman, 2000; OECD, 2001; Sagi et al., 2002).

New fathers are included in many parental leave policies. About one-third of the OECD countries offer some form of paid paternity leave, varying in length from just 2 days to 3 weeks. Parental leaves, which may be taken by either parent, are also available in many of these countries as a supplement to maternity and paternity leaves following the birth of a child. Parental leaves may provide partial payment but are often unpaid time that can be used until the child is 2 or 3 years old (Deven & Moss, 2002; Kamerman, 2000; O'Brien, 2004). Let's look at a few examples of parental leave policies in other countries.

In Canada, the Employment Insurance Act was amended in 2001 to expand paid leave benefits for mothers as well as fathers from 6 months to one year. Mothers can now claim 15 weeks of paid maternity leave (including as much as 8 weeks before giving birth), and either parent can take up to 35 weeks of paid leave (at 55 percent of regular wages). At the same time, the minimum eligibility requirement was reduced to cover women who are employed part-time (as little as 12 hours of work per week, or 600 hours in the previous year), making paid maternity leave available to almost all working mothers in Canada (Marshall, 2003a, 2003b; Rahn & Burch, 2002).

In Israel, all mothers are entitled to 3 months of paid maternity leave following the birth of a child. At the end of this time, they have the option of extending their leave by claiming an additional 9 months of unpaid maternity leave (Sagi et al., 2002).

New mothers in Spain are eligible for a 16-week maternity leave (paid at 100 percent of prior wages). Paternity leaves, by contrast, are only 2 days long, but they are also paid at 100 percent of usual wages. An additional unpaid parental leave is available until children are 3 years old (Kamerman, 2000; O'Brien, 2004).

In Norway, 6 weeks of maternity leave are required to be taken as part of a paid parental leave that may last until the child is 12 months old. New fathers in Norway may take a 2-week unpaid paternity leave, and both parents are allowed to take an additional 12 months of unpaid parental leave.

Swedish fathers may take a 2-week paternity leave that provides approximately 70 percent of regular wages. Maternity leave is available before birth only for women who are ill during their pregnancy, but both parents may take a parental leave (paid at 80 percent of usual wages) until their child is 16 months old. Both parents may also apply for an additional 18 months of unpaid parental leave (Kamerman, 2000; O'Brien, 2004).

In Finland, parents receive a combination of paid maternity leave of up to 12.5 weeks, paid paternity leave of 1 week, and paid parental leave until the child is 26 months, with an additional care leave available up to 36 months. Parents in Finland may also use parental leave payments to pay for in-home care or care in a child care facility up to the age of 36 months (Kamerman, 2000).

Mothers in these countries usually take advantage of the leaves that are available to them, whereas fathers often do not use all of the paid time that they are entitled to take. Even using a portion of potential leave time in Sweden, however, means that fathers are on leave an average of 44 days (Kamerman, 2000).

How do these sorts of parental leave policies affect infants and their families? In Canada, like the United States, a high proportion (60 percent) of mothers with children under the age of 3 years are employed (Statistics Canada, 2003). Following the expansion of the parental leave policy, the median amount of time that Canadian mothers spent caring for their infants at home increased from 6 months in 2000 to 10 months in 2001. Mothers who used parental leave time but returned to work earlier than 9 or 10 months in 2001 frequently had spouses who claimed a portion of paid parental leave as well. This pattern is reflected in a significant increase in the proportion of fathers who used paid parental benefits—3 percent in 2000 as compared with 10 percent in 2001 (Marshall, 2003a, 2003b).

Studies in other countries have found that more generous leaves following childbirth lead to healthier infants and children, as measured by birth weights, infant mortality rates, and rates of breast feeding (Galtry, 2002; Ruhm, 1998). There is also evidence that policies that help parents remain at home with their infants for 6, 9, or 12 months after birth reduce maternal stress and may contribute to infants' cognitive and language development (Hill et al., 2005; Kamerman, 2000). As we will discuss shortly, poor quality child care has been shown to place infants at risk. To the extent that parental leaves enable parents to avoid using inferior child care, they also offer an attractive, direct way to promote their infants' healthy development (Kamerman et al., 2003; Lamb & Ahnert, 2006).

Maternal Employment

The need for nonparental child care in the United States has grown, fueled by steady increases in the rate of participation in the paid labor force by all women, especially mothers of young children. When the Census Bureau began recording labor force participation rates of mothers with infants in 1976, the rate was 31 percent among women who had had a child in the past year. This rate increased or held steady before peaking at 59 percent in 1998. In 2000, the labor force participation rate for mothers of infants dropped to 55 percent and remained at that level in 2002. Full-time employment (35 or more hours per week) is more common than part-time employment (34 percent versus 16 percent) for all mothers of infants except those aged 15 to 19 years, who are more likely to be enrolled in high school (Downs, 2003; Hofferth & Curtin, 2003).

Figures from the U.S. Department of Labor, which reports employment statistics for women with children younger than the age of 3 years, rather than 1 year, show that 57 percent of all women with children younger than 3 participated in the paid labor force in 2004. There are significant differences, however, as a function of marital status and race/ethnicity. With the exception of African American mothers, unmarried women are more likely to be in the paid labor force than are married women. The lowest employment rates overall are found among Hispanic/Latina women, followed by Asian women, white non-Hispanic women, and African American women (U.S. Department of Labor/Bureau of Labor Statistics, 2005).

Child Care Arrangements

Whether they are working full- or part-time, the most basic choice that new parents need to make is whether they want care that is provided by relatives or nonrelatives of their children. Relatives are defined as mothers, fathers, siblings, grandparents, and other relatives (aunts, uncles, cousins). Caregivers in the nonrelative category are in-home babysitters, neighbors, friends, and others providing care in any setting. Some nonrelatives are family child care providers who care for one or more unrelated children in the caregiver's home. Other caregivers in the nonrelative category provide care in an organized child care facility, such as a child care center, nursery school, or preschool (U.S. Census Bureau, 2003; Lamb & Ahnert, 2006).

When parents have a choice between two or more child care settings, their selection may be affected by their beliefs about infants and their development. They may choose a child care provider whose caregiving beliefs and practices are congruent with their own beliefs and practices or they may look for child care providers who can play a complementary role. Establishing a balance between the primary functions of home and child care may be some parents' objective, with parental care emphasizing stress reduction and emotional regulation, while providers' care focuses on cognitive stimulation and learning to participate in a group with other children (Ahnert & Lamb, 2003; Lamb & Ahnert, 2006).

Many infants and toddlers with working parents are cared for by nonrelatives in a family child care home.

Some researchers have asserted that for families of color, nonparental care may represent an opportunity to expose their children to other children of color who are likely to be similar in culture and language background. For other parents, nonparental care may be chosen because it provides early childhood education and enrichment, learning opportunities that their children might not otherwise have (Johnson et al., 2003).

Parents may also choose a child care arrangement for pragmatic reasons, such as the cost and convenience (Hofferth, 1991; Kisker & Maynard, 1991). It is clear that more light needs to be shed on parents' childrearing beliefs and motivations for selecting child care arrangements.

One survey of 324 working mothers 6 months after giving birth showed that the majority (53 percent) desired care provided by their child's father, while approximately one-fourth (24 percent) preferred at-home care provided by a relative or friend. Approximately 10 percent stated a preference for care at home provided by a paid sitter or nanny. As shown in Figure 11.1, however, only a small proportion of mothers were successful in arranging their most preferred type of child care. Besides father-provided care (23 percent), the most commonly used child care arrangements were **family child care homes** (28 percent) and out-of-home care by relatives (20 percent), although these arrangements were not the ones that most mothers had preferred. Child care centers were preferred the least (2 percent) but actually used by about 11 percent of all families in the survey (Riley & Glass, 2002).

The survey also found that a key determinant of whether mothers achieved their most desired child care arrangements was their employment schedule. Mothers who worked evening or night shifts were more likely than mothers who worked daytime hours to use care by family members. Mothers who worked fewer hours were more likely to use a spouse or in-home sitter, whereas mothers working longer hours tended to use family child care homes or day care centers. Families' income per se did not ensure that the preferred child care arrangement was achieved, but mothers with higher levels of education were more successful in achieving a match between their stated preference and their actual child care arrangement. It is possible that these women had more flexible employment options or had family

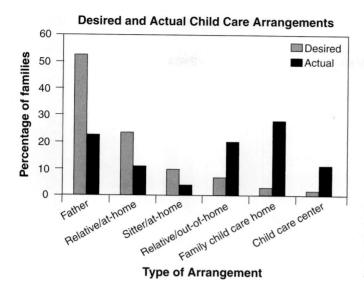

FIGURE 11.1 A large percentage of working mothers in one survey reported differences between their desired and actual child care arrangements.

Source: Riley & Glass, 2002.

members and spouses who were either more willing or more able to participate in providing child care in order to support mothers' employment. Based on their findings, the researchers argue that changes in parental leave policies that reduce the number of hours parents work would enable more families to care for their own infants and to achieve a match between their desired and their actual child care arrangements (Riley & Glass, 2002).

According to the Urban Institute's National Survey of American Families, in 1999, nearly three-quarters (73 percent) of children under age 5 with working parents were cared for by someone other than a parent. This survey, which sampled households with at least one child in 13 U.S. states—Alabama, California, Colorado, Florida, Massachusetts, Michigan, Minnesota, Mississippi, New Jersey, New York, Texas, Washington, and Wisconsin—found that the most frequently used child care arrangements were center-based care (28 percent) and care by relatives (27 percent). In addition, 14 percent of children were cared for in family child care homes, while 4 percent were cared for primarily by nannies or babysitters. Family income and family structure were related to children's primary care arrangements. Children from two-parent households were less likely than children from single-parent homes to be in child care centers. Children from two-parent households were also less likely than children from single-parent households to be cared for by relatives and more likely to be cared for by a parent. There was wide variation across states in the utilization of center-based care, from 37 percent in Alabama to 10 percent in Michigan. When viewed in comparison to historical data, these findings also showed that employed mothers increasingly used center-based care for their youngest preschool children; whereas 6 percent of employed mothers used centers in 1965, the comparable figure by 1993 was 30 percent (Sonenstein et al., 2002).

The very youngest children, those from birth to age 2 years, are more likely to be cared for by relatives than in an organized child care facility. In 1999, fathers provided 20 percent of care for infants under the age of 1 year and 19 percent for 1- to 2-year-old children; in

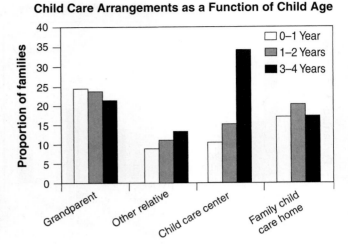

FIGURE 11.2 Child care arrangements vary as a function of child age. Use of child care centers increases dramatically at ages 3 to 4 years.

Source: U.S. Census Bureau, 2003.

some families with children younger than 2 years, parents arrange nonoverlapping work schedules in order to avoid nonparental care entirely. As shown in Figure 11.2, in 1999, the largest proportions of nonparental care for children younger than 2 years were provided by a grandparent or another relative, whereas nonrelative care, especially in an organized center, was more prevalent for 3- to 4-year-old children. (Lamb & Ahnert, 2006; U.S. Census Bureau, 2003).

One of the reasons many parents choose relative care is that nonparental care, especially high-quality care in an organized child care setting, can be very expensive (Helburn & Howes, 1996). Child care costs in the United States vary from state to state, and often differ in rural and urban areas (NACCRRA, 2005). Care for infants is the most expensive of all, with the average annual cost for infants ranging between approximately $4,000 and $14,000 (Mohan, Reef, & Sarkar, 2006; Schulman, 2000). According to the U.S. Census Bureau (2003), the average weekly child care expenditures by families with children under 5 were $94 (approximately $4,888 per year), which represented an average of 8.57 percent of monthly family income. Overall, the average family spends more on infant care than on food each year, and in 49 states average child care fees for two children of any age exceed the average rent cost (Mohan, Reef, & Sarkar, 2006). Child care expenses tend to be lower for poor working families and families with lower levels of parental education, but families with fewer resources also spend a higher percentage of their income on child care (Giannarelli, & Barsimantov, 2000; Mohan, Reef, & Sarkar, 2006; Schulman, 2000).

Even when cost is not a primary consideration, parents of infants may wonder whether their infant will receive enough sensitive, responsive care in a child care center or a family child care home. In our next section, we will consider whether these concerns are supported by evidence gathered from large-scale studies of early child care and its effects on infants and toddlers. We will also examine the characteristics that parents should look for in any nonparental child care arrangement, qualities that are associated with more optimal developmental outcomes.

Effects of Child Care on Infants and Toddlers

One of the most comprehensive sources of information about the effects of early child care on infants and toddlers comes from the National Institute of Child Health and Human Development (NICHD). The **NICHD Study of Early Child Care** was undertaken in 1991 as a 7-year longitudinal study of nearly 1,400 children in 10 sites across the United States. A team of researchers designed the study, ensuring that multiple methods and measures would be used. Information was gathered about the family environment and the characteristics of child care arrangements, such as children's age of entry into nonparental care as well as the quantity, stability, quality, and type of care. Each child care setting was assessed to determine the caregivers' education and training, the child-to-adult ratio, and group size. The multiple methods used include observations, interviews, questionnaires, and standardized tests. In addition, rather than focus on just one domain of development, the NICHD Study of Early Child Care gathered information about children's social, emotional, cognitive, and language development, as well as behavior problems and physical health and development (Lamb & Ahnert, 2006; NICHD Early Child Care Research Network, 2005).

The Sample. To make the findings of the NICHD study as generalizable as possible, a diverse sample of children and families was selected, representing a range of socioeconomic, educational, and racial/ethnic backgrounds in the United States. The resulting sample is 76 percent white non-Hispanic, 13 percent African American, 6 percent Hispanic/Latino, 1 percent Asian/Pacific Islander/Native American, and 4 percent other minorities. Approximately 35 percent of children and families in the sample were living in or near poverty (NICHD Early Child Care Research Network, 2005).

Patterns of Child Care Use. The types of child care included in the study were those chosen by families themselves and reflected the spectrum of child care options available. In keeping with patterns of nonparental child care use that others have reported, a large percentage of infants were cared for by relatives, whereas children older than 2 years were more likely to be in child care centers (NICHD Early Child Care Research Network, 2005).

During the first year of life, children in the NICHD study spent an average of 33 hours per week in nonparental care. There were racial/ethnic differences in the amount of child care, however, with African American infants experiencing the most hours and white non-Hispanic infants receiving the fewest. The majority of infants in the sample entered nonparental care before the age of 4 months, with most being cared for by relatives rather than in a family child care home or a child care center (NICHD Early Child Care Research Network, 2005).

Mothers with the highest incomes were more likely than other mothers to return to work and place their infants in care by the time they were 3 to 5 months old. These infants were more likely than other infants, however, to be cared for at home for the first 15 months after birth. Parents' own beliefs about the effects of early child care affected their decisions about the best arrangements for their infants. Mothers who thought that their children would benefit from child care tended to return to work sooner and to use more hours of formal child care in centers or family child care homes, whereas mothers who were concerned that employment would harm their infants tended to choose informal family-based or in-home options (NICHD Early Child Care Research Network, 2005).

Defining Quality Child Care.   What should parents who are looking for high-quality child care look for? A number of specific definitions and rating systems exist, but as we will see, they share many of the same concerns and focus on many of the same characteristics. Quality of child care is typically measured by examining two kinds of variables. The first, *process* variables, are evident in the degree to which interactions between caregivers and children are stimulating and nurturing and promote children's development. The second type, *structural* variables, include the physical spaces in which children spend their time, the caregiver-to-child ratio, group size, and the education and experience of the caregivers. Although they are defined and measured separately, in most settings these components of quality are strongly linked—high-quality interactions tend to take place in settings that are safe and in which caregivers are well educated about and experienced in child care.

Whether process and structural measures are examined separately or in combination, the quality of the average nonparental child care arrangement has been described by many researchers as poor to mediocre (Helburn & Howes, 1996; Honig, 2002). No one knows with certainty how many young children are in unlicensed care of substandard quality, but one well-known study of 400 child care centers in four states—the Cost, Quality and Child Outcomes in Child Care Centers (CQO) study—was both illuminating and discouraging. The research team found that only 14 percent of the centers provided interactions and care that were of high enough quality to support children's development, and 12 percent were of such low quality that they did not meet children's basic health and safety needs. Infants and toddlers received care that was rated lowest of all; only 8 percent of infant classrooms were judged to be high quality, and 40 percent were actually considered low quality (Cost, Quality, and Child Outcomes Study Team, 1995; National Center for Early Development and Learning, 1997).

A similar study of more than 200 family child care homes in three states—the Study of Children in Family Child Care and Relative Care—found that only 9 percent of family child care homes were providing care that could be considered good, while 56 percent was adequate or custodial, and 35 percent was inadequate (Kontos et al., 1994). Like the CQO study, the Study of Family Child Care and Relative Care also found that the majority of caregivers in both kinds of settings had low levels of formal education and experience in child care.

To address these problems, some early childhood education experts have proposed that federal regulations for child care in the United States be established in order to ensure that all children have access to high-quality nonparental care (Brauner, Gordic, & Zigler, 2004). In the absence of such uniform, widely known, and enforced criteria, however, many parents focus on finding an affordable child care arrangement that will meet their child's basic health and safety needs, while others intentionally look for more expensive options, based on the not-always-valid assumption that high cost is a reliable indicator of program quality (Helburn & Howes, 1996). Regardless of the criteria that they use, many parents do not look specifically for child care that also provides the benefits of high-quality early childhood education—"developmentally-appropriate curricula fostering a child's cognitive, social, and emotional development" (Brauner, Gordic, & Zigler, 2004, p. 3).

Quality of care was a consideration in the NICHD study, which showed that high-quality child care differed from lower quality care in three key ways: 1) a higher frequency of sensitive, responsive interaction between children and caregivers; 2) more adherence to recommended guidelines for group size, child-adult ratios, and aspects of the physical environment; and 3) the presence of caregivers with a higher level of education, specialized training, child care experience, and more accurate beliefs about child development. Children from the highest and the lowest income levels were more likely than children from near-poverty income levels to experience high-quality child care. Unlike affluent parents who could afford to pay for high-quality child care and lower income parents who qualified for subsidized high-quality care, parents living near poverty had considerably fewer economic resources and thus fewer high-quality child care choices (NICHD Early Child Care Research Network, 2005; Shonkoff & Phillips, 2000).

Some of the characteristics of quality—child-to-adult ratios, group size, teacher training, and teacher education—can be assessed through compliance with relevant state regulations. The NICHD study reported that most child care centers included in its sample did not possess all four characteristics. The study found, however, that the greater the number of these characteristics present, the more advanced were children's language comprehension and school readiness and the fewer the number of behavior problems at ages 2 and 3 years (Lamb & Ahnert, 2006; NICHD Early Child Care Research Network, 2005).

The National Association for the Education of Young Children (NAEYC) reviews the quality of child care programs by examining 10 components: child-teacher interactions, curriculum, family-teacher relationships, staff qualifications/professional development, administration, staffing ratios, physical environment, health/safety, nutrition/food service, and program evaluation. Parents looking for high-quality child care can use NAEYC accreditation as a guide during their search, knowing that accredited programs conform to recommendations for age-appropriate adult-to-child ratios, group sizes, teacher training, and teacher education. In NAEYC-accredited programs, teachers are warm, responsive,

In high-quality child care, interactions between caregivers and children are stimulating and nurturing and promote children's development. Structural variables, such as the caregiver-to-child ratio, group size, and the caregivers' education and experience, are also important indicators of quality.

supportive, and show respect for individuality. Teachers in NAEYC-endorsed programs are also likely to demonstrate cultural competence as a result of education and training in the areas of culture, language, and diversity. Staff in NAEYC-accredited programs are adults with recognized training and education; they understand early childhood development and are qualified to implement the program's curriculum. In NAEYC-accredited programs, ratios for the number of adults to children differ across age groups (1:4 for 0 to 12 months; 1:4 or 1:5 for 12 to 24 months, depending on total group size; 1:6 for 24 to 30 months; and 1:7 for 30 to 36 months) (NAEYC, 1995, 2002).

In addition to the measures that we have already discussed, there are a number of formal systems for rating and evaluating the quality of early childhood environments. Among the most frequently used instruments are the Infant/Toddler Environment Rating Scale (Harms, Cryer, & Clifford, 1990), the Early Childhood Environment Rating Scale (Harms, Clifford, & Cryer, 1998), and the Classroom Practice Inventory (Hyson, Hirsh-Pasek, & Rescorla, 1990). These measures are consistent with NICHD definitions, NAEYC accreditation standards, and other well-known guidelines for developmentally appropriate practices (Bredekamp & Copple, 1997; Lamb & Ahnert, 2006).

Many studies have found that high-quality child care tends to produce more positive developmental outcomes than lower quality child care. Program quality is affected by characteristics of families and children, however, including parenting skill, child temperament, and developmental disabilities. There is also variability in the age at which children enter nonparental child care and in the quantity of care they receive each day. As we will see next, the addition of these kinds of child-and-family variables has led to more complex results, but it also has clarified our understanding of the effects of child care during the first 3 years of life.

Effects on the Infant-Parent Relationship.   New parents may worry that full-time child care will negatively affect the infant-parent attachment relationship. The NICHD study provides reassurance for these parents. Child care per se neither jeopardizes nor promotes security of attachment, as measured by the Strange Situation (NICHD Early Child Care Research Network, 1997a, 1997b, 2005; Shonkoff & Phillips, 2000). Study results do indicate certain combinations of early care that were associated with insecure attachment, however. These combinations included poor quality care for more than 10 hours per week and multiple child care arrangements during the first 15 months of life, but only when mothers themselves were less sensitive in their interactions with their infants; infants whose mothers were sensitive were significantly more likely to be securely attached, despite having the same child care arrangements. Conversely, infants whose mothers were less sensitive were less likely to be insecurely attached if they were in high-quality child care (NICHD Early Child Care Research Network, 2005).

Some infants experience a large number of caregiving arrangements and different caregivers as a result of staff turnover, which occurs in child care positions at rates that are among the highest of all occupations in the United States (Shonkoff & Phillips, 2000). Even when there is not high turnover, however, most centers follow a practice of advancing children through different classrooms as they get older, leaving their previous caregivers behind. Some child development experts believe that this practice fails to recognize the importance of the attachment relationship that forms between infants and their primary nonparental caregivers. As an alternative, a small number of child care centers have begun to consider the practice of continuity of caregiver—having infants and toddlers remain with the same primary caregiver(s) during as much of their time in the center as possible (Cryer, Hurwitz, & Wolery, 2003).

There is some evidence from the NICHD study that infants who experience more hours of nonparental care in the first 6 months of life tend to have mothers who are less attentive, less responsive, and less affectionate. Greater amounts of nonparental care at an earlier age was associated with lower levels of positive child-parent interactions at the age of 3 years (Brooks-Gunn, Han, & Waldfogel, 2002). Quality of child care made a difference, however, apart from the amount of time or age of entry into child care. Children in high-quality child care tended to have more positive interactions with nonparental caregivers and also had more positive interactions with their mothers at age 3. Mothers whose children were in high-quality child care tended to show more sensitivity and positive involvement with their children when they were 15 and 36 months old. In the end, however, family variables, such as income, maternal sensitivity, maternal education, marital status, and maternal depression, had a stronger influence on the quality of mother-child interactions than did children's child care experience (Lamb & Ahnert, 2006; Love et al., 2003; NICHD Early Child Care Research Network, 2005).

Researchers involved in a different large-scale study of approximately 760 Israeli infants, however, have obtained a different set of results. Investigators involved in the Haifa Study of Early Child Care found that center care per se increased the likelihood that infants in this large urban area would develop insecure attachment to their mothers, as assessed in the Strange Situation. Infants who were in center care beginning at the age of 3 months were significantly more likely to be insecurely attached than infants who were in group care in a family child care home or in individual care provided by mothers, unpaid relatives, or paid nonrelatives. As has been reported in NICHD studies, the highest rates of insecure attachment were found among infants whose mothers showed low levels of sensitivity toward them. The child care characteristic that appeared to be the principal reason for the elevated incidence of insecure attachment was the higher average infant-to-adult ratio in center care as compared to a family child care home (8:1 versus 4:1) (Sagi et al., 2002).

According to the researchers, center care in Israel is generally of poor quality, when evaluated according to NAEYC criteria, and there is significantly less variability in the quality of center care than is found in the United States. Taken together, these findings suggest that, unlike most U.S. parents, Israeli parents have reason to be concerned about the potentially negative effects of center care for infants and should strongly consider other individual or small-group arrangements for their infants when they return to work.

Effects on Social Development. Consistent with evidence about infant-parent attachment, family and maternal characteristics have been found to exert a stronger influence than child care experience per se on children's social behavior, compliance, and self-control. The most influential aspect of child care experience, as we have already discussed for attachment and infant-parent interaction, is the quality of care provided. Infants in high-quality child care tend to have emotionally positive, sensitive interactions with caregivers and are, in turn, less likely to have behavior problems at 2 and 3 years of age than are children in poor quality child care (NICHD Early Child Care Research Network, 1998; Peisner-Feinberg & Burchinal, 1997; Peisner-Feinberg et al., 2001; Shonkoff & Phillips, 2000).

It has also been reported that children who spend more time in group care tend to display more cooperative behavior than children who spend less time in child care with peers, especially when providers have more than a high school level of education (Lamb & Ahnert, 2006; Loeb et al., 2004; NICHD Early Child Care Research Network, 2004, 2005).

Not all of the findings have been positive, however. One analysis of NICHD data indicated that the more time children spent in nonparental care, the more behavior problems and conflicts with adults they had at 54 months of age and in kindergarten. The effects of maternal sensitivity and family socioeconomic status played an even greater role in children's behavior problems during the transition to kindergarten, but children who had experienced a greater amount of any type of nonparental care still showed more social and emotional problems (NICHD Early Child Care Research Network, 2003, 2005). The reasons for these patterns are not well understood, and some researchers have called for additional study of individual differences, such as temperament or reactivity of the stress-response system, and their influence on the way that early experience in child care affects child development (Crockenberg, 2003; Lamb & Ahnert, 2006).

Children who have higher levels of physical, social, and emotional competence are better prepared for school than children who have difficulty controlling their emotions and relating to peers and teachers. According to current views, these skills are just as important as cognitive and academic readiness (Blair, 2002, 2003; Raver, 2002, 2003.) On the whole, the NICHD study indicates that high-quality child care promotes development in all of these domains, but it also appears that the more time children spend in any type of nonparental child care, the more assertive, aggressive, and disobedient they are in kindergarten. It is unclear, even to many child development experts, how to interpret and respond to these findings. It is possible, for example, that being in child care and amassing large amounts of experience in it causes children to behave in these ways. It is also possible, however, that parents tend to place certain kinds of children in child care from an early age. This might occur if shyer, temperamentally inhibited toddlers are less likely to be placed in nonparental care than are more aggressive, temperamentally uninhibited toddlers. Given the nonexperimental design of the NICHD study, it is not possible to rule out either explanation, but the fact that some children with lots of early child care experience have more behavior problems in kindergarten is a finding that deserves further exploration (Lamb & Ahnert, 2006; NICHD Early Child Care Research Network, 2005).

Effects on Language and Cognitive Development.   As we discussed in Chapter 8, language development is influenced by the family environment and parents' interactions with their children. In high-quality child care, children receive emotionally positive care from caregivers who frequently engage them in stimulating conversations that support and reinforce early language development (Huttenlocher, 1998). The NICHD study has found that children in high-quality child care tend to have better developed language abilities than children in poor quality care at 15, 24, and 36 months, as well as more advanced cognitive abilities at 24 and 54 months (Burchinal et al., 2000; NICHD Early Child Care Research Network, 2000, 2005; NICHD Early Child Care Research Network & Duncan, 2003). By 36 months, children who have been in higher quality child care also tend to show higher levels of school readiness—skills and knowledge that help children do well in school, such as identification of colors, letters, and numbers, as well as counting ability, shape recognition, and the ability to make comparisons (NICHD Early Child Care Research Network, 2005; Peisner-Feinberg & Burchinal, 1997; Peisner-Feinberg et al., 2001).

Positive effects of high-quality center-based care on cognitive growth and school readiness have also been found for low-income children whose mothers were enrolled in welfare-to-work programs (Loeb et al., 2004; Votruba-Drzal, Coley, & Chase-Lansdale, 2004). In fact, there is evidence that high-quality care has an even more profound positive impact on children from lower-income families than it does on children from families with more socioeconomic resources (Brooks-Gunn, 2003; Brooks-Gunn et al., 1993; Fuller et al., 2002; Lamb & Ahnert, 2006; NICHD Early Child Care Research Network, 2005).

One study using data from the NICHD study found that children whose mothers worked typical daytime hours had higher cognitive test scores at 15, 24, and 36 months than children whose mothers had ever worked nonstandard hours, such as night shifts or jobs with variable schedules (Brooks-Gunn, Han, Waldfogel, 2002). This finding is consistent with other research suggesting that long hours of maternal employment in the first year of life may interfere with the time that parents can spend interacting with their infants and stimulating their cognitive and language development (Kamerman et al., 2003). The most negative effects were found when children were placed in lower quality child care after their mothers began working 30 hours or more per week at 6 to 9 months. These negative effects were amplified among children whose mothers who were rated as providing less sensitive care for their infants at 36 months (Brooks-Gunn, Han, & Waldfogel, 2002).

Overall, these findings indicate that early nonparental care is not in itself associated with negative child outcomes. Instead, characteristics of the family, including maternal sensitivity, appear to exert the predominant influence on early development. Nonparental child care can have negative effects on children when the quality is low, and the most harmful situation involves the combination of maternal insensitivity with low quality nonparental child care. High-quality care is expensive, however, and is not universally available. For one group of parents—those whose infants and toddlers have special needs—affordable, high-quality care has often been especially hard to secure (Kelly & Booth, 1999; Shonkoff & Phillips, 2000).

Including Children with Disabilities in Child Care

Children with disabilities or special needs have or are at risk for chronic physical, developmental, behavioral, or emotional conditions and typically need developmental, health, mental health, and related services that extend beyond those generally required by children (Child Care Law Center, 2003). Developmental disabilities may include autism spectrum disorders, cerebral palsy, hearing loss, mental retardation, Down syndrome, spina bifida, and vision impairment (Centers for Disease Control & Prevention, 2005a).

Compared with mothers of typically developing children, mothers of children with disabilities tend to have more difficulty finding appropriate, affordable child care and often return to work later after their children's birth. They also are more likely to work part-time and to choose individual care by a relative instead of group care in a family child care home or child care center (Kelly & Booth, 1999). The greatest challenge in finding care for infants and young children with disabilities is often the availability of child care providers

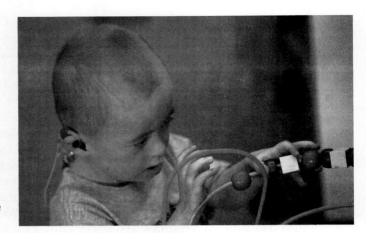

This boy has developmental disabilities, but he attends a child care center with children who are not disabled and is included in all center activities.

who are trained to work with children who have special needs (Wolery & Odom, 2000). Although there is still a need for more child care providers who can work with young children with disabilities, federal legislation enacted since 1990 has led to the expansion of training and graduate programs in early childhood special education.

In 1990, the **Americans with Disabilities Act (ADA)** was passed to protect the civil rights of all individuals with disabilities. With respect to children, the ADA states that children cannot be excluded from services, such as child care centers, private preschools, and other early childhood programs, because of their disability. Children with disabilities are also covered by the federal **Individuals with Disabilities Education Act (IDEA)**. One section of IDEA, referred to as Part C, explicitly covers services provided from birth to 36 months of age; Part C specifies that "to the maximum extent appropriate, children with disabilities including children in public or private institutions or other care facilities, are educated with children who are not disabled, and special classes, separate schooling, or other removal of children with disabilities from the regular educational environment occurs only when the nature or severity of the disability of a child is such that education in regular classes with the use of supplementary aids and services cannot be achieved satisfactorily" (U.S. Department of Education/Office of Special Education Programs, 2001).

According to the U.S. Department of Education's Office of Special Education Programs (2001), approximately 230,000 children age birth to 2 years, or 2 percent of all infants and toddlers in 2000, received services through Part C of IDEA. Approximately 600,000 preschool children, or 5 percent of all 3- to 5-year-olds, received IDEA services in the same year.

Under the provisions of IDEA, children with disabilities in physical, cognitive, communication, or socioemotional development may qualify for **Early Intervention Services (EI or EIS)** that include screening and assessment, family education and training, home visits, health and social services, speech-language therapy, and occupational and physical therapy, as well as assistive technology. Children and their families receive an Individualized Family Service Plan (IFSP) that describes services, providers, locations, and Individualized Education Plan (IEP) goals. In keeping with the concept of inclusion, services involve the family and are provided in the child's natural home and community environment (National Child Care Information Center, 1999).

Despite the progress that has been made in legislating more inclusive policies for children with disabilities, parents of children with special needs still face many challenges, in part because the supply of care for infants and young children with disabilities is still not adequate to meet the demand. In addition, although families living below the poverty level tend to have a higher percentage of children with disabilities or special needs, lower income neighborhoods tend to have fewer child care options for children with special needs than higher income neighborhoods (NACCRRA, 2003; Shonkoff & Phillips, 2000).

Finally, within the child care setting or preschool classroom, different models are used to achieve inclusion, resulting in varying degrees of coordination and collaboration among child care providers and early childhood teachers. In some settings, there is little interaction and coordination, and an external consultant takes one or more children with special needs to a separate area of the classroom or even outside of the regular classroom to work with them on IFSP and IEP goals that may or may not coincide with the activities of the rest of the children in the class. In other cases, the preschool classroom teacher or child care provider collaborates with and coordinates the efforts of a team of specialists who work with the child at different times during the day. A third approach, less commonly used but growing in popularity, employs a co-teaching model with significant classroom roles for both the early childhood teacher and an early childhood special education teacher (Wolery & Odom, 2000).

More research is needed to shed light on the influence of culture on parents' perceptions of children with special needs and inclusion policies and services (Wolery & Odom, 2000). We also need to know more about the quality of care that young children with disabilities receive and the relative effectiveness of different models of care and early childhood special education. The evidence that is available suggests that higher quality care is associated with more advanced development and optimal functioning, just as it is for typically developing infants and toddlers (Booth & Kelly, 1998, 1999; Kelly & Booth, 1999; Shonkoff & Phillips, 2000).

As we conclude our examination of research on early child care, it is important to remember that nearly all of these studies have used observational rather than experimental designs. That is, mothers in the samples have not been randomly assigned to employment versus nonemployment, and type of child care and its quality have not been controlled by researchers. It is likely, therefore, that preexisting differences in family characteristics, including income, education levels, and maternal sensitivity, lead parents to choose different child care arrangements in the first place and contribute to different outcomes across child care settings. Even with this caveat, however, it is clear that the findings of the NICHD longitudinal study and other research on the impact of high versus low quality early child care are generally consistent with the results of studies using experimental designs to evaluate the effects of early interventions.

Early Intervention

As many early childhood experts have noted, the concept of **early intervention** is difficult to define succinctly because it encompasses a wide range of programs and philosophies. In some approaches, the goal is prevention of negative outcomes for children considered to be at risk due to family income, parent characteristics, birth experiences, or aspects of the environment, such as the intervention in Russian Baby Homes that we discussed in Chapter 9 (Groark et al., 2003, 2005). In other interventions, the goal is the amelioration of existing identified conditions, such as developmental disabilities or developmental delays.

Some interventions focus on a specific developmental domain and objective, such as enhancing the quality of mother-infant interactions (Wendland-Carro, Piccinini & Millar, 1999), increasing young children's awareness of nutrition and disease prevention (Williams et al. 1998), or promoting reading and emergent literacy in low-income preschoolers (Weitzman et al., 2004; Whitehurst et al., 1994). Many comprehensive large-scale interventions, including several studies that we will discuss shortly, address multiple developmental outcomes.

Intervention programs may involve direct interaction only with the target child or they may include parents and other family members, either in the home or in controlled child care settings. The timing for initiating interventions is another dimension that varies; some programs begin while the mother is still pregnant, whereas others do not start until after the child is born (Cicchetti & Toth, 2006; Korfmacher, 2002; Lamb & Ahnert, 2006; Powell, 2006; Ramey, Ramey, & Lanzi, 2006; Shonkoff & Phillips, 2000).

Early Intervention through Child Care and Preschool

The strongest conclusions about the impact of early intervention can be made when children are randomly assigned to intervention and control groups, ensuring that there are no preexisting differences between groups at the beginning of the intervention. Let's look now at several of the most frequently cited studies in the early childhood intervention literature.

The High/Scope Perry Preschool Project. The Perry Preschool in Ypsilanti, Michigan, was the setting for an often-cited intervention project, the **High/Scope Perry Preschool Project**, that was carried out in the early 1960s. The target group—approximately 100 low-income African American 3- and 4-year-old children—received $2\frac{1}{2}$ hours of high-quality early childhood education each morning and $1\frac{1}{2}$ hours of home visits each afternoon. Participants in the project were studied longitudinally and compared with a control group of similar children who did not participate in the 30-week preschool program. Initially, there were gains in measured IQ for the intervention group, but these differences diminished within a few years of participation in the program. Other long-lasting advantages for the intervention group were reported, however, including a lower likelihood of being placed in special education in elementary school, higher achievement test scores at age 14, higher rates of graduation from high school, higher earned incomes at age 27, and lower rates of juvenile delinquency and crime (Schweinhart et al., 1993; Weikart, 1998).

The Abecedarian Project and Project CARE. Long-term gains have also been reported in follow-up studies of participants in the **Abecedarian Project**, a study begun in 1972. In this study, approximately 100 low-income, primarily African American children were randomly selected to participate in a full-time, high-quality early childhood education program from the age of 6 weeks until 3 years. Periodic cognitive testing carried out between the ages of 3 and 21 years indicates that children who received the intervention had higher scores than a control group on cognitive and achievement tests, with differences continuing to be found through age 21. Children who were in the intervention group also had lower rates of referral for special education, were less likely to repeat a grade, less likely to become adolescent parents, and more likely to complete high school (Campbell et al., 2001, 2002; Campbell & Ramey, 1994; Ramey & Ramey, 1998a, 1998b; Ramey, Ramey, & Lanzi, 2006). Similar results were found in a subsequent intervention, **Project CARE**, which began in 1978 and combined early child care in a child development center, parent group meetings, and home visiting (Wasik et al., 1990).

The Infant Health and Development Project. In a more recent intervention using a larger sample, the **Infant Health and Development Project**, researchers conducted a longitudinal study of nearly 1,000 preterm, low-birthweight infants (Gross, Spiker, & Haynes, 1997; McCarton et al., 1997). All children participating in the project received health care and other community services, but one-third of the sample (the intervention group) was randomly selected to have home visits and to participate in full-day, high-quality child care in child development centers from birth to age 3. Parents of this subsample also participated in a parent education component. At age 3, children who had participated in the intervention had higher measured intelligence, better vocabulary development, and fewer behavioral problems than children who were not part of the intervention. These gains were not sustained indefinitely, however. By age 8, the intervention group and the comparison group were no longer significantly different (Berlin et al., 1998; Gross, Spiker, & Haynes, 1997).

Early Head Start

In 1994, the Administration on Children, Youth and Families (ACF) established **Early Head Start**, a national intervention program to provide services to low-income pregnant women and families with infants and toddlers. In addition to targeting children and families who meet income eligibility requirements, Early Head Start is guided by a policy of inclusion that requires that at least 10 percent of its programs are made available to children with disabilities, regardless of family income. Early Head Start services may be delivered in center-based or home-based settings, or a combination of these settings, and include quality early childhood education, parenting education, health and mental health care, nutrition education, and family support. The program has grown to over 700 programs serving more than 70,000 children and families across the United States (ACF, 2005; Kamerman, et al., 2003; Powell, 2006).

From the beginning, Early Head Start was intended to be evaluated using a random-assignment design. The Early Head Start Research and Evaluation Project focused on 17 sites and studied 3,000 children and families, half of whom participated in Early Head Start and half of whom were randomly assigned to a control group. An array of assessments of cognitive, language, and social-emotional development were carried out when children were 14, 24, and 36 months old, and families were interviewed periodically about their use of services.

Benefits were found for both home- and center-based services, but the strongest effects were found for programs combining center-based care with home visits. Quality in Early Head Start centers was consistently high, as evaluated by NAEYC criteria. At 14 and 24 months of age, children in Early Head Start were three times more likely to receive their primary nonparental care in a good quality center than children in the control group (ACF,

2003a). As a result, children who participated in Early Head Start during its first 3 years had better outcomes on multiple measures at age 3 than children in the control group. In keeping with other studies of the impact of quality child care on low-income children, more time in center care led to higher levels of cognitive development at 24 and 36 months and higher levels of language development at 36 months. Participation in Early Head Start also contributed to more involved object play and fewer negative interactions with parents (ACF, 2002; Love et al., 2002).

Children participating in Early Head Start were less likely than control group children to experience delays in cognitive and language functioning, but Early Head Start children with disabilities were more likely to receive screening and referral for Part C IDEA services than were control group children. Families of Early Head Start children with disabilities were more likely than other Early Head Start families to be highly involved in the program and to remain in the program longer than other families. This pattern may reflect the parent education and parent support groups that were provided in Early Head Start, as well as specialized training that many Early Head Start staff received to help them identify children who would benefit from a referral for Part C IDEA services. Not all families benefited to the same degree, however; many children in Hispanic/Latino families and children of teen mothers, as well as of children of parents with multiple demographic risk factors (e.g., lower levels of education) had lower functioning in cognitive and language development. These families were more likely than other Early Head Start families to be unaware of their children's disabilities, and their children were the least likely to receive Part C services, suggesting that different approaches may need to be used to help them understand the importance of early identification and intervention (ACF, 2003b).

Benefits were also found for parents who had received Early Head Start services; compared with parents of children in the control group, they were more emotionally supportive and less detached toward their children as well as more likely to report reading to their children every day. Early Head Start parents reported using fewer punitive discipline strategies and were less likely than control group parents to report spanking their children in the previous week. Parents in the Early Head Start group were also more likely to participate in education and job training activities and to be employed than were parents in the control group (Love et al., 2002, 2005; Powell, 2006).

Poverty as a Risk Factor: Implications for Prevention and Intervention

With the notion of prevention rather than intervention in mind, some early childhood experts have asserted that eligibility for IDEA services should be expanded from existing, diagnosed physical or mental conditions to include "family conditions that have a high probability of resulting in a developmental delay, such as significant parental mental illness (particularly maternal depression), parental substance abuse, and significant family violence" (NACCRRA, 2003). If eligibility were expanded in these ways, growing up in an environment of poverty could also be added to the list of risk factors for developmental disabilities and delays because it exerts significant stress on families.

In 2002, 18.5 percent of children under the age of 6 were living in poverty, a figure that is significantly higher than for 18- to 64-year-olds (10.6 percent) and those 65 years and older

Growing up in poverty, especially in an environment of violence, chaos, and instability, exerts stress on families that increases children's risk of developmental delays and disabilities. Children exposed to risks due to earlier and more sustained poverty tend to have lower levels of cognitive and language development than children with briefer exposure.

(10.4 percent). Poverty status also varies as a function of family structure; 48.6 percent of children under 6 living with an unmarried female adult lived in poverty in 2002, as compared with 9.7 percent of children living in married-couple families (Proctor & Dalaker, 2003).

Numerous studies have shown that children living in poverty are more likely than children from higher income families to be exposed to family violence, chaos, and instability, and to live in more dangerous, polluted, and deteriorating neighborhoods. Children living in poverty are also more likely to attend less cognitively stimulating, lower quality child care programs and schools and to have more limited access to books and computers (Evans, 2004). Children exposed to cumulative risks through early and sustained poverty tend to have significantly lower levels of cognitive and language development as well as higher levels of antisocial behavior than children who experience poverty more briefly (Bradley & Corwyn, 2002; Brooks-Gunn & Duncan, 1997; McLoyd, Aikens, & Burton, 2006).

Are these negative outcomes inevitable? Perhaps not, according to one recent study that compared more than 1,000 pairs of 5-year-old monozygotic (identical) and dizygotic (fraternal) twins in England and Wales, all of whom experienced significant socioeconomic deprivation. Some children had more positive outcomes than others and the effects of living in poverty varied as a function of both intrinsic child characteristics and caregiving experience. The researchers found that at least one genetically influenced characteristic—child temperament—appeared to buffer the effects of poverty; they speculate that children with more sociable and outgoing temperaments may have elicited more cognitively stimulating interactions from their child care providers, exchanges that may have contributed to more positive cognitive, language, and behavioral outcomes. Caregiving experience in the family also played a role, however, and children whose mothers showed higher levels of warmth and engaged their children in stimulating activities appeared to promote positive adjustment, even in the face of socioeconomic deprivation (Kim-Cohen et al., 2004). These findings suggest that "if poor families are provided with the means to engage in stimulating activities with their young children, it may be possible to counteract some of the negative effects that living in a socioeconomically impoverished environment has on children's intellectual development" (Kim-Cohen et al., 2004, p. 662).

In addition to the positive influence of child temperament and parental involvement, there is also compelling evidence that child outcomes are enhanced when lower income parents are provided with economic resources, including direct income supplements (McLoyd, 1998, 2005; McLoyd, Aikens, & Burton, 2006; Shonkoff & Phillips, 2000). However, while public policy, such as the Personal Responsibility and Work Opportunity Reconciliation Act of 1996 and Temporary Assistance to Needy Families, requires low-income mothers of infants and toddlers to leave home and enter the paid labor force, there is relatively little support in the United States for providing parents with income supplements per se. As a result, most interventions directly involve infants, toddlers, and their parents in behavioral and educational programs.

Measuring the Impact of Early Childhood Intervention

Does early intervention make a difference? Some critics have raised questions about the use of relatively small sample sizes or the design and methods of some intervention studies. These points do not apply to the Early Head Start Research and Evaluation Project, but some critics have challenged the claim that the Abecedarian Project's results were due to the effects of the first few months of intervention. They assert, instead, that brighter children were, by chance, allocated to the experimental group (Spitz, 1992). While this point can be debated, as noted earlier, the intervention group in that study also had better outcomes in noncognitive domains. Participants in the intervention, for example, were less likely than those in the control group to become teen parents.

Balancing these criticisms, a review of 38 studies of early childhood intervention and education programs, all of which provided high-quality, center-based early childhood education and family-oriented services, suggested that there are often lasting effects on achievement and academic success but few direct and lasting effects on measures of IQ per se (Barnett, 1998). A different review of early intervention programs came to similar conclusions, noting that positive effects of these programs are especially pronounced for lower income children whose parents have lower levels of education. Programs that do not continue as children make the transition to school, however, have relatively limited long-term effects, especially if children continue to live in lower income neighborhoods and attend poor quality schools (Brooks-Gunn, 2003; McLoyd et al., 2006; Ramey, Ramey, & Lanzi, 2006).

Finally, based on their review of the research literature, the primary investigators in the Abecedarian Project identified six principles that underlie most successful interventions in early childhood, including Early Head Start and its predecessor Head Start (Ramey & Ramey, 1998b). *Principle 1* is the principle of developmental timing, in which interventions that begin earlier in development and are of longer duration tend to have larger effects than interventions that are briefer and begin later. According to *Principle 2*, the principle of program intensity, interventions that include more contact hours are most effective, and families who participate most actively tend to receive the greatest benefits. *Principle 3* refers to the superior results achieved through direct rather than intermediary experience; children who receive direct educational interventions have more positive and longer lasting outcomes than children who must wait to receive quality care until their parents have completed training and education interventions.

Program breadth and flexibility comprise *Principle 4*, which states that interventions that employ more services and multiple approaches have larger effects than narrower interventions. In articulating *Principle 5*, the principle of individual differences in program benefits, the review acknowledges that some children and families experience greater benefits than other children and families, even when they are participants in the same intervention. *Principle 6* is the principle of ecological dominion and environmental maintenance of development, which recognizes that positive early experiences must be reinforced with subsequent positive experiences and nurturing environments if early gains are to be maintained.

Still other scholars, as well as the public, have asked whether the cost of interventions in infancy and early childhood is justified by the results. Funding provided for Head Start in 1999 was $4.66 billion, but some would argue that it is unclear whether this was too much or not enough (Shonkoff & Phillips, 2000). The cost of high-quality early intervention programs that incorporate the principles enumerated by Ramey and Ramey (1998b) can surpass $8,000 to $10,000 per child annually. One year of the High/Scope Perry Preschool Project, for example, cost approximately $15,000 per child in 1998 dollars (Barnett, 1998; Shonkoff & Phillips, 2000). For the 100 participants in the Perry Preschool Project, then, the total cost was more than $1 million. If this type of program were provided for tens of thousands of children and their families, how would we know whether the funds were being invested wisely?

A relatively new perspective on this question has been provided through cost-benefit analyses of the High/Scope Perry Preschool Project. By comparing the costs of delivering the program with the value of the program to society as a whole, to taxpayers, and to program participants themselves, these analyses indicate that for every dollar of public funds invested in the intervention, there was a return to the public and participants of $8.74 (Schweinhart et al., 1993). This rate of return reflects savings that accrued, for example, because K-12 education could be provided more efficiently for program participants and with less need for special education or grade retention. There were also savings from the lower incidence of unemployment, welfare use, and criminal behavior by program participants (Barnett, 1998; Ramey, Ramey, & Lanzi, 2006; Shonkoff & Phillips, 2000).

Recently, two Federal Reserve economists performed a different analysis on the Perry Preschool data and concluded that the rate of return directly to the public was actually closer to 12 percent. They note that, not only is this a significantly higher rate than is usually expected from other public expenditures, such as new sports stadiums, but unlike sports stadiums, early childhood interventions can also reduce crime, increase earnings, and potentially break a chain of poverty (Rolnick & Grunewald, 2003). These and similar analyses raise thought-provoking questions about public funding for early childhood programs and will continue to be part of ongoing debates about how to create a better world by "building" better babies.

WRAPPING IT UP: Summary and Conclusion

In this chapter, we focused on societal changes that have occurred since the 1960s and the consequences of those changes for infants, toddlers, and their families. An enormous child care industry has developed and mushroomed to meet the demands created by increasing numbers of women with infants and toddlers participating in the paid labor force. There is now evidence of the harm caused to children by poverty and deprivation, particularly to children under the age of 3 years. However, infants and toddlers are resilient and can benefit, as can their parents, from focused, intensive early interventions.

If we take a look back at the chronology of childhood and child development in the United States (Table 1.1 in Chapter 1), we can see these events in an even broader context. In the mid-1800s, child labor laws began to be passed, on a state-by-state basis, ensuring that children younger than 12 years of age would not work more than 10 hours per day. Similar legislation followed to protect children from physical harm and exploitation. As recently as 1918, compulsory school attendance was not required by law for all U.S. children, but we now recognize that education is a necessity, not a luxury. In 1935, the Social Security Act established a national commitment to provide aid to dependent children, maternal and child health programs, disabled children's programs, and child welfare services.

What does the future hold? A majority of states (38 as of 2002) have established state-funded pre-kindergarten (pre-K) programs for preschoolers, primarily focused on disadvantaged children (Pianta & Rimm-Kaufmann, 2006). In six states—Florida, Georgia, Massachusetts, New York, Oklahoma, and West Virginia—pre-K is more universally available, and all parents may choose to enroll their 4-year-old children. Education and training requirements for pre-K teachers vary across these states, however, as do family and school district participation rates.

One recent evaluation of Oklahoma's universal pre-K program, which was established in 1998 and offers both half-day and full-day programs, showed that families and school districts participate at high rates. Focusing on the pre-K program in Tulsa, Oklahoma, the researchers found that the pre-K student body was both socioeconomically and racially/ethnically diverse. Even more importantly, the evaluation showed that all children benefited from pre-K attendance, especially in pre-reading skills, such as the identification of letters and words. Small gains were also reported for prewriting and spelling skills, as well as early math reasoning and problem-solving abilities (Gormley et al., 2005).

The evaluation does not demonstrate whether the Tulsa pre-K program—or other programs with a similar academic emphasis—is more beneficial than programs such as Early Head Start or its preschool counterpart Head Start. It is unclear whether other states will follow those that have already committed funds to pre-K readiness and whether universal pre-K will become coordinated at the national level. It is also unclear whether pre-K curricula will evolve to give greater attention to other dimensions of school readiness.

What is clear is that we are poised to make use of the knowledge that child development research has produced, particularly since the 1960s (Foster & Kalil, 2005; Huston, 2005). We understand the importance of a dynamic systems perspective, such as the bioecological model articulated by Bronfenbrenner, which highlights the ways in which individuals are affected by, and have an effect on, a complex network of people and contexts (Bronfenbrenner & Morris, 1998). While the complexity of the model helps us consider multiple influences and measures, it reminds us, at the same time, that the task of connecting developmental science to public policy and applications in the field is not a simple one.

What will the future hold? Will more states follow California and offer paid parental leaves? Will there be greater nationwide regulation, coordination, and enforcement of standards for high quality in all early child care settings? In an expanding world, the decisions that we make now will have significant consequences for the entries that appear in a chronology of childhood and child development for the twenty-first century.

THINK ABOUT IT: Questions for Reading and Discussion

1. Do you think that the United States will ever offer paid parental leaves for all parents? Why or why not? What are the pros and cons of paid leave policies, keeping in mind effects on children as well as parents and society?

2. Is child care good or bad for infants and toddlers? How do you know?

3. Have you had any direct experience in a child care setting, either a family child care home or a child care center? If so, how would you evaluate the quality of the program and the care that children received in it?

4. Thinking about all of the people involved—children, parents, and caregivers—what are the advantages and disadvantages of the proposed model of continuity of caregiver? Explain whether you would support this model if it involved your own child or if you were the caregiver.

5. If you could design the optimal intervention for infants and toddlers, what would you include in it and how would you measure the results?

6. What would be gained by legislating universal pre-K education that began before the age of 3 years? What would be the objections to this sort of nationwide initiative?

7. If you were able to shape the future simply by writing a chronology of childhood and child development for the next 25 years, what sorts of entries would you include and why? Do you think that those events will actually occur? Explain.

KEY WORDS

Abecedarian Project (378)	An intervention in which approximately 100 low-income, primarily African American children participated in a full-time, high-quality early childhood program from the age of 6 weeks until 3 years
Americans with Disabilities Act (ADA) (376)	The federal civil rights act protecting individuals with disabilities
Early Head Start (379)	A national intervention program that provides services to low-income pregnant women and families with infants and toddlers
Early intervention (377)	Systematic efforts to either prevent or reduce the adverse developmental effects of family income, parent characteristics, birth experiences, or

aspects of the environment. The strongest conclusions can be made when children are randomly assigned to intervention and control groups

Early Intervention Services (EIS) (376)
Services provided through IDEA, including screening and assessment, family education and training, home visits, health and social services, speech-language therapy, and occupational and physical therapy, as well as assistive technology

Family child care home (366)
Care that is provided for one or more unrelated children in the caregiver's home

Family leave (359)
Job-protected time off from work for a variety of reasons other than the birth of a child

Family and Medical Leave Act (FMLA) (359)
The federal policy that allows certain categories of employees to take a 12-week, job-protected leave to care for a child, spouse, or parent or to take time off due to their own serious health condition

High/Scope Perry Preschool Project (378)
An intervention in which approximately 100 low-income African American preschoolers received high-quality early childhood education and home visits

Individuals with Disabilities Education Act (IDEA) (376)
The federal civil rights act covering children with disabilities; Part C explicitly covers services from birth to 36 months of age

Infant Health and Development Project (379)
An intervention involving nearly 1,000 preterm, low birth weight infants, with one third of the sample randomly selected to have home visits and to participate in full-day, high-quality child care in child development centers from birth to age 3

Maternity leave (359)
A job-protected leave from work for employed women during, and some times before, childbirth

NICHD Study of Early Child Care (369)
A longitudinal, multimethod and multimeasure study of approximately 1,400 children in child care settings across the United States

Parental leave (359)
A job-protected leave that is open to mothers or fathers, typically available as a supplement to maternity and paternity leaves

Paternity leave (359)
A job-protected leave from work for employed men, typically taken after childbirth

Pregnancy Discrimination Act of 1978 (359)
The federal act, passed in 1978, to prohibit employment discrimination on the basis of pregnancy or childbirth

Project CARE (379)
An intervention similar to the Abecedarian Project, in which low-income children participated in a full-time, high-quality early childhood program, supplemented with parent group meetings and home visiting

12

Babies of Today and Tomorrow: Music, Media, and Computers

Our last chapter focuses on three prevalent influences in the lives of infants and toddlers today—music, media, and computers. Only one of these influences, music, is found on the list of Ten Things Every Child Needs, which we discussed briefly in Chapter 9 (Robert R. McCormick Foundation, 1997). As we review current studies and practices in this chapter, consider whether you think that the two other influences, media and computers, *should* be added to this list.

Listening to music is part of a typical day for most (81 percent) children younger than 2 years (Rideout, Vandewater, & Wartella, 2003). If there were a Toddler Top 20, which songs would be on it? According to one informal survey of parents and caregivers, the song at the very top would be "The Itsy Bitsy Spider," while others making the list would include "Pat-A-Cake," "Row, Row, Row Your Boat," and "Twinkle, Twinkle Little Star," (Johnson-Green & Custodero, 2002). These songs (and others shown in Figure 12.1) have been popular for generations, perhaps because they all have in common a simple melody, repetitive rhyming lyrics, and accompanying hand, arm, or whole-body movements that are easy for very young children to discern and imitate. They are also easy for most adults to sing and can be used spontaneously in almost any setting, including during diaper changing, while riding in the car, or during bath time. In this chapter, as we examine the role of music in

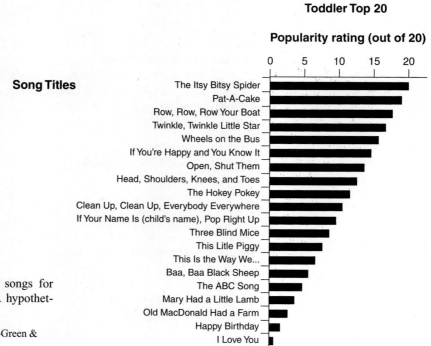

FIGURE 12.1 Popular songs for very young children: A hypothetical Toddler Top 20.

Source: Based on Johnson-Green & Custodero, 2002.

young children's lives, we'll consider infants' and toddlers' ability to perceive the musical world around them as well as their developing ability to be involved in creating music of their own.

As Figure 12.1 shows, one of the titles on our hypothetical Toddler Top 20 is a newer song, "I Love You," which children are likely to hear for the first time while watching *Barney & Friends.* Many mothers and fathers who were themselves brought up watching *Sesame Street* and *Mister Rogers' Neighborhood* now direct their infants and toddlers to educational television programs created specifically for an under-3 audience. As a result, in many households, children younger than 3 not only turn on the TV by themselves and know how to change channels using the remote, but they also have favorite TV programs, TV channels, videos, and DVDs that they ask to watch and are able to start on their own (Anderson & Pempek, 2005; Rideout, Vandewater, & Wartella, 2003). How much television do young children watch, and what are the effects of this activity on their behavior and development?

New and expectant parents are bombarded with advertisements encouraging them to boost their baby's brain by buying classical music CDs and DVDs designed to stimulate the senses of vision and hearing as well as lay a foundation for later language acquisition. It should not be surprising, then, that interactive media have become pervasive in the lives of children in the United States, including those under the age of 3 years, many of whom interact with hybrid products that are part toy, part book, and part computer. Even newborns and young infants are increasingly likely to play with "smart" toys and to fall asleep to the sounds of music by Mozart and other eighteenth century composers being played on twenty-first century "music boxes."

Does Mozart's music have a unique and beneficial impact on infants, as has been asserted by individuals extrapolating from studies of college students (Rauscher, Shaw, & Ky, 1993, 1995)? Do allegedly brain-boosting products influence early development in the ways that their makers claim? Are infants whose parents cannot or choose not to buy and use them at a disadvantage developmentally? How will these experiences affect the babies of today and tomorrow?

Music

As we have discussed in other chapters, the sense of hearing develops in advance of vision and is functioning well at birth. This means that even the very youngest infants are able to perceive an auditory world consisting of speech and nonspeech sounds, the latter of which may be produced by animals and, depending on where the child lives, machines and inanimate objects such as cars, airplanes, doorbells, and kitchen timers. Instrumental music is found in all human cultures and as a result some of the other nonspeech sounds that infants hear are produced by musical instruments. Cultural traditions and the availability of materials influence the size, construction, and purpose of instruments in a society, but nearly all cultures have instruments that can be blown, struck, bowed, or plucked. Given that the propensity to make music exists in all human cultures, many researchers have wondered whether the ability to perceive instrumental and vocal music might have evolved as a fundamental human skill, like the capacity to perceive and acquire language.

As we will discuss shortly, there is reason to believe that infants are born ready to detect the properties of music and songs that they hear (Papousek, 1996; Trehub, 2002) and to use those abilities to make their own nonspeech sounds, which at first may be music only to their parents' ears.

Listening to Music

It seems that it's never too early to listen to and even benefit from music. Before birth, mothers generate a rhythmic "soundtrack" through their heartbeat. Fetuses also hear their mothers' voice and, as we noted in Chapter 8, are able to learn the contours and intonations of their mothers' speech (Moon, Cooper, & Fifer, 1993). Women in the third trimester of pregnancy report that fetuses move and kick in response to music and other audible stimuli (Abrams et al., 1998). Infants in some studies have also responded differently to music that they heard in utero, as compared with other music that they had not heard previously (Hepper, 1991; Wilkin, 1995). Prenatal exposure to music may even stimulate infants' later cognitive and motor development (LaFuente et al., 1997).

Infant-directed music has also been used therapeutically with preterm infants in the neonatal intensive care unit. In a number of studies, it has prevented weight loss, reduced stress, and helped stabilize preterm infants enough to allow them to spend fewer days in the hospital (Caine, 1991; Moore & Standley, 1996; Standley, 1991, 1998b, 1999). These examples may not fit traditional definitions of and experiences with "children's music," but most newborns do not have to wait very long before they hear instrumental and vocal music in more conventional settings.

Music Perception in Infancy.   Researchers studying infants' music perception rely on many of the same procedures that are used to investigate infants' language perception (research methods that we discussed previously in Chapters 2 and 8). In some studies, researchers measure infants' attentiveness, emotional reactions, and motor responsiveness to musical stimuli that are played over loudspeakers. In other studies, a conditioned headturn procedure is used to reward infants with a pleasant visual sight, such as a fun animated toy, if they turn their head in a particular direction after there is a change in a musical soundtrack. Once infants have learned the contingencies involved in the procedure, researchers can present auditory stimuli with varying properties and determine whether they notice the differences. Another method, the headturn preference procedure, involves presenting auditory stimuli on either the left or the right side. Researchers draw infants' attention to one side or the other by flashing a light and then playing music over a speaker located at that spot. If infants look longer when either speaker is playing a particular musical excerpt, researchers infer that the infant recognizes that excerpt. It is difficult to use these procedures with infants younger than 4 months; accordingly, most of the existing studies of music perception have focused on 6- to 12-month-olds (Ilari, 2002; Trehub, 2002).

Numerous studies using these procedures have shown that infants as young as 6 months are usually able to recognize recently heard melodies, despite changes in the pitch or tempo (Ilari, 2002; Trehub, 2002). In other words, if they are first familiarized with a sequence of notes, such as those in the song "Hot Cross Buns," they perceive that melody as familiar the next time it is played, even if it is slower or in a different musical key, as long as the relationship between the notes themselves does not change. When the distance between individual notes changes, however, infants respond as if the melody is a different one.

Infants also retain long-term memories of particular melodies. This has been shown in studies with 6-month-olds, in which infants were able to recognize 30-second excerpts of melodies when they were tested 3 weeks later, provided that the excerpts were not changed (Trainor, Wu, & Tsang, 2004). Slightly older infants are able to store even longer and more complex melodies in memory. In one study, 7-month-olds heard two Mozart sonatas every day for a period of 2 weeks. When they were subsequently presented with either the sonatas that they had previously heard or similar but novel musical passages, they recognized the familiar music and appeared to prefer it instead of the unfamiliar pieces (Saffran, Loman, & Robertson, 2000).

In a different study, 8-month-old infants heard one of two complex classical piano pieces three times a day for a period of 10 days. Two weeks later, when infants were tested using the headturn preference procedure, they showed recognition for the music that they had heard previously by looking longer at the speaker over which that piece was being played than they did when the speaker played unfamiliar music. Infants who had never heard either piece of music showed no difference in looking time (Ilari & Polka, 2006).

Taken together, these findings indicate that well before their first birthday, infants are able to remember both brief and relatively lengthy pieces of music that vary in complexity. These studies do not reveal the basis for infants' auditory perception—the specific information that they remember about the music they have heard. Studies systematically manipulating the properties of musical stimuli may shed light on this early ability.

Infants as young as 4 months of age appear to prefer melodies that adults find pleasant sounding, such as those with consonant rather than dissonant intervals and more regular rhythms (Trehub, 2002). In one study comparing original consonant versions of European folk songs with modified dissonant versions, 4-month-olds looked longer at loudspeakers playing consonant versions and also fussed less and were calmer and more attentive when they heard those renditions (Zentner & Kagan, 1996). By 5 to 6 months of age, infants also discriminate high- and low-pitched sounds and seem to prefer those that are higher pitched (Trainor & Zacharias, 1998). Studies of 6- to 10-month-olds have shown that infants also prefer listening to naturally segmented excerpts of music (those with a pause at the end of a musical phrase) as opposed to excerpts that are unnaturally segmented (with a pause in the middle of a musical phrase) (Jusczyk & Krumhansl, 1993).

If you have ever heard a classical Chinese orchestra, you know that it sounds different from a Western orchestra. Although there are many similarities—such as the existence of families of woodwinds, brasses, strings, and percussion—different instruments as well as different musical scales and styles exist across cultures. By the age of about 12 months, infants know this too and are able to discriminate between features that belong in their own culture's music and features that do not belong. This auditory specialization for music, which is not found in 6-month-old infants, is similar to the specialization for speech sounds that occurs during the second half of the first year of life (Ilari, 2002).

Infants use vision as well as hearing to learn about the sources and properties of music in their environment. This was shown in research in which 7- and 9-month-olds watched side-by-side videos of two musicians playing different musical instruments but heard a soundtrack that matched only one of the instruments. Infants had had little or no prior experience with the instruments included in the videos but looked longer at the video in each pair for which they heard a soundtrack. This finding indicates that they were able to associate the visible physical properties and manner of playing each instrument with the specific sounds of woodwinds, brasses, and strings (Pick et al., 1994). Infants' tactile experience with instruments was not assessed in this study, but it would be interesting to know whether and how such experience would enhance their perceptual learning. Would infants who have toy drums or toy pianos, for example, perform more accurately than infants with less hands-on experience with those instruments?

Infants are sensitive to the rhythmic patterns in music that they hear. In one study with 6- to 9-month-olds, infants were familiarized with a rhythmic pattern consisting of several repetitions of two different tones. Subsequently, when the tones remained the same, but the rhythmic pattern and grouping had changed (e.g., from AAA BBB to AAAB BB or AA ABBB), infants were able to detect those differences (Thorpe & Trehub, 1989; Thorpe et al., 1988). Infants' ability to detect and respond differently to music varying in rhythm and tempo has also been shown in studies comparing lullabies and more playful songs, which we discuss next.

Singing to Infants.   From Baby Mozart to Baby Beluga, there is now a diverse world of music for the very youngest listeners. Parents and caregivers have always sung to infants, of course, usually choosing different songs than they sing in other settings and modifying their singing as the situation demands. Mothers singing their favorite children's songs to their infants tend to use the same pitch level and tempo time after time, unless the infant's state indicates that they need a more or less arousing version (Bergeson & Trehub, 2002; Ilari, 2005).

As shown in Figure 12.2, when parents in one study were asked to sing a song of their choice to their 4- to 18-month-old infants, the most common songs performed were playsongs (e.g., "The Itsy Bitsy Spider"), followed by lullabies (e.g., "Rock-A-Bye Baby"), popular songs (e.g., "Mandy," a song made famous by pop singer Barry Manilow), invented

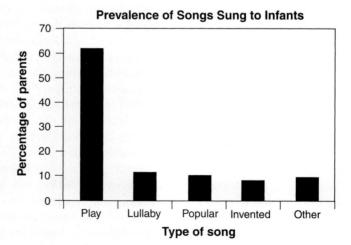

FIGURE 12.2 Out of all songs sung to infants, play-songs appear to be the most prevalent.

Source: Based on information in Trehub, Hill, & Kamenetsky, 1997.

songs (e.g., "It's Bath Time in Canada"), and other songs (including religious and unknown songs). Fathers in this study were less accustomed to singing to their infants than were mothers, which may be one reason that fathers chose to sing more popular and invented songs than traditional children's play songs or lullabies (Trehub et al., 1997).

The presence of an infant appears to elicit a specialized singing style. Mothers and fathers who were asked to sing to their infants and also to sing *as if* their infants were present were judged to be more intense and emotionally expressive in the former condition, regardless of the type of song they chose to sing (O'Neill, Trainor, & Trehub, 2001; Trehub, Hill, & Kamenetsky, 1997; Trehub et al., 1997). Like infant-directed speech, which we discussed in Chapter 8, infant-directed singing is typically slower, higher in pitch, and more emotionally warm than singing that is not directed to infants (Trehub & Trainor, 1998). Older children, even those who are barely 3 years old, also alter their singing style when singing to their infant siblings, using a higher pitch level and a more "smiling" voice than when they cannot see their siblings (Trehub, Unyk, & Henderson, 1994).

Across a wide range of cultures, parents consistently use different kinds of music and songs to influence infants' behavior and states of arousal (Custodero, Britto, & Brooks-Gunn, 2003; Ilari, 2005; Trehub, Unyk, & Trainor, 1993a, 1993b; Unyk et al., 1992). While playsongs are intended to engage infants' attention and stimulate interaction, a quite different genre—the lullaby—is intended to soothe and calm infants as they fall asleep. If infants were able to understand the lyrics of "Rock-A-Bye Baby," which describe breaking tree boughs and falling cradles and babies, they might not find this lullaby very relaxing; fortunately, all they notice is its slow, gliding tempo and their parents' quiet, loving tone of voice.

Adults who hear recordings of lullabies, like "Rock-A-Bye Baby," describe them as "airy and flute-like," "smooth," and "soothing," even when the words have been electronically stripped away. Recordings of playsongs, by contrast, such as "The Itsy Bitsy Spider," tend to be described as "smiling," "brilliant and trumpet-like," "clipped," and "rhythmic" (Rock, Trainor, & Addison, 1999; Trehub et al., 1993a; Unyk et al., 1992). Six- to seven-month-old infants notice these differences as well and respond by showing different behaviors to each. During lullabies, they are more likely to focus their attention on their own bodies and clothing, toys with which they are playing, and other nearby objects, such as pacifiers. When listening to play songs, by contrast, they tend to show more outward-directed behavior, such as looking at their caregiver (Rock, Trainor, & Addison, 1999).

Infants respond positively to the modifications that parents make when singing to them, and they are more attentive when they hear infant-directed singing than when they hear other types of casual singing. This is especially true if the singer is their mother. While recorded performances of unfamiliar adults engaged in infant-directed singing also elicit positive responses from infants, parents need not worry that their own singing is inadequate. Nor should they feel pressured by claims that commercially produced recordings of professional singers are the best way to stimulate their child's brain development. As one expert put it, "No one would suggest replacing maternal verbal interactions with recorded monologues or dialogues by professional actors. By the same token, professional singers are no substitute for live, maternal singing" (Trehub, 2002, p. 21). Instead, infants are likely to benefit most from emotionally rich, spontaneous singing, especially when it reflects and is sensitive to infants' changing states of arousal and emotional needs (Kuhl, Tsao, & Liu, 2003; Trehub, 2002).

Some songs that adults sing with or to children are used for specific routines and tasks. These include personalized versions of "Good Morning" and "Hello, Everybody," songs that signal the beginning of the day to children in group care, as well as the "Clean Up" song that encourages "everybody everywhere" to "do their share" while picking up toys and books in the classroom. Others, such as the "ABC" song, help children establish a foundation for learning the letters of the alphabet. Children who hear parents and other adults sing these songs on a regular basis soon begin to sing along with them (Ringgenberg, 2004). Let's turn now to consider the age at which young children begin to imitate songs that they hear. As we do, we will examine different approaches to music education for very young children.

Making Music

Music education has been part of preschool education in the United States since the nineteenth century, when it was imported from Europe with kindergarten and preschool movements. Frederic Froebel, the founder of kindergarten whom we mentioned in Chapter 1, presented many of his theories about young children's learning in *Mother-Play and Nursery Songs*, a book of songs, verses, games, and instructions to teachers. In Froebel's view, music was not an end in itself but served as a means of educating children, instilling a sense of order, and teaching self-discipline (McDonald & Simons, 1989).

In the 1920s, when child development studies began at child welfare stations in Iowa and elsewhere, researchers investigated music in order to determine the best pitch range for young children's voices. Most people today would probably be surprised to learn that the melody of "Twinkle, Twinkle Little Star" (originally composed in 1914) was modified as a result of this sort of research, repeating the first two lines at the end of the song to make it simpler for young children to sing. Researchers also made recommendations about the content of children's songs, which they asserted should be about common, everyday experiences (McDonald & Simons, 1989).

Today, organizations devoted to supporting development during infancy and early childhood, such as Zero to Three and the National Association for the Education of Young Children (NAEYC), encourage parents to sing to and with their infants and toddlers. They also promote the use of music and singing as a teaching tool in the preschool classroom. Like kindergarten teachers from the nineteenth century, today's early childhood educators recognize that music is a natural and enjoyable way for children to learn. Preschool teachers can pair singing with movement or visual aids, modify familiar tunes in order to teach new vocabulary words, and encourage children to create their own songs and incorporate music into their play (Ringgenberg, 2004).

Learning to Sing.   Like learning to talk, learning to sing does not happen overnight (as shown in Table 12.1). Around the age of 4 to 6 months, infants respond to music and singing with whole-body movements, but these movements are not synchronized to the properties of music that they hear, such as its rhythmic pattern. A period of "vocal contagion" begins at about 6 months of age; infants become so excited by other people's speaking and singing voices that they join in. Parents can encourage these "songs"—and support future speech development—by imitating their infants and responding with positive emotional feedback.

TABLE 12.1   Milestones in Learning to Sing

Age	Milestone
4 to 6 months	Infants respond to music and singing with whole-body movements, usually not synchronized to properties of the music, such as its rhythmic pattern.
6 to 12 months	Infants display "vocal contagion," becoming so excited by other people's singing that they join in. Songs with corresponding gestures that parents and caregivers have used, such as those accompanying "The Itsy Bitsy Spider," become part of the child's performance too.
12 to 18 months	Infants engage in vocal play and experiment with brief but repetitive melodic and rhythmic patterns.
19 to 24 months	Infants create their own spontaneous songs, often while engaged in some other activity, such as playing with toys. Songs often contain recognizable elements of songs that they have heard.
30 to 36 months	Children imitate larger excerpts of songs, although their versions are not always accurate.

Source: Based on McDonald & Simons, 1989.

At 12 to 18 months, infants engage in vocal play and experiment with sound; brief but repetitive melodic and rhythmic patterns begin to appear in these vocalizations, making them sound like excerpts of songs. A listener who does not know the child well may only be able to guess that the child is "singing," whereas parents or other caregivers may be able to recognize bits of songs that the child and parents frequently listen to (such as the theme song from *Barney and Friends* or selections from a CD that is played during most trips in the car).

From 19 to 24 months, infants experiment and create their own spontaneous songs, often while they are engaged in some other activity. Language and vocabulary develop

The National Association for the Education of Young Children promotes the use of music and singing as a teaching tool in the early childhood classroom. These children have a variety of percussion instruments available and are free to explore and use them in small groups or on their own.

rapidly during this period, and around 2 years of age, children's songs are often recognizable as derivations of specific songs. Strangers hearing 2-year-old children singing at the grocery store, for example, are now likely to be able to identify the children's songs, provided that they themselves know them.

Between 30 and 36 months of age, whole parts of songs may be imitated, although children's renditions may not be completely accurate. As children approach the age of 3 years, they are increasingly successful when trying to reproduce the words, rhythm, phrases, and melody of songs they have learned (McDonald & Simons, 1989).

Music education programs for children from birth to 2 years are often designed with parent involvement in mind. Participants in these programs have playful interactions involving music, and parents are able to expand their knowledge of musical songs and games (Trehub, 2002). Typical music activities for infants and toddlers include rocking in time to rhythmic patterns, playing sound-imitation games, personalizing songs to include the child's name, and singing songs that have accompanying actions. Two- to three-year-olds can participate in more complex musical games that involve group actions, such as the "Hokey Pokey," "Two Little Blackbirds," and "Farmer in the Dell," but they may have only limited success in singing or moving together as a group (McDonald & Simons, 1989).

Playing Instruments.   Most infants are exposed to simple percussion instruments—rattles—at an early age, and many toddlers own toy xylophones, drums, or pianos. Whether they own toy instruments or not, all infants seem to enjoy banging with spoons on "drums" made out of high chair trays, plastic bowls, and any overturned container that is available. Infants also enjoy playing with toys that make noise, whether the sounds are produced by mechanical means (as when a ball containing jingle bells is rolled or shaken) or electronic systems (as occurs with devices that can be activated with just the push of a button).

Children younger than 2 years typically interact with musical instruments such as pianos and xylophones by banging on the keys without any discernible rhythm pattern. Considering these tendencies, most early childhood educators recommend providing 2- to 3-year-olds with a variety of music-making materials but caution against musical activities that require children to perform together as a unit (McDonald & Simons, 1989).

Instead, emphasis is usually given to providing very young children with opportunities to explore materials in music-learning centers. In these designated areas of the early childhood classroom, children are able to listen to music, explore musical instruments, and create their own sounds with those instruments in small groups or on their own. Percussion instruments that are often found in these centers include drums, rhythm sticks, sandblocks, woodblocks, tambourines, maracas, bells, cymbals, and gongs. The sounds that emanate from music-learning centers in early childhood classrooms may not always be melodious, but in many approaches to music education, they represent an important stage of development.

Listening to music, playing instruments, singing, and rhythmic movement are major components of most music education programs for young children, but not all forms of music education are alike. The Montessori Method, for example, developed in Italy in the early twentieth century, emphasizes self-directed learning within a predetermined sequence of experiences. In some activities, children as young as $2\frac{1}{2}$ years compare the sounds made by containers filled with different materials, such as sand, dried beans, and flour. In other activities, children learn about the relationship between size and sound by

Some children learn to play a musical instrument at a very young age by using the Suzuki Method—observing others and eventually imitating and playing with them as a group.

trying out a set of bells that gradually increase in size. Montessori's methods have been adapted and interpreted in many different ways over the years, and it is unlikely that many Montessori programs in the United States today follow the entire original music education curriculum (McDonald & Simons, 1989). What may be most important, though, is the continued emphasis on exploration as a fundamental way of learning about music.

A different approach was developed in the 1940s by a Japanese music educator, Shinichi Suzuki. Suzuki Talent Education, often referred to simply as the **Suzuki Method**, is a method for teaching very young children (sometimes as early as 2 to 3 years) to play stringed instruments. Suzuki instructors use games to teach children about pitch and about proper posture, arm position, and bow manipulations, and many of the principles on which it is based can be generalized to music education more generally (McDonald & Simons, 1989). There are, however, a number of unique practices in the Suzuki Method.

The Suzuki Method explicitly compares learning to play an instrument to learning to speak a first language, with the result that imitation and feedback from parents, adults, and other children is the principal method used. Social interaction and being part of a group are also key elements of the Suzuki Method. Before children ever begin to play their own instrument, they attend classes and observe other children who have already begun their lessons.

Suzuki reasoned that, because humans do not learn to read before learning to speak, children learning to play an instrument should do so before learning to read music. Students memorize the pieces they are learning, and written musical notes are not introduced until a satisfactory skill level has been attained.

One consequence of Suzuki's beliefs about the importance of parent involvement is that parents who enroll their children in Suzuki classes are also enrolling themselves. According to Suzuki, mothers must learn to play the instrument first and demonstrate their skills at home so that their children will become interested and insist on playing too. Parents who have learned to play an instrument can reinforce the concepts and skills at home, and because they attend their children's weekly lessons, they are aware of and understand the teacher's instructions. Parents in the Suzuki Method also support their children's development by playing recordings of the pieces that their children are learning, immersing them in the sounds outside of class and aiding their memorization of the music (McDonald & Simons, 1989; Starr, 1976; Suzuki, 1973).

The Suzuki Method enables young children to develop a relatively high level of musical skills earlier than many traditional string instructors even begin formal lessons (Price, 1979). There is relatively little experimental research that clearly supports any one music education approach over all others, however, with respect to ultimate levels of skill development. Not all children are ready to begin an intensive study of an instrument at the age of 2 or 3 years, and not all parents are able to commit their families to a program that assumes that children will practice their instrument 7 days a week. Still, many parents may feel compelled to make an early and significant investment in their children's musical development, increasingly because they have heard about the Mozart Effect. Awareness of this phenomenon has grown since it was first reported in 1993 by researchers studying college students (Rauscher, Shaw, & Ky, 1993). Let's examine the evidence for this well-publicized effect, especially as it pertains to infants and very young children.

The Mozart Effect

The **Mozart Effect** was the name given to findings reported in an experiment with 36 college students who listened to a 10-minute Mozart sonata. When these students took a spatial-temporal test, they scored higher than they had after experiencing 10 minutes of silence or listening to relaxation instructions (Rauscher, Shaw, & Ky, 1993). Some subsequent attempts to replicate this finding have not been successful, but even when it has been reproduced, the effect lasts for only about 10 minutes and appears to be limited to the kind of reasoning required for the spatial-temporal test (Rauscher, Shaw, & Ky, 1995).

As these research findings were disseminated to the general public, and even to professional audiences, however, many people jumped to the conclusion that listening to classical music, especially the music of Mozart, would enhance a wide range of cognitive abilities in both adults and children. There is no experimental evidence to support this conclusion (McKelvie & Low, 2002; Rauscher, 2003), but that has not prevented the proliferation of "brain-boosting" classical music CDs and DVDs, as well as Mozart Effect resources for parents and educators. There are many valid reasons to listen to Mozart and other classical music, and to introduce it to young children, but there is little reason to believe that it will increase their intelligence (Rauscher, 2003).

Parents and educators who wish to enhance children's spatial-temporal ability would do better to provide them with musical *training* (Schellenberg, 2004, 2005). Studies of children aged 3 to 12 years have produced convincing evidence that music instruction results in better performance on spatial-temporal tasks, with the strongest effects occurring for the youngest children (Bilhartz, Bruhn, & Olson, 2000; Gromko & Poorman, 1998; Hetland, 2000; Rauscher, 2003).

In some of these studies, the effects of keyboard instruction have been compared with the effects of singing and with rhythm instruction. In one experiment involving 3- and 4-year-old children enrolled in Head Start, each of these musical experiences was associated with higher scores on spatial tasks than were found among children in a nonmusical control group. The group receiving rhythm instruction performed better than the others on sequencing and arithmetic tests, but no differences were found on tasks involving verbal ability, matching, or memory (Rauscher & LeMieux, 2003).

Other investigations have found that, although spatial-temporal reasoning underlies mathematical abilities, there is only limited support for a direct connection between music instruction and mathematics ability (Rauscher, 2003). Experimental studies of reading ability have failed to produce convincing evidence of a causal relationship between music instruction and reading scores, but there is some correlational support for a link between music instruction and verbal memory ability (Rauscher, 2003).

Although the findings for an effect of music instruction on specific cognitive abilities have been mixed, there is less ambiguous evidence that music training may enhance overall intellectual ability, at least in school-age children (Schellenberg, 2005). In one experiment with 6-year-olds, for example, children were randomly assigned to 36 weeks of music lessons (keyboard or vocal), drama lessons, or no lessons. All of the groups showed increases in scores on standardized IQ tests by the end of the experiment, but the increase was greater for the two music groups (Schellenberg, 2004). Further research is needed in order to understand why and how music has these effects. Is it because music lessons are equivalent to gaining additional schooling? Does the activity help children develop intellectual abilities, such as attention, concentration, and memorization, that contribute to overall IQ? Perhaps the abstract nature of music itself—becoming aware of the relationships that exist among a set of notes in a melody, regardless of the key in which it is played—is involved (Schellenberg, 2005). Ongoing research is examining these alternative hypotheses and may soon shed light on the Music Lesson Effect.

Parents of very young children who wonder whether an early investment in music instruction is worthwhile may find encouragement in studies showing that the earlier children begin music instruction, the longer lasting are the benefits for spatial-temporal reasoning (Rauscher, 2002, 2003; Rauscher et al., 1997; Rauscher & Zupan, 2000). Children in one study who had begun piano instruction before the age of 5, for example, performed better on spatial ability tasks than children who started later and children who had had no music instruction (Costa-Giomi, 1999).

More research is needed, however, to determine whether the benefits found for preschool-age children receiving piano instruction also exist for 2- and 3-year-old Suzuki students and children who begin other forms of music instruction before the age of 3. Regardless of the range of benefits ultimately found, and the age at which they occur, most music educators believe that it is important to employ developmentally appropriate methods and to instill in children (and their parents) an appreciation that music is not just a tool for improving cognitive abilities but is valuable in and of itself (McDonald & Simons, 1989; Ringgenberg, 2004).

Media

Is television valuable in and of itself? Providing entertainment, information, role models, and companionship, television is a staple in most U.S. children's daily media diet. Among children ages 2 to 17, the amount of television viewed per day (approximately 2.5 hours) has remained stable since 1997, even as computers and other media have joined TV sets in a high percentage of homes. A national survey of 1,000 parents of children younger than 6 years found that 99 percent owned at least one television. Nearly half (49 percent) had a video game player, although it was rarely used by children under the age of 2 years. In households where television was used heavily—in which the TV is always left turned on or is on most of the time—children were more likely than in other households to begin watching before the age of 1 (Rideout, Vandewater, & Wartella, 2003; Rideout & Hamel, 2006).

Among older children, television continues to be the medium with which they spend the most time each day (Comstock & Scharrer, 2006; Singer & Singer, 2001; Woodward & Gridina, 2000), but in a typical day children under 2 are more likely to listen to music (81 percent) and read or be read to (71 percent) than they are to watch television (59 percent) or watch videos and DVDs (42 percent). Still, in a typical day, children younger than 2 watch an average of 1 hour and 22 minutes of television and spend approximately the same amount of time (1 hour and 26 minutes) watching videos and DVDs (Rideout, Vandewater, & Wartella, 2003). Is time in front of television screens time well spent?

Some early childhood experts have expressed doubt about this possibility, while others have asserted that the message rather than the medium determines its value (Anderson et al., 2001; Center on Media and Child Health, 2005; Singer & Singer, 2001). Among older children, there are a number of reasons that parents should be concerned about the amount and the content of television being watched (American Academy of Pediatrics Committee on Public Education, 2001). Heavy amounts of television viewing are associated with higher rates of overweight and consumption of unhealthy foods. Limiting the amount of time spent engaged in sedentary screen-based activities has been shown to prevent overweight and obesity, which has increased in recent years among children of all ages (Federal Interagency Forum on Child and Family Statistics, 2005). There is also unambiguous evidence that among older children and adolescents, violent television increases the likelihood of short- and long-term aggressive and violent behavior (Anderson et al., 2003; Comstock & Scharrer, 2006). How does television affect the *youngest* viewers?

Television for Infants and Toddlers

In 2001, the American Academy of Pediatrics (American Academy of Pediatrics Committee on Public Education, 2001) issued a policy statement on children's television viewing, asserting that children younger than 2 years of age should not watch any television, and children older than 2 should be limited to 2 hours of screen time per day. The primary rationale for this recommendation was that very young children benefit most from more active forms of learning, including play and conversations with adults and other children. Results from an experiment that we discussed in Chapter 8 are consistent with this view. In that study, 9-month-old infants who heard Mandarin Chinese that was produced in person by a native speaker were subsequently able to perceive Mandarin phoneme contrasts, but infants who saw only a videotape of the same speaker did not show this ability (Kuhl, Tsao & Liu, 2003).

Judging from the results of the national survey that we mentioned earlier, many parents of very young children may have at least some difficulty following the American Academy of Pediatrics recommendations. Not only is television present in nearly all homes, but

40 percent of children under the age of 3 live in heavy-use households, in which the TV is always or usually on, even if no one is watching. In addition, 30 percent of children under the age of 3 in the survey sample had their own TV in their bedroom, and 58 percent were said to watch TV daily. The survey showed that even many children younger than 2 (26 percent) had a TV in their bedroom, with 43 percent reported to watch TV every day (Rideout Vandewater, & Wartella, 2003; Rideout & Hamel, 2006).

Infant Perception of Video Images.   Most preschool children own a number of videos and DVDs, given to them as gifts or purchased by parents who consider them an important foundation for their children's cognitive development. More than one-fourth (27 percent) of children this age own at least one of the *Baby Einstein* videos designed for children ages 1 to 18 months (Rideout, Vandewater, & Wartella, 2003; Rideout & Hamel, 2006). When infants look at these programs on television screens, what do they see? On one level, they see a flat, two-dimensional surface—the television screen—but that surface is also a representation of people, animals, objects, and events occurring in a three-dimensional world.

Many studies, including some that we have mentioned in previous chapters, have shown that even young infants are able to recognize depictions of real-world entities in pictures and video images. They are also able to differentiate video images from the actual people, objects, and events. Two recent studies with 9-, 14-, and 19-month-old infants, however, show that they do not yet fully understand what the objects displayed on a video screen are (Pierroutsakos & Troseth, 2003). Infants were seated within reaching distance of a video monitor that displayed a video in which a woman presented a series of toys, tapped them on the tabletop shown in the video, and then placed them on the table, which happened to be the same table that the infant's seat was resting on. Some of the toys were stationary, while others could be made to rock or move. While each toy was shown resting, rocking, or moving slowly on the table, the woman's voice said, "Look at the TV" and "Wow, look at that!"

Whereas 9-month-old infants attempted to explore the toys shown on the video monitor, grasping, hitting, patting, and rubbing them as if they were actual objects, 14-month-olds were less likely to do so, and 19-month-olds rarely showed this response. Instead, 14-month-olds and, to an even greater extent, 19-month-olds were more likely to point to the toys shown on the screen. Infants who tried to touch the toys shown in the video did not appear surprised or upset when they failed to do so, suggesting that they may not have expected to be able to grasp them but were still exploring the video images in order to determine what they were (Pierroutsakos & Troseth, 2003).

In fact, the researchers note, it takes many years for children to understand fully the properties of video images. Some 2- and 3-year-olds, for example, interact with televised images of people by talking to them, and children of this age may assert that objects shown in video images would be affected by actions in the room in which the video is being viewed, insisting, for example, that a video image of a ball shown at rest would move if the video monitor were tilted. Taken together, these findings suggest that infants and very young children watching specially produced television programs and "brain-enhancing" videos and DVDs are unlikely to comprehend those materials in the ways that older children and adults would (Garrison & Christakis, 2005; Pierroutsakos & Troseth, 2003).

Infants do perceive many kinds of information in videos, of course, including information about emotion. In Chapter 10, we discussed the phenomena of emotional contagion and social referencing. Two recent studies explored these phenomena further by showing 10- and 12-month-old infants videotapes of a woman reacting to novel objects that had been created by the researchers. The woman first described the objects objectively (e.g., "Look, that's plastic. It has four legs. This thing is red") while displaying neutral emotion. Infants were then given a chance to play with each object before the woman described another object while showing either positive or negative emotions about it. Twelve-month-olds, but not 10-month-olds, responded to the televised displays of negative emotion by showing more negative emotion themselves and by avoiding the objects to which the woman had responded negatively (Mumme & Fernald 2003). These results are consistent with other studies showing that young children perceive and are affected by the emotional experiences of people with whom they spend time. Together, they suggest that parents should be aware that even 1-year-olds, and possibly younger infants, may experience emotional contagion in response to a range of negative emotions that they encounter in television programs, videos, and DVDs, including those that are not intended for child audiences.

Most parents and caregivers do think carefully about the content of programs that their children watch. A national survey of approximately 1,200 parents of children between the ages of 2 and 17 showed that 87 percent of parents of 2- to 5-year-olds had at least "some" concern about television's impact on their children. Regardless of their children's age, large proportions of parents who were surveyed agreed at least "somewhat" with statements about negative effects of television on children, including the belief that watching television decreases time spent reading (86 percent), increases materialism (83 percent), adds to loss of child innocence (77 percent), and increases stereotyped beliefs about gender (71 percent) and race (64 percent) (Woodward & Gridina, 2000). Are these concerns realistic? Let's look now at studies of how television viewing affects behavior and development in very young children.

Young Children's Responses to Television.   Children who live in homes where the television is almost always turned on are not only more likely to spend more time watching television than children in households where television use is not as heavy, but as shown in Figure 12.3, they are also less likely to play outside or read. In keeping with these trends, in heavy-TV homes, the percentage of children over 2 who can read is also lower (24 percent versus 36 percent) than in other homes (Rideout, Vandewater, & Wartella, 2003; Rideout & Hamel, 2006).

Watching television in itself does not necessarily replace or reduce the levels of all other activities. In fact, many children watch television while engaging in other activities, such as play, shifting their attention back and forth (Anderson & Pempek, 2005). The type of television that is watched also influences the way that young children spend their time. One study of 2- and 4-year-old children found that those who watched more hours of entertainment television, such as animated and other programs designed for a child audience without an informative purpose, tended to spend less time reading, whereas children who watched more educational/informative programs did not show a reduction in the amount of time spent reading (Huston et al., 1999). One of the most significant findings about young

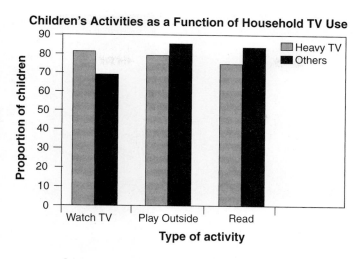

FIGURE 12.3 Children's activities are affected by household TV use.

Source: Based on information in Rideout, Vandewater, & Wartella, 2003.

children and television, therefore, may be that the message *is* more important than the medium.

This was also shown in a longitudinal study of 570 adolescents whose television use had been documented when they were 5 years old. The amount of television children had watched had less of an influence on later behavior and development than the content of programs they had watched (Anderson et al., 2001). Overall, preschoolers who watched more child informative programs with educational and prosocial themes, such as *Sesame Street* and *Mister Rogers' Neighborhood*, tended in adolescence to have higher grades, read more books, and place more value on achievement; they also showed greater creativity and exhibited lower levels of aggression than children who watched violent programs. These findings, although correlational, are in keeping with other studies of the intellectual benefits of educational television for preschool children (Wright et al., 2001).

The longitudinal study also showed, however, that the same programs may influence different children in different ways. Preschoolers who were especially likely to talk about television and incorporate television content into their play tended to show more negative and longer lasting effects of viewing violent programs when they were adolescents. According to the researchers, for these children, the salience and vividness of superheroes and action and adventure themes may have led them to emphasize and practice violent and aggressive actions, increasing the likelihood that they would behave more aggressively throughout childhood and into adolescence (Anderson et al., 2001).

The analyses also showed that, even within the same category, different programs may be associated with different outcomes. Within the informative/educational category, there were differences between *Sesame Street* and *Mister Rogers' Neighborhood*. Different levels of creativity in adolescence among those who watched different educational/informative programs, for example, may have occurred because *Sesame Street* emphasizes and contributes to academic skills and knowledge, whereas *Mister Rogers' Neighborhood* stimulated

This boy is a member of the target audience for Teletubbies, one of the first television programs developed with 2-year-old viewers in mind.

imaginative and creative thinking. Alternatively, as with all correlational research, other explanations should be considered, including the possibility that differences among the children at age 5 drew them to some programs more than others and that children's characteristics were then reinforced—but not caused—by their TV viewing patterns (Anderson et al., 2001).

Parents of very young children monitor and manage their children's television viewing more than parents of older children (Huston et al., 1999). It may not be surprising in light of their influence on very young children's viewing choices, but most parents seem to find that television has more positive than negative effects and tend to believe that it is more helpful than harmful for children's learning. Whereas 70 percent of children 3 and younger were reported to have imitated positive behavior they had seen on television, such as sharing or helping, only 27 percent were reported to have imitated aggressive behavior, such as hitting or kicking (Rideout, Vandewater, & Wartella, 2003; Rideout & Hamel, 2006).

Parents are often aware of the differences between television programs, in part because they watch many of those programs, especially when their children are young. According to one survey, the most popular co-viewed children's programs for parents and preschoolers were *Rugrats, Blues Clues, Barney & Friends*, and *Arthur*. Parents also reported that they encourage their children to watch educational channels and channels produced for child audiences, specifically, the Discovery Channel, PBS, The History Channel, The Learning Channel, and the Disney Channel. The top 10 encouraged children's programs (by the 57 percent of parents who were able to list any programs that they encouraged their children to watch) included *Sesame Street, Blues Clues, Arthur, Barney & Friends, Rugrats*, and *Little Bear*. One program that is made for children, *Power Rangers*, was consistently mentioned as a program that parents did not want their children to watch, presumably due to its themes of action and violence (Woodward & Gridina, 2000).

The first episode of *Sesame Street* was aired on PBS in 1969. Since then, it has been joined on an increasingly crowded television soundstage by a diverse range of human, animal, and uncategorizable performers who appear both on PBS and on a number of cable TV channels that offer programs for preschool children.

One of the most controversial newcomers in the late 1990s was the program *Teletubbies*, developed with 2-year-old viewers in mind. Some parents were critical of the immature language models provided by the four Teletubbies—Tinky Winky, Dipsy, Laa-Laa, and Po. The program was aimed at children who are themselves in early stages of language development, however, and the show's developers deliberately gave each character a style of speaking that represented a particular stage (Teletubbies Frequently Asked Questions, 2002).

Given its young target audience, the pace of *Teletubbies* was designed to be much slower than the pace of programs that most parents enjoy sitting through, such as *Sesame Street*. The plots were also very simple, as seen in these descriptions of two typical episodes. In one, "a pair of boots appears in Teletubbyland," while in the other, "a door appears in Teletubbyland. The Tubbies have great fun opening and closing, knocking on and going through the door." Some parents were uncomfortable with elements of technology that were incorporated into Teletubbyland, including television screens that were built into each Teletubby's stomach. In every episode, one of the Teletubbies' screens turns on and video images of real children are displayed. The program was well received by its intended child audience, many of whom were undoubtedly drawn to the bright primary colors, simple musical melodies, and the Teletubbies' infantlike bodies and facial features.

The slow pace and immature language models in the *Teletubbies* may be one reason that a recent longitudinal study of early television viewing and language outcomes found that watching greater amounts of *Teletubbies* was related to comprehending fewer vocabulary words and having less expressive language at the age of 30 months. Using data provided by parents' diaries of their children's television exposure beginning at the age of 6 months, the researchers also found that children who had watched more of programs designed for older preschool audiences—*Dora the Explorer, Blue's Clues, Arthur, Clifford,* and *Dragon Tales*—had larger receptive vocabularies and higher expressive language scores when they were 30 months old. Children who had watched larger amounts of *Sesame Street* had smaller expressive language, while those who had watched more *Barney & Friends*, a program that we will discuss in greater detail shortly, had more expressive language but comprehended a smaller number of vocabulary words (Linebarger & Walker, 2005). Given that this study was correlational, not experimental, it is not entirely clear how to interpret the results. While it's possible that program content caused children's language to develop—or fail to develop—in particular ways, it is also possible that children were attracted to programs that matched their language abilities. Regardless of the reasons for the observed differences, these intriguing findings deserve follow-up investigation.

Among the still-expanding options for very young viewers are new shows with new names and characters, such as *The Backyardigans* and *Boohbah*. In response to concerns that the downward age trend in children's television has created a new generation of ever younger couch potatoes, themes of physical activity and physical fitness are evident in many of these programs, with most offering fun ways for children to be more active while they are watching (Singer & Singer, 2001).

One of the most physically active characters in children's television since 1993 has been a large purple dinosaur named Barney, a character adored by many 2- and 3-year-olds. As we discuss next, he is also a TV friend from whom they learn.

Barney & Friends

Singer and Singer (1998) evaluated the educational and entertainment value of *Barney & Friends* by studying the content of nearly 70 episodes that were produced between 1993 and 1995. They found that nearly every episode contained many elements that can prepare young children for school, including attention to cognitive skills and knowledge, emotional awareness, prosocial attitudes and behaviors, fine and gross motor skills and physical abilities, music and entertainment, and multicultural awareness.

Singer and Singer also observed 3-year-old children's behaviors while they were watching episodes of *Barney & Friends* in early childhood classrooms. They found that the episodes that had the highest ratings for cognitive content tended to produce the greatest measurable cognitive effects in children, including the acquisition of new vocabulary and high levels of comprehension of the content. The content in the episodes included in the study was diverse, as is true of the program generally, and covered information about colors, animals, pirates, the alphabet, numbers, neighbors and neighborhoods, and music from around the world. The Singers' study showed that the most beneficial group context for learning the content in *Barney & Friends* occurred when children watched the program and then participated in teacher-led activities that reinforced important themes, skills, and vocabulary. Children who merely watched episodes of *Barney & Friends* benefited, albeit not to the same extent that children with a follow-up activity did. Both of the groups that watched *Barney & Friends* benefited more than children in control groups, who were taught the follow-up lessons but did not watch any of the episodes.

Barney's impact was observed in other ways as well. Many children in the Singers' study were observed participating along with Barney in singing, clapping, dancing, and marching during the program. Themes from the episodes were often subsequently incorporated into children's pretend play in the classroom. Children also resonated to the positive emotions displayed in *Barney & Friends*. They held hands, hugged, and sang "I Love You" along with Barney and his friends at the conclusion of each episode. Observations of 2-year-olds watching *Barney & Friends* and playing in the classroom later showed effects that were similar to those found for 3-year-old children. Two-year-olds were attentive during the episodes and subsequently showed a greater tendency to participate in symbolic play and to engage in more prosocial and less aggressive behavior.

Information about the Singers' research and *Barney & Friends* is available on the PBS website (PBSkids.org), along with suggestions for teachers and parents about how to provide children with fun, involving activities to follow up each episode. These activities, like the episodes themselves, reinforce cognitive skills at the same time that they promote pretend play, and the development of language, literacy, and prosocial behavior (see their webpage"Activities for Parents and Children"). Whether children love Barney or merely like him, parents can use these ideas to help get the most out of all of the television programs that their children watch. In general, most experts also recommend that parents of toddlers limit TV time each day, that parents watch with their children so that they can participate together in activities during the show, and that they talk afterward about the positive and negative aspects of the program they have watched (see the PBSKids.org webpage "Getting the Most out of Watching Television with Your Toddler").

Computers

Unlike television, the computer is a medium that was not used by young children's parents during their own infant and toddler years. Nevertheless, the majority (72 percent) of parents of children age 6 and under believe that computers "mostly help" children's learning. Children today are often initiated into using computers by their parents; almost one third (28 percent) had, at age 2 or younger, used a computer while sitting on a parent's lap (Rideout, Vandewater, & Wartella, 2003; Rideout & Hamel, 2006).

Computers in the Home

In households with children 3 years and under, most (71 percent) own computers and more than half (60 percent) are connected to the Internet. One third of children 3 and under (31 percent) have ever used a computer, but regular computer use is relatively light among children in this age range; only 10 percent use a computer for any purpose in a typical day, with nearly all of those children using it to play games (Rideout, Vandewater, & Wartella, 2003; Rideout & Hamel, 2006).

As a result of their experience, even very young children acquire a number of basic computer skills. According to their parents, they know how to turn it on by themselves (11 percent), load a CD-ROM without assistance (10 percent), and use a mouse to point and click (21 percent). Many young children who love Barney, Dora, Blue, and other characters

The majority of households with infants and toddlers own computers, and many young children, like this girl, are initiated into using computers by a parent.

from children's programs know that they can visit their television friends at websites that offer pictures, online computer games, and printable coloring pages. Twenty percent of children between the ages of 4 and 6 as well as 5 percent of children 3 years and under not only know about but also request specific Internet websites like these when using the computer in their home. In fact, according to a survey of parents, by the age of 2 years, 10 percent of children had visited websites for children (Rideout, Vandewater, & Wartella, 2003).

Computers in the Early Childhood Classroom

Early studies of young children's computer use in the preschool classroom addressed some educators' concerns that computers would isolate children from their peers. Observational research has indicated, however, that children tend to prefer using computers in their preschool classroom with peers or a teacher rather than alone. The software that teachers select, and the computer activities that children choose, provide them with numerous opportunities to cooperate as well as to ask questions and share their knowledge and opinions about the games and programs. Some of the 3- to 5-year-old children in one study even became computer experts who spontaneously tutored their classmates and occasionally diagnosed and remedied minor problems with the computer (Rosengren, Gross, & Perlmutter, 1986).

Most early childhood educators now recognize that, as with television, computer technology itself is neither inherently beneficial nor detrimental to children's development (Clements, Nastasi, & Swaminathan, 1993). NAEYC (1996) takes the position that early childhood educators need to evaluate computer software just as they would evaluate books or other classroom materials, taking into account the age, individual, and cultural appropriateness. According to NAEYC and other experts, when computer technology is used appropriately, it can enhance children's cognitive and social development, especially if it is designed to encourage collaboration and communication between two or more children. Ideally, software for children also stimulates their creativity, problem solving, and language skills, while giving them control over the type and pace of activities they perform (Druin, 1999; Druin & Solomon, 1996). Developmentally appropriate uses of technology also include integrating computers into the regular learning environment and reinforcing learning that occurs in other parts of the classroom with more traditional learning tools, including books, art materials, and building toys (NAEYC, 1996).

In the not too distant future, it may become more difficult for early childhood educators to differentiate between traditional learning tools and computers in their classrooms. One reason for the possible confusion is that books may be read on a computer screen, as is now the case for titles in the collection of the International Children's Digital Library (www.ICDLbooks.org). With the click of a mouse, children ages 3 to 13 can read digitized children's books from around the world at an evolving website that is being designed with the help of children. Studies are under way to understand the strategies that school-age children develop when they first begin to use the digital library, and the results may indicate how children themselves think about these resources (Druin et al., 2003).

Another potential source of confusion about how to conceptualize old and new teaching resources is likely to arise because new computers for children are being developed that are not simply boxy machines with glass screens and mice attached to a keyboard. Instead,

Early childhood educators need to evaluate computer software just as they would evaluate other classroom materials. When used appropriately, computers can enhance young children's cognitive and social development, especially if it's designed to encourage collaboration and communication between two or more children.

they resemble books, traditional infant toys, and even stuffed animals (Druin, 1996; Druin & Solomon, 1996; Druin & Hendler, 2000).

Interactive Books and Toys

What is a computer? Although there are some computers and electronic toys that actually look like computers, increasingly, the answer seems to be that a computer is any device that has microchip technology and responds when children act upon it. Parents as well as early childhood educators need to evaluate these new products in light of empirical evidence about their effects on infants and young children.

Interactive Books. **Electronic books** have been developed which are more interactive than ordinary books. Children can read these books by themselves even if they do not yet know how to read. In most electronic books, touching the pages with a special wand activates a voice that reads the text of the story, states the names of objects on the page to which the child is pointing, and asks the child questions about the plot and characters. One potential advantage of many electronic books is that, as children get older, new pages that are even "smarter" can be inserted in place of the original, easier set of pages.

The extent to which educators choose or reject electronic books for their classrooms will be determined, in part, by their effects on young children's literacy skills. Some studies have found that talking books enhance children's phonological awareness, but the experience of using electronic books does not necessarily result in better word reading (Chera & Wood, 2003) or comprehension of the story's meaning (Medwell, 1998). In fact, children may even spend less time reading the text and more time activating other parts of the pages when they use electronic books. It is important, therefore, that nontext elements in electronic books be story-relevant so that they can reinforce key ideas in the text (Labbo & Kuhn, 2000; Wartella, Caplovitz, & Lee, 2004). In addition to illuminating the effects of interactive books on children's reading skills, more research is needed in order to understand whether and how they affect children's ability to make up and tell their own stories.

"Smart" Infant Toys.   Microchip technology has also entered today's toy boxes. For infants as young as 3 months, there are "smart" rattles that not only rattle when shaken but also light up, sing, laugh, and say hello in several languages. Other popular infant toys, like stacking rings, are now available in enhanced versions that respond, literally, with bells and whistles, as well as flashing lights, when the rings are stacked in the correct order. Blocks in one high-tech playset produce beautiful music, including Mozart, when arranged in different orders and with different sides placed into a recessed panel. There are also balls that emit music, letter names, and other sounds as children touch or roll them, and baby gyms in which each touch triggers music, lights, and phrases in foreign languages.

Many manufacturers of these toys claim that they help infants learn more effectively than the traditional versions. Parents and other adults who purchase them may be drawn to the bells and whistles and may enjoy playing with them. They should be aware, however, that there has been almost no independent, systematic research thus far exploring the effects of these toys on infants' development. As a result, we cannot say whether or how activating the smart stacking rings or playing with any toy that is designed to provide reinforcing feedback for only one correct solution influences early exploration, play, and learning (Bergen, 2001).

Interactive Toy Characters.   For young children, including those as young as 1 year, there are interactive stuffed animals that seemingly bring to life favorite television characters such as Barney, Elmo, and the Teletubbies. Interactive Barney, for example, has enough microchip technology to allow him to sing 17 songs and play 12 games in response to a child's squeeze on his hand or foot. When his eyes are covered, he plays peek-a-boo. By buying a special radio transmitter, *Barney & Friends* programs playing on a TV set or VCR can send instructions to the interactive Barney, making him respond to the Barney who appears on screen. With another add-on pack, children can control and communicate with their Barney doll through CD-ROMs playing on a personal computer. Interactive Teletubbies have sensors on their hands and feet and TV-screen tummies that enable them to respond, albeit in more limited ways for their intended users—children between the ages of 1 and 4 years.

All of these technologically loaded toys are more expensive than the original versions, and a fully equipped interactive stuffed animal costs slightly more than $200. Is the expense worth it? Unfortunately, we don't know the answer. Although manufacturers test out these new toys on child focus groups and their parents, there is virtually no systematic, independent empirical research on their impact on early cognitive and social development. Some critics have asserted that many interactive toys and learning products are designed in ways that make the product active and the child simply reactive. They also wonder if playing with programmed, recognizable television characters will limit children's imaginations. Truly interactive products, they argue, should foster creativity and put children in charge to the greatest degree possible (Bergen, 2001; Wartella, Caplovitz, & Lee, 2004).

Some researchers are responding to these concerns by developing toys and games that are more interactive, such as PETS (Personal Electronic Teller of Stories)—robotic animals that children build and then use with accompanying software to tell their own stories. Unlike preprogrammed interactive toy characters, dolls, and stuffed animals, the 7- to 11-year-old children playing with and learning from PETS actually carry out the programming (with the assistance of adults who act as collaborators) and thus determine the course of the story (Montemayor, Druin, & Hendler, 2000; Plaisant et al., 2000). Other related projects have explored ways to enable children to participate in the design of room-size interactive storytelling spaces (AlborziMontemayor, J., Druin, A., & Hendler, J. (2000). PETS: A Personal Electronic Teller of Stories. In A. Druin & J. Hendler (Eds.), *Robots for kids* (pp. 74–108). San Francisco, CA: Morgan Kaufmann. et al., 2000). When the programming procedures used in these settings are adapted for use with younger children, then even 3-year-olds will be able to participate in creating their own truly interactive toys.

This is already beginning to be a reality, as seen in StoryToy, a play system designed for children between 2 and 6 years of age. StoryToy looks like an ordinary farm playset but actually functions like a computer with a touch-sensitive screen. When moved around the play surface, the toy farm animals activate sensors and send signals to start one of several modes of play that vary in terms of how much control and technology the child has available. In free-play mode, for example, the sound system is deactivated, and the technology is turned off, but in other play modes different types of suggestions and feedback are provided when children move the animals around. For example, a cow might say, "I'm hot. Please bring me to the pond so that I can go swimming." When children follow this request, and move the cow to the pond, sounds of splashing water are heard. For older children, many different, open-ended story lines can be chosen and developed during play with the toy farm animals, making it a toy that can develop along with the child's abilities (Fontijn & Mendels, 2005). As these new interactive toys become available, it will be important to investigate their impact on young children's development, for the same reasons that the claims made by today's smart-toy manufacturers need to be tested more thoroughly.

WRAPPING IT UP: Summary and Conclusion

As we have explored the first 3 years of life throughout this book, we have seen that children are born ready to respond to and interact with the people, objects, and events in their world and that these experiences are an important foundation for subsequent development. We know that without adequate prenatal care, good nutrition, safe environments, sensitive and responsive caregivers, and stimulating experiences, infants are at risk for a range of immediate and long-lasting physical, cognitive, social, and emotional problems. We have also seen that infants and young children are resilient and that it is possible to compensate for early deprivation, although it becomes more difficult and more expensive to intervene as time passes. There is great potential to improve the future prospects for the most vulnerable and youngest members of society.

As a society, however, we need to determine how to use the resources and knowledge that we have to promote the well-being of all infants and young children. Concerns about infants and toddlers who have too many smart, bossy toys diminish in significance as we consider that there are still many lower-income children who do not have even one book of their own (Whitehurst, Arnold, Epstein, Angell, Smith, & Fischel, 1994). Debates about whether classical music is beneficial for early intellectual development pale in comparison to the reality that many infants and toddlers spend every day in child care that provides a safe environment but fails to offer a well-rounded, age-appropriate foundation for learning (Brauner, Gordic, & Zigler, 2004). Parents who feel pressure to spend a small fortune on the latest technology-rich toys and learning materials need help, but so do parents who experience stress due to inadequate economic resources, poor or uncertain housing arrangements, and institutions that either ignore or misunderstand different cultural and ethnic backgrounds.

Many parents look to experts for guidance, but the experts too often have knowledge that applies only to specific developmental domains. Trained as scientists, most researchers will not draw conclusions or make recommendations that the available data cannot support, but this may have the unintended result of leaving the door open for unqualified individuals to interpret the findings as they wish. In addition, many academic experts are hesitant to move beyond their laboratories and universities to disseminate their findings to broader audiences or to engage in public policy initiatives, although they may fully endorse the efforts of those who do incorporate these activities into their professional work. It is clear, however, that we need to enlist everyone who has an interest in development from birth to 3 in sharing information across disciplinary and organizational boundaries, as has been suggested by a blue-ribbon panel of early childhood experts (Huston, 2005; Shonkoff & Phillips, 2000). The recommendations that this group produced and published in an important book, *From Neurons to Neighborhoods*, are shown in Table 12.2.

TABLE 12.2   Promoting Healthy Development from Birth to 3

Recommendations

1. Provide the same amount of resources to foster socioemotional school readiness as are now provided to support literacy and numerical skills
2. Evaluate schools' effectiveness in reducing disparities that exist at school entry among children from different socioeconomic and cultural backgrounds
3. Invest resources to address young children's mental health needs by expanding efforts aimed at screening, early detection, treatment, and prevention
4. Establish policies to provide more choices to more parents for allocating responsibility for early child care
5. Coordinate efforts and strategies among private, public, and philanthropic sectors to reduce environmental hazards that are known to pose risks for prenatal and postnatal development
6. Develop funding to improve the quality of early childhood education by enhancing the skills, knowledge, and compensation of nonparental caregivers
7. Review current public investments in child care and early education in order to improve the quality of care that is provided for all young children, including those with developmental disabilities or chronic health conditions
8. Ensure that children who are supported by a working adult do not live in poverty, and eliminate deep, persistent poverty regardless of employment status
9. Document and ensure full implementation of effective interventions
10. Coordinate state and local early childhood policies and agencies, especially those that pertain to mental health services and developmental-behavioral screening for neglected and maltreated children
11. Create broad-based working groups involving professionals from the fields of education, health, and human services; charge them with the task of identifying professional training and development opportunities and challenges for individuals who work with young children and their families

Source: Based on information in Shonkoff and Phillips, 2000.

Researchers supported by the National Institute of Child Health and Human Development, for example, must continue to share their findings not only with scholarly audiences but also through organizations, such as Zero to Three, National Association for the Education of Young Children, and the Children's Defense Fund, that already serve as a bridge between developmental scientists, policy makers, educators, and parents. Parents are ultimately responsible for nurturing and guiding their children from birth to 3 and beyond, but they need and deserve to be educated about the best practices and how to apply them in their own children's lives. If we fail to do this, we risk squandering our greatest resource, children, today as well as tomorrow.

THINK ABOUT IT: Questions for Reading and Discussion

1. What does the Toddler Top 20 and research in the chapter suggest to you about the characteristics of a "good" song for young children? If you wanted to write a new popular children's song, what would you be sure to include in it, and why?

2. How would you respond to a new parent who is considering buying CDs featuring Mozart for Babies in order to make her baby smarter?

3. A parent who has decided that his infant should have music lessons as early as possible comes to you for advice. What would you tell him about the different methods of music instruction for very young children? What should he keep in mind about the early development of the ability to sing and play music?

4. Is television good or bad for infants and toddlers? How do you know?

5. If you wanted to go beyond correlational research to study the effects of television viewing on children younger than 3 years of age, what sort of experiment would you design? What do you think you would find?

6. Many parents disregard the American Academy of Pediatrics recommendations about the use of television with young children. How would you convince parents in heavy-viewing households that they should minimize screen time, especially for children younger than 2 years of age?

7. With computers now in the majority of homes with children 3 years of age and under, is it more or less important than in the past to have computers in child care and early childhood education settings? Explain.

8. What do infants and toddlers gain and lose from interacting with smart books and toys? How might these interactions affect their physical, cognitive, social, and emotional development?

KEY WORDS

Electronic books (409)   Interactive books containing a microchip that enables the reader to activate a voice that reads the text, states the names of objects on the page to which the reader is pointing, and asks the reader questions about the book's contents

Mozart Effect (398)   The name given to findings of an experiment in which college students who listened to a Mozart sonata scored higher than they had after experiencing the same amount of silence or listening to relaxation instructions

Suzuki Method (397)   A system developed in the 1940s by a Japanese music educator who believed that learning to play a musical instrument is like learning to speak a first language

GLOSSARY

Abecedarian Project (378) An intervention in which approximately 100 low-income, primarily African American children participated in a full-time, high-quality early childhood program from the age of 6 weeks until 3 years

Accessibility (295) A dimension of parental involvement that reflects presence and availability to the child

Accommodation (218) Piaget's term for adjusting exploratory actions in response to an object's novel characteristics

Accretion and deletion (187) The apparent appearance and disappearance of elements of a visual stimulus, such as its texture or pattern

Active phase (112) The second phase of labor, with increasingly painful contractions coming more frequently as the cervix opens

Allocentric framework (226) Spatial orientation that is based on external cues in the environment

Americans with Disabilities Act (ADA) (376) The federal civil rights act protecting individuals with disabilities

Amniocentesis (90) A procedure for prenatal diagnosis in which a small sample of fluid is taken from the amniotic sac and used to detect any genetic or chromosomal abnormalities

Amodal properties (197) Properties of events that are not specific to a particular sensory modality, such as the synchrony of a sight and its accompanying sound

Analgesic medication (125) Drugs that reduce pain without eliminating it

Anesthetic medication (125) Drugs that eliminate pain by blocking nerves that send pain signals to the brain

A-not-B error (221) Piaget's term for the tendency, first seen around 8 months of age, for infants to search for objects at locations from which they previously successfully retrieved objects, even thought they saw the object being hidden at a different location

Apgar Score (133) An assessment used at 1 and 5 minutes after birth to provide a profile of the infant's physical health

Arbitrary relations (238) Steps in a sequence that may be performed in any order because they are not logically or practically linked

Archival research (56) Research that replaces the direct observation or assessment of research participants with examination of records or artifacts

Assent (59) Verbal agreement to participate in research, obtained when participants are unable to give informed consent

Assessment of Preterm Infants' Behavior (APIB) (137) A modification of the NBAS that is designed to gauge the effects of interventions and treatments on preterm infants' motor, state, and other neurobehavioral responses (see Brazelton Neonatal Behavioral Assessment Scale)

Assimilation (218) Piaget's term for employing previously used actions to explore an object

Assisted reproductive technology (ART) (74) Fertility treatments in which both egg and sperm are handled

Attachment behaviors (305) Infants' built-in behaviors, such as crying, cooing, smiling, looking at, and reaching for caregivers, that attract attention and elicit care

Attachment Q-Sort (AQS) (307) A rating system that can be used outside of a laboratory setting to assess individual differences in infant-caregiver attachment relationships

Attachment relationship (305) The special relationship that develops over the first year of life between infants and the adults who care for them

Auditory localization (191) The ability to detect the location of sound sources

Autism (281) A syndrome characterized by disordered social interactions and problems with language and communication

Autism spectrum disorder (ASD) (281) A cluster of five related syndromes that vary in terms of language skill deficits, children's IQ, and the appearance and course of symptoms

Autosomes (67) Any of the chromosomes other than the sex-determining chromosomes

Axon (147) A branchlike structure that conveys electrical messages outward from a neuron's cell body and toward the synapse

Babbling (260) Patterned but meaningless sequences of reduplicated sounds, such as strings of syllables

Baby biography (44) Observational records made by parents or other caregivers of an infants' early development

Bayley Scales of Infant Development (BSID) (244) A measure that is used to assess infant intelligence through motor, mental, and behavior rating scales

Bayley Scales of Infant Development-Second Edition (BSID-II) (199) A widely use assessment that includes scales for measuring motor development from birth to 42 months of age

Behavioral state (56) Any of 10 distinct levels of arousal observed in newborn infants, including four awake states, three transition states between sleep and waking, two sleep states, and one transition sleep state

Bidirectional (291) Interactions that involve reciprocal behaviors and responses between social partners

Binocular disparity (190) Slightly different retinal images that are produced when a viewer looks at a single object or visual stimulus

Binocular vision (185) Visual input from two eyes that are aligned and move together

Birth doula (129) A trained layperson who provides nonmedical assistance during labor and delivery

Blastocyst (77) The hollow, spherical structure comprised of approximately 100 identical cells formed through mitosis during the first week after conception

Body mass index (BMI) (143) A measure of weight in relation to height

Brazelton Neonatal Behavioral Assessment Scale (NBAS) (136) A structured examination that is used with infants from birth until the age of 2 months to assess reflexes and social interactive behaviors

Breech presentation (114) A birth in which the infant emerges feet or buttocks first

Case study (44) Also referred to as the clinical method, this is an in-depth examination of a single individual

Categorization (241) The ability to group aspects of the world according to shared attributes

Cephalocaudal principle (79) The pattern of growth in which development begins in the anterior (head) and later occurs in the posterior (tail) of the organism

Certified nurse-midwife (CNM) (128) Registered nurses who are trained to assist during labor and delivery

cesarean delivery (126) A surgical procedure performed when a vaginal delivery would be too dangerous for mother, baby, or both

Chorionic villus sampling (CVS) (90) A procedure for prenatal diagnosis in which cells are collected from the chorion, the fetal membrane that gives rise to the placenta

Chromosomes (67) Physical structures consisting of DNA and supporting proteins

Cohort (49) A particular group or generation of participants, such as infants born in the same year

Cohort effects (50) A problem in cross-sectional research, in which age differences may actually stem from generational, or cohort, differences

Colostrum (167) A thick, yellowish fluid, richer in protein and protective antibodies than the breast milk that is produced a few days after birth

Committed compliance (347) Children's tendency to follow parents' directives and requests with a minimum of prompting and reminding

Complementary feeding (170) The transition from exclusive breastfeeding or formula-feeding to the inclusion of solid food in an infant's diet

Conditioned headturning (54) A technique in which infants are taught to turn their head every time they hear a particular signal—and only when they hear that signal. Once this head-turning response has been conditioned and can be elicited reliably, a different stimulus is presented or alternated with the original signal. Infants who do not turn their head in response to the new stimulus are assumed to be able to discriminate between the signal used in conditioning and the new stimulus, whereas infants who turn their head are thought not to be able to make this discrimination

Cones (183) Photoreceptors in the eye that respond to specific hues, or wavelengths of light

Conscience (346) An internal set of standards that guide behavior

Constrained statistical learning framework (259) The ability to extract recurring patterns from repeated experience with stimuli

Continuous (5) Characterization of development as a gradual, smooth process of change

Coordination of secondary schemes (220) Piaget's fourth substage of the sensorimotor period, in which infants perform two separate schemes in order to produce a desired outcome

Cross-modal perception (196) The ability to transfer information about an object from one sense, such as vision, and use it when encountering the object later using a different sense, such as touch

Cross-sectional research (50) A developmental design in which two or more age groups of participants are compared in terms of their behavior or ability at the same point in time

Deferred imitation (220) The ability to remember and repeat an action that was observed earlier, in the absence of a model for those actions

Dendrites (147) Branchlike structures that convey electrical messages from the synapse and toward a neuron's cell body

Deoxyribonucleic acid (DNA) (67) Strands of molecules that carry the genetic code of a cell

Dependent variable (41) The main behavior or response of interest in a study, this is the researchers' measure of the impact of the independent variable(s)

Depth perception (181) The ability to perceive a three-dimensional world

Dilatation (111) Widening and opening of the cervix during labor

Dishabituation (54) Infants' recovery of attention when a new stimulus is introduced

Disorganized/disoriented attachment (309) An infant-caregiver relationship that may develop when caregivers show contradictory, disrupted, or otherwise unusual emotional communication with their infants; also referred to as Type D

Dizygotic twins (74) Siblings resulting from two different eggs, also known as fraternal (DZ) twins

Down syndrome (70) A congenital syndrome, also referred to as trisomy 21, in which there is an extra chromosome 21; individuals with Down syndrome have distinctive facial features and other physical characteristics and have mild to severe mental retardation

Dyadic synchrony (291) Interactions between infants and caregivers that are characterized by mutual attention and affective matching or regulation

Early Head Start (379) A national intervention program that provides services to low-income pregnant women and families with infants and toddlers

Early intervention (377) Systematic efforts to either prevent or reduce the adverse developmental effects of family income, parent characteristics, birth experiences, or aspects of the environment. The strongest conclusions can be made when children are randomly assigned to intervention and control groups

Early Intervention Services (EIS) (376) Services provided through IDEA, including screening and assessment, family education and training, home visits, health and social services, speech-language therapy, and occupational and physical therapy, as well as assistive technology

Ecological theory of perception (181) A theory that assumes that the visual system perceives meaningful information directly from the properties of the environment

Ectoderm (81) The upper layer of the inner cell mass, which gives rise to the brain and spinal cord, sensory organs, and skin, nails, hair, and teeth

Effacement (112) The thinning out of the cervix during labor

Effectance (292) The feeling of moving between different states, including from a state of nonsynchrony to a state of synchrony

Egocentric (218) Piaget's term for infants' tendency to understand the world through their own sensory and motor acts

Egocentric framework (226) Spatial orientation that is based on one's own body and physical actions

Egocentric speech (230) Verbal behavior that is directed toward oneself rather than others, with the purpose of enhancing concentration and performance during an activity

Electroencephalogram (EEG) (146) A measure of the brain's activity that uses external electrodes placed on the scalp

Electroencephalography (EEG) (52) A measurement of electrical activity and spontaneous natural rhythms in the brain

Electronic books (409) Interactive books containing a microchip that enables the reader to activate a voice that reads the text, states the names of objects on the page to which the reader is pointing, and asks the reader questions about the book's contents

Electronic fetal monitoring (EFM) (124) The use of external or internal sensors to monitor contractions and detect signs of fetal distress

Embryonic stage (79) The second prenatal stage, lasting from 2 weeks to 8 weeks

Emotional contagion (339) A phenomenon in which facial, vocal, or gestural cues of one person give rise to a similar or related state in another person

Emotion regulation (343) A process through which emotions are monitored, appraised, and modified in relation to goals

Enabling relations (238) A logically or practically necessary order between steps in a sequence

Endoderm (81) The lower layer of the inner cell mass, from which the respiratory and digestive systems develop

Engagement (295) A dimension of parental involvement that reflects direct contact and interaction with the child

Episiotomy (126) A procedure in which an incision is made to widen the vaginal opening

Ethnographic research (40) A technique for exploring the interaction of culture and biology, in which researchers from a Western culture make observations or conduct interviews in everyday settings in non-Western cultures

Event sampling (37) A technique in observational research in which a small number of behaviors are identified and the researcher makes a note each time they occur by making a mark on a prepared checklist

Event-related potential (ERP) (53, 236) A measurement of electrical activity resulting in the brain from the presentation of discrete stimuli such as a network of electrodes placed on the scalp's surface

Experience-dependent (149) Aspects of brain development that develop solely as a result of a person's experiences

Experience-expectant (149) Aspects of brain development that "expect" to have certain kinds of stimulation and are ready to develop once they receive it

Experimental design (46) A design that examines the influence of an independent variable on a dependent variable

Explicit memory (236) Conscious awareness of specific information, such as events and facts

Exploratory play (212) Play commonly seen in the first year of life, consisting of repetition of motor movements

External validity (43) The degree to which the findings of one study can be extended, or generalized, to other samples and settings

Failure to thrive (144) Growth stunting that is caused by deprivation of physical contact

Family and Medical Leave Act (FMLA) (359) The federal policy that allows certain categories of employees to take a 12-week, job-protected leave to care for a child, spouse, or parent or to take time off due to their own serious health condition

Family child care home (366) Care that is provided for one or more unrelated children in the caregiver's home

Family leave (359) Job-protected time off from work for a variety of reasons other than the birth of a child

Fetal alcohol syndrome (FAS) (95) A constellation of physical, behavioral, and cognitive abnormalities caused by prenatal exposure to alcohol

Fetal stage (82) The third prenatal stage, lasting from 8 weeks until birth

Fine motor skills (199) Skills, such as grasping small objects, that involve movements of the fingers and hands

Forced-choice preferential looking (184) A research procedure in which infants are shown two visual stimuli simultaneously and the total amount of time they spend looking at each display is compared

Fovea (184) The center of the eye

Functional play (212) Play observed beginning at 12 to 18 months of age that reflects children's understanding of objects' intended uses

Functional-relational play (212) Play observed beginning between 12 and 18 months of age that involves bringing together related objects

Genes (67) Units of hereditary information; each gene is a segment of DNA in a specific location on a chromosome

Germinal stage (77) The first prenatal stage, beginning at conception and ending at approximately 2 weeks

Goodness-of-fit (311) A match between an infant's behaviors and the caregiver's expectations and understanding of those behaviors

Grammar (252) Systems of rules for combining words or signs

Gross motor skills (199) Skills, such as crawling and walking, that involve movements of the whole body and large muscle groups

Guided participation (232) Patterns of social interaction and structured activity during joint problem solving involving people with different levels of skills and knowledge

Habituation (54) The phenomenon in which infants gradually lose interest in a stimulus after repeated presentations

Haptic information (198) Exploratory mouth or hand movements that go well beyond mere tactile contact with an object

High-reactive (330) Infants who respond to novelty by showing extreme degrees of motor activity, fretting, and crying

High/Scope Perry Preschool Project (378) An intervention in which approximately 100 low- income African American preschoolers received high-quality early childhood education and home visits

Holophrase (265) Infants' first one-word utterances that name objects but also communicate other meanings

Implicit memory (236) Unconscious learning, including conditioning and aspects of motor learning

Independent variable (41) Aspects of a research setting that researchers identify or vary, such as presence or absence of an infant's mother, in order to determine their effect on behaviors of interest

Indiscriminate friendliness (303) Behavior that is affectionate and friendly toward all adults, including strangers, without the fear or caution characteristic of normal children; often observed in children adopted from orphanages or other institutional settings

Individuals with Disabilities Education Act (IDEA) (376) The federal civil rights act covering children with disabilities; Part C explicitly covers services from birth to 36 months of age

Infant-directed speech (255) Modifications that adults make when speaking (or signing) to infants, producing language that is shorter, more repetitive, higher-pitched, more variable in pitch, and less semantically and grammatically complex than language addressed to adults

Infant Health and Development Project (379) An intervention involving nearly 1,000 preterm, low birth weight infants, with one third of the sample randomly selected to have home visits and to participate in full-day, high-quality child care in child development centers from birth to age 3

Infant mortality rate (14, 154) Number of deaths per 1,000 live births, usually reported with reference to the age of 1 year

Infant school movement (25) An early nineteenth-century movement, imported to the United States from Europe, in which educators believed that children as young as 18 months could be educated and taught to read

Infantile amnesia (236) The inability that most adults have to recall events that happened before they were about 3 years old

Informed consent (59) A key requirement in ethical research, based on research participants being able to understand the procedures involved in a study and any risks those procedures might entail and knowing that they are free to withdraw or decline to participate without any negative consequences

Inhibited to novelty (330) A constitutionally based tendency to respond to unfamiliar people and places by becoming quiet, vigilant, restrained, and avoidant

Insecure-avoidant attachment (308) An infant-caregiver relationship that may develop when caregivers are overstimulating and intrusive when interacting with their infants; also referred to as Type A

Insecure-resistant attachment (308) An infant-caregiver relationship that may develop when caregivers are rejecting or withdrawn, depressed, and unresponsive to infants' needs and attachment behaviors; also referred to as Type C

Intermodal perception (196) The ability to integrate multiple simultaneous sources of sensory information, such as sights and sounds produced by a single object or event

Internal validity (43) The degree to which differences in the dependent variable are actually due to differences in the independent variable

Internal working model (306) Infants' mental representations of their relationship with their primary caregiver(s)

Joint attention (235) Shared perceptual exploration with another person

Joint attention (269) Nonverbal adjustments in posture, gaze, and head orientation that enable infant-adult dyads to focus their attention together on objects or events

Kinematic depth cues (189) Information about perceptual depth that is carried by motion

Kinesthetic sense (198) A sense that conveys information about the body's position and movement

Labor induction (123) A procedure in which a hormone is administered in order to initiate uterine contractions leading to labor and delivery

Laboratory setting (41) A specially designed research space that enables researchers to control or eliminate the influence of irrelevant or distracting factors

Latent phase (112) The initial phase of the first stage of labor, marked by widely spaced contractions that are not painful

Lexical contrast (274) The ability to learn a new word's meaning by comparing it to words that are already known

Literary evidence (10) Written information, including parents' diaries and letters, childrearing advice written by ministers and doctors, and children's books

Longitudinal research (48) A developmental design in which investigators study the same sample of children (or adults) over time, taking measures of their behavior or ability at specified intervals

Long-term memory (236) Information that is stored and available to be retrieved repeatedly over time

Low birth weight (LBW) (118) A birthweight of less than $5\frac{1}{2}$ lb., or 2,500 grams

Low-reactive (330) Infants who respond to novelty by showing low levels of motor activity and a general absence of crying and fussing

Macrosomic birth (119) A birthweight of more than 8 lb. 13 oz., or 4,000 grams

Magnetic resonance imaging (MRI) (146) An imaging technology that reveals the brain's structure

Maltreatment (149, 301) Neglect, medical neglect, physical abuse, sexual abuse, or psychological abuse

Material culture (10) Physical evidence, such as toys, clothing, furniture, and works of art

Maternal serum alpha fetoprotein (MSAFP) test (89) A screening test in which the level of alpha fetoprotein in the mother's bloodstream is measured; also known as the triple screen because it measures the amount of estriol and HCG present in the mother's blood

Maternity leave (359) A job-protected leave from work for employed women during, and sometimes before, childbirth

Mean length of utterance (MLU) (275) A measure of grammatical development that is based on the number of morphemes in speech

Measurement equivalence (48) Correspondence between the measures, or dependent variables, used at two different points in time

Meiosis (73) The process through which sex cells divide at conception

Mental combinations (220) Piaget's sixth substage of the sensorimotor period, in which infants are able to think about their actions and select schemes in order to achieve a desired outcome

Mental representation (217) The ability to remember and think about objects and events, even when those objects and events are not physically present

Mesoderm (81) The middle layer of the inner cell mass, from which the circulatory and excretory systems, muscles, and skeleton develop

Microgenetic research (50) A developmental design in which participants are observed over a period of time, perhaps 10 or more sessions, with the researchers gathering a rich set of data on which fine-grained analyses can be performed

Micronutrient deficiency (173) A form of malnutrition that occurs when insufficient amounts of minerals and vitamins are consumed in the diet

Mitosis (67) The life-long process of cell division in which a cell divides into two identical cells

Monozygotic twins (74) Siblings resulting from a single egg, also known as identical (MZ) twins

Morphemes (275) Minimal meaningful units in speech, such as words, parts of words, or word endings

Mozart Effect (398) The name given to findings of an experiment in which college students who listened to a Mozart sonata scored higher than they had after experiencing the same amount of silence or listening to relaxation instructions

Multifactorial transmission (71) The interaction of genes and the environment that produces most complex human characteristics

Mutual exclusivity assumption (273) A constraint on learning that guides children to assume that objects will have only one name and to look for a nameless object when they hear a new word

Mutually responsive orientation (MRO) (347) A relationship quality that consists of positive emotions and close cooperative interactions

Myelin (148) A fatty covering that insulates axons and increases the efficiency of neural functioning

Narrative record (37) A detailed description of the range of behaviors researchers observe

Naturalistic observation (37) Studies in which researchers remain relatively passive observers in the sense that, apart from being physically present, they do not intervene in or try to influence the situation

Naturalistic setting (36) Studies in which researchers observe infants in their usual surroundings, such as their own home or their regular child care center

Nature (5) Biological factors influencing development

Neonatal Intensive Care Unit (116) A specialized hospital setting for the care of medically vulnerable infants, including those born preterm and very preterm

Neonatal Intensive Care Unit Network Neurobehavioral Scale (NNNS) (137) A measure designed to assess the functioning of at-risk infants, primarily those believed to have been exposed prenatally to alcohol, cocaine, or other teratogens

Neonate (119) Newborns and infants younger than 1 month of age

Neural tube defects (85) Birth defects that involve abnormal development of the neural tube during the first few weeks of the prenatal period

Neurons (83) Nerve cells in the brain, comprised of a cell body, axons, and dendrites

Neurotransmitters (147) Biochemical substances that transmit information between neurons through release and uptake at synapses

NICHD Study of Early Child Care (369) A longitudinal, multimethod and multimeasure study of approximately 1,400 children in child care settings across the United States

Nurture (5) Environmental and experiential factors influencing development

Object permanence (221) Piaget's term for infants' gradually developing understanding that objects continue to exist even when they are not in sensory or motor contact with them

Oblation (15) Medieval European practice involving the permanent "donation" of an infant or young child to a monastery

Observer bias (38) The phenomenon in which researchers' expectations or beliefs influence the way they record or interpret behavior

Obstetrician (128) A physician trained to assist and perform procedures during labor and delivery

Operational definition (37) A clear, concrete verbal description that enables target behaviors and outcomes to be measured accurately

Optical expansion and contraction (189) The increase and decrease in the size of an object's image on the retina

Orienting response (54) Infants' behavior the first time a stimulus is presented, characterized by momentary cessation of any ongoing activity in order to give close attention to the new stimulus

Overextension (265) A common error in which children use a word to refer to other objects that may be perceptually or functionally similar to the word's correct referent

Overregularization (277) An error in which children apply grammatical morphemes to words for which a language makes an exception to the rule

Ovum (72) Female sex cell

Parental leave (359) A job-protected leave that is open to mothers or fathers, typically available as a supplement to maternity and paternity leaves

Parental reports (55) Data provided about infants' behavior and development by their parents or caregivers

Paternity leave (359) A job-protected leave from work for employed men, typically taken after childbirth

Perceptual magnet effect (258) A phenomenon in which acoustic space is altered as a result of increasing sensitivity to native language phonemes and declining sensitivity to nonnative language phonemes

Phonemes (257) Linguistically meaningful phonetic categories that signal differences in words through combinations of vowels and consonants

Phonetics (257) A set of vowels and consonants that a particular language uses

Phonology (252) Sound patterns of language

Pictorial depth cues (191) Information about perceptual depth that is used in two-dimensional representations of the three-dimensional world, including relative size, linear perspective, texture gradients, and interposition

Placenta (79) A network of blood vessels, formed from cells in the trophoblast and from cells in the uterine lining, the function of which is to convey oxygen and nutrients to the embryo and carry away waste products

Play (212) Activity that is intrinsically motivated, focused on means rather than ends, different from purely exploratory behavior, nonliteral, and free from externally applied rules

Positron emission tomography (PET) (146) An imaging technology that shows the amount of activity in the brain

Postpartum depression (299) A sense of despair and sadness so pervasive that it affects a mother's ability to care for and interact effectively with her baby; approximately 15 percent of new mothers are affected in this way

Practice effect (49) Improvement in participants' performance as a result of the repeated exposure to the measures of those abilities

Pragmatics (252) Using language for particular purposes in specific social contexts

Pregnancy Discrimination Act of 1978 (359) The federal act, passed in 1978, to prohibit employment discrimination on the basis of pregnancy or childbirth

Preimplantation genetic diagnosis (PGD) (88) A procedure in which a biopsy is performed on blastocysts resulting from in vitro fertilization, with the purpose of selecting blastocysts that are not carriers of genetic mutations for disease for transfer to the woman's uterus

Premature rupture of membranes (PROM) (111) Condition occurring when the amniotic sac breaks open before contractions begin

Pretend/symbolic play (215) Play that emerges after 12 months of age, in which children behave in a nonliteral way

Preterm (115) A birth that occurs before 37 weeks gestation

Primary circular reactions (219) Piaget's second substage of the sensorimotor period, in which sensory and motor schemes are activated by chance

Primary emotions (335) A set of emotions—distress, interest, and pleasure—present at birth and differentiating into other emotions during infancy

Project CARE (379) An intervention similar to the Abecedarian Project, in which low-income children participated in a full-time, high-quality early childhood program, supplemented with parent group meetings and home visiting

Proprioceptive sense (198) A sense that conveys information from muscles, tendons, and joints about the body's position and movement

Protein-energy malnutrition (PEM) (172) A form of malnutrition that occurs when insufficient amounts of protein and calories are consumed in the diet

Proximodistal principle (79) The pattern of growth in which development begins in the center of the body and moves toward the extremities of the organism

Quantitative archival evidence (10) Official sources of written information and data, including census data, tax records, and legislative and court records

Quasi-experimental design (45) A design in which researchers collect information about groups of participants that are already formed before the study begins

Random assignment (47) The equivalent of flipping a coin, this technique is used to ensure that each child has an equal chance of being placed into the different groups being compared on a specific dependent variable. As a result of this precaution, potentially important differences across children are distributed across the different groups

Reactive attachment disorder (310) A recently proposed type of attachment that may develop in institutionalized infants who are severely maltreated

Recall memory (238) The ability to remember a previously presented stimulus or event in the absence of ongoing perceptual support

Recognition memory (237) The ability to remember a previously presented stimulus or event when it is presented at a later time

Referential cues (269) Verbal and nonverbal behaviors, such as gaze, facial expression, and head orientation, that reflect an individual's attentional focus, intentions, or expectations

Reflexes (134) Involuntary responses to stimuli, present at birth and gradually diminishing during the first few months of life

Reflex schemes (218) Piaget's first substage of the sensorimotor period, in which infants respond to the world with a limited set of preadapted behaviors

Relational play (212) Play before the age of 12 months that involves unrelated objects

Representational insight (229) Awareness of the relation between a space and a symbol for that space

Research ethics (59) A set of principles and guidelines for conducting acceptable research activities

Responsibility (295) A dimension of parental involvement that reflects participation in tasks such as taking the child to the doctor, arranging play dates, and monitoring activities

Scaffolding (231) The process through which more capable individuals structure tasks to boost less capable individuals' performance

Schemes (218) Piaget's term for actions used to explore and interact with the physical environment

Secondary circular reactions (220) Piaget's third substage of the sensorimotor period, in which infants repeat schemes in order to achieve specific outcomes

Secondary emotions (337) A set of emotions—embarrassment, envy, empathy, pride, shame, and guilt—that emerges during the second and third years of life

Secure attachment relationship (307) An infant-caregiver relationship that develops when caregivers respond quickly and sensitively to their infant's signs of distress and other attachment behaviors; also referred to as Type B

Self-conscious emotions (337) Emotions that involve the comparison of oneself or one's actions to standards and expectations that others hold; also called social emotions

Self-referential language (351) An aspect of the self, seen in children's use of their own name, as well as personal pronouns, such as "me" and "mine"

Semantics (252) Meanings of words or signs

Sensorimotor intelligence (217) Piaget's first stage of cognitive development, from birth to 24 months of age

Sex chromosomes (67) The pair of sex-determining chromosomes that each human possesses: XX in females and XY in males

Sex-linked inheritance (69) Transmission of characteristics via the

mother's X chromosome; sons but not daughters inherit the trait

Shaken baby syndrome (SBS) (151) A form of maltreatment in which an angry or frustrated adult shakes an infant violently, resulting in brain damage or even death

Short-term memory (239) A limited storage system that holds information for only a few seconds if the information is not actively rehearsed

Single-subject research (45) A variation of the case study, in which researchers intervene or study the effects of an experimental manipulation within a single participant

Situation compliance (347) Children's tendency to require prompting and reminding in order to follow parents' directives and requests

Size constancy (189) The ability to perceive an object's actual size correctly, even when it is viewed from different distances

Social referencing (342) Attention that is focused on another person in order to gauge his/her emotional and behavioral response to an ambiguous situation

Sociocultural contexts (230) Settings in which children spend time, including home, child care, and school

Sociodramatic play (216) Cooperative pretend play emerging between 2 and 3 years of age, in which children use verbal skills to coordinate their own actions with those of other children as part of a larger play theme

Sperm (72) Male sex cell

Stagewise (4) Characterization of development as occurring in distinct phases, with qualitative differences between stages

States of arousal (136) Distinct levels of alertness within the general behavioral categories of active sleep, quiet sleep, and wakefulness

Stereoscopic depth information (190) Information about perceptual depth that is produced by binocular disparity

Still-face paradigm (336) A procedure for studying emotional communication and regulation by disrupting the normal verbal and nonverbal signals that parents and infants use to communicate

Strange Situation (307) A laboratory procedure that Ainsworth developed to assess individual differences in infant-caregiver attachment relationships

Sudden infant death syndrome (SIDS) (162) The diagnosis given when an infant younger than 1 year dies and a complete investigation is unable to identify a specific cause

Suzuki Method (397) A system developed in the 1940s by a Japanese music educator who believed that learning to play a musical instrument is like learning to speak a first language

Syllables (260) Combinations of consonants and vowels, such as *baba* and *mama*

Synapses (147) Spaces between neurons, in which biochemical messages are released and absorbed

Synaptogenesis (148) Formation of synapses in a network of neurons

Taxonomic assumption (272) A constraint on learning that guides children to assume that new words should be extended to objects within the same category rather than thematic associates

Telegraphic speech (275) Early two-word and multiword utterances that sound like telegrams because they lack grammatical markers and extra words, such as articles, plural endings, prepositions, and auxiliary verbs

Temperament (324) A theoretical construct consisting of constitutionally based individual differences in emotionality, motor activity, attentiveness, adaptability, and self-regulation

Teratogens (77) Substances, such as alcohol, drugs, nicotine, and radiation, that are known to cause harm to the developing fetus

Tertiary circular reactions (220) Piaget's fifth substage of the sensorimotor period, in which infants try different schemes to discover the effects of those actions

Theory of mind (217) A cognitive achievement that emerges around the age of 3 years, enabling children to understand others' feelings and beliefs

Ultrasound (89) A prenatal diagnostic tool, also referred to as ultrasonography, that uses sound waves to create moving images of the fetus and detect any structural abnormalities

Umbilical cord (81) The structure through which the embryo is connected to the placenta

Underextension (266) An error in which children apply a word only to a specific instance or fail to use it to refer to other referents for which the word would be correct

Uninhibited to novelty (330) A constitutionally based tendency to respond to unfamiliar people and places by showing spontaneous engagement and active interest

Vertex position (112) A birth in which the infant is delivered head first

Very low birth weight (VLBW) (118) A birth weight of less than $3\frac{1}{4}$ lb., or 1,500 grams

Very preterm (115) A birth that occurs before 32 weeks gestation

Vesicles (147) Neurotransmitter storage spaces at the end of the axon

Vestibular sense (198) A sense that conveys information about physical balance and support

Violation-of-expectation procedure (223) A procedure in which infants are shown possible and impossible events in order to test their understanding of physical phenomena and object properties

Visual acuity (183) The smallest spacing that can be perceived between parts of a pattern

Visual cortex (184) The area of the brain that processes visual information

Visual fixation (53) Infants' looking behavior at stimuli presented in laboratory settings

Visual preference method (53) A technique in which infants' looking behavior is used to determine their ability to perceive and notice differences between stimuli presented in a laboratory setting

Visual self-recognition (350) An early aspect of the self, measured by children's understanding that when they look in a mirror, the reflection that they see is their own

Whole object assumption (271) A constraint on learning that guides children to assume that new words refer to whole objects rather than actions, spatial location, or parts or features of objects

Zone of proximal development (ZPD) (231) Vygotsky's term for the distance between a child's ability to solve a problem alone and how much better the child can solve the problem when guided or assisted by a more capable individual

Zygote (73) The cell that results when an ovum is fertilized by a sperm cell

REFERENCES

Abbott, J.S.C. (1834/1972). *The mother at home; or, the principles of maternal duty familiarly illustrated.* New York: Arno Press & The New York Times.

Abel, E.L., & Kruger, M. (2002). Physician attitudes concerning legal coercion of pregnant alcohol and drug abusers. *American Journal of Obstetrics & Gynecology. 186*(4):768–772.

Abramovitch, R., Corter, C., Pepler, D.J., & Stanhope, L. (1986). Sibling and peer interaction: A final follow-up and a comparison. *Child Development, 57,* 217–229.

Abrams, R.M., Griffiths, S.K., Huang, X., Sain, J., Langford, G., & Gerhardt, K.J. (1998). Fetal music perception: The role of sound transmission. *Music Perception, 15,* 307–317.

Acredolo, L.P. (1978). Development of spatial orientation in infancy. *Developmental Psychology, 14,* 224–234.

Acredolo, L.P. (1990). Behavioral approaches to spatial orientation in infancy. In A. Diamond (Ed.), *The development and neural bases of higher cognitive functions* (pp. 596–607). New York: New York Academy of Sciences.

Acredolo, L.P., & Goodwyn, S.W. (1988). Symbolic gesturing in normal infants. *Child Development, 59,* 450–466.

Acredolo, L.P., & Goodwyn, S.W. (1990). Sign language in babies: The significance of symbolic gesturing for understanding language development. In R. Vasta (Ed.), *Annals of Child Development,* (Vol. 7, pp. 1–42). London: Jessica Kingsley Publishers.

Activities for Parents and Children. (2002). Retrieved November 18, 2002, from http://pbskids.org/barney/pareduc/parents/activities.html.

Adam, E.K., Gunnar, M.R., & Tanaka, A. (2004). Adult attachment, parent emotion, and observed parenting behavior: Mediator and moderator models. *Child Development, 75,* 110–122.

Adams, R.J., Courage, M.L., & Mercer, M.E. (1991). Deficiencies in human neonates' color vision: Photoreceptoral and neural explanations. *Behavioural Brain Research, 43,* 109–114.

Adams, R.J., Courage, M.L., & Mercer, M.E. (1994). Systematic measurement of human neonatal color vision. *Vision Research, 34,* 1691–1701.

Adibi, J.J., Perera, F.P., Jedrychowski, W., Camann, D.E., Barr, D., & Whyatt, R.M. (2003). Prenatal exposures to phthalates among women in New York City and Krakow, Poland. *Environmental Health Perspectives, 111,* 1719–1722.

ACF (Administration for Children and Families/U.S. Department of Health and Human Services). (2002). *Early Head Start benefits children and families.* Retrieved on September 1, 2005, from http://www.acf.hhs.gov/programs/core/ongoing_research/ehs/ehs_intro.html

ACF (Administration for Children and Families/U.S. Department of Health and Human Services). (2003a). *Research to practice: Child care.* Retrieved on September 1, 2005, from http://www.acf.hhs.gov/programs/core/ongoing_research/ehs/ehs_intro.html

ACF (Administration for Children and Families/U.S. Department of Health and Human Services). (2003b). *Research to practice: Children with disabilities in Early Head Start.* Retrieved on September 1, 2005, from http://www.acf.hhs.gov/programs/core/ongoing_research/ehs/ehs_intro.html

ACF (Administration on Children, Youth and Families/U.S. Department of Health and Human Services). (2005). About Early Head Start. Retrieved on September 1, 2005, from http://www.headstartinfo.org/infocenter/ehs_tkit3.htm

Adolph, K.E. (1995). Psychophysical assessment of toddlers' ability to cope with slopes. *Journal of Experimental Psychology, 21,* 734–750.

Adolph, K.E. (1997). Learning in the development of infant locomotion. *Monographs of the Society for Research in Child Development, 62*(3, Serial No. 251).

Adolph, K.E. (2000). Specificity of learning: Why infants fall over a veritable cliff. *Psychological Science, 11,* 290–295.

Adolph, K.E., & Berger, S.E. (2006). Motor development. In W. Damon & R. Lerner (Series Eds.) & D. Kuhn & R. Siegler (Vol. Eds.), *Handbook of child psychology: Vol. 2. Cognition, perception, and language* (6th ed., pp. 161–213). New York: Wiley.

Adolph, K.E., Vereijken, B., & Denny, M.A. (1998). Learning to crawl. *Child Development, 69,* 1299–1312.

Adolph, K.E., Vereijken, B., & Shrout, P.E. (2003). What changes in infant walking and why. *Child Development, 74,* 475–497.

Ahluwalia, I.B., & Daniel, K.L. (2001). Are women with recent live births aware of the benefits of folic acid? *Morbidity and Mortality Weekly Report, 50(RR06),* 3–14.

Ahmed, S.F., & Hughes, I.A. (2002). The genetics of male undermasculinization. *Clinical Endocrinology, 56,* 1–18.

Ahnert, L., & Lamb, M.E. (2003). Shared care: Establishing a balance between home and child care settings. *Child Development, 74,* 1044–1049.

Ahnert, L, Gunnar, M.R., Lamb, M.E., & Barthel, M. (2004). Transition to child care: Associations with infant-mother attachment, infant negative emotion, and cortisol elevations. *Child Development, 75,* 639–650.

Ainsworth, M.D.S. (1967). *Infancy in Uganda: Infant care and growth of love.* Baltimore: Johns Hopkins University Press.

Ainsworth, M.D.S., & Bell, S.M. (1969). Some contemporary patterns of mother-infant interaction in the feeding situation. In A.Ambrose (Ed.), *Stimulation in early infancy* (pp. 133–170). London: Academic Press.

Ainsworth, M.D.S., Bell, S.M., & Stayton, D.J. (1972). Individual differences in the development of some attachment behaviors. *Merrill-Palmer Quarterly, 18,* 123–143.

Ainsworth, M.D.S., Blehar, M.C., Waters, E., & Wall, S. (1978). *Patterns of attachment: A psychological study of the strange situation.* Oxford, UK: Erlbaum.

Akhtar, N., & Tomasello, M. (2000). The social nature of words and word learning. In R.M., Golinkoff, K. Hirsh-Pasek, L. Bloom, L.B. Smith, A.L. Woodward, N. Akhtar, et al., *Becoming a word learner: A debate on lexical acquisition* (pp. 115–135). New York: Oxford University Press.

Akhtar, N., Dunham, F., & Dunham, P. J. (1991). Directive interactions and early vocabulary development: The role of joint attentional focus. *Journal of Child Language, 18,* 41–49.

Aksan, N., & Kochanska, G. (2005). Conscience in childhood: Old questions, new answers. *Developmental Psychology, 41,* 506–516.

Aksoy, S., & Slobin, D.I. (1985). The acquisition of Turkish. In D.I. Slobin (Ed.), *The crosslinguistic study of language acquisition* (Vol. 1, pp. 15–68). Hillsdale, NJ: Erlbaum.

Alan Guttmacher Institute. (1999). *Sharing responsibility: Women, society, and abortion worldwide.* New York: AGI.

Alanese, A., Hamill, G., Jones, J., Skuse, D.H., Matthews, D.R., & Stanhope, R. (1994). Reversibility of physiological growth hormone secretion in children with psychosocial dwarfism. *Clinical Endocrinology, 40,* 687–692.

Alborzi, H., Druin, A., Montemayor, J., Sherman, L., Taxen, G., Best, J., et al. (2000). Designing StoryRooms: Interactive storytelling spaces for children. Symposium on Designing Interactive Systems Archive. *Proceedings of the Conference on Designing Interactive Systems: Processes, Practices, Methods, and Techniques* (pp. 95–104).

Alexander, J.M., McIntire, D.D., & Leveno, K.J. (2001). Prolonged pregnancy: Induction of labor and Cesarean births. *Obstetrics & Gynecology, 97,* 911–915.

Alliance to End Childhood Lead Poisoning. (2002). About lead poisoning. Retrieved June 3, 2004, from http://www.aeclp.org

Allison, A. (1996). Producing mothers. In A.E. Imamura (Ed.), *Re-imaging Japanese women* (pp. 135–155). Berkeley, CA: University of California Press.

Als, H., Butler, S., Kosta, S., & McAnulty, G. (2005). The Assessment of Preterm Infants' Behavior (APIB): Furthering the understanding and measurement of neurodevelopmental competence in preterm and full-term infants. *Mental Retardation and Developmental Disabilities Research Reviews. Special Issue: Neurodevelopmental Assessment of the Fetus and Young Infant, 11,* 94–102.

Als, H., Lester, B.M., Tronick, E., & Brazelton, T.B. (1982). Towards a research instrument for the assessment of preterm infants' behavior (APIB). In H.E. Fitzgerald, B.M. Lester, & M.W. Yogman (Eds.), *Theory and research in behavioral pediatrics* (Vol. 1, pp. 65–132). New York: Plenum.

Als, H., Gilkerson, L., Duffy, F.H., McAnulty, G.B., Buehler, D.M., Vandenberg, K., et al. (2003). A three-center, randomized, controlled trial of individualized developmental care for very low birth weight preterm infants: Medical, neurodevelopmental, parenting, and caregiving effects. *Developmental and Behavioral Pediatrics, 24,* 399–408.

Alvarez, J.O., Caceda, J., Woolley, T.W., Carley, K.W., Baiocchi, N., Caravedo, L., et al. (1993). A longitudinal study of dental caries in the primary teeth of children who suffered from infant malnutrition. *Journal of Dental Research, 72,* 1573–1576.

American Academy of Pediatrics. (1994). Prenatal genetic diagnosis for pediatricians, *Pediatrics, 93,* 1010–1015.

American Academy of Pediatrics Committee on Fetus and Newborn. (1996). Use and abuse of the Apgar score. *Pediatrics, 98,* 141–142.

American Academy of Pediatrics. (1999a). Fetal therapy—Ethical considerations. *Pediatrics, 103,* 1061–1063.

American Academy of Pediatrics. (1999b). Folic acid for the prevention of neural tube defects. *Pediatrics, 104,* 325–327.

American Academy of Pediatrics. (2000a). Changing concepts of Sudden Infant Death Syndrome: Implications for infant sleeping environment and sleep position. *Pediatrics, 105,* 650–656.

American Academy of Pediatrics. (2000b). Fetal alcohol syndrome and alcohol-related neurodevelopmental disorders. *Pediatrics, 106,* 358–361.

American Academy of Pediatrics. (2000c). Molecular genetic testing in pediatric practice: A subject review. *Pediatrics, 106,* 1494–1497.

American Academy of Pediatrics. (2000d). Prevention and management of pain and stress in the neonate. *Pediatrics, 105,* 454–461.

American Academy of Pediatrics. (2000e). Use of psychoactive medication during pregnancy and possible effects on the fetus and newborn. *Pediatrics, 105,* 880–887.

American Academy of Pediatrics. (2001). The prenatal visit. *Pediatrics, 107,* 1456–1458.

American Academy of Pediatrics Committee on Child Abuse and Neglect. (1993). Shaken Baby Syndrome: Inflicted cerebral trauma. *Pediatrics, 92,* 872–875.

American Academy of Pediatrics Committee on Children with Disabilities. (2001). Developmental surveillance and screening of infants and young children. *Pediatrics, 108,* 192–196.

American Academy of Pediatrics Committee on Environmental Health (1997). Noise: A hazard for the fetus and newborn. *Pediatrics, 100,* 724–726.

American Academy of Pediatrics Committee on Environmental Health.

(1998). Screening for elevated blood levels. *Pediatrics, 101,* 1072–1078.

American Academy of Pediatrics Committee on Fetus and Newborn. (2005). *Underwater births. Pediatrics, 115,* 1413–1414.

American Academy of Pediatrics Committee on Fetus and Newborn, American College of Obstetricians and Gynecologists, and Committee on Obstetric Practice. (2006). The Apgar score. *Pediatrics, 117,* 1444–1447.

American Academy of Pediatrics Committee on Fetus and Newborn, Committee on Drugs, Section on Anesthesiology, Section on Surgery. (2000). Prevention and management of pain and stress in the neonate. *Pediatrics, 105,* 454–461.

American Academy of Pediatrics Committee on Genetics. (1996). Newborn screening fact sheets. *Pediatrics, 98,* 473–501.

American Academy of Pediatrics/Committee on Injury and Poison Prevention. (1993). Drowning in infants, children, and adolescents. *Pediatrics, 92,* 292–294.

American Academy of Pediatrics Committee on Injury and Poison Prevention. (2001a). Falls from heights: Windows, roofs, and balconies. *Pediatrics, 107,* 1188–1191.

American Academy of Pediatrics Committee on Injury and Poison Prevention. (2001b). Injuries associated with infant walkers. *Pediatrics, 108,* 790–792.

American Academy of Pediatrics Committee on Nutrition. (1999a). Calcium requirements of infants, children, and adolescents. *Pediatrics, 104,* 1152–1157.

American Academy of Pediatrics Committee on Nutrition. (1999b). Iron fortification of infant formulas. *Pediatrics, 104,* 119–123.

American Academy of Pediatrics Committee on Pediatric AIDS. (1995). Perinatal human immunodeficiency virus testing. *Pediatrics, 95,* 303–307.

American Academy of Pediatrics Committee on Practice and Ambulatory Medicine and Section on Ophthalmology. (2002a). Use of photoscreening for children's vision screening. *Pediatrics, 109,* 524–525.

American Academy of Pediatrics Committee on Public Education. (2001). Children, adolescents, and television. *Pediatrics, 107,* 423–426.

American Academy of Pediatrics Committee on Sports Medicine. (1988). Infant exercise programs. *Pediatrics, 82,* 800.

American Academy of Pediatrics Section on Ophthalmology. (2002b). Red reflex examination in infants. *Pediatrics, 109,* 980–981.

American Academy of Pediatrics, Shelov, S.P., & Hannemann, R.E. (Eds.). (1998). *Caring for your baby and young child: Birth to age 5.* New York: Bantam Doubleday Dell.

American Academy of Pediatrics Subcommittee on Hyperbilirubinemia. (1994). Management of hyperbilirubinemia in the healthy term newborn. *Pediatrics, 94,* 558–565.

American Academy of Pediatrics Subcommittee on Hyperbilirubinemia. (2004). Management of hyperbilirubinemia in the newborn infant 35 or more weeks of gestation. *Pediatrics, 114,* 297–316.

American Academy of Pediatrics Task Force on Newborn and Infant Hearing. (1999). Newborn and infant hearing loss: Detection and intervention. *Pediatrics, 103,* 527–530.

American Academy of Pediatrics/Work Group on Breastfeeding. (1997). Breastfeeding and the use of human milk. *Pediatrics, 100,* 1035–1039.

American College of Obstetricians and Gynecologists. (1994). Exercise during pregnancy and the postpartum period. *ACOG Technical Bulletin, 189.*

American College of Obstetricians and Gynecologists. (1996). Maternal serum screening. *ACOG Technical Bulletin, 228.*

American College of Obstetricians and Gynecologists. (1997). Routine ultrasound in low-risk pregnancy. *ACOG Practice Patterns, 59,* 273–278.

American College of Obstetricians and Gynecologists. (1999). Scheduled cesarean delivery and the prevention of vertical transmission of HIV infection. Committee Opinion, Number 219.

American College of Obstetricians and Gynecologists. (2000). Perinatal viral and parasitic infections. *ACOG Practice Bulletin, Number 20.*

American College of Obstetricians and Gynecologists. (2003). Exercise during pregnancy and the postpartum period. *Clinical Obstetrics and Gynecology, 46,* 496–499.

American College of Obstetricians and Gynecologists Committee on Obstetric Practice. (2002). ACOG committee opinion. Mode of term singleton breech delivery. *International Journal of Gynecology and Obstetrics, 77,* 65–66.

Ames, E. W. (1997). *The development of Romanian orphan children adopted to Canada.* Burnaby, BC: Simon Fraser University.

Anderson, C.A. Berkowitz, L., Donnerstein, E., Huesmann, L.R., Johnson, J.D., Linz, D., Malamuth, N.M., & Wartella, E. (2003). The influence of media violence on youth. *Psychological Science in the Public Interest, 4, 81–110.*

Anderson, D.R., & Pempek, T.A. (2005). Television and very young children. *American Behavioral Scientist, 48,* 505–522.

Anderson, D.R., Huston, A.C., Schmitt, K.L., Linebarger, D.L., & Wright, J.C. (2001). Early childhood television viewing and adolescent behavior: The recontact study. *Monographs of the Society for Research in Child Development, 66*(1, Serial No. 264).

Andersson, K., Bohlin, G., & Hagekull, B. (1999). Early temperament and stranger wariness as predictors of social inhibition in 2-year-olds. *British Journal of Developmental Psychology, 17,* 421–434.

Anglin, J.M. (1977). *Word, object and conceptual development.* New York: Norton.

Anisfeld, M. (1996). Only tongue protrusion modeling is matched by neonates. *Developmental Review, 16,* 149–161.

Apgar, V. (1953). A proposal for a new method of evaluation of the newborn infant. *Current Research in Anesthesia and Analgesia, 32,* 260–267.

Ariès, P. (1962). *Centuries of childhood: A social history of family life* (R. Baldick, Transl.). New York: Knopf.

Arnett, J.J. (2000). Emerging adulthood: A theory of development from the late teens through the twenties. *American Psychologist, 55,* 469–480.

Arterberry, M.E., & Yonas, A. (1995). Perception of structure from motion by 2-month-old infants. *Investigative Ophthalmology and Visual Science Supplements, 36(4),* 909.

Arterberry, M.E., Yonas, A., & Bensen, A.S. (1989). Self-produced locomotion and the development of responsiveness to linear perspective and texture gradients. *Developmental Psychology, 25,* 976–982.

Asendorpf, J.B., & Baudonniere, P.M. (1993). Self-awareness and other-awareness: Mirror self-recognition and synchronic imitation among unfamiliar peers. *Developmental Psychology, 29,* 88–95.

Ashby, L. (1985). Partial promises and semi-visible youths: The Depression and World War II. In J.M. Hawes, & N.R. Hiner (Eds.), *American childhood: A research guide and historical handbook* (pp. 489–531). Westport, CT: Greenwood Press.

Asher, L.J., & Lenhoff, D.R. (2001). Family and Medical Leave: Making time for family is everyone's business. *The Future of Children, 11*(1), 115–121.

Ashmead, D.H., & Perlmutter, M. (1980). Infant memory in everyday life. In M. Perlmutter (Ed.), *New directions for child development: Vol. 10. Children's memory* (pp. 1–16). San Francisco: Jossey-Bass.

Aslin, R.N. (1981). Development of smooth pursuit in human infants. In D.F. Fisher, R.A. Monty, & J.W. Senders (Eds.), *Eye movements: Cognition and visual perception* (pp. 31–51). Hillsdale, NJ: Erlbaum.

Aslin, R.N., Jusczyk, P.W., & Pisoni, D.B. (1998). Speech and auditory processing during infancy: Constraints on and precursors to language. In W. Damon (Ed.) & D. Kuhn & R.S. Siegler (Vol. Eds.), *Handbook of child psychology* (5th ed.): *Vol. 2.: Cognition,*

perception, and language (pp. 147–198). New York: Wiley.

Atella, L.D., DiPietro, J., Smith, B.A., & St. James-Roberts, I. (2003). More than meets the eye: Parental and infant contributors to maternal and paternal reports of early infant difficultness. *Parenting: Science and Practice, 3,* 265–284.

Atkinson, L., Chisholm, V.C., Scott, B., Goldberg, S., Blackwell, J., Dickens, S., & Tam, F. (1995). Cognitive coping, affective stress, and maternal sensitivity: Mothers of children with Down syndrome. *Developmental Psychology, 31,* 668–676.

Atkinson, L., Chisholm, V.C., Scott, B., Goldberg, S., Vaughn, B.E., Blackwell, J., Dickens, S., & Tam, F. (1999). Maternal sensitivity, child functional level, and attachment in Down syndrome. In J.I. Vondra & D. Barnett (Eds.), Atypical attachment in infancy and early childhood among children at developmental risk. *Monographs of the Society for Research in Child Development, 64*(3, Serial No. 258), 45–66.

Au, T.K., & Glusman, M. (1990). The principle of mutual exclusivity in word learning: To honor or not to honor? *Child Development, 61,* 1474–1490.

Au, T.K., Dapretto, M., & Song, Y. (1994). Input vs. constraints: Early word acquisition in Korean and English. *Journal of Memory and Language, 33,* 567–582.

Star Tribune (eds.). (2002, Feb. 27). "Baby's Alzheimer's screening adds to genetic ethics debate." *StarTribune,* pp. A1, A9.

Baddeley, A.D. (1986). *Working memory.* Oxford, UK: Clarendon.

Baddeley, A.D. (1992). Working memory. *Science, 255,* 556–559.

Bahrick, L.E. (1987). Infants' intermodal perception of two levels of temporal structure in natural events. *Infant Behavior and Development, 10,* 387–416.

Bahrick, L.E., & Watson, J.S. (1985). Detection of intermodal proprioceptive-visual contingency as a potential basis of self-perception in infancy. *Developmental Psychology, 21,* 963–973.

Bahrick, L.E., Netto, D.S., & Hernandez-Reif, M. (1998). Intermodal perception of adult and child faces and voices by infants. *Child Development, 69,* 1263–1275.

Bai, D.L., & Bertenthal, B.I. (1992). Locomotor status and the development of spatial search skills. *Child Development, 63,* 215–226.

Bailey, W.T. (1995). A longitudinal study of fathers' involvement with young children: Infancy to age 5 years. *Journal of Genetic Psychology, 155,* 331–339.

Baillargeon, R. (1993). The object concept revisited: New directions in the investigation of infants' physical knowledge. In C.E. Granrud (Ed.), *Visual perception and cognition in infancy* (pp. 265–315). Hillsdale, NJ: Erlbaum.

Baillargeon, R. (1994a). How do infants learn about the physical world? *Current Directions in Psychological Science, 3,* 133–140.

Baillargeon, R. (1994b). Physical reasoning in young infants: Seeking explanations for impossible events. *British Journal of Developmental Psychology, 12,* 9–33.

Baillargeon, R. (1995). A model of physical reasoning in infancy. In C. Rovee-Collier, & L.P. Lipsitt (Eds.), *Advances in infancy research* (Vol. 9, pp. 305–371). Norwood, NJ: Ablex.

Baillargeon, R. (1999). Young infants' expectations about hidden objects: A reply to three challenges. *Developmental Science, 2,* 115–132.

Baillargeon, R., Spelke, E.S., & Wasserman, S. (1985). Object permanence in five-month-old infants. *Cognition, 20,* 191–208.

Bakker, E., & Wyndaele, J.J. (2000). Changes in the toilet training of children during the last 60 years: The cause of an increase in lower urinary tract dysfunction? *British Journal of Urology International, 86*(3), 248–252.

Baldwin, D.A. (1991). Infants' contribution to the achievement of joint reference. *Child Development, 62,* 875–890.

Baldwin, D.A. (1993a). Early referential understanding; Infants' ability to recognize referential acts for what they are. *Developmental Psychology, 29,* 832–843.

Baldwin, D.A. (1993b). Infants' ability to consult the speaker for clues to word reference. *Journal of Child Language, 20,* 394–419.

Baldwin, D.A., & Tomasello, (1998). Word learning: A window on early pragmatic understanding. In E.V. Clark (Ed.), *Proceedings of the 29th Annual Child Language Research Forum* (pp. 3–23). Stanford, CA: Center for the Study of Language and Information.

Baldwin, D.A., Markman, E.M., & Melartin, R. (1989). Infants' inferential abilities: Evidence from exploratory play. Paper presented at the Biennial Meeting of the Society for Research in Child Development, Kansas City, MO.

Baldwin, D.A., Markman, E.M., Bill, B., Desjardins, R.N., Irwin, R.N., & Tidball, G. (1996). Infants' reliance on a social criterion for establishing word-object relations. *Child Development, 67,* 3135–3153.

Baldwin, E.N. (2001). A current summary of breastfeeding legislation in the U.S. Retrieved October 11, 2002, from http://www.lalecheleague.org/LawMain.html

Baltimore, D. (2001). Our genome unveiled. *Nature, 409,* 814–816.

Baranek, G.T. (1999). Autism during infancy: A retrospective video analysis of sensory-motor and social behaviors at 9-12 months of age. *Journal of Autism & Developmental Disorders, 29,* 213–224.

Barlow, W.E., Davis, R.L., Glasser, J.W., Rhodes, P.H., Thompson, R.S., Mullooly, J.P., Black, S.B., Shinefield, H.R., Ward, J.I., Marcy, S.M., DeStefano, F., Chen, R.T., Immanuel, V., Pearson, J.A., Vadheim, C.M., Rebolledo, V., Christakis, D., Benson, P.J., & Lewis, N. (2001). The risk of seizures after receipt of whole-cell pertussis or measles, mumps, and rubella vaccine. *New England Journal of Medicine, 345,* 656–661.

Barnard, K.E., & Solchany, J. (2002). Mothering. In M.H. Bornstein (Ed.), *Handbook of parenting: Vol. 3 Status and social conditions of parenting* (2nd ed., pp. 3–25). Mahwah, NJ: Erlbaum.

Barnett, D., Ganiban, J., & Cicchetti, D. (1999). Maltreatment, negative expressivity, and the development of Type D attachments from 12 to 24 months of age. In J.I. Vondra & D. Barnett (Eds.), *Atypical attachment in infancy and early childhood among children at developmental risk. Monographs of the Society for Research in Child Development, 64*(3, Serial No. 258), 97–118.

Barnett, W.S. (1998). Long-term cognitive and academic effects of early childhood education on children in poverty. *Preventive Medicine, 27,* 204–207.

Baron-Cohen, S. (1989). Perceptual role-taking and protodeclarative pointing in autism. *British Journal of Developmental Psychology, 7,* 113–127.

Barrett, K.C., & Campos, J.J. (1987). Perspectives on emotional development II.: A functionalist approach to emotions. In J.D. Osofsky (ed.), *Handbook of infant development* (2nd ed., pp. 555–578). New York: Wiley.

Barrett, K.C., & Nelson-Goens, G.C. (1997). Emotion communication and the development of the social emotions. *New Directions for Child Development, No. 77.* 69–88.

Bates, E., & Goodman, J.C. (2001). On the inseparability of grammar and the lexicon: Evidence from acquisition. In M. Tomasello & E. Bates (Eds.), *Language development: The essential readings. Essential readings in developmental psychology* (pp. 134–162). Malden, MA: Blackwell.

Bates, E., Benigni, L., Bretherton, I., Camaioni, L., & Volterra, V. (1979). *The emergence of symbols: Cognition and communication in infancy.* New York: Academic Press.

Bates, E., Bretherton, I., & Snyder, L. (1988). *From first words to grammar: Individual differences and dissociable mechanisms.* Cambridge: Cambridge University Press.

Bates, E., Dale, P., & Thal, D. (1995). Individual differences and their implications for theories of language development. In P. Fletcher & B. MacWhinney (Eds.), *The handbook of child language* (pp. 96–151). Oxford, UK: Blackwell.

Bates, E., Marchman, V., Thal, D., Fenson, L., Dale, P., Reznick, J.S., et al. (1994). Developmental and stylistic variation in the composition of early vocabulary. *Journal of Child Language, 21,* 85–124.

Bates, J., Freeland, C., & Lounsbury, M. (1979). Measurement of infant difficultness. *Child Development, 50,* 794–803.

Bates, J.E., Bayles, K., Bennett, D.S., Ridge, B., & Brown, M.M. (1991). Origins of externalizing behavior problems at eight years of age. In D. Pepler & K. Rubin (Eds.), *Development and treatment of childhood aggression* (pp. 93–120). Hillsdale, NJ: Erlbaum.

Bauer, P.J. (1996). What do infants recall of their lives? Memory for specific events by one- to two-year-olds. *American Psychologist, 51,* 29–41.

Bauer, P.J. (2002). Long-term recall memory: Behavioral and neuro-developmental changes in the first 2 years of life. *Current Directions in Psychological Science, 11,* 137–141.

Bauer, P.J. (2005). New developments in the study of infant memory. In D.M. Teti (Ed.), *Handbook of research methods in developmental psychology* (pp. 467–488). Oxford, UK: Blackwell.

Bauer, P.J. (2006). Event memory. In W. Damon & R. Lerner (Eds.) & D. Kuhn & R. Siegler (Vol. Eds.), *Handbook of child psychology: Vol. 2. Cognition, perception, and language* (6th ed., pp. 373–425). New York: Wiley.

Bauer, P.J., Wenner, J.A., Dropik, P.L., & Wewerka, S.S. (2000). Parameters of remembering and forgetting in the transition from infancy to early childhood. *Monographs of the Society for Research in Child Development, 65*(4, Serial No. 263).

Bauer, P.J., Wiebe, S.A., Waters, J.M., & Bangston, S.K. (2001). Reexposure breeds recall: Effects of experience on 9-month-olds' ordered recall. *Journal of Experimental Child Psychology, 80,* 174–200.

Bauer, P.J., Wiebe, S.A., Carver, L.J., Waters, J.M., & Nelson, C.A. (2003).

Developments in long-term explicit memory late in the first year of life: Behavioral and electrophysiological indices. *Psychological Science, 14,* 629–635.

Baydar, N., Greek, A., & Brooks-Gunn, J. (1997). A longitudinal study of the effects of the birth of a sibling during the first 6 months of life. *Journal of Marriage and the Family, 59,* 939–956.

Baydar, N., Hyle, P., & Brooks-Gunn, J. (1997). A longitudinal study of the effects of the birth of a sibling during preschool and early grade school years. *Journal of Marriage and the Family, 59,* 957–965.

Baydar, N., McCann, M., Williams, R., Vesper, E., & McKinney, P. (1997). *WIC Infant Feeding Practices Study.* Washington, DC: U.S. Department of Agriculture.

Bayley, N. (1949). Consistency and variability in the growth of intelligence from birth to eighteen years. *Journal of Genetic Psychology, 75,* 165–196.

Bayley, N. (1969). *Bayley Scales of Infant Development.* New York: Psychological Corporation.

Bayley, N. (1993). *Bayley Scales of Infant Development: II.* New York: Psychological Corporation.

Beales, J.G. (1982). The assessment and management of pain in children. In P. Karoly, D.D. Steffer, & O'Grady (Eds.), *Child health psychology: Concepts and issues* (pp. 154–179). New York: Pergamon Press.

Beales, R.W., Jr. (1985). The child in seventeenth-century America. In J.M. Hawes, & N.R. Hiner (Eds.). (1985). *American childhood: A research guide and historical handbook* (pp. 15–56). Westport, CT: Greenwood Press.

Beauchamp, G.K., Cowart, B.L., Mennella, J.A., & Marsh, R.R. (1994). Infant salt taste: Developmental, methodological and contextual factors. *Developmental Psychobiology, 27,* 353–365.

Beck, L.F., Morrow, B., Lipscomb, L.E., Johnson, C.H., Gaffield, M., Rogers, M., & Gilbert, B.C. (2002). Prevalence of selected maternal behaviors and ex-periences, pregnancy risk assessment monitoring system (PRAMS), 1999. *Morbidity and Mortality Weekly Report, 51,* 1–26.

Beers, S.R., & De Bellis, M.D. (2002). Neuropsychological function in children with maltreatment-related post-traumatic stress disorder. *American Journal of Psychiatry, 159,* 483–486.

Behrend, D.A. (1995). Processes involved in the initial mapping of verb meanings. In M. Tomasello & W. Merriman (Eds.), *Beyond names for things: Children's acquisition of verbs* (pp. 251–273). Hillsdale, NJ: Erlbaum.

Behrend, D.A., Scofield, J., & Kleinknecht, E.E. (2001). Beyond fast mapping: Young children's extensions of novel words and novel facts. *Developmental Psychology, 37,* 698–705.

Behrman, R.E., & Butler, A.S. (2006). *Preterm birth: Causes, consequences, and prevention.* Washington, DC: Institute of Medicine.

Behrman, R.E, Kliegman, R., & Jenson, H.B. (Eds.). (2000). *Nelson textbook of pediatrics* (16th ed.). Philadelphia: W.B. Saunders.

Beilin, Y. (2002). Advances in labor analgesia. *Mount Sinai Journal of Medicine, 69,* 38–44.

Bell, M.A., & Wolfe, C.D. (2004). Emotion and cognition: An intricately bound developmental process. *Child Development, 75,* 366–370.

Bellinger, D.C. (2005). Teratogen update: Lead and pregnancy. *Birth Defects Research and Clinical Molecular Teratology, 73,* 409–420.

Belsky, J. (1996). Parent, infant, and so-cial-contextual antecedents of father-son attachment security. *Developmental Psychology, 32,* 905–913.

Belsky, J., & Rovine, M. (1987). Temperament and attachment security in the strange situation: An empirical rapprochement. *Child Development, 58,* 787–795.

Belsky, J., Campbell, S.B., Cohn, J.F., & Moore, G. (1996). Instability of infant-parent attachment security. *Developmental Psychology, 32,* 921–924.

Benshushan, A., & Schenker, J.G. (1998). The right to an heir in the era of assisted reproduction. *Human Reproduction, 13,* 1407–1410.

Bergen, D. (2001). Learning in the robotic world: Active or reactive? *Childhood Education, 77,* 249–250.

Berger, S.E., & Adolph, K.E. (2003). Infants use handrails as tools in a locomotor task. *Developmental Psychology, 39,* 594–605.

Berger, S.E., Adolph, K.E., & Lobo, S.A. (2005). Out of the toolbox: Toddlers differentiate wobbly and wooden handrails. *Child Development, 76,* 1294–1307.

Bergeson, T.R., & Trehub, S.E. (2002). Absolute pitch and tempo in mothers' songs to infants. *Psychological Science, 13,* 71–74.

Berkeley, G. (1901/1709). *An essay toward a new theory of vision.* Oxford, UK: Clarendon.

Berko, J. (1958). The child's learning of English morphology. *Word, 14,* 150–177.

Berkowitz, G.S., Wetmur, J.G., Birman-Deych, E., Obel, J., Lapinski, R.H., Godbold, J.H., Holzman, I.R., & Wolff, M.S. (2004). In utero pesticide exposure, maternal paraoxonase activity, and head circumference. *Environmental Health Perspectives, 112,* 388–391.

Berlin, L.J., Brooks-Gunn, J., McCarton, C., & McCormick, M.C. (1998). The effectiveness of early intervention: Examining risk factors and pathways to enhanced development. *Preventive Medicine, 27,* 238–245.

Berrol, S. (1985). Ethnicity and American children. In J.M. Hawes, & N.R. Hiner (Eds.), *American childhood: A research guide and historical handbook* (pp. 343–375). Westport, CT: Greenwood Press.

Bertenthal, B.I., & Clifton, R.K. (1998). Perception and action. In W. Damon (Editor-in-Chief), D. Kuhn, & R.S. Siegler (Vol. Eds.), *Handbook of Child Psychology: Vol. 2. Cognition, perception, and language* (5th ed., pp. 51–102). New York: Wiley.

Bertenthal, B.I., & Fischer, K.W. (1978). Development of self-recognition in the infant. *Developmental Psychology, 14,* 44–50.

Berthier, N., DeBlois, S., Poirier, C.R., Novak, M.A., & Clifton, R.K. (2000). What's behind the door? Two- and three-year-olds reason about unseen events. *Developmental Psychology, 36,* 394–401.

Berthier, N.E. (1996). Learning to reach: A mathematical model. *Developmental Psychology, 32,* 811–823.

Best, C. T., McRoberts, G. W., & Sithole, N. M. (1988). Examination of the perceptual re-organization for speech contrasts: Zulu click discrimination by English-speaking adults and infants. *Journal of Experimental Psychology: Human Perception and Performance, 14,* 345–360.

Bhatia, T.K., & Ritchie, W.C. (1999). The bilingual child: Some issues and perspectives. In W. C. Ritchie & T. K. Bhatia (Eds.), *Handbook of child language acquisition* (pp. 569–643). San Diego: Academic Press.

Bhutta, A.T., Cleves, M.A., Casey, P.H., Cradock, M.M., & Anand, K.J.S. (2002). Cognitive and behavioral outcomes of school-aged children who were born preterm: A meta-analysis. *JAMA, 288,* 728–737.

Bhutta, Z.A., Darmstadt, G.L., Hasan, B.S., & Haws, R.A. (2005). Community-based interventions for improving perinatal and neonatal health outcomes in developing countries: A review of the evidence. *Pediatrics, 115,* 519–617.

Biederman, J., Hirshfeld-Becker, D.R., Rosenbaum, J.F., Herot, C., Friedman, D., Snidman, N., et al. (2001). Further evidence of association between behavioral inhibition and social anxiety in children. *American Journal of Psychiatry, 158,* 1673–1679.

Bilhartz, T.D., Bruhn, R.A., & Olson, J.E. (2000). The effect of early music training on child cognitive development. *Journal of Applied Developmental Psychology, 20*(4), 615–636.

Birch, E.E., Garfield, S., Hoffman, D.R., Uauy, R., & Birch, D.G. (2000). A randomized controlled trial of early dietary supply of longchain polyunsaturated fatty acids and mental development in term infants. *Developmental Medicine and Child Neurology, 42,* 174–181.

Bishop, D.V.M., Price, T.S., Dale, P.S., & Plomin, R. (2003). Outcomes of early language delay: II. Etiology of transient and persistent language difficulties. *Journal of Speech, Language, and Hearing Research, 46,* 561–575.

Black, J.E. (1998). How a child builds its brain: Some lessons from animal studies of neural plasticity. *Preventive Medicine, 27,* 168–171.

Blair, C. (2002). School readiness: Integrating cognition and emotion in a neurobiological conceptualization of child functioning at school entry. *American Psychologist, 57,* 111–127.

Blair, C. (2003). *Self-regulation and school readiness.* EDO-PS-03-7. Champaign, IL: Clearinghouse on Elementary and Early Childhood Education.

Blake, J., & de Boysson-Bardies, B. (1992). Patterns in babbling: A cross linguistic study. *Journal of Child Language, 19,* 51–74.

Blass, E.M., & Hoffmeyer, L.B. (1991). Sucrose as an analgesic for newborn infants. *Pediatrics, 87,* 215–218.

Blehar, M.C., Lieberman, A.F., & Ainsworth, M.D.S (1977). Early face-to-face interaction and its relations to later infant-mother attachment. *Child Development, 48,* 182–194.

Block, J. (1976). Issues, problems and pitfalls in assessing sex differences: A critical review of "The Psychology of Sex Differences." *Merrill-Palmer Quarterly, 22,* 283–340.

Bloom, K., Russell, A., & Wassenberg, K. (1987). Turn-taking affects the quality of infant vocalization. *Journal of Child Language, 14,* 211–227.

Bloom, L. (1970). *Language development: Form and function in emerging grammars.* Cambridge, MA: MIT Press.

Bloom, L. (1973). *One word at a time: The use of single word utterances before syntax.* The Hague: Mouton.

Bloom, L. (1993). *The transition from infancy to language.* New York: Cambridge University Press.

Bloom, L. (1998). Language acquisition in its developmental context. In W. Damon (Ed.) & D. Kuhn & R.S. Siegler (Vol. Eds.), *Handbook of child psychology* (5th ed.): *Vol. 2. Cognition, perception, and language* (pp. 309–370). New York: Wiley.

Bloom, L., Tinker, E., & Margulis, C. (1993). The words children learn: Evidence against a noun bias in children's vocabularies. *Cognitive Development, 8,* 431–450.

Bloom, P. (2000). *How children learn the meanings of words.* Cambridge, MA: MIT Press.

Boccia, M., & Campos, J.J. (1989). Maternal emotional signals, social referencing, and infants' reactions to strangers. In N. Eisenberg (Ed.), *New directions for child development* (Vol. 44, pp. 25–49). San Francisco: Jossey-Bass.

Bodrova, E., & Leong, D.J. (1996). *Tools of the mind: The Vygotskian approach to early childhood education.* Englewood Cliffs, NJ: Prentice Hall.

Bodrova, E., & Leong, D.J. (1998). Adult influences on play. In D.P. Fromberg & D. Bergen (Eds.), *Play from birth to twelve and beyond: Contexts, perspectives, and meanings.* (pp. 277–282). New York: Garland Publishing.

Bojczyk, K.E., & Corbetta, D. (2004). Object retrieval in the 1st year of life: Learning effects of task exposure and box transparency. *Developmental Psychology, 40,* 54–66.

Bokhorst, C.L., Bakermans-Kranenburg, M.J., Fearon, R.M. P., van IJzendoorn, M.H., Fonagy, P., & Schuengel, C. (2003). The importance of shared environment in mother-infant attachment security: A behavioral genetic study. *Child Development, 74,* 1769–1782.

Booth, C.L., & Kelly, J.F. (1998). Child care characteristics of infants with and without special needs: Comparisons and concerns. *Early Childhood Research Quarterly, 13,* 603–622.

Booth, C.L., & Kelly, J.F. (1999). Child care and employment in relation to infants' disabilities and risk factors. *American Journal on Mental Retardation, 104,* 117–130.

Bornstein, M., Gaughran, J., & Segui, I. (1991). Multimethod assessment of infant temperament: Mother questionnaire and mother and observer reports evaluated and compared at five months using the infant temperament measure. *International Journal of Behavioral Development, 14,* 131–151.

Bornstein, M.H. (1985). How infant and mother jointly contribute to developing cognitive competence in the child. *Proceedings of the National Academy of Science, 82,* 7470–7473.

Bornstein, M.H. (1988). Mothers, infants, and the development of cognitive competence. In H.E. Fitzgerald, B.M. Lester, & M.W. Yogman (Eds.), *Theory and research in behavioral pediatrics* (Vol. 4, pp. 67–99). New York: Plenum.

Bornstein, M.H. (1989). Information processing (habituation) in infancy and stability in cognitive development. *Human Development, 32,* 129–136.

Bornstein, M.H. (2006). Parenting science and practice. In W. Damon & R. Lerner (Eds.) & K.A. Renninger & I.E. Sigel (Vol. Eds.), *Handbook of child psychology: Vol. 4. Child psychology in practice* (6th ed., pp. 893–949). New York: Wiley.

Bornstein, M.H., & Cote, L.R. (2004). Mothers' parenting cognitions in cultures of origin, acculturating cultures, and cultures of destination. *Child Development, 75,* 221–235.

Bornstein, M.H., & Lamb, M. E. (1992). *Development in infancy: An introduction* (3rd ed.). New York: McGraw-Hill.

Bornstein, M.H., & Tamis-LeMonda, C. (1994). Antecedents of information-processing skills in infants: Habituation, novelty responsiveness, and cross-modal transfer. *Infant Behavior and Development, 17,* 371–380.

Bornstein, M.H., Haynes, O.M., O'Reilly, A.W., & Painter, K. (1996). Solitary and collaborative pretense play in early childhood: Sources of individual variation in the development of representational competence. *Child Development, 67,* 2910–2929.

Bornstein, M.H., Haynes, O.M., Pascual, L., Painter, K.M., & Galperin, C. (1999). Play in two societies: Pervasiveness of process, specificity of structure. *Child Development, 70,* 317–331.

Bornstein, M.H., Slater, A., Brown, E., Roberts, E., & Barrett, J. (1997). Stability of mental development from infancy to later childhood: Three "waves" of research. In. G. Bremner, A. Slater,, & G. Butterworth (Eds.), *Infant development: Recent advances* (pp. 191–215). East Sussex, UK: Psychology Press.

Borst, C.G. (1995). *Catching babies: The professionalization of childbirth, 1870–1920.* Cambridge, MA: Harvard University Press.

Borstelmann, L. J. (1983). Children before psychology: Ideas about children from antiquity to the late 1800s. In P. H. Mussen (Ed.) & W. Kessen (Vol. Ed.), *Handbook of Child Psychology* (4th ed.): *Vol. 1. History, theory, and methods.* New York: Wiley.

Boswell, J. (1988). *The kindness of strangers: The abandonment of children in Western Europe from late antiquity to the Renaissance.* Chicago: University of Chicago Press.

Bowden, K., Kessler, D., Pinette, M., & Wilson, E. (2003). Underwater birth: Missing the evidence or missing the point? *Pediatrics, 112,* 972–973.

Bowlby, J. (1969/1982). *Attachment and loss: Vol. 1. Attachment.* (2nd ed.). New York: Basic Books.

Bowlby, J. (1973). *Attachment and loss: Vol. 2. Separation: Anxiety and anger.* New York: Basic Books.

Bowlby, J. (1980). *Attachment and loss: Vol. 3. Loss: Sadness and depression.* New York: Basic Books.

Bowlby, J. (1988). *A secure base: Parent-child attachment and healthy human development.* New York: Basic Books.

Bradley, R.A., & Montagu, A. (1996). *Husband-coached childbirth: The Bradley method of natural childbirth* (4th ed). New York: Bantam.

Bradley, R.H., & Corwyn, R.F. (2002). Socioeconomic status and child development. *Annual Review of Psychology, 53,* 371–399.

Brankston, G.N., Mitchell, B.F., Ryan, E.A., & Okun, N.B. (2004). Resistance exercise decreases the need for insulin in overweight women with gestational diabetes mellitus. *American Journal of Obstetrics and Gynecology, 190,* 188–193.

Branum, A.M., & Schoendorf, K.C. (2002). Changing patterns of low birthweight and preterm birth in the United States, 1981–1998. *Paediatric and Perinatal Epidemiology, 16,* 8–15.

Brauner, J., Gordic, B., & Zigler, E. (2004). Putting the child back into child care: Combining care and education for children ages 3–5. *Social Policy Report, 18*(3).

Braungart-Rieker, J.M., Garwood, M.M., Powers, B.P., & Notaro, P.C. (1998). Infant affect and affect regulation during the still-face paradigm with mothers and fathers: The role of infant characteristics and parental sensitivity. *Developmental Psychology, 34,* 1428–1437.

Brayfield, A. (1995). Juggling jobs and kids: The impact of employment schedules on fathers' caring for children. *Journal of Marriage and the Family, 57,* 321–332.

Brazelton, T.B., & Nugent, J.K. (1995). *Neonatal Behavioral Assessment Scale*(3rd ed.). Cambridge, UK: Cambridge University Press.

Brazelton, T.B., Christophersen, E.R., Frauman, A.C., Gorski, P.A., Poole, J.M., Stadtler, A.C., et al. (1999). Instruction, timeliness, and medical influences affecting toilet training. *Pediatrics, 103,* 1353–1358.

Bredekamp, S., & Copple, C. (1997). *Developmentally appropriate practice in early childhood programs* (Rev. ed.). Washington, DC: National Association for the Education of Young Children.

Bremner, R.H., Barnard, J., Hareven, T.K., & Mennell, R. (Eds.). (1970). *Children and youth in America: A documentary history: Vol. I, 1600–1865.* Cambridge, MA: Harvard University Press.

Bremner, R.H., Barnard, J., Hareven, T.K., & Mennell, R. (Eds.). (1971). *Children and youth in America: A documentary history: Vol. II, 1866–1932.* Cambridge, MA: Harvard University Press.

Brenner, R.A., Simons-Morton, B.G., Bhaskar, B., Revenis, M., Das, A., & Clemens, J.D. (2003). Infant-parent bed sharing in an inner-city population. *Archives of Pediatrics and Adolescent Medicine, 157,* 33–39.

Brent, R.L. (2004). Utilization of animal studies to determine the effects and human risks of environmental toxicants (drugs, chemicals, and physical agents). *Pediatrics, 113,* 984–995.

Brent, R.L., & Weitzman, M. (2004). The current state of knowledge about the effects, risks, and science of children's environmental exposures. *Pediatrics, 113,* 1158–1166.

Bretherton, I. (1992). The origins of attachment theory: John Bowlby and Mary Ainsworth. *Developmental Psychology, 28,* 759–775.

Bretherton, I., Fritz, J., Zahn-Waxler, C., & Ridgeway, D. (1986). Learning to talk about emotions: A functionalist perspective. *Child Development, 57,* 529–548.

Brewer, J., & Hunter, A. (1989). *Multimethod research: A synthesis of styles.* Newbury Park, CA: Sage.

Bridges, L.J., Denham, S.A., & Ganiban, J.M. (2004). Definitional issues in emotion regulation research. *Child Development, 75,* 340–345.

Brody, G.H. (1998). Sibling relationship quality: Its causes and consequences. *Annual Review of Psychology, 49,* 1–24.

Brody, J.E. (1999, Aug. 3). Success of toilet training still a matter of time. *The New York Times On the Web.* Retrieved September 30, 2000, from http://www.nytimes.com/library/national/science/080399hth-brody-children.html

Bronfenbrenner, U., & Morris, P.A. (1998). The ecology of developmental processes. In W. Damon (Ed.) & R. M. Lerner (Vol. Ed.), *Handbook of Child Psychology: Vol. 1. Theoretical models of human development* (pp. 993–1028). New York: Wiley.

Brooks, R., & Meltzoff, A.N. (2002). The importance of eyes: How infants interpret adult looking behavior. *Developmental Psychology, 38,* 958–966.

Brooks, R., & Meltzoff, A.N. (2005). The development of gaze following and its relation to language. *Developmental Science, 8,* 535–543.

Brooks-Gunn, J. (2003). Do you believe in magic?: What we can expect from early childhood intervention programs. *Social Policy Report, 17*(1).

Brooks-Gunn, J., & Duncan, G.J. (1997). The effects of poverty on children and youth. *The Future of Children, 7*(2), 55–71.

Brooks-Gunn, J., Han, W.J., & Waldfogel, J. (2002). Maternal employment and child cognitive outcomes in the first three years of life: The NICHD Study of Early Child Care. *Child Development, 73,* 1052–1072.

Brooks-Gunn, J., Klebanov, P.K., Liaw, F., & Spiker, D. (1993). Enhancing the development of low birth weight, premature infants: Changes in cognition and behavior over the first three years. *Child Development, 64,* 736–753.

Brown, A. (2000). U.S. Consumer Product Safety Commission response to *The Future of Children* issue on unintentional injuries in childhood. Retrieved October 11, 2002, from http://www.futureofchildren.org/cpsc.htm

Brown, J.R., & Dunn, J. (1996). Continuities in emotional understanding from 3 to 6 years. *Child Development, 67,* 789–802.

Brown, R. (1973). *A first language: The early stages.* Cambridge, MA: Harvard University Press.

Brown, R., & Hanlon, C. (1970). Derivational complexity and order of acquisition in child speech. In J. R. Hayes (Ed.), *Cognition and the development of language* (pp. 155–207). New York: Wiley.

Brown, R.W. (1957). Linguistic determinism and the parts of speech. *Journal of Abnormal and Social Psychology, 55,* 1–5.

Bruner, J.P., Tulipan, N., Paschall, R.L., Boehm, F.H., Walsh, W.F., Silva, S.R., Hernanz-Schulman, M., Lowe, L.H., & Reed, G.W. (1999). Fetal surgery for myelomeningocele and the incidence of shunt-dependent hydrocephalus. *JAMA, 282,* 1819–1825.

Bucklin, B.A., Chestnut, D.H., & Hawkins, J.L. (2002). Intrathecal opioids versus epidural local anesthetics for labor analgesia: A meta-analysis.

Regional Anesthesis and Pain Medicine, 27, 23–30.

Bugental, D.B., & Grusec, J.E. (2006). Socialization processes. In W. Damon & R. Lerner (Eds.) & N. Eisenberg (Vol. Ed.), *Handbook of child psychology: Vol. 3. Social, emotional, and personality development* (6th ed., pp. 366–428). New York: Wiley.

Burchinal, M.R., Roberts, J.E., Riggins, R., Jr., Zeisel, S.A., Neebe, E., & Bryant, D. (2000). Relating quality of center-based child care to early cognitive and language development longitudinally. *Child Development, 71,* 339–357.

Buriel, R. (1993). Childrearing orientations in Mexican American families: The influence of generation and Sociocultural factors. *Journal of Marriage and the Family, 55,* 987–1000.

Bushnell, E.W., McKenzie, B.E., Lawrence, D.A., & Connell, S. (1995). The spatial coding strategies of one-year-old infants in a locomotor search task. *Child Development 66,* 937–958.

Busjahn, A., Knoblauch, H., Faulhaber, H., Aydin, A., Uhlmann, R., Tuomilehto, J., et al. (2000). A region on chromosome 3 is linked to dizygotic twinning. *Nature Genetics, 26,* 398–399.

Buss, A.H. (1995). *Personality, temperament, social behavior, and the self.* Boston: Allyn & Bacon.

Buss, K.A., & Goldsmith, H.H. (1998). Fear and anger regulation in infancy: Effects on the temporal dynamics of affective expression. *Child Development, 69,* 359–374.

Buss, K.A., & Plomin, R. (1984). *Temperament: Early developing personality traits.* Hillsdale, NJ: Erlbaum.

Buss, K.A., Davidson, R.J., Kalin, N.H., & Goldsmith, H.H. (2004). Context-specific freezing and associated physiological reactivity as a dysregulated fear response. *Developmental Psychology, 40,* 583–594.

Buss, K.A., Malmstadt, Schumacher, J., Dolski, I., Kalin, N.H., Goldsmith, H.H., & Davidson, R.J. (2003). Right frontal brain activity, cortisol, and withdrawal behavior in 6-month-old infants. *Behavioral Neuroscience, 117,* 11–20.

Butler, S.C., Berthier, N.E., & Clifton, R.K. (2002). Two-year-olds' search strategies and visual tracking in a hidden displacement task. *Developmental Psychology, 38,* 581–590.

Butterworth, G., & Hicks, L. (1977). Visual proprioception and postural stability in infancy: A developmental study. *Perception, 6,* 255–262.

Byrne, J.P., Crowther, C.A., & Moss, J.R. (2000). A randomised controlled trial comparing birthing centre care with delivery suite care in Adelaide, Australia. *Australian and New Zealand Journal of Obstetrics and Gynaecology, 40,* 268–274.

Cabrera, N.J., & Garcia Coll, C. (2004). Latino fathers: Uncharted territory in need of much exploration. In M.E. Lamb (Ed.), *The role of the father in child development* (4th ed., pp. 98–120). New York: Wiley.

Cabrera, N.J., Tamis-LeMonda, C.S., Bradley, R.H., Hofferth, S., & Lamb, M.E. (2000). Fatherhood in the twenty-first century. *Child Development, 71,* 127–136.

Cahan, E., Mechling, J., Sutton-Smith, B., & White, S.H. (1993). The elusive historical child: Ways of knowing the child of history and psychology. In G. H. Elder, Jr., J. Modell, & R.D. Parke (Eds.), *Children in time and place: Developmental and historical insights* (pp. 192–223). New York: Cambridge University Press.

Caine, J. (1991). The effect of music on the selected stress behaviors, weight, caloric and formula intake, and length of hospital stay of premature and low birth weight neonates in a newborn intensive care unit. *Journal of Music Therapy, 28,* 180–192.

Cairns, R. B. (1998) The making of developmental psychology. In W. Damon (Ed.) & R.M. Lerner (Vol. Ed.), *Handbook of child psychology (5th ed.): Vol. 1. Theoretical models of human development* (pp. 25–105). New York: Wiley.

Calvert, K. (1992). *Children in the house: The material culture of early childhood, 1600–1900.* Boston: Northeastern University Press.

Cammu, H., Martens, G., Ruyssinck, G., & Amy, J.J. (2002). Outcome after elective labor induction in nulliparous women: A matched cohort study. *American Journal of Obstetrics and Gynecology, 186,* 240–244.

Campbell, F.A., & Ramey, C.T. (1994). Effects of early intervention on intellectual and academic achievement: A follow-up study of children from low-income families. *Child Development, 65,* 684–698.

Campbell, F.A., Pungello, E.P., Miller-Johnson, S., Burchinal, M., & Ramey, C.T. (2001). The development of cognitive and academic abilities: Growth curves from an early childhood educational experiment. *Developmental Psychology, 37,* 231–242.

Campbell, F.A., Ramey, C.T., Pungello, E.P., Sparling, J., & Miller-Johnson, S. (2002). Early childhood education: Young adult outcomes from the Abecedarian Project. *Applied Developmental Science, 6,* 42–57.

Campbell, S.B., Cohn, J.F., & Meyers, T. (1995). Depression in first-time mothers: Mother-infant interaction and depression chronicity. *Developmental Psychology, 31,* 349–357.

Campos, J.J., Campos, R.G., & Barrett, K.C. (1989). Emergent themes in the study of emotional development and emotion regulation. *Developmental Psychology, 25,* 394–402.

Campos, J.J., Frankel, C.B., & Camras, L. (2004). On the nature of emotion regulation. *Child Development, 75,* 377–394.

Campos, J.J., Mumme, D.L., Kermoian, R., & Campos, R.G. (1994). A functionalist perspective on the nature of emotion. In Fox, N.A. (Ed.), The development of emotion regulation: Biological and behavioral considerations. *Monographs of the Society for Research in Child Development, 59*(2–3, Serial No. 240), 284–303.

Camras, L.A., Lambrecht L., & Michel, G.F. (1996). Infant "surprise" expressions as coordinative motor structures. *Journal of Nonverbal Behavior, 20,* 183–195.

Canfield, R.L., Smith, E.G., Brezsnyak, M.P., & Snow, K.L. (1997). Information processing through the first year of life: A longitudinal study using the visual expectation paradigm. *Monographs of the Society for Research in Child Development, 62*(2, Serial No. 250).

Cantor, D., Waldfogel, J., Kerwin, J., Wright, M., Levin, K., Rauch, J., et al. (2001). *Balancing the needs of families and employers: Family and Medical Leave surveys, 2000 update.* Rockville, MD: Westat.

Cao, X.Y., Jiang, X.M., Dou, Z.H., Rakeman, M.A., Zhang, M.L., O'Donnell, K., et al. (1994). Timing of vulnerability of the brain to iodine deficiency in endemic cretinism. *New England Journal of Medicine, 331,* 1739–1744.

Capps, L., Sigman, M., & Mundy, P. (1994). Attachment security in children with autism. *Development and Psychopathology, 6,* 249–261.

Carey, S., & Bartlett, E. (1978). Acquiring a single new word. *Papers and Reports on Child Language Development, 15,* 17–29.

Carey, W., & McDevitt, S. (1978). Revision of the infant temperament questionnaire. *Pediatrics, 61,* 735–739.

Carlson, A., Lino, M., Gerrior, S., & Basiotis, P.P. (2001). Report card on the diet quality of children ages 2 to 9. *Nutrition Insight, 25.* Alexandria, VA: USDA Center for Nutrition Policy and Promotion.

Carlson, E.A. (1998). A prospective longitudinal study of attachment disorganization/disorientation. *Child Development, 69,* 1107–1128.

Carlson, E.A., Sroufe, L.A., & Egeland, B. (2004). The construction of experience: A longitudinal study of representation and behavior. *Child Development, 75,* 66–83.

Carlson, M., & Earls, F. (1997). Psychological and neuroendocrinological sequelae of early social deprivation in institutionalized children in Romania. *Annals of the New York Academy of Sciences, 807,* 419–426.

Carlson, M., Dragomir, C., Earls, F., Farrell, M., Macovei, O., Nystrom, P., & Sparling, J. (1995). Effects of social deprivation on cortisol regulation in institutionalized Romanian infants. *Society of Neuroscience Abstracts, 21,* 524.

Carpenter, M., Nagell, K., & Tomasello, M. (1998). Social cognition, joint attention, and communicative competence from 9 to 15 months of age. *Monographs of the Society for Research in Child Development, 63*(4, Serial No. 255).

Carter, A.S., Garrity-Rokous, F.E., Chazan-Cohen, R., Little, C., & Briggs-Gowan, M.J. (2001). Maternal depression and comorbidity: Predicting early parenting, attachment security, and toddler social-emotional problems and competencies. *Journal of the American Academy of Child and Adolescent Psychiatry, 40,* 18–26.

Carty, H., & Ratcliffe, J. (1995). The shaken infant syndrome. *BMJ, 310,* 344–345.

Casasola, M., Cohen, L.B., & Chiarello, E. (2003). Six-month-old infants' categorization of containment spatial relations. *Child Development, 74,* 679–693.

Casper, L.M., & O'Connell, M. (1998). Work, income, the economy, and married fathers as child care providers. *Demography, 35,* 243–250.

Casper, M.J. (1998). *The making of the unborn patient: A social anatomy of fetal surgery.* New Brunswick, NJ: Rutgers University Press.

Caspi, A. (1998). Personality development across the life course. In W. Damon (Series Ed.) & N. Eisenberg (Vol. Ed.), *Handbook of child psychology: Vol. 3. Social, emotional, and personality development* (5th ed., pp. 311–388). New York: Wiley.

Caspi, A. (2000). The child is father of the man: Personality continuities from childhood to adulthood. *Journal of Personality and Social Psychology, 78,* 158–172.

Caspi, A., & Shiner, R.L. (2006). Personality development. In W. Damon & R. Lerner (Eds.) & N. Eisenberg (Vol. Ed.), *Handbook of child psychology: Vol. 3. Social, emotional, and personality development* (6th ed., pp. 300–365). New York: Wiley.

Caspi, A., & Silva, P.A. (1995). Temperamental qualities at age three predict personality traits in young adulthood: Longitudinal evidence from a birth cohort. *Child Development, 66,* 486–498.

Caspi, A., Moffitt, T.E., Morgan, J., Rutter, M., Taylor, A., Arseneault, L., Tully, L., Jacobs, C., Kim-Cohen, J., & Polo-Tomas, M. (2004). Maternal expressed emotion predicts children's antisocial behavior problems: Using monozygotic-twin differences to identify environmental effects on behavioral development. *Developmental Psychology, 40,* 149–161.

Cassidy, J. (1994). Emotion regulation: Influences of attachment relationships. In Fox, N.A. (Ed.), The development of emotion regulation: Biological and behavioral considerations. *Monographs of the Society for Research in Child Development, 59*(2–3, Serial No. 240), 228–249.

Caughey, A.B., & Musci, T.J. (2004). Complications of term pregnancies beyond 37 weeks of gestation. *Obstetrics & Gynecology,103,* 57–62.

Center on Media and Child Health. (2005). *The effects of electronic media on children ages zero to six: A history of research.* Menlo Park, CA: The Henry J. Kaiser Family Foundation.

Centers for Disease Control and Prevention. (1995). Ectopic pregnancy, United States, 1990–1992. *Morbidity and Mortality Weekly Report, 44,* 46–48.

Centers for Disease Control and Prevention. (2000a). Birth defects. *National Vital Statistics Reports, 50*(5).

Centers for Disease Control and Prevention. (2000b). Blood levels in young children, United States and selected states, 1996–1999. *Morbidity & Mortality Weekly Report, 49,* 1133–1137.

Centers for Disease Control and Prevention. (2000c). Contribution of assisted reproductive technology and ovulation-inducing drugs to triplet and higher-order multiple births, United States, 1980–1997. *Morbidity and Mortality Weekly Report, 49,* 535–538.

Centers for Disease Control and Prevention. (2000d). Neural tube defect surveillance and folic acid intervention—Texas-Mexico border, 1993–1998. *Morbidity and Mortality Weekly Report, 49,* 1–4.

Centers for Disease Control and Prevention. (2000e). Public Health Service Task Force recommendations for the use of antiretroviral drugs in pregnant women infected with HIV-1 for maternal health and for reducing perinatal HIV-1 transmission in the United States. Revisions to the 1998 recommendations. *Morbidity and Mortality Weekly Report, 47*(RR–2), 1–30.

Centers for Disease Control and Prevention. (2001). *1999 Assisted reproductive technology success rates: National summary and fertility clinic reports.* Atlanta, GA.

Centers for Disease Control and Prevention. (2002b). Birth defects: Having a healthy pregnancy. Retrieved December 4, 2004, from http://www.cdc.gov/ncbddd/bd/abc.htm

Centers for Disease Control and Prevention. (2002c). Childhood lead poisoning. Retrieved September 10, 2003, from http://www.cdc.gov/nceh/lead/factsheets/childhoodlead.htm

Centers for Disease Control and Prevention. (2002d). Infant mortality and low birth weight among black and white infants: United States, 1980–2000. *Morbidity & Mortality Weekly Report, 51,* 589–592.

Centers for Disease Control and Prevention. (2002e). Progress toward elimination of perinatal HIV infection, Michigan, 1993–2000. *Morbidity and Mortality Weekly Report, 51,* 93–97.

Centers for Disease Control and Prevention. (2002f). Public Health Service Task Force recommendations for use of antiretroviral drugs in pregnant HIV-1-infected women for maternal health and interventions to reduce perinatal HIV-1 transmission in the United States. Revisions to the 1998 recommendations. *Morbidity and Mortality Weekly Report, 51*(RR18), 1–38.

Centers for Disease Control and Prevention. (2002g). Racial and ethnic disparities in infant mortality rates: 60 largest U.S. cities, 1995–1998. *Morbidity & Mortality Weekly Report, 51,* 329–332, 343.

Centers for Disease Control and Prevention. (2002h). Use of assisted reproductive technology—United States, 1996 and 1998. *Morbidity and Mortality Weekly Report, 51,* 97–101.

Centers for Disease Control and Prevention. (2002i). West Nile virus and breastfeeding. *Morbidity & Mortality Weekly Report, 51,* 877–878.

Centers for Disease Control and Prevention. (2003). *Assisted reproductive technology (ART) report.* Washington, DC: Author, Department of Health and Human Services.

Centers for Disease Control and Prevention. (2004). Spina bifida and anencephaly before and after folic acid mandate: United States, 1995–1996 and 1999–2000. *Morbidity & Mortality Weekly Report, 53,* 362–365.

Centers for Disease Control and Prevention. (2005a). Developmental disabilities. Retrieved December 28, 2005 from http://www.cdc.gov/ncbddd/dd/aic/resources/

Centers for Disease Control and Prevention. (2005b). Measles: United States, 2004. *Morbidity & Mortality Weekly Report, 54,* 1229–1231.

Centers for Disease Control and Prevention. (2005c). Pertussis: United States, 2001–2003. *Morbidity & Mortality Weekly Report, 54,* 1283–1286.

Centers for Disease Control and Prevention. (2005d). Progress toward interruption of wild poliovirus transmission: Worldwide, January 2004–March 2005. *Morbidity & Mortality Weekly Report, 54,* 408–412.

Centers for Disease Control and Prevention. (2005e). Racial/ethnic disparities in infant mortality: United States, 1995–2002. *Morbidity & Mortality Weekly Report, 54,* 553–556.

Centers for Disease Control and Prevention. (2005f). Recommended childhood and adolescent immunization schedule: United States, 2006. *Morbidity & Mortality Weekly Report, 54,* Q1–Q4.

Centers for Disease Control and Prevention. (2005g). Varicella-related deaths: United States, January 2003–June 2004. *Morbidity & Mortality Weekly Report, 54,* 272–274.

Centers for Disease Control and Prevention. (2005h). 2005 National immunization survey. Retrieved November 30, 2006, from http://www.cdc.gov/breastfeeding/data/NNIS_data/data_2005.htm

Centers for Disease Control for Prevention. (2006). Improved national prevalence estimates for 18 selected major birth defects: United States, 1999–2001. *Morbidity & Mortality Weekly Report, 54,* 1301–1305.

Chahin, J., Villarruel, F.A., & Viramontez, R.A. (1999). Dichos y refranes: The transmission of cultural values and beliefs. In H.P. McAdoo (Ed.), *Family ethnicity: Strength in diversity* (2nd ed., pp. 153–167). Thousand Oaks, CA: Sage.

Chamayou, S., Alecci, C., Ragolia, C., Giambona, A., Siciliano, S., Maggio, A., Fichera, M., & Guglielmino, A. (2002). Successful application of preimplantation genetic diagnosis for B-thalassaemia and sickle cell anaemia in Italy. *Human Reproduction, 17,* 1158–1165.

Chan, L.Y., Leung, T.Y., Fok, W.Y., Chan, L.W., & Lau, T.K. (2002). High incidence of obstetric interventions after successful external cephalic version. *BJOG, 109,* 627–631.

Chandra, A., Martinez, G.M., Mosher, W.D., Abma, J.C., & Jones, J. (2005). Fertility, family planning, and reproductive health of U.S. women: Data from the 2002 National Survey of Family Growth. National Center for Health Statistics. *Vital Health Statistics, 23*(25).

Chen, A., & Rogan, W.J. (2004). Breastfeeding and the risk of postneonatal death in the United States. *Pediatrics, 113,* e435–e439.

Chera, P., & Wood, C. (2003). Animated multimedia "talking books" can promote phonological awareness in children beginning to read. *Learning and Instruction, 13,* 33–52.

Chess, S., & Thomas, A. (1996). *Temperament: Theory and practice.* Philadelphia: Brunner/Mazel.

Child Care Law Center. (2003). *Caring for children with special needs: The Americans with Disabilities Act (ADA) and child care.* San Francisco: CCLC.Children's Environmental Health Initiative. (2002). Children's environmental health. Retrieved September 1, 2003, from http://www.env.duke.edu/cehi/health/ lead.htm

Chiriboga, C.A., Brust, J.C.M., Bateman, D., & Hauser, W.A. (1999). Dose-response effect of fetal cocaine exposure on newborn neurologic function. *Pediatrics, 103,* 79–85.

Chisholm, K. (1998). A three year follow-up of attachment and indiscriminate friendliness in children adopted from Romanian orphanages. *Child Development, 69,* 1092–1106.

Chisholm, K., Carter, M., Ames, E.W., & Morison, S.J. (1995). Attachment security and indiscriminately friendly behavior in children adopted from Romanian orphanages. *Development and Psychopathology, 7,* 283–294.

Choi, S., & Gopnik, A. (1995). Early acquisition of verbs in Korean: A cross-linguistic study. *Journal of Child Language, 22,* 497–529.

Chomsky, N. (1958). Review of *Verbal Behavior* by B. F. Skinner. *Language, 35,* 26–58.

Chomsky, N. (1965). *Aspects of the theory of syntax.* Cambridge, MA: MIT Press.

Chomsky, N. (1980). Rules and representations. *Behavioral and Brain Sciences, 3,* 1–61.

Chomsky, N. (1986). *Knowledge of language: Its nature, origin, and use.* New York: Praeger.

Chomsky, N. (1995). *The minimalist program.* Cambridge, MA: MIT Press.

Chugani, H.T., Behen, M.E., Muzik, O., Juhasz, C., Nagy, F., & Chugani, D.C. (2001). Local brain functional activity following early deprivation: A study of postinstitutionalized Romanian orphans. *Neuroimage, 14,* 1290–1301.

Cicchetti, D., & Toth, S.L. (2006). Developmental psychopathology and preventive intervention. In W. Damon & R. Lerner (Eds.) & K.A. Renninger & I.E. Sigel (Vol. Eds.), *Handbook of child psychology: Vol. 4. Child psychology in practice* (6th ed., pp. 497–547). New York: Wiley.

Cicero, S., Curcio, P., Papageorghiou, A., Sonek, J., & Nicolaides, K. (2001). Absence of nasal bone in fetuses with trisomy 21 at 11–14 weeks of gestation: An observational study. *Lancet, 358,* 1665–1667.

Clapp, J. (1996). Morphometric and neurodevelopmental outcome at age five years of the offspring of women who continued to exercise regularly throughout pregnancy. *Journal of Pediatrics, 129,* 856–863.

Clark, J.E., & Phillips, S.J. (1993). A longitudinal study of interlimb coordination in the first year of independent walking: A dynamical systems analysis. *Child Development, 64,* 1143–1157.

Clarke-Stewart, K., Fitzpatrick, M., Allhusen, V., & Goldberg, W. (2000). Measuring difficult temperament the easy way. *Developmental and Behavioral Pediatrics, 21,* 207–223.

Clarkson, M.G. (1996). Infants' perception of intensity: Spectral profiles. *Infant Behavior and Development, 19,* 181–190.

Clarkson, M.G., & Montgomery, C.R. (2000, July). Precision of infants' localization of brief sounds. Paper presented at the Biennial International Conference on Infancy Studies, Brighton, UK.

Clarkson, M.G., Martin, R.L., & Miciek, S.G. (1996). Infants' perception of pitch: Number of harmonics. *Infant Behavior and Development, 19,* 191–197.

Clements, D.H., Nastasi, B.K., & Swaminathan, S. (1993). Young children and computers: Crossroads and directions from research. *Young Children, 48,* 56–64.

Clifton, R.K., Muir, D., Ashmead, D.H., & Clarkson, M.G. (1993). Is visually guided reaching in early infancy a myth? *Child Development, 64,* 1099–1110.

Clifton, R.K., Rochat, P., Litovsky, R.Y., & Perris, E.E. (1991). Object representation guides infants' reaching in the dark. *Journal of Experimental Psychology: Human Perception and Performance, 17,* 323–329.

Clifton, R.K., Rochat, P., Robin, D.J., & Berthier, N.E. (1994). Multimodal perception in human infants. *Journal of Experimental Psychology: Human Perception and Performance, 20,* 876–886.

Cohen, L.B., & Cashon, C.H. (2006). Infant cognition. In W. Damon & R. Lerner (Eds.) & D. Kuhn & R. Siegler (Vol. Eds.), *Handbook of child psychology: Vol. 2. Cognition, perception, and language* (6th ed., pp. 214–251). New York: Wiley.

Cohen, N.L., & Tomlinson-Keasey, C. (1980). The effects of peers and mothers on toddlers' play. *Child Development, 51,* 921–924.

Cohen, R., Mrtek, M.B., & Mrtek, R.G. (1995). Comparison of maternal absenteeism and infant illness rates among breastfeeding and formula-feeding women in two corporations. *American Journal of Health Promotion, 10,* 148–153.

Cohen, R.D. (1985). Child-saving and progressivism, 1885–1915. In J.M. Hawes, & N. R. Hiner (Eds.), *American childhood: A research guide and historical handbook* (pp. 273–309). Westport, CT: Greenwood Press.

Cohn, J.F., & Tronick, E.Z. (1983). Three-month-old infants' reaction to simulated maternal depression. *Child Development, 54,* 185–193.

Cohn, J.F., & Tronick, E.Z. (1987). Mother-infant face-to-face interaction: The sequence of dyadic states. *Developmental Psychology, 23,* 66–77.

Coie, J.D., & Dodge, K.A. (1998). Aggression and antisocial behavior. In W. Damon (Series Ed.) & N. Eisenberg (Vol. Ed.), *Handbook of child psychology: Vol. 3. Social, emotional, and personality development* (5th ed., pp. 779–862). New York: Wiley.

Cole, P.M., Barrett, K.C., & Zahn-Waxler, C. (1992). Emotion displays in two-year-olds during mishaps. *Child Development, 63,* 314–324.

Cole, P.M., Martin, S.E., & Dennis, T.A. (2004). Emotion regulation as a scientific construct: Methodological challenges and directions for child development research. *Child Development, 75,* 317–333.

Colombo, J. (1993). *Infant cognition: Predicting later intellectual functioning.* Thousand Oaks, CA: Sage.

Colombo, J. (2001). The development of visual attention in infancy. *Annual Review of Psychology, 52,* 337–367.

Colombo, J. (2002). Infant attention grows up: The emergence of a developmental cognitive neuroscience perspective. *Current Directions in Psychological Science, 11,* 196–200.

Colombo, J., & Janowsky, J.S. (1998). A cognitive neuroscience approach to individual differences in infant cognition. In J.E. Richards (Ed.), *Cognitive neuroscience of attention* (pp. 363–391). Mahwah, NJ: Erlbaum.

Colombo, J., & Mitchell, D.W. (1990). Individual and developmental differences in infant visual attention. In J. Colombo & J.W. Fagen (Eds.), *Individual differences in infancy* (pp. 193–227). Hillsdale, NJ: Erlbaum.

Colombo, J., Richman, W.A., Shaddy, D.J., Greenhoot, A.F., & Maikranz, J. (2001). HR-defined phases of attention, look duration, and infant performance in the paired-comparison paradigm. *Child Development, 72,* 1605–1616.

Colón, A.R., & Colón, P.A. (2001). *A history of children: A socio-cultural survey across millennia.* Westport, CT: Greenwood Press.

Colón, J.M. (1997). Assisted reproductive technologies. In M.L. Sipski, & C.J. Alexander (Eds.), *Sexual function in people with disability and chronic illness: A health professional's guide* (pp. 557–575). Gaithersburg, MD: Aspen Publishers.

Committee on Fetus and Newborn. (2005). Underwater births. *Pediatrics, 115,* 1413–1414.

Committee on Fetus and Newborn, American Academy of Pediatrics, and Committee on Obstetric Practice, American College of Obstetricians and Gynecologists. (1996). Use and abuse of the Apgar score. *Pediatrics, 98,* 141–142.

Comstock, G., & Scharrer, E. (2006). Media and popular culture. In W. Damon & R. Lerner (Eds.) & D. Kuhn & R. Siegler (Vol. Eds.), *Handbook of child psychology: Vol. 2. Cognition, perception, and language* (6th ed., pp. 817–863). New York: Wiley.

Connolly, K.J., & Dalgleish, M. (1989). The emergence of a tool-using skill in infancy. *Developmental Psychology, 25*, 894–912.

Cooper, R.P., & Aslin, R.N. (1990). Preference for infant-directed speech in the first month after birth. *Child Development, 61*, 1584–1595.

Cooper, R.P., & Aslin, R.N. (1994). Developmental differences in infant attention to the spectral properties of infant-directed speech. *Child Development, 65*, 1663–1677.

Corbetta, D., & Bojczyk, K.E. (2002). Infants return to two-handed reaching when they are learning to walk. *Journal of Motor Behavior, 34*, 83–95.

Cosans, C. (2004). The meaning of natural childbirth. *Perspectives in Biology and Medicine, 47*, 266–272.

Cost, Quality, and Child Outcomes Study Team. (1995). Cost, quality, and child outcomes in child care centers: Key findings and recommendations. *Young Children, 50*(4), 40–44.

Costa-Giomi, E. (1999). The effects of three years of piano instruction on children's cognitive development. *Journal of Research in Music Education, 47*, 198–212.

Courage, M.L., Edison, S.C., & Howe, M.L. (2004). Variability in the early development of visual self-recognition. *Infant Behavior & Development, 27*, 509–532.

Crago, M., Annahatak, B., & Ningiuruvik, L. (1993). Changing patterns of language socialization in Inuit homes. *Anthropology and Educational Quarterly, 24*, 205–223.

Crain, W. (2000). *Theories of development: Concepts and applications.* Upper Saddle River, NJ: Prentice Hall.

Cravens, H. (1985). Child-saving in the age of professionalism, 1915–1930. In J.M. Hawes, & N.R. Hiner (Eds.). (1985). *American childhood: A research guide and historical handbook* (pp. 415–488). Westport, CT: Greenwood Press.

Crockenberg, S.C. (2003). Rescuing the baby from the bathwater: How gender and temperament (may) influence how child care affects child development. *Child Development, 74*, 1034–1038.

Crook, C.K. (1978). Taste perception in the newborn infant. *Infant Behavior and Development, 1*, 52–69.

Cryer, D., Hurwitz, S., & Wolery, M. (2003). *Continuity of caregiver for infants and toddlers.* EDO-PS-03-17. Champaign, IL: Clearinghouse on Elementary and Early Childhood Education.

Cummings, E.M., & Davies, P.T. (1999). Depressed parents and family functioning: Interpersonal effects and children's functioning and development. In T. Joiner & J.C. Coyne (Eds.), *Advances in interpersonal approaches: The interactional nature of depression* (pp. 299–327). Washington, DC: American Psychological Association Press.

Cunniff, C., & Committee on Genetics. (2004). Pediatrics prenatal screening and diagnosis for pediatricians. *Pediatrics, 114*, 889–894.

Cunningham, D., Xiao, Q., Chatterjee, A., Sulik, K., Juriloff, D., Elder, F., et al. (2002). exma: An X-linked insertional mutation that disrupts forebrain and eye development. *Mammalian Genome, 13*, 179–185.

Cunningham, M., Cox, E.O., American Academy of Pediatrics/Committee on Practice and Ambulatory Medicine, & Section on Otolaryngology and Bronchoesophagology. (2003). Hearing assessment in infants and children: Recommendations beyond neonatal screening. *Pediatrics, 111*, 436–440.

Curtiss, S. (1977). *Genie.* New York: Academic Press.

Custodero, L., Britto, P.R., & Brooks-Gunn, J. (2003). Musical lives: A collective portrait of American parents and their young children. *Applied Developmental Psychology, 24*, 553–572.

Dale, P.S., Price, T.S., Bishop, D.V.M., & Plomin, R. (2003). Outcomes of early language delay: I. Predicting persistent and transient language difficulties at 3 and 4 years. *Journal of Speech, Language, and Hearing Research, 46*, 544–560.

Dale, P.S., Simonoff, E., Bishop, D.V.M., Eley, T.C., Oliver, B., Price, T.S., et al. (1998). Genetic influence on language delay in two-year-old children. *Nature Neuroscience, 1*, 324–328.

Damewood, M. D. (2001). Ethical implications of a new application of preimplantation diagnosis. *JAMA, 285*, 3143–3144.

Darwin, C. (1877). A biographical sketch of an infant. *Mind, 2*, 285–294.

Davis-Floyd, R.E. (1994). The technocratic body: American childbirth as cultural expression. *Social Science and Medicine, 38*, 1125–1140.

Dawson, G. (1994). Frontal electroencephalographic correlates of individual differences in emotion expression in infants: A brain systems perspective on emotion. In Fox, N.A. (Ed.), The development of emotion regulation: Biological and behavioral considerations. *Monographs of the Society for Research in Child Development, 59*(2–3, Serial No. 240), 135–151.

Dawson, G., & Ashman, S.B. (2000). On the origins of a vulnerability to depression: The influence of the early social environment on the development of psychobiological systems related to risk for affective disorder. In C.A. Nelson (Ed.), The effects of early adversity on neurobehavioral development. *The Minnesota Symposia on Child Psychology* (Vol. 31, pp. 245–279). Mahwah, NJ: Erlbaum.

Dawson, G., Panagiotides, H., Klinger, L.G., & Spieker, S. (1997). Infants of depressed and nondepressed mothers exhibit differences in frontal brain electrical activity during the expression of negative emotions. *Developmental Psychology, 33*, 650–656.

Dawson, G., Meltzoff, A. N., Osterling, J., Rinaldi, J., & Brown, E. (1998). Children with autism fail to orient to naturally occurring social stimuli. *Journal of Autism & Developmental Disorders, 28*, 479–485.

Dawson, G., Munson, J., Estes, A., Osterling, J., McPartland, J., Toth, K., et al. (2002). Neurocognitive function and joint attention ability in young children with autism spectrum disorder versus developmental delay. *Child Development, 73*, 345–358.

Dawson, G., Frey, K., Self, J., Panagiotides, H., Hessl, D., Yamada, E., and Rinaldi, J. (1999). Frontal brain electrical activity in infants of depressed and nondepressed mothers: Relation to variations in infant behavior. *Development and Psychopathology, 11,* 589–605.Dawson, G., Toth, K., Abbott, R., Osterling, J., Munson, J., Estes, A., & Liaw, J. (2004). Early social attention impairments in autism: Social orienting, joint attention, and attention to distress. *Developmental Psychology, 40,* 271–283.

De Bellis M.D., Keshavan, M.S., Clark, D.B., Caseey, B.J., Giedd, J.B., Boring, A.M., Frustaci, K., & Ryan, N.D. (1999). Developmental traumatology, Part 2: Brain development. *Biological Psychiatry, 45,* 1271–1284.

de Haan, M., & Nelson, C.A. (1997). Recognition of the mother's face by six-month-old infants: A neurobehavioral study. *Child Development, 68,* 187–210.

De Mause, L. (1974). *The history of childhood.* New York: Psychohistory Press.

de Villiers, J.G., & de Villiers, P.A. (1973). A cross-sectional study of the acquisition of grammataical morphemes. *Journal of Psycholinguistic Research, 2,* 267–278.

de Villiers, P.A., & de Villiers, J.G. (1978). *Language acquisition.* Cambridge, MA: Harvard University Press.

De Wolff, M.S., & van IJzendoorn, M.H. (1997). Sensitivity and attachment: A meta-analysis on parental antecedents of infant attachment. *Child Development, 68,* 571–591.

DeCasper, A.J., & Fifer, W.P. (1980). Of human bonding: Newborns prefer their mother's voices. *Science, 208,* 174–176.

DeCasper, A.J., & Spence, M.J. (1986). Prenatal maternal speech influences newborns' perception of speech sounds. *Infant Behavior and Development, 9,* 133–150.

DeCasper, A.J., Lecanuet, J.P., Busnel, M.C., Granier-Deferre, C., & Maugeais, R. (1994). Fetal reactions to recurrent maternal speech. *Infant Behavior and Development, 17,* 159–164.

DeHart, G.B. (1999). Conflict and averted conflict in preschoolers' interactions with siblings and friends. In W.A. Collins, & B. Laursen (Eds.), Relationships as developmental contexts. *The Minnesota Symposia on Child Psychology* (Vol. 30, pp. 281–303). Mahwah, NJ: Erlbaum.

Delaney-Black, V., Covington, C., Templin, T., Ager, J., Martier, S., & Sokol, R. (1998). Prenatal cocaine exposure and child behavior. *Pediatrics, 102,* 945–950.

DeLoache, J., & Gottlieb, A. (2000). *A world of babies: Imagined childcare guides for seven societies.* New York: Cambridge University Press.

DeLoache, J.S. (1987). Rapid change in the symbolic functioning of very young children. *Science, 238*(4833), 1556–1557.

DeLoache, J.S. (1991). Symbolic functioning in very young children: Understanding of pictures and models. *Child Development, 62,* 736–752.

DeLoache, J.S. (1995). Early understanding and use of symbols: The model model. *Current Directions in Psychological Science, 4,* 109–113.

DeLoache, J.S. (2000). Dual representation and young children's use of scale models. *Child Development, 71,* 329–338.

DeLoache, J.S., & Brown, A.L. (1983). Very young children's memory for the location of objects in a large-scale environment. *Child Development, 54,* 888–897.

DeLoache, J.S., & Burns, N.M. (1994). Early understanding of the representational function of pictures. *Cognition, 52,* 83–110.

DeLoache, J.S., Pierroutsakos, S.L., Uttal, D.H., Rosengren, K.S., & Gottlieb, A. (1998). Grasping the nature of pictures. *Psychological Science, 9,* 205–210.

Deloukas, P., Matthews, L.H., Ashurst, J., Burton, J., Gilbert, J.G., Jones, M., et al. (2001). The DNA sequence and comparative analysis of human chromosome 20. *Nature, 414,* 865–871.

Dennis, C., & Gallagher, R. (2001). *The human genome.* New York: Palgrave.

Department of Health and Human Services. (2001). *Women and smoking: A report of the Surgeon General.* Washington, DC: U.S. Department of Health and Human Services.

Derryberry, D., & Rothbart, M.K. (1997). Reactive and effortful processes in the organization of temperament. *Development and Psychopathology, 9,* 633–652.

deUngria, M., Rao, R., Wobken, J.D., Luciana, M., Nelson, C.A., & Georgieff, M.K. (2000). Perinatal iron deficiency decreases cytochrome c oxidase (CytOx) activity in selected regions of neonatal rat brain. *Pediatric Research, 48,* 169–176.

Deven, F., & Moss, P. (2002). Leave arrangements for parents: overview and future outlook. *Community, Work and Family, 5,* 237–256.

Diamond, A. (1991). Neuropsychological insights into the meaning of object concept development. In S. Carey & R. Gelman (Eds.), *Biology and knowledge: Structural constraints on development* (pp. 37–80). Hillsdale, NJ: Erlbaum.

Diamond, A. (1998). Understanding the A-not-B error: Working memory vs. reinforced response, or active trace vs. latent trace. *Developmental Science, 1,* 185–189.

Diamond, A., Werker, J.F., & Lalonde, C. (1994). Toward understanding commonalities in the development of object search, detour navigation, categorization, and speech perception. In G. Dawson, & K. Fischer (Eds.), *Human behavior and the developing brain* (pp. 380–426). New York: Guildford Press.

DiPietro, J., Hilton, S., Hawkins, M., Costigan, K., & Pressman, E. (2002). Maternal stress and affect influence fetal neurobehavioral development. *Developmental Psychology, 38,* 659–668.

DiPietro, J.A. (2004). The role of prenatal maternal stress in child development. *Current Directions in Psychological Science, 13,* 71–74.

DiPietro, J.A., Hodgson, D.M., Costigan, K.A., & Johnson, T.R.B. (1996). Fetal antecedents of infant temperament. *Child Development, 67,* 2568–2583.

Dodge, K.A., Coie, J.D., & Lynam, D. (2006). Aggression and antisocial behavior in youth. In W. Damon & R. Lerner (Eds.) & N. Eisenberg (Vol. Ed.), *Handbook of child psychology: Vol. 3. Social, emotional, and personality development* (6th ed., pp. 719–788). New York: Wiley.

Donald, A., & Muthu, V. (2002). No evidence that MMR vaccine is associated with autism or bowel disease. *Clinical Evidence, 7,* 331–340.

Donzella, B., Gunnar, M.R., Krueger, W.K., & Alwin, J. (2000). Cortisol and vagal tone responses to competitive challenge in preschoolers: Associations with temperament. *Developmental Psychiology, 37,* 209–220.

Dore, J., Franklin, M., Miller, R., & Ramer, A. (1976). Transitional phenomena in early language acquisition. *Journal of Child Langauge, 3,* 13–28.

Doulas of North America. (2002). *What is a doula?* Retrieved January 10, 2003, from http://www.dona.org/faq.html

Douvan, E. (1985). The age of narcissism, 1963–1982. In J.M. Hawes, & N. R. Hiner (Eds.), *American childhood: A research guide and historical handbook* (pp. 587–617). Westport, CT: Greenwood Press.

Downs, B. (2003). Fertility of American women: June 2002. *Current Population Reports, P20–548.* Washington, DC: U.S. Census Bureau.

Dreher, M.C., Nugent, K., & Hudgins, R. (1994). Prenatal marijuana exposure and neonatal outcomes in Jamaica: An ethnographic study. *Pediatrics, 93,* 254–260.

Dromi, E. (1986). The one-word period as a stage in language development: quantitative and qualitative accounts. In I. Levin (Ed.), *Stage and structure: Reopening the debate* (pp. 220–245). Norwood, NJ: Ablex.

Druin, A. (Ed.). (1999). *The design of children's technology.* San Francisco, CA: Morgan Kaufmann Publishers.

Druin, A., & Hendler, J. (Eds.). (2000). *Robots for kids: Exploring new technologies for learning.* San Diego, CA: Morgan Kaufmann Publishers.

Druin, A., & Solomon, C. (1996). *Designing multimedia environments for children: Computers, creativity, and kids.* New York: Wiley.

Druin, A., Bederson, B.B., Weeks, A., Farber, A., Grosjean, J., Guha, N.L., et al. (2003, May 5). The International Children's Digital Library: Description and analysis of first use. Sustaining Digital Resources: Web-Wise 2003, 8(5). Retrieved March 28, 2005, from http://outreach.lib.uic.edu/www/issues/issue8_5/druin/index.html

Dunham, I., et al. (1999). The DNA sequence of human chromosome 22. *Nature, 402,* 489–495.

Dunn, J. (1998). Siblings, emotion and the development of understanding. In S. Bråten (Ed.), *Intersubjective communication and emotion in early ontogeny. Studies in emotion and social interaction,* 2nd series (pp. 158–168). New York: Cambridge University Press.

Dunn, J. (2002). Sibling relationships. In P.K. Smith & C.H. Hart (Eds.), *Blackwell handbook of childhood social development. Blackwell handbooks of developmental psychology* (pp. 223–237). Malden, MA: Blackwell.

Dunn, J., & Brown, J. (1996). Children's family relationships between two and five: Developmental changes and individual differences. *Social Development, 5,* 230–250.

Dunn, J., & Kendrick, C. (1982). Siblings and their mothers: Developing relationships within the family. In M.E. Lamb & B. Sutton-Smith (Eds.), *Sibling relationships: Their nature and significance across the lifespan* (pp. 39–60). Hillsdale, NJ: Erlbaum.

Dunn, J., & Munn, P. (1985). Becoming a family member: Family conflict and the development of social understanding in the second year. *Child Development, 56,* 480–492.

Dunn, J., & Shatz, M. (1989). Becoming a conversationalist despite (or because of) having an older sibling. *Child Development, 60,* 399–410.

Dunn, J., Brown, J., & Beardsall, L., (1991). Family talk about feeling states and children's later understanding of others' emotions. *Developmental Psychology, 27,* 448–455.

Dunn, J., Kendrick, C., & MacNamee, R. (1981). The reaction of first-born children to the birth of a sibling: Mothers' reports. *Journal of Child Psychology and Psychiatry, 22,* 1–18.

Eberhard, J., & Geissbuhler, V. (2000). Influence of alternative birth methods on traditional birth management. *Fetal Diagnosis and Therapy, 15,* 283–290.

Ebrahim, S.H., & Gfroerer, J. (2003). Pregnancy-related substance use in the United States during 1996–1998. *Obstetrics and Gynecology, 101,* 374–379.

Ebrahim, S.H., Decoufle, P., & Palakathodi, A.S. (2000). Combined tobacco and alcohol use by pregnant and reproductive-aged women in the United States. *Obstetrics & Gynecology, 96,* 767–771.

Ebrahim, S.H., Diekman, S.T., Floyd, L., & Decoufle, P. (1999). Comparison of binge drinking among pregnant and nonpregnant women, United States, 1991–1996. *American Journal of Obstetrics and Gynecology, 180,* 1–7.

Eckenrode, J., Ganzel, B., Henderson, C.R., Smith, E., Olds, D.L., Powers, J., Cole, R., Kitzman, H., & Sidora, K. (2000). Preventing child abuse and neglect with a program of nurse home visitation. *JAMA, 284,* 1385–1391.

Ecker, J.L., Chen, K.T., Cohen, A.P., Riley, L.E., & Lieberman, E.S. (2001). Increased risk of cesarean delivery with advancing maternal age: Indications and associated factors in nulliparous women. *American Journal of Obstetrics and Gynecology, 185,* 883–887.

Eckerman, C.O., & Didow, S.M. (1989). Toddlers' social coordinations: Changing responses to another's invitation to play. *Developmental Psychology, 25,* 794–804.

Edwards, M. (1999). Pollution in the former Soviet Union: Lethal legacy. *National Geographic, 186*(2), pp. 70–115.

Effer, S.B., Moutquin, J.M., Farine, D., Saigal, S., Nimrod, C., Kelly, E., & Niyonsenga, T. (2002). Neonatal survival rates in 860 singleton live births at 24 and 25 weeks gestational age. *BJOG, 109,* 740–745.

Egeland, B., Jacobvitz, D., & Sroufe, L.A. (1988). Breaking the cycle of abuse. *Child Development, 59,* 1080–1088.

Ehrenberg, H.M., Dierker, L., Milluzzi, C., & Mercer, B.M. (2003). Low maternal weight, failure to thrive in pregnancy, and adverse pregnancy outcomes. *American Journal of Obstetrics and Gynecology, 189,* 1726–1730.

Eimas, P.D., & Corbit, J.D. (1973). Selective adaptation of linguistic feature detectors. *Cognitive Psychology, 4,* 99–109.

Eimas, P.D., Siqueland, E.R., Jusczyk, P., & Vigorito, J. (1971). Speech perception in infants. *Science, 171,* 303–306.

Eisenberg, A., Murkoff, H.E., & Hathaway, S.E. (1991). *What to expect when you're expecting.* New York: Workman Publishing.

Eisenberg, N., & Spinrad, T.L. (2004). Emotion–related regulation: Sharpening the definition. *Child Development, 75,* 334–339.

Eisenberg, N., Fabes, R.A., & Spinrad, T.L. (2006). Prosocial development. In W. Damon & R. Lerner (Eds.) & N. Eisenberg (Vol. Ed.), *Handbook of child psychology: Vol. 3. Social, emotional, and personality development* (6th ed., pp. 646–718). New York: Wiley.

Elder, G.H., Jr. (1974). *Children of the Great Depression: Social change in life experience.* Chicago: University of Chicago Press.

Elder, G.H., Jr., & Hareven, T.K. (1993). Rising above life's disadvantage: From the Great Depression to war. In G.H. Elder, Jr., J. Modell, & R.D. Parke (Eds.). *Children in time and place: Developmental and historical insights* (pp. 47–72). New York: Cambridge University Press.

Elder, G.H., Jr., Modell, J., & Parke, R.D. (Eds.). (1993). *Children in time and place: Developmental and histor-*

ical insights. New York: Cambridge University Press.

Ellemberg, D., Lewis, T.L., Maurer, D., & Brent, H.P. (2000). Influence of monocular deprivation during infancy on the later development of spatial and temporal vision. *Vision Research, 40,* 3283–3295.

Emde, R.N. (1992). Individual meaning and increasing complexity: Contributions of Sigmund Freud and René Spitz to developmental psychology. *Developmental Psychology, 28,* 347–359.

Emde, R.N., Biringen, A., Clyman, R.B., & Oppenheim, D. (1991). The moral self in infancy: Affective core and procedural knowledge. *Developmental Review, 11,* 251–270.

Engle, P.L. & Breaux, C. (1998). Fathers' involvement with children: Perspectives from developing countries. *Social Policy Report, XII*(1), 1–21.

Ennouri, K., & Bloch, H. (1996). Visual control of hand approach movements in newborns. *British Journal of Developmental Psychology, 14,* 327–338.

Eppler, M.A., Adolph, K.E., & Weiner, T. (1996). The developmental relationship between infants' exploration and action on sloping surfaces. *Infant Behavior and Development, 19,* 259–264.

Erickson, M.F., & Egeland, B. (1996). Child neglect. In J. Briere, & L. Berliner (Eds.), *The APSAC handbook on child maltreatment* (pp. 4–20). Thousand Oaks, CA: Sage.

Erickson, M.F., Korfmacher, J., & Egeland, B. (1992). Attachments past and present: Implications for therapeutic intervention with mother-infant dyads. *Development and Psychopathology, 4,* 495–507.

Erickson, M.F., Sroufe, L.A., & Egeland, B. (1985). The relationship between quality of attachment and behavior problems in a high risk sample. In I. Bretherton & E. Waters (Eds.), Growing points in attachment theory and research. *Monographs of the Society for Research in Child Development, 50*(1/2, Serial No. 209), 147–166.

Erikson, E.H. (1950). *Childhood and society.* New York: Norton.

Erting, C.J., Prezioso, C., & O'Grandy Hynes, M. (1990). The interactional context of deaf mother-infant communication. In V. Voltera & C.J. Erting (Eds.), *From gesture to language in hearing and deaf children* (pp. 97–106). Berlin: Springer.

ESHRE PGD Consortium Steering Committee. (2002). ESHRE Preimplantation Genetic Diagnosis Consortium: Data collection III (May 2001). *Human Reproduction, 17,* 233–246.

ESHRE Task Force on Ethics and Law. (2002). Gamete and embryo donation. *Human Reproduction, 17,* 1407–1408.

Eskenazi, B., & Castorina, R. (1999). Association of prenatal maternal or postnatal child environmental tobacco smoke exposure and neurodevelopmental and behavioral problems in children. *Environmental Health Perspectives, 107,* 991–1000.

Evans, G.W. (2004). The environment of childhood poverty. *American Psychologist, 59,* 77–92.

Evans, M.I., Harrison, M.R., Flake, A.W., & Johnson, M.P. (2002). Fetal therapy. *Clinical Obstetrics & Gynaecology, 16,* 671–683.

Evans, M.J., Gurer, C., Loike, J.D., Wilmut, I., Schnieke, A.E., Schon, E.A., et al. (1999). Mitochondrial DNA genotypes in nuclear transfer-derived cloned sheep. *Nature Genetics, 23,* 90–93.

Eyler, F.D., Behnke, M., Conlon, M., Woods, N.S., & Wobie, K. (1998). Birth outcome from a prospective, matched study of crack/cocaine use: II. Interactive and does effects on neurobehavioral assessment. *Pediatrics, 101,* 237–241.

Fagot, B.I., & Hagan, R. (1991). Observations of parent reactions to sex-stereotyped behavior. *Child Development, 62,* 617–628.

Fantz, R.L. (1961). The origin of form perception. *Scientific American, 204,* 66–72.

Fantz, R.L. (1963). Pattern vision in newborn infants. *Science, 140,* 296–297.

Fantz, R.L., Fagan, J.F., & Miranda, S.B. (1975). Early visual selectivity. In

L.B. Cohen & P. Salapatek (Eds.), *Infant perception: From sensation to cognition* (Vol. 1, pp. 249–345). New York: Academic Press.

Farley, T.F., Hambidge, S.J., & Daley, M.F. (2002). Association of low maternal education with neural tube defects in Colorado, 1989–1998. *Public Health, 116,* 89–94.

Farver, J.M., & Howes, C. (1993). Cultural differences in American and Mexican mother-child pretend play. *Merrill-Palmer Quarterly, 39,* 344–358.

Farver, J.M., & Wimbarti, S. (1995). Indonesian toddlers' social play with their mothers and older siblings. *Child Development, 66,* 1493–1513.

Farver, J.M., Kim, Y.K., & Lee, Y. (1995). Cultural differences in Korean- and Anglo- American preschoolers' social interaction and play behaviors. *Child Development, 66,* 1088–1099.

Federal Interagency Forum on Child and Family Statistics. (2005). *America's children: Key national indicators of well-being, 2005.* Retrieved November 4, 2005, from http://childstats.gov/americaschildren/

Feinbloom, R.I. (1993). *Pregnancy, birth, and the early months: A complete guide* (2nd ed.). Reading, MA: Perseus Books.

Feldman, R. (2006). Biological rhythms to social rhythms: Physiological precursors of mother-infant synchrony. *Developmental Psychology, 41,* 175–188.

Feldman, R., Eidelman, A.I., & Rotenberg, N. (2004). Parenting stress, infant emotion regulation, maternal sensitivity, and the cognitive development of triplets: A model for parent and child influences in a unique ecology. *Child Development, 75,* 1774–1791.

Fenson, L., Bates, E., Dale, P.S., Goodman, J., Reznick, J.S., & Thal, D. (2000). Measuring variability in early child language: Don't shoot the messenger. *Child Development, 71,* 323–328.

Fenson, L., Dale, P.S., Reznick, J.S., Bates, E., Thal, D.J., & Pethick, S.J. (1994). Variability in early communicative development. *Monographs of the Society for Research in Child Development, 59*(5, Serial No. 242).

Ferber, S.G., & Makhoul, I.R. (2004). The effect of skin-to-skin contact (kangaroo care) shortly after birth on the neurobehavioral responses of the term newborn: A randomized, controlled trial. *Pediatrics, 113,* 858–865.

Fernald, A. (1984). The perceptual and affective salience of mothers' speech to infants. In L. Feagans, C. Garvey, & R. Golinkoff (Eds.), *The origins and growth of communication* (pp. 5–29). Norwood, NJ: Ablex.

Fernald, A. (1985). Four-month-old infants prefer to listen to motherese. *Infant Behavior and Development, 8,* 181–195.

Fernald, A. (1992). Human maternal vocalizations to infants as biologically relevant signals: An evolutionary perspective. In J.H. Barkow, L. Cosmides, & J. Tooby (Eds.), *The adapted mind: Evolutionary psychology and the generation of culture* (pp. 391–428). New York: Oxford University Press.

Fernald, A. (1993). Approval and disapproval: Infant responsiveness to vocal affect in familiar and unfamiliar languages. *Child Development, 64,* 657–674.

Fernald, A., & Kuhl, P.K. (1987). Acoustic determinants of infant preference for motherese speech. *Infant Behavior and Development, 10*(3), 279–293.

Fernald, A., & Mazzie, C. (1991). Prosody and focus in speech to infants and adults. *Developmental Psychology, 27,* 209–221.

Fernald, A., & Morikawa, H. (1993). Common themes and cultural variations in Japanese and American mothers' speech to infants. *Child Development, 64,* 637–656.

Fernald, A., & O'Neill, D.K. (1993). Peekaboo across cultures: How mothers and infants play with voices, faces, and expectations. In K. MacDonald (Ed.), *Parent-child play* (pp. 259–285). Albany, NY: State University of New York Press.

Fernald, A., & Simon, T. (1984). Expanded intonation contours in mothers' speech to newborns. *Developmental Psychology, 20,* 104–113.

Fernald, A., Perfors, A., & Marchman, V.A. (2006). Picking up speed in understanding: Speech processing efficiency and vocabulary growth across the 2nd year. *Developmental Psychology, 42,* 98–116.

Fernald, A., Pinto, J.P., Swingley, D., Weinberg, A., & McRoberts, G.W. (1998). Rapid gains in speed of verbal processing by infants in the 2nd year. *Psychological Science, 9,* 228–231.

Field, T. (1998b). Maternal depression effects on infants and early interventions. *Preventive Medicine, 27,* 200-203.

Field, T. (1994). The effects of mother's physical and emotional unavailability on emotion regulation. In Fox, N.A. (Ed.), The development of emotion regulation: Biological and behavioral considerations. *Monographs of the Society for Research in Child Development, 59*(2–3, Serial No. 240), 208–227.

Field, T. (1995). Infant massage therapy. In T.M. Field (Ed.), *Touch in early development* (pp. 105–114). Mahwah, NJ: Erlbaum.

Field, T. (1998a). Early interventions for infants of depressed mothers. *Pediatrics, 102,* 1305–1310.

Field, T., Hernandez-Reif, M., & Freedman, J. (2004). Stimulation programs for preterm infants. *Social Policy Report, 18*(1), 1–19.

Field, T., Diego, M., Hernandez-Reif, M., Schanberg, S., & Kuhn, C. (2003). Depressed mothers who are "good interaction" partners versus those who are withdrawn or intrusive. *Infant Behavior & Development, 26,* 238–252.

Field, T., Fox, N.A., Pickens, J., Nawrocki, T., & Soutollo, D. (1995). Right frontal EEG activation in 3- to 6-month-old infants of depressed mothers. *Developmental Psychology, 31,* 358–363.

Field, T., Schanberg, S., Scafidi, F., Bower, C., Vega-Lahr, N., Garcia, R., et al. (1986). Tactile/kinesthetic stimulation effects on preterm neonates. *Pediatrics, 77,* 654–658.

Field, T., Grizzle, N., Scafidi, F., Abrams, S., Rchardson, S., Kuhn, C., & Schanberg, S. (1996). Massage therapy for infants of depressed mothers. *Infant Behavior and Development, 19,* 107–112.

Field, T., Healy, B., Goldstein, S., Perry, S., Bendell, D., Schanberg, S., Zimmerman, E.A., & Kuhn, C. (1988). Infants of depressed mothers show "depressed" behavior even with nondepressed adults. *Child Development, 59,* 1569–1579.

Field, T.M., Woodson, R., Greenberg, R., & Cohen, D. (1982). Discrimination and imitation of facial expression by neonates. *Science, 218,* 179–181.

Field, T.M., Woodson, R., Cohen, D., Greenberg, R., Garcia, R., & Collins, K. (1983). Discrimination and imitation of facial expressions by term and preterm neonates. *Infant Behavior and Development, 9,* 473–478.

Fields, J. (2003). Children's living arrangements and characteristics: March 2002. *Current Population Reports, P20–547.* Washington, DC: U.S. Census Bureau.

Filipek, P.A., Accardo, P.J., Ashwal, S., Baranek, G. T., Cook, E. H., Dawson, G., et al. (2000). Practice parameter: Screening and diagnosis of autism: Report of the Quality Standards Subcommittee of the American Academy of Neurology and the Child Neurology Society. *Neurology, 55,* 468–479.

Finkelstein, B. (1985). Casting networks of good influence: The reconstruction of childhood in the United States, 1790–1870. In J.M. Hawes, & N.R. Hiner (Eds.). *American childhood: A research guide and historical handbook* (pp. 111–152). Westport, CT: Greenwood Press.

Fisher, L., Ames, E.W., Chisholm, K., & Savoie, L. (1997). Problems reported by parents of Romanian orphans adopted to British Columbia. *International Journal of Behavioral Development, 20,* 67–82.

Fivush, R., & Fromhoff, F.A. (1988). Style and structure in mother-child conversations about the past. *Discourse Processes, 11,* 337–355.

Fivush, R., Brotman, M., Buckner, J.P., & Goodman, S. (2000). Gender differences in parent-child emotion narratives. *Sex Roles, 42,* 233–254.

Flanagan, K.D., & Park, J. (2005). *American Indian and Alaska Native children: Findings from the base year of the Early Childhood Longitudinal Study, birth cohort (ECLS-B).* Washington, DC: U.S. Department of Education.

Flavell, J.H., Miller, P.H., & Miller, S.A. (2002). *Cognitive development* (4e). Upper Saddle River, NJ: Prentice Hall.

Flege, J.E. (1989). Chinese subjects' perception of the word-final English /t/-/d/ contrast: Before and after training. *Journal of the Acoustical Society of America, 86,* 1684–1697.

Fleming, P.J., Blair, P.S., Pollard, K., Platt, M.W., Leach, C., Smith, I., et al. (1999). Pacifier use and sudden infant death syndrome: Results from the CESDI/SUDI case control study. *Archives of Disease in Childhood, 81,* 112–116.

Fletcher, K.L., Huffman, L.F., Bray, N.W., & Grupe, L.A. (1998). The use of the microgenetic method with children with disabilities: Discovering competence. *Early Education and Development, 9,* 357–373.

Flom, R. & Pick, A.D. (2003). Verbal encouragement and joint attention in 18-month-old infants. *Infant Behavior & Development, 26,* 121–134.

Fogel, A., Nwokah, E., & Karns, J. (1993). Parent-infant games as dynamic social systems. In K. MacDonald (Ed.), *Parent-child play.* Albany, NY: State University of New York Press.

Fogel, A., Dickson, K.L., Hsu, H.C., Messinger, D., Nelson-Goens, G.C., & Nwokah, E. (1997). Communication of smiling and laughter in mother-infant play: Research on emotion from a dynamic systems perspective. *New Directions for Child Development, No. 77,* 5–24.

Folven, R.J., & Bonvillian, J.D. (1991). The transition from nonreferential to referential language in children acquiring American Sign Language. *Developmental Psychology, 27,* 806–816.

Fombonne, E., & Chakrabati, S. (2001). No evidence for a new variant of measles-mumps-rubella-induced autism. *Pediatrics, 108,* 58–66.

Fontaine, P., Adam, P., & Svendsen, K.H. (2002). Should intrathecal narcotics be used as a sole labor analgesic? A prospective comparison of spinal opioids and epidural bupivacaine. *Journal of Family Practice, 51,* 630–635.

Fontanel, B., & d'Harcourt, C. (1997). *Babies: History, art, and folklore.* New York: Harry N. Abrams.

Fontijn, W., & Mendels, P. (2005). StoryToy the interactive storytelling toy. Proceedings of the Second International Workshop on Pervasive Gaming Applications. Retrieved December, 22, 2005, from http://www.ipsi.fraunhofer.ed/ambiente/pergames2005/allpapers.htm

Forman, D.R., Aksan, N., & Kochanska, G. (2004). Toddlers' responsive imitation predicts preschool-age conscience. *Psychological Science, 15,* 699–704.

Foster, E.M., & Kalil, A. (2005). Developmental psychology and public policy: Progress and prospects. *Developmental Psychology, 41,* 827–832.

Fox, M.A., Connolly, B.A., & Snyder, T.D. (2005). *Youth indicators, 2005: Trends in the well-being of American youth* (NCES 2005050). Washington, DC: U.S. Department of Education, National Center for Education Statistics.

Fox, M.K., Pac, S., Devaney, B., & Jankowski, L. (2004). Feeding Infants and Toddlers study: What foods are infants and toddlers eating? *Journal of the American Dietetic Association, 104,* 22–30.

Fox, N.A., Kimmerly, N.L., & Schafer, W.D. (1991). Attachment to mother/attachment to father: A meta-analysis. *Child Development, 62,* 210–225.

Franco, P., Scaillet, S., Wermenbol, V., Valente, F., Grosswasser, J., & Kahn,

A. (2000). The influence of a pacifier on infants' arousals from sleep. *The Journal of Pediatrics, 136,* 775–779.

Frank, D.A., Brown, J., Johnson, S., & Cabral, H. (2002). Forgotten fathers: An exploratory study of mothers' report of drug and alcohol problems among fathers of urban newborns. *Neurotoxicology & Teratology, 24,* 339–347.

Frank, D.A., Jacobs, R.R., Beeghly, M., Augustyn, M., Bellinger, D., Cabral, H., et al. (2002). Level of prenatal cocaine exposure and scores on the Bayley Scales of Infant Development: Modifying effects of caregiver, early intervention, and birth weight. *Pediatrics, 110,* 1143–1152.

Frankenburg, W., Dodds, J.B., & Archer, P. (1990). *Denver II: Technical manual.* Denver: Denver Developmental Materials.

Frasier, D. (1991). *On the day you were born.* Orlando, FL: Harcourt Brace & Co.

Freed, J. (2004, April 10). Rare disorder robs toddler of pain. Associated Press.

Freud, S. (1910). The origin and development of psychoanalysis. *American Journal of Psychology, 21,* 181–218.

Freudigman, K.A., & Thoman, E.B. (1998). Infants' earliest sleep/wake organization differs as a function of delivery mode. *Developmental Psychobiology, 32,* 293–304.

Frick, J.E., Colombo, J., & Saxon, T.F. (1999). Individual and developmental differences in disengagement of fixation in early infancy. *Child Development, 70,* 537–548.

Frick, P.J. (2004). Integrating research on temperament and childhood psychopathology: Its pitfalls and promise. *Journal of Clinical Child and Adolescent Psychology, 33,* 2–7.

Friedlmeier, W., & Trommsdorff, G. (1999). Emotion regulation in early childhood: A cross-cultural comparison between German and Japanese toddlers. *Journal of Cross-Cultural Psychology, 30,* 684–711.

Fujioka, T., Fujioka, A., Tan, N., Chowdhury, G., Mouri, H., Sakata, Y., et al.

(2001). Mild prenatal stress enhances learning performance in the non-adopted rat offspring. *Neuroscience, 103,* 301–307.

Fuller, B., Kagan, S.L., Caspary, G.L., & Gauthier, C.A. (2002). Welfare reform and child care options for low-income families. *The Future of Children, 12*(1), 97–119.

Furman, L., Taylor, G., Minich, N., & Hack, M. (2003). The effect of maternal milk on neonatal morbidity of very low-birth-weight infants. *Archives of Pediatrics and Adolescent Medicine, 157,* 66–71.

Galtry, J. (2002). Child Health: An underplayed variable in parental leave policy debates? *Community, Work, & Family, 5,* 257–278.

Ganchrow, J.R., Steiner, J.E., & Daher, M. (1983). Neonatal facial expressions in response to different qualities and intensities of gustatory stimuli. *Infant Behavior and Development, 6,* 473–484.

Gardiner, H.W., Mutter, J.D., & Kosmitzki, C. (2002). *Lives across cultures: Cross-cultural human development* (2nd ed.). Boston: Allyn & Bacon.

Gardner, L.I. (1972). Deprivation dwarfism. *Scientific American, 227,* 76–82.

Garner, B.P. (1998). Play development from birth to age four. In D.P. Fromberg & D. Bergen (Eds.), *Play from birth to twelve and beyond: Contexts, perspectives, and meaning* (pp. 137–145). New York: Garland.

Garrison, M.M., & Christakis, D.A. (2005). *A teacher in the living room? Educational media for babies, toddlers and preschoolers.* Menlo Park, CA: The Henry J. Kaiser Family Foundation.

Gawande, A. (2004, Jan. 12). The mop-up: Eradicating polio from the planet, one child at a time. *The New Yorker,* pp. 34–40.

Geissbuhler, V., & Eberhard, J. (2000). Waterbirths: A comparative study. A prospective study on more than 2,000 waterbirths. *Fetal Diagnosis and Therapy, 15,* 291–300.

Geissbuhler, V., & Eberhard, J. (2005). Experience of pain and analgesia with

water and land births. *Journal of Psychosomatic Obstetrics and Gynaecology, 26,* 127–133.

Geissbuhler, V., Stein, S., & Eberhard, J. (2004). Waterbirths compared with landbirths: An observational study of nine years. *Journal of Perinatal Medicine, 32,* 308–314.

Gelman, S.A., & Kalish, C.W. (2006). Conceptual development. In W. Damon & R. Lerner (Eds.) & D. Kuhn & R. Siegler (Vol. Eds.), *Handbook of child psychology: Vol. 2. Cognition, perception, and language* (6th ed., pp. 687–733). New York: Wiley.

Gelman, S.A., & Taylor, M. (1984). How two-year-old children interpret proper and common names for unfamiliar objects. *Child Development, 55,* 1535–1540.

Gentner, D. (1982). Why nouns are learned before verbs: Linguistic relativity versus natural partitioning. In S. Kuczaj (Ed.), *Language development: Language, cognition and culture* (pp. 301–334). Hillsdale, NJ: Erlbaum.

George, V.K., Li, H., Teloken, C., Grignon, D.J., Lawrence, W.D., & Dhabuwala, C.B. (1996). Effects of long-term cocaine exposure on spermatogenesis and fertility in peripubertal male rats. *Journal of Urology, 155,* 327–331.

Gesell, A. (1946). The ontogenesis of infant behavior. In L. Carmichael (Ed.), *Manual of child psychology.* New York: Wiley.

Gesell, A. (1954). The ontogenesis of infant behavior. In L. Carmichael (Ed.), *Manual of child psychology* (2nd ed.). New York: Wiley.

Getting the Most out of Watching Television with Your Toddler. (2002). Retrieved November 18, 2002, from http://pbskids/org/barney/pareduc/ parents/philosophy.html

Gianino, A., & Tronick, E.Z. (1988). The mutual regulation model: The infant's self and interactive regulation and coping defensive capacities. In T.M. Field, P.M. McCabe, & N. Schneiderman (Eds.), *Stress and coping across development* (pp. 47–68). Hillsdale, NJ: Erlbaum.

Giannarelli, L., & Barsimantov, J. (2000). Child care expenses of America's families. *Assessing the New Federalism*. Washington, DC: Urban Institute. Retrieved August 15, 2005, from http://www.urban.org/url.cfm?ID=310028

Gibson, E.J. (1969). *Principles of perceptual learning and development*. New York: Appleton-Century-Crofts.

Gibson, E.J. (1984). Perceptual development from an ecological approach. In M. Lamb, A. Brown, & B. Rogoff (Eds.), *Advances in developmental psychology* (Vol. 3, pp. 243–285). Hillsdale, NJ: Erlbaum.

Gibson, E.J., & Walk, R.D. (1960). The visual cliff. *Scientific American, 202,* 64–71.

Gibson, E.J., & Walker, A.S. (1984). Development of knowledge of visual-tactual affordances of substance. *Child Development, 55,* 453–460.

Gibson, E.J., Riccio, G., Schmuckler, M.A., Stoffregen, T.A., Rosenberg, D., & Taormina, J. (1987). Detection of the traversability of surfaces by crawling and walking infants. *Journal of Experimental Psychology: Human Perception and Performance, 13,* 533–544.

Gibson, J.J. (1966). *The senses considered as perceptual systems*. Boston: Houghton Mifflin.

Gibson, J.J. (1979). *The ecological approach to visual perception*. Boston: Houghton Mifflin.

Gilbert, R. (2002). Water birth: a near-drowning experience. *Pediatrics, 110,* 409.

Gilbert, R., & Tookey, P. (1999). Perinatal mortality and morbidity among babies delivered in water: Surveillance study and postal survey. *BMJ, 319,* 483–487.

Gilbert, S.F. (2000). *Developmental biology* (6th ed.). Sunderland, MA: Sinauer Associates.

Gill, J.H. (2002). *Native American worldviews: An introduction*. Amherst, NY: Humanity Books.

Gleitman, L. (1990). The structural sources of verb meanings. *Language Acquisition, 1,* 3–55.

Gohlke B.D., Khadilkar, V.V., Skuse, D.H., & Stanhope, R. (1998). Recognition of children with psychosocial short stature. *Journal of Pediatric Endocrinology and Metabolism, 11,* 509–517.

Gold, S.J. (1999). Continuity and change among Vietnamese families. In H.P. McAdoo (Ed.), *Family ethnicity: Strength in diversity* (2nd ed., pp. 225–234). Thousand Oaks, CA: Sage.

Goldberg, J., & Falcone, T. (1999). Effect of diethylstilbestrol on reproductive function. *Fertility & Sterility, 72,* 1–7.

Goldberg, J., Holtz, D., Hyslop, T., & Tolosa, J.E. (2002). Has the use of routine episiotomy decreased? Examination of episiotomy rates from 1983 to 2000. *Obstetrics & Gynecology, 99,* 395–400.

Goldenberg, R.L., & Jobe, A.H. (2001). Prospects for research in reproductive health and birth outcomes. *JAMA, 285,* 633–639.

Goldfield, B. (1987). The contributions of child and caregiver to referential and expressive language. *Applied Psycholinguistics, 8,* 267–280.

Goldfield, B.A. (1993). Noun bias in maternal speech to one-year-olds. *Journal of Child Language, 20,* 85–99.

Goldfield, B.A., & Reznick, J.S. (1990). Early lexical acquisition: Rate, content and the vocabulary spurt. *Journal of Child Language, 17,* 171–183.

Goldin-Meadow, S. (2000). Beyond words: The importance of gesture to researchers and learners. *Child Development, 71,* 231–239.

Goldin-Meadow, S. (2006). Nonverbal communication: The hand's role in talking and thinking. In W. Damon & R. Lerner (Eds.) & D. Kuhn & R. Siegler (Vol. Eds.), *Handbook of child psychology: Vol. 2. Cognition, perception, and language* (6th ed., pp. 336–369). New York: Wiley.

Goldin-Meadow, S., & Mylander, C. (1983). Gestural communication in deaf children: Noneffect of parental input on language development. *Science, 221,* 372–374.

Goldin-Meadow, S., & Mylander, C. (1984). Gestural communication in deaf children: The effects and non-effects of parental input on early language devel-

opment. *Monographs of the Society for Research in Child Development, 49,* (3–4, Serial No. 207).

Goldin-Meadow, S., & Mylander, C. (1998). Spontaneous sign systems created by deaf children in two cultures. *Nature, 391,* 279–281.

Goldin-Meadow, S., Gelman, S.A., & Mylander, C. (2005). Expressing generic concepts with and without a language model. *Cognition, 96,* 109–126.

Goldman, L., Falk, H., Landrigan, P.J., Balk, S.J., Reigart, J.R., & Etzel, R.A. (2004). Environmental pediatrics and its impact on government health policy. *Pediatrics, 113,* 1146–1157.

Goldsmith, H.H. (1996). Studying temperament via construction of the Toddler Behavior Assessment Questionnaire. *Child Development, 67,* 218–235.

Goldsmith, H.H., & Campos, J.J. (1990). The structure of infant temperamental dispositions to experience fear and pleasure: A psychometric perspective. *Child Development, 61,* 1944–1964.

Goldsmith, H.H., & Davidson, R.J. (2004). Disambiguating the components of emotion regulation. *Child Development, 75,* 361–365.

Goldsmith, H.H., Buss, A.H., Plomin, R., Rothbart, M.K., Thomas, A., Chess, S., Hinde, R.A., McCall, R.B. (1987). Roundtable: What is temperament? Four approaches. *Child Development, 58,* 505–529.

Golinkoff, R.M., Hirsh-Pasek, K., Bailey, L.M., & Wenger, N.R. (1992). Young children and adults use lexical principles to learn new nouns. *Developmental Psychology, 28,* 99–108.

Golinkoff, R.M., Hirsh-Pasek,K., Cauley, K.M., & Gordon, L. (1987). The eyes have it: Lexical and syntactic comprehension in a new paradigm. *Journal of Child Language, 14,* 23–45.

Golinkoff, R.M., Shuff-Bailey, M., Olguin, R., & Ruan, W. (1995). Young children extend novel words at the basic level: Evidence for the principle of categorical scope. *Developmental Psychology, 31,* 494–507.

Golinkoff, R.M., Hirsh-Pasek, K., Mervis, C.B., Frawley, W.B., & Parillo, M. (1995). Lexical principles can be extended to the acquisition of verbs. In M. Tomasello & W. Merriman (Eds.), *Beyond names for things: Children's acquisition of verbs* (pp. 185–221). Hillsdale, NJ: Erlbaum.

Gonzalez, E., Fekany-Lee, K., Carmany-Rampey, A., Erter, C., Topczewski, J., Wright, C.V.E., & Solnica-Krezel, L. (2000). Head and trunk in zebrafish arise via coinhibition of BMP signaling by *bozozok* and *chordino*. *Genes & Development, 14,* 3087–3092.

Goodluck, C.T. (1999). Necessary social work roles and knowledge with Native American: Indian Child Welfare Act. In McAdoo, H.P. (Ed.), *Family ethnicity: Strength in diversity* (2nd ed., pp. 293–300). Thousand Oaks, CA: Sage.

Goodman, S.H., & Gotlib, I.H. (1999). Risk for psychopathology in the children of depressed mothers: A developmental model for understanding mechanisms of transmission. *Psychological Review, 106,* 458–490.

Goodwyn, S.W., & Acredolo, L.P. (1998). Encouraging symbolic gestures: A new perspective on the relationship between gesture and speech. In J. M. Iverson & S. Goldin-Meadow (Eds.), *The nature and functions of gesture in children's communication* (pp. 61–73). San Francisco: Jossey-Bass.

Goodwyn, S.W., Acredolo, L.P., & Brown, C.A. (2000). Impact of symbolic gesturing on early language development. *Journal of Nonverbal Behavior, 24,* 81–103.

Gormley, W.T., Jr., Gayer, T., Phillips, D., & Dawson, B. (2005). The effects of universal pre-K on cognitive development. *Developmental Psychology, 41,* 872–884.

Gottesman, I.I. (2001). Psychopathology through a life span-genetic prism. *American Psychologist, 56,* 867–878.

Gottlieb, A. (2000). Luring your child into this life: A Beng path for infant care. In J. DeLoache & A. Gottlieb (Eds.), *A world of babies: Imagined childcare guides for seven societies* (pp. 55–89). New York: Cambridge University Press.

Gottlieb, L.N., & Mendelson, M.J. (1990). Parental support and firstborn girls' adaptation to the birth of a sibling. *Journal of Applied Developmental Psychology, 11,* 29–48.

Goubet, N., & Clifton, R.K. (1998). Object and event representation in 6 1/2-month-old infants. *Developmental Psychology, 34,* 63–76.

Grab, D., Paulus, W.E., Bommer, A., Buck, G., & Terinde, R. (1999). Treatment of fetal erythroblastosis by intravascular transfusions: Outcome at 6 years. *Obstetrics and Gynecology, 93,* 165–168.

Gralinski, J.H., & Kopp, C.B. (1993). Everyday rules for behavior: Mothers' requests to young children. *Developmental Psychology, 29,* 573–584.

Grammatopoulos, D.K., & Hillhouse, E.W. (1999). Role of corticotropin-releasing hormone in onset of labour. *Lancet, 354,* 1546–1549.

Grandjean, H., Larroque, D., & Levi, S. (1999). The performance of routine ultrasonic screening of pregnancies in the Eurofetus study. *American Journal of Obstetrics and Gynecology, 181,* 446–454.

Grandjean, P., Weihe, P., White, R.F., Debes, F., Araki, S., Yokoyama, K., et al. (1997). Cognitive deficit in 7-year-old children with prenatal exposure to methylmercury. *Neurotoxicology and Teratology, 19,* 417–428.

Granrud, C.E., Yonas, A., Smith, I.M., Arterberry, M.E., Blicksman, M.L., & Sorknes, A.C. (1984). Infants' sensitivity to accretion and deletion of texture as information for depth at an edge. *Child Development, 55,* 1630–1636.

Gray, L., Watt, L. & Blass, E. (2000). Skin-to-skin contact is analgesic in healthy newborns. *Pediatrics, 105,* 1–6.

Groark, C.J., McCall, R.B., Muhamedrahimov, R.J., Nikiforova, N.V., & Palmov, O.I. (2003). *The effects of improving caregiving on early development.* Pittsburgh, PA: Office of Child Development, University of Pittsburgh.

Groark, C.J., McCall, R.B., Muhamedrahimov, R.J., Nikiforova, N.V., Palmov, O.I., & Fish, L. (2005). The developmental consequences of improvements in social-emotional environments in St. Petersburg (Russia) orphanages. Paper presented at the Biennial Meeting of the Society for Research in Child Development, Atlanta, GA.

Gromko, J.E., & Poorman, A.S. (1998). The effect of music training on preschoolers' spatial-temporal task performance. *Journal of Research in Music Education, 46,* 173–181.

Gross, R.T., Spiker, D., Haynes, C.W. (Eds.). (1997). *Helping low birth weight, premature babies: The Infant Health and Development Program.* Stanford, CA: Stanford University Press.

Grossmann, K.E., Grossmann, K., & Zimmermann, P. (1999). A wider view of attachment and exploration: Stability and change during the years of immaturity. In J. Cassidy & P.R. Shaver (Eds.), *Handbook of attachment: Theory, research, and clinical applications* (pp. 760–787). New York: Guilford Press.

Guesry, P. (1998). The role of nutrition in brain development. *Preventive Medicine, 27,* 189–194.

Guise, J., Palda, V., Westhoff, C., Chan, B.K.S., Helfand, M., & Lieu, T.A. (2003). The effectiveness of primary care-based interventions to promote breastfeeding: Systematic evidence review and meta-analysis for the U.S. Preventive Services Task Force. *Annals of Family Medicine, 1,* 70–80.

Gunderson, V.M., Yonas, A., Sargent, P.L., & Grant-Webster, K.S. (1993). Infant macaque monkeys respond to pictorial depth. *Psychological Science, 4,* 93–98.

Gunnar, M., & Van Dulman, M. (Fall, 2003). Are behavior problems tied to early life experiences? *International Adoption News,* pp. 1, 6.

Gunnar, M.R. (1994). Psychoendocrine studies of temperament and stress in early childhood: Expanding current models. In J.E. Bates & T.D. Wachs (Eds.), *Temperament, individual differences at the interface of biology and behavior* (pp. 175–198). Washington, DC: American Psychological Association Press.

Gunnar, M.R. (2000). Early adversity and the development of stress reactivity and regulation. In C. Nelson (Ed.), *Minnesota Symposium on Child Psychology: Vol. 31. The effects of adversity on neurobehavioral development* (pp. 163–200). Mahwah, NJ: Erlbaum.

Gunnar, M.R., Malone, S., & Fisch, R.O. (1985). The psychology of stress and coping in the human neonate: Studies of adrenocortical activity in response to aversive stimulation. In T.M. Field, P.M. McCabe, & N. Schneiderman (Eds.), *Stress and coping* (pp. 179–196). Hillsdale, NJ: Erlbaum.

Gunnar, M.R., Mangelsdorf, S., Larson, M.C., & Hertsgaard, L. (1989). Attachment, temperament, and adrenocortical activity in infancy: A study of psychoendocrine regulation. *Developmental Psychology, 25,* 355–363.

Gunnar, M.R., Larson, M., Hertsgaard, L., Harris, M., & Broderson, L. (1992). The stressfulness of separation among 9-month-old infants: Effects of social context variable and infant temperament. *Child Development, 63,* 290–303.

Hack, M., Klein, N.K., & Taylor, H.G. (1995). Long-term developmental outcomes of low birth weight infants. *The Future of Children: Low Birth Weight, 5(1),* 19–34. Los Altos, CA: Center for the Future of Children. The David and Lucile Packard Foundation.

Hack, M., Breslau, N., Aram, D., Weissman, B., Klein, N., & Borawski-Clark, E. (1992). The effect of very low birth weight and social risk on neurocognitive abilities at school age. *Journal of Developmental and Behavioral Pediatrics, 13,* 412–420.

Haddow, J.E., Palomaki, G.E., Allan, W.C., Williams, J.R., Knight, G.J., Gagnon, J., et al. (1999). Maternal thyroid deficiency during pregnancy and subsequent neuropsychological development of the child. *New England Journal of Medicine, 341,* 549–555.

Hadjikhani, N., Chabris, C.F., Joseph, R.M., Clark, J., McGrath, L., Aharon, I., et al. (2004). Early visual cortex organization in autism: An fMRI study. *Neuroreport: For Rapid Communication of Neuroscience Research, 15,* 267–270.

Haehl, V., Vardaxis, V., & Ulrich, B. (2000). Learning to cruise: Bernstein's theory applied to skill acquisition during infancy. *Human Movement Science, 19,* 685–715.

Hagekull, B. (1994). Infant temperament and early childhood functioning: Possible relations to the Five-Factor Model. In C.J. Halverson, Jr., G.A. Kohnstamm, & R.P. Martin (Eds.), *The developing structure of temperament and personality* (pp. 227–240). Hillsdale, NJ: Erlbaum.

Hagekull, B., & Bohlin, G. (2003). Early temperament and attachment as predictors of the Five Factor Model of personality. *Attachment & Human Development, 5,* 2–18.

Haith, M.M., & Benson, J.B. (1998). Infant cognition. In W. Damon (Editor-in-Chief), D. Kuhn, & R.S. Siegler (Vol. Eds.), *Handbook of child psychology: Vol. 2. Cognition, perception, and language* (5th ed., pp. 199–254). New York: Wiley.

Hakuta, K. (1986). *Mirror of language: The debate on bilingualism.* New York: Basic Books.

Hale, C.M., & Tager-Flusberg, H. (2005). Social communication with children with autism: The relationship between theory of mind and discourse development. *Autism, 9,* 157–178.

Halgunseth, L.C. (2004). Continuing research on Latino families: El pasado y el futuro. In M. Coleman & L.H. Ganong (Eds.), *Handbook of contemporary families: Considering the past, contemplating the future* (pp. 333–351). Thousand Oaks, CA: Sage.

Hall, D.G., & Waxman, S.R. (2004). *Weaving a lexicon.* Cambridge, MA: MIT Press.

Hall, D.G., Lee, S.C., & Belanger, J. (2001). Young children's use of syntactic cues to learn proper names and count nouns. *Developmental Psychology, 37,* 298–307.

Halpern, S.A. (1988). *American pediatrics: The social dynamics of professionalism, 1880–1980.* Berkeley, CA: University of California Press.

Halverson, H.M. (1931). An experimental study of prehension in infants by means of systematic cinema records. *Genetic Psychology Monographs, 10,* 107–286.

Halverson, H.M. (1932). A further study of grasping. *Journal of Genetic Psychology, 7,* 34–64.

Hamilton, B.E., Martin, J.A., Ventura, S.J., Sutton, P.D., & Menacker, F. (2005). Births: Preliminary data for 2004. *National Vital Statistics Reports, 54*(8). Hyattsville, MD: National Center for Health Statistics.

Hampson, J., & Nelson, K. (1993). The relation of maternal language to variation in rate and style of language acquisition. *Journal of Child Language, 20,* 313–342.

Hannah, M.E., Hannah, W.J., Hodnett, E.D., Chalmers, B., Kung, R., Willan, A., et al. (2002). Outcomes at 3 months after planned cesarean vs. planned vaginal delivery for breech presentation at term: The international randomized Term Breech Trial. *JAMA, 10;287(14),* 1822–1831

Hannah, M.E., Hannah, W.J., Hellmann, J., Hewson, S., Milner, R., & Willan, A. (1992). Induction of labor as compared with serial antenatal monitoring in post-term pregnancy. A randomized controlled trial. The Canadian Multicenter Post-term Pregnancy Trial Group. *New England Journal of Medicine, 326,* 1587–1592.

Hareven, T. (1985). Historical change in the family and the life course: Implications for child development. In Smuts, A.B., & Hagen, J.W. (Eds.), History and research in child development. *Monographs of the Society for Research in Child Development, 50* (4–5, Serial No. 211), 8–23.

Hareven, T. K. (2000). *Families, history, and social change.* Boulder, CO: Westview Press.

Harjo, S.S. (1999). The American Indian experience. In H.P. McAdoo (Ed.), *Family ethnicity: Strength in diversity* (2nd ed., pp. 63–71). Thousand Oaks, CA: Sage.

Harms, T., Clifford, R.M., & Cryer, D. (1998). *Early Childhood Environment Rating Scale—Revised (ECERS-R).* New York: Teachers College Press.

Harms, T., Cryer, D., & Clifford, R.M. (1990). *Infant/Toddler Environment*

Rating Scale. New York, NY: Teachers College Press.

Harris, B. (1979). Whatever happened to little Albert? *American Psychologist, 34,* 151–160.

Harris, G. (1997). Development of taste perception and appetite regulation. In G. Bremner, A. Slater, & G. Butterworth (Eds.), *Infant development: Recent advances* (pp. 9–30). East Sussex, UK: Psychology Press.

Harris, G., Thomas, A., & Booth, D.A. (1990). Development of salt taste in infancy. *Developmental Psychology, 26,* 534–538.

Harris, L.J. (1985). James Mark Baldwin on the origins of right- and left-handedness: the story of an experiment that mattered. In Smuts, A.B., & Hagen, J.W. (Eds.), History and research in child development. *Monographs of the Society for Research in Child Development, 50*(4–5, Serial No. 211), 44–64.

Harris, P.L., & Kavanaugh, R.D. (1993). Young children's understanding of pretense. *Monographs of the Society for Research in Child Development, 58* (1, Serial No. 231).

Harrison, M.R., Keller, R.I., Hawgood, S.B., Kitterman, J.A., Sandberg, P.L., Farmer, D.L., et al. (2003). A randomized trial of fetal endoscopic tracheal occlusion for severe fetal congenital diaphragmatic hernia. *New England Journal of Medicine, 349,* 1916–1924.

Harrist, A.W., & Waugh, R.M. (2002). Dyadic synchrony: Its structure and function in children's development. *Developmental Review, 11,* 555–592.

Hart, B., & Risley, T.R. (1995). *Meaningful differences in the everyday experience of young American children.* Baltimore: Paul H. Brookes Publishing.

Hart, B., & Risley, T.R. (1999). *The social world of children learning to talk.* Baltimore: Paul H. Brookes Publishing.

Harter, S. (1998). The development of self-representations. In W. Damon (Series Ed.) & N. Eisenberg (Vol. Ed.), *Handbook of child psychology: Vol. 3. Social, emotional, and person-*

ality development (5th ed., pp. 553–617). New York: Wiley.

Harter, S. (2006). The self. In W. Damon & R. Lerner (Eds.) & N. Eisenberg (Vol. Ed.), *Handbook of child psychology: Vol. 3. Social, emotional, and personality development* (6th ed., pp. 505–570). New York: Wiley.

Hartup, W.W. (1989). Social relationships and their developmental significance. *American Psychologist, 44,* 120–126.

Hartup, W.W. (1996). The company they keep: Friendships and their developmental significance. *Child Development, 67,* 1–13.

Harwood, R., Leyendecker, B., Carlson, V., Asencio, M., & Miller, A. (2002). Parenting among Latino families in the U.S. In M.H. Bornstein (Ed.), *Handbook of parenting: Vol. 4. Social conditions and applied parenting* (2nd ed., pp. 21–46). Mahwah, NJ: Erlbaum.

Harwood, R.L., Miller, J.G., & Irizarry, N.L. (1995). *Culture and attachment.* New York: Guilford Press.

Harwood, R.L., Schöelmerich, A., Schulze, P.A., & Gonzalez, Z. (1999). Cultural differences in maternal beliefs and behaviors: A study of middle-class Anglo and Puerto Rican mother-infant pairs in four everyday situations. *Child Development, 70,* 1005–1016.

Harwood, R.L., Schöelmerich, A., Ventura-Cook, E., Schulze, P.A., & Wilson, S.P. (1996). Culture and class influences on Anglo and Puerto Rican mothers' beliefs regarding long-term socialization goals and child behavior. *Child Development, 67,* 2446–2461.

Hastings, P.D., & Rubin, K.H. (1999). Predicting mothers' beliefs about preschool-aged children's social behavior: Evidence for maternal attitudes moderating child effects. *Child Development, 70,* 722–741.

Hatchett, S.J., & Jackson, J.S. (1999). African American extended kin systems: An empirical assessment in the National Survey of Black Americans. In H.P. McAdoo (Ed.), *Family ethnicity: Strength in diversity* (2nd ed., (pp. 171–190). Thousand Oaks, CA: Sage.

Hattori, M., Fujiyama, A., Taylor, T.D., Watanabe, H., Yada, T., Park, H.S., et al. (2000). The DNA sequence of human chromosome 21. *Nature, 405,* 311–319.

Hauck, F.R., Omojokun, O.O., & Siadaty, M.S. (2005). Do pacifiers reduce the risk of sudden infant death syndrome? A meta-analysis. *Pediatrics, 116,* e716–e723.

Hauck, F.R. Moore, C.M., Herman, S.M., Donovan, M., Kalelkar, M., Christoffel, K.K., et al. (2002). The contribution of prone sleeping to the racial disparity in sudden infant death syndrome: The Chicago Infant Mortality Study. *Pediatrics, 110,* 772–780.

Hauser, M.D., Newport, E.L., & Aslin, R.N. (2001). Segmentation of the speech stream in a nonhuman primate: Statistical learning in cotton-top tamarins. *Cognition, 78,* B53–B64.

Hausman, B.L. (2005). Risky business:Framing childbirth in hospital settings. *Journal of Medicine and Humanities, 26,* 23–38.

Haviland, J.M., & Lelwica, M. (1987). The induced affect response: 10-week-old infants' responses to three emotional expressions. *Developmental Psychology, 23,* 97–104.

Hawes, J.M., & Hiner, N.R. (Eds.). (1985). *American childhood: A research guide and historical handbook.* Westport, CT: Greenwood Press.

Hay, D.F., Pawlby, S., Angold, A., Harold, G.T., & Sharp, D. (2003). Pathways to violence in the children of mothers who were depressed postpartum. *Developmental Psychology, 39,* 1083–1094.

Hayne, H., Barr, R., & Herbert, J. (2003). The effect of prior practice on memory reactivation and generalization. *Child Development, 74,* 1615–1627.

Hediger, M.L., Overpeck, M.D., Ruan, W.J., & Troendle, J.F. (2002). Birthweight and gestational age effects on motor and social development. *Paediatric and Perinatal Epidemiology, 16,* 33–46.

Hedrick, D., Prather, E., & Tobin, A. (1984). *The Sequenced Inventory of Communication Development.* Seattle: University of Washington Press.

Heibeck, T.H., & Markman, E.M. (1987). Word learning in children: An examination of fast mapping. *Child Development, 58,* 1021–1034.

Heikkila, M., Peltoketo, H., & Vainio, S. (2001). Wnts and the female reproductive system. *Journal of Experimental Zoology, 290,* 616–623.

Helburn, S.W., & Howes, C. (1996). Child care cost and quality. *The Future of Children, 6*(2), 62–82.

Held, R., Birch, E.E., & Gwiazda, J. (1980). Stereoacuity of human infants. *Proceedings of the National Academy of Sciences, 77,* 5572–5574.

Helfand, W. H., Lazarus, J., & Theerman, P. (2001). ". . . So that others may walk": The March of Dimes. *American Journal of Public Health, 91*(8), 1190.

Hepper, P.G. (1991). An example of fetal learning before and after birth. *Irish Journal of Psychology, 12,* 95–107.

Hernandez, D.J. (1997). Child development and the social demography of childhood. *Child Development, 68,* 149–169.

Herrera, C., & Dunn, J. (1997). Early experiences with family conflict: Implications for arguments with a close friend. *Developmental Psychology, 33,* 869–881.

Hertsgaard, L., Gunnar, M., Erickson, M.F., & Nachmias, M. (1995). Adrenocortical responses to the strange situation in infants with disorganized/disoriented attachment relationships. *Child Development, 66,* 1100–1106.

Hetland, L. (2000). Learning to make music enhances spatial reasoning. *Journal of Aestheetic Education, 34,* 179–238.

Hetzel, B. S. (1999). Iodine deficiency and fetal brain damage. *New England Journal of Medicine, 331(26),* 1770–1771.

Hewlett, B.S. (1987). Intimate fathers: Patterns of paternal holding among Aka pygmies. In M.E. Lamb (Ed.), *The father's role: Cross-cultural perspectives* (pp. 295–330). Hillsdale, NJ: Erlbaum.

Hewlett, B.S. (2004). Fathers in forager, farmer, and pastoral cutlures. In M.E. Lamb (Ed.), *The role of the father in child development* (4th ed., pp. 182–195). New York: Wiley.

Hewlett, B.S., Lamb, M.E., Shannon, D., Leyendecker, B., & Schölmerich, A. (1998). Culture and early infancy among central African foragers and farmers. *Developmental Psychology, 34,* 653–661.

Hiatt, S., Campos, J.J., & Emde, R.N. (1979). Facial patterning and infant emotional expression: Happiness, surprise and fear. *Child Development, 50,* 1020–1035.

Hildyard, K.L., & Wolfe, D.A. (2002). Child neglect: Developmental issues and outcomes. *Child Abuse and Neglect, 26,* 679–695.

Hill, J.A. (1998). Miscarriage risk factors and causes: What we know now. *OBG Management, 10,* 58–68.

Hill, N.E., Bush, K.R., & Roosa, M.W. (2003). Parenting and family socialization strategies and children's mental health: Low-income Mexican-American and Euro-American mothers and children. *Child Development, 74,* 189–204.

Hinds, T.S., West, W.L., Knight, E.M., & Harland, B.F. (1996). The effect of caffeine on pregnancy outcome variables. *Nutrition Reviews, 54,* 203–207.

Hirsh-Pasek, K., & Golinkoff, R. (1991). Language comprehension: A new look at some old themes. In N. Krasnegor, D. Rumbaugh, R. Schieffelbusch, & M. Studdert-Kennedy (Eds.), *Biological and behavioral determinants of language development* (pp. 301–320). Hillsdale, NJ: Erlbaum.

Hirsh-Pasek, K., & Golinkoff, R. (1996). *The origins of grammar: Evidence from early language comprehension.* Cambridge, MA: MIT Press.

Hirsh-Pasek, K., Trieman, R., & Schneiderman, M. (1984). Brown and Hanlon revisited: Mothers' sensitivity to ungrammatical forms. *Journal of Child Language, 11,* 81–88.

Ho, D.Y.F. (1987). Fatherhood in Chinese culture. In M.E. Lamb (Ed.), *The father's role: Cross-cultural perspectives* (pp. 227–245). Hillsdale, NJ: Erlbaum.

Hodges, C.A., Ilagan, A., Jennings, D., Keri, R., Nilson, J., & Hunt, P.A. (2002). Experimental evidence that changes in oocyte growth influence meiotic chromosome segregation. *Human Reproduction, 17,* 1171–1180.

Hodnett, E.D. (2001). Home-like versus conventional institutional settings for birth. *Cochrane Database Syst Review, 4,* CD000012.

Hodnett, E.D., Lowe, N.K., Hannah, M.E., Willan, A.R., Stevens, B., Weston, J.A., Ohlsson, A., Gafni, A., Muir, H.A., Myhr, T.L., & Stremler, R. (2002). Effectiveness of nurses as providers of birth labor support in North American hospitals. *JAMA, 288,* 1373–1381.

Hoff, E., (2003). The specificity of environmental influence: Socioeconomic status affects early vocabulary development via maternal speech. *Child Development, 74,* 1368–1378.

Hofferth, S.L. (1991). *National Child Care Survey, 1990.* Washington, DC: The Urban Institute.

Hofferth, S.L., & Curtin, S.C. (2003). The impact of parental leave on maternal return to work after childbirth in the United States. *OECD Social, Employment and Migration Working Papers No. 7,* 1–26.

Hofferth, S.L., Brayfield, A., Deich, S., & Holcomb, P. (1991). *National Child Care Survey 1990.* Washington, DC: The Urban Institute.

Hoff-Ginsberg, E. (1997). *Language development.* Pacific Grove, CA: Brooks/Cole.

Hofmeyr, G.J. (2002). Interventions to help external cephalic version for breech presentation at term. *Cochrane Database of Systematic Reviews, 2,* CD000184.

Hollich, G.J., Hirsh-Pasek, K., & Golinkoff, R.M. (2000). Breaking the language barrier: An emergentist coalition model for the origins of word learning. *Monographs of the Society for Research in Child Development, Serial No. 262, 65(3).*

Holowka, S., & Petitto, L.A. (2002). Left hemisphere cerebral specialization for babies while babbling. *Science, 297,* 1515.

Holowka, S., Brosseau-Lapré, F., & Petitto, L.A. (2002). Semantic and conceptual knowledge underlying bilingual babies' first signs and words. *Language Learning, 52,* 205–262.

Holzman, C., Bullen, B., Fisher, R., Paneth, N., & Reuss, L. (2001). Pregnancy outcomes land community health: the POUCH study of preterm delivery. *Paediatric and Perinatal Epidemiology, 15(Suppl 2),* 136–158.

Homer, C., Davis, G., Petocz, P., Barclay, L., Matha, D., & Chapman, M. (2000). Birth centre or labour ward? A comparison of the clinical outcomes of low-risk women in a NSW hospital. *Australian Journal of Advanced Nursing, 18,* 8–12.

Homer, C.S., Davis, G.K., Cooke, M., & Barclay, L.M. (2002). Women's experiences of continuity of midwifery care in a randomised controlled trial in Australia. *Midwifery, 18,* 102–112.

Honein, M.A., Paulozzi, L.J., Mathews, T.J., Erickson, J.D., & Wong, L.C. (2001). Impact of folic acid fortification of the US food supply on the occurrence of neural tube defects. *JAMA, 285,* 2981–2986.

Honig, A.S. (2002). Research on quality in infant-toddler programs. EDO-PS-02-19. Champaign, IL: Clearinghouse on Elementary and Early Childhood Education.

Hood, B., & Willatts, P. (1986). Reaching in the dark to an object's remembered position: Evidence for object permanence in 5-month-old infants. *British Journal of Developmental Psychology, 4,* 57–65.

Hood, B., Cole-Davies, V., & Dias, M. (2003). Looking and search measures of object knowledge in preschool children. *Developmental Psychology, 39,* 61–70.

Hopkins, B., & Rönnqvist, L. (2002). Facilitating postural control: Effects on the reaching behavior of 6-month-old infants. *Developmental Psychobiology, 40,* 168–182.

Hopkins, B., & Westra, T. (1990). Motor development, maternal expectations and the role of handling. *Infant Behavior and Development, 13,* 117–122.

Horbar, J.D., & Lucey, J.F. (1995). Evaluation of neonatal intensive care technologies. *The Future of Children: Low Birth Weight, 5(1),* 139–161. Los Al-

tos, CA: Center for the Future of Children, The David and Lucile Packard Foundation.

Hornik, R., Risenhoover, N., & Gunnar, M. (1987). The effects of maternal positive, neutral, and negative affective communications on infant responses to new toys. *Child Development, 58,* 937–944.

Horst, J.S., Oakes, L.M., & Madole, K.L. (2005). What does it look like and what can it do? Category structure influences how infants categorize. *Child Development, 76,* 614–631.

Hossain, Z., & Roopnarine, J.L. (1994). African-American fathers' involvement with infants: Relationship to their functional style, support, education, and income. *Infant Behavior and Development, 17,* 175–184.

Hossain, Z., Field, T., Pickens, J., Gonzalez, A., Malphurs, J., & DelValle, C. (1994). Infants of depressed mothers interact better with their nondepressed fathers. *Infant Mental Health Journal, 15,* 348–357.

Howe, C.M. (Spring 1998). Teething: The El Nino of childhood. *Not For Kids Only, 1*(2), p. 1.

Howe, N., & Ross, H.S. (1990). Socialization, perspective-taking, and sibling relationship. *Developmental Psychology, 26,* 160–165.

Howes, C. (1983). Patterns of friendship. *Child Development, 54,* 1041–1053.

Howes, C. (1985). Sharing fantasy: Social pretend play in toddlers. *Child Development 56,* 1253–1258.

Howes, C. (1988). Peer interaction of young children. *Monographs of the Society for Research in Child Development, 53*(1, Serial No. 217).

Howes, C. (1996). The earliest friendships. In W.M. Bukowski, A.F., Newcomb, & W.W. Hartup (Eds.), *The company they keep: Friendship in childhood and adolescence* (pp. 66–86). Boston: Cambridge University Press.

Howes, C. (1999). Attachment relationships in the context of multiple caregivers. In J. Cassidy & P.R. Shaver (Eds.), *Handbook of attachment theory and research* (pp. 671–687). New York: Guilford Press.

Howes, C., & Farver, J. (1987). Toddlers' responses to the distress of their peers. *Journal of Applied Developmental Psychology, 8,* 441–452.

Howes, C., & Matheson, C.C. (1992). Sequences in the development of competent play with peers: Social and social pretend play. *Developmental Psychology, 28,* 961–974.

Howes, C., & Unger, O.A. (1989). Play with peers in child care settings. In M.Bloch & A. Pellegrini (Eds.), *The ecological contexts of children's play* (pp. 104–119). Norwood, NJ: Ablex.

Howse, J.L. (2001). March of Dimes commitment to solving the problem of prematurity. *Paediatric and Perinatal Epidemiology, 15*(Suppl 2), 1–2.

Hsu, H.-C., & Fogel, A. (2003a). Social regulatory effects of infant nondistress vocalization on maternal behavior. *Developmental Psychology, 39,* 976–991.

Hsu, H.-C., & Fogel, A. (2003b). Stability and transitions in mother-infant face-to-face communication during the first 6 months: A microhistorical approach. *Developmental Psychology, 39,* 1061–1082.

Hubbs-Tait, L., Nation, J.R., Krebs, N.F., & Bellinger, D.C. (2005). Neurotoxicants, micronutrients, and social environments: Individual and combined effects on children's development. *Psychological Science in the Public Interest, 6,* 57–121.

Hubert, N.C., Wachs, T.D., Peters-Martin, P., & Gandour, M.J. (1982). The study of early temperament: Measurement and conceptual issues. *Child Development, 53,* 571–600.

Huizink, A., Mulder, E., & Buitelaar, J. (2004). Prenatal stress and risk for psychopathology: Specific effects or induction of general susceptibility? *Psychological Bulletin, 130,* 115–142.

Huizink, A., Robles de Medina, P., Mulder, E., Visser, G., & Buitelaar, J. (2002). Psychological measures of prenatal stress as predictors of infant temperament. *Journal of the American Academy of Chlid & Adolescent Psychiatry, 41,* 1078–1085.

Hulbert, A. (Winter 1999). The century of the child. *Wilson Quarterly, 23*(1), 14–29.

Hulbert, A. (2003). *Raising America: Experts, parents, and a century of advice about children.* New York: Alfred A. Knopf.

Huston, A.C. (2005). Connecting the science of child development to public policy. *Social Policy Report, 19*(4), 1–19.

Huston, A.C., Wright, J.C., Marquis, J., & Green, S.B. (1999). How young children spend their time: Television and other activities. *Developmental Psychology, 35,* 912–925.

Huttenlocher, J. (1998). Language input and language growth. *Preventive Medicine, 27,* 195–199.

Huttenlocher, J., & Smiley, P. (1987). Early word meanings: The case of object names. *Cognitive Psychology, 19,* 63–89.

Huttenlocher, J., Levine, S., & Vevea, J. (1998). Environmental input and cognitive growth: JA study using time-period comparisons. *Child Development, 69,* 1012–1029.

Huttenlocher, J., Vasilyeva, M., Cymerman, E., & Levine, S. (2002). Language input at home and at school: Relation to child syntax. *Cognitive Psychology, 45,* 337–374.

Huttenlocher, J., Haight, W., Bryk, A., Seltzer, M., & Lyons, T. (1991). Early vocabulary growth: Relation to language input and gender. *Developmental Psychology, 27,* 236–248.

Hutton, E.K., Hannah, M.E., & Barrett, J. (2002). Use of external cephalic version for breech pregnancy and mode of delivery for breech and twin pregnancy: A survey of Canadian practitioners. *Journal of Obstetrics and Gynaecology Canada, 24,* 804–810.

Hwang, V., Shofer, F.S., Durbin, D.R., & Baren, J.M. (2003). Prevalence of traumatic injuries in drowning and near drowning in children and adolescents. *Archives of Pediatrics and Adolescent Medicine, 157,* 50–53.

Hyson, M.C., Hirsh–Pasek, K., & Rescorla, L. (1990). The classroom practices inventory: An observation instrument based on the NAEYC's guidelines for developmentally appropriate practices for 4- and 5-year old children. *Early Childhood Research Quarterly, 5,* 475–494.

Iams, J.D., Newman, R.B., Thom, E.A., Goldenberg, R.L., Mueller-Heubach, E., Moawas, A., et al. (2002). Frequency of uterine contractions and the risk of spontaneous preterm delivery. *New England Journal of Medicine, 346,* 250–255.

Ianzito, C. (2004, June 8). Parents who keep their children close. *Washington Post,* p. C10.

Ilari, B. (2004). Music cognition in infancy: Infants' preferences and long-term memory for complex music. *Dissertation Abstracts International Section A: Humanities and Social Sciences, 64*(12–A), 4262.

Ilari, B. (2005). On musical parenting of young children: Musical beliefs and behaviors of mothers and infants. *Early Child Development and Care, 175,* 647–660.

Ilari, B., & Polka, L. (2006). Music cognition in early infancy: infants' preferences and long-term memory for Ravel. *International Journal of Music Education, 24,* 7–20.

Ilari, B.S. (2002). Music perception and cognition in the first year of life. *Early Child Development and Care, 172,* 311–322.

Imai, M., & Gentner, D. (1997). A crosslinguistic study of early word meaning: Universal ontology and linguistic influence. *Cognition, 62,* 169–200.

Immigration and Naturalization Service. (1998). *Immigrant orphans admitted to the United States by country of origin or region of birth 1989–1998.* Washington, DC: U.S. Department of Justice.

Ingersoll, E.W., Thoman, E.B. (1999). Sleep/wake states of preterm infants: Stability, developmental change, diurnal variation, and relation with caregiving activity. *Child Development, 70,* 1–10.

Institute of Medicine Immunization Safety Review Committee. (2004). *Immunization safety review: Vaccines and autism.* Washington, DC: National Academies Press.

International Genome Sequencing Consortium. (2001). Initial sequencing and analysis of the human genome. *Nature, 409,* 860–921.

Ip, S., Chung, M., Kulig, J., O'Brien, R., Sege, R., Glicken, S., et al. (2004). An evidence-based review of important issues concerning neonatal hyperbilirubinemia. *Pediatrics, 113,* 130–153.

Ireton, H., & Thwing, E. (1974). *The Minnesota Child Development Inventory.* Minneapolis: Behavior Science Systems.

Isabella, R.A., & Belsky, J. (1991). Interactional synchrony and the origins of infant-mother attachment: A replication study. *Child Development, 62,* 373–384.

Ispa, J.M.. Fine, M.A., Halgunseth, L.C., Harper, S., Robinson, J., Boyce, L., Brooks-Gunn, J., & Brady-Smith, C. (2004). Maternal intrusiveness, maternal warmth, and mother-toddler relationship outcomes: Variations across low-income ethnic and acculturation groups. *Child Development, 75,* 1613–1631.

Iverson, P., & Kuhl, P.K. (1995). Mapping the perceptual magnet effect for speech using signal detection theory and multidimensional scaling. *Journal of the Acoustical Society of America, 97,* 553–562.

Iverson, P., Kuhl, P.K., Akahane-Yamada, R., Diesch, E., Tohkura, Y., Kettermann, A., et al. (2003). A perceptual interference account of acquisition difficulties for non-native phonemes. *Cognition, 87,* B47–B57.

Iyasu, S., Randall, L.L., Welty, T.K., Hsia, J., Kinney, H.C., Mandell, F., McClain, M., Randall, B., Habbe, D., Wilson, H., & Willinger, M. (2002). Risk factors for sudden infant death syndrome among Northern Plains Indians. *JAMA, 288,* 2717–2723.

Izard, C.E. (1977). *Human Emotions.* New York: Plenum Press.

Izard, C.E. (1979). *The Maximally Discriminative Facial Movement Coding System (MAX).* Newark, DE:

Instructional Resources Center, University of Delaware.

Izard, C.E., & Malatesta, C.Z. (1987). Perspectives on emotional development: I. Differential emotions theory of emotional development. In J.D. Osofsky (Ed.), *Handbook of infant development* (2nd ed., pp. 494–554). New York: Wiley.

Izard, C.E., Hembree, E.A., & Huebner, R.R. (1987). Infants' emotion expressions to acute pain: Developmental change and stability of individual differences. *Developmental Psychology, 23,* 105–113.

Izard, C.E., Hembree, E.A., Dougherty, L.M., & Spizzirri, C. (1983). Changes in 2- to 19-month-old infants' responses to acute pain. *Developmental Psychology, 19,* 418–426.

Izard, C.E., Huebner, R., Risser, D., McGinnes, G., & Dougherty, L. (1980). The young infant's ability to produce discrete emotion expressions. *Developmental Psychology, 16,* 132–140.

Izard, C.E., Fantauzzo, C.A., Castle, J.M., Haynes, O.M., Rayias, M.F., & Putnam, P.H. (1995). The ontogeny and significance of infants' facial expressions in the first 9 months of life. *Developmental Psychology, 31,* 997–1013.

Jacobs, S., Sokol, J., & Ohlsson, A. (2002). The newborn individualized developmental care and assessment program is not supported by meta-analyses of the data. *Journal of Pediatrics, 140,* 699–706.

Jacobson, J.L., & Jacobson, S.W. (1996). Intellectual impairment in children exposed to poly-cholorinated biphenyls in utero. *New England Journal of Medicine, 335,* 783–789.

Jacobson, S.W., & Jacobson, J.L. (2000). Teratogenic insult and neurobehavioral function in infancy and childhood. In C.A. Nelson (Ed.), *The effects of early adversity on neurobehavioral development: The Minnesota Symposia on Child Psychology.* (Vol. 31, pp. 61–112). Mahwah, NJ: Erlbaum.

Jaffe, J., Beebe, B., Feldstein, S., Crown, C.L., & Jasnow, M.D. (2001).

Rhythms of dialogue in infancy. *Monographs of the Society for Research in Child Development, 66*(2, Serial No. 265).

Jahromi, L.B., Putnam, S.P., & Stifter, C.A. (2004). Maternal regulation of infant reactivity from 2 to 6 months. *Developmental Psychology, 40,* 477–487.

Jankowiak, W. (1992). Father-child relations in urban China. In B.S. Hewlett (Ed.), *Father-child relations: Cultural and biosocial contexts* (pp. 345–363). New York: Aldine de Gruyter.

Jankowski, J.J., Rose, S.A., & Feldman, J.F. (2001). Modifying the distribution of attention in infants. *Child Development, 72,* 339–351.

Janni, W., Schiessl, B., Peschers, U., Huber, S., Strobl, B., Hantschmann, P., et al. (2002). The prognostic impact of a prolonged second stage of labor on maternal and fetal outcome. *Acta Obstetricia et Gynecologica Scandinavica, 81,* 214–221.

Jedrychowski, W., Bendkowska, I., Flak, E., Penar, A., Jacek, R., Kaim, I., et al. (2004). Estimated risk for altered fetal growth resulting from exposure to fine particles during pregnancy: An epidemiologic prospective cohort study in Poland. *Environmental Health Perspectives, 112,* 1398–1402.

Ji, B.T., Shu, X.O., Linet, M.S., Zheng, W. Wacholder, S., Gao, Y.T., et al. (1997). Paternal cigarette smoking and the risk of childhood cancer among offspring of nonsmoking mothers. *Journal of the National Cancer Institute, 89,* 238–244.

Johanson, R.B., & Menon, B.K. (2000). Vacuum extraction versus forceps for assisted vaginal delivery. *Cochrane Database System Review, 2,* CD000224.

Johnson, D.E. (2000). Medical and developmental sequelae of early childhood institutionalization in Eastern European adoptees, In C.A. Nelson (Ed.), *Minnesota Symposium on Child Psychology: Vol. 31. The effects of adversity on neurobehavioral development* (pp. 113–162). Mahwah, NJ: Erlbaum.

Johnson, D.E., Miller, L.C., Iverson, S., Thomas, W., Franchino, B., Dole, K., et al. (1993). Post-placement catch-up growth in Romanian orphans with psychosocial short stature. *Pediatric Research, 33,* 89A.

Johnson, D.J., Jaeger, E., Randolph, S.M., Cauce, A.M., Ward, J., & National Institute of Child Health and Human Development Early Child Care Research Network. (2003). Studying the effects of early child care experiences on the development of children of color in the United States: Toward a more inclusive research agenda. *Child Development, 74,* 1227–1244.

Johnson, M.H. (1997a). Building a brain. In *Developmental cognitive neuroscience: An introduction* (pp. 23–67). London: Blackwell.

Johnson, M.H. (1998). The neural basis of cognitive development. In D. Kuhn & R.S. Siegler (Eds.), *Handbook of Child Psychology* (5th ed.): *Vol. 2. Cognition, perception, and language* (pp. 1–49). New York: Wiley.

Johnson, M.H. (2000). Functional brain development in infants: Elements of an interactive specialization framework. *Child Development, 71,* 75–81.

Johnson, M.H. (2001). Functional brain development in humans. *Nature Reviews Neuroscience, 2,* 475–483.

Johnson, M.H. (2005). Developmental neuroscience, psychophysiology, and genetics. In M.H. Bornstein, & M.E. Lamb (Eds.), *Developmental science: An advanced textbook* (pp. 187–222). Mahwah, NJ: Lawrence Erlbaum Associates.

Johnson, S.P. (1997b). Young infants' perception of object unity: Implications for development of attentional and cognitive skills. *Current Directions in Psychological Science, 6,* 5–11.

Johnson, S.P., & Aslin, R.N. (1995). Perception of object unity in 2-month-old infants. *Developmental Psychology, 31,* 739–745.

Johnson, S.P., & Aslin, R.N. (1996). Perception of object unity in young infants: The roles of motion, depth, and orientation. *Cognitive Development, 11*, 161–180.

Johnson, S.P., & Mason, U. (2002). Perception of kinetic illusory contours by two-month-old infants. *Child Development, 73*, 22–34.

Johnson, S.P., Bremner, J.G., Slater, A., Mason, U., Foster, K., & Cheshire, A. (2003). Infants' perception of object trajectories. *Child Development, 74*, 94–108.

Johnson-Green, E., & Custodero, L.A. (September, 2002). The toddler top 40: Musical preferences of babies, toddlers, and their parents. *Zero to Three, 25*, 47–48.

Johnston, R.B., Jr., Williams, M.A., Hogue, C.J., & Mattison, D.R. (2001). Overview: New perspectives on the stubborn challenge of preterm birth. *Paediatric and Perinatal Epidemiology, 15*(Suppl. 2) 3–6.

Johnston, S.L., & Openshaw, P.J.M. (2001). The protective effect of childhood infections. *BMJ, 322*, 376–377.

Jones, K.L., & Smith, D.W. (1973). Recognition of the fetal alcohol syndrome in early infancy. *Lancet, 2*, 999–1001.

Jones, N.A., Field, T., Fox, N.A., Lundy, B., & Davalos, M. (1997). EEG activation in one-month-old infants of depressed mothers. *Development and Psychopathology, 9*, 491–505.

Jones, S.S. (1996). Imitation or exploration? Young infants' matching of adults' oral gestures. *Child Development, 67*, 1952–1969.

Juffer, F., & Rosenboom, L.G. (1997). Infant-mother attachment of internationally adopted children in the Netherlands. *International Journal of Behavioral Development, 20*, 93–107.

Juffer, F., & van IJzendoorn, M.H. (2005). Behavior problems and mental health referrals of international adoptees: A meta-analysis. *JAMA, 293*, 2501–2515.

Jusczyk, P.W., & Hohne, E.A. (1997). Infants' memory for spoken words. *Science, 277*, 1984–1986.

Jusczyk, P.W., & Krumhansl, C.L. (1993). Pitch and rhythmic patterns affecting infants' sensitivity to musical phrase structure. *Journal of Experimental Psychology: Human Perception and Performance, 19*, 627–640.

Jusczyk, P.W., Hohne, E.A., Jusczyk, A.M., & Redanz, N.J. (1993). Do infants remember voices? *Journal of the Acoustical Society of America, 93*, 2373.

Kagan, J. (1994). On the nature of emotion. In Fox, N.A. (Ed.), The development of emotion regulation: Biological and behavioral considerations. *Monographs of the Society for Research in Child Development, 59*(2–3, Serial No. 240), 7–24.

Kagan, J. (1998). Biology and the child. In W. Damon (Series Ed.) & N. Eisenberg (Vol. Ed.), *Handbook of child psychology: Vol. 3. Social, emotional, and personality development* (5th ed., pp. 177–235). New York: Wiley.

Kagan, J., & Fox, N.A. (2006). Biology, culture, and temperamental biases. In W. Damon & R. Lerner (Eds.) & N. Eisenberg (Vol. Ed.), *Handbook of child psychology: Vol. 3. Social, emotional, and personality development* (6th ed., pp. 167–225). New York: Wiley.

Kagan, J., & Snidman, N. (1991a). Infant predictors of inhibited and uninhibited profiles. *Psychological Science, 2*, 40–44.

Kagan, J., & Snidman, N. (1991b). Temperamental factors in human development. *American Psychologist, 48*, 856–862.

Kagan, J., & Snidman, N. (1999). Early childhood predictors of adult anxiety disorders. *Journal of Biological Psychiatry, 46*, 1536–1541.

Kagan, J., Reznick, J.S., & Snidman, N. (1988). Biological bases of childhood shyness. *Science, 240*, 167–171.

Kagan, J., Snidman, N., & Arcus, D. (1998). Childhood derivatives of high and low reactivity in infancy. *Child Development, 69*, 1483–1493.

Källen, B. (2004). Neonate characteristics after maternal use of antidepressants in late pregnancy. *Archives of Pediatrics & Adolescent Medicine, 158*, 312–316.

Kamerman, S.B. (2000). Parental leave policies: An essential ingredient in early childhood education and care policies. *Social Policy Report, 14*(2), 1–16.

Kamerman, S.B., Neuman, M., Waldfogel, J., & Brooks-Gunn, J. (2003). Social policies, family types and child outcomes in selected OECD countries. *OECD Social, Employment and Migration Working Papers No. 6*, 1–55.

Kant, I. (1924/1781). *Critique of pure reason* (F. M. Muller, Transl.). New York: Macmillan.

Kaplan, P.S., Goldstein, M.H., Huckeby, E.R., Owren, M.J., & Cooper, R.P. (1995). Dishabituation of visual attention by infant- versus adult-directed speech: Effects of frequency modulation and spectral composition. *Infant Behavior and Development, 18*, 209–223.

Karraker, K.H., & Coleman, P. (2002). Infants' characteristics and behaviors help shape their environments. In H.E. Fitzgerald, K.H. Karraker, & T. Luster (Eds.), *Infant development: Ecological perspectives* (pp. 165–191). New York: RoutledgeFalmer.

Karrass, J., & Braungart-Rieker, J.M. (2004). Infant negative emotionality and attachment: Implications for preschool intelligence. *International Journal of Behavioral Development, 28*, 221–229.

Karrass, J., Braungart-Rieker, J.M., Mullins, J., & Lefever, J.B. (2002). Processes in language acquisition: The roles of gender, attention, and maternal encouragement of attention over time. *Journal of Child Language, 29*, 519–543.

Kasari, C., Sigman, M., Mundy, P., & Yirmiya, N. (1990). Affective sharing in the context of joint attention interactions of normal, autistic, and mentally retarded children. *Journal of Autism and Developmental Disorders, 20*, 87–100.

Katz, N., Baker, E., & Macnamara, J. (1974). What's in a name? A study of how children learn common and proper names. *Child Development, 45*, 469–473.

Kaufman, R.H. (1982). Structural changes of the genital tract associated with in utero exposure to diethylstilbestrol. *Obstetrics and Gynecology Annual, 11*, 187–202.

Kaufmann-Hayoz, R., Kaufmann, F., & Stucki, M. (1986). Kinetic contours in infants' visual perception. *Child Development, 57,* 292–299.

Kavanaugh, R.D., & Engel, S. (1998). The development of pretense and narrative in early childhood. In O.N. Saracho, & B. Spodek, (Eds.), *Multiple perspectives on play in early childhood education* (pp. 81–99). Albany, NY: State University of New York Press.

Kavanaugh, R.D., Eizenman, D.R., & Harris, P.L. (1997). Young children's understanding of pretense expressions of independent agency. *Developmental Psychology, 33,* 764–770.

Kawasaki, N. Nishimura, H. Yoshimura, T. Okamura, H. (2002). A diminished intrapartum amniotic fluid index is a predictive marker of possible adverse neonatal outcome when associated with prolonged labor. *Gynecologic and Obstetric Investigation,53,* 1–5.

Kay, M.A. (1982). *Anthropology of human birth.* Philadelphia: F.A. Davis Co.

Keating, M.B., McKenzie, B.E., & Day, R.H. (1986). Spatial localization in infancy: Position constancy in a square and circular room with and without a landmark. *Child Development, 57,* 115–124.

Keenan, P. (2000). Benefits of massage therapy and use of a doula during labor and childbirth. *Alternative Therapies in Health and Medicine, 6,* 66–74.

Keller, H., Lohaus, A., Kuensemueller, P., Abels, M., Yosvi, R.D., Voelker, S., et al. (2004a). The bio-culture of parenting: Evidence from five cultural communities. *Parenting: Science and Practice, 4,* 25–50.

Keller, H., Yovsi, R., Borke, J., Kärtner, J., Jensen, H., & Papaligoura, Z. (2004b). Developmental consequences of early parenting experiences: Self-recognition and self-regulation in three cultural communities. *Child Development, 75,* 1745–1760.

Kelley, S.A., Brownell, C.A., & Campbell, S.B. (2000). Mastery motivation and self-evaluative affect in toddlers: Longitudinal relations with maternal behavior. *Child Development, 71,* 1061–1071.

Kellman, P.J. (1984). Perception of three-dimensional form by human infants. *Perception and Psychophysics, 36,* 353–358.

Kellman, P.J., & Arterberry, M.E. (1998). *The cradle of knowledge: Development of perception in infancy.* Cambridge, MA: MIT Press.

Kellman, P.J., & Arterberry, M.E. (2006). Infant visual perception. In W. Damon & R. Lerner (Eds.) D. Kuhn & R. Siegler (Vol. Eds.), *Handbook of child psychology: Vol. 2. Cognition, perception, and language* (6th ed., pp. 109–160). New York: Wiley.

Kellman, P.J., & Banks, M.S. (1998). Infant visual perception. In W. Damon (Editor-in-Chief), D.Kuhn, & R.S. Siegler (Vol. Eds.), *Handbook of Child Psychology: Vol. 2. Cognition, perception, and language* (5th ed., pp. 103–146). New York: Wiley.

Kellman, P.J., & Short, K.R. (1987). Development of three-dimensional form perception. *Journal of Experimental Psychology: Human Perception and Performance, 13,* 545–557.

Kellman, P.J., & Spelke, E.S. (1983). Perception of partly occluded objects in infancy. *Cognitive Psychology, 15,* 483–448.

Kellman, P.J., & von Hofsten, C. (1992). The world of the moving infant: Perception of motion, stability, and space. *Advances in Infancy Research, 7,* 147–184.

Kelly, J.F., & Booth, C.L. (1999). Child care for infants with special needs: Issues and applications. *Infants and Young Children, 12,* 26–33.

Kemler Nelson, D.G., Hirsh-Pasek, K., Jusczyk, P.W., & Cassidy, K.W. (1989). How the prosodic cues in motherese might assist language learning. *Journal of Child Language, 16(1),* 55–68.

Kennedy, H.P., & Shannon, M.T. (2004). Keeping birth normal: Research findings on midwifery care during childbirth. *Journal of Obstetrical and Gynecological Neonatal Nursing, 33,* 554–560.

Kent, R., & Miolo, G. (1995). Phonetic abilities in the first year of life. In P. Fletcher & B MacWhinney (Eds.), *The handbook of child language* (pp. 302–334). Oxford, UK: Blackwell.

Kessen, W. (1979). The American child and other cultural inventions. *American Psychologist, 34,* 815–820.

Kiang, L., Moreno, A.J., & Robinson, J.L. (2004). Maternal preconceptions about parenting predict child temperament, maternal sensitivity, and children's empathy. *Developmental Psychology, 40,* 1081–1092.

Kim-Cohen, J., Moffitt, T.E., Caspi, A., & Taylor, A. (2004). Genetic and environmental processes in young children's resilience and vulnerability to socioeconomic deprivation. *Child Development, 75,* 651–668.

Kinney, H.C., Randall, L.L., Sleeper, L.A., Willinger, M., Belliveau, R.A., Zec, N., et al. (2003). Serotonergic brainstem abnormalities in Northern Plains Indians with the sudden infant death syndrome. *Journal of Neuropathology and Experimental Neruology, 62,* 1178–1191.

Kisilevsky, B.S. Hains, S.M.J., Lee, K., Xie, X., Huang, H., Ye, H.H., et al. (2003). Effects of experience on fetal voice recognition. *Psychological Science, 14,* 220–224.

Kisker, E., & Maynard, R. (1991). Quality, cost and parental choice of child care. In D.M. Blau (Ed.), *The economics of child care* (pp. 127–143). New York: Russell Sage Foundation.

Kjos, S. (1999). Gestational diabetes mellitus. *New England Journal of Medicine, 341,* 1749–1756.

Klaus, M.H., & Kennell, J.H. (1997). The doula: An essential ingredient of childbirth rediscovered. *Acta Paediatr, 86,* 1034–1036.

Klein, M.C., Gauthier, R.J., Jorgensen, S.H., Robbins, J.M., Kaczorowski, J., Johnson, B., et al. (1992). Does episiotomy prevent perineal trauma and pelvic floor relaxation? *The Online Journal of Current Clinical Trials, 106,* 375–377.

Klein, P. J., & Meltzoff, A. N. (1999). Long-term memory, forgetting, and deferred imitation in 12-month-old infants. *Developmental Science, 2,* 102–113.

Kleiner, K.A. (1987). Amplitude and phase spectra as indices of infants' pattern preferences. *Infant Behavior and Development, 10,* 45–55.

Kleiner, K.A., & Banks, M.S. (1987). Stimulus energy does not account for 2-month-olds' face preferences. *Journal of Experimental Psychology: Human Perception and Performance, 13,* 594–600.

Klemmt, L., & Scialli, A.R. (2005). The transport of chemicals in semen. *Birth Defects Research. Part B, Developmental and Reproductive Toxicology, 74,* 119–131.

Klin, A., Volkmar, F.R., & Sparrow, S. (1992). Autistic social dysfunction: Some limitations of the theory of mind hypothesis. *Journal of Child Psychology and Psychiatry, 33,* 861–876.

Klonoff-Cohen, H., & Lam-Kruglick, P. (2001). Maternal and paternal recreational drug use and sudden infant death syndrome. *Archives of Pediatric and Adolescent Medicine, 155,* 765–770.

Kochanek, K.D., Murphy, S.L., Anderson, R.N., & Scott, C. (2004). Deaths: Final data for 2002. *National Vital Statistics Reports, 53*(5), 1–116.

Kochanska, G. (2002). Mutually responsive orientation between mothers and their young children: A context for the early development of conscience. *Current Directions in Psychological Science, 11,* 191–195.

Kochanska, G., & Murray, K.T. (2000). Mother-child mutually responsive orientation and conscience development: From toddler to early school age. *Child Development, 71,* 417–431.

Kochanska, G., & Radke-Yarrow, M. (1992). Inhibition in toddlerhood and the dynamics of the child's interaction with an unfamiliar peer at age five. *Child Development, 63,* 325–335.

Kochanska, G., Coy, K.C., & Murray, K.T. (2001). The development of self-regulation in the first four years of life. *Child Development, 72,* 1091–1111.

Kochanska, G., Coy, K.C., Tjebkes, T.L., & Husarek, S.J. (1998). Individual dif-

ferences in emotionality in infancy. *Child Development, 69,* 375–390.

Koester, L.S. (1995). Face-to-face interactions between hearing mothers and their deaf infants. *Infant Behavior & Development, 18,* 145–153.

Koester, L.S., Traci, M.A., Brooks, L.R., Karkowski, A.M., & Smith-Gray, S. (2004). In Meadow-Orlans, K.P., Spencer, P.E., Koester, L.S. *The world of deaf infants: A longitudinal study* (pp. 40–56). New York: Oxford University Press.

Koffka, K. (1935). *Principles of Gestalt Psychology.* New York: Harcourt, Brace & World.

Kofman, O. (2002). The role of prenatal stress in the etiology of developmental behavioral disorders. *Neuroscience and Biobehavioral Reviews, 26,* 457–470.

Kogan, M.D., Alexander, G.R., Jack, B.W., & Allen, M.C. (1998). The association between adequacy of prenatal care utilization and subsequent pediatric care utilization in the United States. *Pediatrics, 102,* 25–30.

Koivurova, S., Hartikainen, A., Gissler, M., Hemminki, E., Sovio, U., & Jarvelin, M. (2002). Neonatal outcome and congenital malformations in children born after in-vitro fertilization. *Human Reproduction, 17,* 1391–1398.

Kojima, Y. (1999). Mothers' adjustment to the birth of a second child: A longitudinal study on use of verbal and nonverbal behaviors toward two children. *Psychological Reports, 84,* 141–144.

Kolata, G. (March 3, 1999). $50,000 offered to tall, smart egg donor. *New York Times.*

Kontos, S., Howes, C., Shinn, M., & Galinsky, E. (1994). *Quality in family child care and relative care.* New York: Teachers College Press.

Kopp, C.B. (1989). Regulation of distress and negative emotions: A developmental view. *Developmental Psychology, 25,* 343–354.

Koren, G., Pastuszak, A., & Ito, S. (1998). Drugs in pregnancy. *New England Journal of Medicine, 338,* 1128–1137.

Korfmacher, J. (2002). Early childhood interventions: Now what? In H.E. Fitzgerald, K. H. Karraker, & T. Luster

(Eds.), *Infant development: Ecological perspectives* (pp, 275–294). New York: RoutledgeFalmer.

Korn, S.J. (1984). Continuities and discontinuities in difficult/easy temperament: From infancy to young adulthood. *Merrill-Palmer Quarterly, 30,* 189–199.

Kramer, L., & Gottman, J.M. (1992). Becoming a sibling: "With a little help from my friends." *Developmental Psychology, 28,* 685–699.

Kramer, MS. Chalmers, B. Hodnett, ED. Sevkovskaya, Z. Dzikovich, I. Shapiro, S. et al. (2001). Promotion of Breastfeeding Intervention Trial (PROBIT): A randomized trial in the Republic of Belarus. *Journal of the American Medical Association, 285,* 413–420.

Kramer, M.S., Goulet, L., Lydon, J., Sequin, L., McNamara, H., Dassa, C., et al. (2001). Socio-economic disparities in preterm birth: Causal path ways and mechanism. *Paediatric and Perinatal Epidemiology, 15*(Suppl. 2), 104–123.

Kreider, R.M. (2003). Adopted children and stepchildren: 2000. *Census 2000 Special Reports, CENSR-6RV.* Washington, DC: U.S. Census Bureau.

Kreppner, K. (1988). Changes in parent-child relationships with the birth of the second child. *Marriage and Family Review, 12,* 157–181.

Kuczmarski, R.J., Ogden, C.L., Grummer-Strawn, L.M., Flegal, K.M., Guo, S.S., Wei, R., et al. (2000). CDC growth charts: United States. *Advance data from vital and health statistics, No. 314.* Hyattsville, MD: National Center for Health Statistics.

Kuhl, P.K. (1979). Speech perception in early infancy: Perceptual constancy for spectrally dissimilar vowel categories. *Journal of the Acoustical Society of America, 66,* 1668–1679.

Kuhl, P.K. (1981). Discrimination of speech by nonhuman animals: Basic auditory sensitivities conducive to the perception of speech-sound categories. *Journal of the Acoustical Society of America, 70,* 340–349.

Kuhl, P.K. (1987). Perception of speech and sound in early infancy. In P. Salapatek & L. Cohen (Eds.), *Handbook of infant perception: Vol. 1. From sensation of perception* (pp. 275–382). Orlando, FL: Academic Press.

Kuhl, P.K. (1991). Human adults and human infants show a "perceptual magnet effect" for the prototypes of speech categories, monkeys do not. *Perception & Psychophysics, 50,* 93–107.

Kuhl, P.K. (2000). A new view of language acquisition. *Proceedings of the National Academy of Sciences, 97,* 11850–11857.

Kuhl, P.K. (2004). Early language acquisition: Cracking the speech code. *Nature Reviews Neuroscience, 5,* 831–843.

Kuhl, P.K., & Miller (1982). Discrimination of auditory target dimensions in the presence or absence of variation in a second dimension by infants. *Perception & Psychophysics, 31,* 279–292.

Kuhl, P.K., Tsao, F.M., & Liu, H.M. (2003) Foreign-language experience in infancy: Effects of short-term exposure and social interaction on phonetic learning. *Proceedings of the National Academy of Sciences, 100,* 9096–9101.

Kuhl, P.K., Coffey-Corina, S., Padden, D., & Dawson, G. (2005a). Links between social and linguistic processing of speech in preschool children with autism: Behavioral and electrophysiological measures. *Developmental Science, 8,* F1–F12.

Kuhl, P.K., Conboy, B.T., Padden, D., Nelson, T., & Pruitt, J. (2005b). Early speech perception and later language development: Implications for the "critical period." *Language Learning and Development, 1,* 237–264.

Kuhl, P.K., Williams, K.A., Lacerda, F., Stevens, K.N., & Lindblom, B. (1992). Linguistic experience alters phonetic perception in infants by 6 months of age. *Science, 255,* 606–608.

Kuhl, P.K., Andruski, J.E., Chistovich, I.A., Chistovich, L.A., Kozhevnikova, E.V., Ryskina, E.I., Stolyarova, E.I., Sundberg, U., & Lacerda, F. (1997). Cross-language analysis of phonetic units in language addressed to infants. *Science, 277,* 684–686.

Kurki, T., Hiilesmaa, V., Raitasalo, R., Mattila, H., & Ylikorkala, O. (2000). Depression and anxiety in early pregnancy and risk for preeclampsia. *Obstetrics and Gynecology, 95,* 487–490.

Labbo, L.D., & Kuhn, M.R. (2000). Weaving chains of affect and cognition: A young child's understanding of CD-ROM talking books. *Journal of Literacy Research, 32,* 187–210.

Labrell, F. (1994). A typical interaction between fathers and toddlers: Teasing. *Early Development and Parenting, 3,* 125–130.

LaFuente, M.J., Grifol, R., Segarra, J., Soriano, J., Gorba, M.A., & Montesinos, A. (1997). Effects of the Firstart method of prenatal stimulation on psychomotor development: The first six months. *Pre- and Peri-Natal Psychology Journal, 11,* 151–162.

Lahey, B.B. (2004). Commentary: Role of temperament in developmental models of psychopathology. *Journal of Clinical Child and Adolescent Psychology, 33,* 88–93.

Laible, D. (2004a). Mother-child discourse about a child's past behavior at 30 months and early socioemotional development at age 3. *Merrill-Palmer Quarterly, 50,* 159–180.

Laible, D. (2004b). Mother-child discourse in two contexts: Links with child temperament, attachment security, and socioemotional competence. *Developmental Psychology, 40,* 979–992.

Laible, D.J., & Thompson, R.A. (2000). Mother-child discourse, attachment security, shared positive affect, and early conscience development. *Child Development, 71,* 1424–1440.

Lamb, M.E. (1987). Predictive implications of individual differences in attachment. *Journal of Consulting and Clinical Psychology, 55,* 817–824.

Lamb, M.E. (1997). The development of father-infant relationships. In M.E. Lamb (Ed.), *The role of the father in child development* (3rd ed., pp. 104–120). New York: Wiley.

Lamb, M.E., & Ahnert, L. (2006). Nonparental child care: Context, concepts, correlates, and consequences. In W. Damon & R. Lerner (Eds.) & K.A. Renninger & I.E. Sigel (Vol. Eds.), *Handbook of child psychology: Vol. 4.* *Child psychology in practice* (6th ed., pp. 950–1016). New York: Wiley.

Lamb, M.E., & Lewis, C. (2004). The development and significance of father-child relationships in two-parent families. In M.E. Lamb (Ed.), *The role of the father in child development* (4th ed., pp. 272–306). Hoboken, NJ: Wiley.

Lamb, S., & Zakhireh, B. (1997). Toddlers' attention to the distress of peers in a daycare setting. *Early Education & Development, 8,* 105–118.

Lambert, E.B., & Clyde, M. (2003). Putting Vygotsky to the test. In J.L. Roopnarine (Series Ed.) & D. E. Lytle (Vol. Ed.), *Play and educational theory and practice. Play & culture studies* (Vol. 5, pp. 59–98). Westport, CT: Praeger.

Lampl, M., Johnson, M.L., & Frongillo, E.A., Jr. (2001). Mixed distribution analysis identifies saltation and stasis growth. *Annals of Human Biology, 28,* 403–411.

Lampl, M., Veldhuis, J.D., & Johnson, M.L. (1992). Saltation and stasis: A model of human growth. *Science, 258,* 801–803.

Landy, H.J., & Keith, L.G. (1998). The vanishing twin: a review. *Human Reproduction Update, 4,* 177–183.

Langer, A., Campero, L., Garcia, C., & Reynoso, S. (1998). Effects of psychosocial support during labour and childbirth on breastfeeding, medical interventions, and mothers' wellbeing in a Mexican public hospital: A randomised clinical trial. *British Journal of Obstetrics and Gynaecology, 105,* 1056–1063.

Larson, M.C., White, B.P., Cochran, A., Donzella, B., & Gunnar, M.R. (1998). Dampening of the cortisol response to handling at 3 months in human infants and its relation to sleep, circadian cortisol activity, and behavioral distress. *Developmental Psychobiology, 33,* 327–337.

Laursen, B., Hartup, W.W., & Koplas, A.L. (1996). Towards understanding peer conflict. *Merrill-Palmer Quarterly, 35,* 281–297.

Lavelli, M., & Fogel, A. (2005). Developmental changes in the relationship between the infant's attention and emotion during early face-to-face communication: The 2-month-transition. *Developmental Psychology, 41,* 265–280.

Lavelli, M., Pantoja, A.P.F., Hsu, H., & Messinger, D. (in press). Using microgenetic designs to study change processes: A relational-historical approach. In D. M. Teti (Ed.), *Handbook of research methods in developmental psychology.* Baltimore, MD: Blackwell.

Lederman, S.A., Rauh, V., Weiss, L., Stein, J.L., Hoepner, L.A., Becker, M., et al. (2004). The effects of the World Trade Center event on birth outcomes among term deliveries at three lower Manhattan hospitals. *Environmental Health Perspectives, 112,* 1772–1778.

Lee, C.L., & Bates, J.E. (1985). Mother-child interaction at age two years and perceived difficult temperament. *Child Development, 56,* 1314–1325.

Lee, D.N., & Aronson, E. (1974). Visual proprioceptive control of standing in human infants. *Perception & Psychophysics, 15,* 529–532.

Lee, K.S., Perlman, M., Ballantyne, M., Elliott, I., & To, T. (1995). Association between duration of neonatal hospital stay and readmission rate. *The Journal of Pediatrics, 127,* 758–766.

Leiferman, J.A., & Evenson, K.R. (2003). The effect of regular leisure physical activity on birth outcomes. *Maternal and Child Health Journal, 7,* 59–64.

Lemery, K.S., Goldsmith, H.H., Klinnert, M.D., & Mrazek, D.A. (1999). Developmental models of infant and childhood temperament. *Developmental Psychology, 35,* 189–204.

Lenneberg, E.H., Rebelsky, F.G., & Nichols, I.A. (1965). The vocalizations of infants born to deaf and hearing parents. *Human Development, 8,* 23–27.

Leonard, C.H., Clyman, R.I., Piecuch, R.E., Juster, R.P., Ballard, R.A., & Behle, M.B. (1990). Effect of medical and social risk factors on outcome of prematurity and very low birth weight. *Journal of Pediatrics, 116,* 620–626.

LePecq, J., & Lafaite, M. (1989). The early development of position constancy in a no-landmark environment. *British Journal of Developmental Psychology, 7,* 289–306.

Leslie, A.M. (1987). Pretense and representation: The origins of "theory of mind." *Psychological Review, 94,* 412–426.

Leslie, A.M., & Roth, D. (1993). What autism teaches us about metarepresentation . In S. Baron-Cohen, H. Tager-Flusberg & D. Cohen (Eds.), *Understanding other minds: Perspectives from autism* (pp. 83–111). Oxford, UK: Oxford University Press.

Lester, B.M., Tronick, E.A., Mayes, L., et al. (1994). Neurodevelopmental consortium, the NICHD Neonatal research network. A neurodevelopmental follow-up battery for substance exposed infants. *Pediatric Research, 35,* 23A.

Lester, B.M., Tronick, E.Z., LaGasse, L., Seifer, R., Bauer, C.R., Shankaran, S., et al. (2002). The Maternal Lifestyle Study: Effects of substance exposure during pregnancy on neurodevelopmental outcome in 1-month-old infants. *Pediatrics, 110,* 1182–1192.

Lester, B.M., Tronick, E.Z., LaGasse, L., Seifer, R., Bauer, C.R., Shankaran, S., et al. (2004). Summary statistics of Neonatal Intensive Care Unit Network Neurobehavioral Scale scores from the Maternal Lifestyle Study: A quasi-normative sample. *Pediatrics, 113,* 668–675.

Levine, E.M., Ghai, V., Barton, J.J., & Strom, C.M. (2001). Mode of delivery and risk of respiratory disease in newborns. *Obstetrics & Gynecology, 97,* 439–442.

LeVine, R.A., Dixon, S., LeVine, S., Richman, A., Leiderman, P.H., Keefer, C.H., & Brazelton, T.B. (1994). *Child care and culture: Lessons from Africa.* Cambridge: Cambridge University Press.

Levitt, P., Reinoso, B., Jones, L. (1998). The critical impact of early cellular environment on neuronal development. *Preventive Medicine, 27*(2), 180–183.

Lewis, C. (1997). Fathers and preschoolers. In M.E. Lamb (Ed.), *The role of the father in child development* (3rd ed., pp. 121–142). New York: Wiley.

Lewis, C.T., Mathews, T.J., & Heuser, R.L. (1996). Prenatal care in the United States, 1980–1994. National Center for Health Statistics. *Vital Health Statistics, 21(54).*

Lewis, M. (1995). Self-conscious emotions. *American Scientist, 83,* 68–78.

Lewis, M. (2000). The emergence of human emotions. In M. Lewis & J. M. Haviland-Jones (Eds.), *Handbook of emotions* (2nd ed., pp. 265–280). New York: Guilford Press.Lewis, M., & Brooks-Gunn, J. (1979). *Social cognition and the acquisition of self.* New York: Plenum.

Lewis, M., & Ramsay, D.S. (2004). Development of self-recognition, personal pronoun use, and pretend play during the 2nd year. *Child Development, 75,* 1821–1831.

Lewis, M., & Ramsay, D. (1997). Stress reactivity and self-recognition. *Child Development, 68,* 621–629.

Lewis, M.D., & Stieben, J. (2004). Emotion regulation in the brain: Conceptual issues and directions for developmental research. *Child Development, 75,* 371–376.

Lewkowicz, D.J. (2000). The development of intersensory temporal perception: An epigenetic systems/limitation view. *Psychological Bulletin, 126,* 281–308.

Li, H., George, V.K., Bianco, F.J., Jr., Lawrence, W.D., & Dhabuwala, C.B. (1997). Histopathological changes in the testes of prepubertal male rats after chronic administration of cocaine. *Journal of Environmental Pathology, Toxicology, and Oncology, 16,* 67–71.

Lickliter, R., & Bahrick, L.E. (2000). The development of infant intersensory perception: Advantages of a comparative convergent-operations approach. *Psychological Bulletin, 126,* 260–280.

Lieberman, A.F., & Zeanah, C.H. (1995). Disorders of attachment in infancy. *Infant Psychiatry, 4,* 571–587.

Lieu, J. E. C., & Feinstein, A. R. (2002). Effect of gestational and passive smoke exposure on ear infections in children. *Archives of Pediatrics & Adolescent Medicine, 156,* 147–154.

Liittschwager, J. C., & Markman, E. M. (1994). Sixteen- and 24-month-olds' use of mutual exclusivity as a default assumption in second label learning. *Developmental Psychology, 30,* 955–968.

Lillard, A.S., & Witherington, D.C. (2004). Mothers' behavior modifications during pretense and their possible signal value for toddlers. *Developmental Psychology, 40,* 95–113.

Lin, C., & Liu, W.T. (1999). Intergenerational relationships among Chinese immigrant families from Taiwan. In H.P. McAdoo (Ed.), *Family ethnicity: Strength in diversity* (2nd ed., pp. 235–251). Thousand Oaks, CA: Sage.

Lindegren, M.L., Byers, R.H., Jr., Thomas, P., Davis, S.F., Caldwell, B., Roger, M., et al. (1999). Trends in perinatal transmission of HIV/AIDS in the United States. *JAMA, 282,* 531–538.

Linebarger, D.L., & Walker, D. (2005). Infants' and toddlers' television viewing and language outcomes. *American Behavioral Scientist, 48,* 624–645.

Liu, H.M., Kuhl, P.K., & Tsao, F.M. (2003). An association between mothers' speech clarity and infants' speech discrimination skills. *Developmental Science, 6,* F1–F10.

Liu, X., Jiang, Q., Mansfield, S.G., Puttaraju, M., Zhang, Y., Zhu, W., et al. (2002). Partial correction of endogenous DeltaF508 CFTR in human cystic fibrosis airway epithelia by spliceosome-mediated RNA trans-splicing. *Nature Biotechnology, 20,* 47–52.

Lively, S., Logan, J.S., & Pisoni, D.B. (1993). Training Japanese listeners to identify English /r/ and /l/. II. The role of phonetic environment and talker variability in learning new perceptual categories. *Journal of the Acoustical Society of America, 94,* 1242–1255.

Lively, S., Pisoni, D.B., Yamada, R.A., Tohkura, Y., & Yamada, T. (1994). Training Japanese listeners to identify English /r/ and /l/. III. Long-term retention of new phonetic categories. *Journal of the Acoustical Society of America, 94,* 2076–2087.

Lloyd, B., & Goodwin, R. (1995). Let's pretend: Casting the characters and setting the scene. *British Journal of Developmental Psychology, 13,* 261–270.

Lo, Y.M., Hjelm, N.M., Fidler, C., Sargent, I.L., Murphy, M.F., Chamberlain, P.F., et al. (1998). Prenatal diagnosis of fetal RhD status by molecular analysis of maternal plasma. *New England Journal of Medicine, 339,* 1734–1738.

Locke, J.L. (1983). *Phonological acquisition and change.* New York: Academic Press.

Lockman, J.J. (2000). A perception-action perspective on tool use development. *Child Development, 71,* 137–144.

Loeb, S., Fuller, B., Kagan, S.L., & Carrol, B. (2004). Child care in poor communities: Early learning effects of type, quality, and stability. *Child Development, 75,* 47–65.

Logan, J.S., Lively, S.E., & Pisoni, D.B. (1991). Training Japanese listeners to identify English /r/ and /l/: A first report. *Journal of the Acoustical Society of America, 89,* 874–886.

Lord, C., Rutter, M., & LeCouteur, A. (1994). Autism Diagnostic Interview-Revised: A revised version of a diagnostic interview for caregivers of individuals with possible pervasive developmental disorders. *Journal of Autism and Developmental Disorders, 24,* 659–685.

Lord, C., Risi, S., Lambrecht, L., Cook, E.H., Leventhal, B.L., DiLavore, P.S., et al. (2000). The Autism Diagnostic Observation Schedule-Generic: A standard measure of social and communication deficits associated with the spectrum of autism. *Journal of Autism and Developmental Disorders, 30,* 205–223.

Lott, K.R. (2002). Oral healthcare for infants. *Dentistry Today, 21,* 64–67.

Louis, J., Cannard, C., Bastuji, H., & Challamel, M.J. (1997). Sleep ontogenesis revisited: A longitudinal 24-hour home polygraphic study on 15 normal infants during the first two years of life. *Sleep, 20,* 323–333.

Lovaas, O.I., & Smith, T. (1989). A comprehensive behavioral theory of autistic children: Paradigm for research and treatment. *Journal of Behavior Therapy and Experimental Psychiatry, 20,* 17–29.

Love, J.M., Harrison, L., Sagi-Schwartz, A., van IJzendoorn, M.H., Ross, C., Ungerer, J.A., et al. (2003). Child care quality matters: How conclusions may vary with context. *Child Development, 74,* 1021–1033.

Love, J.M., Kisker, E.E., Ross, C.M., Brooks-Gunn, J., Schochet, P.Z., Boller, K., et al. (2002). *Making a difference in the lives of infants and toddlers and their families: The impacts of Early Head Start* (Report prepared for the Administration for Children and Families, U.S. Department of Health and Human Services). Princeton: NJ: Mathematica Policy Research.

Love, J.M., Kisker, E.E., Ross, C., Raikes, H., Constantine, J., Boller, K., et al. (2005). The effectiveness of Early Head Start for 3-year-old children and their parents: Lessons for policy and programs. *Developmental Psychology, 41,* 885–901.

Loveland, K., & Landry, S. (1986). Joint attention and language in autism and developmental language delay. *Journal of Autism and Developmental Disorders, 16,* 335–349.

Low, W.A. & Clift, V.A. (1984). *Encyclopedia of Black America.* New York: Da Capo Press.

Lubic, R.W. (2002). Introduction to international efforts. Retrieved October 12, 2003, from http://www.BirthCenters.org

Lyons-Ruth, K., Bronfman, E., & Parsons, E. (1999). Maternal frightened, frightening, or atypical behavior and disorganized infant attachment patterns. In J.I. Vondra & D. Barnett (Eds.), Atypical attachment in infancy and early childhood among children at developmental risk. *Monographs of the Society for Research in Child Development, 64*(3, Serial No. 258), 67–96.

Lytle, D.E. (Ed.). (2003). *Play and Educational Theory and Practice: Play &*

Culture Studies (Vol. 5). Westport, CT: Praeger.

Lytton, H., & Romney, D.M. (1991). Parents' differential socialization of boys and girl: A meta-analysis. *Psychological Bulletin, 109,* 267–296.

Macfie, J., Cicchetti, D., & Toth, S.L. (2001). The development of dissociation in maltreated preschool-aged children. *Development and Psychopathology, 13,* 233–254.

Macnamara, J. (1982). *Names for things.* Cambridge, MA: MIT Press.

MacWhinney, B., & Snow, C.E. (1990). The Child Language Data Exchange System: An update. *Journal of Child Language, 17,* 457–472.

MacWhinney, B., & Snow, C.E. (1985). The Child Language Data Exchange System. *Journal of Child Language, 12,* 271–296.

Madole, K.L., Oakes, L.M., & Cohen, L.B. (1993). Developmental changes in infants' attention to function and form-function correlations. *Cognitive Development, 8,* 189–209.

Main, M., & Solomon, J. (1986). Discovery of a disorganized disoriented attachment pattern. In T.B. Brazelton & M.W. Yogman (Eds.), Affective development in infancy (pp. 95–124). Norwood, NJ: Ablex.

Main, M., & Solomon, J. (1990). Procedures for identifying infants as disorganized/disoriented during the Ainsworth Strange Situation. In M. Greenberg, D. Cicchetti, & E.M. Cummings (Eds.), *Attachment in the preschool years: Theory, research, and intervention* (pp. 121–160). Chicago: University of Chicago Press.

Makin, J.W., & Porter, R.H. (1989). Attractiveness of lactating females' breast odors to neonates. *Child Development, 60,* 803–810.

Malatesta, C.Z., & Haviland, J.M. (1982). Learning display rules: The socialization of emotion expression in infancy. *Child Development, 53,* 991–1003.

Malatesta, C.Z., Culver, C., Tesman, J.R., & Shepard, B. (1989). The development of emotion expression during the first two years of life. *Monographs of the Society for Research in Child Development, 54*(1–2, Serial No. 219).

Malloy, M.H., & Freeman, D.H. (2004). Age at death, season, and day of death as indicators of the effect of the Back to Sleep Program on Sudden Infant Death Syndrome in the United States, 1992–1999. *Archives of Pediatrics & Adolescent Medicine, 158,* 359–365.

Malone, F.D., Canick, J.A., Ball, R.H., Nyberg, D.A., Comstock, C.H., Bukowski, R., et al. (2005). First-trimester of second-trimester screening, or both, for Down's Syndrome. *New England Journal of Medicine, 353,* 2001–2011.

Malpani, A., Malpani, A., & Modi, D. (2002). Preimplantation sex selection for family balancing in India. *Human Reproduction, 17,* 11–12.

Malphurs, J., Larrain, C., Field, T., Pickens, J., Peláez-Nogueras, M., Yando, R., et al. (1996). Altering withdrawn and intrusive interaction behaviors of depressed mothers. *Infant Mental Health Journal, 17,* 152–160.

Mandel, D. R., Jusczyk, P. W., & Pisoni, D. B. (1995). Infants' recognition of the sound patterns of their own names. *Psychological Science, 6,* 314–317.

Mandler, J.M. (1988). How to build a baby: On the development of an accessible representational system. *Cognitive Development, 3,* 113–136.

Mandler, J.M. (1992). How to build a baby. II. Conceptual primitives. *Psychological Review, 99,* 587–604.

Mandler, J.M. (1998). Representation. In W. Damon (Editor-in-Chief), D. Kuhn, & R.S. Siegler (Vol. Eds.), *Handbook of child psychology: Vol. 2. Cognition, perception, and language* (5th ed., pp. 255–308). New York: Wiley.

Mandler, J.M., & McDonough, L. (1993). Concept formation in infancy. *Cognitive Development, 8,* 237–264.

Mandler, J.M., & McDonough, L. (1996). Drinking and driving don't mix: Inductive generalization in infancy. *Cognition, 59,* 307–335.

Mandler, J.M., & McDonough, L. (1998). On developing a knowledge base in infancy. *Developmental Psychology, 34,* 1274–1288.

Mangan, P., Franklin, A., Tignor, T., Bolling, L., & Nadel, L. (1994). Development of spatial memory abilities in young children. *Society for Neuroscience Abstracts, 20,* 363.

Mangelsdorf, S.C. (1992). Developmental changes in infant-stranger interaction. *Infant Behavior and Development, 15,* 191–208.

Mangelsdorf, S.C., & Frosch, C.A. (1999). Temperament and attachment: One construction or two? In H.W. Reese (Ed.), *Advances in child development and behavior* (pp. 181–220). San Diego, CA: Academic.

Mangelsdorf, S.C., Shapiro, J.R., & Marzolf, D. (1995). Developmental and temperamental differences in emotion regulation in infancy. *Child Development, 66,* 1817–1828.

Mangelsdorf, S.C., Gunnar, M., Kestenbaum, R., Lang, S., & Andreas, D. (1990). Infant proneness-to-distress temperament, maternal personality, and mother-infant attachment: Associations and goodness of fit. *Child Development, 61,* 820–831.

Mangelsdorf, S.C., Plunkett, J.W., Dedrick, C.F., Berlin, M., Meisels, S.J., McHale, J.L., et al. (1996). Attachment security in very low birth weight infants. *Developmental Psychology, 32,* 914–920.

Maratsos, M. (1998). The acquisition of grammar. In W. Damon (Ed.) & D. Kuhn & R.S. Siegler (Vol. Eds.), *Handbook of child psychology* (5th ed.): *Vol. 2. Cognition, perception, and language* (pp. 421–466). New York: Wiley.

March of Dimes. (2002). *HIV and AIDS in pregnancy.* Retrieved October 2, 2005, from http://www.modimes.org

Marcovitch, S., & Zelazo, P.D. (1999). The A-not-B error: Results from a logistic meta-analysis. *Child Development, 70,* 1297–1313.

Marcus, G.F., Vijayan, S., Bandi Rao, S., & Vishton, P.M. (1999). Rule learning by seven-month-old infants. *Science, 283,* 77–80.

Marcus, G.F., Pinker, S., Ullman, M., Hollander, M., Rosen, T.J., & Xu, F. (1992). Overregularization in language acquisition. *Monographs of the Society for Research in Child Development, 57*(4, Serial No. 228).

Markman, E.M. (1989). *Categorization and naming in children: Problems of induction.* Cambridge, MA: MIT Press.

Markman, E.M., & Hutchinson, J.E. (1984). Children's sensitivity to constraints on word meaning: Taxonomic versus thematic relations. *Cognitive Psychology, 16,* 1–27.

Marlier, L., & Schaal, B. (2005). Human newborns prefer human milk: Conspecific milk odor is attractive without postnatal exposure. *Child Development, 76,* 155–168.

Marlier, L., Schaal, B., & Soussignan, R. (1998). Bottle-fed neonates prefer an odor experienced in utero to an odor experienced postnatally in the feeding context. *Developmental Psychobiology, 33,* 133–145.

Marshall, K. (2003a). Benefiting from extended parental leave. *Perspectives on Labour and Income, 4*(3), 5–11. Statistics Canada, Cat. No. 75-001-XIE.

Marsiglio, W. (Ed.). (1993). Contemporary scholarship on fatherhood: Culture, identity, and conduct. *Journal of Family Issues, 14(Special issue), 484–509.*

Martin, G.B., & Clark, R.D. (1982). Distress crying in neonates: Species and peer specificity. *Developmental Psychology, 18,* 3–9.

Martin, J.A., MacDorman, M.F., Mathews, T.J. (1997). Triplet births: trends and outcomes, 1971–94. *Vital Health Statistics, 21*(55). Hyattsville, MD: National Center for Health Statistics.

Martin, J.A., Park, M.M., & Sutton, P.D. (2002). Births: Preliminary data for 2001. *National Vital Statistics Reports, 50*(10). Hyattsville, MD: National Center for Health Statistics.

Martin, J.A., Hamilton, B.E., Ventura, S.J., Menacker, F., & Park, M.M. (2002). Births: Final data for 2000. *National Vital Statistics Reports,* 50(5). Hyattsville, MD: National Center for Health Statistics.

Martin, J.A., Hamilton, B.E., Sutton, P.D., Ventura, S.J., Menacker, F., & Munson, M.L. (2005). Births: Final data for 2003. *National Vital Statistics Reports, 54*(2). Hyattsville, MD: National Center for Health Statistics.

Martinez, E.A. (1999). Mexican American/Chicano families: Parenting as diverse as the families themselves. In McAdoo, H.P. (Ed.), *Family ethnicity: Strength in diversity* (2nd ed., pp. 121–134). Thousand Oaks, CA: Sage.

Masataka, N. (1992). Motherese in a signed language. *Infant Behavior and Development, 15,* 453–460.

Masataka, N. (1996). Perception of motherese in a signed language by 6-month-old deaf infants. *Developmental Psychology, 32,* 874–879.

Masataka, N. (1998). Perception of motherese in Japanese Sign Language by 6-month-old hearing infants. *Developmental Psychology, 34,* 241–246.

Masur, E. (1982). Mothers' responses to infants' object-related gestures: Influences on lexical development. *Journal of Child Language, 9,* 23–30.

Mathews, T.J. (2003). Trends in spina bifida and anencephalus in the United States, 1991–2002. National Center for Health Statistics eStat. Retrieved December 10, 2005, from http://www .cdc.gov/nchs/products/pubs/pubd/ hestats/spine_anen.htm

Mathews, T.J., Hamilton, B.E. (2002). Mean age of mother, 1970–2000. *National Vital Statistics Reports, 51*(1). Hyattsville, MD: National Center for Health Statistics.

Mathews, T.J., MacDorman, M.F., & Menacker, F. (2001). Infant mortality statistics from the 1999 period linked birth/infant death data set. *National Vital Statistics Reports, 50*(4). Hyattsville, MD: National Center for Health Statistics.

Mathews, T.J., MacDorman, M.F., & Menacker, F. (2002). Infant mortality statistics from the 1999 period linked birth/infant death data set. *National Vital Statistics Reports, 50(4).* Hy-attsville, MD: National Center for Health Statistics.

Mathews, T.J., Menacker, F., & MacDorman, M.F. (2002). Infant mortality statistics from the 2000 period linked birth/infant death data set. *National Vital Statistics Reports, 50(12).* Hyattsville, MD: National Center for Health Statistics.

Matthews, A., Ellis, A.E., & Nelson, C.A. (1996). Development of preterm and full-term infant ability on AB, recall memory, transparent barrier detour, and means-end tasks. *Child Development, 67,* 2658–2676.

Maurer, D., Lewis, T.L., Brent, H.P., & Levin, A.V. (1999). Rapid improvement in the acuity of infants after visual input. *Science, 286,* 108–110.

Maynard, A.E. (2002). Cultural teaching: The development of teaching skills in Maya sibling interactions. *Child Development, 73,* 969–982.

McAdoo, H.P. (Ed.). (1999). *Family ethnicity: Strength in diversity* (2nd ed.). Thousand Oaks, CA: Sage.

McCall, R.B., & Carriger, M.S. (1993). A meta-analysis of infant habituation and recognition memory performance as predictors of later IQ. *Child Development, 64,* 57–79.

McCarton, C.M., Brooks-Gunn, J., Wallace, I.F., & Bauer, C.R. (1997). Results at age 8 years of early intervention for low-birth-weight premature infants: The infant health and development program. *Journal of the American Medical Association, 277,* 126–132.

McComas, J., & Field, J. (1984). Does early crawling experience affect infants' emerging spatial orientation abilities? *New Zealand Journal of Psychology, 13,* 63–68.

McCraw, R.K. (1989). Recent innovations in childbirth. Dangerous proposals, harmless fads, or wave of the future? *Journal of Nurse-Midwifery, 34,* 206–210.

McCreath, K.J., Howcroft, J., Campbell, K.H., Colman, A., Schnieke, A.E., & Kind, A.J. (2000). Production of gene-targeted sheep by nuclear transfer from cultured somatic cells. *Nature, 405,* 1066–1069.

McDonald, D.T., & Simons, G.M. (1989). *Musical growth and development: Birth through six.* New York: Schirmer Books.

McEachin, J.J., Smith, T., & Lovaas, O.I. (1993). Long-term outcome for children with autism who received early intensive behavioral treatment. *American Journal on Mental Retardation, 97,* 359–372.

McGraw, M.B. (1935). *Growth: A study of Johnny and Jimmy.* New York: Appleton-Century.

McGraw, M.B. (1940). Neuromuscular development of the human infant as exemplified in the achievement of erect locomotion. *Journal of Pediatrics, 17,* 747–771.

McKelvie, P., & Low, J. (2002). Listening to Mozart does not improve children's spatial ability: Final curtains for the Mozart effect. *British Journal of Developmental Psychology, 20*(2), 241–258.

McLoyd, V.C. (1998). Socioeconomic disadvantage and child development. *American Psychologist, 53,* 185–204.

McLoyd, V.C. (2005). Economic context and childhood experience: Making the case for why and how race matters in children's development. Master lecture given at the Biennial Meeting of the Society for Research in Child Development, Atlanta, GA.

McLoyd, V.C., Aikens, N.L., & Burton, L.M. (2006). Childhood poverty, policy, and practice. In W. Damon & R. Lerner (Eds.) & K.A. Renninger & I.E. Sigel (Vol. Eds.), *Handbook of child psychology: Vol. 4. Child psychology in practice* (6th ed., pp. 700–775). New York: Wiley.

Mead, M. (1928). *Coming of age in Samoa.* New York: Morrow.

Mead, M. (1930). *Growing up in New Guinea.* New York: Blue Ribbon.

Meadows, M. (2001). Pregnancy and the drug dilemma. FDA Consumer Magazine. Retrieved January 12, 2002, from http://www.fda.gov/fdac/features/2001/301_preg.html

Medoff-Cooper, B., McGrath, J.M., & Shults, J.J. (2002). Feeding patterns of full-term and preterm infants at forty weeks postconceptional age. *Journal of Developmental and Behavioral Pediatrics, 23,* 231–236.

Medwell, J. (1998). The Talking Books Project: Some further insights into the use of talking books to develop reading. *Reading, 32,* 3–8.

Meier, P. (1999, March 14). Childbirth pioneer: Dr. Martha Ripley crusaded for safer childbirth and healthier infants and founded Ripley Maternity Hospital in 1886. *StarTribune,* pp. E1, E5.

Meltzoff, A.N. (1988a). Infant imitation and memory: Nine-month-olds in immediate and deferred acts. *Child Development, 59,* 217–225.

Meltzoff, A.N. (1988b). Infant imitation after a 1-week delay: Long-term memory for novel acts and multiple stimuli. *Developmental Psychology, 24,* 470–476.

Meltzoff, A.N., & Borton, R.W. (1979). Intermodal matching by human neonates. *Nature, 282,* 403–404.

Meltzoff, A.N, & Moore, M.K. (1983). Newborn infants imitate adult facial gestures. *Child Development, 54,* 702–719.

Mennella, J.A., & Beauchamp, G.K. (1991). Maternal diet alters the sensory qualities of human milk and the nursling's behavior. *Pediatrics, 88,* 737–744.

Mennella, J.A., & Beauchamp, G.K. (1999). Experience with a flavor in mother's milk momdifies the infant's acceptance of flavored cereal. *Developmental Psychobiology, 35,* 197–203.

Mennella, J.A., & Beauchamp, G.K. (2002). Flavor experiences curing formula feeding are related to preferences during childhood. *Early Human Development, 68,* 71–82.

Mennella, J.A., Jagnow, C.P., & Beauchamp, G.K. (2001). Prenatal and postnatal flavor learning by human infants. *Pediatrics, 107,* E88–E93.

Merewood, A., Mehta, S.D., Chamberlain, L.B., Philipp, B.L., & Bauchner, H. (2005). Breastfeeding rates in US baby-friendly hospitals: Results of a national survey. *Pediatrics, 116,* 628–634.

Merriman, W.E., & Bowman, L.L. (1989). The mutual exclusivity bias in children's word learning. *Monographs of the Society for Research in Child Development, 54*(Serial No. 220).

Merriman, W.E., & Schuster, J.M. (1991). Young children's disambiguation of object name reference. *Child Development, 62,* 1288–1301.

Merten, S., Dratva, J., & Ackermann-Liebrich, U. (2005). Do baby-friendly hospitals influence breastfeeding duration on a national level? *Pediatrics, 116,* e702–e708.

Messer, D.J. (1981). The identification of names in maternal speech to infants. *Journal of Psychholinguistic Research, 10,* 69–77.

Messinger, D.S., & Fogel, A. (1998). Give and take: The development of conventional infant gestures. *Merrill-Palmer Quarterly, 44,* 566–590.

Messinger, D.S., Bauer, C.R., Das, A., Seifer, R., Lester, B.M., LaGasse, L.L., et al. (2004). The Maternal Lifestyle Study: Cognitive, motor, and behavioral outcomes of cocaine-exposed and opiate-exposed infants through three years of age. *Pediatrics, 113,* 1677–1685.

Miller, P.J., Fung, H., & Mintz, J. (1996). Self-construction through narrative practices: A Chinese and American comparison of early socialization. *Ethos, 24,* 237–280.

Miller, P.J., Wiley, A.R., Fung, H., & Liang, C.H. (1997). Personal storytelling as a medium of socialization in Chinese and American families. *Child Development, 68,* 557–568.

Miller, P.J., Mintz, J., Hoogstra, L., Fung, H., & Potts, R. (1992). The narrated self: Young children's construction of self in relation to others in conversational stories of personal experience. *Merrill-Palmer Quarterly, 38,* 45–67.

Miller, S.A. (1998). *Developmental research methods* (2nd ed.). Upper Saddle River, NJ: Prentice Hall.

Minami, M., & McCabe, A. (1995). Rice balls and bear hunts: Japanese and North American family narrative patterns. *Journal of Child Language, 22,* 423–445.

Miotti, P.G., Taha, T.E.T., Kumwenda, N.I., Broadhead, R., Mtimavalye, L.A., Van der Hoeven, L., et al. (1999). HIV transmission through breastfeeding: A study in Malawi. *JAMA, 282,* 744–749.

Mirande, A. (1988). Chicano fathers: Traditional perceptions and current realities. In P. Bronstein & C/P Cowan (Eds.), *Fatherhood today: Men's changing role in the family* (pp. 93–106). New York: Wiley.

Mirmiran, M., Kok, J.H., Boer, K., & Wolf, H. (1992). Perinatal development of human circadian rhythms: Role of the fetal biological clock. *Neuroscience Biobehavioral Review, 16,* 371–378.

Mitchell, E.A., Thach, B.T., Thompson, J.M., & Williams, S. (1999). Changing infants' sleep position increases risk of sudden infant death syndrome. *Archives of Pediatrics & Adolescent Medicine, 153,* 1136–1141.

Mitka, M. (2000). Neonatal screening varies by state of birth. *JAMA, 284,* 2044–2046.

Mix, K.S., Huttenlocher, J., & Levine, S.C. (2002). Multiple cues for quantification in infancy: Is number one of them? *Psychological Bulletin, 128,* 278–294.

Miyake, K., Campos, J., Kagan, J., & Bradshaw, D. (1986). Issues in socioemotional development in Japan. In H. Azuma, K. Hakuta, & H. Stevenson (Eds.), *Kodomo: Child development and education in Japan* (pp. 238–261). San Francisco: Freeman.

Moe, V., & Smith, L. (2003). The relation of prenatal substance exposure and infant recognition memory to later cognitive competence. *Infant Behavior & Development, 26,* 87–99.

Mohan, E., Reef, G., Sarkar, M. (2006). *Breaking the Piggy Bank: Parents and the High Cost of Child Care.* Arlington, VA: National Association of Child Care Resource and Referral Agencies.

Montemayor, J., Druin, A., & Hendler, J. (2000). PETS: A personal electronic teller of stories. In A. Druin & J.

Hendler (Eds.), *Robots for kids* (pp. 74–108). San Francisco: Morgan Kaufmann Publishers.

Montgomery, C.R., & Clarkson, M.G. (1997). Infants' perception of pitch: Masking by low- and high-frequency noises. *Journal of the Acoustical Society of America, 102,* 3665–3672.

Moon, C., Cooper, R.P., & Fifer, W.P. (1993). Two-day-olds prefer their native language. *Infant Behavior and Development, 16,* 495–500.

Moon, R.Y., Patel, K.M., & Shaefer, S.J. (2000). Sudden infant death syndrome in child care settings. *Pediatrics, 106,* 295–300.

Moore, G.A., & Calkins, S.D. (2004). Infants' vagal regulation in the still-face paradigm is related to dyadic coordination of mother-infant interaction. *Developmental Psychology, 40,* 1068–1080.

Moore, G.A., Cohn, J.F., & Campbell, S.B. (1997). Mothers' affective behavior with infant siblings: Stability and change. *Developmental Psychology, 33,* 856–860.

Moore, G.A., Cohn, J.F., & Campbell, S.B. (2001). Infant responses to maternal still-face at 6 months differentially predict externalizing and internalizing behaviors at 18 months. *Developmental Psychology, 37,* 706–714.

Moore, M.K., & Meltzoff, A.N. (2004). Object permanence after a 24-hr delay and leaving the locale of disappearance: The role of memory, space, and identity. *Developmental Psychology, 40,* 606–620.

Moore, R., & Standley, J. (1996). Therapeutic effects of music and mother's voice on premature infants. *Pediatric Nursing, 21,* 509–514.

Moran, G.F., & Vinovskis, M.A. (1985). The great care of godly parents: Early childhood in Puritan New England. In Smuts, A.B., & Hagen, J. W. (Eds.), History and research in child development (pp. 24–37). *Monographs of the Society for Research in Child Development, 50*(4–5, Serial No. 211).

Morelli, G.A., Rogoff, B., Oppenheim, D., & Goldsmith, D. (1992). Cultural

variation in infants' sleeping arrangements: Questions of independence. *Developmental Psychology, 28,* 604–613.

Morison, S.J., Ames, E.W., & Chisholm, K. (1995). The development of children adopted from Romanian orphanages. *Merrill-Palmer Quarterly, 41,* 411–430.

Morrongiello, B.A., Fenwick, K.D., Hillier, L., & Chance, G. (1994). Sound localization in newborn human infants. *Developmental Psychobiology, 27,* 519–538.

Mortensen, E.L., Michaelsen, K.F., Sanders, S.A., & Reinisch, J.M. (2002). The association between duration of breastfeeding and adult intelligence. *JAMA, 287,* 2365–2371.

Moses, L.J., Baldwin, D.A., Rosicky, J.G., & Tidball, G. (2001). Evidenc for referential understanding in the emotions domain at twelve and eighteen months. *Child Development, 72,* 718–735.

Moss, W., Darmstadt, G.L., Marsh, D.R., Black, R.E., & Santosham, M. (2002). Research priorities for the reduction of perinatal and neonatal morbidity and mortality in developing country communities. *Journal of Perinatology, 22,* 484–495.

Mouradian, L.E., & Als, H. (1994). The influence of neonatal intensive care unit caregiving practices on motor functioning of preterm infants. *The American Journal of Occupational Therapy, 48,* 527–533.

Mouradian, L.E., Als, H., & Coster, W.J. (2000). Neurobehavioral functioning of healthy preterm infants of varying gestational ages. *Developmental and Behavioral Pediatrics, 21,* 408–416.

Mouradian, W.E., Wehr, E., & Crall, J.J. (2000). Disparities in children's oral health and access to dental care. *JAMA, 284,* 2625–2631.

Muir, D., & Hains, S. (2004). The u-shaped developmental function for auditory localization. *Journal of Cognition and Development, 5,* 123–130.

Muir, D., Abraham, W., Forbes, B., Harris, L. (1979). The ontogenesis of an auditory localization response from birth to four months of age. *Canadian Journal of Psychology, 33,* 320–333.

Muir, D.W., Clifton, R.K., Clarkson, M.G. (1989). The development of a human auditory localization response: a U-shaped function. *Canadian Journal of Psychology, 43,* 199–216.

Mulder, E., Robles de Medina, P., Huizink, A., Van den Bergh, B., Buitelaar, J., & Visser, G. (2002). Prenatal maternal stress: Effects on pregnancy and the (unborn) child. *Early Human Development, 70,* 3–14.

Mumme, D.L., & Fernald, A. (2003). The infant as onlooker: Learning from emotional reactions observed in a television scenario. *Child Development, 74,* 221–237.

Mumme, D.L., Fernald, A., & Herrera, C. (1996). Infants' responses to facial and vocal emotional signals in a social referencing paradigm. *Child Development, 67,* 3219–3237.

Munakata, Y. (1998). Infant perseveration and implications for object permanence theories: A PDP model of the AB task. *Developmental Science, 1,* 161–184.

Munakata, Y., McClelland, J., Johnson, M., & Siegler, R. (1997). Rethinking infant knowledge: Toward an adaptive process account of successes and failures in object permanence tasks. *Psychological Review, 104,* 686–713.

Mundy, P., Sigman, M., Ungerer, J., & Sherman, T. (1986). Defining the social deficits in autism: The contribution of nonverbal communication measures. *Journal of Child Psychology and Psychiatry, 27,* 657–669.

Murray, L., & Trevarthen, C. (1985). Emotional regulation of interactions between two-month-olds and their mothers. In T.M. Field & N.A. Fox (Eds.), *Social perception in infants* (pp. 177–197). Norwood, NJ: Ablex.

Murray, L., Fiori-Cowley, A., Hooper, R., & Cooper, P. (1996). The impact of postnatal depression and associated adversity on early mother-infant interactions and later infant outcome. *Child Development, 67,* 2512–2526.

Myers, M.M., Fifer, W. P., Schaeffer, L., Sahni, R., Ohira-Kist, K., Stark, R.I.,

et al., (1998). Effects of sleeping position and time after feeding on the organization of sleep/wake states in prematurely born infants. *Sleep, 21,* 343–350.

NACCRRA. (2003). Issue paper: Reauthorization of the Individuals with Disabilities Education Act. Retrieved August 29, 2005, from http://www.naccrra.org/policy

NACCRRA. (2005). Child care in America. Retrieved September 1, 2005, from http://www.naccrra.org

Nachmias, M., Gunnar, M., Mangelsdorf, S., Parritz, R.H., & Buss, K. (1996). Behavioral inhibition and stress reactivity: The moderating role of attachment security. *Child Development, 67,* 508–522.

NAEYC. (1995). *NAEYC position statement. Where we stand: Many languages, many cultures: Respecting and responding to diversity.* Adapted from *Responding to linguistic and cultural diversity: Recommendations for effective early childhood education.* Washington, DC: NAEYC.

NAEYC. (1996). *NAEYC position statement on technology and young children: Ages 3 through 8.* Washington, DC: NAEYC.

NAEYC. (2002). NAEYC accreditation. Retrieved on October 23, 2002, from http://www.naeyc.org

Naigles, L. G. (1990). Children use syntax to learn verb meanings. *Journal of Child Language, 17,* 357–374.

Naigles, L.G. (1996). The use of multiple frames in verb learning via syntactic bootstrapping. *Cognition, 58, 221–251.*

Nanez, J. (1988). Perception of impending collision in 3- to 6-week-old infants. *Infant Behavior and Development, 11,* 447–463.

Nanez, J., & Yonas, A. (1994). Effects of luminance and texture motion on infant defensive reactions to optical collision. *Infant Behavior and Development, 17,* 165–174.

Napier, K., & Meister, K. (2000). *Growing healthy kids: A parents' guide to infant and child nutrition.* New York: American Council on Science and Health.

National Association for Sport and Physical Education. (2002). *Active start guidelines for exercise for infants and toddlers.* Reston, VA: NASPE.

National Association of Childbearing Centers. (2002). The birth center concept. Retrieved January 12, 2002, from http://www.birthcenters.org

National Center for Biotechnology Information. (2002). Genes and disease. Retrieved January 12, 2002, from http://www.ncbi.nlm.nih.gov/disease/

National Center for Early Development and Learning (1997). Quality in child care centers, *Briefs, 1*(1). Chapel Hill, NC: Frank Porter Graham Child Development Center.

National Center for Education in Maternal and Child Health. (2002). *Bright futures in practice: Nutrition pocket guide.* Washington, DC: Georgetown University.

National Center for Education Statistics. (2004). Participation in undergraduate education. Washington, DC: Author. Retrieved November 1, 2005, from http://nces.gov

National Center for Health Statistics. (2000). Prenatal care. *National Vital Statistics Report, 48(3).* Hyattsville, MD.

National Center for Health Statistics. (2001). Births/natality. *National Vital Statistics Reports, 50(5).* Hyattsville, MD.

National Center for Health Statistics. (2002). *Health, United States, 2002. With chartbook on trends in the health of Americans.* Hyattsville, MD.

National Center for Health Statistics. (2003). *Health, United States, 2003. With chartbook on trends in the health of Americans.* Hyattsville, MD.

National Center for Health Statistics. (2005). *Health, United States, 2005. With chartbook on trends in the health of Americans.* Hyattsville, MD.

National Center on Shaken Baby Syndrome. (2002). SBS questions. Retrieved January 10, 2003, from http://www.dontshake.com/sbsquestions.html

National Child Abuse and Neglect Data System. (2004). *Summary of key findings from calendar year 2000.*

Retrieved January 10, 2006, from http://www.calib.com/nccanch/pubs/factsheets/canstats.cfm

National Child Care Information Center. (1999). Inclusive child care—Quality child care for all children. *Child Care Bulletin* (Jan./Feb., Issue 21). Retrieved September 1, 2005, from http://www.nccic.org/ccb/issue21.html

National Highway Traffic Safety Administration. (2002). Retrieved January 12, 2002, from http://www.nhtsa.dot.gov

National Institute of Neurological Disorders and Stroke (2001). NINDS spina bifida information. Retrieved December 10, 2005, from http://www.ninds.nih.gov/disorders/spina_bifida/spina_bifida.htm

NICHD (National Institute of Child Health and Human Development) Early Child Care Research Network. (1997a). The effects of infant child care on infant-mother attachment security: Results of the NICHD Study of Early Child Care. *Child Development, 68,* 860–879.

NICHD (National Institute of Child Health and Human Development) Early Child Care Research Network. (1997b). Child care in the first year of life. *Merrill-Palmer Quarterly, 43,* 340–360.

NICHD (National Institute of Child Health and Human Development) Early Child Care Research Network. (1998). Early child care and self-control, compliance and problem behavior at twenty-four and thirty-six months. *Child Development, 69,* 1145–1170.

NICHD (National Institute of Child Health and Human Development) Early Child Care Research Network. (2000). The relation of child care to cognitive and language development. *Child Development, 71,* 960–980.

NICHD (National Institute of Child Health and Human Development) Early Child Care Research Network. (2003). Does amount of time spent in child care predict socioemotional adjustment during the transition to kindergarten? *Child Development, 74,* 976–1005.

NICHD (National Institute of Child Health and Human Development) Early Child Care Research Network.

(2004). Trajectories of physical aggression from toddlerhood to middle childhood. *Monographs of the Society for Research in Child Development, 69*(4, Serial No. 278).

NICHD (National Institute of Child Health and Human Development) Early Child Care Research Network. (2005). *Child care and child development: Results from the NICHD Study of Early Child Care and Youth Development.* New York: Guilford Press.

NICHD (National Institute of Child Health and Human Development) Early Child Care Research Network & Duncan, G.J. (2003). Modeling the impacts of child care quality on children's preschool cognitive development. *Child Development, 74,* 1454–1475.

National Institute on Drug Abuse. (1996). *National Pregnancy and Health Survey* (pp. 93–3819). Rockville, MD: National Institutes of Health.

National Institute on Drug Abuse. (2002). Heroin: Abuse and addiction. Retrieved August 26, 2004, from http://www.nida.nih.gov/ResearchReports/heroin/heroin4.html

National Institute on Occupational Safety and Health. (2002). The effects of workplace hazards on male reproductive health. *DHHS (NIOSH) Publication No. 96–132.* Washington, DC: National Institute on Occupational Safety and Health.

National Organization on Fetal Alcohol Syndrome. (2002). What is Fetal Alcohol Syndrome? Retrieved January 12, 2002, from http://www.nofas.org/main/stats.htm

National SIDS Resource Center. (2002). What is SIDS? Retrieved January 10, 2003, from http://www.circsol.com/SIDS/SIDSFACT.HTM

Nazzi, T., Jusczyk, P. W., & Johnson, E. K. (2000). Language discrimination by English-learning 5-month-olds: Effects of rhythm and familiarity. *Journal of Memory & Language, 43,* 1–19.

Neisser, U. (1991). Two perceptually given aspects of the self and their development. *Developmental Review, 11,* 197–209.

Neisser, U. (1993). The self perceived. In U. Neisser (Ed.), *The perceived self: Ecological and interpersonal sources of self-knowledge* (pp. 3–24). New York: Cambridge University Press.

Nelson, C.A. (1987). The recognition of facial expression in the first two years of life: Mechanisms of development. *Child Development, 58,* 889–909.

Nelson, C.A. (1994). Neural correlates of recognition memory in the first postnatal year. In G. Dawson, & K. Fischer (Eds.), *Human behavior and the developing brain* (pp. 269–313). New York: Guildford Press.

Nelson, C.A. (1995). The ontogeny of human memory: A cognitive neuroscience perspective. *Developmental Psychology, 31,* 723–738.

Nelson, C.A. (1997). The neurobiological basis of early memory development. In N. Cowan (Ed.), *The development of memory in childhood* (pp. 41–82). Hove, UK: Psychology Press.

Nelson, C.A. (1998). The nature of early memory. *Preventive Medicine, 27,* 172–179.

Nelson, C.A., & Bloom, F.E. (1997). Child development and neuroscience. *Child Development, 68,* 970–987.

Nelson, C.A., & Horowitz, F.D. (1983). The perception of facial expressions and stimulus motion by 2- and 5-month-old infants using holographic stimuli. *Child Development, 56,* 868–877.

Nelson, C.A., & Monk, C.S. (2001). The use of event-related potentials in the study of cognitive development. In C.A. Nelson & M. Luciana (Eds.), *Handbook of developmental cognitive neuroscience* (pp. 125–136). Cambridge, MA: MIT Press.

Nelson, C.A., & Webb, S.J. (2002). A cognitive neuroscience perspective on early memory development. In M. de Haan & M.H. Johnson (Eds.), *The cognitive neuroscience of development* (pp. 99–125). London: Psychology Press.

Nelson, C.A., Thomas, K.M., & de Haan, M. (2006). Neural bases of cognitive development. In W. Damon & R. Lerner (Eds.) & D. Kuhn & R. Siegler (Vol. Eds.), *Handbook of child psychology: Vol. 2. Cognition, percep-*

tion, and language (6th ed., pp. 3–57). New York: Wiley.

Nelson, K. (1993). Events, narratives, memory: What develops? In C.A. Nelson (Ed.), *Memory and affect. Minnesota Symposia on Child Psychology* (Vol. 26, pp. 1–24). Hillsdale, NJ: Erlbaum.

Nelson, K. (1975). The nominal shift in semantic-syntactic development. *Cognitive Psychology, 7,* 461–479.

Nelson, K. (1973). Structure and strategy in learning to talk. *Monographs of the Society for Research in Child Language Development, 38*(149). Nelson, K., Hampson, J., & Shaw, L. (1993). Nouns in early lexicons: Evidence, explanations and implications. *Journal of Child Language, 20,* 61–84.

Newcombe, N., & Huttenlocher, J. (2006). Development of spatial cognition. In W. Damon & R. Lerner (Eds.) & D. Kuhn & R. Siegler (Vol. Eds.), *Handbook of child psychology: Vol. 2. Cognition, perception, and language* (6th ed., pp. 734–776). New York: Wiley.

Newcombe, N., Huttenlocher, J., Drummey, A.B., & Wiley, J.G. (1998). The development of spatial location coding: Place learning and dead reckoning in the second and third years. *Cognitive Development, 13,* 185–201.

Newcombe, N.S., Sluzenski, J., & Huttenlocher, J. (2005). Preexisting knowledge versus on-line learning: What do young infants really know about spatial location? *Psychological Science, 16,* 222–227.

Newport, E.L., & Aslin, R.N. (2000). Innately constrained learning: Blending old and new approaches to language acquisition. In S.C. Howell, S.A. Fish, & T. Keith-Lucas (Eds.), *Proceedings of the 24th Boston University Conference on Language Development* (pp. 1–21). Somerville, MA: Cascadilla Press.

Nguyen, S., Kushel, C., & Teele, R. (2002). Water birth: A near-drowning experience. *Pediatrics, 110,* 411–413.

NIH/NIMH Human Genetics Initiative (2005). *Identifying autism susceptibility genes.* Retrieved October 18, 2005, from http://www.nimh.nih.gov/press/autismgenetics.cfm

Nikodem, V.C. (2004). Immersion in water in pregnancy, labour and childbirth. In *The Cochrane Library* (Issue 1). Chichester, UK: Wiley

Nolan, M. (1995). Supporting women in labour: The doula's role. *Modern Midwife, 5,* 12–15.

Noymer, A. (2002). The March of Dimes. *American Journal of Public Health, 92*(2), 158.

Nsamenang, B.A. (1992). Perceptions of parenting among the Nso of Cameroon. *Father-child relations: Cultural and biosocial contexts* (pp. 321–344). New York: de Gruyter.

Nwokah, E., & Fogel, A. (1993). Laughter in mother-infant emotional communication. *Humor: International Journal of Humor Research, 6,* 137–161.

Nwokah, E.E., Hsu, H., Davies, P., & Fogel, A. (1999). The integration of laughter and speech in vocal communication: A dynamic systems perspective. *Journal of Speech and Hearing Research, 42,* 880–894.

O'Brien, M. (2004). Social science and public policy perspectives on fatherhood in the European Union. In M.E. Lamb (Ed.), *The role of the father in child development* (4th ed., pp. 121–145). New York: Wiley.

O'Connell, M. (1990). Maternity leave arrangements: 1961–1985. In *Work and Family Patterns of American Women. Current Population Reports,* Special Studies series P–23, no. 165. Washington, DC: U.S. Census Bureau.

O'Connor, T., Bredenkamp, D., Rutter, M., and The English and Romanian Adoptees (ERA) Study Team (1999). Attachment disturbances and disorders in children exposed to early severe deprivation. *Infant Mental Health Journal, 20,* 10–29.

O'Connor, T., Rutter, M., Beckett, C., Keaveney, L., Kreppner, J.M., and The English and Romanian Adoptees (ERA) Study Team. (2000). The effects of global severe privation on cognitive competence: Extension and longitudinal follow-up. *Child Development, 71,* 376–390.

O'Neill, C., Trainor, L.J., & Trehub, S.E. (2001). Infants' responsiveness to fathers' singing. *Music Perception, 18,* 409–425.

Oakes, L.M., & Madole, K.L. (2000). The future of infant categorization research: A process-oriented approach. *Child Development, 71,* 119–126.

Oakes, L.M., Coppage, D.J., & Dingel, A. (1997). By land or by sea: The role of perceptual similarity in infants' categorization of animals. *Developmental Psychology, 33,* 396–407.

Ochs, E., & Schieffelin, B. (1984). Language acquisition and socialization: Three developmental stories and their implications. In R. Schweder & R. Levine (Eds.), *Culture theory: Essays in mind, self and emotion* (pp. 276–320). New York: Cambridge University Press.

OECD. (2001). *Starting strong: Early childhood education and care.* Paris, France: OECD.

Offit, P.A., Quarles, J., Gerber, M.A., Hackett, C.J., Marcuse, E.K., Kollman, T.R., Gellin, B.G., & Landry, S. (2002). Addressing parents' concerns: Do multiple vaccines overwhelm or weaken the infant's immune system? *Pediatrics, 109,* 124–129.

Ogonuki, N., Inoue, K., Yamamoto, Y., Noguchi, Y., Tanemura, T., Suzuki, O., et al. (2002). Early death of mice cloned from somatic cells. *Nature Genetics, 30,* 253–254.

Oken, E., Wright, R.O., Kleinman, K.P., Bellinger, D., Amarasiriwardena, C.J., et al. (2005). Maternal fish consumption, hair mercury, and infant cognition in a U.S. cohort. *Environmental Health Perspectives, 113,* 1376–1380.

Olds, D.L., Henderson, C.R., Klitzman, H.J., Eckenrode, J.J., Cole, R.E., & Tatelbaum, R.C. (1999). Prenatal and infancy home visitation by nurses: Recent findings. *The Future of Children, 9,* 44–65.

Oller, D.K., & Eilers, R.E. (1988). The role of audition in infant babbling. *Child Development, 59,* 441–449.

Oshima-Takane, Y., Goodz, E., & Derevensky, J.L. (1996). Birth order effects on early language development: Do secondborn children learn from overheard speech? *Child Development, 67,* 621–634.

Oster, H., Hegley, D., & Nagel, L. (1992). Adult judgments and fine-grained analysis of infant facial expressions: Testing the validity of a priori coding formulas. *Developmental Psychology, 28,* 1115–1131.

Osterling, J., & Dawson, G. (1994). Early recognition of children with autism: A study of first birthday home videotapes. *Journal of Autism & Developmental Disorders, 24,* 247–257.

Ou, Y.S., & McAdoo, H.P. (1999). The ethnic socialization of Chinese American children. In H.P. McAdoo (Ed.), *Family ethnicity: Strength in diversity* (2nd ed., pp. 252–276). Thousand Oaks, CA: Sage.

Overpeck, M.D., Brenner, R.A., Trumble, A.C., Smith, G.S.. MacDorman, M.F., & Berendes, H.W. (1999). Infant injury deaths with unknown intent: What else do we know? *Injury Prevention, 5,* 272–275.

Oviatt, S. (1982). Inferring what words mean: Early development in infants' comprehension of common object names. *Child Development, 53,* 274–277.

Owen, C.G., Whincup, P.H., Odoki, K., Gilg, J.A., & Cook, D.G. (2002). Infant feeding and blood cholesterol: A study in adolescents and a systematic review. *Pediatrics,* 110, 597–608.

Owen, D. (2000, Aug. 21 & 22). The chosen one. *The New Yorker,* pp. 106–116, 118–119.

Owens, M.D. (1984). Pain in infancy: Conceptual and methodological issues. *Pain, 20,* 218–230.

Owens, R.E., Jr. (1984). *Language development: An introduction.* Columbus, OH: Charles E. Merrill Publishing.

Özcaliskan, S., & Goldin-Meadow, S. (2005a). Do parents lead their children by the hand? *Journal of Child Language, 32,* 481–505.

Özcaliskan, S., & Goldin-Meadow, S. (2005b). Gesture is at the cutting edge of early language development. *Cognition, 96,* B101–B113.

Palmer, C.F. (1989). The discriminating nature of infants' exploratory actions. *Developmental Psychology, 25,* 885–893.

Palmer, S. (1998). Shaken Baby Syndrome. Retrieved January 10, 2003, from http://thearc.org/faqs/Shaken.html

Pandis, G.K., Papageorghiou, A.T., Ramanathan, V.G., Thompson, M.O., & Nicolaides, K.H. (2001). Preinduction sonographic measurement of cervical length in the prediction of successful induction of labor. *Ultrasound in Obstetrics and Gynecology, 18,* 623–628.

Pang, J.W.Y., Heffelfinger, J.D., Huang, G.J., Benedetti, T.J., & Weiss, N.S. (2002). Outcomes of planned home births in Washington state: 1989–1996. *Obstetrics & Gynecology, 100,* 253–259.

Pantoja, A.P.F., Nelson-Goens, G.C. & Fogel, A. (2001). A dynamical systems approach to the study of early emotional development in the context of mother-infant communication (pp. 901–920). In A.F. Kalverboer & A.Gramsbergen (Eds), *Brain and Behavior in Human Development.* Dordrecht, The Netherlands: Kluwer Academic Publishers.

Papousek, H. (1996). Musicality in infancy research: Biological and cultural origins of early musicality. In I. Deliege, & J. Sloboda (Eds*.), Musical beginnings: Origins and development of musical competence* (pp. 37–87). Oxford: Oxford University Press.

Parke, R.D. (2002). Fathers and families. In M.H. Bornstein (Ed.), *Handbook of parenting: Vol. 3. Status and social conditions of parenting* (2nd ed., pp. 27–73). Mahwah, NJ: Erlbaum.

Parke, R.D., & Buriel, R. (2006). Socialization in the family: Ethnic and ecological perspectives. In W. Damon & R. Lerner (Eds.) & N. Eisenberg (Vol. Ed.), *Handbook of child psychology: Vol. 3. Social, emotional, and personality development* (6th ed., pp. 429–504). New York: Wiley.

Parke, R.D., Dennis, J., Flyr, M.L., Morris, K.L., Killian, C., McDowell, D.J.,

et al. (2004). Fathering and children's peer relationships. In M.E. Lamb (Ed.), *The role of the father in child development* (4th ed., pp. 307–340). New York: Wiley.

Parker, L., Pearce, M.S., Dickinson, H.O., Aitkin, M., & Craft, A.W. (1999). Stillbirths among offspring of male radiation workers at Sellafield nuclear reprocessing plant. *Lancet, 354,* 1407–1414.

Pauen, S. (2002). Evidence for knowledge-based category discrimination in infancy. *Child Development, 73,* 1016–1033.

Pawliuk, R., Westerman, K.A., Fabry, M.E., Payen, E., Tighe, R., Bouhassira, E.E., et al. (2001). Correction of sickle cell disease in transgenic mouse models by gene therapy. *Science, 294,* 2368–2371.

Peek, G.J., & Elliott, M.J. (2004). Fetal surgery for congenital diaphragmatic hernia. *Pediatrics, 113,* 1810–1811.

Pegg, J.E., Werker, J.F., & McLeod, P.J. (1992). Preference for infant-directed over adult-directed speech: Evidence from 7-week-old infants. *Infant Behavior and Development, 15,* 325–345.

Peisner-Feinberg, E.S., & Burchinal, M.R. (1997). Relations between preschool children's child-care experiences and concurrent development: The Cost, Quality, and Outcomes Study. *Merrill-Palmer Quarterly, 43,* 451–477.

Peisner-Feinberg, E.S., Burchinal, M.R., Clifford, R.M., Culkin, M.L., Howes, C., Kagan, S.L., et al. (2001). The relation of preschool child-care quality to children's cognitive and social developmental trajectories through second grade. *Child Development, 72,* 1534–1553.

Peláez-Nogueras, M., Field, T.M., Hossain, Z., & Pickens, J. (1996). Depressed mothers' touching increases infants' positive affect and attention in still-face interactions. *Child Development, 67,* 1780–1792.

Peláez-Nogueras, M., Field, T., Cigales, M., Gonzalez, A., & Clasky, S. (1995). Infants of depressed mothers show less "depressed" behavior with their nursery teachers. *Infant Mental Health Journal, 15,* 358–367.

Pellegrini, A.D. (1998). Rough-and-tumble play from childhood through adolescence. In D.P. Fromberg & D. Bergen (Eds.*), Play from birth to twelve and beyond: Contexts, perspectives, and meaning* (pp. 401–408). New York: Garland.

Pellegrini, A.D., & Smith, P.K. (1998). Physical activity play: The nature and function of a neglected aspect of play. *Child Development, 69,* 577–598.

Perera, F.P., Rauh, V., Tsai, W.Y., Kinney, P., Camman, D., Barr, D.B., et al. (2002). Effects of transplacental exposure to environmental pollutants on birth outcomes in a multiethnic population. *Environmntal Health Perspectives, 111,* 201–205.

Perera, F.P., Rauh, V., Whyatt, R.M., Tsai, W.Y., Bernert, J.T., Andrews, H., et al. (2004a). Molecular evidence of an interaction between prenatal environmental exposures and birth outcomes in a multiethnic population. *Environmental Health Perspectives, 112,* 626–630.

Perera, F.P., Tang, D., Tu, Y.H., Cruz, L.A., Borjas, M., Bernert, T., et al. (2004b). Biomarkers in maternal and newborn blood indicate heightened fetal susceptibility to procarcinogenic DNA damage. *Environmental Health Perspectives, 112,* 1133–1136.

Perry, B.D., & Pollard, R. (1998). Homeostasis, stress, trauma, and adaptation: A neurodevelopmental view of childhood trauma. *Child and Adolescent Psychiatric Clinics of North America, 7,* 33–51.

Pérusse, D. (2003b). New maternity and parental benefits. *Perspectives on Labour and Income, 4*(3), 12–15, Statistics Canada, Cat. No. 75-001-XIE.

Pesonen, A.K., Räikkönen, K., Keskivaara, P., & Keltikangas-Järvinen, L. (2002). Difficult temperament in childhood and adulthood: Continuity from maternal perceptions to self-ratings over 17 years. *Personality and Individual Differences, 34,* 19–31.

Peters, J.W.B., Koot, H.M., Grunau, R.E., de Boer, J., van Druenen, M.J., Tibboel, D., et al. (2003). Neonatal facial coding system for assessing postoperative pain in infants: Item reduction is valid and feasible. *The Clinical Journal of Pain, 19,* 353–363.

Petitto, L.A. & Kovelman, I. (2003). The bilingual paradox: How signing-speaking bilingual children help us to resolve it and teach us about the brain's mechanisms underlying all language acquisition. *Learning Languages, 8,* 5–18.

Petitto, L.A., & Marentette, P. (1991). Babbling in the manual mode: Evidence for the ontogeny of language. *Science, 251,* 1493–1496.

Petitto, L.A., Holowka, S., Sergio, L.E., Levy, B., & Ostry, D. J. (2004). Baby hands that move to the rhythm of language: Hearing babies acquiring sign language babble silently on the hands. *Cognition, 93,* 43–73.

Petitto, L.A., Holowka, S., Sergio, & Ostry, D.J. (2001). Language rhythms in baby hand movements: Hearing babies born to deaf parents babble silently with their hands. *Nature, 413,* 35–36.

Petitto, L.A., Zatorre, R.J., Gauna, K., NIkelski, E.J., Dostie, D., & Evans, A.C. (2000). Speech-like cerebral activity in profoundly deaf people processing signed languages: Implications for the neural basis of human language. *Proceedings of the National Academy of Sciences, 97,* 13961–13966.

Petrova, A., Gnedko, T., Maistrova, I., Zafranskaya, M., & Dainiak, N. (1997). Morbidity in a large cohort study of children born to mothers exposed to radiation from Chernobyl. *Stem Cells, 15*(Suppl. 2), 141–150.

Petterson, S., & Albers, A.B. (2001). Effects of poverty and maternal depression on early child development. *Child Development, 72,* 1794–1813.

Phipps, M.G., Blume, J.D., & DeMonner, S.M. (2002). Young maternal age associated with increased risk of postnatal death. *Obstetrics and Gynecology, 100,* 481–486.

Piaget, J. (1936/1952). *The origins of intelligence in children.* New York: Norton.

Piaget, J. (1937/1971). *The construction of reality in the child.* New York: Ballantine.

Piaget, J. (1946/1962). *Play, dreams and imitation in childhood.* New York: Norton.

Piaget, J. (1954). *The construction of reality in the child.* New York: Basic Books.

Pianta, R.C., & Rimm-Kaufmann, S. (2006). The social ecology of the transition to school: Classrooms, families, and children. In K. McCarthy & D. Phillips (Eds.), *Handbook of early child development* (pp. 490–507). Oxford, UK: Blackwell.

Pick, A.D., Gross, D., Heinrichs, M., Love, M., & Palmer, C. (1994). Development of perception of the unity of musical events. *Cognitive Development, 9,* 355–375.

Pierroutsakos, S.L., & Troseth, G.L. (2003). Video verité: Infants' manual investigation of objects on video. *Infant Behavior & Development, 26,* 183–199.

Pilu, G., & Hobbins, J.C. (2002). Sonography of fetal cerebrospinal anomalies. *Prenatal Diagnosis, 22,* 321–330.

Pinker, S. (1994). *The language instinct: How the mind creates langauge.* New York: William Morrow.

Pipp, S., Fischer, K.W., & Jennings, S. (1987). Acquisition of self- and mother knowledge in infancy. *Developmental Psychology, 23,* 86–96.

Plaisant, C., Druin, A., Lathan, C., Dakhane, K. Edwards, K., Vice, J.M., & Montemayor, J. (2000). A storytelling robot for pediatric rehabilitation. *Proceedings of ASSETS'00.* New York: Association for Computing Machinery.

Pleck, J.H. (1997). Paternal involvement: Levels, sources, and consequences. In M.E. Lamb (Ed.), *The role of the father in child development* (pp. 66–103). New York: Wiley.

Pleck, J.H., & Masciadrelli, B.P. (2004). Paternal involvement by U.S. residential fathers: Levels, sources, and consequences. In M.E. Lamb (Ed.), *The role of the father in child development* (4th ed., pp. 272–306). New York: Wiley.

Polka, L., & Bohn, O.S. (1996). Cross-language comparison of vowel perception in English-learning and German-learning infants. *Journal of the Acoustical Society of America, 100,* 577–592.

Polka, L., & Werker, J. F. (1994). Developmental changes in perception of nonnative vowel contrasts. *Journal of Experimental Psychology: Human Perception and Performance, 20,* 421–435.

Pollack, L.A. (1983). *Forgotten children: Parent-child relations from 1500 to 1900.* New York: Cambridge University Press.

Pollitt, E., Gorman, K.S., Engle, P.L., Martorell, R., & Rivera, J. (1993). Early supplementary feeding and cognition. *Monographs of the Society for Research in Child Development, 58*(7, Serial No. 235).

Pollitt, E., Golub, M., Gorman, K., Gratham-McGregor, S., Levitsky, D., Schürch, B., et al. (1996). A reconceptualization of the effects of undernutrition on children's biological, psychosocial, and behavioral development. *Social Policy Report, 10*(5), 1–28.

Population Reference Bureau/Child Trends (2002). *KIDS COUNT international data sheet summary.* Washington, DC: PRB/CT.

Porter, M.L., & Dennis, B.L. (2002). Hyperbilirubinemia in the term newborn. *American Family Physician, 65,* 599–606.

Porter, R.H., & Winberg, J. (1999). Unique salience of maternal breast odors for newborn infants. *Neuroscience and Biobehavioral Reviews, 23,* 439–449.

Porter, R.H., Makin, J.W., Davis, L.B., & Christensen, K.M. (1992). Breastfed infants respond to olfactory cues from their own mothers and unfamiliar lactating females. *Infant Behavior and Development, 15,* 85–93.

Posada, G., Carbonell, O.A., Alzate, G., & Plata, S.J. (2004). Through Colombian lenses: Ethnographic and conventional analyses of maternal care and their associations with secure base behavior. *Developmental Psychology, 40,* 508–518.

Posada, G., Gao, Y, Posada, R., Tascon, M., Schoelmerich, A., Sagi, A., et al. (1995). The secure-base phenomenon across cultures: Children's behavior, mothers' preferences, and experts' concepts. In E. Waters, B.E. Vaughn, G., Posada, & K. Kondo-Ikemura (Eds.), Caregiving, cultural, and cognitive perspectives on secure-base behavior and working models: New growing points in attachment theory and research. *Monographs of the Society for Research in Child Development, 60* (Serial No. 244), 27–48.

Powell, D.R. (2006). Families and early childhood interventions. In W. Damon & R. Lerner (Eds.) & K.A. Renninger & I.E. Sigel (Vol. Eds.), *Handbook of child psychology: Vol. 4. Child psychology in practice* (6th ed., pp. 548–591). New York: Wiley.

Pretorius, E., Naudé, H., & Van Vuuren, C.J. (2002). Can cultural behavior have a negative impact on the development of visual integration pathways? *Early Child Development and Care, 172,* 173–181.

Price, C.V.G. (1979). A model for the implementation of a Suzuki violin program for the day-care center environment: An evaluation of its effectiveness and impact. *Dissertation Abstracts International, 40,* 5357A.

Proctor, B.D., & Dalaker, J. (2003). Poverty in the United States: 2002. *Current Population Reports, P60–222.* Washington, DC: U.S. Census Bureau.

Pruett, K. (1987). *The nurturing father.* New York: Warner Books.

Pye, C. (1986). Quiche Mayan speech to children. *Journal of Child Language, 13,* 85–100.

Quinn, P.C., Eimas, P.D., & Rosenkranz, S.L. (1993). Evidence for representations of perceptually similar natural categories by 3-month-old and 4-month-old infants. *Perception, 22,* 463–475.

Radin, N. (1994). Primary-caregiving fathers in intact families. In A.E. Gottfried & A.W. Gottfried (Eds.), *Redefining families: Implications for children's development* (pp. 11–54). New York: Plenum.

Rahn, S.L., & Burch, H.A. (2002). Paid maternal and parental leave legislation and primary prevention. *The Social Policy Journal, 1,* 75–86.

Raje, N., & Anderson, K. (1999). Thalidomide: A revival story. *New England Journal of Medicine, 341,* 1606–1609.

Rakison, D.H., & Poulin-Dubois, D. (2002). You go this way and I'll go that way: Developmental changes in infants' detection of correlations among static and dynamic features in motion events. *Child Development, 73,* 682–699.

Ramey, C.T., & Campbell, F.A. (1991). Poverty, early childhood education, and academic competence. In A. Huston (Ed.), *Children reared in poverty* (pp. 190–221). Cambridge, UK: Cambridge University Press.

Ramey, C.T., & Ramey, S.L. (1998a). Early intervention and early experience. *American Psychologist, 53,* 109–120.

Ramey, C.T., & Ramey, S.L. (1998b). Prevention of intellectual disabilities: Early interventions to improve cognitive development. *Preventive Medicine, 27,* 224–232.

Ramey, C.T., Ramey, S.L., & Lanzi, R.G. (2006). Children's health and education. In W. Damon & R. Lerner (Eds.) & K.A. Renninger & I.E. Sigel (Vol. Eds.), *Handbook of child psychology: Vol. 4. Child psychology in practice* (6th ed., pp. 864–892). New York: Wiley.

Ramey, C.T., Campbell, F.A., Burchinal, M., Skinner, M. L., Gardner, D. M., & Ramey, S. L. (2000). Persistent effects of early childhood education on high-risk children and their mothers. *Applied Developmental Science, 4,* 2–14.

Ramus, F., Hauser, M.D., Miller, C., Morris, D., & Mehler, J. (2001). Language discrimination by human newborns and by cotton-top tamarin monkeys. In M. Tomasello & E. Bates (Eds.), *Language development: The essential readings* (pp. 34–41). Malden, MA: Blackwell.

Rao, M.R., Hediger, M.L., Levine, R.J., Naficy, A.B., & Vi, K.T. (2002). Effect of breastfeeding on cognitive development of infants born small for gestational age. *Acta Paediatrica, 91*, 267–274.

Rao, R., & Georgieff, M.K. (2000) Early nutrition and brain development. In C.A. Nelson (Ed.), The effects of early adversity on neurobehavioral development. *The Minnesota symposia on child psychology, 31*, 1–30. Mahwah, NJ: Lawrence Erlbaum Associates.

Rao, R., & Georgieff, M.K. (2001). Neonatal iron nutrition. *Seminars in Neonatology, 6*, 425–435.

Rapin, I. (1997). Autism. *New England Journal of Medicine, 337*, 97–104.

Rattaz, C., Goubet, N., Bullinger, A. (2005). The calming effect of a familiar odor on full-term newborns. *Journal of Developmental & Behavioral Pediatrics, 26*, 86–92.

Rauscher, F.H. (2002). Mozart and the mind: Factual and fictional effects of musical enrichment. In J. Aronson (Ed.), *Improving academic achievement: Impact of psychological factors on education* (pp. 267–278). San Diego: Academic Press.

Rauscher, F.H. (2003). Can music instruction affect children's cognitive development? *ERIC Digest, EDO-PS-03-12.*

Rauscher, F.H., & LeMieux, M.T. (2003, April). *Piano, rhythm, and singing instruction improve different aspects of spatial-temporal reasoning in Head Start children.* Poster presented at the annual meeting of the Cognitive Neuroscience Society, New York.

Rauscher, F.H., & Zupan, M. (2000). Classroom keyboard instruction improves kindergarten children's spatial-temporal performance: A field experiment. *Early Childhood Research Quarterly, 15*, 215–228.

Rauscher, F.H., Shaw, G.L., & Ky, K.N. (1993). Music and spatial task performance. *Nature, 365*, 611.

Rauscher, F.H., Shaw, G.L., & Ky, K.N. (1995). Listening to Mozart enhances spatial-temporal reasoning: Towards a neurophysiological basis. *Neuroscience Letters, 185*, 44–47.

Rauscher, F.H., Shaw, G.L., Levine, L.J., Wright, E.L., Dennis, W.R., & Newcomb, R.L. (1997). Music training causes long-term enhancement of preschool children's spatial-temporal reasoning. *Neurological Research, 19*(1), 1–8.

Raver, C.C. (2002). Emotions matter: Making the case for the role of young children's emotional development for early school readiness. *Social Policy Report, 16*(3), 3–19.

Raver, C.C. (2003). *Young children's emotional development and school readiness.* EDO-PS-03-8. Champaign, IL: Clearinghouse on Elementary and Early Childhood Education.

Rayburn, W.F., & Zhang, J. (2002). Rising rates of labor induction: Present concerns and future strategies. *Obstetrics & Gynecology, 100*, 164–167.

Reddy, U.M., & Mennuti, M.T. (2006). Incorporating first-trimester Down Syndrome studies into prenatal screening. *Obstetrics & Gynecology, 107*, 167–173.

Reis, H.T., & Collins, W.A. (2004). Relationships, human behavior, and psychological science. *Current Directions in Psychological Science, 13*, 233–237.

Reissland, N., & Snow, D. (1996). Maternal pitch height in ordinary and play situations. *Journal of Child Language, 23*, 269–278.

Repacholi, B.M., & Gopnik, A. (1997). Early reasoning about desires: Evidence from 14- and 18-month-olds. *Developmental Psychology, 33*, 12–21.

Repka, M.X. (2002). Eye drops and patches both in fact work for amblyopia. *BMJ, 324*, 1397.

Repka, M.X., Beck, R.W., Holmes, J.M., Birch, E.E., Chandler, D.L., Cotter, S.A., et al. (2003). A randomized trial of patching regimens for treatment of moderate amblyopia in children. *Archives of Ophthalmology, 121*, 603–611.

Rescorla, L. (1989). The Language Development Survey: A screening tool for delayed language in toddlers. *Journal of Speech and Hearing Disorders, 54*, 587–599.

Rescorla, L, & Alley, A. (2001). Validation of the Language Development Survey (LDS): A parent report tool for identifying language delay in toddlers. *Journal of Speech, Language, and Hearing Research, 44*, 434–445.

Rescorla, L.A. (1980). Overextension in early language development. *Journal of Child Language, 7*, 321–335.

Reynell, J., & Gruber, C. (1990). *Reynell Developmental Language Scales—U.S. Edition.* Los Angeles: Western Psychological Services.

Reynolds, A.J., & Robertson, D.L. (2003). School-based early intervention and later child maltreatment in the Chicago Longitudinal Study. *Child Development, 74*, 3–26.

Reznick, J.S., Corley, R., & Robinson, J. (1997). A longitudinal twin study of intelligence in the second year. *Monographs of the Society for Research in Child Development, 62*(1, Serial No. 250).

Reznick, J.S., Fueser, J., & Bosquet, M. (1998). Self-corrected reaching in a three-location delayed-response search task. *Psychological Science, 9*, 66–70.

Ricci, C.M., & Beal, C.R. (2002). The effect of interactive media on children's story memory. *Journal of Educational Psychology, 94*, 138–144.

Richman, A.L., Miller, P.M., & LeVine, R.A. (1992). Cultural and educational variations in maternal responsiveness. *Developmental Psychology, 28*, 614–621.

Richter, L., & Richter, D.M. (2001). Exposure to parental tobacco and alcohol use: Effects on children's health and development. *American Journal of Orthopsychiatry, 71*, 182–203.

Rideout, V.J., & Hamel, E. (2006). *The media family: Electronic media in the lives of infants, toddlers, preschoolers, and their parents.* Menlo Park, CA: The Henry J. Kaiser Family Foundation.

Rideout, V.J., Vandewater, E.A., & Wartella, E.A. (2003). *Zero to six: Electronic media in the lives of infants, toddlers and preschoolers.* Menlo Park, CA: The Henry J. Kaiser Family Foundation.

Rieser, J.J. (1979). Spatial orientation of six-month-old infants. *Child Development, 50*, 1078–1087.

Riley, L.A., & Glass, J.L. (2002). You can't always get what you want–Infant care preferences and use among employed mothers. *Journal of Marriage and Family, 64,* 2–15.

Ringgenberg, S. (2004). Singing as a teaching tool. Early Years Are Learning Years, Release # 04/1. Washington, DC: National Association for the Education of Young Children. Retrieved March 29, 2006, from http://www.naeyc.org/ece/2004/01.asp

Rivera-Gaxiola, M., Silva-Pereyra, J., & Kuhl, P.K. (2005). Brain potentials to native and non-native speech contrasts in 7- and 11-month-old American infants. *Developmental Science, 8,* 162–172.

Robboy, S.J., Noller, K.L., O'Brien, P., Kaufman, R.H., Townsend, D., Barnes, A.B., et al. (1984). Increased incidence of cervical and vaginal dysplasia in 3,980 diethylstilbestrol-exposed young women: experience of the National Collaborative Diethylstilbestrol Adenosis Project. *JAMA, 252,* 2979–2983.

Robert R. McCormick Foundation. (1997). *Ten Things Every Child Needs.* Chicago: McCormick Foundation.

Robin, D.J., Berthier, N.E., & Clifton, R.K. (1996). Infants' predictive reaching for moving objects in the dark. *Developmental Psychology, 32,* 824–835.

Rochat, P. (1989). Object manipulation and exploration in 2- to 5-month-old infants. *Developmental Psychology, 25,* 871–884.

Rochat, P., & Senders, S.J. (1991). Active touch in infancy: Action systems in development. In M.J.S. Weiss & P.R. Zelazo (Eds.), *Newborn attention: Biological constraints and the influence of experience* (pp. 412–442). Norwood, NJ: Ablex.

Rochat, P., Querido, J. G., & Striano, T. (1999). Emerging sensitivity to the timing and structure of protoconversation in early infancy. *Developmental Psychology, 35,* 950–957.

Rock, A.M.L., Trainor, L.J., & Addison, T.L. (1999). Distinctive messages in infant-directed lullabies and playsongs. *Developmental Psychology, 35,* 527–534.

Rogoff, B. (1998). Cognition as a collaborative process. In W. Damon (Editor-in-Chief), D. Kuhn, & R.S. Siegler (Vol. Eds.), *Handbook of child psychology: Vol. 2. Cognition, perception, and language* (5th ed., pp. 679–744). New York: Wiley.

Rogoff, B., & Morelli, G. (1989). Perspectives on children's development from cultural psychology. *American Psychologist, 44,* 343–348.

Rogoff, B., Mistry, J., Göncü, A., & Mosier, C. (1993). Guided participation in cultural activity by toddlers and caregivers. *Monographs of the Society for Research in Child Development, 58*(8, Serial No. 236).

Rogoff, B., Topping, K., Baker-Sennett, J., & Lacasa, P. (2002). Mutual contributions of individuals, partners, and institutions: Planning to remember in Girl Scout cookie sales. *Social Development, 11,* 266–289.

Rolnick, A., & Grunewald, R. (2003). The ABCs of ECD: A Discussion on the Economics of Early Childhood Development. *The Region, 17(4),* 6–11.

Romero, R., Gómez, R., Chaiworapongsa, T., Conoscenti, G., Kim, J.C., & Kim, Y.M. (2001). The role of infection in preterm labour and delivery. *Paediatric and Perinatal Epidemiology, 15*(Suppl. 2), 41–56.

Rönnqvist, L., & von Hofsten, C. (1994). Neonatal finger and arm movements as determined by a social and an object context. *Early Development & Parenting, 3,* 81–94.

Rooks, J.P. (1997). *Midwifery and childbirth in America.* Philadelphia: Temple University Press.

Rooks, J.P., Weatherby, N.L., Ernst, E.K.M., Stapleton, S., Rosen, D., & Rosenfiled, A. (1989). Outcomes of care in birth centers: The National Birth Center Study. *New England Journal of Medicine, 321,* 1804–1811.

Roopnarine, J.L. (2004). African American and African Caribbean fathers: Level, quality, and meaning of involvement. In M.E. Lamb (Ed.), *The role of the father in child development* (4th ed., pp. 58–97). New York: Wiley.

Roopnarine, J.L., Johnson, J.E., & Hooper, F.H. (Eds.). (1994). *Children's play in diverse cultures.* Albany, NY: State University of New York Press.

Roopnarine, J.L., Lasker, J., Sacks, M., & Stores, M. (1998). The cultural contexts of children's play. In O.N. Saracho, & B. Spodek (Eds.), *Multiple perspectives on play in early childhood education* (pp. 194–219). Albany, NY: State University of New York Press.

Rose, S.A. (1981). Developmental changes in infants' retention of visual stimuli. *Child Development, 52,* 227–233.

Rose, S.A., & Feldman, J.F. (1995). Prediction of IQ and specific cognitive abilities at 11 years from infancy measures. *Developmental Psychology, 31,* 685–696.

Rose, S.A., & Feldman, J.F. (1997). Memory and speed: Their role in the relation of infant information processing to later IQ. *Child Development, 68,* 630–641.

Rose, S.A., & Feldman, J.F. (2000). The relation of very low birthweight to basic cognitive skills in infancy and childhood. In C.A. Nelson (Ed.), *The effects of early adversity on neurobehavioral development: The Minnesota Symposia on Child Psychology* (Vol. 31, pp. 31–59). Mahwah, NJ: Erlbaum.

Rose, S.A., Feldman, J.F., & Jankowski, J.J. (2001). Visual short-term memory in the first year of life: Capacity and recency effects. *Developmental Psychology, 37,* 539–549.

Rose, S.A., Feldman, J.F., & Jankowski, J.J. (2002). Processing speed in the 1st year of life: A longitudinal study of preterm and full-term infants. *Developmental Psychology, 38,* 895–902.

Rose, S.A., Feldman, J.F., Jankowski, J.J., & Van Rossem, R. (2005). Pathways from prematurity and infant abilities to later cognition. *Child Development, 76,* 1172–1184.

Rosengren, K.S., Gross, D., & Perlmutter, M. (1986). Preschool children's computing activity. *ERIC document ED 264–953. Resources in Education.* Available at http://www.eric.ed.gov

Ross-Sheehy, S., Oakes, L.M., & Luck, S.J. (2003). The development of visual short-term memory capacity in infants. *Child Development, 74,* 1807–1822.

Rothbart, M.K. (1981). Measurement of temperament in infancy. *Child Development, 52,* 569–578.

Rothbart, M.K. (2004). Commentary: Differentiated measures of temperament and multiple pathways to childhood disorders. *Journal of Clinical Child and Adolescent Psychology, 33,* 82–87.

Rothbart, M.K., & Bates, J.E. (1998). Temperament. In W. Damon (Series Ed.) & N. Eisenberg (Vol. Ed.), *Handbook of child psychology: Vol. 3. Social, emotional, and personality development* (5th ed., pp. 105–176). New York: Wiley.

Rothbart, M.K., & Bates, J.E. (2006). Temperament. In W. Damon & R. Lerner (Series Eds.) & N. Eisenberg (Vol. Ed.), *Handbook of child psychology: Vol. 3. Social, emotional, and personality development* (6th ed., pp. 99–166). New York: Wiley.

Rothbart, M.K., & Derryberry, D. (1981). Development of individual differences in temperament. In M.E. Lamb & A.L. Brown (Eds.), *Advances in developmental psychology* (Vol. 1, pp. 37–86). Hillsdale, NJ: Erlbaum.

Rothbart, M.K., Ahadi, S.A., & Evans, S.A. (2000). Temperament and personality: Origins and outcomes. *Journal of Personality and Social Psychology, 78,* 122–135.

Rothbart, M.K., Derryberry, D., & Hershey, K. (2000). Stability of temperament in childhood: Laboratory infant assessment to parent report at seven years. In V.J. Molfese & D.L. Molfese (Eds.), *Temperament and personality development across the life span* (pp. 85–119). Hillsdale, NJ: Erlbaum.

Rothbart, M.K., Ahadi, S.A., & Hershey, K.L.(1994). Temperament and social behavior in childhood. *Merrill-Palmer Quarterly, 40,* 21–39.

Rothbart, M.K., Ahadi, S.A., Hershey, K., & Fisher, P. (2001). Investigations of temperament at three to seven years:

The Children's Behavior Questionnaire. *Child Development, 72,* 1394–1408.

Rothman, K.J., Moore, L.L., Singer, M.R., Nguyen, U.S., Mannino, S., & Milunsky, A. (1995). Teratogenicity of high vitamin A intake. *New England Journal of Medicine, 333,* 1369–1373.

Rovee-Collier, C. (1999). The development of infant memory. *Current Directions in Psychological Science, 8,* 80–85.

Rovee-Collier, C., Hartshorn, K., & DiRubbo, M. (1999). Long-term maintenance of infant memory. *Developmental Psychobiology, 35,* 91–102.

Rubin, K.H., Bukowski, W., & Parker, J.G. (1998). Peer interactions, relationships, and groups. In W. Damon (Series Ed.) & N. Eisenberg (Vol. Ed.), *Handbook of child psychology: Vol. 3. Social, emotional, and personality development* (5th ed., pp. 619–700). New York: Wiley.

Rubin, K.H., Bukowski, W., & Parker, J.G. (2006). Peer interactions, relationships, and groups. In W. Damon & R. Lerner (Eds.) & N. Eisenberg (Vol. Ed.), *Handbook of child psychology: Vol. 3. Social, emotional, and personality development* (6th ed., pp. 571–645). New York: Wiley.

Rubin, K.H., Fein, G.G., & Vandenberg, B. (1983). Play. In E.M. Hetherington (Vol. Ed.) & P.H. Mussen (Series Ed.), *Handbook of child psychology* (Vol. 4, pp. 693–741). New York: Wiley.

Ruda, M.A., Ling, Q-D., Hohmann, A.G., Peng, Y.B., & Tachibana, T. (2000). Altered nociceptive neuronal circuits after neonatal peripheral inflammation. *Science, 289,* 628–630.

Ruhm, C.J. (1998). Parental leave and child health. NBER Working Paper No. W6554. Cambridge, MA: National Bureau of Economic Research.

Rush, J., Burlock, S., Lambert, K., Loosley-Millman, M., Hutchinson, B., & Enkin, M. (1996). The effects of whirlpool baths in labor: A randomized controlled trial. *Birth, 23,* 136–143.

Rutter, M. (1998). Developmental catch-up, and deficit, following adoption after severe global early privation. English

and Romanian Adoptees (ERA) Study Team. *Journal of Child Psychology & Psychiatry, 39,* 465–476.

Rutter, M. (2000). Resilience reconsidered: Conceptual considerations, empirical findings, and policy implications. In J.P. Shonkoff & S.J. Meisels (Eds.), *Handbook of early childhood intervention,* (2th ed., pp. 651–682). New York: Cambridge University Press.

Rutter, M., and the English and Romanian Adoptees (ERA) Study Team. (1998). Developmental catch-up, and deficit, following adoption after severe global early privation. *Journal of Child Psychology and Psychiatry, 39,* 465–476.

Rutter, M., Kreppner, J., & O'Connor, T. (2001). Specificty and heterogeneity in children's responses to profound institutional privation. *British Journal of Psychiatry, 179,* 97–103.

Rutter, M., Andersen-Wood, L., Beckett, C., Bredenkamp, D., Castle, J., Groothues, C., Kreppner, J., Keaveney, L., Lord, C., & O'Connor, T.G. (1999). Quasi-autistic patterns following severe early global privation. English and Romanian Adoptees (ERA) Study Team. *Journal of Child Psychology and Psychiatry, 40,* 537–549.

Rymer, R. (1993). *An abused child: Flight from silence.* New York: HarperCollins.

Saarni, C., Mumme, D.L., & Campos, J.J. (1998). Emotional development: Action, communication, and understanding. In W. Damon (Series Ed.) & N. Eisenberg (Vol. Ed.), *Handbook of child psychology: Vol. 3. Social, emotional, and personality development* (5th ed., pp. 237–309). New York: Wiley.

Saffran, J.R. (2003). Statistical language learning: Mehanisms and constraints. *Current Directions in Psychological Science, 12,* 110–114.

Saffran, J.R., & Thiessen, E.D. (2003). Pattern induction by infant language learners. *Developmental Psychology, 39,* 484–494.

Saffran, J.R., Aslin, R.N., Newport, E.L. (1996). Statistical learning by 8-month-old infants. *Science, 274,* 1926–1928.

Saffran, J.R., Loman, M.M., & Robertson, R.R.W. (2000). Infant memory for musical experiences. *Cognition, 77,* B15–B23.

Saffran, J.R., Werker, J.F., & Werner, L.A. (2006). The infant's auditory world: Hearing, speech, and the beginnings of language. In W. Damon & R. Lerner (Eds.) & D. Kuhn & R. Siegler (Vol. Eds.), *Handbook of child psychology: Vol. 2. Cognition, perception, and language* (6th ed., pp. 58–108). New York: Wiley.

Sagi, A., Koren-Karie, N., Gini, M., Ziv, Y., & Joels, T. (2002). Shedding further light on the effects of various types and quality of early child care on infant-mother attachment relationship: The Haifa Study of Early Child Care. *Child Development, 73,* 1166–1186.

Sagi, A., van IJzendoorn, M.H., Aviezer, O., Donnell, F., & Mayseless, O. (1994). Sleeping out of home in a kibbutz communal arrangement: It makes a difference for infant-mother attachment. *Child Development, 65,* 992–1004.

Sagi, A., Lamb, M.E., Lewkowicz, K.S., Shoham, R., Dvir, R., & Estes, D. (1985). Security of infant-mother, -father, and –metapelet attachments among kibbutz-reared Israeli children. In I. Bretherton & E. Waters (Eds.), Growing points of attachment theory and research. *Monographs of the Society for Research in Child Development, 50*(1/2, Serial No. 209), 257–275.

Sagi, A., van IJzendoorn, M.H., Aviezer, O., Donnell, F., Koren-Karie, N., Joels, T., & Harel, Y. (1995). Attachments in a multiple-caregiver and multiple-infant environment: The case of the Israeli kibbutzim. In E. Waters, B.E. Vaughn, G., Posada, & K. Kondo-Ikemura (Eds.), Caregiving, cultural, and cognitive perspectives on secure-base behavior and working models: New growing points in attachment theory and research. *Monographs of the Society for Research in Child Development, 60* (Serial No. 244), 71–91.

Salsberry, P.J., & Reagan, P.B. (2005). Dyanmics of early childhood overweight. *Pediatrics, 116,* 1329–1338.

Samuels, H.R. (1980). The effect of an older sibling on infant locomotor exploration of a new environment. *Child Development, 51,* 607–609.

Sanchez-Ramos, L., Olivier, F., Delke, I., & Kaunitz, A.M. (2003). Labor induction versus expectant management for postterm pregnancies: A systematic review with meta-analysis. *Obstetrics & Gynecology, 101,* 1312–1318.

Sanders, C., Diego, M., Fernandez, M., Field, T., Hernandez-Reif, M., Roca, A. (2002). EEG asymmetry responses to lavender and rosemary aromas in adults and infants. *International Journal of Neuroscience, 112,* 1305–1320.

Santos, I., Victora, C.G., Martines, J., Goncalves, H., Gigante, H.P., Valle, N.J., et al. (2001). Nutrition counselling increases weight gain among Brazilian children. *Journal of Nutrition, 131,* 2866–2873.

Santos, I.S., Victora, C.G., Huttly, S., & Carvalhal, J. B. (1998). Caffeine intake and low birthweight: A population-based case-control study. *American Journal of Epidemiology, 147,* 620–627.

Satcher, D. (2000). *Oral health in America: A report of the Surgeon General.* Washington, DC: U.S. Department of Health and Human Services.

Savulescu, J., & Dahl, E. (2000). Sex selection and preimplantation diagnosis: A response to the Ethics Committee of the American Society of Reproductive Medicine. *Human Reproduction, 15,* 1879–1880.

Sayle, A.E., Savitz, D.A., Thorp, J.M., Hertz-Picciotto, I., & Wilcox, A.J. (2001). Sexual activity during late pregnancy and risk of preterm delivery. *Obstetrics & Gynecology, 97,* 283–289.

Schaal, B., Marlier, L., & Soussignan, R. (1998). Olfactory function in the human fetus: Evidence from selective neonatal responsiveness to the odor of amniotic fluid. *Behavioral Neuroscience, 112,* 1438–1449.

Schaal, B., Marlier, L., Soussignan, R. (2000). Human foetuses learn odours from their pregnant mother's diet. *Chemical Senses, 25,* 729–737.

Scheers, N.J., Rutherford, G.W., & Kemp, J.S. (2003). Where should infants sleep? A comparison of risk for suffocation of infants sleeping in cribs, adult beds, and other sleeping locations. *Pediatrics, 112,* 883–889.

Schellenberg, E.G. (2004). Music lessons enhance IQ. *Psychological Science, 15,* 511–514.

Schellenberg, E.G. (2005). Music and cognitive abilities. *Current Directions in Psychological Science, 14,* 317–320.

Schenker, J. G., & Ezra, Y. (1994). Complications of assisted reproductive techniques. *Fertility and Sterility, 61,* 411–422.

Schieffelin, B.B. (1990). *The give and take of everyday life: Language socialization of Kaluli children.* Cambridge, UK: Cambridge University Press.

Schieve, L.A., Peterson, H.B., Meikle, S.F., Jeng, G., Danel, I., Burnett, N. M., et al. (1999). Live-birth rates and multiple-birth risk using in vitro fertilization. *JAMA, 282,* 1832–1838.

Schieve, L.A., Cogswell, M.E., Scanlon, K.S., Perry, G., Ferre, C., Blackmore-Price, C., et al. (2000). Prepregnancy body mass index and pregnancy weight gain: Associations with preterm delivery. *Obstetrics & Gynecology, 96,* 194–200.

Schlossman, S. (1985). Perils of popularization: The founding of *Parents Magazine.* In A. Smuts & J.W. Hagen (Eds.), History and research in child development (pp. 65–77). *Monographs of the Society for Research in Child Development, 50*(4–5, Serial No. 211).

Schmidt, L.A., Fox, N.A., Rubin, K.H., Sternberg, E.M., Gold, P.W., Smith, C.C., & Schulkin, J. (1997). Behavioral and neuroendocrine responses in shy children. *Developmental Psychobiology, 30,* 127–140.

Schmidt, L.A., Fox, N.A., Schulkin, J., & Gold, P.W. (1999). Behavioral and psychophysiological correlates of self-presentation in temperamentally shy children. *Developmental Psychobiology, 35,* 119–135.

Schmidt, N., Abelsen, B., & Olan, P. (2002). Deliveries in maternity homes in Norway: Results from a 2-year prospective study. *Acta Obstetr Gynecol Scand, 81,* 731–737.

Schmitt, B.D. (1991). *Your child's health: The parents' guide to symptoms, emergencies, common illnesses, behavior, and school problems.* New York: Bantam Books.

Schmuckler, M. (1996). Development of visually guided locomotion: Barrier crossing by toddlers. *Ecological Psychology, 8,* 209–236.

Schmuckler, M.A., & Fairhall, J.L. (2001). Visual-proprioceptive intermodal perception using point light displays. *Child Development, 72,* 949–962.

Schmuckler, M.A., & Gibson, E.J. (1989). The effect of imposed optical flow on guided locomotion in young walkers. *British Journal of Developmental Psychology, 7,* 193–206.

Schneider, W., & Bjorklund, D.F. (1998). Memory. In W. Damon (Editor-in-Chief), D. Kuhn, & R.S. Siegler (Vol. Eds*.), Handbook of child psychology: Vol. 2. Cognition, perception, and language* (5th ed., pp. 467–522). New York: Wiley.

Schnieke, A.E., Kind, A.J., Ritchie, W.A., Mycock, K., Scott, A.R., Ritchie, M., Wilmut, I., Colman, A., & Campbell, K.H. (1997). Human factor IX transgenic sheep produced by transfer of nuclei from transfectee fetal fibroblasts. *Science, 278,* 2130–2133.

Schnitzer, P.G., & Ewigman, B.G. (2005). Child deaths resulting from inflicted injuries: Household risk factors ad perpetrator characteristics. *Pediatrics, 116,* e687–e693.

Schott, J.J., Benson, D.W., Basson, C.T., Pease, W., Silberbach, G.M., Moak, J.P., et al. (1998). Congenital heart disease caused by mutations in the transcription factor NKX2-5. *Science, 281,* 108–111.

Schroeter, K. (2004). Water births: A naked emperor. *Pediatrics, 114,* 855–858.

Schulman, K. (2000). *The high cost of child care puts quality care out of reach for many families.* Washington, DC: Children's Defense Fund.

Schulz, C.B. (1985). Children and childhood in the eighteenth century. In J.M. Hawes, & N.R. Hiner (Eds.), *American childhood: A research guide and historical handbook* (pp. 57–109). Westport, CT: Greenwood Press.

Schwartz, C.E., Snidman, N., & Kagan, J. (1999). Adolescent social anxiety as an outcome of inhibited temperament in childhood. *Journal of the American Academy of Child and Adolescent Psychiatry, 38,* 1008–1015.

Schwartz, R.G., & Leonard, L.B. (1980). Words, objects, and actions in early lexical acquisition. *Papers and Reports in Child Language Development, 19,* 29–36.

Schweinhart, L., Barnes, H., Weikart, D., Barnett, W.S., & Epstein, A. (1993). *Significant benefits: Vol. 10. The High/Scope Perry Preschool study through age 27.* Ypsilanti, MI: High/Scope Press.

Scott, K.D., Berkowitz, G., & Klaus, M. (1999). A comparison of intermittent and continuous support during labor: A meta-analysis. *American Journal of Obstetrics and Gynecology, 180,* 1054–1059.

Scott, K.D., Klaus, P.H., & Klaus, M.H. (1999). The obstetrical and postpartum benefits of continuous support during childbirth. *Journal of Women's Health and Gender Based Medicine, 8,* 1257–1264.

Search Institute. (2000a). 40 developmental assets for infants. Retrieved September 4, 2005, from http://www.search-institute.org/assets/infants .html.

Search Institute. (2000b). 40 developmental assets for toddlers. Retrieved September 4, 2005, from http://www.search-institute.org/assets/toddlers .html

Sears, R.R. (1975). Your ancients revisited: A history of child development. In E.M Hetherington (Ed.), *Review of child development research* (Vol. 5, pp. 1–73). Chicago: University of Chicago Press.

Seifer, R., & Dickstein, S. (2000). Parental mental illness and infant development. In C.H. Zeanah, Jr. (Ed.), *Handbook of infant mental health* (2nd ed., pp. 145–160). New York: Guilford Press.

Seifer, R., & Schiller, M. (1995). The role of parenting sensitivity, infant temperament, and dyadic interaction in attachment theory and assessment. In E. Waters, B.E. Vaughn, G., Posada, & K. Kondo-Ikemura (Eds.), Caregiving, cultural, and cognitive perspectives on secure-base behavior and working models: New growing points in attachment theory and research. *Monographs of the Society for Research in Child Development, 60* (2/3, Serial No. 244), 146–174.

Seifer, R., Schiller, M., Sameroff, A.J., Resnick, S., & Riordan, K. (1996). Attachment, maternal sensitivity, and temperament during the first year of life. *Developmental Psychology, 32,* 3–11.

Seifer, R., LaGasse, L.L., Lester, B., Bauer, C.R., Shankaran, S., Bada, H.S., et al. (2004). Attachment status in children prenatally exposed to cocaine and other substances. *Child Development, 75,* 850–868.

Seiner, S.A., & Gelfand, D.M. (1995). Effects of mothers' simulated withdrawal and depressed affect on mother-toddler interactions. *Child Development, 66,* 1519–1528.Selman, P. (2002). Intercountry adoption in the new millennium: the "quiet migration" revisited. *Population Research and Policy Review, 21,* 205–225.

Senghas, A., & Coppola, M. (2001). Children creating language: How Nicaraguan Sign Language acquired a spatial grammar. *Psychological Science, 12,* 323–328.

Senghas, A., Kita, S., & Özyurek, A. (2004). Children creating core properties of language: Evidence from an emerging sign language in Nicaragua. *Science, 305,* 1779–1782.

Serbin, L.A., Moller, L.C., Gulko, J., Powlishta, K.K., & Colburne, K.A. (1994). The emergence of sex segregation in toddler playgroups. *New Di-*

rections in *Child Development, 65,* 7–17.

Seress, L. (2001). Morphological changes of the human hippocampal formation from midgestation to early childhood. In C.A. Nelson & M. Luciana (Eds.), *Handbook of developmental cognitive neuroscience* (pp. 45–58). Cambridge, MA: MIT Press.

Sharma, S.K., Alexander, J.M., Messick, G., Bloom, S.L., McIntire, D.D., Wiley, J., & Leveno, K.J. (2002). Cesarean delivery: A randomized trial of epidural analgesia versus intravenous meperidine analgesia during labor in nulliparous women. *Anesthesiology, 96,* 546–551.

Sharon, T., & DeLoache, J.S. (2003). The role of perseveration in children's symbolic understanding and skill. *Developmental Science, 6,* 289–297.

Shaw, D.S., & Vondra, J.I. (1995). Infant attachment security and maternal predictors of early behavior problems: A longitudinal study of low-income families. *Journal of Abnormal Child Psychology, 23,* 335–357.

Shea, S.L., & Aslin, R.N. (1990). Oculomotor responses to step-ramp targets by young human infants. *Vision Research, 30,* 1077–1092.

Shepard, T.H., Brent, R.L., Friedman, J. M., Jones, K.L., Miller, R.K., Moore, C.A., & Polifka, J. E. (2002). Update on new developments in the study of human teratogens. *Teratology, 65,* 153–161.

Shin, T., Kraemer, D., Pryor, J., Liu, L., Rugila, J., Howe, L., et al. (2002). Cell biology: A cat cloned by nuclear transplantation. *Nature, 415,* 859.

Shinn, M.W. (1900/1985). *The biography of a baby.* Reading, MA: Addison-Wesley.

Shonkoff, J.P., & Phillips, D.A. (Eds.). (2000). *From neurons to neighborhoods: The science of early childhood development.* Committee on Integrating the Science of Early Childhood Development. Board on Children, Youth, and Families, Commission on Behavioral and Social Sciences and Education. Washington, DC: National Academy Press.

Shore, C. (1995). *Individual differences in language development.* Thousand Oaks, CA: Sage.

Shore, C.M. (Ed.). (2004). *The many faces of childhood: Diversity in development.* Boston: Pearson Education.

Shu, X.O., Perentesis, J.P., Wen, W., Buckley, J.D., Boyle, E., Ross, J.A., et al. (2004). Parental exposure to medications and hydrocarbons and ras mutations in children with acute lymphoblastic leukemia: A report from the Children's Oncology Group. *Cancer Epidemiology, Biomarkers and Prevention, 13,* 1230–1235.

Shwalb, D.W., Shwalb, B.J., & Shoji, J. (1996). Japanese mothers' ideas about infants and temperament. In S. Harkness & C.M. Super (Eds.), *Parents' cultural belief systems: Their origins, expressions, and consequences* (pp. 169–191). New York: Guilford Press.

Shwalb, D.W., Nakawaza, J., Yamamoto, T., & Hyun, J.H. (2004). Fathering in Japanese, Chinese, and Korean cultures: A review of the research literature. In M.E. Lamb (Ed.), *The role of the father in child development* (4th ed., pp. 146–181). New York: Wiley.

Shwe, H.I., & Markman, E.M. (1997). Young children's appreciation of the mental impact of their communication signals. *Developmental Psychology, 33,* 630–636.

Shweder, R.A., Goodnow, J.J., Hatano, G., LeVine, R.A., Markus, H.R., & Miller, P.J. (2006). The cultural psychology of development: One mind, many mentalities. In W. Damon & R. Lerner (Eds.) & R.M. Lerner (Vol. Eds.), *Handbook of child psychology: Vol. 1. Theoretical models of human development* (6th ed., pp. 716–792). New York: Wiley.

Siddiqui, A. (1995). Object size as a determinant of grasping in infancy. *Journal of Genetic Psychology, 156,* 345–358.

Siegel, A.C., & Burton, R.V. (1999). Effects of babywalkers on motor and mental development in human infants. *Journal of Developmental and Behavioral Pediatrics, 20,* 355–361.

Siegler, R.S. (1996). *Emerging minds: The process of change in children's thinking.* New York: Oxford University Press.

Siegler, R.S. (2006). Microgenetic analyses of learning. In W. Damon & R. Lerner (Eds.) & D. Kuhn & R. Siegler (Vol. Eds.), *Handbook of child psychology: Vol. 2. Cognition, perception, and language* (6th ed., pp. 464–510). New York: Wiley.

Siegler, R.S. & Crowley, K. (1991). The microgenetic method: A direct means for studying cognitive development. *American Psychologist, 46,* 606–620.

Sigman, M., & Ruskin, E. (1999). Social competence in children with autism, Down Syndrome and other developmental delays: A longitudinal study. *Monographs of the Society for Research in Child Development, 64*(1, Serial No. 256).

Silverman, W.K., & Ollendick, T.H. (Eds.). (1999). *Developmental issues in the clinical treatment of children.* Needham Heights, MA: Allyn & Bacon.

Silvey, L.E. (1999). Firstborn American Indian daughters: Struggles to reclaim cultural and self-identity. In H.P. McAdoo (Ed.), *Family ethnicity: Strength in diversity* (2nd ed., pp. 72–93). Thousand Oaks, CA: Sage.

Simon, T. J., Hespos, S. J., & Rochat, P. (1995). Do infants understand simple arithmetic? A replication of Wynn (1992). *Cognitive Development, 10,* 253–269.

Simons, S.H.P., van Dijk, M., Anand, K.S., Roofthooft, D., van Lingen, R., & Tibboel, D. (2003). Do we still hurt newborn babies: A prospective study of procedural pain and analgesia in neonates. *Archives of Pediatrics & Adolescent Medicine, 157,* 1058–1064.

Simpson, J. L. (1999). Fetal surgery for myelomeningocele: Promise, progress, and problems. *JAMA, 282,* 1873–1874.

Sinal, S.H., Petree, A.R., Herman-Giddens, M., Rogers, M.K., Enand, C., & DuRant, R.H. (2000). Is race or ethnicity a predictive factor in shaken baby syndrome? *Child Abuse & Neglect, 24,* 1241–1246.

Singer, D.G., & Singer, J.L. (Eds.). (2001). *Handbook of children and the media.* Thousand Oaks, CA: Sage.

Singer, J.L., & Singer, D.G. (1998). Barney & Friends as entertainment and education: Evaluating the quality and effectiveness of a television series for preschool children. In J. K. Asamen, & G.L. Berry (Eds.), *Research paradigms, television, and social behavior* (pp. 305–367). Thousand Oaks, CA: Sage.

Singer, L.T., Arendt, R.E., Minnes, S., Farkas, K., Salvator, A., Kirchner, H.L., et al. (2002). Cognitive and motor outcomes of cocaine-exposed infants. *JAMA, 287,* 1952–1960.

Singhal A, Cole, T.J., Fewtrell, M., & Lucas, A. (2004). Breastmilk feeding and lipoprotein profile in adolescents born preterm: follow-up of a prospective randomised study. *The Lancet, 363,* 1571–1578.

Sirois, S., & Mareschal, D. (2002). Models of habituation in infancy. *Trends in Cognitive Sciences, 6,* 293–298.

Skinner, B.F. (1957). *Verbal behavior.* New York: Appleton.

Skuse, D.H. (1985). Non-organic failure to thrive: A reappraisal. *Archives of the Diseases of Childhood, 60,* 173–178.

Slater, A. (1997). Visual perception and its organisation in early infancy. In G. Bremner, A. Slater, & G. Butterworth (Eds.), *Infant development: Recent advances* (pp. 31–53). East Sussex, UK: Psychology Press.

Slater, A., & Butterworth, G. (1997). Perception of social stimuli: Face perception and imitation. In G. Bremner, A. Slater, & G. Butterworth (Eds.), *Infant development: Recent advances* (pp. 223–245). East Sussex, UK: Psychology Press.

Slater, A., & Morison, V. (1985). Shape constancy and slant perception at birth. *Perception, 14,* 337–344.

Slater, A., & Morison, V. (Eds.). (1991). *Visual attention and memory at birth.* Norwood, NJ: Ablex.

Slater, A., Mattock, A., & Brown, E. (1990). Size constancy at birth: Newborn infants' responses to retinal and real size. *Journal of Experimental Child Psychology, 49,* 314–322.

Slater, A., Johnson, S.P., Brown, E., & Badenoch, M. (1996). Newborn infants' perception of partly occluded objects. *Infant Behavior and Development, 19,* 145–148.

Slobin, D.I. (1992). Introduction. In D.I. Slobin (Ed.), *The crosslinguistic study of language acquisition* (Vol. 2, pp. 1–14). Hillsdale, NJ: Erlbaum.

Slobin, D.I. (Ed.). (1985). *The crosslinguistic study of language acquisition* (Vol. 2). Hillsdale, NJ: Erlbaum.

Small, M.F. (1998). *Our babies, ourselves: How biology and culture shape the way we parent.* New York: Anchor Books.

Smetana, J.G. (1984). Toddlers' social interactions regarding moral and conventional transgressions. *Child Development, 55,* 1767–1776.

Smith, B.A., & Blass, E.M. (1996). Taste-mediated calming in premature, preterm, and full-term human infants. *Developmental Psychology, 32,* 1084–1089.

Smith, B.L. (1982). Some observations concerning premeaningful vocalizations: hearing-impaired infants. *Journal of Speech and Hearing Disorders, 47,* 439–442.

Smith, G.C.S., Pell, J.P., Cameron, A.D., & Dobbie, R. (2002). Risk of perinatal death associated with labor after previous Caesarean delivery in uncomplicated term pregnancies. *JAMA, 287,* 2684–2690.

Smith, K., & Bachu, A. (1999). Women's labor force attachment patterns and maternity leave: A review of the literature. *Population Division Working Paper No. 32.* Washington, DC: U.S. Bureau of the Census.

Smith, K., Downs, B., & O'Connell, M. (2001). Maternity leave and employment patterns: 1961–1995. *Current Population Reports P70(79)* (pp. 1–21). Washington, DC: U.S. Bureau of the Census.

Smith, L.B. (2000). Learning how to learn words. In R.M., Golinkoff, K. Hirsh-Pasek, L. Bloom, L.B. Smith, A.L. Woodward, N. Akhtar, et al.,

Becoming a word learner: A debate on lexical acquisition (pp. 51–80). New York: Oxford University Press.

Smith-Hefner, N.J. (1988). The linguistic socialization of Javanese children in two communities. *Anthropological Linguistics, 30,* 166–198.

Smuts, A.B., & Hagen, J.W. (Eds.) (1985). History and research in child development. *Monographs of the Society for Research in Child Development, 50*(4–5, Serial No. 211).

Snow, C. E. (1972). Mothers' speech to children learning language. *Child Development, 43,* 549–565.

Social Security Administration. (2006). *Popular baby names, 1880–2005.* Retrieved July 19, 2006, from http://www.ssa.gov/OACT/babynames/

Society for Research in Child Development (2000). Ethical standards for research with children. *SRCD Directory of Members, 1999–2000* (pp. 283–284). Ann Arbor, MI: SRCD.

Soja, N.N. (1992). Inferences about the meanings of nouns: The relationship between perception and syntax. *Cognitive Development, 7,* 29–45.

Soken, N.H., & Pick, A.D. (1992). Intermodal perception of happy and angry expressive behaviors by seven-month-old infants. *Child Development, 63,* 787–795.

Soken, N.H., & Pick, A.D. (1999). Infants' perception of dynamic affective expressions: Do infants distinguish specific expressions? *Child Development, 70,* 1275–1282

Sonenstein, F.L., Gates, G.J., Schmidt, S., & Bolshun, N. (2002). Primary child care arrangements of employed parents: Findings from the 1999 National Survey of America's Families. *Occasional Paper Number 59.* Washington, DC: The Urban Institute.

Sorce, J.F., Emde, R.N., Campos, J.J., & Klinnert, M.D. (1985). Maternal emotional signaling: Its effects on the visual cliff behavior of 1-year-olds. *Developmental Psychology, 21,* 195–200. [cited in Harris, 1989]

Spangler, G., & Grossmann, K.E. (1993). Biobehavioral organization in securely and insecurely attached infants. *Child Development, 64,* 1439–1450.

Spelke, E.S. (1990). Principles of object perception. *Cognitive Science, 14,* 29–56.

Spelke, E.S., & Newport, E.L. (1998). Nativism, empiricism, and the development of knowledge. In W. Damon (Editor-in-Chief) & R.M. Lerner (Vol. Ed.), *Handbook of child psychology: Vol. 1. Theoretical models of human development* (5th ed., pp. 275–340). New York: Wiley.

Spelke, E.S., Breinlinger, K., Jacobson, K., & Phillips, A. (1993). Gestalt relations and object perception: A developmental study. *Perception, 22,* 1483–1501.

Spelke, E.S., Breinlinger, K., Macomber, J., & Jacobson, K. (1992). Origins of knowledge. *Psychological Review, 99,* 605–632.

Spencer, J.P., Smith, L.B., & Thelen, E. (2001). Tests of a dynamic systems account of the A-not-B error: The influence of prior experience on the spatial memory abilities of two-year-olds. *Child Development, 72,* 1327–1346.

Spitz, H.H. (1992). Does the Carolina Abecedarian Early Intervention Project prevent sociocultural mental retardation? *Intelligence, 16,* 225–237.

Spitz, R. (1945). Hospitalism. An inquiry into the genesis of psychiatric conditions in early childhood. In A. Freud, H. Hartmann, & E. Kris (Eds.), *The psychoanalytic study of the child* (pp. 53–74). New York: International Universities Press.

Sroufe, L.A. (1979). The coherence of individual development: Early care, attachment, and subsequent developmental issues. *American Psychologist, 34,* 834–841.

Sroufe, L.A. (1983). Infant-caregiver attachment and patterns of adaptation in preschool: The roots of maladaptation and competence. In M. Perlmutter (Ed.), *Development and policy concerning children with special needs. Minnesota Symposia on Child Psychologoy,* (Vol. 16, pp. 41–83). Hillsdale, NJ: Erlbaum.

Sroufe, L.A., & Fleeson, J. (1986). Attachment and the construction of relationships. In W. Hartup & Z. Rubin (Eds.), *Relationships and development* (pp. 57–72). Hillsdale, NJ: Erlbaum.

Sroufe, L.A., Carlson, E., & Shulman, S. (1993). Individuals in relationships: Development from infancy through adolescence. In D.C. Funder, R.D. Parke, C. Tomlinson-Keasey, & K. Widaman (Jeds.), *Studying lives through time: Personality and development* (pp. 315–342). Washington, DC: American Psychological Association Press.

Sroufe, L.A., Egeland, B., & Carlson, E. (1999). One social world: The integrated development of parent-child and peer relationships. In W.A. Collins & B. Laursen (Eds.), *Minnesota Symposium on Child Psychology: Vol. 30. Relationships as developmental contexts* (pp. 241–262). Mahwah, NJ: Erlbaum.

St. James-Roberts, I., & Plewis, I. (1996). Individual differences, daily fluctuations, and developmental changes in amounts of infant waking, fussing, crying, feeding, and sleeping. *Child Development, 67,* 2527–2540.

Stack, D.M., & Muir, D.W. (1990). Tactile stimulation as a component of social interchange: New interpretations for the still-face effect. *British Journal of Developmental Psychology, 8,* 131–145.

Stack, D.M., & Muir, D.W. (1992). Adult tactile stimulation during face-to-face interactions modulates five-month-olds' affect and attention. *Child Development, 63,* 1509–1525.

Stack, D.M., Muir, D.W., Sherriff, F., Roman, J. (1989). Development of infant reaching in the dark to luminous objects and 'invisible sounds'. *Perception, 18,* 69–82.

Stams, G.J., Juffer, F., & van IJzendoorn, M.H. (2002). Maternal sensitivity, infant attachment, and temperament in early childhood predict adjustment in middle childhood: The case of adopted children and their biologically unrelated parents. *Developmental Psychology, 38,* 806–821.

Standley, J.M. (1998a). Pre and perinatal growth and development: Implications of music benefits for premature infants. *International Journal of Music Education, 31,* 1–13.

Standley, J.M. (1998b). The effect of music and multimodal stimulation on physiological and developmental responses of premature infants in neonatal intensive care. *Pediatric Nursing, 24,* 532–538.

Standley, J.M. (1999). Music therapy in the NICU: Pacifier activated lullabies (PAL) for reinforcement of nonnutritive sucking. *International Journal of Arts Medicine, 6,* 17–21.

Standley, J.M. (1991). The role of music in the pacification/stimulation of premature infants with low birthweights. *Music Therapy Perspectives, 9,* 19–25.

Stansbury, K., & Gunnar, M.R. (1994). Adrenocortical activity and emotion regulation. In Fox, N.A. (Ed.), The development of emotion regulation: Biological and behavioral considerations. *Monographs of the Society for Research in Child Development, 59*(2–3, Serial No. 240), 108–134.

Starr, W. (1976). *The Suzuki violinist.* Knoxville, TN: Kingston Ellis Press.

Statistics Canada. (2003). The people: Household and family life: Stress. In: Statistics Canada. Canada e-book. Ottawa, Ontario: Statistics Canada; 2003. Retrieved December 22, 2005, from http://142.206.72.67/02/02d/02d_005_e.htm

Stein, B.E., Meredith, M.A., & Wallace, M.T. (1994). Development and neural basis of multisensory integration. In D.J. Lewkowicz & R. Lickliter (Ed.), *The development of intersensory perception: Comparative perspectives* (pp. 81–105). Hillsdale, NJ: Erlbaum.

Steiner, J.E. (1979). Human facial expressions in response to taste and smell stimulation. In H.W. Reese & L.P.J. Lipsitt (Eds.), *Advances in child development and behavior* (Vol. 13, pp. 257–295). New York: Academic Press.

Stenberg, C., & Campos, J.J. (1990). The development of anger expressions in infancy. In N. Stein, T. Trabasso, & B.

Leventhal (Eds.), *Concepts in emotion* (pp. 518–530). Hillsdale, NJ: Erlbaum.

Stenberg, C., Campos, J.J., & Emde, R.N. (1983). The facial expression of anger in seven month old infants. *Child Development, 54,* 178–184.

Steptoe, P.C., & Edwards, R. G. (1978). Birth after re-implantation of a human embryo. *Lancet, 2,* 366.

Stewart, R.B. (1983). Sibling attachment relationship: Child-infant interactions in the strange situation. *Developmental Psychology, 19,* 192–199.

Stewart, R.B., & Marvin, R.S. (1984). Sibling relations: The role of conceptual perspective-taking in the ontogeny of sibling caregiving. *Child Development, 55,* 1322–1332.

Stilson, S.R., & Harding, C.G. (1997). Early social context as it relates to symbolic play: A longitudinal investigation. *Merrill-Palmer Quarterly, 43,* 682–693.

Stipek, D., Recchia, S., & McClintic, S. (1992). Self-evaluation in young children. *Monographs of the Society for Research in Child Development, 57*(1, Serial No. 226).

Stoffregen, T., Adolph, K.E., Thelen, E., Gorday, K.M., & Sheng, Y.Y. (1997). Toddlers' postural adaptations to different support surfaces. *Motor Control, 1,* 119–137.

Stone, P.W., Zwanziger, J., Hinton Walker, P., & Buenting, J. (2000). Economic analysis of two models of low-risk maternity care: A freestanding birth center compared to traditional care. *Res Nurs Health, 23,* 279–289.

Streri, A. (1987). Tactile discrimination of shape and intermodal transfer in two- to three-month-old infants. *British Journal of Developmental Psychology, 5,* 213–220.

Streri, A., & Molina, M. (1993). Visual-tactual and tactual-visual transfer between objects and pictures in 2-month-old infants. *Perception, 22,* 1299–1318.

Strickland, C.E., & Ambrose, A.M. (1985). The baby boom, prosperity, and the changing worlds of children, 1945–1963. In J.M. Hawes & N.R. Hiner (Eds.), *American childhood: A research guide and historical handbook* (pp. 533–585). Westport, CT: Greenwood Press.

Sturner, R., Layton, T., Evans, A., Heller, J., Funk, S., & Machon, M. (1994). Preschool speech and language screening: A review of currently available tests. *American Journal of Speech-Language Pathology, 3,* 25–36.

Suárez, Z.E. (1999). Cuban Americans in exile: Myths and reality. In H.P. McAdoo (Ed.), *Family ethnicity: Strength in diversity* (2nd ed., pp. 135–152). Thousand Oaks, CA: Sage.

Suddendorf, T. (2003). Early representational insight: Twenty-four-month-olds can use a photo to find an object in the world. *Child Development, 74,* 896–904.

Sun, L.C., & Roopnarine, J.L. (1996). Mother-infant, father-infant interaction and involvement in childcare and household labor among Taiwanese families. *Infant Behavior and Development, 19,* 121–129.

Suomi, S. J. (1991). Early stress and adult emotional reactivity in rhesus monkeys. In D. Barker (Ed.), *The childhood environment and adult disease* (Ciba Foundation Symposium #156, pp. 171–188). Chichester, UK: Wiley.

Super, C. (1976). Environmental effects on motor development: The case of African infant precocity. *Developmental Medicine and Child Neurology, 18,* 561–567.

Super, C.M., Harkness, S., van Tijen, N., van der Vlugt, E., Fintelman, M., & Dijkstra, J. (1996). The three R's of Dutch childrearing and the socialization of infant arousal. In S. Harkness & C.M. Super (Eds.), *Parents' cultural belief systems: Their origins, expressions, and consequences* (pp. 447–466). New York: Guilford Press.

Susman-Stillman, A, Kalkoske, M., Egeland, B., & Waldman, I. (1996). Infant temperament and maternal sensitivity as predictors of attachment security. *Infant Behavior and Development, 19,* 33–47.

Sutton, L.N., Adzick, N.S., Bilaniuk, L.T., Johnson, M.P., Cromblehome, T.M., & Flake, A.W. (1999). Improvement in hindbrain herniation demonstrated by serial fetal magnetic resonance imaging following fetal surgery for myelomeningocele. *JAMA, 282,* 1826–1831.

Sutton-Smith, B. (1997). *The ambiguity of play.* Cambridge, MA: Harvard University Press.

Suzuki, S.(1973). Children can develop their ability to the highest standard. In E. Mills, & T.C. Murphy (Eds.), *The Suzuki concept: An introduction to a successful method for early music education* (pp. 9–16). Berkeley, CA: Diablo Press.

Swan SH. (2000). Intrauterine exposure to diethylstilbestrol: Long-term effects in humans. *APMIS, 108,* 793–804.

Sylvester, K. (2001). Caring for our youngest: Public attitudes in the United States. *The Future of Children, 11*(1), 53–61.

Taddio, A. Katz, J. Ilersich, AL. Koren, G. (1997). Effect of neonatal circumcision on pain response during subsequent routine vaccination. *Lancet, 349,* 599–603.

Taddio, A. Goldbach, M. Ipp, M. Stevens, B. Koren, G. (1995). Effect of neonatal circumcision on pain response during vaccination in boys. *Lancet, 345,* 291–292.

Tager-Flusberg, H. (1993). What language reveals about the understanding of minds in children with autism. In S. Baron-Cohen, H. Tager-Flusberg, & D. Cohen (Eds.), *Understanding other minds: Perspectives from autism* (pp. 138–157). Oxford, UK: Oxford University Press.

Tager-Flusberg, H. (2004). Strategies for conducting research on language in autism. *Journal of Autism and Developmental Disorders, 34,* 75–80.

Tamis-LeMonda, C.S., & Bornstein, M.H. (1996). Variation in children's exploratory, nonsymbolic, and symbolic play: An exploratory multidimensional framework. In C Rovee-Collier & L.P. Lipsitt (Eds.), *Advances in infancy research* (Vol. 10, pp. 37–78). Norwood, NJ: Ablex.

Tamis-LeMonda, C.S., Bornstein, M. H., & Baumwell, L. (2001). Maternal responsiveness and children's achievement of language milestones. *Child Development, 72,* 748–767.

Tamis-LeMonda, C.S., Chen, L.A., & Bornstein, M.H. (1997). Mothers' knowledge about children's play and language development: Short-term stability and interrelations. *Developmental Psychology, 34,* 115–124.

Tamis-LeMonda, C.S., Damast, A.M., & Bornstein, M.H. (1994). What do mothers know about the developmental nature of play? *Infant Behavior and Development, 17,* 341–345.

Tamis-LeMonda, C.S., Shannon, J.D., Cabrera, N.J., & Lamb, M.E. (2004). Fathers and mothers at play with their 2- and 3-year-olds: Contributions to language and cognitive development. *Child Development, 75,* 1806–1820.

Tamis-LeMonda, C.S., Bornstein, M.H., Cyphers, L., Toda, S., & Ogino, M. (1992). Language and play at one year: A comparison of toddlers and mothers in the United States and Japan. *International Journal of Behavioral Development, 15,* 19–42.

Task Force on Sudden Infant Death Syndrome. (2005). The changing concept of sudden infant death syndrome: Diagnostic coding shifts, controversies regarding the sleep environment, and new variables to consider in reducing risk. *Pediatrics, 116,* 1245–1255.

Taylor, H.S. (2000). The role of HOX genes in the development and function of the female reproductive tract. *Seminars in Reproductive Medicine, 18,* 81–89.

Taylor, I. (1990). *Psycholinguistics.* Englewood Cliffs, NJ: Prentice Hall.

Teletubbies Frequently Asked Questions. (2002). Retrieved November 20, 2002, from http://www.bbc.co/uk/cbeebies/teltubbies/information/faq/

Teller, D.Y., Peeples, D.R., & Sekel, M. (1978). Discrimination of chromatic from white light by 2-month-old infants. *Vision Research, 18,* 41–48.

Teti, D.M. (2002). Sibling relationships. In J. McHale & W. Grolnick (Eds.), *Interiors: Retrospect and prospect in*

the psychological study of families (pp. 193–224). Mahwah, NJ: Erlbaum.

Teti, D.M., & Ablard, K.E. (1989). Security of attachment and infant-sibling relationships: A laboratory study. *Child Development, 60,* 1519–1528.

Teti, D.M., & Teti, L.O. (1996). Infant-parent relationships. In N. Canzetti & S. Duck (Eds.), *A lifetime of relationships* (pp. 77–104). Pacific Grove, CA: Brooks/Cole.

Teti, D.M., Gelfand, D.M., Messinger, D.S., & Isabella, R. (1995). Maternal depression and the quality of early attachment: An examination of infants, preschoolers, and their mothers. *Developmental Psychology, 31,* 364–376.

Teti, D.M., Sakin, J., Kucera, E., Corns, K.M., & Eiden, R.D. (1996). And baby makes four: Predictors of attachment security among preschool-aged firstborns during the transition to siblinghood. *Child Development, 67,* 579–596.

Tew, M., & Damstra-Wijmenga, S.M.I. (1991). The safest birth attendants: Recent Dutch evidence. *Midwifery, 7,* 55–65.

Thacker, S.B., Addiss, D.G., Goodman, R.A., Holloway, B.R., & Spencer, H.C. (1992). Infectious diseases and injuries in child day care: Opportunities for healthier children. *JAMA, 268,* 1720–1726.

The Future of Children. (2000). Unintentional injuries in childhood: Executive summary. *The Future of Children, 10(1),* 2–7.

The Infant Health and Development Program. (1990). Enhancing the outcomes of low-birth-weight premature infants. *Journal of the American Medical Association, 263,* 3035–3042.

Thelen, E., & Smith, L. (1994). *A dynamic systems approach to the development of cognition and action.* Cambridge, MA: MIT Press.

Thelen, E., Fisher, D.M., & Ridley-Johnson, R. (1984). The relationship between physical growth and a newborn reflex. *Infant Behavior and Development, 7,* 479–493.

Thiessen, E.D., & Saffran, J.R. (2003). When cues collilde: Use of stress and

statistical cues to word boundaries by 7- to 9-month-old infants. *Developmental Psychology, 39,* 706–716.

Thiessen, E.D., Hill, E.A., & Saffran, J.R. (2005). Infant-directed speech facilitates word segmentation. *Infancy, 7,* 53–71.

Thoman, E.B. (1990). Sleeping and waking states in infants: A functional perspective. *Neuroscience and Biobehavioral Review, 14,* 93–107.

Thomas, A., & Chess, S. (1977). *Temperament and development.* New York: Brunner/Mazel.Thomas, A., & Chess, S. (1982). Temperamental differences in infants and young children. In *Temperamental differences in infants and young children* (pp. 168–175). Ciba Foundation Symposium. London: Pitman.

Thomas, A., Chess, S., & Birch, H.G. (1968). *Temperament and behavior disorders in children.* New York: New York University Press.

Thomas, A., Chess, S., & Birch, H.G., Hertzig, M.E., & Korn, S. (1963). *Behavioral individuality in early childhood.* New York: New York University Press.

Thompson, R.A. (1990). Vulnerability in research: A developmental perspective on research risk. *Child Development, 61,* 1–16.

Thompson, R.A. (1994). Emotion regulation: A theme in search of definition. In Fox, N.A. (Ed.), The development of emotion regulation: Biological and behavioral considerations. *Monographs of the Society for Research in Child Development, 59*(2–3, Serial No. 240), 25–52.

Thompson, R.A. (1998). Early sociopersonality development. In W. Damon (Editor-in-Chief) & N.Eisenberg (Vol. Ed.), *Handbook of child psychology* (5th ed.): *Vol. 3. Social, emotional, and personality development* (pp. 25–104). New York: Wiley.

Thompson, R.A. (2006). The development of the person: Social understanding, relationships, conscience, self. In W. Damon & R. Lerner (Eds.) & N. Eisenberg (Vol. Ed.),

Handbook of child psychology: Vol. 3. Social, emotional, and personality development (6th ed., pp. 24–98). New York: Wiley.

Thompson, R.A. (2001). Development in the first years of life. *The Future of Children, 11*(1), 21–33.

Thorpe, L.A., & Trehub, S.E. (1989). Duration illusion and auditory grouping in infancy. *Developmental Psychology, 25*, 122–127.

Thorpe, L.A., Trehub, S.E., Morrongiello, B.A., & Bull, D. (1988). Perceptual grouping by infants and preschool children. *Developmental Psychology, 24*, 484–491.

Timmons, P.M., Rigby, P.W. J., & Poirer, F. (2001). The murine seminiferous cycle is pre-figured in the Sertoli cells of the embryonic testis. *Development, 129*, 635–647.

Tobin, J.J., Wu, D.Y.H., & Davidson, D.H. (1989). *Preschool in three cultures: Japan, China, and the United States.* New Haven, CT: Yale University Press.

Tomasello, M. (2000). Do young children have adult syntactic competence? *Cognition, 74*, 209–253.

Tomasello, M. (2006). Acquiring linguistic constructions. In W. Damon & R. Lerner (Eds.) & D. Kuhn & R. Siegler (Vol. Eds.), *Handbook of child psychology: Vol. 2. Cognition, perception, and language* (6th ed., pp. 255–298). New York: Wiley.

Tomasello, M., & Barton, M. (1994). Learning words in non-ostensive context. *Developmental Psychology, 30*, 639–650.

Tomasello, M., & Farrar, J. (1986). Joint attention and early language. *Child Development, 57*, 1454–1463.

Tomasello, M., Kruger, A.C., & Ratner, H.H. (1993). Cultural learning. *Behavioral and Brain Sciences, 16*, 495– 552.

Tong, S., Baghurst, P.A., Sawyer, M.G., Burns, J., & McMichael, A.J. (1998). Declining blood lead levels and changes in cognitive function during childhood: The Port Pirie cohort study. *JAMA, 280*, 1915–1919.

Tournaye, H., & Van Steirteghem, A. (1997). Intracytoplasmic sperm injection: ICSI concerns do not outweigh its benefits. *Journal of NIH Research, 9*, 35, 39–40.

Towner, D., & Loewy, R.S. (2002). Ethics of preimplantation diagnosis for a woman destined to develop early-onset Alzheimer disease. *JAMA, 287*, 1038–1040.

Townsend, N.W. (1997). Men, migration, and households in Botswana: An exploration of connections over time and space. *Journal of Southern African Studies, 23*, 405–420.

Trainor, L.J., & Zacharias, C.A. (1998). Infants prefer higher-pitched singing. *Infant Behavior and Development, 21*, 799–806.

Trainor, L.J., Austin, C.M., & Desjardins, R.N. (2000). Is infant-directed speech prosody a result of the vocal expression of emotion? *Psychological Science, 11*, 188–195.

Trainor, L.J., Wu, L., & Tsang, C.D. (2004). Long-term memory for music: Infants remember tempo and timbre. *Developmental Science, 7*, 289–296.

Travis, L.L., & Sigman, M.D. (2000). A developmental approach to autism. In A.J. Sameroff, M. Lewis, & S.M. Miller (Eds.), *Handbook of developmental psychopathology* (2nd ed., pp. 641–655). New York: Plenum.

Trehub, S.E. (September, 2002). Mothers are musical mentors. *Zero to Three, 23*, 19–20.

Trehub, S.E., & Trainor, L. (1998). Singing to infants: Lullabies and play songs. *Advances in Infancy Research, 12*, 43–77.

Trehub, S.E., Hill, D.S., & Kamenetsky, S.B. (1997). Parents' sung performances for infants. *Canadian Journal of Experimental Psychology, 51*, 385–396.

Trehub, S.E., Unyk, A.M., & Henderson, J.L. (1994). Children's songs to infant siblings: Parallels with speech. *Journal of Child Language, 21*, 735– 744.

Trehub, S.E., Unyk, A.M., Trainor, L.J. (1993a). Adults identify infant-directed music across cultures. *Infant Behavior and Development, 16*, 193–211.

Trehub, S.E., Unyk, A.M., Trainor, L.J. (1993b). Maternal singing in cross-cultural perspective. *Infant Behavior and Development, 16*, 285–295.

Trehub, S.E., Unyk, A.M., Kamenetsky, S.G., Hill, D.S., Trainor, L.J., Henderson, J.L., & Saraza, M. (1997). Mothers' and fathers' singing to infants. *Developmental Psychology, 33*, 500– 507.

Trimble, E.L, (2001). Update on diethylstilbestrol. *Obstetrics and Gynecological Survey, 56*, 187–189.

Tronick, E.Z., & Weinberg, M.K. (1997). Depressed mothers and infants: Failure to form dyadic states of consciousness. In L. Murray & P.J. Cooper (Eds.), *Postpartum depression and child development* (pp. 54–81). New York: Guilford Press.

Tröster, H., & Brambring, M. (1993). Early motor development in blind infants. *Journal of Applied Developmental Psychology, 14*, 83–106.

Tröster, H., & Brambring, M. (1994). The play behavior and play materials of blind and sighted infants and preschoolers. *Journal of Visual Impairment & Blindness, 88*, 421–432.

Tsao, F.M., Liu, H.M., & Kuhl, P.K. (2004). Speech perception in infancy predicts language development in the second year of life: A longitudinal study. *Child Development, 75*, 1067–1084.

Tudge, J.R., Lee, S., Putnam, S. (1998). Young children's play in socio-cultural context: South Korea and the United States. In S. Reifel (Series Ed.), *Play and Culture Studies* (Vol. 1, pp. 77–90). Stamford, CT: Ablex.

U.S. Bureau of the Census. (1999). *Current population reports: Growth in single fathers outpaces growth in single mothers.* (Series P20, No. 1344). Washington, DC: U.S. Government Printing Office.

U.S. Census Bureau. (2003). Who's minding the kids? Child care arrangements: Spring 1999. *Current Population Reports, Detailed Tables (PPL–168).* Washington, DC: U.S. Bureau of the Census.

U.S. Consumer Product Safety Commission. (No date). *The safe nursery: A booklet to help avoid injuries from nursery furniture and equipment. CPSC 202.* Washington, DC: USCPSC.

U.S. Department of Agriculture. (2002). *How WIC helps.* Retrieved January 10, 2003, from http://www.fns.usda.gov/wic/ProgramInfo/howwichelps.htm

U.S. Department of Education/Office of Special Education Programs. (2001). *Twenty-fourth Annual Report to Congress on the Implementation of the Individuals with Disabilities Education Act.* Washington, DC: U.S. Department of Education.

U.S. Department of Health and Human Services. (2000). *Healthy people 2010: Understanding and improving health.* Washington, DC: U.S. Government Printing Office.

U.S. Department of Health and Human Services. (2000, Nov. 27). *HHS Fact Sheet: HHS on the forefront of autism research.* Retrieved May 2, 2001, from http://www.hhs.gov/news/press/2001pres/01fsautism.html

U.S. Department of Health and Human Services. (2001). *The Surgeon General's call to action to prevent and decrease overweight and obesity.* Rockville, MD: U.S. Department of Health and Human Services, Public Health Service, Office of the Surgeon General.

U.S. Department of Labor. (2005). Federal vs. state Family and Medical Leave laws. Retrieved on August 23, 2005, from http://www.dol.gov/esa/programs/whd/state/fmla/index.htm

U.S. Department of Labor/Bureau of Labor Statistics. (2005). *Women in the labor force: A databook.* Washington, DC: Bureau of Labor Statistics.

Uller, C., Carey, S., Huntley-Fenner, G., & Klatt, L. (1999). What representations might underlie infant numerical knowledge? *Cognitive Development, 14,* 1–36.

UNICEF. (2002). *The state of the world's children, 2002.* New York: UNICEF.

UNICEF. (2006). *The state of the world's children, 2006: Excluded and invisible.* New York: UNICEF.

United States Food and Drug Administration. (1996). Folic acid fortification

fact sheet. Retrieved September 10, 2001, from http://www.cfsan.fda.gov/~dms/wh-folic.html

Unyk, A.M., Trehub, S.E., Trainor, L.J., & Schellenberg, G. (1992). Lullabies and simplicity: A cross-cultural perspective. *Psychology of Music, 20,* 15–28.

Uygur, D. Kis, S. Tuncer, R. Ozcan, F. Erkaya, S. (2002). Risk factors and infant outcomes associated with umbilical cord prolapse. *International Journal of Gynaecology and Obstetrics, 78,* 127–130.

Uzgiris, I.C., & Hunt, J.M. (1975). *Assessment in infancy: Ordinal scales of psychological development.* Urbana, IL: University of Illinois Press.

Vainio, S., Heikkiia, M., Kispert, A., Chin, N., & McMahon, A. P. (1999). Female development in mammals is regulated by Wnt-4 signalling. *Nature, 397,* 405–409.

Valenzuela, M. (1997). Maternal sensitivity in a developing society: The context of urban poverty and infant chronic undernutrition. *Developmental Psychology, 33,* 845–855.

Vance, M.R. (2006). Summary of breastfeeding legislation in the U.S. Retrieved May 12, 2006, from http://www.lalecheleague.org/Law/summary.html

Van de Velde, M., Vercauteren, M., & Vandermeersch, E. (2001). Fetal heart rate abnormalities after regional analgesia for labor pain: The effect of intrathecal opioids. *Regional Anesthia and Pain Medicine, 26,* 257–262.

Van de Walle, G.A., & Spelke, E.S. (1996). Spatiotemporal integration and object perception in infancy: Perceiving unity versus form. *Child Development, 67,* 2621–2640.

van den Boom, D.C. (1989). Neonatal irritability and the development of attachment. In G.A. Kohnstamm, J.E. Bates, & M.K. Rothbart (Eds.), *Temperament in childhood* (pp. 299–318). Chichester, UK: Wiley.

van den Boom, D.C. (1994). The influence of temperament and mothering on attachment and exploration: An experimental manipulation of sensitive responsiveness among lower-class

mothers with irritable infants. *Child Development, 65,* 1457–1477.

van den Boom, D.C. (2001). First attachments: Theory and research. In G. Bremner, & A. Fogel (Eds.), *Blackwell handbook of infant development* (pp. 296–325). Oxford, UK: Blackwell.

van der Meer, A.L.H., van der Weel, F.R., & Lee, D.N. (1995). The functional significance of arm movements in neonates. *Science, 267,* 693–695.

Van der Molen, M.W., & Molenaar, P.C.M. (1994). Cognitive psychophysiology: A window to cognitive development and brain maturation. In G. Dawson, & K. Fischer (Eds.), *Human behavior and the developing brain* (pp. 456–490). New York: Guildford Press.

van IJzendoorn, M.H., Dijkstra, J., & Bus, A.G. (1995). Attachment, intelligence, and language: A meta-analysis. *Social Development, 4,* 115–128.

van IJzendoorn, M.H., Schuengel, C., & Bakermans-Kranenburg, M.J. (1999). Disorganized attachment in early childhood: Meta-analysis of precursors, concomitants, and sequelae. *Development and Psychopathology, 11,* 225–249.

van IJzendoorn, M.H., Goldberg, S., Kroonenberg, P.M., & Frenkel, O.J. (1992). The relative effects of maternal and child problems on the quality of attachment: A meta-analysis of attachment in clinical samples. *Child Development, 63,* 840–858.

van IJzendoorn, M.H., Moran, G., Belsky, J., Pederson, D., Bakermans-Krannburg, M.J., & Kneppers, K. (2000). *Child Development, 71,* 1086–1098.

Varendi, H., Porter, R.H., & Winberg, J. (1992). Attractiveness of amniotic fluid odor: Evidence of prenatal olfactory learning? *Acta paediatrica, 85,* 1223–1227.

Varendi, H., Christensson, K., Porter, R.H., & Winberg, J. (1998). Soothing effect of amniotic fluid smell in newborn infants. *Early Human Development, 51,* 47–55.

Vaughn, B.E., & Bost, K.K. (1999). Attachment and temperament: Redundant, independent, or interacting influences on interpersonal adaptation and personality development? In J. Cassidy & P.R. Shaver (Eds.), *Handbook of attachment: Theory, research, and clinical applications* (pp. 198–225). New York: Guilford Press.

Vaughn, B.E., Stevenson-Hinde, J., Waters, E., Kotsaftis, A., Lefaver, G.B., Shouldice, A., Trudel, M., & Belsky, J. (1992). Attachment security and temperament in infancy in early childhood. *Developmental Psychology, 28,* 463–473.

Venter, J.C., Adams, M.D., Myers, E.W., Li, P.W., Mural, R.J., Sutton, G.G., et al. (2001). The sequence of the human genome. *Science, 291,* 1304–1351.

Ventura, S.J., Hamilton, B.E., Mathews, T.J., & Chandra, A. (2003). Trends and variations in smoking during pregnancy and low birth weight: Evidence from the birth certificate, 1990–2000. *Pediatrics, 111,* 1176–1180.

Verlinsky, Y., Rechitsky, S., Schoolcraft, W., Strom, C., & Kuliev, A. (2001). Preimplantation diagnosis for Fanconi anemia combined with HLA matching. *JAMA, 285,* 3130–3133.

Verlinsky, Y., Rechitsky, S., Verlinsky, O., Masciangelo, C., Lederer, K., & Kuliev, A. (2002). Preimplantation diagnosis for early-onset Alzheimer disease caused by V717L mutation. *JAMA, 287,* 1018–1021.

Verschueren, K., Marcoen, A., & Schoefs, V. (1996). The internal working model of the self, attachment, and competence in five-year-olds. *Child Development, 67,* 2493–2511.

Vestergaard, M., Wisborg, K., Henriksen, T.B., Secher, N.J., Ostergaard, J.R., & Olsen, J. (2005). Prenatal exposure to cigarettes, alcohol, and coffee and the risk for febrile seizures. *Pediatrics, 116,* 1089–1094.

Volden, J., & Lord, C. (1991). Neologisms and idiosyncratic language in autistic speakers. *Journal of Autism and Developmental Disorders, 21,* 109–131.

Volling, B.L., McElwain, N.L., & Miller, A.L. (2002). Emotion regulation in context: The jealousy complex between young siblings and its relations with child and family characteristics. *Child Development, 73,* 581–600.

von Hofsten, C. (1983). Foundations for perceptual development. In L.P. Lipsitt & C.K. Rovee-Collier (Eds.), *Advances in infancy research* (Vol. 2, pp. 241–264). Norwood, NJ: Ablex.

von Hofsten, C. (1991). Structure of early reaching movements: A longitudinal study. *Journal of Motor Behavior, 23,* 280–292.

Vondra, J.I., & Barnett, D. (Eds.). (1999). Atypical attachment in infancy and early childhood among children at developmental risk. *Monographs of the Society for Research in Child Development, 64*(3, Serial No. 258).

Vondra, J.I., Hommerding, K.D., & Shaw, D.S. (1999). Stability and change in infant attachment in a low-income sample. In J.I. Vondra, J.I. & D. Barnett (Eds.), Atypical attachment in infancy and early childhood among children at developmental risk. *Monographs of the Society for Research in Child Development, 64*(3, Serial No. 258), 119–144.

Votruba-Drzal, E., Coley, R.L., & Chase-Lansdale, P.L. (2004). Child care and low-income children's development: Direct and moderated effects. *Child Development, 75,* 296–312.

Vygotsky, L.S. (1933/1978). The role of play in development (M. Lopez-Morillas, trans.). In M. Cole, V. John-Steiner, S. Scribner, & E. Souberman (Eds.), *L.S. Vygotsky: Mind in society.* Cambridge, MA: Harvard University Press.

Vygotsky, L.S. (1934/1986). *Thought and language* (A. Kozulin, transl.). Cambridge, MA: MIT Press.

Wachs, T.D., & Bates, J.E. (2001). Temperament. In G. Bremner, & A. Fogel (Eds.), *Blackwell handbook of infant development* (pp. 465–501). Oxford, UK: Blackwells.

Wakeley, A., Rivera, S., & Langer, J. (2000a). Can young infants add and subtract? *Child Development, 71,* 1525–1534.

Wakeley, A., Rivera, S., & Langer, J. (2000b). Not proved: Reply to Wynn. *Child Development, 71,* 1537–1539.

Wakschlag, L.S., Chase-Lansdale, P.L., & Brooks-Gunn, J. (1996). Not just "ghosts in the nursery": Contemporaneous intergenerational relationships and parenting in young African-American families. *Child Development, 67,* 2131–2147.

Waldfogel, J. (September 2001). Family and medical leave: Evidence from the 2000 surveys. *Monthly Labor Review,* pp. 17–23.

Walk, R.D., & Gibson, E.J. (1961). A comparative and analytical study of visual depth perception. *Psychology Monographs, 75*(15).

Walker-Andrews, A.S. (1986). Intermodal perception of expressive behaviors: Relation of eye and voice? *Devel- opmental Psychology, 22,* 373–377.

Walker, C.N., & O'Brien, B. (1999). The relationship between method of pain management during labor and birth outcomes. *Clinical Nursing Research, 8,* 119–134.

Walker, J.R. (1996). Funding child rearing: Child allowance and parental leave. *The Future of Children, 6*(2), 5–25.

Wang, Q. (2004). The emergence of cultural self-construct: Autobiographical memory and self-description in American and Chinese children. *Developmental Psychology, 40,* 3–15.

Ward, M.J., Vaughn, B.E., & Robb, M.D. (1988). Social-emotional adaptation and infant-mother attachment in siblings: Role of the mother in cross-sibling consistency. *Child Development, 59,* 643–651.

Warren. S.L., Gunnar, M.R., Kagan, J., Anders, T.F., Simmens, S.J., Rones, M., et al. (2003). Maternal panic disorder: Infant temperament, neurophysiology, and parenting behaviors. *Journal of the American Academy of Child and Adolescent Psychiatry, 42,* 814–825.

Wartella, E., Caplovitz, A.G., & Lee, J.H. (2004). From Baby Einstein to Leapfrog, from Doom to the Sims, from instant messaging to Internet chat rooms: Public interest in the role of interactive media in children's lives. *Social Policy Report, 18*(4), 1–19.

Wasik, B.H., Ramey, C.T., Bryant, D.M., & Sparling, J.J. (1990). A longitudinal study of two early intervention strategies: Project CARE. *Child Development, 61,* 1682–1696.

Waters, E. (1995). Appendix A. The Attachment Q-set (Version 3). In E. Waters, B.E. Vaughn, G., Posada & K. Kondo-Ikemura (Eds.), Caregiving, cultural, and cognitive perspectives on secure-base behavior and working models: New growing points in attachment theory and research. *Monographs of the Society for Research in Child Development, 60* (Serial No. 244), 234–246.

Waters, E., & Deane, K.E. (1985). Defining and assessing individual differences in attachment relationships: Q-methodology and the organization of behavior in infancy and early childhood. In I. Bretherton & E. Waters (Eds.), Growing points of attachment theory and research. *Monographs of the Society for Research in Child Development, 50*(1/2, Serial No. 209), 41–65.

Watkins, M.L., Rasmussen, S.A., Honein, M.A., Botto, L.D., & Moore, C.A. (2003). Maternal obesity and risk for birth defects. *Pediatrics, 111,* 1152–1158.

Watson, J.B. (1928). *Psychological care of infant and child.* New York: Norton.

Watson, J.B., & Rayner, R.A. (1920). Conditional emotional reactions. *Journal of Experimental Psychology, 3,* 1–14.

Watson, J.D., & Crick, F.H.C. (1953). Molecular structure of nucleic acids. *Nature, 171,* 737–738.

Waxman, S.R., & Lidz, J.L. (2006). Early word learning. In W. Damon & R. Lerner (Eds.) & D. Kuhn & R. Siegler (Vol. Eds.), *Handbook of child psychology: Vol. 2. Cognition, perception, and language* (6th ed., pp. 299–335). New York: Wiley.

Waxman, S.R., & Hall, D.G. (1993). The development of a linkage between count nouns and object categories: Evidence from fifteen- to twenty-one-month-old infants. *Child Development, 64,* 1224–1241.

Waxman, S.R., & Kosowski, T.D. (1990). Nouns mark category relations: Toddlers' and preschoolers' word learning biases. *Child Development, 61,* 1461–1473.

Waxman, S.R., & Markow, D.B. (1995). Words as invitations to form categories: Evidence from 12- to 13-month-old infants. *Cognitive Psychology, 29,* 257–302.

Waxman, S.R., & Senghas, A. (1992). Relations among word meaning in early lexical development. *Developmental Psychology, 34,* 1289–1309.

Weeks, J.D., & Kozak, L.J. (2001). Trends in the use of episiotomy in the United States: 1980–1998. *Birth, 28,* 152–160.

Weikart, D.P. (1998). Changing early childhood development through educational intervention. *Preventive Medicine, 27,* 233–237.

Weinberg, M.K., & Tronick, E.Z. (1994). Beyond the face: An empirical study of infant affective configurations of facial, vocal, gestural, and regulatory behaviors. *Child Development, 60,* 85–92.

Weinberg, M.K., & Tronick, E.Z. (1996). Infant affective reactions to the resumption of maternal interaction after stillface. *Child Development, 67,* 905–914.

Weinberg, M.K., Tronick, E.Z., Cohn, J.F., & Olson, K.L. (1999). Gender differences in emotional expressivity and selfregulation during early infancy. *Developmental Psychology, 35,* 175–188.

Weitzman, C.C., Roy, L., Walls, T., & Tomlin, R. (2004). More evidence for Reach Out and Read: A home-based study. *Pediatrics, 113,* 1248–1253.

Wellman, H., & Wooley, J. (1990). From simple desires to ordinary beliefs: The early development of everyday psychology. *Cognition, 35,* 245–275.

Wellman, H., Harris, P.L., Banerjee, M., & Sinclair, A. (1995). Early understanding of emotion: Evidence from natural language. *Cognition and Emotion, 9,* 117–149.

Wellman, H.M., Cross, D., & Bartsch, K. (1986). A meta-analysis of research on Stage 4 object permanence: The A-not-B error. *Monographs of the Society for Research in Child Development, 51(3,* Serial No. 214).

Wendland-Carro, J., Piccinini, C.A., & Millar, W.S. (1999). The role of an early intervention on enhancing the quality of mother-infant interaction. *Child Development, 70,* 713–721.

Werker, J.F., & Lalonde, C.E. (1988). Cross-language speech perception: Initial capabilities and developmental change. *Developmental Psychology, 24,* 672–683.

Werker, J.F., & McLeod, P.J. (1989). Infant preference for both male and female infant-directed talk: A developmental study of attentional and affective responsiveness. *Canadian Journal of Psychology, 43,* 230–246.

Werker, J.F., & Tees, R.C. (1984). Cross-language speech perception: Evidence for perceptual re-organization during the first year of life. *Infant Behavior and Development, 7,* 49–63.

Werker, J.F., Pegg, J.E., & McLeod, P.J. (1994). A cross-language investigation of infant preference for infant-directed communication. *Infant Behavior and Development, 17,* 323–333.

Werner, E. (2000). Protective factors and resilience. In J.P. Shonkoff & S.J. Meisels (Eds.), *Handbook of early childhood intervention* (2nd ed., pp. 115–132). New York: Cambridge University Press.

Werner, E., Dawson, G., Osterling, J., & Dinno, N. (2000). Recognition of autism spectrum disorder before one year of age: A retrospective study based on home videotapes. *Journal of Autism & Developmental Disorders, 30,* 157–162.

Werner, E., Dawson, G., Osterling, J., & Dinno, N. (2000). Recognition of autism spectrum disorder before one year of age: A retrospective study based on home videotapes. *Journal of Autism and Developmental Disorders, 30,* 157–162.

Wertsch, J. (1979). From social interaction to higher psychological processes. *Human Development, 22,* 1–22.

Wertsch, J. (1985). *Vygotsky and the social formation of mind.* Cambridge, MA: Harvard University Press.

Wertsch, J.V., & Tulviste, P. (1992). L.S. Vygotsky and contemporary developmental psychology. *Developmental Psychology, 28,* 548–557.

White, B., Gunnar, M.R., Larson, M.C., Donzella, B., & Barr, R.G. (2000). Behavioral and physiological responsivity, sleep, and patterns of daily cortisol production in infants with and without colic. *Child Development, 71,* 862–877.

Whitehurst, G.J., Arnold, D.S., Epstein, J.N., Angell, A.L., Smith, M., & Fischel, J.E. (1994). A picture book reading intervention in day care and home for children from low-income families. *Developmental Psychology, 30,* 679–689.

Whiting, J.W.M., Child, I.L., Lambert, W.W., Fischer, A.M., Fischer, J.L., Nydegger, C., et al. (1966). *Field guide for a study of socialization: Six cultures series (Vol. 1).* New York: Wiley.

Whitney, M.P., & Thoman, E.B. (1994). Sleep in premature and fullterm infants from 24-hour home recordings. *Infant Behavior & Development, 17,* 223–234.

Whyatt, R.M., Rauh, V., Barr, D.B., Camann, D.E., Andrews, H.F., Garfinkel, R., et al. (2004). Prenatal insecticide exposures, birth weight and length among an urban minority cohort. *Environmental Health Perspectives, 112,* 1125–1132.

Widdowson, E.M. (1951). Mental contentment and physical growth. *Lancet, 1,* 1316–1318.

Wiggins, P. (2000). Shaken Baby Syndrome: What caregivers need to know. *Texas Child Care, 23(4),* 16–19.

Wilkin, P. (1995). A comparison of fetal and newborn responses to music and sound stimuli with and without daily exposure to a specific piece of music. *Bulletin of the Council for Research in Music Education, 27,* 163–169.

Willatts, P. (1997). Beyond the "couch potato" infant: How infants use their knowledge to regulate action, solve problems, and achieve goals. In G. Bremner, A. Slater,, & G. Butterworth (Eds.), *Infant development: Recent advances* (pp. 109–135). East Sussex, UK: Psychology Press.

Williams, C.L., Squillace, M.M., Bollella, M.C., Brotanek, J., Campanaro, L., D'Agostino, C., et al. (1998). *Healthy Start*: A comprehensive health education program for preschool children. *Preventive Medicine, 27,* 216–223.

Williams, K., & Umberson, D. (1999). Medical technology and childbirth: Experiences of expectant mothers and fathers. *Sex Roles, 41,* 147–168.

Willinger, M., Ko, C.W., Hoffman, H.J., Kessler, R.C., & Corwin, M.J. (2000). Factors associated with caregivers' choice of infant sleep position, 1994–1998: The National Infant Sleep Position Study. *JAMA, 283,* 2135–2142.

Willinger, M., Ko, C.W., Hoffman, H.J., Kessler, R.C., & Corwin, M.J. (2003). Trends in infant bed sharing in the United States, 1993–2000: The National Infant Sleep Position Study. *Archives of Pediatrics and Adolescent Medicine, 157,* 43–49.

Wilson, D.A., & Sullivan, R.M. (1994). Neurobiology of associative learning in the neonate: Early olfactory learning. *Behavioral and Neural Biology, 61,* 1–18.

Wilson, R.D. (2002). Prenatal evaluation for fetal surgery. *Current Opinions in Obstetrical Gynecology, 14,* 187–193.

Winikoff, B., Castle, M A., & Laukaran, V. H. (Eds.). (1988). *Feeding infants in four societies: Causes and consequences of mothers' choices.* New York: Greenwood Press.

Winston, F.K., Chen, I.G., Elliott, M.R., Arbogast, K.B., & Durbin, D.R. (2004). Recent trends in child restraint practices in the United States. *Pediatrics, 113,* e458–e464.

Witherington, D.C., Campo, J.J., & Hertenstein, M.J. (2001). Principles of emotion and its development in infancy. In G. Bremner & A. Fogel (Eds.), *Blackwell handbook of infant development* (pp. 427–464). Oxford, UK: Blackwell.

Wolery, R.A., & Odom, S.L. (2000). *An administrator's guide to preschool inclusion.* Chapel Hill, NC: University of North Carolina, FPG Child Development Center, Early Childhood Research Institute on Inclusion.

Wolf, A.W., Lozoff, B., Latz, S., Paludetto, R. (1996). Parental theories in the management of young children's sleep in Japan, Italy, and the United States. In S. Harkness, & C. M. Super (Eds.), *Parents' cultural belief systems: Their origins, expressions, and consequences* (pp. 364–384). New York: Guilford Press.

Wolfsberg, T.G., McEntyre, J., & Schuler, G. D. (2001). Guide to the draft human genome. *Nature, 409,* 824–826.

Wood, D., Bruner, J., & Ross, G. (1976). The role of tutoring in problem solving. *Journal of Child Psychology and Psychiatry, 17,* 89–100.

Woodward, A.L. (2000). Constraining the problem space in early word learning. In R. Golinkoff, K. Hirsh-Pasek, N. Bloom, G. Hollich, L. Smith, A.L. Woodward, Akhtar, L., Tomasello, M., & Hollich, G. (Eds.), *Becoming a word learner: A debate on lexical acquisition* (pp. 81–114). Oxford: Oxford University Press.

Woodward, A.L., & Markman, E.M. (1998). Early word learning. In W. Damon (Ed.) & D. Kuhn & R.S. Siegler (Vol. Eds.), *Handbook of child psychology* (5th ed.): *Vol. 2. Cognition, perception, and language* (pp. 371–420). New York: Wiley.

Woodward, A.L., Markman, E.M., & Fitzsimmons, C.M. (1994). Rapid word learning in 13- and 18-month-olds. *Developmental Psychology, 30,* 553–566.

Woodward, E.H., & Gridina, N. (2000). *Media in the home, 2000: The fifth annual survey of parents and children.* Philadelphia, PA: The Annenberg Public Policy Center of the University of Pennsylvania. Available at http://www

.appcpenn.org/mediainhome/survey/survey7.pdf

Woodward, J., & Kelly, S.M. (2004). A pilot study for a randomized controlled trial of waterbirth versus land birth. *BJOG, 111,* 537–545.

World Health Organization. (1996). Safe use of iodized oil to prevent iodine deficiency in pregnant women. *Bulletin of the World Health Organization, 74,* 1–3.

World Health Organization. (2000). WHO Global Data Bank on Breastfeeding. Retrieved December 10, 2002, from http://www.who.int/nut/db_bfd.htm

Word Health Organization. (2001a). Assessment of iodine deficiency disorders and monitoring their elimination: A guide for programme managers (2nd ed.). Geneva: WHO.

World Health Organization. (2001b). Micronutrient deficiencies: Combating vitamin A deficiency. Retrieved December 10, 2002, from http://www.who.int/nut/vad.htm.

World Health Organization. (2002). Complementary feeding: A review of scientific evidence. Retrieved January 10, 2003, from http://www.who.int/child-adolescent-health/NUTRTION/complementary.htm

World Health Organization. (2002). Micronutrient deficiencies. Retrieved December 10, 2002, from http://www.who.int/nut/#mic

World Health Organization/PAHO Consultation on CVS. (1999). Evaluation of chorionic villus sampling safety. *Prenatal Diagnosis, 19,* 97–99.

Wren, C., Birrell, G., & Hawthorne, G. (2003). Cardiovascular malformations in infants of diabetic mothers. *Heart, 89,* 1217–1220.

Wright, A.L., & Schanler, R.J. (2001). The resurgence of breastfeeding at the end of the second millennium. *The Journal of Nutrition, 131,* 421S–425S.

Wright, C.A., George, T.P., Burke, R., Gelfand, D.M., & Teti, D.M. (2000). Early maternal depression and children's adjustment to school. *Child Study Journal, 30,* 153–168.

Wright, J., Huston, A.C., Murphy, K.C., St. Peters, M., Piñon, M., Scantlin, R., et al. (2001). The relations of early television viewing to school readiness and vocabulary of children from low-income families: The Early Window Project. *Child Development, 72,* 1347–1366.

Wynn, K. (1992). Evidence against empiricist accounts of the origins of numerical knowledge. *Mind and Language, 7,* 315–332.

Wynn, K. (1996). Infants' individuation and enumeration of actions. *Psychological Science, 7,* 164–169.

Wynn, K. (2000). Findings of addition and subtraction in infants are robust and consistent: Reply to Wakeley, Rivera, and Langer. *Child Development, 71,* 1535–1536.

Xu, K., Shi, Z.M., Veeck, L.L., Hughes, M.R., & Rosenwaks, Z. (1999). First unaffected pregnancy using preimplantation genetic diagnosis for sickle cell anemia. *JAMA, 281,* 1701–1706.

Yang, Q., Khoury, M.J., & Mannino, D. (1997). Trends and patterns of birth defects and genetic diseases associated mortality in United States, 1979–1992: An analysis of multiple-cause mortality data. *Genetic Epidemiology, 14,* 493–505.

Yavas, M. (1995). Phonological selectivity in the first fifty words of a bilingual child. *Language and Speech, 38,* 189–202.

Yazigi, R.A., Odem, R.R., & Polakoski, K.L. (1991). Demonstration of specific binding of cocaine to human spermatozoa. *JAMA, 266,* 1956–1959.

Yearbook of Immigration Statistics 2004. (2004). Department of Homeland Security. Retrieved November 4, 2005, from http://uscis.gov/graphics/shared/statistics/yearbook/YrBk04Im.htm

Yeung, W.J., Sandberg, J.F., Davis-Kean, P., & Hofferth, S.L. (2001). Children's time with fathers in intact families. *Journal of Marriage and the Family, 63,* 136–154.

Yoshinaga-Itano, C., Sedey, A.L., Coulter, D.K., & Mehl, A.L. (1998). Language of early- and later-identified children with hearing loss. *Pediatrics, 102,* 1161–1171.

Young, K.T. (1990). American conceptions of infant development from 1955 to 1984: What the experts are telling parents. *Child Development, 61,* 17–28.

Youngblade, L.M., & Dunn, J. (1995). Individual differences in young children's pretend play with mother and sibling: Links to relationships and understanding of other people's feelings and beliefs. *Child Development, 66,* 1472–1492.

Younger, B. (1985). The segregation of items into categories by ten-month-old infants. *Child Development, 56,* 1574–1583.

Zeanah, C.H. (2000). Disturbances of attachment in young childre adopted from institutions. *Developmental and Behavioral Pediatrics, 21,* 230–236.

Zeanah, C.H., & Boris, N.W. (2000). Disturbances and disorders of attachment in early childhood. In C.H. Zeanah (Ed.), *Handbook of infant mental health* (2nd ed., pp. 353–368). New York: Guilford Press.

Zeanah, C.H., & Emde, R.N. (1994). Attachment disorders in infancy. In M. Rutter, L. Hersov, & E. Taylor (Eds.), *Child and adolescent psychiatry: Modern approaches* (pp. 490–504). Oxford, UK: Blackwell.

Zeanah, C.H., & Fox, N.A. (2004). Temperament and attachment disorders. *Journal of Clinical Child and Adolescent Psychology, 33,* 32–41.

Zeanah, C.H., Boris, N.W., & Larrieu, J.A. (1997). Infant development and developmental risk: A review of the past 10 years. *Journal of the American Academy of Child and Adolescent Psychiatry, 36,* 165–178.

Zeanah, C.H., Nelson, C.A., Fox, N.A., Smyke, A.T., Marshall, P., Parker, S.W., & Koga, S. (2003). Designing research to study the effects of institutionalization on brain and behavioral development: The Bucharest Early Intervention Project. *Development and Psychopathology,15,* 885– 907.

Zelazo, P.D., Reznick, J.S., & Spinazzola, J. (1998). Representational flexibility and response control in a multi-step, mutilocation search task. *Developmental Psychology, 34*, 203–214.

Zelazo, P.R., Zelazo, N.A., & Kolb, S. (1972). Walking in the newborn. *Science, 176*, 314–315.

Zentner, M.R., & Kagan, J. (1996). Perception of music by infants. *Nature, 383*, 29.

Zhang, J., Bernasko, J.W., Leybovich, E., Fahs, M., & Hatch, M.C. (1996). Continuous labor support from labor attendant for primiparous owmen: A meta-analysis. *Obstetrics and Gynecology, 88*, 739–744.

Zhang, J., Meikle, S., Grainger, D.A., & Trumble, A. (2002). Multifetal pregnancy in older women and perinatal outcomes. *Fertility and Sterility, 78*, 562–568.

Zhang, Y., Kuhl, P.K., Imada, T., Kotani, M., & Tohkura, Y. (2005). Effects of language experience: Neural commitment to language-specific auditory patterns. *NeuroImage, 26*, 703–720.

Zhao, Y., Sheng, H.Z., Amini, R., Grinberg, A., Lee, E., Huang, S., et al. (1999). Control of hippocampal morphogenesis and neuronal differentiation by the LIM homeobox gene Lhx5. *Science, 284*, 1155–1158.

Zimmerman, I., Steiner, V., & Pond, P. (1991). *Preschool Language Scale—3*. San Antonio, TX: Psychological Corp.

Zimmerman, R., Huch, A., & Huch, R. (1993). Water birth: Is it safe? *Journal of Perinatal Medicine, 21*, 5–11.

Zukow-Goldring, P. (2002). Sibling caregiving. In M.H. Bornstein (Ed.), Handbook of parenting: Vol. 3. Status and social conditions of parenting (2nd ed., pp. 253–286). Mahwah, NJ: Erlbaum.

INDEX

Page numbers in **bold** indicate key word definitions.

Answer Key

Questions by Duane Bolin and Luke Holzmann
Edited by Amber Densmer Baker

Solution Concept and Design by Amber Densmer Baker

ISBN: 978-1-935570-03-5

Avyx, Inc.
8032 South Grant Way
Littleton, CO 80122
USA
303-483-0140
www.avyx.com

Table of Contents

Answer Key

This page intentionally left blank.

Welcome to the MathTacular 4 Workbook Answer Key!

Do you remember word problems in math class when you were growing up? Did you love them, or did you sometimes find yourself staring at the page until the words blurred together, wondering where to begin? If only someone had given you a "plan of attack" that worked every time...

Well, that's what we've done here. We hope the instruction in this program will give you and your children the tools you need to overcome Word Problem Intimidation. Take a few minutes to review the Simple Steps to Solve Word Problems located on the inside back cover of this book. These are the same steps Detective Justin Time presents on the DVD, which will teach your little problem solvers how to determine what each problem is asking, and how to pull the relevant information out of that daunting block of words. The more you and your children work through these steps, the more second-nature they will become, and before long, it will seem as though those pesky word problems have finally met their match.

How to use this workbook set with the MathTacular 4 DVD:

In order to understand the MathTacular 4 story, we recommend you begin by watching the first few scenes on the DVD. We'll introduce you to our hero, Detective Justin Time, and the task before him: to assist Amber Waves with her Word Puzzler woes, and eventually rescue her pork-napped pig, Polly Esther.

As each chapter of the story unfolds, our heroes encounter word problems—the same **Sample** word problems found at the beginning of each chapter in the Workbook. Before we solve the problem on the DVD, Detective Time will first ask your children to try to solve the problem on their own in their book. Keep in mind that the DVD will stop on its own (unless you've selected "Play All") to give them time to do so. Even if they've never done this type of word problem before, have them give it their best shot. When they're done, go back to the DVD, press "Continue" and the heroes in our story will walk them through the solution to the word problem.

Once you've solved the Sample problem, Detective Time will give your children an opportunity to work on the **Practice Problems** that complete each chapter in this book. When they're finished, have your children compare their answers to the answers found in this **Answer Key**. Once they've finished all of the additional word problems in a particular section, continue watching the DVD and move on to the next type of word problem—and the next part of the adventure!

Be sure to check out the handy **Tool Kit** (see page 163 of the Workbook) that contains lists of Clue Words, Units and Measurements and other nuggets that will help your children solve the problems in this program.

Pacing: Please review the list of skills provided after each chapter title on the Table of Contents. This program covers a very wide range of mathematical skills—probably some your younger children have yet to learn in math class. But that's okay! Your children will probably enjoy the story line of the DVD (which is why we've included the "Play All" feature), and may pick up a few things as they watch our heroes solve each word problem. We encourage you to incorporate the problems in the Workbook as you cover each skill in your own math curriculum.

MathTacular 4 ▲ Answer Key ▲ Introduction ▲ i

About the Answer Key

We created this Answer Key to complete the MathTacular 4 program. Not only does it contain the solution to every problem presented in the Student Workbook, but we've mapped out all of the steps it will take your student to solve each and every word problem—start to finish. By showing your children how we arrived at our answer, we can not only demonstrate how to logically think through a problem to find a solution, but also gently redirect your children's thinking should it veer off course, and help them figure out where they might have gone wrong. However, just as there are many ways to stuff a taco, there are also sometimes several ways to arrive at the same answer to a word problem. If your children discover a different path to solve a problem than one we present here, applaud them! Some of our answers even include a separate box that describes an "Alternate Way to Solve" a particular problem. Please do not require your children to always mimic our process—sometimes the way they've processed the information will make more sense to them, and as long as their math and the answer they find checks out, we're happy.

Even though they may deem it worse than a trip to the dentist, **please encourage your children to always show their work**. When they don't and they miss an answer, they will probably also miss the opportunity to learn from where their thinking went awry when they check the solution in this book. In addition, some teachers and professors in their future may give partial credit on tests if they can figure out where your child went wrong—credit they'll miss out on if they're not in the habit of showing their work.

A Wide Range of Skills: Since we believe that anyone can learn to conquer word problems, we have designed this program to cover a very wide scope of mathematical skills. While there's a good chance that younger students haven't yet studied, say, fractions or ratios in their math curriculum, they will probably still enjoy watching our heroes work through the word problems to find the clues that lead them to Polly Esther, and they will probably absorb some of the mathematical concepts they'll experience along the way. If you'd like to take it a step further, you can read through the solutions to the tougher problems in the Answer Key, and then see if your children can work out the problem independently. Keep in mind that if you still have many more years of math study in your future, you'll be able to use this program again and again. You'll be able to introduce more of the extra problems in this workbook as your children learn to master new topics in their math curriculum. Whether MathTacular 4 is one of your fun Friday activities or you simply revisit it periodically as you learn new skills in your own math curriculum, we hope this program will become one of your favorite learning tools for years to come.

Final Important Fact About Word Problems: Please remind your children that, regardless of length, most word problems are like newspaper articles—they present the facts. If a word problem didn't specifically give certain information, you probably don't need to know it in order to solve the problem. So, say a problem only gives information about Bernardo belly dancing on Monday, Wednesday and Friday. It's safe to assume, then, that Bernardo did *not* belly dance the rest of the week. Help your children succeed by encouraging them to take these problems at face value.

Calculators? Of course, it is always your choice whether you'd like your children to use a calculator when they're working on mathematical computations. While it's always good "mental exercise" for your children to practice basic math facts, remember that pulling the right information out of a word problem and then correctly building a math problem with that information (that will take you to the *right* answer) is a daunting and complicated task in itself. We encourage you to use this program to first mold the problem solving skills it takes to tackle word problems, and only require calculator-free math when it isn't an added burden. (How much "chicken-scratching" *does* it take to solve $265.30 \div 14$? Or are you reaching for your calculator too?)

Simple Addition

Sample Problem

Hannah has four goats. ~~Their names are Loretta, Ignatius, Kimberly, and Bob. Kimberly was Hannah's favorite. Loretta and Bob were the two oldest goats.~~ At the County Fair, Hannah bought three more goats from her friend Amy. ~~These goats are named Tim, Phil, and Wayne.~~ How many goats does she have now?

4 goats
+ 3 goats
7 goats

Amy now has 7 goats.

Practice Problem #1

Ronald the Raccoon loves to steal garbage from the neighborhood trash cans. On Tuesdays, he visits three trash cans. On Thursdays, he visits six other trash cans. Ronald is considering going out on Saturday night to visit an additional twelve trash cans. ~~If he starts out at 8:00 pm, he figures he can be done by 11:30 pm.~~ If he does go out on Saturday as planned, how many trash cans will Ronald visit altogether each week?

3 trash cans
6 trash cans
+ 12 trash cans
21 trash cans

Ronald will visit 21 trash cans.

Practice Problem #2

Cashew and her brother Samson went fishing down by the Ol' Waterin' Hole. ~~Cashew had her brand new Bezco rod and reel. Samson was using a tuning fork on which he'd tied a piece of string.~~ In the first hour, Cashew landed 27 striped bass, while Samson only managed to wrangle four giant tuna. In the second hour, Cashew caught an additional 12 striped bass, and Samson hauled in 29 Atlantic Salmon. ~~Since they wanted to catch a 3 p.m. matinee of "Aluminum Man," they headed home with their catch.~~ How many fish did they catch in all?

27 (fish)
4 (fish)
12 (fish)
+ 29 (fish)
72 (fish)

They caught 72 fish in all.

Practice Problem #3

Bo Jest works for "A Clown a Day Keeps the Blues Away" Circus. ~~He was recently promoted from "The Cotton Candy Guy" to "The Guy Who Puts the Clowns in the Tiny Car." Wanting to impress his boss, he promises to fit more clowns into the tiny car than ever before.~~ On his first day, Bo shoves 12 clowns into the tiny car. Then he has an epiphany. After coating the clowns in peanut oil, Bo is able to slide an additional 7 clowns into the car. Still not satisfied, Bo grabs a plunger and a shoe horn and is finally able to squeeze 5 more clowns into the tiny car. How many clowns total did he fit into the tiny car?

$$\begin{array}{r} 12 \text{ clowns} \\ 7 \text{ clowns} \\ + 5 \text{ clowns} \\ \hline 24 \text{ clowns} \end{array}$$

He fit 24 clowns into the car.

Practice Problem #4

~~Roger works at a factory and earns $11.27 an hour maintaining the bolt making machine. The machine has a maximum output capacity of 225 bolts per day.~~ Unfortunately, it breaks down often. On Monday the machine was able to spit out 217 bolts before falling apart. ~~It took Roger until the factory closed on Thursday night to get the machine up and running again.~~ On Friday the machine made another 192 bolts before it completely fell apart. How many bolts did the machine manage to make that week?

$$\begin{array}{r} 217 \text{ bolts} \\ + 192 \text{ bolts} \\ \hline 409 \text{ bolts} \end{array}$$

The machine made 409 bolts.

Practice Problem #5

~~It was lab day at the Practicum for Underwater Terrestrial Research of Invertebrate Digestion: P.U.T.R.I.D. Sandy, Sunny, and Al were in a group.~~ Sandy's tapeworm had collected 0.03 L of digestive fluid. Sunny was only able to extract 0.16 L of digestive fluid from his starfish. And Al's three-pound Grouper had a shockingly low level of liquid with only 0.59 L. The lab sheet asked: How many Liters of digestive fluid are there in your three specimens altogether? What should the lab partners write down as their answer?

$$\begin{array}{r} 0.03 \text{ L} \\ 0.16 \text{ L} \\ + 0.59 \text{ L} \\ \hline 0.78 \text{ L} \end{array}$$

There are 0.78 L of digestive fluid altogether.

Less Than

Simple Subtraction

Sample Problem

Dagmar Olsen loves flapjacks. ~~Yesterday, he ate 17 flapjacks~~ ~~for breakfast. Mysteriously, Dagmar's tummy started to ache~~ ~~shortly thereafter. He went to the doctor, and~~ the nurse told him he ~~was 47 inches tall and~~ weighed 273 pounds. ~~Yesterday,~~ Dagmar's best friend, Elton ~~Noberto, ate 3 bowls of "You Can't~~ ~~Beat Wheat" cereal. Later that day, Elton went to the doctor~~ ~~for a check-up. The nurse told him he was 61 inches tall and~~ weighed 126 pounds <u>less than</u> Dagmar Olsen. <u>How much does</u> <u>Elton Norberto weigh?</u>

- 126 pounds

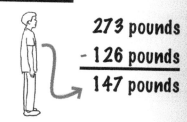

```
  273 pounds
- 126 pounds
  147 pounds
```

Elton Norberto weighs 147 pounds.

Practice Problem #1

~~Custer and Buster were very competitive twin hedgehogs.~~ ~~One fine Saturday, they agreed to saddle up their horses and~~ ~~compete to see who could ride the farthest that day. At the~~ ~~crack of 10 a.m., Buster broke out to an early lead and soon~~ ~~left Custer in the dust. At Tuna Fork, Buster took the High~~ ~~Road and kept his lightning-quick pace. When Custer reached~~ ~~the Fork, he could see from the tracks in the dust that the only~~ ~~chance he'd have would be to go down the Low Road.~~ When night fell, Buster had traveled an amazing 293 miles. Due to an unfortunate incident at Little Bighorn, Custer ended up traveling 154 miles <u>less than</u> Buster that day. <u>How many miles did</u> <u>Custer travel that fateful Saturday?</u>

```
Buster   →  293 miles
- 154 miles  - 154 miles
Custer   ←  139 miles
```

Custer traveled 139 miles.

2

Practice Problem #2

Iglopuk, an Inuit entrepreneur from Gnome, Alaska, took a cab from the Miami airport to the Everglades. When he jumped in the cab, it was a blazing 98 degrees inside! The cabbie apologized for the heat but confessed that his air conditioner had been broken for a week. Without skipping a beat, Iglopuk opened his bag and flipped on the air conditioner he'd made out of an old VCR, baling wire and a used A/B switch. By the time the cab reached the Everglades, it was 32 degrees cooler inside the cab than it had been at the airport. What temperature was it inside the cab when they got to the Everglades?

```
  98 degrees
- 32 degrees
  66 degrees
```

It was 66 degrees inside the cab when they reached the Everglades.

Practice Problem #3

Nevil the Rat knows that there are 37 treats on the third shelf of the bookcase. As a sensible rat, he loves treats, food, and just about anything he can put in his mouth and digest. After three days of failed attempts, he is finally able to get to the third shelf by climbing up the pile of laundry to the chair, the chair to the windowsill, and, with nothing more than a dangerous lateral leap, to the shelf and his prize. Hungry from his climb, Nevil promptly consumes 18 of the treats until he is discovered, scolded and put back in his cage. How many treats are left for Nevil's next excursion?

```
  37 treats
- 18 treats
  19 treats
```

Nevil has 19 treats left.

Practice Problem #4

~~Granny and Fanny were the lone contestants in the final~~ ~~round of the Ultimate Speed Knitting Championship. At the~~ ~~bell, their needles clicked and whirred into a blur—some even~~ ~~thought they saw smoke rising from Granny's hands! The~~ ~~match was expected to be close, but unfortunately, Fanny's~~ ~~patented Yarn Unwinder 5000 jammed in the final seconds and~~ ~~Granny blew past her to the finish.~~ Final scarf measurements confirmed that Granny had knit an astonishing 163 feet, while Fanny had only knit 124 feet. How much longer was Granny's championship-winning scarf?

163 feet
- 124 feet
39 feet longer

Granny's scarf was
39 feet longer.

Practice Problem #5

~~It was an unusually dark and stormy night. In fact, Luke could not remember the last~~ ~~time the annual Ocho de Mayo celebration had been rained out. As he wandered home,~~ his mind went back to '88, when he was crowned King Burrito. He had put away 60 burritos ~~in~~ ~~only 30 minutes that year.~~ In '89 he had eaten 12 fewer burritos, ~~but he had also just recov-~~ ~~ered from a serious bout with rickets—just enough of a handicap to allow Miz Chalupa to~~ ~~steal his crown.~~ Finally, in '90, he once again reigned supreme…Burrito Supreme, that is. That year, Miz Chalupa could only gulp down 10 fewer burritos than Luke had the previous year. ~~Since that time, Luke's reign earned him the nickname "Ol' Iron Stomach."~~ How many burritos did Miz Chalupa eat in '90?

'88 = 60 burritos   '89 = 12 fewer than '88   '90 = 10 fewer than '89

'89 = 12 fewer than 60 burritos   '90 = 10 fewer than 48 burritos
'89 = 60 burritos - 12 burritos   '90 = 48 burritos - 10 burritos
'89 = 48 burritos   '90 = 38 burritos

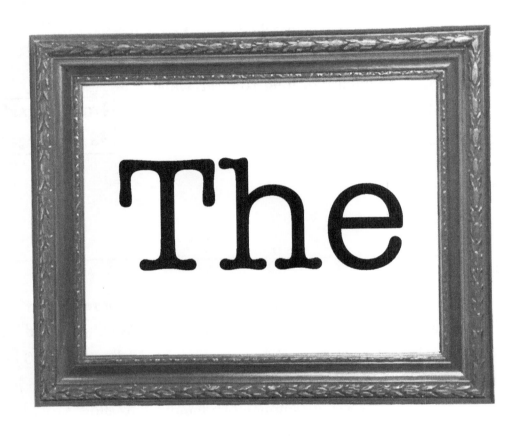

Trail Mix

Addition / Subtraction Two-Step Problems

Sample Problem

A beaver and an otter were creating a trail ~~from the beaver's dam to the otter's apartment.~~ ~~The beaver was 7 years old and the otter was almost 12.~~ The first① morning, they were able to blaze a trail 62 feet long. ~~That afternoon, it rained so they took the rest of the day off, as well as the next morning.~~ The next② afternoon, the otter and the beaver created 17 <u>fewer</u> feet of new trail ~~than they had the previous morning.~~ <u>How many feet of trail did the beaver and the otter create on that afternoon?</u> <u>How many feet of trail did they finish in total?</u>

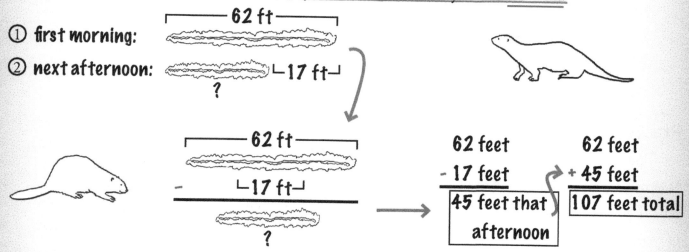

① first morning: ⌐——— 62 ft ———⌐

② next afternoon: └17 ft┘ ?

62 ft ⌐———————⌐ — └17 ft┘ ?

62 feet
− 17 feet
─────────
45 feet that afternoon

62 feet
+ 45 feet
─────────
107 feet total

Practice Problem #1

~~Rolando Fitzgerald was arguably the most handsome brother of the circus act, The Famous Five Fitzgeralds. Seriously, neither Orlando nor Lorando nor Randolfo could hold a candle to his rugged good looks. Only his youngest brother, Pete, had the same flowing locks and golden skin tone that made the lasses swoon.~~ Rolando also stood an impressive 195 cm tall. Pete, on the other hand, was 45 cm <u>shorter</u>. ~~However, Pete knew that his height was particularly suited to jumping. He could spring into the air, turn somersaults, and land on the head of a pin…or, occasionally, the head of a brother. Pete once sprang into the air, did a double back flip, and landed squarely on the freshly-combed locks of Rolando.~~ With Pete standing on Rolando's head, <u>what was the total height of the two brothers?</u>

Rolando ⟶ 195 cm
− 45 cm   − 45 cm
─────────   ─────────
Pete ⟶   150 cm

Rolando ⟶ 195 cm
+ Pete ⟶   + 150 cm
─────────────────────
Total Height   345 cm

Practice Problem #1 (continued)

Alternate Way to Solve:

Rolando | 195 cm
Pete ↓ | + 195 cm − 45 cm
_____
390 cm − 45 cm = 345 cm

Practice Problem #2

~~The competition was stiff at this year's Merry Men (and Women) Marksmanship Tryouts for the local Renaissance Fair.~~ Each contestant shoots 5 arrows at a target. A bull's-eye is worth 10 points, which means it is possible to score a maximum of 50 points. Ms. Marion's first three arrows scored a 7, a 6 and a 6. For her last two arrows, she readjusted her stance, tightened the bow stabilizer and scored an 8 and a 9. What is the difference between the points Ms. Marion scored and the total points possible?

7 points
6 points
6 points
8 points
+ 9 points
_____
36 total points

50 points (possible)
− 36 points (total)
_____
14 point difference

Alternate Way to Solve:

Arrow	Points Possible		Score		Difference
#1:	10	—	7	=	3
#2:	10	—	6	=	4
#3:	10	—	6	=	4
#4:	10	—	8	=	2
#5:	10	—	9	=	1
				Total:	14 points

There is a 14 point difference between Ms. Marion's score and the total possible points.

Practice Problem #3

Gillian loves to play with the hose. ~~She loves to fill up buckets and dump them out so she can fill them up again.~~ Gillian's new green bucket can hold 6 gallons. She also has a one-gallon milk jug and a two-gallon detergent bottle. If Gillian emptied both① the milk jug and the detergent bottle into her green bucket, how much water would be in the bucket?② How much more water would Gillian need to pour into her bucket if she wanted to fill it to the brim?

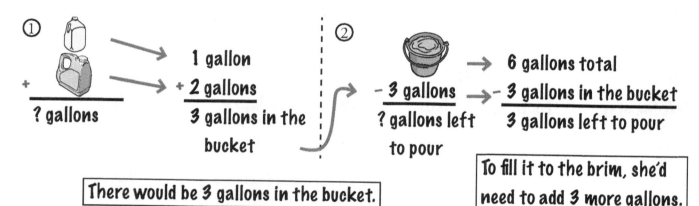

There would be 3 gallons in the bucket.

To fill it to the brim, she'd need to add 3 more gallons.

Practice Problem #4

Earl has wanted an Atlantic Coast Limited Edition 2% Sharkskin Full-Body swimsuit for years. ~~Unfortunately, the cost is a little outside of his price range. Exactly $3.27 outside, in fact.~~ So of course Earl was excited when Atlantic Coast offered a $3.59 mail-in rebate. Since stamps still cost only $0.32 at that time, the suit was finally within his budget. If the normal price for the suit is $302.99, how much money will Earl spend, factoring in the cost of the stamp?

$302.99 (price)
− $3.59 (rebate)
$299.40 (new price)
↓
$299.40 (new price)
+ $0.32 (stamp)
$299.72 total cost

Earl will spend $299.72.

Practice Problem #5

~~Dave E. Jones, the one-eyed fish, thought his chances were pretty good for winning the~~ ~~Moat Mile. The first fish to successfully complete 12 laps around the castle's moat would~~ ~~win. Since the tragic welding accident, Dave E. swam in circles so he could keep an eye on~~ ~~everything around him—and he thought these spins would lead him to an easy victory. Of~~ ~~course, all of the other fish believed his circular reasoning was somewhat faulty. Nonetheless,~~ ~~Dave E. stepped up his training regimen so that he now practices 3 days per week.~~ He swam an astounding 100 laps during practice on Monday. On Wednesday, he swam 12 <u>fewer</u> laps than on Monday. On Friday, he swam 7 <u>fewer</u> laps than he had on Wednesday. <u>How many</u> <u>total laps did he swim this week?</u>

Monday =	100 laps	100 laps	100 laps
Wednesday =	Monday - 12 laps =	100 laps - 12 laps =	88 laps
Friday =	Wednesday - 7 laps =	88 laps - 7 laps =	+ 81 laps
		Total laps for the week:	269 laps

Bearing Fruit

Simple Multiplication

Sample Problem

Chef Justin Time fixed three bowls of fresh fruit for his friend Amber Waves. In each bowl, he put three pieces of fruit: three apples in the first bowl, three oranges in the second bowl, and three bananas in the third bowl. How many pieces of fruit are there in all?

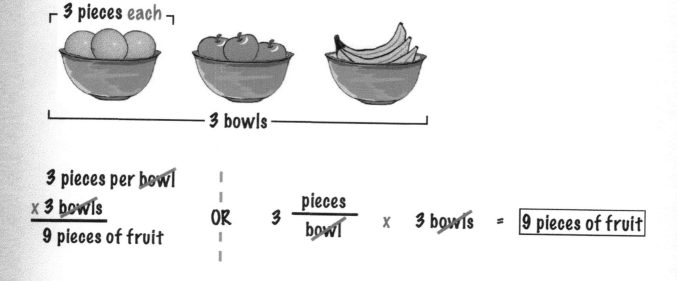

┌ **3 pieces each** ┐

3 bowls

3 pieces per bowl
x 3 bowls
───────────
9 pieces of fruit

OR

$3 \dfrac{\text{pieces}}{\text{bowl}} \times 3 \text{ bowls} =$ **9 pieces of fruit**

Practice Problem #1

As Oscar was about to jump off of a particularly large tree root, he noticed a very old bottle. ~~Rubbing the side of the bottle to remove the dirt on the label, Oscar was shocked to see a note pop out of the top of the bottle, which read: "Bearer of this note entitled to three wishes. Wishes for more wishes are not allowed. Void where prohibited. Results may vary." After a bit of thought, he decided that his first wish would be—not for more wishes, exactly—but to find more bottles just like the one he had just found. Feeling smug at his brilliance, Oscar started home.~~ Along the way, he found 7 more bottles, each with a note entitling the finder to three wishes. How many wishes total did Oscar earn today?

1 bottle + 7 bottles = 8 bottles in all

$\dfrac{8 \text{ bottles}}{1} \times 3 \dfrac{\text{wishes}}{\text{bottle}} =$ **24 wishes**

> **Remember:**
>
> $8 \text{ bottles} = \dfrac{8 \text{ bottles}}{1}$
>
> …because any number divided by 1 is the same number.

Simple Multiplication

Practice Problem #2

Mr. Sutton, the beloved math teacher at Little Quirky High School, is very particular. Every Monday is Spirit Day, and every Spirit Day, Mr. Sutton wears his bright blue pants. Also, Mr. Sutton coaches the school's pickleball team that plays on Wednesdays, so every Wednesday, he again wears the blue pants. Therefore, on Sundays and Tuesdays each week, Mrs. Sutton runs a load of laundry to make sure the favorite blue pants are ready for the upcoming event. If today is September 1st, how many times will Mrs. Sutton wash the blue pants in the 16 weeks before Christmas Break begins?

$$\frac{16 \text{ weeks}}{1} \times 2 \frac{\text{washes}}{\text{week}} = \boxed{32 \text{ washes}}$$

Practice Problem #3

After being duly sworn in as the new President of the Board of Shady Acres Convalescent Retreat, Old Man Jenkins made good on his campaign promise to provide all guests with a goodie bag of treats. He decided each goodie bag would contain 1 toothbrush, 5 tea bags, 2 decks of cards, 1 jar of Bran Nuggets, 1 pair of trifocals, and a collapsible cane to keep the young whippersnappers in line. After five hours of work, two naps, and a trip to China Buffet for the Early Bird Special, Old Man Jenkins had assembled 87 goodie bags for the residents of Shady Acres. How many tea bags did he use?

$$\frac{87 \text{ goodie bags}}{1} \times 5 \frac{\text{tea bags}}{\text{goodie bag}} = \boxed{435 \text{ tea bags}}$$

Practice Problem #4

Tayler loves to help in the nursery at church. Every Sunday, Tayler has helped watch Zoé, Camden, Brandon and Madison. Each baby plays with three toys each week, and each week when the children go home, Tayler washes all of the toys and puts them away. How many toys has Tayler washed in the past four weeks?

For each week...

4 babies
x 3 toys per baby
12 toys

In the past 4 weeks...

12 toys per week
x 4 weeks
48 toys in the
    past four weeks

4

> Tayler has washed 48 toys in the past four weeks.

Practice Problem #5

On Friday nights, Kevin and his friends spend their evening at Ted and Harry's Arcade. This week Kevin was busy mowing lawns, so he arrives at the arcade with $10.00 to spend. Kevin's favorite game is Bowler Ball because he can win 8 tickets for each game he plays. If every Bowler Ball game costs $0.50, how much money will he spend to play 9 games? Does he have enough money to play 9 games?

① $0.50 per game
x   9 games
$4.50 spent on
    games

② $10.00 > $4.50 → so yes, Kevin has enough money to play 9 games.

Split the Bill

Simple Division

Sample Problem

At last month's Metropolis Detectives' Association meeting, 8 detectives ate Beef Fajitas (not Pork Rind Casserole). The recipe called for 4 pounds of beef, 4 green peppers, 2 large onions, and 16 flour tortillas. The total for the ingredients was $16. The detectives split the cost of the groceries evenly. How much did each detective pay?

$16 ÷ 8 = $2 per

Practice Problem #1

Kelly left her weekly Snickerdoodle troop meeting clutching the cookie order form. She had big plans. Her heart was set on going to Camp Pinecone again this year. Last year, she had met her best friend, Valorie, there, and the two had spent a blissful week building hummingbird feeders, learning to weave baskets underwater, and making up silly songs until all hours of the night. Her troop leader had told Kelly that if she could sell 270 cookies, she'd earn the troop's scholarship and wouldn't have to pay the usual $175 for the trip. If each box contains 18 cookies, how many boxes will Kelly need to sell to win the scholarship?

```
                    15 boxes
18 cookies ) 270 cookies
per box   - 18
            90
           -90
            0
```

She needs to sell 15 boxes of cookies.

Practice Problem #2

Old Man Jenkins wanted to split his fortune evenly amongst his 42 descendants. And that was no easy task, for his fortune amounted to a whopping $1,915,200. It was a testament to clipping coupons and avoiding infomercials about salad spinners and grills named after that famous rollerpolo player. If you were one of Old Man Jenkins' descendants, how much would you stand to inherit if he suddenly met his demise?

```
                        $45,600
42 descendants ) $1,915,200
                 -168
                  235
                 -210
                  252
                 -252
                    0
```

$45,600 per descendant

Practice Problem #3

~~Delbert emerged from Swanson's Corner Truck Stop grinning like a 5 year old on his birthday.~~ He plopped back into the driver's seat and revealed the bag of 100 licorice ropes he'd purchased inside. Mama gave him a look of reproach as he started <u>dividing</u> the ropes <u>evenly</u> among his cheering fan base—the <u>five kids</u> in the back seat. ~~Knowing that the older kids, Delbert Jr., Katarina, Isabella and Norm, could pace themselves, Mama started to worry that Delbert would spoil the baby's dinner with his little treat.~~ <u>How many licorice ropes did Delbert give to baby Maude?</u>

$$\begin{array}{r} \boxed{20 \text{ ropes per kid}} \\ 5 \text{ kids } \overline{)\ 100 \text{ ropes}} \\ -\ 10 \\ \hline 00 \\ -\ 0 \\ \hline 0 \end{array}$$

Practice Problem #4

~~Bubbly Betty and her band of bodacious balloon bursters bopped onto the grounds of the biggest Balloon Bashing Bout since '56. The bunch of beauties had been training biweekly for months, and now quietly eyed the Big Bad Boomer trophy with humble admiration. They knew that they'd need to be at the top of their game if they stood a chance to win the competition.~~ In order for Betty's band to beat the best time, each of the 4 team members would need to burst an <u>equal share</u> of the competition-sized balloon bouquet. When their match began, Betty's bunch was blown away when they realized that their balloon bundle held an unprecedented 256 balloons. <u>How many balloons should each balloon burster bash?</u>

$$\begin{array}{r} \boxed{64 \text{ balloons ea.}} \\ 4 \text{ bursters } \overline{)\ 256 \text{ balloons}} \\ -24 \\ \hline 16 \\ -16 \\ \hline 0 \end{array}$$

Practice Problem #5

~~Leon looked about and then popped a stray jelly bean into his mouth. As much fun as looking for eggs in the town's yearly Egg Hunt had been a few years ago, he'd recently taken a shine to helping the adults get everything ready the night before—mostly because Mrs. Waddlekins (the Egg Hunt Head Honcho) told him he could snack on as much of the leftover candy as he wanted.~~ His current task is to <u>evenly</u> <u>separate</u> a fresh bag of 192 jellybeans into two dozen plastic eggs. When Leon completes his task, <u>how many jelly beans will each plastic egg hold?</u>

$$\begin{array}{r} \boxed{8 \text{ jellybeans ea.}} \\ 24 \text{ eggs } \overline{)\ 192 \text{ jellybeans}} \\ -192 \\ \hline 0 \end{array}$$

2 dozen eggs = 24 eggs

Donut Dilemma

Multiplication / Division Two-Step Problems

Sample Problem

Old Man Jenkins bought 7 boxes of Squish Custard donuts at the Inconvenience Store. He paid $35.99 for the donuts, which he thought was way too much for an old man on a fixed income. There were 13 donuts in each box. If Mr. Jenkins gives one donut to each person at Shady Acres, <u>how many people will get a free donut?</u>

Old Man Jenkins needed to take a 3-hour nap after carrying the donuts. If the total weight of the donuts was 728 grams and each donut was the same weight, <u>how much did each donut weigh?</u>

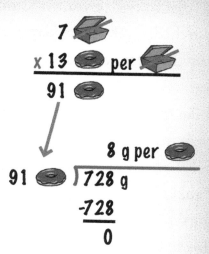

$$\begin{array}{r} 7 \\ \times\ 13 \\ \hline 91 \end{array}$$

$$\begin{array}{r} 8 \text{ g per} \\ 91\ )\overline{728}\text{ g} \\ -728 \\ \hline 0 \end{array}$$

> **91 people will get a free donut. Each donut weighs 8 grams.**

Practice Problem #1

Dolly the Llama loved mashed potatoes. At exactly 6:23 a.m. every day, her human, Farmer Kip, would fill up his wagon with 56 pounds of potatoes and bring them to the barn where his 4 children would divide them into 7 <u>equal</u> piles. Then, Farmer Kip's wife, Linda, would take 2 piles of potatoes and mash them up with butter and garlic for Dolly's breakfast. <u>How many pounds of mashed potatoes does Dolly the Llama eat for breakfast each morning?</u>

56 pounds ÷ 7 piles = 8 pounds per pile

$$\begin{array}{r} 8 \text{ pounds per pile} \\ \times\ 2 \text{ piles} \\ \hline 16 \text{ pounds in} \\ \text{Dolly's breakfast} \end{array}$$

> **Dolly ate 16 pounds of potatoes for breakfast.**

Multiplication/Division Two-Step Problems

Practice Problem #2

~~Sadly, twelve years of drought had left Jackrabbit Hill
parched. In the glory days, rabbits would've spent all day guiding their canoes and kayaks down Jackrabbit Hill's many waterways. Over the last dozen years, though,~~ the rabbits could only
hike their way down the 8 dry creek beds that wound their
way from the summit to the base of the hill. ~~But that would
all change today.~~ Chugging along up the side of the hill were 4
tanker trucks, each filled with 1,250 gallons of water. ~~The rabbits' plan was to erect a giant water tower, fill it with the water
from the trucks, and then release the water into the creeks.~~ If
the rabbits divide the water equally between the creeks, how
many gallons of water will each creek have?

1,250 gallons per ~~truck~~
x   4 ~~trucks~~
5,000 gallons of water

5,000 gallons ÷ 8 creek beds = 625 gallons per creek bed

Each creek will have
625 gallons of water.

Practice Problem #3

~~Chris Gibson opened the door and took a deep breath of
the fresh sparkling air. Ah, Spring. Today was the opening day
of his Sherwood Forest Petting Zoo. He turned on his heel and
decided it was time to wake the critters. Since the weather had
been so warm yesterday,~~ he'd asked his new assistant, Marty, to
put two of the new water bowls he'd ordered last week in each
of the seven cages. ~~Well, the new water bowls looked fine and
dandy, but after a moment's observation, Chris decided that the
newness of the water bowls made the food bowls look particularly slobbery and shabby. As he sauntered back to his office,
he remembered that the Woodland Creature Supply Company
also offered food bowls that were the same price as water bowls,
and that~~ he had paid $265.30 for the new bowls. What price
did Chris Gibson pay per bowl for the new set of water bowls?

7 ~~cages~~
x 2 bowls per ~~cage~~
14 bowls (left in the
cages yesterday)

$18.95
14 bowls) $265.30

$18.95 per bowl

Practice Problem #4

~~The incident was as unfortunate as unfortunate incidents~~ ~~can come. Along his daily roll, Old Man Jenkins somehow~~ ~~managed to high-center his All-Terrain Motor Seat 3000 on an~~ ~~unusually large stone. But that wasn't the worst of it. After dis-~~ ~~mounting to assess the situation, he then proceeded to snap his~~ ~~only cane in two while trying to pry said stone from beneath~~ ~~the Motor Seat. Now, seat-less, cane-less, and frustrated as all~~ ~~get-out,~~ Old Man Jenkins had to hobble down to Canes R Us to see about replacing his third cane that month. He finally settled on a 3-foot model ~~with a mother-of-pearl handle, but~~ ~~again left the store empty-handed when the clerk told him the~~ ~~cane cost $185!~~ He wobbled home and eventually found the exact same cane on eBuy for $135. Still skeptical about the price, he did a little cipherin' and discovered that the price per inch of the eBuy cane still wasn't a great deal. <u>How much did the eBuy cane cost per inch?</u>

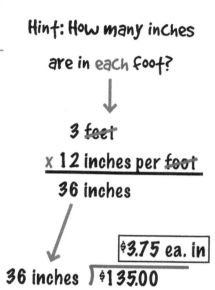

Hint: How many inches are in each foot?

↓

3 ~~feet~~
x 12 inches per ~~foot~~
36 inches

↓

$3.75 ea. in

36 inches) $135.00

Practice Problem #5

~~The ants of Grassy Knoll had foraged well that sum-~~ ~~mer. Matilda, the queen ant, sat back one late summer after-~~ ~~noon and surveyed their winter stock piles.~~ According to the accounting department, <u>each</u> of the 4 foraging battalions had contributed 37,829,996 morsels of food to the storehouses that season. ~~Knowing it was time to divert workers to prepare the~~ ~~hill for winter, Matilda glanced again over the current roster~~ ~~and found~~ there were 2,789 ants currently living in the hill. If Matilda stopped all foraging efforts now and <u>divided</u> the stored food <u>evenly</u> between the ants, <u>how many morsels of food would each ant have to eat that winter?</u>

37,829,996 morsels per ~~battalion~~

x   4 ~~battalions~~
151,319,984 morsels

151,319,984 morsels ÷ 2,789 ants = 54,256 morsels per ant

Each ant would have 54,256 morsels of food to eat.

Divvy It Up

Sample Problem

Bubba is the Official Fill-Up Man at the local FASCAR track. ~~On race day, he leaves home at 7:00 a.m. and arrives at the FASCAR track at 7:37 a.m.~~ Bubba's tank has 247 liters of high-quality FASCAR fuel.

~~Halfway through the race, Gordon Jeffers pulls his car up to Bubba's tank for a fill-up. He is followed by Ernie Dalehard, Stewart Tonay and John Jimmyson. Each driver requests 70 liters of gas, but Bubba does not have that much gas!~~ Bubba <u>divides</u> the gas <u>evenly</u> between the four drivers. ~~Gordon Jeffers eventually wins in a photo finish.~~ <u>How much gas did Bubba pass to each of the four drivers?</u> <u>How much gas did he have left at the end of the day?</u>

$$
\begin{array}{r}
61\ R\ 3\ L \\
4\overline{)247\ L} \\
-24 \\
\hline
07 \\
-\ 4 \\
\hline
3
\end{array}
$$

61 L to each driver
3 L left over

Practice Problem #1

~~Times were rough on the high seas for the dread pirate Plaidbeard. His old crew had dipped a little too freely into the buried treasure when that new-fangled iPaddle hit the market, and now they all spent their days rowing about the harbor in their little skiffs, and generally not doing anything.~~ Now, strapped for cash, Plaidbeard was forced to hire the cheapest labor he could find—14 landlubbers who clearly had left their sea legs back on the dock. And therein lay Plaidbeard's dilemma: ~~Each scurvy knave needed 3 seasickness pills, but~~ Plaidbeard had only purchased a small generic bottle of seasickness medication with 30 pills in it—not enough to give each sick crew member a full dose. ~~Deciding that a partial dose was better than nothing,~~ Plaidbeard <u>divides</u> the pills <u>evenly</u> amongst his crew. <u>How many pills does each crew member get?</u> <u>How many pills will be left over?</u>

$$
\begin{array}{r}
2\ R\ 2\ \text{pills} \\
14\ \text{members}\overline{)30\ \text{pills}} \\
-28 \\
\hline
2
\end{array}
$$

2 pills each
2 pills left over

Quotient and Remainder

Practice Problem #2

~~Captain Johan Beagleman pulled his convoy of wagons to a halt at a crossroads in Inner Mongolia.~~ There were 22 wagons in his convoy carrying a variety of meats, cheeses, spices and pre-owned auto parts. The road ahead split into 4 different paths. But which one would lead them to riches of the Lost City of Pyrite? ~~There was no way to be sure of the right path, and yet it was just as dangerous to wait at the crossroads with their goods for scouting parties to return with information. What if a wild pack of former vegetarians got a craving for Inner Mongolian BBQ? Praying that he was making the right decision,~~ Beagleman grabbed his bullhorn and announced that he would send an <u>equal</u> number of wagons down each trail, leaving the fewest number of wagons to guard the goods. <u>How many wagons would go down each trail?</u> <u>How many would remain to protect their goods?</u>

$$\begin{array}{r} 5\,R\,2 \\ 4\text{ paths } \overline{)\,22\text{ wagons}} \\ \underline{-20} \\ 2 \end{array}$$

| 5 wagons down each path |
| 2 wagons left to guard |

Practice Problem #3

Marjorie ~~was proud of her efforts to date. With a lot of hard work, she'd~~ been able to secure 40 local donors to kick-start her Save the Owls campaign. She had promised the local donors that, should she secure a national sponsor, she would return to <u>each</u> of them an <u>equal</u> portion of the money, while using whatever was left over to build an owl sanctuary on the roof of the local Smoothie Joint. ~~Impressed by Marjorie's campaign, the Onomatopoeia Wouldn'twannabeya League of Superheroes~~ (O.W.L.S.) donated $2,190 in Susan B. Anthony coins as the first national sponsor of Marjorie's campaign. True to her word, she split the coins equally amongst the local supporters. If each coin is worth $1, <u>how much did each supporter receive?</u> <u>How many coins were left over for the rooftop owl sanctuary?</u>

$$\begin{array}{r} \$54\,R\,\$30 \\ 40\text{ donors } \overline{)\,\$2{,}190} \\ \underline{-200} \\ 190 \\ \underline{-160} \\ 30 \end{array}$$

| $54 to each donor |
| $30 (or 30 coins) left for sanctuary |

Practice Problem #4

Vladimir Eclair scratched his head. ~~Dear, sweet Mrs. Witt~~ ~~had hired him to build a picket fence around her prized petunia~~ ~~patch, but had insisted that she order the pickets herself from~~ ~~her son's woodworking company. In hopes of avoiding mis-~~ ~~hap, he had tried to be very clear that~~ he would need 3 pickets per foot of fence she'd like him to build. And while she had sounded confident at the time, he was baffled when her son's company later delivered only 23 pickets. How many whole feet of fence is Vladimir Eclair able to build? How many pickets were left over?

$$\begin{array}{r} 7\ R\ 2 \\ 3\ \text{pickets} \overline{)\ 23\ \text{pickets}} \\ \text{per foot} \quad -\underline{21} \\ 2 \end{array}$$

| 7 feet of fence |
| 2 pickets left over |

Practice Problem #5

Juan Pablo ~~sighed. Due to a shocking rock-paper-scissors~~ ~~upset, he now~~ had Albino Duck duty—~~his least favorite job~~ ~~at the nature preserve.~~ ~~Not only did the~~ 173 ducks ~~tend to be~~ ~~complaining prima donnas, it was also the height of summer~~ ~~which meant~~ he had to coat every one of them with a generous dollop of duck lotion—~~Duck Protection Factor 300—to keep~~ ~~their sensitive skin from frying and creating one massive order~~ ~~of Duck L'Orange.~~ As Juan Pablo grabbed a tub of lotion tubes, he realized there were only 513 small tubes of lotion left. If he coats each duck equally, how many tubes of duck lotion will each duck receive? How much will be left over?

$$\begin{array}{r} 2\ R\ 167 \\ 173\ \text{ducks} \overline{)\ 513\ \text{tubes}} \\ -\underline{346} \\ 167 \end{array}$$

| 2 tubes per duck |
| 167 tubes left over |

Parts of a Whole

fractions

Sample Problem

Babs Anchorpants loves to swim. ~~Her favorite swimmin' hole is Porcupine Pond. Each morning at 6:00 a.m., Babs throws herself into the pond and~~ swims 12 laps as fast as she can. ~~Each lap is 10 yards long. Unfortunately for Babs, she swims really…really…slow.~~ It takes Babs 1 hour to complete her workout. ~~At 7:00 a.m. Babs' arch-nemesis, Bubbles McGee, shows up. Bubbles says she can swim faster than Babs. Babs says, "Prove it, Bubbles!" Bubbles dives in and when all is said and swam,~~ Bubbles completed 12 laps in 1/5 of the time it took Babs. How long did it take Bubbles to swim 12 laps in Porcupine Pond? How much longer did it take Babs to swim those dozen laps?

$$\frac{1}{5} \quad \text{X} \quad \frac{60}{1} \text{ min} \quad = \quad \frac{60}{5} \quad = \quad 12 \text{ minutes}$$

or

$$\frac{1}{5} \quad = \quad 0.2 \quad \text{X} \quad 60 \text{ min} \quad = \quad 12 \text{ minutes}$$

$$60 \text{ min} \quad - \quad 12 \text{ min} \quad = \quad 48 \text{ minutes}$$

> It took Bubbles 12 minutes to swim 12 laps.
> It took Babs 48 minutes longer to swim the same 12 laps.

Practice Problem #1

~~Stanley the Singing Frog tossed the end of his scarf over his shoulder, picked up the microphone and began to belt out an a cappella version of "It Ain't Easy Being Green." Tonight's show at La Cantina Loco was the final show of the year. As he looked back over the past 365 days,~~ Stanley could scarcely believe this was his 300th performance of the year. ~~Stanley's stage stamina was the envy of all the other singing animal performers, including Rice & Beans, the singing mouse duo from Monterrey. As hard as they had tried,~~ Rice & Beans had been able to perform only two-thirds the number of shows Stanley had over the course of the previous year. How many shows had Rice & Beans performed?

$$\frac{2}{3} \quad \text{X} \quad \frac{300}{1} \text{ shows} \quad = \quad \frac{600 \text{ shows}}{3} \quad = \quad \boxed{200 \text{ shows}}$$

Alternate Way to Solve:

$$2 \quad \text{X} \quad \frac{1}{3} \quad \text{X} \quad \frac{300}{1} \text{ shows} \quad = \quad 2 \text{ x} \quad \frac{300}{3} \text{ shows} \quad = \quad 2 \text{ x } 100 \text{ shows} \quad = \quad \boxed{200 \text{ shows}}$$

Practice Problem #2

~~The clock struck 11 p.m. and~~ Biff and Squash suddenly realized they were famished. ~~Even though they had arrived for dinner in the dorm cafeteria promptly at 6:07 p.m., their meal of mystery meat and mushy peas just wasn't going to make it for that long night of presentation preparation ahead of them. Now, after 28 minutes of sheer anticipation (and excavating a spot in the teenage-boy-carnage on the dorm room floor),~~ the two sat with a Cheese Monster pizza between them, lovingly cut into 12 equal slices. ~~Unfortunately, they soon realized that their eyes had been bigger than their stomachs.~~ While Biff did manage to eat 1/3 of the pizza, Squash could only put away 1/4 of it. How many pieces did each lad eat?

8

Biff: $\dfrac{1}{3}$ x $\dfrac{12}{1}$ slices   = $\dfrac{12\ \text{slices}}{3}$ = | 4 slices |

Squash: $\dfrac{1}{4}$ x $\dfrac{12}{1}$ slices   = $\dfrac{12\ \text{slices}}{4}$ = | 3 slices |

Practice Problem #3

~~Percival the otter loved clams. So when he stumbled across a rickety shack in a forgotten part of the wharf with a sign that read "Bucket of Clams—$5," he thought he'd struck gold. After seating himself at a small table and placing his order, Babs, the waitress, heaved the most enormous bucket of clams he'd ever seen onto his table.~~ Babs noticed the otter's eyes bulge as she did so, and informed Percival that each bucket held 175 clams. ~~Undaunted, Percival flipped onto his back, pulled his trusty pet rock out of his pocket and began to crack open the clams on his stomach.~~ After giving it his best effort, Percival finally gave up when he'd finished 4/5 of the clams. How many clams did Percival eat?

$\dfrac{4}{5}$ x $\dfrac{175}{1}$ clams   = $\dfrac{700\ \text{clams}}{5}$ =   140 clams

Alternate Way to Solve:

4 x $\dfrac{1}{5}$ x $\dfrac{175}{1}$ clams   = 4 x $\dfrac{175}{5}$ clams   =   4 x 35 clams   = | 140 clams |

Practice Problem #4

~~Gracie stared out the window, daydreaming as she watched the last student skip to her car~~ ~~after dress rehearsal. Her young swans were only 1 day away from their debut performance~~ ~~of "People Lake" and she knew it was simply going to be the best ballet performance the~~ ~~swans on this side of the pond had ever seen. She hoped that all of the money she had spent~~ ~~sponsoring this year's event would translate into a packed house for tomorrow night's show.~~ Gracie figured that, of the 80 available seats, 5/8 of them would need to be filled in order for her to break even. How many seats need to be filled at tomorrow night's performance for Gracie's production to break even?

$$\frac{5}{8} \ \times \ \frac{80}{1} \text{ seats} \ = \ \frac{400 \text{ seats}}{8} \ = \ \boxed{50 \text{ seats}}$$

Alternate Way to Solve:

$$5 \ \times \ \frac{1}{8} \ \times \ \frac{80}{1} \text{ seats} \ = \ 5 \times \frac{80}{8} \text{ seats} \ = \ 5 \times 10 \text{ seats} \ = \ \boxed{50 \text{ seats}}$$

Practice Problem #5

Polly Popsicle, ~~owner of the Fabulous Frozen Treats Company looked over the results~~ ~~from that year's springtime treat survey. As it had been a surprisingly warm spring, she~~ had received a whopping 320 responses to her "My Top Treat" survey. One quarter of the respondents had selected Frosted Gooeys as their treat of choice while 5/16 preferred the Icy Sours. The remaining 7/16 of those surveyed had voted for Crunchy Gum Gum Yummers as their favorite snack—~~which explained why Yummers sales had spiked in the last month.~~ How many votes did each treat receive?

Frosted Gooeys:	$\frac{1}{4}$	$\times$	$\frac{320}{1}$ votes	$=$	$\frac{320 \text{ votes}}{4}$	$= \boxed{80 \text{ votes}}$
Icy Sours:	$\frac{5}{16}$	$\times$	$\frac{320}{1}$ votes	$=$	$\frac{1600 \text{ votes}}{16}$	$= \boxed{100 \text{ votes}}$
Crunchy Gum Gum Yummers:	$\frac{7}{16}$	$\times$	$\frac{320}{1}$ votes	$=$	$\frac{2240 \text{ votes}}{16}$	$= \boxed{140 \text{ votes}}$

(...and since 80 votes + 100 votes + 140 votes = 320 votes, our answers check out!)

Practice Problem #5 (continued)

Alternate Way to Solve:

Frosted Gooeys: $\dfrac{1}{4}$ x $\dfrac{320}{1}$ votes   = $\dfrac{320 \text{ votes}}{4}$ =   80 votes

$\dfrac{1}{16}$ of $\dfrac{320}{1}$ votes   = $\dfrac{1}{16}$ x $\dfrac{320}{1}$ votes   =   20 votes

Icy Sours: $\dfrac{5}{16}$: 5 x $\dfrac{1}{16}$ x $\dfrac{320}{1}$ votes   =   5 x 20 votes   =   100 votes

Crunchy Gum
Gum Yummers: $\dfrac{7}{16}$: 7 x $\dfrac{1}{16}$ x $\dfrac{320}{1}$ votes   =   7 x 20 votes   =   140 votes

A Walk Around the Cement Pond

Perimeter

Sample Problem

Bubbles McGee loves to swim at the cement pond of Muddy Waters. It is a large rectangle that is 100 meters long and 50 meters wide. ~~Bubbles invites Babs Anchorpants to a swimming party at the pond. But Bubbles' invitation was a ruse to lure Babs into another competition. Bubbles says that she can swim to the other side of the pond and back faster than Babs can walk around it.~~

~~Bubbles' best friend, Wanda, starts the race. Unbeknownst to Bubbles, Babs walks much faster than she swims. Although Bubbles took only 2 minutes to swim,~~ Babs walked around the pond ~~in 5/9 of that time.~~ How far did Babs walk on her trip around the cement pond?

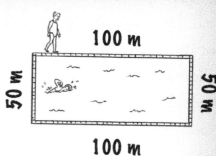

100 m
50 m
50 m
100 m

$P = 2(l) + 2(w)$

$P = 2(100\text{ m}) + 2(50\text{ m})$

$P = 200\text{ m} + 100\text{ m}$

$P = 300\text{ m}$

Babs walked 300 m.

⑨

Practice Problem #1

The Sicilian Lovers of Oregon Pizzassociation (S.L.O.P.) were holding their 30th biannual fundraiser. ~~However, this year, the stakes were high. If every one of their 348 members did not sell at least 83 jars of pizza sauce, their grand plans to build the world's largest Sicilian pizza would never be realized.~~ The pizza would be the size of a football field: 360 feet long by 160 feet wide. ~~A pizza that size would need truck-loads of toppings,~~ and a thick crust to go all the way around each of its four sides. Assuming the fundraiser is successful and the members of S.L.O.P are able to build their dream pizza, how many feet of crust will they need to frame their edible work of art?

$P = l + l + w + w$

$P = 360\text{ ft} + 360\text{ ft} + 160\text{ ft} + 160\text{ ft}$

$P = \boxed{1,040\text{ feet of crust}}$

Practice Problem #2

Clem ~~just had to win the Square Dance competition this~~ ~~year. He simply could not face the prospect of being runner-up~~ ~~for the 4th year in a row. So he~~ decided to turn his garage into a home studio where he could practice to his heart's content. ~~To figure out how much wood he'd need to construct a dance~~ ~~floor, he knew he would need to measure his garage. With his~~ ~~trusty meter stick,~~ he measured the first wall and found it was 32 meters long. ~~But when he measured each of the other walls,~~ ~~the strangest thing happened. Each wall measured the same as~~ ~~the first!~~ His garage was a true square! ~~Could anything be more~~ ~~perfect for square dancing?~~ In his excitement, he danced a jig along all four walls of the garage. How many meters did Clem jig in his excitement?

Hint: since all four sides of a square are the same length, we can use the following formula to find the perimeter.

$P = 4(l)$

$P = 4(32\,m)$

$P = 128\,m$

or

$P = l + l + w + w$

$P = 32m + 32m + 32m + 32m$

$P = \boxed{128\,m}$

Practice Problem #3

The cattle wranglers were exhausted. ~~Yet one of them would~~ ~~have to keep watch. It wasn't fair, of course, that they had been~~ ~~working since sun-up to retrieve the dozen cows that had man-~~ ~~aged to escape from the ranch. Luckily, they had stumbled~~ ~~across three sections of fence abandoned on the prairie.~~ The longest section was 65 feet long. The other two sections were both 60 feet. ~~Racing to beat dusk,~~ the wranglers used the fence sections to create a triangular pen for the wayward cattle. ~~Now~~ ~~the youngest, Joe Bob, had been chosen to take the first watch.~~ To help keep his eyes open, Joe Bob decided to walk around and around the cow's pen. How many feet will Joe Bob walk each time he walks all the way around the triangular pen?

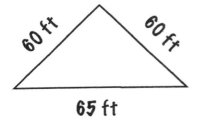

$P = l + l + l$

$P = 60\,ft + 60\,ft + 65\,ft$

$P = \boxed{185\,ft}$

Practice Problem #4

Half of the kids on the playground wanted to play Department of Defense. The other half, however, wanted to play Duck, Duck, Goose. As class president, Mildred suggested that they should use some old boards to construct a pentagon-shaped clubhouse for the Department of Defense, and the Duck, Duck, Goose crowd could play around the outside of the clubhouse. Since everyone thought this was a grand compromise, Joey Badabing found five large boards. One measured 16 feet long. Two others were exactly 23 feet long. The last two were 17 feet and 18 feet long, respectively. As soon as they had arranged the boards into a rough pentagon for the clubhouse, the rest of the kids began to run around the clubhouse, shouting "Duck!"… "Duck!"… "Goose!" How many feet did the children run each time they went around the clubhouse?

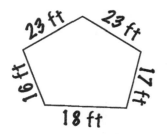

P = | + | + | + | + |

P = 16 ft + 23 ft + 23 ft + 17 ft + 18 ft

P = 97 ft

Practice Problem #5

King Bubbaloo was always concerned about security. Several years ago, he worried that the 50-ft. high stone walls would not be enough to protect the kingdom if they were attacked. So all of his subjects banded together to build a rectangular moat around the castle that was 150 yards long and 100 yards wide. After years of hard labor, the moat was finally finished and filled with water from the local spring. To celebrate, King Bubbaloo allowed the workers to swim in the moat—which turned out to be so much fun that King Bubbaloo added a couple of slides and turned his prized defense mechanism into a waterpark. Every year now, King Bubbaloo holds a Swimming of the Moat race to encourage his subjects to stay physically fit. To complete one lap around the moat, how far must one swim?

150 yd

100 yd   100 yd

150 yd

P = | + | + | + |

P = 150 yd + 100 yd + 150 yd + 100 yd

P = 500 yd

Bits and Pieces

Fraction Two-Step Problems

Sample Problem

Juan and Wanda grabbed all of their allowance money and headed off to The Pawn Shop. ~~Juan saw an electric guitar that was $60.00, but he did not have enough money to buy it. Wanda found an electric waffle maker that was on sale for only $5.00. They shopped until 11:00 a.m. and then they went next door to have lunch at The Prawn Shop. Juan had a Big Prawn sandwich, and Wanda had Prawn Nuggets. Since Juan had bought Wanda's lunch last Thursday, Wanda paid for both of their lunches today. After lunch, they headed back to The Pawn Shop,~~ where Juan ended up spending 3/5 <u>of</u> his money on barbecue tongs that cost $30.00. <u>How much money did Juan have to start with?</u>

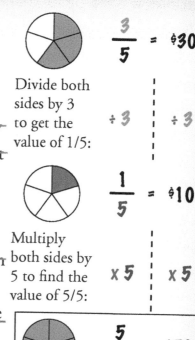

Divide both sides by 3 to get the value of 1/5:

Multiply both sides by 5 to find the value of 5/5:

Practice Problem #1

The day broke bright and sunny. Esteban was smiling at 6 a.m. as his feet hit the floor, ready to start a new day. ~~Yesterday had been rough. The Sisters of Infinite Mercy had worked him hard all day long, but today he would have some free time, and he began to wonder what he should do with it. That new "Tae Kwan Do Tiger" movie was out, but of course, his miniature golf game could use some work, too. He decided to mull over the options while he fixed the weight bench at the convent. Five hours later, the Sisters of Infinite Mercy were again pumping iron and Esteban headed to the theater. Unfortunately, the movie was sold out,~~ so he ended up spending 2/3 <u>of</u> his free time watching a 120-minute documentary about Alpaca farming in the Andes. <u>In all, how much free time did Esteban have that day?</u>

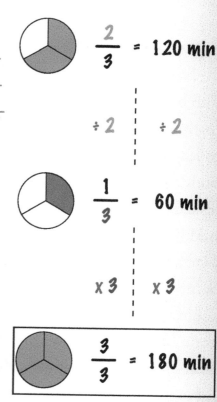

fraction Two-Step Problems

Practice Problem #2

Delores was fed up. ~~She slammed the trunk and jumped in the driver's seat. Although it was already 5:30 p.m., she knew if she kept the pedal to the metal she could make Phuntown by sundown. Anything was better than Littletown, but really, Megalopolis was her final destination. After a stop for several bites to eat at Phuntown's More Than You Should Eat Buffet, Delores decided to turn in so she could start early in the morning.~~ The next day, Delores drove the final 500 miles to the big city, which was 4/5 of the distance between Littletown and Megalopolis. ~~However, upon her arrival, she realized she'd made a huge mistake: what opportunity was there for a professional shepherdess in the big city? She vowed to drive straight home to Littletown the next morning.~~ How many miles in total will Dolores drive to return home to Littletown from Megalopolis?

① $\dfrac{4}{5}$ = 500 mi

$\div 4$ ┊ $\div 4$

② $\dfrac{1}{5}$ = 125 mi

$\times 5$ ┊ $\times 5$

③ $\boxed{\dfrac{5}{5} = 625\ mi}$

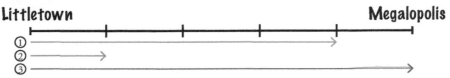

Littletown ─────────────────── Megalopolis
① ⟶
② ⟶
③ ⟶

Practice Problem #3

Norm's first experience with his new Scrubadub Whirlyjet Tub hadn't gone well. ~~He'd filled it to the brim with scalding hot water, and even though the temperature caused him to leap back out again at lightning speed, it wasn't before his body mass had displaced a significant portion of water…which leaked through poor Mrs. Kaplansky's ceiling, right in the middle of "Squeal or No Squeal." And yes, she squealed. But Norm had changed a few things since then. He had to, as the Scrubadub Whirlyjet Tub is the only device known to man that could remove the muck that Norm accumulated on his body as a mechanic at the local Quickky Lube.~~ He now filled the tub with 40 gallons ~~of significantly-cooler~~ water, which filled the tub only 5/8 of the way to capacity. What is the total capacity of Norm's Scrubadub Whirlyjet Tub?

$\dfrac{5}{8}$ = 40 gallons

$\div 5$ ┊ $\div 5$

$\dfrac{1}{8}$ = 8 gallons

$\times 8$ ┊ $\times 8$

$\boxed{\dfrac{8}{8} = 64\ gallons}$

Practice Problem #4

Bubba wanted to do something special for his rollerpolo team. ~~Not only had the Holy Rollers completely turned their season around, they had finally beaten their rivals, the Rusty Buckets, in the championship game.~~ Now, here they sat, basking in the glory of ~~very small trophies and~~ a medium-sized cash prize. Counting the money, Bubba decided to order $25 worth of pizza to celebrate. ~~After their bellies were full, Bubba figured he'd better use the remaining funds to restock the first aid supplies.~~ If Bubba had spent 5/6 of the money on pizza, how much money did he have to start with?

$$\frac{5}{6} = \$25$$

$$\div 5 \quad \vdots \quad \div 5$$

$$\frac{1}{6} = \$5$$

$$\times 6 \quad \vdots \quad \times 6$$

$$\boxed{\frac{6}{6} = \$30}$$

Practice Problem #5

~~Archibald sighed. Once again, Joan—the enormous sow who was new to the farm—beat him to the slop. Even though Archibald was a gentleman and more than happy to let ladies go first, most ladies didn't throw their weight around the barnyard, demanding to be called "Joan of Pork."~~ And they certainly didn't eat 45 pounds of slop in a sitting the way Joan did—5/16 of the total slop available, and way more than her fair share. ~~Even though the Farm Arbitration Team (F.A.T.) once confronted Joan about her inconsiderate eating habits, Joan continued in her selfish ways.~~ On a typical day, how many pounds of slop in total did the pigs have to share?

$$\frac{5}{16} = 45 \text{ pounds}$$

$$\div 5 \quad \vdots \quad \div 5$$

$$\frac{1}{16} = 9 \text{ pounds}$$

$$\times 16 \quad \vdots \quad \times 16$$

$$\boxed{\frac{16}{16} = 144 \text{ pounds}}$$

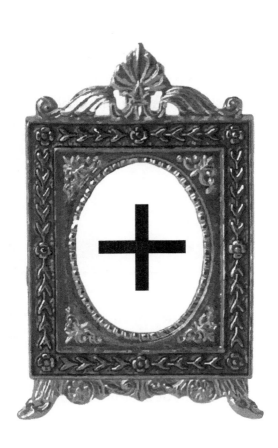

Field of Dreams

Perimeter/Area Two-Step Problems

Sample Problem

Otar-Lina and Brakabrik are foreign exchange students from the Republic of Yoothmanistan. ~~Their homeland is 3,047 miles away from where they are staying in Denver, Colorado, USA.~~ Their favorite sport from their homeland is called Whammyball. The relatively-unknown game is played on a rectangular field. In their homeland, there is a brand new Whammyball stadium, the floor of which measures 120.5 yards by 80.2 yards. The field is regulation size and lies within the stadium floor, with a 10.7 yard margin all around it. ~~Brakabrik's favorite Whammyball team won the championship last year by a score of 456.8 to 379.2.~~ What is the area of a regulation Whammyball field?

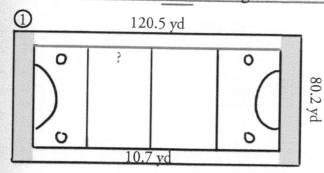

120.5 - 10.7 - 10.7 = 99.1 yd

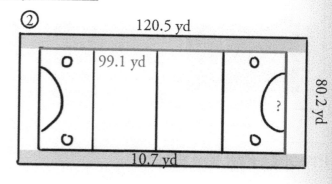

80.2 - 10.7 - 10.7 = 58.8 yd

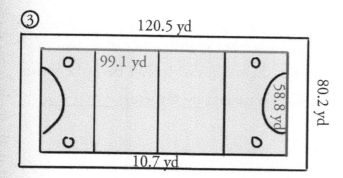

A = l x w

A = yd x yd = yd²

A = 99.1 yd x 58.8 yd = $\boxed{5,827.08 \text{ yd}^2}$

Perimeter/Area Two-Step Problems

Practice Problem #1

~~Presentation was so critical. How many times had Chef Legume told his students that?~~ ~~But in this week's competition, it appeared someone had finally listened. Sauntering over to~~ ~~a beautifully formed Molten Brownie Diet-Destroyer on a bone-white plate, Chef Legume~~ ~~beamed.~~ The plate measured 20 cm by 30 cm, which left a tasteful 2.5 cm margin between the edge of the plate and the side of chocolatey bliss. ~~With his mind made up that this dish~~ ~~had earned the Fuchsia Ribbon, Chef Legume turned over the name card and was shocked~~ ~~to find that Larry, the brash American who insisted upon deep frying everything was respon-~~ ~~sible for this week's winning entry.~~ What was the total <u>area</u> of Larry's brownie creation?

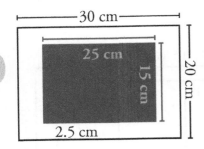

20 cm - 2.5 cm - 2.5 cm = 15 cm

30 cm - 2.5 cm - 2.5 cm = 25 cm

A = l x w

A = 15 cm x 25 cm = $\boxed{375 \text{ cm}^2}$

Practice Problem #2

Lanky Linda ~~tugged on the sheet again, only to pull the top part away from the head-~~ ~~board. How could this be? She and her mother had made a special trip to Crates and Cribs~~ ~~just before she came back to college and had carefully purchased sheets for her enormous new~~ ~~bed. Then, like a water-filled sponge, it struck her:~~ she must have grabbed her little sister's new sheets by mistake! No wonder when she laid the flat sheet out on the her bed, there was a half-meter margin on each side. If Linda's bed measures 6 meters by 4 meters, <u>what was the</u> <u>area of her little sister's sheet?</u>

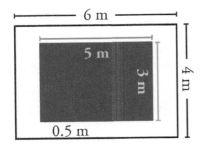

6 m - 0.5 m - 0.5 m = 5 m

4 m - 0.5 m - 0.5 m = 3 m

A = l x w

A = 5 m x 3 m = $\boxed{15 \text{ m}^2}$

Practice Problem #3

Rowland handed his picture to the kid behind the counter at Frames Galore. ~~After a moment's contemplation, he opted for the deluxe framing package, thinking to himself, "If I'm going to be framed, I might as well get the deluxe treatment."~~ Rowland knew his picture measured 4 inches by 6 inches, and that the deluxe package included a one-inch mat that would add an inch on each side of the picture. What is the area of Rowland's matted picture?

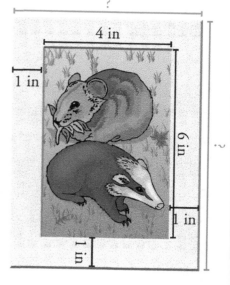

$$4 \text{ in} + 1 \text{ in} + 1 \text{ in} = 6 \text{ in}$$
$$6 \text{ in} + 1 \text{ in} + 1 \text{ in} = 8 \text{ in}$$
$$A = l \times w$$
$$A = 6 \text{ in} \times 8 \text{ in} = \boxed{48 \text{ in}^2}$$

Practice Problem #4

Farmer Frank was excited about winning the off-season football lottery. Winning the contest meant he would be able to use the local football field to grow crops in the off-season. ~~He didn't need the whole field though, that was for sure.~~ The entire field measured 360 feet by 160 feet. After much thought, Farmer Frank decided that he'd leave a 30 foot margin around all four sides of his planting area. ~~With his mind made up, he started planting beets along the 50-yard line, carrots and beans along the 40-yard line, and watermelon along the 30-yard line. He finished off his crop by filling the rest of the planting space with corn.~~ If Farmer Frank decided to build a fence around the portion of planted field, how many feet of fencing would he need to buy?

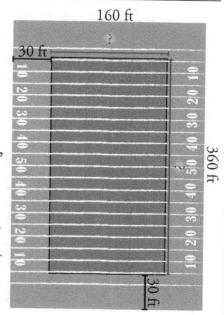

$$160 \text{ ft} - 30 \text{ ft} - 30 \text{ ft} = 100 \text{ ft}$$
$$360 \text{ ft} - 30 \text{ ft} - 30 \text{ ft} = 300 \text{ ft}$$

$$P = l + l + w + w$$
$$P = 100 \text{ ft} + 100 \text{ ft} + 300 \text{ ft} + 300 \text{ ft} = \boxed{800 \text{ ft}}$$

Practice Problem #5

Challenge: ~~The rug propped up between the old ping-pong table and the faded kayak at the yard sale was a thing of beauty. Sure, the edges were mostly frayed and there was one long stirp of binding trailing in the grass, but it had been years since Elsie had seen the elusive "small woodland animals playing badminton" pattern anywhere, and her cutting-edge designer sense told her it was about to make a big come-back. Since she~~ had perfected the art of replacing rug bindings, she made her purchase and hurried back to her shop to lay the rug out on the floor and assess the damage. In her workroom which was 10 meters long and had an area of 50 square meters, Elsie straightened the rug and found that there was a 1 meter margin between each wall and all four edges of the carpet. How many meters of binding tape should Elsie buy to replace the binding on all four edges of the carpet?

11

10 m

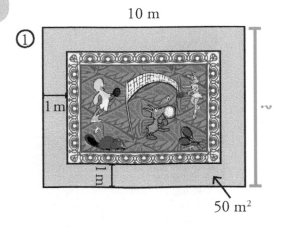

①

1 m

50 m²

$$\frac{A = l \times w}{}$$

$$\frac{A}{l} = w$$

$$\frac{50 \text{ m}^2}{10 \text{ m}} = 5 \text{ m}$$

10 m

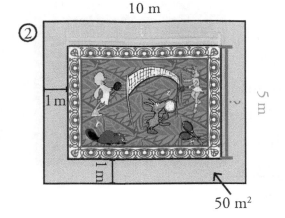

②

1 m

5 m

1 m

50 m²

10 m − 1 m − 1 m = 8 m

5 m − 1 m − 1 m = 3 m

P = l + l + w + w

P = 8 m + 8 m + 3 m + 3 m = **22 m**

Pour Me
▲
Volume

Sample Problem

A pig owner, a detective, and an accountant were sitting at a table in the accountant's office one day. They had a 1 liter bottle of water. They poured water from the bottle into a small rectangular container until it was full. If the small rectangular container measures 10 cm long by 5 cm wide by 5 cm tall, how much water is left in the bottle?

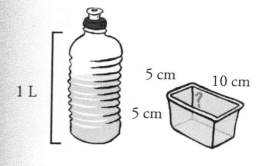

$V = l \times w \times h$

$V = 10 \text{ cm} \times 5 \text{ cm} \times 5 \text{ cm} = 250 \text{ cm}^3$

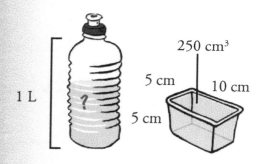

$1 \text{ L} - 250 \text{ cm}^3 = ?$ $\boxed{1 \text{ L} = 1000 \text{ cm}^3}$

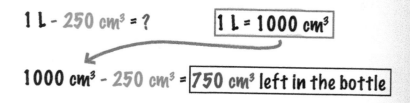

$1000 \text{ cm}^3 - 250 \text{ cm}^3 = \boxed{750 \text{ cm}^3 \text{ left in the bottle}}$

Practice Problem #1

~~Lord Elroy planted his foot firmly on the final step and heaved himself onto the ledge.~~ ~~He stared in wonder at the bubbling cauldron in front of him, knowing he didn't have much~~ ~~time. The flying squirrels would soon pick up his scent, and if the villagers of Pfuddyduddy~~ ~~were to have any chance at recovery from the Beriberi Plague, he would have to fill his rect-~~ ~~angular, water-tight container with the healing waters of the Cauldron of Pfire quickly. As~~ ~~he pulled the custom-made piece of Supperware from his bag,~~ he wondered if the 20 cm by 10 cm by 6 cm box would really hold enough Pfirewater to save all of the villagers. ~~Quickly~~ ~~dismissing his doubts, he dipped the container in the cauldron, snapped on the lid, and beat~~ ~~a hasty retreat.~~ How many liters of Pfirewater did the custom-made Supperware container hold?

12

20 cm

10 cm

6 cm

?

$$V = l \times w \times h$$
$$V = 20 \text{ cm} \times 10 \text{ cm} \times 6 \text{ cm} = 1200 \text{ cm}^3$$

$$\boxed{1 \text{ L} = 1000 \text{ cm}^3}$$

$$1200 \text{ cm}^3 \times \frac{1 \text{ L}}{1000 \text{ cm}^3} = \frac{1200 \text{ L}}{1000} = \boxed{1.2 \text{ L}}$$

Practice Problem #2

~~Larry, the host of the Deep Fried Goodness Show, needed~~ ~~to clean out his deep fryer prior to filming this season's finale.~~ ~~The last episode had been a disaster. The remnants of his Fried~~ ~~Catfish Surprise had clung to his Deep Fried Flan like a dryer~~ ~~sheet to his favorite pair of stretchy pants, and now the fryer~~ ~~was a fishy, flan-y mess! Luckily,~~ Larry had invented the oil change basket years ago. The 5-inch square basket was only 2.31 inches deep, ~~but if you simply dipped it into the fryer,~~ ~~it would fill with oil that you could dispose of at the nearest~~ ~~Biohazard Reclamation Site. Refill with fresh oil and you're~~ ~~back in the deep frying business.~~ How many cubic inches of oil does Larry's oil change basket hold?

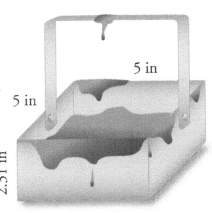

5 in

5 in

2.31 in

$$V = l \times w \times h$$
$$V = 5 \text{ in} \times 5 \text{ in} \times 2.31 \text{ in}$$
$$V = \boxed{57.75 \text{ in}^3}$$

Practice Problem #3

~~Jackrabbit Hill was alive with the sounds of rushing water, canoe paddles slapping the water, and young rabbits laughing as they navigated the Hill's 8 creeks. One rabbit in particular was making a lot of noise.~~ Simon Bigears had decided to attempt the first ever solo navigation of ~~Carrot Creek—Jackrabbit Hill's longest and fiercest waterway. Simon let out squeal after squeal, as his canoe bopped up and down through the rapids. What a "hare"-raising adventure! In fact,~~ Simon's canoe would probably sail right into the air if it weren't for the super-secret compartment he had designed in its hull. Measuring 1.5 m by 40 cm by 20 cm, the compartment held just enough water to serve as ballast to keep his canoe in the water and on track. How many liters of water did Simon's super-secret canoe compartment hold?

20 cm   1.5 m   150 cm

40 cm

$1 \text{ m} = 100 \text{ cm}$ → multiply by 10^2 or 100*

$1.5 \times 100 = 150 \text{ cm}$

$V = l \times w \times h$

$V = 150 \text{ cm} \times 20 \text{ cm} \times 40 \text{ cm} = 120{,}000 \text{ cm}^3$

$1 \text{ L} = 1000 \text{ cm}^3$

$120{,}000 \text{ cm}^3 \times \dfrac{1 \text{ L}}{1000 \text{ cm}^3} = \dfrac{120{,}000 \text{ L}}{1000} = \boxed{120 \text{ L}}$

12

*See the "Unit Conversions in the Metric System" instruction in the Tool Kit for more information.

Practice Problem #4

Ben Beagle paced silently along the side of the pool. ~~In his day, he had been quite the sprinter.~~ He could doggie paddle the 30 meter length of the pool faster than anyone around. ~~But that was then, and this is now. Today he walked the deck of the Canine Aquatic Temple (C.A.T.) as the new pool manager—the King of the C.A.T., the Poobah of the Pool. And today he knew that he needed to get water in the pool before sundown, or there would be some seriously disappointed puppies when the C.A.T. opened for the season tomorrow.~~ Ben measured the width of the pool and then it's depth to find that both measured 10 meters. What is the volume of the pool in cubic centimeters? How many liters of water will Ben need to fill the pool?

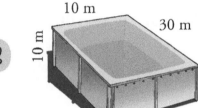

10 m
30 m
10 m

$$\boxed{1 \text{ m} = 100 \text{ cm}} \longrightarrow \text{multiply by } 10^2 \text{ or } 100$$

$$10 \text{ m}: 10 \times 10^2 = 10 \times 100 = 1000 \text{ cm}$$
$$30 \text{ m}: 30 \times 10^2 = 30 \times 100 = 3000 \text{ cm}$$

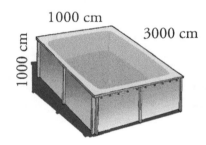

1000 cm
3000 cm
1000 cm

$$V = l \times w \times h$$
$$V = 3000 \text{ cm} \times 1000 \text{ cm} \times 1000 \text{ cm} = \boxed{3,000,000,000 \text{ cm}^3}$$

$$\boxed{1 \text{ L} = 1000 \text{ cm}^3}$$

$$3,000,000,000 \text{ cm}^3 \times \frac{1 \text{ L}}{1000 \text{ cm}^3} = \frac{3,000,000,000 \text{ L}}{1000} = \boxed{3,000,000 \text{ L}}$$

Practice Problem #5

Trent Trout and his wife, Sally Salmon, were out shopping for a new home. ~~They had given up the wild stream life years ago and, pooling their savings, they had purchased a beginner tank from a couple of catfish who were retiring to the coast. Now with their son, Little Bobby Bass, in the picture, their beginner tank was just too crowded. Since they both wanted a large family, they decided to take a tour of the~~ ① ⓐ XL GigaGlass model, which measured 10 m long by 6 m wide by 5 m deep. ~~Although they both loved it, the XL model was just outside their budget.~~ So they settled for the ⓑ L model instead, which was the same depth as the XL but exactly ④ 1 m shorter in both length and width. How many liters of water will they need to fill their new GigaGlass L model tank?

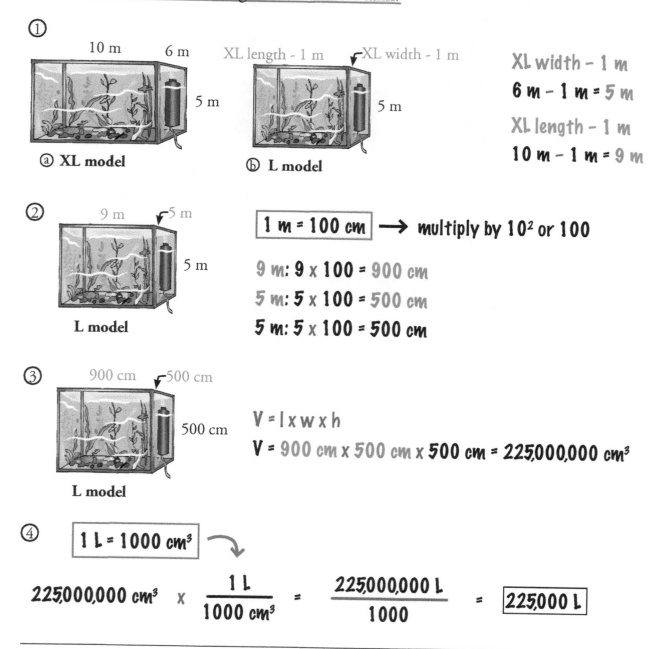

①

10 m   6 m   XL length - 1 m   XL width - 1 m

5 m   5 m

ⓐ XL model   ⓑ L model

XL width – 1 m
6 m – 1 m = 5 m
XL length – 1 m
10 m – 1 m = 9 m

②

9 m   5 m

5 m

L model

1 m = 100 cm → multiply by 10² or 100

9 m: 9 × 100 = 900 cm
5 m: 5 × 100 = 500 cm
5 m: 5 × 100 = 500 cm

③

900 cm   500 cm

500 cm

L model

V = l x w x h
V = 900 cm x 500 cm x 500 cm = 225,000,000 cm³

④

1 L = 1000 cm³

225,000,000 cm³ x $\frac{1 \text{ L}}{1000 \text{ cm}^3}$ = $\frac{225,000,000 \text{ L}}{1000}$ = 225,000 L

12

Sample Problem

Carmelita Huevos bought 360 limes for ③$175.00. ~~Since the temperature during rainy season had averaged 78 degrees Fahrenheit, the limes were 50% bigger than they were the last year.~~ She packed the limes in small, green bags of ① 3 limes <u>each</u>. She gave them to her brother, Jose, and he sold all the bags of ② limes at $3.00 <u>per</u> bag. <u>How much money did she make?</u>

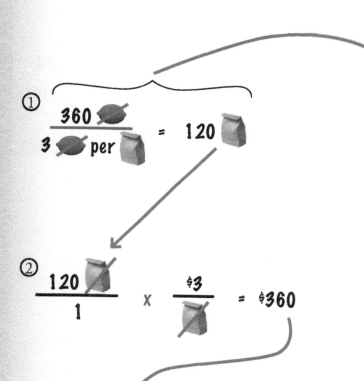

① $\dfrac{360 \text{🍋}}{3 \text{🍋 per} \text{🛍}} = 120 \text{🛍}$

② $\dfrac{120 \text{🛍}}{1} \times \dfrac{\$3}{\text{🛍}} = \$360$

③ $\begin{array}{r} \$360 \\ -\ \$175 \\ \hline \$185 \end{array}$

| Carmelita made $185 (profit). |

Why this works:

360 limes ÷ 3 limes per bag:

$$360 \text{🍋} \div \dfrac{3 \text{🍋}}{1 \text{🛍}}$$

Dividing by a fraction is the same thing as multiplying by the reciprocal....

$$\dfrac{360 \text{🍋}}{1} \times \dfrac{1 \text{🛍}}{3 \text{🍋}}$$

$$\dfrac{360 \text{🛍}}{3} = 120 \text{🛍}$$

13

Multi-Step Problems

Practice Problem #1

Akbar ~~was starting to panic. When he had~~ purchased the 120 acres of forest for the Big Project, he hadn't done his research. Now, the night before the Big Project broke ground, he finds out that ① 2/3 <u>of</u> the trees in the forest housed endangered pygmy flying squirrels, and he wouldn't be able to use them. Akbar knew that only ② 100 trees grew on <u>each</u> acre, and that this new development wouldn't leave him with enough trees. ~~When his cell phone rang, he knew it was Big Jimmy calling to find out how many trucks he'd need to haul away the harvested trees.~~ If Big Jimmy's trucks can carry ③ 50 trees <u>per</u> truck, <u>how many trucks will Akbar need to remove the trees he can cut down for the Big Project?</u>

① **Akbar can NOT use 2/3 of the trees.**

$$\frac{2}{3} \text{ of } 120 \text{ acres} = \frac{2}{3} \times 120 \text{ acres} = \frac{240 \text{ acres}}{3} = 80 \text{ acres}$$

120 acres – 80 acres = **40 acres of trees** (that he **WILL** use)

② **40 acres, 100 trees on each acre**

$$\frac{40 \text{ acres}}{1} \times \frac{100 \text{ trees}}{1 \text{ acre}} = \frac{4{,}000 \text{ trees}}{1} = \textbf{4{,}000 trees}$$

③ **4,000 trees, 50 trees per truck**

$$\frac{4{,}000 \text{ trees}}{1} \div \frac{50 \text{ trees}}{1 \text{ truck}}$$

$$\frac{4{,}000 \text{ trees}}{1} \times \frac{1 \text{ truck}}{50 \text{ trees}} = \frac{4{,}000}{50} \text{ trucks} = \boxed{\textbf{80 trucks}}$$

OR:

$$\frac{4{,}000 \text{ trees}}{50 \text{ trees per truck}} = \textbf{80 trucks}$$

13

Practice Problem #2

It was finally the first sunny day Monty Chaney had seen in weeks. The sunshine meant that Paul, the owner of Four Burly Boys Concrete Company, would bring his crew to finish the concrete work around Monty's house. That day, Austin poured a patio slab that measured 10 yards by 30 yards, while his brother, Brian, poured a sidewalk that measured 30 yards by 2 yards. Out front, Adam finished the driveway which measured 15 yards by 18 yards. At the end of the day, Monty paid Paul $3,010 for the work, and Paul paid his workers $3 for each square yard of concrete that they poured. How much money did Paul have left over at the end of the day?

Think Backward: Money left over → Total – what he paid his workers

Workers are paid by the square yard, so how many square yards did each pour?

① **How many square yards did each worker pour?**

Worker	Measurements	Area Poured
Austin	10 yd x 30 yd	= 300 yd^2
Brian	30 yd x 2 yd	= 60 yd^2
Adam	15 yd x 18 yd	= 270 yd^2

② **Paul paid $3 for each square yard...**

Worker	Area Poured	X	$3 per square yard	=	Total $ earned
Austin	$\dfrac{300\ yd^2}{1}$	X	$\dfrac{\$3}{1\ yd^2}$	=	$900
Brian	$\dfrac{60\ yd^2}{1}$	X	$\dfrac{\$3}{1\ yd^2}$	=	$180
Adam	$\dfrac{270\ yd^2}{1}$	X	$\dfrac{\$3}{1\ yd^2}$	=	+ $810

Total paid: $1,890

③ **Monty paid $3,010, how much did Paul have left over?**

$3010 – $1,890 = $1120 left over

> **Alternate Way to Solve:**
> Add the total square yards after Step 1 (= 630 yd^2). Then multiply that figure by $3 per square yard:
> 630 yd^2 x $3 per yd^2 = $1,890

Practice Problem #3

Ben Beagle smiled contentedly as he reached for the bank's door. He had just wrapped up the most successful week in Canine Aquatic Temple (C.A.T.) history. On Monday, the C.A.T. had opened its doors at 8 a.m. By the end of the day, there had been a record 427 visitors! Tuesday through Friday had seen daily attendance decreases by exactly 12 visitors each day, compared to the previous day. With each visitor paying an entrance fee of $1.25, Ben Beagle now had an enormous amount of money. But unbeknownst to Ben, had just stepped into the middle of a bank robbery in progress. Five flying squirrels, wearing tunics made out of what appeared to be dish towels, stood at the counter, brandishing rubber-band guns. Once they saw Ben, the squirrels snatched the money from Ben's grasp, and exited the bank in a flash. If the squirrels split the money equally, how much would each squirrel receive?

Think Backward: Split money equally ⟶ Total money ÷ 5 squirrels

Total money? ⟶ Each visitor paid $1.25, so how many visitors in all?

①

Day:	Number of Visitors:			
Monday	427			427
Tuesday	Mon. – 12	427 – 12	=	415
Wednesday	Tue. – 12	415 – 12	=	403
Thursday	Wed. – 12	403 – 12	=	391
Friday	Thurs. – 12	391 – 12	=	379

Total Number of Visitors: 2,015

② **Each visitor paid $1.25**

2,015 x $1.25 = $2,518.75 total

③ **5 squirrels split the money equally**

$2,518.75 ÷ 5 squirrels = $503.75 per squirrel

Practice Problem #4

~~Old Man Jenkins waited impatiently by the mailbox. If it didn't come today, he would be~~ ~~in a pickle. That afternoon, the residents of Shady Acres would all gather at the local croquet~~ ~~field for the Biannual Crankypants Walk-a-thon.~~ Old Man Jenkins' sponsors had promised that for every kilometer he walked today, he would earn $57 to put towards this year's Senility Ball. But if his new cane didn't arrive soon, he wouldn't be able to walk even one of the square croquet field's 125 m sides. ~~Just as he thought all hope was lost, Babs' mail truck~~ ~~screeched to a halt in front of him, and she handed him a package from eBuy. The package~~ ~~measured 25 in by 5 in by 3 in and contained his fancy new cane!~~ Arriving at the field in the nick of time, Old Man Jenkins walked at a brisk pace and circled the entire field 8 times before the walk ended. How much money did Old Man Jenkins earn for the Senility Ball?

Think Backwards: How much money did he earn? → ③ $57 per kilometer
How far did he walk? → ②8 times ①around a square croquet field that has 125 m sides

13

125 m

125 m

① **What is the perimeter of the croquet field?**

$P = l + l + w + w$

$P = 125\ m + 125\ m + 125\ m + 125\ m = 500\ m$

...in kilometers? | 1 km = 1000 m | → divide by 10^3 or 1000*
$500\ m \div 1000 = 0.5\ km$ The perimeter is 0.5 km.

② **8 times** around the perimeter
$8 \times 0.5\ km = 4\ km$ He walked 4 km in all.

③ **$57 for every** kilometer, 4 km in all

$$\frac{\$57}{1\ km} \times \frac{4\ km}{1} = \boxed{\$228\ total\ profit}$$

*See the "Unit Conversions in the Metric System" instruction in the Tool Kit for more information.

Multi-Step Problems

Practice Problem #5

~~The penguins at the Gubba Bump Fish Company were exhausted. The guy in the red suit was working their flippers to the cartilage. There were no happy feet on the ice that day, yet they persevered.~~ The waddle of penguins diligently stuffed ①10 fish in <u>every</u> box—no exceptions. At the end of the day, the guy in the red suit sailed away with a ship packed with 488 boxes of fish. He promised to sell as many individual fish as he could and send ④<u>3/8 ③of the</u> proceeds back to the penguins. If the guy in the red suit ②sells 7/8 of the fish for $2 <u>each</u>, <u>how much will the penguins earn for their hard labor?</u>

Since we know the price of each individual fish, we'll need to figure out how many individual fish there were in all, and how many of those fish he actually sold.

① **10 fish in every box, 488 boxes**

$$\frac{10 \text{ fish}}{1 \text{ box}} \times \frac{488 \text{ boxes}}{1} = \frac{4,880 \text{ fish}}{1} = 4,880 \text{ total individual fish}$$

② **He sold 7/8 of all the fish: 7/8 of 4,880 fish = number of fish sold**

$$\frac{7}{8} \times \frac{4,880 \text{ fish}}{1} = \frac{34,160}{8} \text{ fish} = 4,270 \text{ fish sold}$$

③ **4,270 fish sold for $2 each**

4,270 x $2 = $8,540 **total profit**

④ **3/8 of the profit back to the penguins**

$$\frac{3}{8} \times \frac{\$8,540}{1} = \frac{\$25,620}{8} = \$3,202.50$$

| The penguins earned $3,202.50 for their labor. |

13

Fishin' Whole

Sample Problem

Clem and Bobby Ray went fishing in the creek behind Old Man Jenkins' place. ~~Clem caught 2 striped bass and 3 trout. Bobby caught 4 bluefin tuna. He also caught an electric eel. Since it was past 7:00 p.m. they fried up their catch for dinner.~~ Clem just happened to have 2/3 of a quart of "Fried Right" cooking oil ~~in the back of his 1972 El Cheapo. Bobby Ray suggested that it might be wise to save some of the oil for breakfast in the morning.~~ So Clem used 3/7 of the oil to fry the fish. ~~They ended up throwing the eel back in the creek. The next morning, Bobby Ray and Clem headed home to watch the 10:00 a.m. FASCAR race on TV.~~ How much oil did Clem use to fry the fish the night they camped by the creek behind Old Man Jenkins' place?

$$\frac{3}{7} \text{ of } \frac{2}{3} = \frac{3}{7} \times \frac{2}{3} = \frac{6}{21} \longrightarrow \frac{6}{21} \div \frac{3}{3} = \frac{2}{7}$$

> **Clem used 2/7 of the oil to fry the fish.**

Practice Problem #1

~~As Clem and Bobby Ray settled into the couch for some serious FASCAR viewing, they discussed the ever-changing world of FASCAR politics.~~ With 93 drivers on the FASCAR circuit, ~~the competitive field was bigger than ever.~~ For today's race, though, only 2/3 of the drivers qualified for the race. ~~As the race was reaching its climax, Ernie Dalehard made a last-ditch effort to catch Stuart Tonay. But just as his car was moving faster than a buttered squirrel down an aluminum drain spout, he blew a tire, which led to a series of collisions. Thankfully, no drivers were injured, although~~ the collisions did knock 1/2 of the drivers out of the race. What fraction of all of the drivers in the circuit finished the race? How many drivers were knocked out of the race?

93 drivers

① **If 1/2 of the drivers were out, then 1/2 of those competing actually finished:**

$$\frac{1}{2} \text{ of } \frac{2}{3} = \frac{1}{2} \times \frac{2}{3} = \frac{2}{6} \longrightarrow \frac{2}{6} \div \frac{2}{2} = \frac{1}{3}$$

> **1/3 of the 93 drivers finished the race.**   ...which means 1/3 were also knocked out...

②

$$\frac{1}{3} \text{ of } 93 \text{ drivers} = \frac{1}{3} \times \frac{93}{1} = \frac{93}{3} = \boxed{31 \text{ drivers were knocked out}}$$

Practice Problem #2

Bummed by the outcome of the FASCAR race, Clem and Bobby Ray decided to grab some snacks and head on down to the cement pond for some fun in the sun. Clem found 5/8 of a bag of Tater Chips behind the couch, ~~and Bobby Ray still had half of a can of Academia nuts in the glove compartment of Clem's El Cheapo. Since they knew the cement pond around the pond would be warm, the good ole boys fashioned some flip flops out of work boots that had been run over by the lawn mower and 3 yards of string. After a quick dip, Clem and Bobby Ray had a snack and then a nap.~~ If Clem ate 5/6 of the remaining Tater Chips, what fraction of the whole bag did he eat?

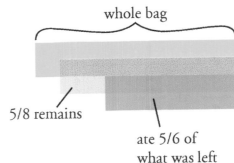

whole bag

5/8 remains

ate 5/6 of
what was left

$$\frac{5}{6} \text{ of the remaining } \frac{5}{8} = \frac{5}{6} \times \frac{5}{8} = \frac{25}{48}$$

Clem ate 25/48 of the whole bag of Tater Chips.

Practice Problem #3

~~Contrary to popular belief, Clem and Bobby Ray were a tad forgetful at times. And yep, they both neglected to apply sunscreen prior to their pool-side adventure, so that evening, both were sunburned like a couple of crispy critters. In fact, Clem and Bobby Ray sported two of the reddest necks you're likely to ever see. Needing to cool off in the shade the next day, they decided to go to the new release of "Alabama Jones and the Lost City of Tarnation."~~ At the theater, Bobby Ray bought the 5-gallon Gutbuster Tub O' Popcorn, but since the Gutbuster came with free refills, he only saw about 4/5 of the movie on account of his numerous trips back to the snack bar. ~~Due to the gastronomic consequences of his allergy to partially-hydrogenated coconut oil,~~ Clem also spent a significant amount of time away from the big screen. In fact, he saw only 2/3 of what Bobby Ray saw. What fraction of the movie did Clem see?

Bobby Ray = 4/5 of the movie

Clem = 2/3 of Bobby Ray's portion

$$\frac{2}{3} \text{ of } \frac{4}{5} = \frac{2}{3} \times \frac{4}{5} = \frac{8}{15}$$

Clem saw 8/15 of the movie.

Practice Problem #4

~~After the movie, Clem and Bobby Ray joined up with their friend, Earl, who had won four tickets to that night's tractor pull at the local fairgrounds. The tractor pull started promptly at half past seven. Crowd favorite "Crazy Jake" was driving his silver and cyan Dear Johan tractor. With 1,100 horsepower at his disposal, "Crazy Jake" managed to pull the sled~~ 9/10 ~~of the way to the finish line. Although "Crazy Jake" had set the bar high, newcomer Rascal Rollins felt up to the challenge. In his 1,200-horsepower Massive Fergeysohn trac-tor, Rascal put the pedal to the metal and very nearly won the competition. When the dust settled, though,~~ Rascal had only pulled the sled 8/9 of the distance "Crazy Jake" had. What fraction of the track did Rascal Rollins pull the sled?

Crazy Jake = 9/10 of the whole way

Rascal = 8/9 of Crazy Jake's distance

$$\frac{8}{9} \text{ of } \frac{9}{10} = \frac{8}{9} \times \frac{9}{10} = \frac{72}{90}$$

$$\frac{72}{90} \div \frac{9}{9} = \frac{8}{10}$$

$$\frac{8}{10} \div \frac{2}{2} = \frac{4}{5}$$

Rascal Rollins pulled the sled 4/5 of the way to the finish line.

14

Practice Problem #5

~~After 3 non-stop hours of loud engines, Clem and Bobby Ray yearned for some peace and quiet. So, after dropping Earl off at the Podunk Laundromat, Clem and Bobby Ray headed over to the Barns & Yokel bookstore for a poetry reading. …Unfortunately, the fun came to a screeching halt when Professor Angie Lou from the local college took the stage and read an epic poem about gladiators…in Greek.~~ Clem was distraught by the lack of rhyme and understood only about 2/3 of the words. Bobby Ray, despite being a fan of gladiators, only understood 2/7 of the words Clem understood. What fraction of the gladiator poem's words did Bobby Ray understand?

Clem = 2/3 of the words in the poem

Bobby Ray = 2/7 of the words Clem understood

$$\frac{2}{7} \text{ of } \frac{2}{3} = \frac{2}{7} \times \frac{2}{3} = \frac{4}{21}$$

Bobby Ray understood 4/21 of the words in the poem.

Shopping Spree

Advanced Frations: Multi-Step Problems

Sample Problem

~~Granny and Gramps keep all of their money in their mattress. Lately, Gramps has been having some problems with his back which may have something to do with the hundreds of rolls of quarters on his side of the bed. They decided they had to spend that money as quickly as possible to save Gramps' back.~~ At the mall, Gramps gave 2/3 ① of the money to Granny, ③ ④ ~~so she could buy a Z-Box 180 and a big screen Plazmatic TV.~~ Gramps spent 1/2 ② of the remaining money ⑤ ~~on a pedicure and a sea kelp facial. When they met back at the car,~~ they still had $425.00 <u>left</u> in the trunk, ~~which was way more than enough for breakfast at the We Wouldn't Steer You Wrong Steakhouse.~~ <u>How much money did Granny and Gramps have to start with?</u>

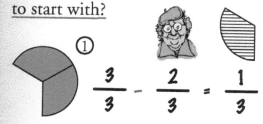

$$\frac{3}{3} - \frac{2}{3} = \frac{1}{3}$$

② $\frac{1}{2}$ of $\frac{1}{3} = \frac{1}{2} \times \frac{1}{3} = \frac{1}{6}$

15

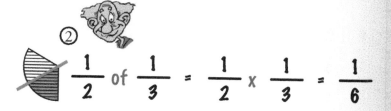

③
$$\frac{2}{3} \times \frac{2}{2} = \frac{4}{6}$$
$$+ \frac{1}{6}$$
_____

$$+ \frac{1}{6}$$
_____
$$\frac{5}{6}$$ spent altogether

④ All: $1 \rightarrow \frac{6}{6}$

Spent: $\frac{5}{6} \quad \frac{5}{6}$

Left: $\quad - \frac{5}{6}$
_____
$$\frac{1}{6}$$

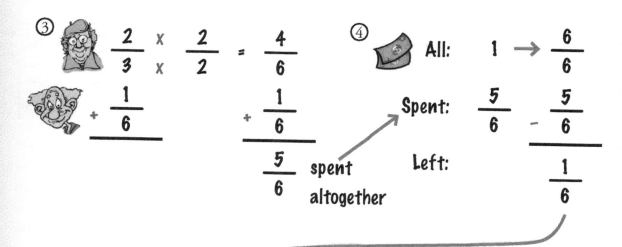

All: $\frac{6}{6} =$

Left: $\frac{1}{6} = 425.00

⑤

$425.00 \times 6 = $2,550.00$

All: $\frac{6}{6} = $2,550.00$

Granny and Gramps had $2,550.00 to start with.

Advanced Frations: Multi-Step Problems

Practice Problem #1

~~Seth and Maggie could not believe they had spent the entire morning collecting golf balls.~~ ~~Seth thought the golfers at Cataract Country Club must be the worst golfers on the planet.~~ ~~Maggie agreed that they couldn't hit the broad side of a barn with a softball…let alone a golf~~ ~~ball. When they returned home, they sorted the golf balls they had found.~~ Seth put 7/8 of the golf balls into a box on the upper shelf. Maggie took 1/3 of the remaining golf balls and put them in a basket to sell at their Lemonade/Used Golf Ball Stand, ~~and left the rest in a~~ ~~bucket in the garage. Later that afternoon, Mary Ellen stopped by their stand for a glass of~~ ~~lemonade and some used golf balls. As luck would have it, she~~ needed 6 golf balls and that's exactly how many golf balls Maggie had in her basket. How many golf balls total did Seth and Maggie find that day?

① **If Seth put 7/8 of the golf balls away, what fraction remained?**

$$\frac{8}{8} - \frac{7}{8} = \frac{1}{8}$$

② **Maggie put 1/3 of the remaining golf balls in her basket.**

$$\frac{1}{3} \text{ of } \frac{1}{8} = \frac{1}{3} \times \frac{1}{8} = \frac{1}{24}$$

Maggie put 1/24 of all the golf balls in her basket.

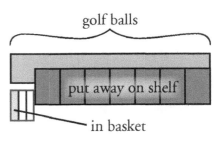

③ **All: $1 = \frac{24}{24}$**

Left: $\frac{1}{24} = 6$ balls

6 balls x 24 = 144 balls

> Seth and Maggie found
> a total of 144 golf balls.

15

Practice Problem #2

Ella Funt was the smartest girl on her street. ~~Her memory was simply amazing. To the astonishment of all the parents on Peanut Drive, she had successfully memorized all 24 license plates of the cars parked along both sides of the street. Mr. Bailey was so impressed that he awarded Ella a free afternoon at the zoo.~~ Since they were her favorite animal, Ella planned to spend the ① last 3/4 of her time with the pachyderms, which meant she had to plan the rest of her time carefully. As soon as she got to the zoo, she spent ② 1/4 of the time before her pachyderm appointment with the monkeys. After the monkeys, she realized she still had ② 24 minutes before she was due at the Pachyderm Palace. How many minutes total did Ella plan to spend at the zoo?

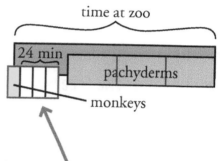

time at zoo

24 min

pachyderms

monkeys

① 3/4 of her time with the pachyderms means that 1/4 of her time at the zoo was free time.

$$\frac{4}{4} - \frac{3}{4} = \frac{1}{4}$$

② If she spent 1/4 of her free time with the monkeys, then she still had 3/4 of her free time left over. If there were 24 minutes left before her pachyderm appointment, then:

$$\frac{3}{4} \text{ of free time} = 24 \text{ minutes}$$

③ How many total minutes (4/4) of free time did she have?

$$\frac{1}{4} \text{ of free time} = 24 \text{ minutes} \div 3 = 8 \text{ minutes}$$

8 minutes x 4 = 32 minutes of free time in all

④ If her free time was only 1/4 of the total time she spent at the zoo, then how many minutes is 4/4 of her total time equal to?

32 minutes x 4 = 128 minutes

> Ella planned to spend
> 128 minutes at the zoo.

Or, in hours and minutes: 1 hour = 60 min

$$\frac{128 \text{ min}}{1} \times \frac{1 \text{ hr}}{60 \text{ min}} = \frac{128}{60} = 2 \text{ hr R8}$$

2 hours 8 minutes

15

Advanced Frations: Multi-Step Problems

Practice Problem #3

Luigi had never seen so much pepperoni. One little typo on the order form…that's all it took. And now here he was, knee-deep in pepperoni. Thinking quickly, he packaged up ①5/6 of it and, with the help of a shoe horn and a logging chain, managed to get it in the freezer. Still faced with a mound of pepperoni on his front counter, Luigi decided to put ②2/7 of what was left on the 40 pizzas about to leave the shop for the Alfresco wedding. When his brother, Donato, had finally left the shop with the wedding pizzas, Luigi took a deep breath and considered the ③45 pounds of pepperoni still sitting on the counter. What could he do with it? He had no idea. All he knew was that he would never make such an ordering mistake again. How many pounds of pepperoni did he order in total?

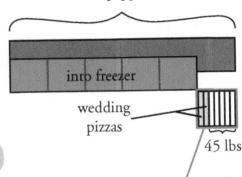

total pepperoni

into freezer

wedding pizzas

45 lbs

① If he put 5/6 of the pepperoni in the freezer, then 1/6 of the pepperoni was left out of the freezer.

$$\frac{6}{6} - \frac{5}{6} = \frac{1}{6}$$

② If 2/7 of the left out pepperoni went on wedding pizzas, what fraction of left out pepperoni is equal to 45 lbs?

$$\frac{7}{7} - \frac{2}{7} = \frac{5}{7} \longrightarrow = 45 \text{ lbs}$$

③ If 5/7 = 45 lbs, then what is 1/7 equal to?

$$\frac{1}{7} = 45 \text{ lbs} \div 5 = 9 \text{ lbs}$$

④ … and then 7/7?

9 lbs x 7 = 63 lbs $\frac{7}{7} = \frac{63 \text{ lbs}}{\text{left out}}$

⑤ If 7/7 or 63 lbs = 1/6 of all of the pepperoni, then what are 6/6 equal to?

63 lbs x 6 = 378 lbs

Luigi ordered 378 total pounds of pepperoni.

15

Practice Problem #4

~~When the carrot harvest was complete, many of the rabbits wanted to throw a party to celebrate their great fortune. Peter, however, insisted that they work even harder to store as much of the harvest as possible for the lean winter months. Under Peter's constant heck-ling,~~ the rabbits managed to ①store away 8/9 of the harvest in the form of carrot sticks, carrot juice, canned carrots, and delicious carrot cake. Proud of how hard they hard worked, Peter decided that they would ②cook 1/5 of the remaining carrots into a stew for a party that eve-ning. As for the ③88 pounds of leftover carrots, ~~he divided them equally amongst the 11 rabbit families and sent them each home after the party with food for the next month.~~ How many pounds of carrots in total did the rabbits harvest?

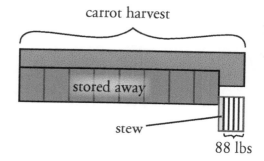

carrot harvest

stored away

stew

88 lbs

① **If the rabbits stored away 8/9 of the carrots, what fraction of all the carrots were left out?**

$$\frac{9}{9} - \frac{8}{9} = \frac{1}{9}$$

② **If 1/5 of the carrots that were left out were used in stew, what fraction remained?**

$$\frac{5}{5} - \frac{1}{5} = \frac{4}{5} \longrightarrow = 88 \text{ lbs}$$

③ **If 4/5 = 88 lbs, then what is 1/5 equal to?**

$$\frac{1}{5} = 88 \text{ lbs} \div 4 = 22 \text{ lbs}$$

④ **... and then 5/5?**

$$22 \text{ lbs} \times 5 = 110 \text{ lbs} \qquad \frac{5}{5} = \frac{110 \text{ lbs}}{\text{left out}}$$

⑤ **If 5/5 or 110 lbs = 1/9 of all of the carrots, then what is 9/9 equal to?**

110 lbs x 9 = 990 lbs

The rabbits harvested 990 lbs of carrots total.

Alternate Way to Solve:

If 1/5 went into the stew, then 4/5 = 88 lbs. So how many lbs = 1/5?
1/5 = 88 ÷ 4 = 22 lbs
1/5 of 1/9 = 22 lbs.   So: 1/5 x 1/9 = 1/45 = 22 lbs
So how many lbs = 45/45?   45/45 = 45 x 22 lbs = 990 lbs.

Practice Problem #5

~~Talk about irony.~~ Vincent couldn't believe he'd spent ① 6/7 of his birthday money ~~on the new Buzzer Blade 3750 remote control airplane, only to get it snagged in a tree during its inaugural flight. The unfortunate incident sent Vincent back to the hobby store where~~ he ended up spending ② 1/4 of the remaining money on repairs. Now, here he sat, wondering if he should spend the ③ $27 he had left on flying lessons. <u>How much birthday money had Vincent received in total?</u>

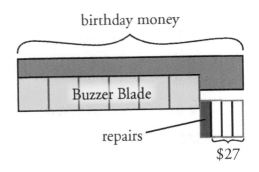

birthday money

Buzzer Blade

repairs

$27

① **If Vincent spent 6/7 of his birthday money on the plane, what fraction of all the money remained?**

$$\frac{7}{7} - \frac{6}{7} = \frac{1}{7}$$

15

② **If he spent 1/4 of the remaining money on repairs, what fraction did he have left?**

$$\frac{4}{4} - \frac{1}{4} = \frac{3}{4} \longrightarrow = \$27$$

③ **If 3/4 = $27, then what is 1/4 equal to?**

$$\frac{1}{4} = \$27 \div 3 = \$9$$

④ **... and then 4/4?**

$$\$9 \times 4 = \$36 \qquad \frac{4}{4} = \$36 \text{ remained after plane purchase}$$

⑤ **If 4/4 or $36 = 1/7 of all of the money, then what is 7/7 equal to?**

$36 \times 7 = $252

Vincent had received $252 in birthday money.

Alternate Way to Solve:
If 1/4 went to repairs, then 3/4 = $27. So how many $ = 1/4?
1/4 = $27 ÷ 3 = $9
1/4 of 1/7 = $9   So: 1/4 x 1/7 = 1/28 = $9
So how many $ = 28/28?   28/28 = 28 x $9 = $252

Recipe for Trouble
Ratios

Sample Problem

Every New Year's Eve, Aunt Mabel makes her "extra special" egg nog. ~~Uncle Emmett brings his secret-recipe fruitcake. It is rumored (since it's a secret) that Uncle Emmett's fruitcake recipe calls for 3 cups of dates and 4 ounces of persimmons.~~ Aunt Mabel's recipe, on the other hand, is actually posted on the bulletin board at the local Quik-E-Mart. In addition to the eggs, sugar, and nutmeg, you must carefully mix in 2 liters of buttermilk for every 7 liters of heavy cream. ~~This year, Uncle Emmett made 2 fruitcakes.~~ Not to be outdone, Aunt Mabel made an extra-large batch of egg nog. If she used 6 liters of buttermilk, how many liters of heavy cream did she need?

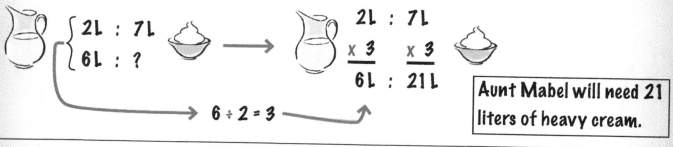

2L : 7L
6L : ?

6 ÷ 2 = 3

2L : 7L
× 3   × 3
6L : 21L

Aunt Mabel will need 21 liters of heavy cream.

Practice Problem #1

Old Man Jenkins won 3 tickets to the local taping of his favorite cooking show, "The Deep Fried Goodness Show." ~~Since he owed them a debt of gratitude for fixing one of his canes, Old Man Jenkins decided to take Clem and Bobby Ray to the show. As luck would have it, Larry, the host, was cooking up something special today. With his demonstration table piled high with foot-long hot dogs, buttermilk, corn on the cob, tapioca pudding and water chestnuts, Larry could only be making one thing: his world-famous deep-fried foot-long tapioca corn-on-the-cob dogs! The boys, of course, were already salivating.~~ As Larry began to cook, he explained that the key to the recipe was to use 4 cups of tapioca pudding for every 3 ears of corn. When all was said and fried, the platter Larry laid before the camera was a work of art. If Larry used two dozen ears of corn, how many cups of tapioca pudding must he have used?

2 dozen ears = 24 ears

4 cups : 3 ears
? : 24 ears

24 ÷ 3 = 8

4 cups : 3 ears
× 8   × 8
32 cups : 24 ears

Practice Problem #2

The un-civil war between the primates and the pachyderms was getting out of hand. ~~Jane, the zookeeper, was at her wits' end. Not only did the animals' monkey business upset the children visiting the zoo, but it was getting messy.~~ For every 2 bananas the apes threw at the pachyderms, the elephants would return fire with a machine-gun like barrage of 37 pea-nuts. ~~When you took into consideration the ice cream spilled by terrified children fleeing the scene, it's no surprise the battle ground between the two warring factions had become known as the "Banana Split." Now, after a long night of peace talks between the two enclosures, Jane thought she had finally made some progress, until just as she was turning away, first one banana, then another, whizzed by her head.~~ If the monkeys opened the day with a volley of 22 bananas, the elephants would return fire with how many peanuts?

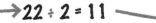

$$\begin{cases} \text{2 bananas} : \text{37 peanuts} \\ \text{22 bananas} : ? \end{cases}$$

2 bananas : 37 peanuts
      x 11   x 11
22 bananas : 407 peanuts

→ 22 ÷ 2 = 11 →

Practice Problem #3

Jethro was proud of his new invention. ~~Using only duct tape, the blades off of Clem's old lawnmower, and a hubcap from a Specific Motors sedan, Jethro had fashioned the world's first pizza cutter that could~~—with a solitary press on the Jethcut 2000—turn a pizza into 12 perfectly-symmetrical slices. ~~Now, Jethro knew that most families (who only ate one or two pizzas at a time) wouldn't have use for a Jethcut 2000. But what about the institu-tions? Prisons, the old folks' homes, the schools, and other places with lots of inmates? Jethro believed those were the places where the efficiencies gained by using the Jethcut 2000 could make a real difference. To test his new product, he decided to give it a whirl at Shady Acres' weekly pizza day. Norm, Shady Acres' head chef, was a bit skeptical at first, but he soon became a believer as he witnessed~~ Jethro turn 47 pizzas into how many perfectly-symmetrical slices?

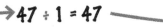

$$\begin{cases} \text{1 pizza} : \text{12 slices} \\ \text{47 pizzas} : ? \end{cases}$$

1 pizza : 12 slices
     x 47   x 47
47 pizzas : 564 slices

→ 47 ÷ 1 = 47 →

Practice Problem #4

~~When Cletus told Earlene they were going to honeymoon in Lost Bagels, she assumed they would be flying there immediately after the wedding. You can imagine her disappointment when Cletus, instead, had one of his buddies drive his dilapidated old Potomac Flytrap up to the front of City Hall. With about a hundred tin cans tied to the bumper, they hit the highway in a cacophony, backfires and screeching tires. What annoyed Earlene more than anything was that, every time they stopped for gas, Cletus had her get out and put more oil in the engine.~~ The Flytrap's heyday—if it ever had one—was long gone and it now used 2 quarts of oil <u>for every</u> 40 gallons of gas. ~~Three days~~ and 280 gallons of gas later, the newly-wed couple finally pulled into The Philly, the most-famous resort in Lost Bagels. Suddenly it didn't matter that Earlene had put <u>how many quarts of oil into the Flytrap over the course of the trip?</u>

  2 qt of oil : 40 gal of gas
                      ? : 280 gal

2 qt of oil : 40 gal of gas
    x 7   x 7
|14 quarts| : 280 gal

280 ÷ 40 = 7

Practice Problem #5

The vendors at the ~~87th Annual~~ Eastminister Dog Show were ecstatic. Attendance was the highest it had ever been in the show's history. And these pooches were hungry! Not surprisingly, Catsicles were outselling Squirrel Pops. In fact, the vendors were selling 5 Catsicles <u>for every</u> 3 Squirrel Pops. ~~After "New Tricks for Old Dogs," the last seminar of the show,~~ the vendors packed up their carts and totaled their sales for the weekend. All in all, the vendors had sold 129 Squirrel Pops. <u>How many Catsicles had they sold?</u>

  5 Catsicles : 3 Squirrel Pops
                       ? : 129 Squirrel Pops

5 Catsicles : 3 Squirrel Pops
   x 43   x 43
|215 Catsicles| : 129 Squirrel Pops

129 ÷ 3 = 43

16

Sample Problem

The Cowtippers Organization of Washington (C.O.W.) had 724 members as of January 1, 2007. ~~This represented a 43.2% increase over their 2006 membership numbers. The C.O.W. leadership attributes the skyrocketing membership numbers to a very successful advertising campaign sponsored by the Pork Is Great Society (P.I.G.S.).~~ In April 2007, each member tipped exactly one cow. 137 members tipped a Jersey cow. 406 members tipped a Guernsey cow. The rest of the members tipped Polled Herefords. What percentage of the members tipped a Polled Hereford?

All: 724

137

− 406

181

$$\frac{181}{724} = 0.25$$

$$0.25 \times 100 = 25\%$$

25% of members tipped a Polled Hereford.

Practice Problem #1

The smoke-filled room was filled with the usual sounds of dogs playing poker: chips clicking, tails wagging, growling, licking…you get the picture. This was the final round, so Rover decided to go all in. Scruffy and Scraps folded. That left Bruce. Calling Rover's bluff, Bruce also went all in. In total, there were 200 chips in the middle of the table. Scruffy and Scraps each had 25 chips in the pile. If Bruce had 70 chips in the pile, what percentage of the chips were Rover's?

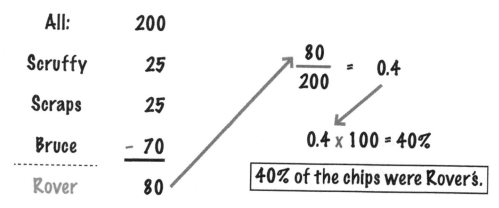

All: 200

Scruffy   25

Scraps   25

Bruce   − 70

Rover   80

$$\frac{80}{200} = 0.4$$

$$0.4 \times 100 = 40\%$$

40% of the chips were Rover's.

Famous Painting *Dogs Playing Poker*: Brown & Bigelow, an advertising firm, asked artist C.M. Coolige to paint the "Dogs Playing Poker" series.

17

Practice Problem #2

Plaidbeard shook his head as he surveyed the deck of his ship. It had been a rough fort-night at sea. Of the 14 landlubbers he had hired to man his ship, two had succumbed to seasickness, and had been dropped off during their last raid. Three others had joined his new parrot in an attempted mutiny and had been forced to walk the plank. Adding insult to injury, two others had gotten into his private stash of gummy bears and had been swiftly thrown into the brig. ~~So here he stood, captain of a skeleton crew of misfits, 1,000 miles from home. Oh, he knew that—if he ever made it home—this would make a whale of a pirate tale. But that was a big "if" at the moment.~~ He did not like his chances. After all, he had only what percentage of his crew left?

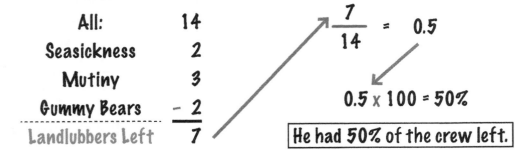

All:	14
Seasickness	2
Mutiny	3
Gummy Bears	- 2
Landlubbers Left	7

$$\frac{7}{14} = 0.5$$

$$0.5 \times 100 = 50\%$$

He had 50% of the crew left.

Practice Problem #3

Fog and Tad sat by the side of the stream, talking about their favorite things. Fog, of course, could speak at length about his button collection. With the addition of the three ivory buttons he had recently purchased at Scott the Skunk's swap meet, Fog now had a total of 1,250 buttons. Tad was floored. He could not believe Fog would spend so much money on buttons for his collection. Fog explained, though, that he hadn't spent money on most of them. For example, 625 of them had been gifts from his Aunt Mildred. In addition, 500 of his buttons had come from clothes his parents had given to him over his lifetime. Yes, he had purchased the remaining buttons in his collection, but that only amounted to what percentage of his collection?

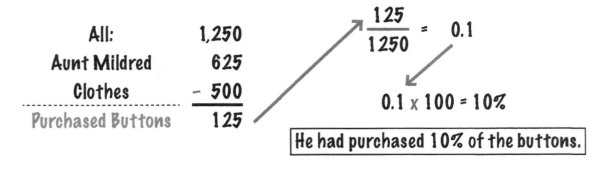

All:	1,250
Aunt Mildred	625
Clothes	- 500
Purchased Buttons	125

$$\frac{125}{1250} = 0.1$$

$$0.1 \times 100 = 10\%$$

He had purchased 10% of the buttons.

Practice Problem #4

Ronald the Raccoon was in the zone. ~~Although he usually only hit 21 trash cans each week, it was getting toward the end of summer and that meant it was high time to start storing some food away for the winter.~~ So, with that goal in mind, this week Ronald raided 50 trash cans. Ten of the trash cans were chock full of pizza left over from the Alfresco wedding. He also found 12 trash cans with leftover Squirrel Pops behind Eastminster Kennel Club. To date, though, the best find had to be the 8 trash cans full of pre-packaged Bran Nuggets he discovered behind Shady Acres. Although the <u>remaining</u> trash cans were devoid of good eats, Ronald had accumulated more than enough food for the foreseeable future. <u>What percentage of the trash cans Ronald the Raccoon visited did not contain treats?</u>

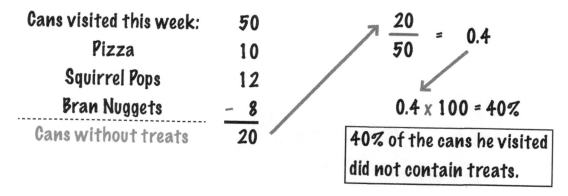

Cans visited this week:	50
Pizza	10
Squirrel Pops	12
Bran Nuggets	– 8
Cans without treats	20

$$\frac{20}{50} = 0.4$$

$$0.4 \times 100 = 40\%$$

40% of the cans he visited did not contain treats.

Practice Problem #5

Geezer McDougall was in a real pickle. ~~Here it was, the 15th of the month, and he was burning through his funds like he was made of money.~~ Of course, he wasn't wealthy. Indeed, he was on a fixed income of $300 per month. His room and board at Shady Acres was $150 per month. When you figured he usually spent $90 per month on tuba lessons, that didn't leave a whole lot of discretionary income. ~~The last couple of weeks, he had taken each of the Dombrowski sisters on a date to the local cinema. Now he was almost broke.~~ He sure wished <u>that more than what percentage of his fixed income was discretionary?</u>

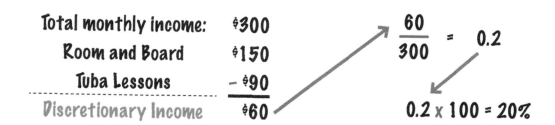

Total monthly income:	$300
Room and Board	$150
Tuba Lessons	– $90
Discretionary Income	$60

$$\frac{60}{300} = 0.2$$

$$0.2 \times 100 = 20\%$$

20% of his income is discretionary.

Mean Jumpers

Averages

Sample Problem

Hank, Rodney, and Mr. Jeepers were at the carnival one evening, when the barker challenged them to participate in a game of Hillbilly Hopscotch. ~~Never one to back down, Hank stepped up right away. Rodney and Mr. Jeepers tried to slip away, but two large clowns forced them to Hank's side. Mr. Jeepers went first and then, Hank, emboldened by Mr. Jeepers' sudden burst of team spirit, sprang through the air like a jungle cat. Rodney, never one to be outdone by his friends, leaped forward like he was shot out of a cannon. The crowd cheered and much cotton candy was consumed forthwith.~~ The average of all three jumps was 13 feet. If the average of Rodney's and Hank's jumps was 14.5 feet, how far did Mr. Jeepers jump?

① 13 ft x 3 = 39 ft

② 14.5 ft x 2 = 29 ft

} x {

To find the average or mean of, say, three numbers, add the numbers together and then divide by three. If a problem gives you information about an average, you'll need to "work backwards" (so multiply, then subtract) to answer the question.

③

39 ft

− 29 ft
_____

10 ft

} −

18

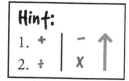

Hint:
1. + | − ↑
2. ÷ | x

Averages

Practice Problem #1

Cletus had driven Earlene batty on their trip to Lost Bagels. ~~Not only did he have to add oil every time they stopped for gas, but Cletus also made her keep an eagle eye out for the cheapest gas. He kept saying they had to stay within budget if they were going to be able to afford the More-Than-You-Should-Eat Buffet.~~ For example, as they traveled through Alabammy, they had to stop for gas three times. On <u>average</u>, they ended up paying $3.67 per gallon for gas there. Their first stop had been in Mobeel, where they paid $3.73 per gallon. From there, they made it all the way to Montgumry, where they paid $3.70 per gallon. Earlene had earned her spot at the buffet, though when they passed through Tuskaloosey and she noticed a <u>Quick-E Mart selling gas for how much?</u>

① $\dfrac{\text{Mobeel + Montgumry + Tuskaloosey}}{3} = \$3.67$

$\cancel{3}\left(\dfrac{\text{Mobeel + Montgumry + Tuskaloosey}}{\cancel{3}}\right) = \$3.67 \times 3$

Mobeel + Montgumry + Tuskaloosey = $11.01

②
	$11.01
Mobeel	$3.73
Montgumry	− $3.70
Tuskaloosey	$3.58

Tuskaloosey had gas for sale for $3.58 per gallon.

Practice Problem #2

A tear ran down Percival's cheek as the Yellowhound bus passed the "Now Leaving San Berdu" sign on the outskirts of town. ~~His time in San Berdu had been clam-tastic, but he understood that all good things must come to an end. When the fickle climate changes of El Dino caused the price of a bucket of clams at the Clam Pit to hit $20, he knew it was time to move on. Not knowing exactly when his next meal would be once he left town, Percival had decided to make his last week in San Berdu one to remember.~~ On Monday, Wednesday and Friday, he had eaten an <u>average</u> of 75 clams each day. On Tuesday and Thursday, ~~which were always half-price clam days,~~ he had eaten an <u>average</u> of 125 clams each day. Taking into consideration all five days he ate clams, <u>how many clams on average did Percival eat each day?</u>

① M, W, F: 75 × 3 = 225   225
② T, Th: 125 × 2 = 250   + 250
   M, T, W, Th, F   475

③ $\dfrac{475}{5} = 95$

Percival ate an average of 95 clams each day.

18

Practice Problem #3

Buoyed by last season's championship victory, Bubba's Holy Rollers rollerpolo team started the new season on fire. Indeed, their righteous mallets connected on every strike and left their opponents in shambles. ①Over the course of their first three games, the Holy Rollers averaged ②14 goals per game. In the first two games—a doubleheader against the Salon Sweepers—the Holy Rollers averaged 10 goals per game. But then, in just their third game of the season, the Holy Rollers faced their arch-nemesis, the Rusty Buckets, in a grudge match repeat of last season's championship. With the Rusty-Bucket-intimidation-factor no longer a threat, the Holy Rollers—fueled by nine years of pent-up frustration—steamrolled their opponent, scoring how many goals in a lopsided shutout victory?

① $$\frac{\text{Game 1} + \text{Game 2} + \text{Game 3}}{3} = 14 \text{ points}$$

$$\cancel{3}\left(\frac{\text{Game 1} + \text{Game 2} + \text{Game 3}}{\cancel{3}}\right) = 14 \times 3$$

Game 1 + Game 2 + Game 3 = 42 points

②

	42
Game 1	10
Game 2	− 10
Game 3	22

> The Holy Rollers scored 22 points against the Rusty Buckets.

Practice Problem #4

Bruce stared across the stream with a lump in his throat. ~~He knew the magnitude of the challenge before him. It was time for his beaver crew to show what they were made of.~~ If they ①were going to complete this dam on time, they would need to average 100 feet of new construction every day for the next five days. ~~Bruce knew…Dam."~~ Enlivened by Bruce's ukulele ②playing, the beaver crew averaged 110 feet of new construction each day for the first four days. ~~Proud of his crew's efforts, Bruce told them that they would likely be able to finish early on the last day.~~ How many more feet of new construction was left to complete the final day?

① 100 ft per day x 5 days = 500 ft in all

② $$\frac{\text{Day 1} + \text{Day 2} + \text{Day 3} + \text{Day 4}}{4} = 110 \text{ feet}$$

$$\cancel{4}\left(\frac{\text{Day 1} + \text{Day 2} + \text{Day 3} + \text{Day 4}}{\cancel{4}}\right) = 110 \times 4$$

Day 1 + Day 2 + Day 3 + Day 4 = 440

③

In all	500
First 4 days	− 440
Left	60

> The beavers had 60 feet of dam left to build on Day 5.

Practice Problem #5

The Dombrowski sisters had struck gold. ~~In an effort to repair some of Shady Acres' exercise equipment before this year's Senility Ball, the sisters had been scouring magazines for the perfect fundraiser…and they'd finally found it: the Curmudgeon 5000. Not only was it an telephone that would also wake the user in time to do those all-important things, like taking medication and getting to the restaurant in time for the Early Bird Special, it also came with "whippersnapper" features, such as auto-emailing children and grandchildren when they hadn't visited for X number of days.~~ To reach their goal, the sisters needed to sell an average ① of 20 Curmudgeon 5000s per day for the next six days, and so far, the residents of Shady ② Acres snapped them up like bran flakes. Over the first four days, the sisters sold an average ④ of 25 units each day. For each of the final two days, how many units do they need to sell on average to meet their goal?

① **20 units per day x 6 days = 120 units in all**

③ In all   120
    First 4 days   − 100
    Left   20

② $\dfrac{\text{Day 1 + Day 2 + Day 3 + Day 4}}{4}$ = **25 units**

$\cancel{4}\left(\dfrac{\text{Day 1 + Day 2 + Day 3 + Day 4}}{\cancel{4}}\right)$ = **25 x 4**

Day 1 + Day 2 + Day 3 + Day 4 = 100 units

④ $\dfrac{20 \text{ units}}{2 \text{ days}}$ = **10 units per day**

The sisters needed to sell an average of 10 units per day for the final two days in order to meet their goal.

18

fuel for Thought

Sample Problem

FASCAR racing teams are always pushing the limits of technology in their unending pursuit of speed. FASCAR driver Gordon Jeffers is using a corn-based racing fuel. He can now drive ① 120 km on 12L of "Gas on the Cob." Ernie Dalehard, on the other hand, is experimenting with a new fuel distilled from cooking oils. Using "French Fry Fuel," Ernie is able to travel ② 90km on 10L of fuel. ~~Perhaps most impressive, though, is Stewart Tonay's mixture of guava juice, lima beans, and oatmeal—combined with the battery power of 4,762 "AAA" batteries. This enables Stewart to drive an astounding 150km on only 5L.~~ ③ How far can Gordon Jeffers travel on 15L of "Gas on the Cob"? ④ How much "French Fry Fuel" will Ernie Dalehard use if he travels 54km?

① **To compare or calculate rates, reduce one side of the ratio to 1:**

$$120 \text{ km} : 12 \text{ L}$$
$$\div 12 \qquad \div 12$$
$$10 \text{ km} : 1 \text{ L}$$

$$90 \text{ km} : 10 \text{ L}$$
$$\div 10 \qquad \div 10$$
$$9 \text{ km} : 1 \text{ L}$$

② **On the DVD, our heroes could see from the problem what they would need to multiply the ratio by in order to solve the problem. If you can't quite tell, you can also use the unit conversion method described on page 168 in the Tool Kit to help you.**

Remember, you can also express ratios as fractions:

> Since this represents a ratio, you can write the fraction with either value in the denominator. Be sure you write it so your units will cancel in the next step.

$$10 \text{ km} : 1 \text{ L} \longrightarrow \frac{10 \text{ km}}{1 \text{ L}}$$

$$9 \text{ km} : 1 \text{ L} \longrightarrow \frac{9 \text{ km}}{1 \text{ L}}$$

③ **So if Gordon Jeffers uses 15 L of "Gas on the Cob":**

$$\frac{15 \cancel{L}}{1} \times \frac{10 \text{ km}}{1 \cancel{L}} = 150 \text{ km}$$

④ **And if Ernie Dalehard travels 54 km:**

$$\frac{54 \cancel{\text{km}}}{1} \times \frac{1 \text{ L}}{9 \cancel{\text{km}}} = \frac{54}{9} \text{ L} = 6 \text{ L}$$

> Gordon Jeffers can travel **150 km** on **15 L** of "Gas on the Cob."
> Ernie Dalehard will use **6 L** of "French Fry Fuel" to travel **54 km.**

Rates

Practice Problem #1

Ben Thayer got a brand-new lawnmower for his 16th birthday. ~~It wasn't exactly the set of wheels he had been hoping for, but his parents wanted him to put it to good use making money for college.~~ Ben's best friend, Doug Thatt, got a used lawnmower for his birthday just two weeks later. Since Ben's mower was new, he could mow ②4 lawns with a full, 2-gallon tank of gas. Doug's mower, on the other hand, was ~~3 years~~ older than Ben's and could only mow ③3 lawns with a full, 2-gallon tank of gas. If Ben Thayer and Doug Thatt go into business together and evenly split ① a 10-gallon can of gas, ④how many lawns will they be able to mow together?

① **If they evenly split a 10-gallon can of gas, how much gas did each boy use?**

   10 gallons of gas ÷ 2 boys = 5 gallons per boy

② **Ben can mow 4 lawns on a 2-gallon tank of gas.**

   4 lawns : 2 gallons $\longrightarrow$ $\dfrac{4 \text{ lawns}}{2 \text{ gallons}}$

   $\dfrac{5 \cancel{\text{gallons}}}{1} \times \dfrac{4 \text{ lawns}}{2 \cancel{\text{gallons}}} = \dfrac{20}{2} \text{ lawns} = 10 \text{ lawns}$

③ **Doug can mow 3 lawns on a 2-gallon tank of gas.**

   3 lawns : 2 gallons $\longrightarrow$ $\dfrac{3 \text{ lawns}}{2 \text{ gallons}}$

   $\dfrac{5 \cancel{\text{gallons}}}{1} \times \dfrac{3 \text{ lawns}}{2 \cancel{\text{gallons}}} = \dfrac{15}{2} \text{ lawns} = 7.5 \text{ lawns}$

④ **To find how many lawns they can mow together:**

   Ben + Doug = what they can mow together
   10 lawns + 7.5 lawns = 17.5 lawns

   Ben and Doug can mow 17.5 lawns together.

19

Practice Problem #2

Wayne Bruce was tired of life as a secret superhero. Not only were his superhero duties starting to put a damper on his social calendar, they were also starting to put a serious dent in his wallet. The ① Wombatmobile could only travel 12 miles on a full, 24-gallon tank of gas—a fact that had never concerned Wayne until he had bought his new, day-job commuter vehicle, the Gasmizer Deluxe. Unlike the Wombatmobile, the ② Gasmizer Deluxe could travel an astounding 320 miles on a full, 8-gallon tank of gas. Wayne's dilemma reached a climax when the Wombat Signal sounded, alerting him to a problem in ⓑ Tunnelton—960 miles away. He knew he'd probably miss the features of his superhero car, but he cringed at the thought of how much gas it would take to drive the Wombatmobile all the way to Tunnelton. What a conundrum! <u>How much gas would Wayne need if he drove the Wombatmobile to Tunnelton? How much gas would he need if he drove the Gasmizer Deluxe instead?</u>

① **Wombatmobile:**

ⓐ 12 mi : 24 gal

÷ 12   ÷ 12

1 mi : 2 gal → $\dfrac{2\ \text{gallons}}{1\ \text{mile}}$

ⓑ **Tunnelton is 960 miles away.**

$$\dfrac{960\ \cancel{\text{miles}}}{1} \times \dfrac{2\ \text{gallons}}{1\ \cancel{\text{mile}}} = 1{,}920\ \text{gallons}$$

② **Gasmizer Deluxe:**

ⓐ 320 mi : 8 gal

÷ 8   ÷ 8

40 mi : 1 gal → $\dfrac{40\ \text{miles}}{1\ \text{mile}}$

ⓑ $\dfrac{960\ \cancel{\text{miles}}}{1} \times \dfrac{1\ \text{gallon}}{40\ \cancel{\text{miles}}} = \dfrac{960}{40}\ \text{gallons} = 24\ \text{gallons}$

Alternate Way to Solve:

If you have a calculator, you don't *have* to reduce the ratio first. Reducing simply makes the mathematical computations easier.

$$\dfrac{960\ \cancel{\text{miles}}}{1} \times \dfrac{24\ \text{gallons}}{12\ \cancel{\text{miles}}} = \dfrac{23{,}040}{12}\ \text{gal} = 1{,}920\ \text{gallons}$$

$$\dfrac{960\ \cancel{\text{miles}}}{1} \times \dfrac{8\ \text{gallons}}{320\ \cancel{\text{miles}}} = \dfrac{7{,}680}{320}\ \text{gal} = 24\ \text{gallons}$$

The Wombatmobile will require 1,920 gallons of gas.

The Gasmizer Deluxe will require 24 gallons of gas.

19

Practice Problem #3

As a college student, Professor Stodgypants had done his dissertation on the comparative slithering capabilities of the Fang Viper and the common snail. His careful observations had revealed that a Fang Viper ① could cover 95 meters in 5 seconds. ~~The common snail, on the other hand, took 15 minutes to cover the same amount of ground.~~ Little did he know that his research would one day save his life. One fateful Saturday morning, while he was trimming his prize petunias, he heard the tell-tale (or is that tell-tail?) rattle of a Fang Viper. Slowly turning, he spotted the snake aggressively coiled approximately ② 133 meters away. His mind raced as he computed how long it would take him to reach the safety of his garden shed, which stood directly behind him. As he leapt toward the shed, a huge smile spread across his face, for he knew he could make it there in 6 seconds—and that it would take the Fang Viper how long to travel the 133 meters to his current position?

① **95 m : 5 s**

$\div 5 \quad \div 5$

19 m : 1 s

$$\frac{19 \text{ meters}}{1 \text{ second}}$$

② $\dfrac{133 \text{ meters}}{1} \times \dfrac{1 \text{ second}}{19 \text{ meters}} = \dfrac{133}{19}$ **seconds = 7 seconds**

> It would take the
> Fang Viper 7 seconds
> to travel the 133 m.

Practice Problem #4

Eileen had beaten the odds and she had the aluminum medal to show for it. ~~Ever since she was 13 years old, she had loved running, but it was not easy for her. You see, she had one leg that was 4 centimeters shorter than the other. Despite this physical limitation,~~ Eileen kept at it and eventually broke records, running an amazing ① 120 meters in only 12 seconds during the state championship race. Her win at the state level meant that she would compete at Nationals next month in San Berdu. At the national level, however, the race would cover ② 180 meters, which was the international standard. If Eileen maintains her state championship pace, how long will it take her to run the 180-meter national championship race?

① **120 m : 12 s**

$\div 12 \quad \div 12$

10 m : 1 s

$$\frac{10 \text{ meters}}{1 \text{ second}}$$

② $\dfrac{180 \text{ meters}}{1} \times \dfrac{1 \text{ second}}{10 \text{ meters}} = \dfrac{180}{10}$ **seconds = 18 seconds**

> It will take Eileen
> 18 seconds to run
> the 180 meters.

Practice Problem #5

Since Bobby Ray had gone to Tuskaloosey for the holiday weekend, Clem called Dutch to see if he wanted to come over to watch FASCAR on TV. Dutch got all excited and said he'd be over in two shakes of a dog's tail. That satisfied Clem, who looked around his place and decided it was not quite ready for guests yet. Mainly, he knew he needed to secure grape soda. Usually, ① Clem would drink a six-pack of grape soda over the course of a 3-hour FASCAR race. He also knew that ② Dutch had a reputation for being able to drink a cool dozen grape sodas during a race. Well, this weekend was the ⓑ 24-hour FASCAR marathon, and that meant that Clem needed more grape soda—a lot of it, actually. In fact, he was completely out of grape soda presently. ③ If Clem runs to the store, how many (individual) grape sodas does he need to buy to last Dutch and himself the entire FASCAR marathon?

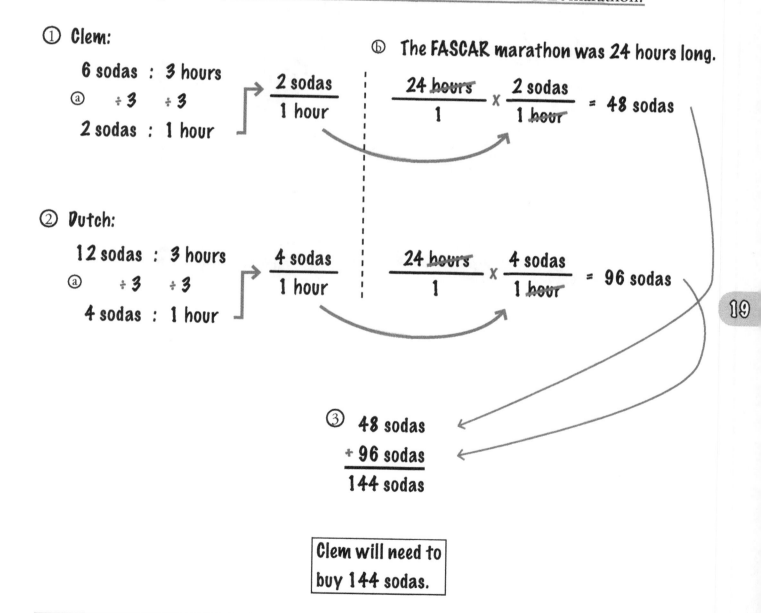

① **Clem:**

6 sodas : 3 hours

ⓐ ÷3   ÷3

2 sodas : 1 hour

$\dfrac{2 \text{ sodas}}{1 \text{ hour}}$

ⓑ **The FASCAR marathon was 24 hours long.**

$\dfrac{24 \text{ hours}}{1} \times \dfrac{2 \text{ sodas}}{1 \text{ hour}} = 48 \text{ sodas}$

② **Dutch:**

12 sodas : 3 hours

ⓐ ÷3   ÷3

4 sodas : 1 hour

$\dfrac{4 \text{ sodas}}{1 \text{ hour}}$

$\dfrac{24 \text{ hours}}{1} \times \dfrac{4 \text{ sodas}}{1 \text{ hour}} = 96 \text{ sodas}$

③ 48 sodas
  + 96 sodas
  144 sodas

Clem will need to buy 144 sodas.

19

Snack Time

Algebra

Sample Problem

At the FASCAR concession stand, a small popcorn costs x. A Super Mega Jumbo soda pop costs three <u>times</u> as much as a small popcorn. A FASCAR "value" meal, which consists of a Carburetor Chicken sandwich, Tire Tread fries, and a Super Mega Jumbo soda pop, costs $8 <u>more</u> than a Super Mega Jumbo soda pop alone. If the FASCAR "value" meal costs $14, <u>how much would it cost to buy a small popcorn and a Super Mega Jumbo soda pop?</u>

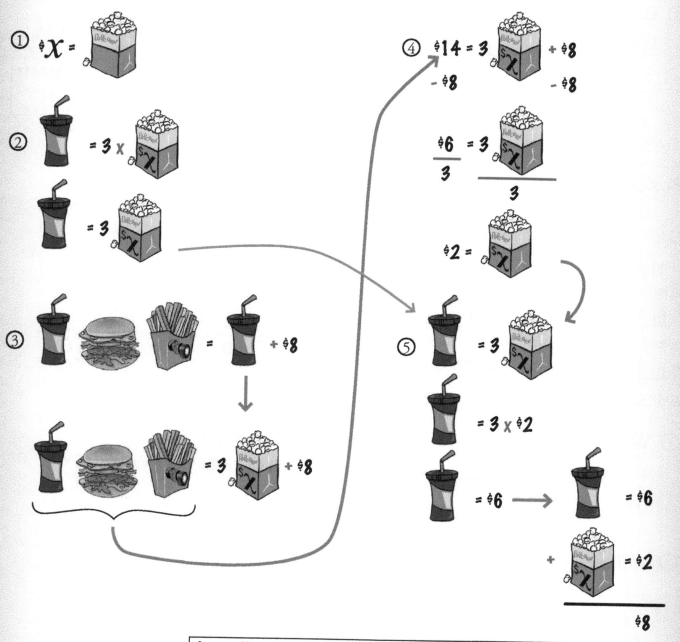

A small popcorn and a Super Mega Jumbo soda pop cost $8.

Algebra

Practice Problem #1

Lord Sudsbury's day had turned out better than expected. ~~The Duchess of Winch, …in anticipation for this very day.~~ The Earl of Hurl, who ended up hitting **X** targets that day, was blown away by Lord Sudsbury's shooting prowess, as he hit **3 times** the number of targets as the Earl. When the gun smoke finally cleared, the two sportsmen had hit a total of **24 targets** that day. Later, when the Duchess pressed for details of who had hit how many targets, how did Lord Sudsbury proudly reply?

① Earl = x
    Lord = $3x$

② Earl + Lord = Total Targets
    $x + 3x = 24$
    $\dfrac{4x}{4} = \dfrac{24}{4}$
    $x = 6$

③ Earl = x = 6
    Lord = $3x$ = 3 (6) = 18

> Lord Sudsbury had hit 18 targets and the Earl had hit 6 targets.

Practice Problem #2

~~Diligently following the advice of their expensive P.R. consultant, the three billy goats Gruff were working hard to overcome their bad reputations…~~ William, the eldest, headed straight to Flor Mart where he stationed himself by the entrance and successfully greeted **X** customers. Will, the middle brother, found a nice spot by the local watering hole and greeted **5 more** individuals than his older brother. Pedro, the youngest, went to Barns & Yokel, which was packed due to the release of the latest Hairy Otter book, and managed to greet **9 more** Field residents than William. If the three goats greeted a total of **74 residents**, how many residents did each Gruff greet individually?

① **William** = x
    Will = $x + 5$
    Pedro = $x + 9$

② **William + Will + Pedro = Total Residents**
    $x + (x + 5) + (x + 9)$ = 74 residents
    $3x + 14$ = 74 residents
    $- 14$ $- 14$
    $\dfrac{3x}{3} = \dfrac{60}{3}$
    x = 20 residents

③ **William** = x = 20
    Will = $x + 5$ = (20) + 5 = 25
    Pedro = $x + 9$ = (20) + 9 = 29

> **William greeted 20 residents, Will greeted 25 residents, and Pedro greeted 29 residents.**

Practice Problem #3

As the annual Ocho de Mayo celebration had been rained out yesterday, the townsfolk decided to go ahead with the festivities tonight, since the sky was clear. ~~Luke would, of course, try to defend his title as King Burrito~~... Miz Chalupa①, on the other hand, had gone to the More-Than-You-Should-Eat Buffet. As a result, tonight she was only able to wolf down *x* burritos.ⓐ Taco Johan, still feeling the effects of seasickness, was only able to eat 2 <u>more</u> burritos than Miz Chalupa. All of this worked inⓑ Luke's favor, and "Ol' Iron Stomach" managed to put away 11 <u>more</u> burritos than Taco Johan. If the contestants ate② 90 burritos <u>all together</u>③, <u>how many did each contestant eat individually?</u>

① **Miz Chalupa** = x

  ⓐ Taco Johan = $x + 2$

  ⓑ **Luke** = Taco Johan + 11 = $(x + 2) + 11$

② **Miz Chalupa** + Taco Johan + **Luke** = **Total Burritos**

$$x + (x + 2) + ((x + 2) + 11) = 90 \text{ burritos}$$
$$x + x + 2 + x + 2 + 11 = 90 \text{ burritos}$$
$$3x + 15 = 90 \text{ burritos}$$
$$\underline{-15 \quad -15}$$
$$\frac{3x}{3} = \frac{75}{3}$$
$$x = 25 \text{ burritos}$$

③ **Miz Chalupa** = x = **25 burritos**

  Taco Johan = $x + 2$ = (25) + 2 = 27 burritos

  Luke = Taco Johan + 11 = (27) + 11 = 38 burritos

> **Miz Chalupa ate 25 burritos, Taco Johan ate 27, and Luke ate 38 burritos.**

20

Practice Problem #4

The feud between the flying squirrels, the beagles and the badgers hit a fever pitch in the summer of '74. It had all started when the flying squirrels mocked the beagles for being afraid to ride The Whipporwill, the largest roller coaster in the amusement park. In response, the beagles challenged the squirrels to a roller coaster ride-off, ~~and before long, it became a~~ ~~3-way battle. Of course, the wily badgers' craftiness soon became apparent. The flying squir-~~ ~~rels and the beagles kept losing their place in line to various and sundry badger tricks, includ-~~ ~~ing the ol' buttered squirrel gag and the occasional cry of "Fetch!"~~ When the park finally closed, the flying squirrels had ridden The Whipporwill x times, and the beagles, who were a little less easily fooled, had ridden the coaster twice as often as the squirrels. As nobody had distracted the badgers from the game, they rode the coaster an impressive three times more than the flying squirrels. If all three groups rode the coaster a total of 42 times all together, how many times did each group ride individually?

① **Flying Squirrels** = x

ⓐ **Beagles** = 2 x **Squirrels** = $2x$

ⓑ **Badgers** = 3 x **Squirrels** = $3x$

② **Flying Squirrels + Beagles + Badgers = Total Rides**

$$x + 2x + 3x = 42 \text{ rides}$$
$$x + (x + x) + (x + x + x) = 42 \text{ rides}$$
$$\frac{6x}{6} = \frac{42}{6} \text{ rides}$$
$$x = 7 \text{ rides}$$

> The flying squirrels rode the roller coaster 7 times, the beagles rode 14 times and the badgers rode 21 times.

③ **Flying Squirrels** = x = **7 rides**

Beagles = 2 x **Squirrels** = $2x$ = 2 x **7 rides** = 14 rides

Badgers = 3 x **Squirrels** = $3x$ = 3 x **7 rides** = 21 rides

Practice Problem #5

The pig, the chicken and the sheep met at the diner for dinner last Tuesday night. Out of respect for their fellow dinner guests—and to help make this barnyard word problem "udderly ridiculous"—they didn't order bacon, eggs or lamb chops. Instead, they each ordered the tofu plate. However, the ①chicken, who was never a big fan of tofu anyway, only pecked around her plate and ate only x pieces of tofu. The ⓐsheep, unbeknownst to the others, had just started a low-soy diet, yet still managed to eat 7 more pieces of tofu than the chicken had eaten. The ⓑpig, true to his form, finished his plate as well as the leftovers from the others, for a grand total of ②3 times the amount of tofu as the chicken. If the chicken, the pig and the sheep ate a ③total of 47 pieces of tofu altogether, how many pieces of tofu did each eat individually?

① **chicken** = x

ⓐ **sheep** = **chicken** + 7 = x + 7

ⓑ **pig** = 3 x **chicken** = $3x$

②   **chicken** + **sheep** + **pig** = **Total pieces of tofu**

$$x + (x + 7) + 3x = 47 \text{ pieces}$$
$$x + (x + 7) + (x + x + x) = 47 \text{ pieces}$$
$$5x + 7 = 47 \text{ pieces}$$
$$\underline{ -7 \quad\quad -7}$$
$$\frac{5x}{5} = \frac{40}{5} \text{ pieces}$$
$$x = 8 \text{ pieces}$$

> The chicken ate **8 pieces** of tofu, the sheep ate **15 pieces**, and the pig ate **24 pieces** of tofu.

③ **chicken** = x = **8 pieces**

   sheep = **chicken** + 7 = x + 7 = 8 + 7 = **15 pieces**

   pig = 3 x **chicken** = $3x$ = 3 (8 pieces) = 24 pieces

Road Trip

Speed

Sample Problem

Ernie Dalehard left Daytona Beach at ②9:45 a.m. With his windows rolled down, he sang Mason-Dixon Chicken songs at the top of his lungs. Since he had plenty of beef jerky in the glove box and a Super Mega Jumbo soda pop in the cup holder, he did not have to make any stops until he reached the final destination in Miami at 2:15 p.m. The trip computer on his car computed his average speed on the trip as 95 km/hr. Based on Ernie's trip data, ①how far apart are Daytona Beach and Miami?

① **Use algebra to find the formula equal to distance.**

$$Speed = \frac{Distance}{Time}$$

$$T \times S = \frac{D}{\cancel{T}} \times \cancel{T}$$

$$T \times S = D$$

③ $\quad$ 4.5 hr x S = D

② **Convert the time information into hours:**

1 hr $\quad$ 11:45-12:45 $\quad$ 1 hr
10:45-11:45 $\qquad\qquad$ 12:45-1:45

1 hr $\;$ 9:45-10:45 $\qquad\qquad\qquad$ 1:45-2:15 $\;$ 1/2 hr

9:45 to 2:15 = 4 1/2 hours = 4.5 hours

Add the information about speed to the equation:

$$4.5 \text{ hr} \times 95 \frac{km}{hr} = D$$

$$\frac{4.5 \cancel{hr}}{1} \times 95 \frac{km}{\cancel{hr}} = D$$

$$4.5 \times 95 \text{ km} = D$$

$$427.5 \text{ km} = D$$

> **Daytona Beach is 427.5 km from Miami.**

21

Practice Problem #1

Barry McGuire, the '70s solo artist who recorded the hit album "Bullfrogs and Butterflies," had to get to Kalamazoo to launch his third farewell tour by ⓶7 p.m. tonight. He glanced at his watch and grimaced. ⓷It was already 12:45. If he were going to make it to the concert on time, he'd need to cover the 30 miles between Chicken Junction and Kalamazoo in a hurry. Thankfully, he'd just tuned up his Harley Mo-ped. He quickly loaded his trusty old guitar into the kid trailer attached to the back, and coasted down the driveway at 1 p.m. ⓵How fast would he need to travel—on average—to make it to the concert on time?

① **We need to figure out his speed, so the original formula for speed will work this time.**

$$S = \frac{D}{T}$$

② **Convert the time information to hours:**

1 p.m. - 2 p.m.:	1 hr
2 p.m. - 3 p.m.:	1 hr
3 p.m. - 4 p.m.:	1 hr
4 p.m. - 5 p.m.:	1 hr
5 p.m. - 6 p.m.:	1 hr
6 p.m. - 7 p.m.:	+ 1 hr
	6 hrs

③ **We also know information about distance from the problem.**

$$S = \frac{30 \text{ mi}}{6 \text{ hrs}}$$

$$S = 5 \frac{\text{mi}}{\text{hr}}$$

> **Barry would need to maintain an average a speed of 5 miles per hour to make it to the concert on time.**

21

Practice Problem #2

Lulabelle and Bessy were on the lam. At ③ 10:15 a.m., they had hijacked the Udderly Fantastic milk truck and hit the road looking for adventure. ~~They soon found it, as two local policemen on motorcycles gave chase. While Lulabelle drove the milk truck through a series of evasive maneuvers, Bessy threw 8 glass bottles of milk onto the pavement behind the truck, creating a minefield of glass shards that soon deflated both policemen's tires. Confident that they would now make a clean getaway, the bovine bandits put the pedal to the metal and headed due south.~~ Lulabelle and Bessy maintained an average speed of ② 90 km/hr. They figured they'd be safe as soon as they reached at Granny Bossy's farm, 360 km away from the scene of the crime. ① <u>At approximately what time will these cows-gone-bad reach Granny's farm?</u>

① **Use algebra to find the formula equal to time.**

$$S = \frac{D}{T}$$

$$T \times S = \frac{D}{T} \times T$$

$$T \times S = D$$

$$\frac{T \times S}{S} = \frac{D}{S}$$

$$\boxed{T = \frac{D}{S}}$$

② **Plug in information from the problem:**

$$T = \frac{D}{S}$$

$$T = \frac{360 \text{ km}}{90 \text{ km/hr}}$$

$$T = 4 \text{ hr}$$

③ **So what time will it be, 4 hours from 10:15 a.m.?**

10:15 a.m. – 11:15 a.m.	1 hr
11:15 a.m. – 12:15 p.m.	1 hr
12:15 p.m. – 1:15 p.m.	1 hr
1:15 p.m. – 2:15 p.m.	1 hr

Lulabelle and Bessy will arrive at Granny's farm at 2:15 p.m.

21

Speed

Practice Problem #3

Yoga Bear and his lil' buddy, Bubbaloo, set off into the wilderness at promptly ②6 a.m. They went in search of the Golden Pikanik Basket, which they believed they would find at the base of Mount Smoky, approximately ③16 miles away. At 2 p.m., they reached Mount Smoky, only to find newly-constructed condominiums and a beaver lodge. Disappointed and hungry, the bears sat down to rest, since they were also tired from ①maintaining a grueling pace of what speed throughout the forest on their journey?

① We need to figure out his speed, so the original formula for speed will work this time.

$$S = \frac{D}{T}$$

② Convert the time information to hours:

6 a.m. - 7 a.m.	1 hr	10 a.m. - 11 a.m.	1 hr
7 a.m. - 8 a.m.	1 hr	11. a.m. - 12 p.m.	1 hr
8 a.m. - 9 a.m.	1 hr	12 p.m. - 1 p.m.	1 hr
9 a.m. - 10 a.m.	1 hr	1 p.m. - 2 p.m.	+ 1 hr
			8 hrs

③ We also know information about distance from the problem.

$$S = \frac{16 \text{ mi}}{8 \text{ hrs}}$$

$$S = 2 \frac{\text{mi}}{\text{hr}}$$

> Yoga Bear and Bubbaloo maintained a speed of 2 miles per hour.

Practice Problem #4

The train chugged steadily along the track. It had left Cellulite Station ~~with its cargo of three-dozen Thighblaster 4000s~~ at 7:30 a.m. Traveling at only 20 miles per hour through the Hefty Mountains, it was due in Saggy Bottom at 8 p.m. <u>How far is it between Cellulite Station and Saggy Bottom?</u>

① **Use algebra to find the formula equal to distance.**

$$\text{Speed} = \frac{\text{Distance}}{\text{Time}}$$

$$T \times S = \frac{D}{\cancel{T}} \times \cancel{T}$$

$$T \times S = D$$

② **Convert the time information to hours:**

7:30 a.m. - 7:30 p.m.:	12 hrs
7:30 p.m. - 8 p.m.:	+ 0.5 hrs
	12.5 hrs

③ **Plug the information about speed into the equation:**

$T \times S = D$

12.5 ~~hrs~~ x 20 mi/~~hr~~ = D

250 mi = D

> 250 miles lie between Cellulite Station and Saggy Bottom.

Practice Problem #5

Challenge! Roscoe and Rita were on the run. The all-camp game of Capture the Flag was getting intense, and these two camp veterans had just snatched the flag from the hollow of a tree down by the creek. Finalizing their plans to divide and conquer, Rita dashed off due west with flag tucked into the pocket of her hoodie—all except the required "5 inches of visibility," that is. Roscoe watched her go, and then turned and ran due east for ② 10 minutes at 600 feet per minute. Unfortunately, Rita was tagged after running for only 8 minutes at 500 feet per minute. ① <u>How many feet will Roscoe have to run back (to the west) to recapture the flag from where Rita was tagged?</u>

Ro: 10 minutes at 600 ft/min   Ri: 8 minutes at 500 ft/min

?

③

① **Use algebra to find the formula equal to distance.**

$$\text{Speed} = \frac{\text{Distance}}{\text{Time}}$$

$$T \times S = \frac{D}{\cancel{T}} \times \cancel{T}$$

$$T \times S = D$$

② **Plug information for each player into the equation to find how far each ran.**

ⓐ Roscoe:

$$T \times S = D$$

$$10 \,\cancel{min} \times 600 \; ft/\cancel{min} = 6{,}000 \; ft$$

ⓑ Rita:

$$T \times S = D$$

$$8 \,\cancel{min} \times 500 \; ft/\cancel{min} = 4{,}000 \; ft$$

21

③ **Since Roscoe needs to run the entire way back to the tree and then continue to finish the distance that Rita ran, add the two distances together:**

Roscoe + Rita = Total Distance

6,000 ft + 4,000 ft = **10,000 ft**

Roscoe will need to run **10,000 ft** to recapture the flag.

Water Torture

Sample Problem

Gordon and Horatio could not believe that they had water duty the first day at camp. ~~There were 27 scouts in their troop, so they would need to refill the bucket 5 times that day.~~ At the well, they used a jug to fill the bucket. After emptying 20 jugs of water into the bucket, it was 5/8 full. Gordon dumped another 8 jugs into the bucket and then the jug slipped out of his hand and into the well. Luckily, Horatio had a cup with him. After 10 cups, the bucket was finally full. The boys lugged the bucket of water back down the hill. Gordon told the camp director that he had lost the jug down the well and the camp director replied, "you'll just have to use that cup from now on." How many cups will the bucket hold?

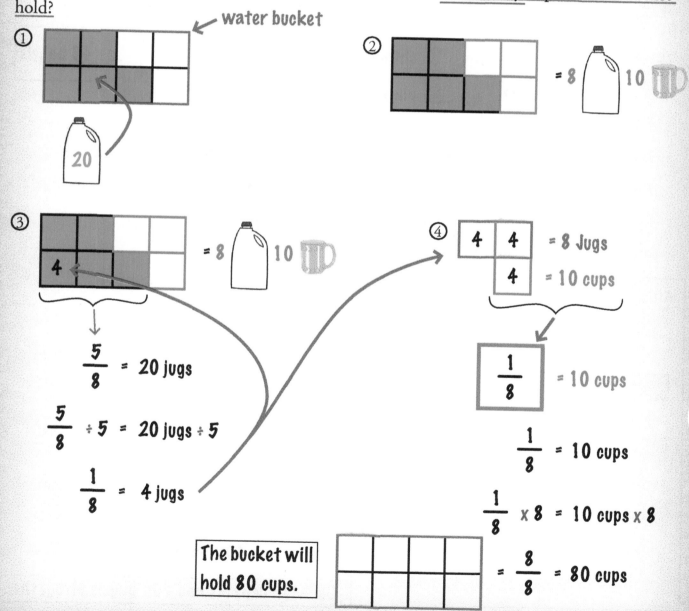

$$\frac{5}{8} = 20 \text{ jugs}$$

$$\frac{5}{8} \div 5 = 20 \text{ jugs} \div 5$$

$$\frac{1}{8} = 4 \text{ jugs}$$

$$\frac{1}{8} = 10 \text{ cups}$$

$$\frac{1}{8} = 10 \text{ cups}$$

$$\frac{1}{8} \times 8 = 10 \text{ cups} \times 8$$

$$= \frac{8}{8} = 80 \text{ cups}$$

The bucket will hold 80 cups.

Practice Problem #1

After winning the door prize at this year's Senility Ball, Old Man Jenkins decided to treat the residents of Shady Acres to some free bagels. He hobbled down to Beagle's Bagels and asked for as many bagels as his fixed income would allow. The girl with pink hair behind the counter filled a large box full of bagels and sent Old Man Jenkins on his way. When he got to Shady Acres and opened the box, he saw that ②1/4 of the bagels were sesame. There were also ③48 more cinnamon bagels than sesame bagels. The ④remaining 152 bagels were plain. ①How many bagels were there altogether?

all of the bagels

$\frac{1}{4}$ = sesame   152 = plain

$\frac{1}{4}$ + 48 = cinnamon

① **Let's say:** all of the bagels = x

We also know:

② sesame = **1/4 of all of the bagels** = $\boxed{\frac{1}{4} \, x}$

③ **cinnamon = sesame + 48 bagels** = $\boxed{\frac{1}{4} \, x + 48 \text{ bagels}}$

④ **plain = 152 bagels**

- -

Set up an equation that is equal to all of the bagels:

sesame + cinnamon + plain = all of the bagels

$$\frac{1}{4} \, x + \left(\frac{1}{4} \, x + 48 \text{ bagels}\right) + (152 \text{ bagels}) = x$$

$$\frac{1}{4} \, x + \frac{1}{4} \, x + 48 \text{ bagels} + 152 \text{ bagels} = x$$

Remember: $\frac{2}{2} = 1$

$\frac{2}{4} \, x \longrightarrow$

$$\frac{1}{2} \, x + 200 \text{ bagels} = \frac{2}{2} \, x$$

$$-\frac{1}{2} \, x \qquad\qquad -\frac{1}{2} \, x$$

$$200 \text{ bagels} = \frac{1}{2} \, x$$

To divide by a fraction, simply multiply by the reciprocal.

$$\frac{2}{1} (200 \text{ bagels}) = \left(\frac{1}{2} \, x\right) \frac{2}{1}$$

$$400 \text{ bagels} = x$$

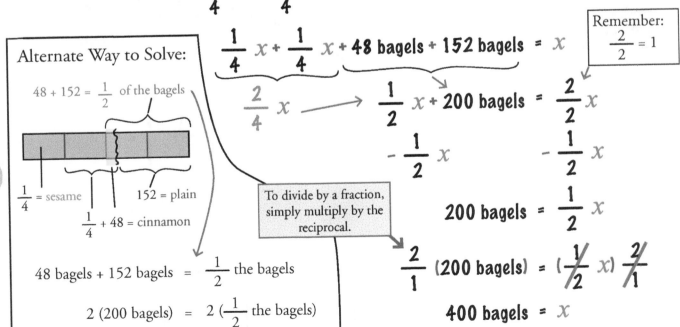

Alternate Way to Solve:

$48 + 152 = \frac{1}{2}$ of the bagels

$\frac{1}{4}$ = sesame   152 = plain

$\frac{1}{4}$ + 48 = cinnamon

$$48 \text{ bagels} + 152 \text{ bagels} = \frac{1}{2} \text{ the bagels}$$

$$2 (200 \text{ bagels}) = 2 \left(\frac{1}{2} \text{ the bagels}\right)$$

$$400 \text{ bagels} = \text{ all of the bagels}$$

Old Man Jenkins had 400 bagels altogether.

22

Practice Problem #2

Bobby Jo spent ⓑ 2/5 of his weekly take-home pay on video games for his Z-Box 180, and ⓒ 1/2 of the remainder he used on a Thighblaster 4000. ⓓ He spent $12 more on the video games than he spent on the Thighblaster 4000. ⓐ How much money (after taxes) does Bobby Jo make each week?

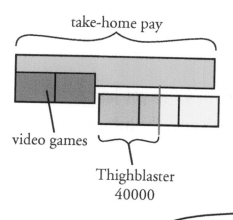

take-home pay

video games

Thighblaster 40000

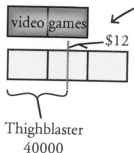

video games

$12

Thighblaster 40000

ⓐ **Let's say:** take-home pay = x

We also know:

ⓑ **video games = 2/5** of take-home pay **= 2/5** x

ⓒ Thighblaster **= 1/2** of remaining **= 1/2 x 3/5** x

[remaining **= 5/5** x **– 2/5** x **= 3/5** x]

ⓓ **video games =** Thighblaster **+ $12**

① **First, simplify the value for the** Thighblaster.

$$\text{Thighblaster} = \frac{1}{2} \times \frac{3}{5}\, x = \frac{3}{10}\, x$$

② **Since the final equation contains a dollar amount, plug the other information you know into that equation:**

video games = Thighblaster **+ $12**

$$\left(\frac{2}{5}\, x\right) = \left(\frac{3}{10}\, x\right) + \$12$$

$$-\frac{3}{10}\, x \quad -\frac{3}{10}\, x$$

$$\frac{2}{5}\, x - \frac{3}{10}\, x = \$12$$

$$\frac{4}{10}\, x - \frac{3}{10}\, x = \$12$$

$$\frac{1}{10}\, x = \$12$$

$$\frac{10}{1}\left(\frac{1}{10}\, x\right) = (\$12)\frac{10}{1}$$

$$x = \$120$$

Bobby Jo makes $120 in take-home pay each week.

22

Practice Problem #3

Hillary and John were running against one another for class president. ⓑHillary earned 1/4 <u>of</u> the votes while ©John earned 1/3 <u>of</u> the votes. The winner of the election, however, turned out to be a write-in candidate named ⓓRuss Parole, who won with a <u>total</u> of 45 votes. If Hillary, John and Russ were the only 3 candidates, ⓐ<u>how many votes were cast altogether?</u> ②<u>How many votes each did Hillary and John receive?</u>

ⓐ **Let's say:** all the votes = x

We also know:

ⓑ **Hillary = 1/4 of all the votes = 1/4 x** ⎫
ⓒ **John = 1/3 of all the votes = 1/3 x** ⎭

ⓓ **Russ Parole = 45 votes**

② **Plug the value you just found for x back into the information you know for each incumbent:**

$$\text{Hillary} = \frac{1}{4}x$$

$$= \frac{1}{4}(108 \text{ votes})$$

$$= 27 \text{ votes}$$

$$\text{John} = \frac{1}{3}x$$

$$= \frac{1}{3}(108 \text{ votes})$$

$$= 36 \text{ votes}$$

① **Set up an equation that is equal to all the votes:**

Hillary + John + Russ Parole = all the votes

$$\frac{1}{4}x + (\frac{1}{3}x) + (45 \text{ votes}) = x$$

$$(\frac{1}{4} \times \frac{3}{3})x + (\frac{1}{3} \times \frac{4}{4})x + 45 \text{ votes} = x$$

(Find a common denominator.)

$$\frac{3}{12}x + \frac{4}{12}x + 45 \text{ votes} = x$$

$$\frac{7}{12}x + 45 \text{ votes} = \frac{12}{12}x$$

(Remember, any number divided by itself is equal to 1.)

$$-\frac{7}{12}x \qquad -\frac{7}{12}x$$

$$45 \text{ votes} = \frac{5}{12}x$$

$$\frac{12}{5}(45 \text{ votes}) = (\frac{5}{12}x)\frac{12}{5}$$

$$\frac{540 \text{ votes}}{5} = x$$

$$108 \text{ votes} = x$$

Out of 108 total votes, Hillary received 27 votes and John received 36 votes.

Practice Problem #4

Duke read ⓑ2/5 of his ice cream truck repair manual on Monday. On ⓒTuesday, he read another ⓓ420 pages. If Duke still has 1/2 of the ice cream truck repair manual to read, ⓐhow many pages total are there in the book?

ⓐ **Let's say:** total pages = x

We also know:

ⓑ **Monday = 2/5** of the total pages = **2/5** x

ⓒ **Tuesday = 420 pages**

ⓓ **He still has 1/2** of the total pages **left to read.**

- -

① **Since we know information about the first 1/2 of the manual, we can set up an equation equal to 1/2 x:**

$$\text{Monday + Tuesday} = \frac{1}{2} x$$

$$\frac{2}{5} x + 420 \text{ pages} = \frac{1}{2} x$$

$$-\frac{2}{5} x \quad -\frac{2}{5} x$$

$$420 \text{ pages} = \frac{1}{2} x - \frac{2}{5} x$$

$$420 \text{ pages} = \left(\frac{1}{2} \times \frac{5}{5}\right) x - \left(\frac{2}{5} \times \frac{2}{2}\right) x$$

$$420 \text{ pages} = \frac{5}{10} x - \frac{4}{10} x$$

$$\frac{10}{1}(420 \text{ pages}) = \left(\frac{1}{10} x\right) \frac{10}{1}$$

$$4200 \text{ pages} = x$$

The ice cream truck repair manual is 4200 pages long.

Practice Problem #5

When Vince turned 16 this past Saturday, ~~he took all $422 in his savings account~~ and bought a used 1975 Hi-Way Croozer. ~~He got such a good deal on it because the gas gauge is broken and the dealer did not know how large the gas tank was. With the help of his Uncle Cooter, Vince set about the task of determining how much gas the Croozer would hold.~~ Thanks to Uncle Cooter's home-made 'T'aint Full Yet device, the fellas determined that the tank was ⓑ 1/5 full when they began their experiment. Vince grabbed his can of gas and, after ⓓ adding 7 gallons to the tank, the tank was now ⓒ 2/3 full. Vince said, "Eureka! I've got it!" ⓐ How many gallons will the Croozer's tank hold?

ⓐ **Let's say:**   a full tank $= x$

We also know:

ⓑ **Start of the experiment** = **1/5** of a full tank = **1/5** x

ⓒ **End of the experiment** = **2/3** of a full tank = **2/3** x

ⓓ **Gas added** = **7 gallons**

- -

① **Set up an equation to describe the "experiment":**

$$\text{Start} + \text{Gas} = \text{End}$$

$$\frac{1}{5}x + 7 \text{ gallons} = \frac{2}{3}x$$

$$-\frac{1}{5}x \qquad\qquad -\frac{1}{5}x$$

$$7 \text{ gallons} = \frac{2}{3}x - \frac{1}{5}x$$

$$7 \text{ gallons} = \left(\frac{2}{3} \times \frac{5}{5}\right)x - \left(\frac{1}{5} \times \frac{3}{3}\right)x$$

$$7 \text{ gallons} = \frac{10}{15}x - \frac{3}{15}x$$

$$7 \text{ gallons} = \frac{7}{15}x$$

$$\frac{15}{7}(7 \text{ gallons}) = \left(\frac{7}{15}x\right)\frac{15}{7}$$

$$\frac{105 \text{ gallons}}{7} = x$$

$$15 \text{ gallons} = x$$

ⓐ 22

The Croozer's tank will hold 15 gallons of gas.

Heavy Thinkers

Algebra Challenges

Sample Problem

Private Sanders, Wendy, and Mr. McDonald were all headed to the 49th floor of the Fast Food Administration. They wished to share an elevator, but a sign in the elevator read: "Maximum Capacity: 100 kg." They compared weights and were astounded to learn that Private Sanders weighed twice as much as Mr. McDonald. Wendy weighed only 4 kg less than Private Sanders. The average of their weights was 32 kg. Can they all safely ride the elevator together? How much does each person weigh?

① **Total weight:** 3 x 32 kg = 96 kg → 100 kg > 96 kg → | Yes, all three can ride safely in the elevator together.

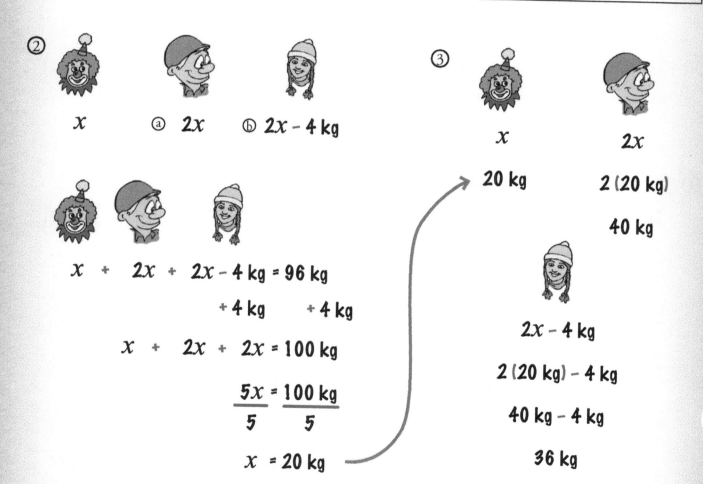

②

x ⓐ $2x$ ⓑ $2x - 4$ kg

$x + 2x + 2x - 4$ kg $= 96$ kg

$ + 4$ kg $ + 4$ kg

$x + 2x + 2x = 100$ kg

$\dfrac{5x}{5} = \dfrac{100 \text{ kg}}{5}$

$x = 20$ kg

③

x $2x$

20 kg   2 (20 kg)

$ $ 40 kg

$2x - 4$ kg

2 (20 kg) – 4 kg

40 kg – 4 kg

36 kg

Mr. McDonald weighs 20 kg, Private Sanders weighs 40 kg, and Wendy weighs 36 kg.

Practice Problem #1

Mr. Whitherby, Sammy, and a guy everyone just called The Conductor met at El Huevo Loco for 2-for-1 burrito night. Although they had intended simply to have a quick snack before catching a matinee of "The Chalupa Always Rings Twice," the trio of friends would soon be responsible for eating ⓐ2/3 <u>of</u> the 90 burritos served that evening at El Huevo Loco. It all started when The Conductor bet Mr. Witherby that he could eat the most burritos. Sammy quickly jumped into the fray and before long, belts were being loosened and burritos were being devoured like juicy gossip at the water cooler. ⓑThe Conductor made good on his bet, eating <u>twice</u> as many burritos as Mr. Witherby. ⓒSammy ate 4 <u>more</u> burritos than Mr. Witherby, despite the fact that this was his first experience with a mass ingestion contest. <u>How many burritos did each amigo eat?</u>

We know:

ⓐ **They ate 2/3 of 90 burritos= 2/3 x 90 burritos**

ⓑ **The Conductor: 2 x Witherby** $= 2x$

ⓒ **Sammy: 4 burritos + Witherby** $= 4 \text{ burritos} + x = x + 4 \text{ burritos}$

ⓓ **So if: Witherby $= x$ Then...**

- -

① **Set up an equation that is equal to all the burritos they ate.**

The Conductor + Sammy + Witherby = the burritos they ate

$$(2x) + (x + 4 \text{ burritos}) + x = \frac{2}{3} \times 90 \text{ burritos}$$

$$2x + x + 4 \text{ burritos} + x = 60 \text{ burritos}$$

$$\underline{- 4 \text{ burritos}} \qquad \underline{- 4 \text{ burritos}}$$

$$2x + x + x = 56 \text{ burritos}$$

$$4x = 56 \text{ burritos}$$

$$\frac{4x}{4} = \frac{56 \text{ burritos}}{4}$$

$$x = 14 \text{ burritos}$$

② **The Conductor: $2x = 2 \times 14$ burritos = 28 burritos**

Sammy: $x + 4 = 14$ burritos + 4 burritos = 18 burritos

Witherby: $x = 14$ burritos

> **The Conductor ate 28 burritos, Sammy ate 18 burritos, and Witherby ate 14 burritos.**

Practice Problem #2

The aardvarks were so close. They could see the lights of Lost Bagels shimmering in the distance ahead. Their trip across the desert had been an arduous one, yet they had managed to cover an ①<u>average</u> of 12.5 miles per day over the four days of the trip. The ⓐfirst day had been the hardest. The hot sun was so oppressing that they had managed only x miles that day. The ⓑfollowing day, however, was cloudy and they covered <u>twice</u> as many miles as the first day. On the ⓒthird day, it rained but they still managed to travel 2 ⓓ<u>more</u> miles than they had on the previous day. And then, today, with Lost Bagels on the horizon, they had given it their all and cranked out <u>4 more</u> miles than the day before. ①<u>How many miles did the aardvarks travel altogether?</u> ④<u>How many miles did they travel each day?</u>

① **How many miles did they travel altogether?**
   They averaged 12.5 miles per day for 4 days:
   ~~12.5 mi/day~~ × ~~4 days~~ = 50 miles | They traveled 50 miles altogether. |

② ⓐ **Day 1:** x **miles**   ⓒ **Day 3: 2 mi + Day 2 = 2 mi + $2x$ = $2x$ + 2 mi**

   ⓑ **Day 2: 2 x Day 1 = $2x$**   ⓓ **Day 4: 4 mi + Day 3 = 4 mi + ($2x$ + 2 mi) = $2x$ + 6 mi**

③ **Since we know they traveled 50 miles altogether, set up**
   an equation equal to the total miles they traveled.

$$\text{Day 1} + \text{Day 2} + \text{Day 3} + \text{Day 4} = \text{total miles}$$
$$x + (2x) + (2x + 2\text{ mi}) + (2x + 6\text{ mi}) = 50\text{ mi}$$
$$x + 2x + 2x + 2x + 8\text{ mi} = 50\text{ mi}$$
$$-8\text{ mi} \qquad -8\text{ mi}$$
$$x + 2x + 2x + 2x = 42\text{ mi}$$
$$7x = 42\text{ mi}$$
$$\frac{7x}{7} = \frac{42\text{ mi}}{7}$$
$$x = 6\text{ mi}$$

④ **Day 1:** x **= 6 mi** ←

   Day 2: $2x$ = 2 (6 mi) = 12 mi

   Day 3: $2x$ + 2 mi = 2 (6 mi) + 2 mi = 14 mi

   Day 4: $2x$ + 6 mi = 2 (6 mi) + 6 mi = 12 mi + 6 mi = 18 mi

| Day 1 they traveled 6 miles, Day 2 they traveled 12 miles, Day 3 they traveled 14 miles and Day 4 they traveled 18 miles. |

Practice Problem #3

Their first morning at Camp Pinecone, the Snickerdoodle girls had been distraught to find that their favorite Capture the Flag battle grounds had been decimated by last summer's forest fire, and the whole area needed to be replanted. To spur the camp into action, Kelly's cabin renamed themselves the Mongoose Horde, and challenged the other cabins to a tree-planting competition. One thing led to another, and by the time the forest floor settled, the girls at Camp Pinecone had planted ① 3/4 of the camp's 4,360 pinecones in the burned-out area. The ⓐ Woodchucks had planted a total of **x** pinecones. The ⓑ Platypus Clan's tag-team approach helped them plant three times as many pinecones as the Woodchucks. But the ⓒ Mongoose Horde's automatic 'cone catapult had launched ① twice the number of pinecones as the Platypus Clan into prime planting space. ④ How many pinecones had the girls planted altogether? How many pinecones did each cabin plant?

① **How many pinecones did they plant** altogether?
   planted 3/4 of 4,360 pinecones:
   3/4 x 4,360 pinecones = 3,270 pinecones

> They planted 3,270 pinecones altogether.

② ⓐ Woodchucks: **x pinecones**

   ⓑ Platypus Clan: **3 times Woodchucks = 3x**

   ⓒ Mongoose Horde: **2 x Platypus Clan = 2 x 3x = 6x**

③ **Since we know they planted 3,270 pinecones altogether, set up an equation equal to the total number of pinecones they planted.**

$$\text{Woodchucks} + \text{Platypus} + \text{Mongoose} = \text{total pinecones}$$
$$x + (3x) + (6x) = 3,270 \text{ pinecones}$$
$$x + 3x + 6x = 3,270 \text{ pinecones}$$
$$\frac{10x}{10} = \frac{3,270 \text{ pinecones}}{10}$$
$$x = 327 \text{ pinecones}$$

> The Woodchucks planted 327 pinecones, the Platypus Clan planted 981 pinecones, and the Mongoose Horde planed 1,962 pinecones.

④ Woodchucks: **x pinecones = 327 pinecones**

   Platypus Clan: **3x = 3 (327 pinecones) = 981 pinecones**

   Mongoose Horde: **6x = 6 (327 pinecones) = 1,962 pinecones**

23

Practice Problem #4

Thelma, Bertha, Velma and Dominique drove to Vern's Seaworthy Crafts to rent a boat to celebrate their graduation from beauty school. Vern warned the ladies that his boats had a strict weight limit of 500 pounds—even one pound over and the boat would sink to the bottom like a lead balloon. …On the way to the docks, Thelma, who weighed 3 pounds more than Bertha, told the others that they would show that mean ol' Vern a thing or two about beauty-school graduates and sailing. Velma, who weighed 10 pounds less than Thelma, sniffed loudly and glared in Vern's general direction. Only Dominique, who weighed 7 pounds less than Velma seemed concerned about Vern's warning. If the average weight of the four friends was 130 pounds, what will happen when the sailing beauties board ship? How much does each lady weigh?

① **How much do the 4 friends weigh altogether?**
   average weight x # of friends = total weight:
   130 lbs x 4 = 520 lbs ⟶ **520 lbs > 500 lbs** ⟶ | The boat will sink when they board ship! |

② ⓐ Thelma: **Bertha + 3 lbs** | = $x + 3$ lbs
   ⓑ Velma: **Thelma − 10 lbs** | = $(x + 3$ lbs$) − 10$ lbs
   ⓒ Dominique: **Velma − 7 lbs** | = $[(x + 3$ lbs$) − 10$ lbs$] − 7$ lbs

   Since the problem didn't provide information for Bertha, let's say... | Bertha = x lbs |

③ **Since we know their total weight is 520 lbs, set up an equation equal to the total weight of the friends.**

$$\text{Bertha} + \text{Thelma} + \text{Velma} + \text{Dominique} = \text{total weight}$$
$$x + (x + 3 \text{ lbs}) + (x + 3 \text{ lbs}) − 10 \text{ lbs} + [(x + 3 \text{ lbs}) − 10 \text{ lbs}] − 7 \text{ lbs} = 520 \text{ lbs}$$
$$4x + (3 \text{ lbs} + 3 \text{ lbs} + 3 \text{ lbs}) − 10 \text{ lbs} − 10 \text{ lbs} − 7 \text{ lbs} = 520 \text{ lbs}$$
$$4x + 9 \text{ lbs} − 27 \text{ lbs} = 520 \text{ lbs}$$
$$4x − 18 \text{ lbs} = 520 \text{ lbs}$$
$$+ 18 \text{ lbs} \qquad + 18 \text{ lbs}$$
$$\frac{4x}{4} = \frac{538 \text{ lbs}}{4}$$
$$x = 134.5 \text{ lbs} ⟶$$

23

④ **Use the information you found for x to solve the following:**

Thelma: **Bertha + 3 lbs** = x + 3 lbs
Velma: **Thelma – 10 lbs** = (x + 3 lbs) – 10 lbs
Dominique: **Velma – 7 lbs** = [(x + 3 lbs) – 10 lbs] – 7 lbs

Bertha: x = 134.5 lbs

Bertha weighs 134.5 lbs,
Thelma weighs 137.5 lbs,
Velma weighs 127.5 lbs and
Dominique weighs 120.5 lb.

Option 1:

Thelma: x + 3 lbs = 134.5 lbs + 3 lbs = 137.5 lbs

Velma: (x + 3 lbs) – 10 lbs = (134.5 lbs + 3 lbs) – 10 lbs
= 137.5 lbs – 10 lbs = 127.5 lbs

Dominique: [(x + 3 lbs) – 10 lbs] – 7 lbs = [(134.5 lbs + 3 lbs) – 10 lbs] – 7 lbs
= [137.5 lbs – 10 lbs] – 7 lbs
= 127.5 lbs – 7 lbs
= 120.5 lbs

Option 2:

Thelma: x + 3 lbs = 134.5 lbs + 3 lbs = 137.5 lbs

Velma: Thelma – 10 lbs = 137.5 lbs – 10 lbs = 127.5 lbs

Dominique: Velma – 7 lbs = 127.5 lbs – 7 lbs = 120.5 lbs

A word of caution: If you solve using the Option 2 method, be aware that any computational errors you make will trickle down into other answers—even if you perform the rest of the math flawlessly. For example, if you mistakenly add 0.3 lbs instead of 3 lbs:

Thelma: x + 3 lbs = 134.5 lbs + 3 lbs = 134.8 lbs ✗

Velma: Thelma – 10 lbs = 134.8 lbs – 10 lbs = 124.8 lbs ✗

Dominique: Velma – 7 lbs = 124.8 lbs – 7 lbs = 117.8 lbs ✗

Even though the process is more cumbersome, you will not risk such an extreme "trickle-down" effect with the Option 1 method. If you notice your final answers are still incorrect, check the value you're using for x…

Practice Problem #5

There was once an old lady who lived in a shoe. ~~It was a used size-7 athletic sneaker and smelled something awful.~~ It was also quite cramped since the old lady had 3 kids living with her. ~~After winning the 50/50 raffle at a local football game, the old lady met with a local realtor, who helped her move up to a brand spankin' new size 13 mountain boot.~~ The kids, whose ① average shoe size was an 8, were ecstatic. Little Toeny, who had the smallest feet, loved to slide down the laces of his new house. His older brother, ⓑ Archie, who wore shoes two sizes larger than Little Toeny, loved to play with their dog, Bunion, and he often tried to teach Bunion to heel. The eldest child, ⓒ Naillie, had the largest feet of all—a full two sizes larger than Archie. Naillie was quite straight-laced and would never, ever stick out her tongue. If the old lady spends the rest of her raffle winnings on new shoes for the three kids, ④ what size should she purchase for each?

① **First, let's "undo" the average to find the total sum of the kids' shoe sizes:**

average shoe size x number of kids = sum

size 8 x 3 = 24

② **Since the problem didn't provide specific information for Toeny, let's say:**

ⓐ Toeny: x

ⓑ Archie: Toeny + 2 = $x + 2$

ⓒ Naillie: Archie + 2 = $(x + 2) + 2$

③ **Since we know sum of their shoe sizes is 24, set up an equation to find the sum of the "shoe size formulas" for each kid.**

Toeny + Archie + Naillie = sum

$$x + (x + 2) + [(x + 2) + 2] = 24$$
$$3x + 6 = 24$$
$$-6 \quad\quad -6$$
$$\frac{3x}{3} = \frac{18}{3}$$
$$x = \text{size } 6$$

④ **Plug the information for x back into each equation:**

ⓐ Toeny: x = size 6

ⓑ Archie: $x + 2 = 6 + 2$ = size 8

ⓒ Naillie: $(x + 2) + 2 = 6 + 4$ = size 10

> She should purchase a size 6 for Toeny, a size 8 for Archie and a size 10 for Naillie.

23

Sample Problem

A detective spent ② 1/6 of his money on a Mason-Dixon Chickens CD. He spent 3/5 of the remainder on overpriced coffee drinks that he can't even pronounce. If the ① coffee cost $11 more than the CD, how much money did he spend altogether?

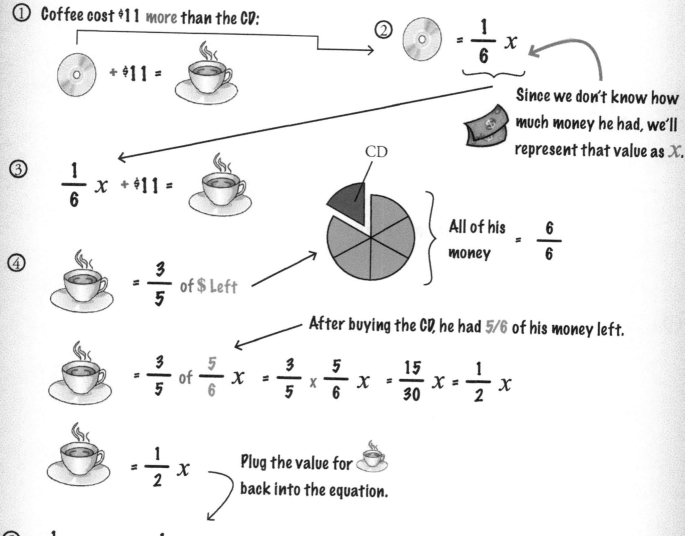

① Coffee cost $11 more than the CD:

② 🖸 $= \dfrac{1}{6} x$

Since we don't know how much money he had, we'll represent that value as x.

③ $\dfrac{1}{6} x + \$11 =$ ☕

CD

All of his money $= \dfrac{6}{6}$

④ ☕ $= \dfrac{3}{5}$ of $ Left

After buying the CD, he had 5/6 of his money left.

☕ $= \dfrac{3}{5}$ of $\dfrac{5}{6} x = \dfrac{3}{5} \times \dfrac{5}{6} x = \dfrac{15}{30} x = \dfrac{1}{2} x$

☕ $= \dfrac{1}{2} x$

Plug the value for ☕ back into the equation.

⑤ $\dfrac{1}{6} x + \$11 = \dfrac{1}{2} x$

$-\dfrac{1}{6} x \qquad -\dfrac{1}{6} x$

$\$11 = \dfrac{1}{2} x - \dfrac{1}{6} x$

$\$11 = \left(\dfrac{1}{2} \times \dfrac{3}{3} \right) x + \dfrac{1}{6} x$

$\$11 = \dfrac{3}{6} x - \dfrac{1}{6} x$

$\$11 = \dfrac{2}{6} x = \dfrac{1}{3} x$

$\dfrac{3}{1} (\$11) = \left(\dfrac{1}{\cancel{3}} x \right) \dfrac{\cancel{3}}{\cancel{1}}$

$\$33 = x$

24

fraction Challenges

$33 = x$ ← So he had $33 to start with. Let's use that value to find the cost of the individual items he purchased.

⑥ $= \dfrac{1}{6}$ $x = \dfrac{1}{6} \times \$33 = \dfrac{\$33}{6} = \$5.50$

⑦ $33.00

 $- 5.50$

——————

$27.50   He had $27.50 left after he purchased the CD.

⑧ $= \dfrac{3}{5}$ of $ Left

 $= \dfrac{3}{5} \times \$27.50 = \$16.50$ He spent $16.50 on coffee.

⑨ $16.50

$+ 5.50$

——————

$22.00

He spent $22 altogether.

24

Practice Problem #1

Luke stepped out onto the balcony of his hotel room. ~~There, hundreds of feet … Like a bloodhound,~~ Luke caught the trail and was soon standing before the beach-side burrito vendor. He spent 3/4 of his money on 3 Burrito Locos and 6 Chalupas Grandes. When he was finished, he was still hungry. The Chalupas Grandes had been more delicious than he ever could have imagined. If a Burrito Loco costs 3 times as much as a Chalupa Grande, how many Chalupas Grandes could Luke buy with the rest of his money?

① **Luke spent 3/4 of his money, so:** $\dfrac{4}{4} - \dfrac{3}{4} = \dfrac{1}{4}$ **of his money was left**

② **So if he spent 3/4 of his money on 3 B.L. and 6 C.G.…**

$$\frac{3}{4} = 3\ \text{B.L.} + 6\ \text{C.G.}$$

③ **…divide both sides by 3 to determine how much he could buy with 1/4 of his money:**

$$\frac{\frac{3}{4}}{3} = \frac{3\ \text{B.L.}}{3} + \frac{6\ \text{C.G.}}{3}$$

$$\frac{1}{4} = 1\ \text{B.L.} + 2\ \text{C.G.}$$

④ **Since a Burrito Loco costs 3 times as much as a Chalupa Grande…**

$$\frac{1}{4} = 1\ \text{B.L.} + 2\ \text{C.G.}$$

$$\frac{1}{4} = 3\ \text{C.G.} + 2\ \text{C.G.}$$

$$\frac{1}{4} = 5\ \text{C.G.}$$

> 1 B.L. = 3 x 1 C.G.
> 1 B.L. = 3 C.G.

> **He could buy 5 Chalupas Grandes.**

24

Practice Problem #2

When Vladimir parted ways with Mrs. Witt, he spent ① 1/5 of his money on a cab ride into town. Since he was still a little embarrassed about that incident with the spray cheese in the local convenience store, Vlad (that's what his friends call him) spent ② 1/2 of the remainder an ingenious disguise, which consisted of a large red handkerchief, a clown nose, a puffy shirt, sandals and knee socks. When he looked in his wallet, he realized he had exactly ③ $14 left, which would be just enough for the Early Bird Special at the Cow Palace. ④ How much money did Vladimir have to start with?

We know:

① **1/5 of his money = cab ride** → $\dfrac{5}{5} - \dfrac{1}{5} = \dfrac{4}{5}$ **of his money remained**

② **1/2 of the remainder = disguise**

$$\frac{1}{2} \times \frac{4}{5} = \frac{4}{10} = \frac{2}{5} = \text{disguise}$$

③ **If he spent 1/2 of the remainder on the disguise, the other 1/2 of the remainder was left in his wallet, so:**

$$\frac{2}{5} = \$14$$

④ **If we can figure out how much money is equal to 1/5, we can use that information to figure out how much 5/5 (or all) of his money is equal to:**

$$\frac{\frac{2}{5}}{2} = \frac{\$14}{2}$$

$$\frac{1}{5} = \$7$$

→ $5 \times \dfrac{1}{5} = \$7 \times 5$

$$\frac{5}{5} = \$35$$

> **Alternate Way to Solve:**
> 1/5 = cab ride
> 1/2 of 4/5 = disguise ⎫
> the other 1/2 = $14 ⎬
> So 2/2 = $28 = 4/5 ⎭
>
> $28 = 4/5
> ÷ 4   ÷ 4
> $7 = 1/5
> 5 x $7 = 1/5 x 5
> $35 = 5/5

> **Vladimir had $35 to start with.**

24

Practice Problem #3

Professor Stodgypants had finally saved up enough money to go on his dream trip to Africa. At long last he would finally be able to study the rare African Bolin Constrictor in its natural habitat. Upon arrival in Port Squeezy, Professor Stodgypants was delighted to find that food and lodging was much less expensive than he had feared. In fact, he only spent ⓐ1/3 of his money during the first week of his stay. After the novelty of the area had worn off, he spent even less—only ⓑ1/5—of his money in the second week. If he ©spent $1,600 altogether, how much money did he have total in his vacation fund?

① Since we need to know how much money he had in his vacation fund, let's say that all of the money in his vacation fund equals x.

② We know:
ⓐ Week 1: spent 1/3 of his money = 1/3 x
ⓑ Week 2: spent 1/5 of his money = 1/5 x
© He spent $1,600 altogether.

③ Since we know information about his spending habits, set up an equation equal to the amount he spent.

$$\text{Week 1} + \text{Week 2} = \text{amount spent}$$

$$\frac{1}{3}x + \frac{1}{5}x = \$1,600$$

$$\left(\frac{1}{3} \times \frac{5}{5}\right)x + \left(\frac{1}{5} \times \frac{3}{3}\right)x = \$1,600$$

$$\frac{5}{15}x + \frac{3}{15}x = \$1,600$$

$$\frac{\cancel{15}}{\cancel{8}}\left(\frac{\cancel{8}}{\cancel{15}}x\right) = (\$1,600)\frac{15}{8}$$

$$x = \frac{\$24,000}{8}$$

$$x = \$3,000$$

He had $3,000 total in his vacation fund.

24

Practice Problem #4

Johan Sebastian Guttenberg knew the end was near. ~~His solo trip to the Equator had been a miserable failure, in his opinion. ...and his profuse sweating had left him dehydrated.~~ In his final moments of clear thinking, he used a pen made out of a coconut to write a Last Will and Testament on a piece of bleached monkey-hide. His last wishes were for all his posses-sions to be sold, with ⓐ 3/5 of the money going to his wife and the ⓑ remainder divided equally between his 4 offspring. If, after his inevitable demise, his ⓒ children each receive $800, ② how much will his wife receive?

We could work through this problem repeatedly saying "all of the money" or part "of the money", but to simplify things, let's use x to represent all of the money.

① **We know:**

ⓐ **Wife: receives 3/5 of the money = 3/5 x**

ⓑ **Kids: remaining money divided equally → 4 kids**

$$\frac{5}{5} x - \frac{3}{5} x = \frac{2}{5} x$$

$$\frac{2}{5} x \div 4 = \frac{2}{5} x \div \frac{4}{1} = \frac{2}{5} x \times \frac{1}{4} = \frac{2}{20} x \div \frac{2}{2} = \frac{1}{10} x$$

ⓒ **Each child receives $800...which is equal to 1/10 of the money.**

So if $800 = 1/10 x, how much money is equal to 10/10 (or all) of the money?

$$10 (\$800) = \frac{1}{10} x \times \frac{10}{1}$$

$$\$8,000 = \frac{10}{10} x$$

$$\$8,000 = x$$

② **So if his wife receives 3/5 of the money...**

$$\frac{3}{5} x = \frac{3}{5} \times \$8,000 = \frac{\$24,000}{5} = \$4,800$$ | **His wife will receive $4,800.**

Practice Problem #5

Jethro could scarcely believe his eyes. ~~There, in his hands, was a letter from the largest venture capital firm in all of Podunk.~~ ...and emptied its contents into his trouser pocket. At Bobby Ray's garage sale, Jethro hit the mother lode. He spent 3/5 ⓐ of his money on 6 hubcaps and 8 lawn mower blades. He figured that with the ⓑ rest of his money he could buy another 12 hubcaps. However, if he spends all of the rest of his money on lawn mower blades only, how many lawn mower blades can he buy?

Again, to un-clutter the math below, let's say that all of his money equals x.

① **We know:**

ⓐ He spent **3/5** of the money on **6 hubcaps** and **8 lawn mower blades**:

$$\frac{3}{5}x = 6 \text{ hubcaps} + 8 \text{ blades}$$

ⓑ He could spend the rest of the money on **12 hubcaps**:

$$\frac{5}{5}x - \frac{3}{5}x = \frac{2}{5}x \quad \rightarrow \quad \frac{\frac{2}{5}x}{2} = \frac{12 \text{ hubcaps}}{2}$$

$$\frac{1}{5}x = 6 \text{ hubcaps}$$

② **If he could spend 1/5 of his money on 6 hubcaps, then we can replace "6 hubcaps" in the equation about what he spent with 1/5 x:**

$$\frac{3}{5}x = 6 \text{ hubcaps} + 8 \text{ blades}$$

$$\frac{3}{5}x = \frac{1}{5}x + 8 \text{ blades}$$

$$-\frac{1}{5}x \quad -\frac{1}{5}x$$

$$\frac{2}{5}x = 8 \text{ blades}$$

③ **If he had 2/5 of his money left after his initial purchase (ⓑ), and 2/5 will buy 8 lawn mower blades, then:**

> He can buy **8 lawn mower blades** with his remaining money.

24

Bait and Switch

Ratio Challenges

Sample Problem

Lil' Johnny took his dad's fishing tackle box to school for show-and-tell yesterday. Aside from the fact that Lil' Johnny is now grounded from varmint hunting for a full week, his presentation to his class was a great success. His classmates were particularly interested in the many fishing lures his dad has. The kids counted and discovered that ② 1/5 of the lures in the tackle box were purple. The remaining lures were either orange or green. The ratio of the number of orange lures to the number of green lures was ⓐ 2:3. If there were ⓑ 12 green lures in the tackle box, <u>how many purple lures were there?</u>

①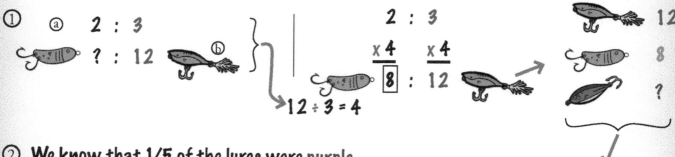

② We know that 1/5 of the lures were purple, so that means that 4/5 of the lures were either orange or green.

③ Since we know there were 8 orange lures and 12 green lures, then we know there are 20 orange or green lures... which is equal to 4/5 of the lures.

$$8 + 12 = 20$$

④ If we can figure out how many lures is equal to 1/5 of the lures, we'll know how many purple lures he had. So if:

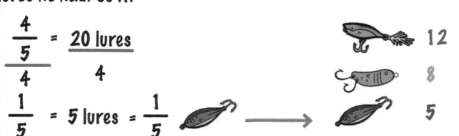

Lil' Johnny had 5 purple lures.

25

Practice Problem #1

Bubbly Betty, Blondie and Blind Barb were biding their time by the bayou before bopping into Boonieville's next Balloon Bashing Bout. Each of the bodacious beauties was burdened with a basic task to ensure their next bout went off with, well…a bang. The bulk of their round went as planned and before long, Betty's band had beat the opposition and won not only the trophy but prize money as well. Bubbly Betty, Blondie and Blind Barb decided to split the bucks in a ratio of 6:5:3, respectively. If Blondie's cut is $45, how much money in total did they win?

① First, use the ratio to determine each lady's portion of the winnings.

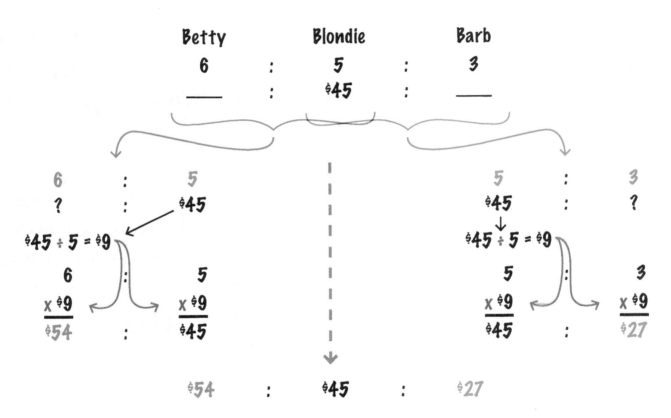

	Betty		Blondie		Barb
	6	:	5	:	3
	___	:	$45	:	___

	6	:	5				5	:	3
	?	:	$45				$45	:	?
	$45 ÷ 5 = $9						$45 ÷ 5 = $9		
	6		5				5		3
	x $9		x $9				x $9		x $9
	$54	:	$45				$45	:	$27

$54 : $45 : $27

② Add the amounts they each won together to determine how much they won in total.

$54
$45
+ $27
―――
$126

They won $126 altogether.

Practice Problem #2

A moose and a beaver were reclining next to a stream. As they were debating the relative merits of hunting vs. gathering, they heard an odd tinkling sound coming from the stream. When they sat up to investigate, they were amazed to see a steady stream of bottles of Uncle Geezer's Old Tyme Root Beer floating lazily down the stream. Every so often, the bottles would collide with each other and small stones in the stream, making an extraordinarily enjoyable tinkling sound. The moose and the beaver quickly waded into the stream and began to collect the bottles of root beer. Since he was bigger, the moose retrieved more bottles than the beaver in a ratio of ①7:5. If there were ②72 bottles total in the stream, ④how many more bottles did the moose retrieve than the beaver?

① The ratio tells us that every time the moose picked up 7 bottles, the beaver picked up 5 bottles.

So how many bottles did they pick up in a single "round"?

Moose		Beaver		Total:
7 bottles	+	5 bottles	=	12 bottles

② If they picked up 12 bottles each time, how many times did they pick up bottles in order to pick up a total of 72 bottles?

72 bottles ÷ 12 bottles = 6 times

③ So by their 6th "round", how many bottles had they each picked up?

Moose		Beaver		Total:
7 bottles	+	5 bottles	=	12 bottles
x 6		x 6		x 6
42 bottles	+	30 bottles	=	72 bottles

④ The question asks: "how many more bottles did the moose retrieve...?"

Moose		Beaver		
42 bottles	–	30 bottles	=	12 bottles

The moose retrieved 12 more bottles than the beaver.

25

Practice Problem #3

Kentuckiana Jones tossed his pencil and protractor aside and raised his map in frustration. "Blast these trigonometric roadblocks!" he shouted. "I'll never find the Lost City of Phuntabulous at this rate." On the verge of giving up, KJ noticed a peculiar shape taking form on his map as he held it up to the light. There, hidden beneath layers of dirt and grime, was what he had been searching for: the key to the map! It resembled a ① triangle, the length of whose sides were in a ratio of 4:3:5. Using his slide rule, tweezers, and an old popsicle stick, KJ determined that the ② perimeter of the triangle measured 48 cm. KJ knew that the shortest side of the triangle represented the most direct route to the Lost City, so he needed to find out how long that shortest side was. <u>What is the length of the shortest side of the map scale triangle?</u>

① **The length of the sides of the scale triangle are in a 4:3:5 ratio.**

So similar a triangle whose sides measured: ...would have a perimeter of:

Side 1		Side 2		Side 3		Perimeter:
4 cm	+	3 cm	+	5 cm	=	12 cm

② **The perimeter (or the total length of the sides) of the triangle on the map is 48 cm.**
So how many times bigger is the map triangle from our similar, smaller triangle?

Side 1		Side 2		Side 3		Perimeter:	ⓑ
4 cm	+	3 cm	+	5 cm	=	12 cm	
× 4		× 4		ⓒ × 4		ⓐ × ?	4 times
16 cm	+	12 cm	+	20 cm	=	48 cm	12 cm ⟌ 48 cm
							− 48
							0

The length of the shortest side is 12 cm.

KJ rejoiced when he discovered that he is currently at one end of the triangle's shortest side. If the map's scale ratio is 1 cm : 5 mi, <u>how many miles away is the Lost City?</u>

1 cm : 5 mi
12 cm : ?

1 cm : 5 mi
× 12   × 12
12 cm : **60 mi**

The Lost City is 60 miles away.

→ 12 ÷ 1 = 12 ←

Practice Problem #4

Ever since their trip to Lost Bagels, Cletus and Earlene have enjoyed collecting funny bumper stickers. Cletus' favorite is the one that says "Hard Work Never Killed Anyone BUT WHY TAKE THE CHANCE?" Earlene prefers the one that says "What if the Hokey Pokey *is* what it's all about?" Recently, they've been engaged in a bit of competitive collecting to see who can find the funniest bumper stickers. The ratio of the number of Cletus' bumper stickers to the number of Earlene's bumper stickers is currently 5:2. Cletus has 27 more bumper stickers than Earlene. How many bumper stickers should Cletus give to Earlene so that the ratio of the number of his bumper stickers to her bumper stickers will be 3:4?

① Before we can figure out how many stickers Cletus should give to Earlene, let's first determine how many bumper stickers he'd need to give her each round in order for the ratio to be 3:4.

According to the two ratios, Cletus would need to give Earlene 2 stickers each round for the ratio to be 3:4.

$$5 : 2$$
$$-2 \downarrow +2$$
$$3 : 4$$

② If he gives her 2 stickers each round, we'll need to know how many rounds have passed, so we can multiply that value times 2. So how many rounds has it taken him to collect 27 more bumper stickers?

Well, how many more bumper stickers did he have after the first "round" (according to the first ratio)?

5:3   5 – 2 = 3 more

So each round, Cletus will advance by an additional 3 bumper stickers.

Round		Ratio		Difference:	
1:		5 :	2	3 stickers	
2:	x 2	10 :	4	6 stickers	⟩ + 3
3:	x 3	15 :	6	9 stickers	⟩ + 3

③ How many rounds will it take before he has 27 more bumper stickers?

$$27 \text{ stickers} \div 3 \frac{\text{stickers}}{\text{round}} = 27 \cancel{\text{stickers}} \times \frac{1}{3} \frac{\text{round}}{\cancel{\text{stickers}}} = 9 \text{ rounds}$$

④ So if he gives her 2 stickers each round, by the 9th round:

$$9 \cancel{\text{rounds}} \times 2 \frac{\text{stickers}}{\cancel{\text{round}}} = 18 \text{ stickers}$$

Cletus needs to give Earlene 18 of his bumper stickers.

25

Practice Problem #5

To get in shape for bass fishin' season, Clem and Bobby Ray have embarked upon an ambitious new diet and exercise program. First, they no longer use the TV remote. If they want to change the channel, they take turns getting off the couch to change it manually. Second, they only eat donuts without sprinkles. Finally, and most importantly, they no longer go back for thirds (or fourths or fifths) at the More Than You Should Eat Buffet. As of this morning's weigh-in, 1/6 of Clem's weight is equal to 1/9 of Bobby Ray's weight. What is the ratio of Clem's weight to Bobby Ray's weight?

① Let's start with the equation the problem set up for us. It's almost a ratio already, but we need to convert the fractions into whole number values:

$$\frac{1}{6} \text{ of Clem} = \frac{1}{9} \text{ of Bobby Ray}$$

$$\frac{6}{1}\left(\frac{1}{6}\text{Clem}\right) = \left(\frac{1}{9}\text{Bobby Ray}\right)\frac{6}{1}$$

$$\text{Clem} = \frac{6}{9}\text{Bobby Ray}$$

$$\text{Clem} = \frac{2}{3}\text{Bobby Ray}$$

Clem's weight is 2/3 the weight of Bobby Ray, so the ratio of their weights is 2:3.

The ratio of Clem's weight to Bobby Ray's weight is 2:3.

Beefing Up

Percentage Challenges

Sample Problem

On January 1, 2007, the Pork Is Great Society (P.I.G.S.) had ⓐ1200 members, 60% of which were cows ~~and 40% of which were chickens~~. During Fair Week, the P.I.G.S. executed a very successful New Member Campaign, which resulted in the addition of ⓑ400 new members. After the new P.I.G.S. members were sworn in during a secret ceremony, President-elect Bo Vine noted that the percentage of members who were cows had fallen to ⓒ50%. ⓛHow many of the new P.I.G.S. members sworn in during the secret ceremony after Fair Week were cows?

① Since we need to know how many of the new members were cows, let's write down what we know from the problem about cows:

ⓐ Before: **60% of 1200 =**

ⓑ **+ 400**
_____
1600
↓
(joined during fair week)

ⓒ After: **50% of 1600 =**

② Before:

60% = 0.6

0.6 × 1200 = 720

(720 members were cows before)

After:

50% = 0.5

0.5 × 1600 = 800

(800 members were cows after)

③

After   **800**

− Before   **− 720**
_____
Joined during: **80 cows**

> 80 of the members that joined during fair week were cows.

Percentage Challenges

Practice Problem #1

Jethro was excited, finally, to be selling his Jethcut 2000 door-to-door. This morning, his plan was to visit the Dombrowski sisters at Shady Acres and then head on over to Moneytree Lane to try to sell as many units as possible. As luck would have it, each of the ⒜two Dombrowski sisters wanted her own Jethcut 2000. Since they were his first customers of the day, he sold them each one Jethcut 2000 at only 10% over cost. When he hit Moneytree Lane, though, the money really started rolling in. By lunchtime, he had sold an additional ⒝three units, each at 35% over cost. If Jethro received $1,875 from his sales, what is the cost price of a Jethcut 2000?

① **Since we need to know the cost price of a Jethcut 2000, let's say that value is equal to 100%. So if he sold units at 10% and 35% over cost:**

ⓐ **Dombrowski:** $100\% + 10\% = 110\%$

ⓑ **Moneytree Lane:** $100\% + 35\% = 135\%$

② **He sold 2 units at the Dombrowski price and 3 units at the Moneytree Lane price:**

$$D + D + ML + ML + ML = \$1,875$$
$$110\% + 110\% + 135\% + 135\% + 135\% = \$1,875$$
$$\frac{625\%}{625} = \frac{\$1,875}{625}$$
$$100\,(1\%) = (\$3)\,100$$
$$100\% = \$300$$

Alternate Way to Solve:

If Cost Price = x, then:
Dombrowski: $2(\text{cost} + 10\% \text{ of cost}) = 2(x + 10\%x)$
Moneytree: $3(\text{cost} + 35\% \text{ of cost}) = 3(x + 35\%x)$

$$2(x + 10\%x) + 3(x + 35\%x) = \$1,875$$
$$2(x + 0.1x) + 3(x + 0.35x) = \$1,875$$
$$2(1.1x) + 3(1.35x) = \$1,875$$
$$2.2x + 4.05x = \$1,875$$
$$\frac{6.25x}{6.25} = \frac{\$1,875}{6.25}$$
$$x = \$300$$

> The cost price of a Jethcut 2000 is $300.

26

Practice Problem #2

The fans at the FASCAR track were on their feet. It was the last race and it had come down to a dogfight between Ernie Dalehard and Stewart Tonay. Since all of the other drivers had fallen by the wayside, all the fans in the stands had split their support between the two frontrunners. (a) 60% of the fans were cheering for Stewart Tonay, and there were ② 250 more Stewart Tonay fans than Ernie Dalehard fans. How many fans total were at the race?

① **Since we need to find the total number of fans, let's say that "all of the fans" equals 100%. From the problem:**

(a) Stewart Tonay: 60%

(b) So: Ernie Dalehard: 100% – 60% = 40%

② **We also know:**

Ernie Dalehard + **250 fans** = Stewart Tonay

$$40\% + 250 \text{ fans} = 60\%$$
$$-40\% \quad -40\%$$
$$5 (250 \text{ fans}) = (20\%) 5 \quad \leftarrow \textbf{Multiply by 5 to find 100\%}$$
$$1,250 \text{ fans} = 100\%$$

There were 1,250 total fans at the race.

Alternate Way to Solve:

If the difference between the number of Ernie Dalehard fans and Stewart Tonay fans is 250, then what is the difference between 60% and 40%?

60% – 40% = 20%   So: 5 (20%) = (250 fans) 5

100% = 1,250 fans

26

Practice Problem #3

On his first day on the job as "The Guy Who Puts the Clowns in the Tiny Car," Bo Jest crammed 24 clowns into the tiny car. ...Bo returned to the circus the following day and, after a litany of promises and a few bribes, managed to fit a whopping 36 clowns into the tiny car without incident.② <u>What percent more clowns did Bo Jest fit into the tiny car today than yesterday?</u>

① **If he fit 36 clowns today and only 24 clowns yesterday, then he fit:**

36 clowns – 24 clowns = 12 more clowns today than yesterday

② **Since we need to know what percent more (than 24 clowns) ... we can say that 24 clowns equals to 100%.**

So what percentage of 24 clowns is 12 clowns?

$$\frac{12 \text{ clowns}}{24 \text{ clowns}} = 0.5 = 50\%$$

> **Bo Jest fit 50% more clowns today than yesterday.**

Practice Problem #4

Delbert was really frustrated. The ol' paycheck just didn't go as far as it used to. For example, he cashed his check today and immediately had to <u>spend</u> 10% of his pay on diapers for Maude. As if that weren't enough, he then had to spend 20% of the <u>remainder</u> on tutus for Katarina and Isabella. <u>When he looked into his wallet, Delbert could hardly believe that he only had what percentage of his pay left?</u>

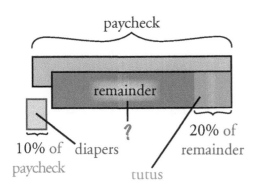

paycheck

remainder

?

10% of diapers
paycheck

20% of remainder

tutus

① **100% cashed paycheck**
 – 10% diapers
 90% remained

② **He spent 20% of the remainder on tutus:**

90% x 20% = 0.18

or 18% of his paycheck on tutus

③ **paycheck – diapers – tutus = what he has left**
 100% – 10% – 18% = 72% of his paycheck left

> **Delbert had 72% of his paycheck left.**

26

Practice Problem #5

Cletus and Earlene's bumper sticker collection had grown to enormous proportions in the last couple of months. Out of all the new additions to his collection, Cletus thought the best was the one that read "Just say NO to negativity." Earlene's most recent favorite was the one that read "National Spellling Bee Runer-Up." Altogether, the two now had a total of ④ 500 bumper stickers. ① Earlene now has 24% more bumper stickers than Cletus. ⑤ Cletus thinks its unfair that Earlene now has how many more bumper stickers than he has?

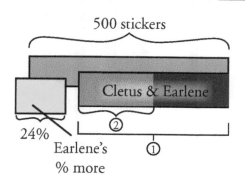

500 stickers

Cletus & Earlene

②

24% Earlene's % more ①

In order to find out how many more stickers Earlene has, we first need to figure out how many stickers they each have.

In order to do that, we'll need to determine what % of 500 stickers belong to Earlene, and what % belong to Cletus.

① Since Cletus + Earlene + ~~24%~~ = 100%:

$$100\%$$
$$- ~~24\%~~ \text{ (Earlene's \% more)}$$
$$76\%: \text{ 1/2 of which = Cletus, 1/2 = Earlene}$$

② 50% of 76% = Cletus or Earlene
50% x 76% = Cletus or Earlene
0.38 = 38% = Cletus or Earlene

③ 38% + ~~24%~~ = all of Earlene's stickers
62% = all of Earlene

④ 38% of 500 stickers = Cletus
38% x 500 stickers = Cletus
190 stickers = Cletus

62% of 500 stickers = all of Earlene
62% x 500 stickers = all of Earlene
310 stickers = all of Earlene

⑤ Earlene – Cletus = Earlene's amount more
310 stickers – 190 stickers = Earlene's amt more
120 stickers = Earlene's amount more

Earlene now has 120 more bumper stickers than Cletus.

Alternate Way to Solve:
If you recognized that:
Cletus + Earlene + 24% = 500
and that you need to find this amount,
then you could simply find: 24% of 500:
24% x 500 = 0.24 x 500 = 120 stickers

26

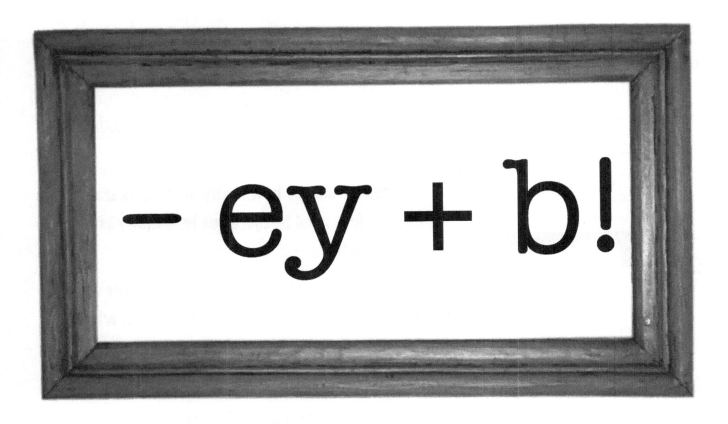

Okay, Master Problem Solvers, have you noticed that the Word Puzzler has left one final message for you, sprinkled through the pages of this Answer Key? A rebus is a puzzle or riddle made up of pictures or symbols that represent words. As one of your final challenges, flip back through the pages of the Answer Key to locate all of the clues, and then decipher the message in the space below.

Answer located on the final page of the Tool Kit.

Horse Thief

Speed Challenges

Sample Problem

On the day of his most famous bank robbery, Smitty ~~Werben Jaeger Man Jensen took~~ ~~$723.47 from the vault in the Tumblewood bank. Smitty stole the fastest horse he could~~ ~~find, a noble steed named Frank~~ …took 6 hours to cover the first 3/4 of his trip at an average of 12 mi/hr …~~money bag ripped and 2/3 of the coins fell out. Fearing that there might~~ ~~be a posse in pursuit, Smitty refused to stop for the fallen loot.~~ …arrived at exactly 6:00 p.m. If Smitty averaged 18 mi/hr during the last 1/4 of his trip, <u>what time did he leave Tumblewood?</u>

① 6 hours 12 mi/hr

72 mi

18 mi/hr

② 24 mi

T — 24 mi | 24 mi | 24 mi | 24 mi — C

③ 1 hr 20 min

This line represents the distance between Tumblewood and Cactopolis.

Since we know information about 3/4 and about 1/4 of his trip, divide the line into quarters.

① The first 3/4 of the trip: took 6 hours, average speed of 12 mi/hr. So how far did he travel?

$T \times S = D$

6 hr × 12 mi/hr = 72 mi

② If we know the distance for 3/4 of the trip, divide by 3 to figure out the distance for 1/4 of the trip.
72 mi ÷ 3 = 24 mi

③ If he went 24 miles for the last 1/4 of the trip, divide by the speed to figure out how long it took him to travel that distance:

$$\frac{T \times S}{S} = \frac{D}{S}$$

$$\frac{1}{3} \times 60 \text{ min} = \frac{60}{3} = 20 \text{ min}$$

$$T = \frac{D}{S} = \frac{24 \text{ mi}}{18 \text{ mi/hr}} = 1 \text{ R } 6 \text{ hr} = 1\frac{6}{18} \text{ hr} = 1\frac{1}{3} \text{ hr} \qquad = 1 \text{ hr } 20 \text{ min}$$

④ Since we know how long it took for him to travel both the first 3/4 and the last 1/4 of the trip, we can add those two values together to see how long the trip took.

6 hr + 1 hr 20 min = 7 hr 20 min

④ So if he arrived in Cactopolis at 6:00 p.m., subtract 7 hr 20 min to find out when he left Tumblewood.   6:00 p.m. – 7 hr 20 min = 10:40 a.m. | He left Tumblewood at 10:40 a.m. |

Practice Problem #1

Angelique and Dusty both drove a distance of 240 miles from their home in Ramal to the airport in Louisville. Given the price of gas, Dusty thought driving separately was a waste, but Angelique insisted it was necessary because she still had to get a pedicure. As a result, Angelique started her trip one hour later than Dusty. However, due to her lead foot and the massive engine in her Urban Suburban, Angelique actually reached the airport at the exact same time Dusty did. If Angelique's average speed was 80 miles per hour, <u>what was Dusty's average speed?</u>

To find Dusty's speed, we need to know how far (D) he traveled, and how long (T) it took him to get there.

$$S = \frac{D}{T}$$

We know:
They both traveled 240 mi, so: D = 240 mi
Angelique: S = 80 mi/hr
   she left one hour after Dusty, so Dusty's T = Angelique's T + 1 hr

① **So how long (T) was Angelique's drive?**

$$T = \frac{D}{S} = \frac{240 \text{ mi}}{80 \text{ mi/hr}} = \frac{240 \text{ mi}}{1} \times \frac{1 \text{ hr}}{80 \text{ mi}} = 3 \text{ hr}$$

To find the formula equal to time:

$$S = \frac{D}{T}$$

$$T \times S = \frac{D}{T} \times T$$

$$T \times S = D$$

$$\frac{T \times S}{S} = \frac{D}{S}$$

$$\boxed{T = \frac{D}{S}}$$

② **So Dusty's speed:**

$$S = \frac{D}{T} = \frac{240 \text{ mi}}{\text{Ang. T + 1 hr}} = \frac{240 \text{ mi}}{3 \text{ hr} + 1 \text{ hr}} = \frac{240 \text{ mi}}{4 \text{ hr}} = 60 \text{ mi/hr}$$

Dusty's average speed was 60 mi/hr.

27

Practice Problem #2

Back on shore again, Plaidbeard the Pirate piled his crew into his new Minibus XL and drove them 80 miles from the docks to Parrotopolis to have lunch at China Buffet. For the first 40 minutes of the trip, Plaidbeard drove an average speed of 75 miles per hour. But then he saw a policeman on a motorcycle and thought it best to slow down just a bit. The rest of the way to China Buffet, he drove at an average speed of 72 miles per hour. If Plaidbeard and his crew left the docks at high noon, what time did they arrive at Parrotopolis?

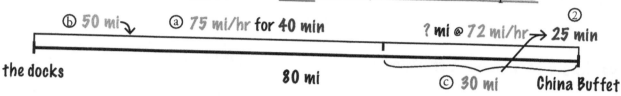

ⓐ **75 mi/hr for 40 min**   **? mi @ 72 mi/hr → 25 min** ②

ⓑ 50 mi ↓

the docks   80 mi   ⓒ 30 mi   China Buffet

① We know the entire length of the trip was 80 miles. If we can figure out how many miles they went at 75 mi/hr (ⓑ), a little subtraction (ⓒ) will help us figure out how many miles they went at 72 mi/hr.

ⓐ So if they went 75 mi/hr for 40 minutes, let's first convert minutes into hours so we can use the time information in our formula.

$$\frac{40 \text{ min}}{1} \times \frac{1 \text{ hr}}{60 \text{ min}} = \frac{40}{60} \text{ hr} = \frac{2}{3} \text{ hr}$$

ⓑ $D = T \times S = \frac{2}{3} \text{ hr} \times \frac{75 \text{ mi}}{1 \text{ hr}} = \frac{150}{3} \text{ mi} = 50 \text{ mi}$

ⓒ 80 mi − 50 mi = 30 mi left to go

② Use the formula to find how long (T) it took to go 30 miles at 72 mi/hr.

$$T = \frac{D}{S} = \frac{30 \text{ mi}}{72 \text{ mi/hr}} = \frac{30 \text{ mi}}{1} \times \frac{1 \text{ hr}}{72 \text{ mi}} \times \frac{60 \text{ min}}{1 \text{ hr}} = 25 \text{ min}$$

↳ to convert to minutes

③ So to find the total time of the trip:

First leg + Second leg = total time

40 min + 25 min = 65 min or 1 hr 5 min

④ But the question asks what time they arrived, so if they left at high noon:

12:00 + 1 hr 5 min = 1:05 p.m.

Plaidbeard and his crew arrived at China Buffet at 1:05 p.m.

27

Practice Problem #3

After the FASCAR season was over, Ernie Dalehard invited Stuart Tonay to go camping.① Unbeknownst to Stewart, Ernie had modified the engine in his RV so he could make the 180 km drive to the campground faster than Stewart. Despite Ernie's souped-up RV—and the fact that Stewart ended up leaving town ⓐ 40 minutes after Ernie—Stewart's superior driving skills (and the inherent superiority of his Specific Motors RV) got him to the campground a full 20 minutes before Ernie. If Ernie Dalehard's average speed in his modified RV was ⓑ 60 km/hr,② what was Stewart Tonay's average speed?

① **We know both drivers traveled 180 km.** $D = 180 \text{ km}$

② **We need to know Stuart's speed, so what does the problem tell us about Stuart?**

$S = \dfrac{D}{T}$

ⓐ **He started 40 min after Ernie, and arrived 20 min before:**

40 min + 20 min = 60 min → So his trip was 60 min (1 hr) shorter than Ernie's.

ⓑ **So how long (T) was Ernie's trip?**

$$T = \frac{D}{S} = \frac{180 \text{ km}}{60 \text{ km/hr}} = \frac{180 \text{ km}}{1} \times \frac{1 \text{ hr}}{60 \text{ km}} = 3 \text{ hr}$$

③ **Stuart's trip was 1 hr shorter than Ernie's:**

Stuart's time = 3 hr – 1 hr = 2 hr

④ **So Stuart's speed:**

$$S = \frac{D}{T} = \frac{180 \text{ km}}{2 \text{ hr}} = 90 \text{ km/hr}$$

> **Stuart Tonay's average speed was 90 km/hr.**

27

Practice Problem #4

On their first anniversary, Cletus and Earlene drove back to Lost Bagels to relive their honeymoon. On the way there, they averaged 30 miles per hour over the course of the 210-mile trip. As they were packing to go home, they suddenly remembered the new season of The Deep Fried Goodness Show would start that night. So, in order to make it home in time for the early airing, Cletus put the pedal to the metal and averaged 70 miles per hour on the return trip. What was their average speed for the whole trip?

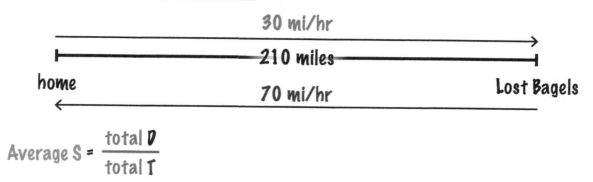

Average S = $\dfrac{\text{total } D}{\text{total } T}$

① **What was their total distance?**

210 mi x 2 = 420 mi

② **How long was their trip to Lost Bagels?**

$T = \dfrac{D}{S} = \dfrac{210 \text{ mi}}{30 \text{ mi/hr}} = \dfrac{210 \text{ mi}}{1} \times \dfrac{1 \text{ hr}}{30 \text{ mi}} = 7 \text{ hr}$

> Cletus and Earlene's average speed for the entire trip was 42 mi/hr.

③ **How long was their trip home?**

$T = \dfrac{D}{S} = \dfrac{210 \text{ mi}}{70 \text{ mi/hr}} = \dfrac{210 \text{ mi}}{1} \times \dfrac{1 \text{ hr}}{70 \text{ mi}} = 3 \text{ hr}$

④ **So total time:**   7 hr + 3 hr = 10 hr

⑤ **Apply the information about distance and time to the formula:**

Average S = $\dfrac{\text{total } D}{\text{total } T} = \dfrac{420 \text{ mi}}{10 \text{ hr}} = 42 \text{ mi/hr}$

27

Practice Problem #5

At high noon, Ethan jumped on his Hogley Favoriteson motorcycle and began the 40 mile journey from Frogtown to Podunk. At the exact same time, Noah mounted his trusty steed, Buttercup, and left Podunk and heads toward Frogtown. If Ethan travels at 30 miles per hour and Noah squeezes 6 miles per hour out of Buttercup, how far apart will they be at 12:30 p.m.?

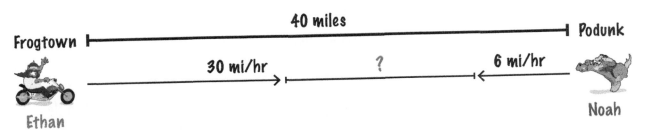

① We know they both left at high noon, and it's now 12:30 p.m.

12:30 p.m. – 12:00 p.m. = 30 minutes or $\frac{1}{2}$ hour of travel time.

② Use the information about speed and time to determine the distance they each traveled.

$$D = T \times S$$

ⓐ Ethan:

$$D = \frac{1}{2} \, hr \times \frac{30 \, mi}{1 \, hr} = \frac{30}{2} \, mi = 15 \, mi$$

ⓑ Noah:

$$D = \frac{1}{2} \, hr \times \frac{6 \, mi}{1 \, hr} = \frac{6}{2} \, mi = 3 \, mi$$

③ So: Total distance – Ethan's distance – Noah's distance = distance apart

40 mi – 15 mi – 3 mi = 22 mi

Ethan and Noah are 22 miles apart.

27

Notes

Notes

Notes

Notes

Notes

Notes